Percentage Points of the *t*-distribution

d.f.	1 T = 0.4 2 T = 0.8	0.25 0.5	0.1 0.2	0.05 0.1	0.025 0.05	0.01 0.02	0.005 0.01	0.0025 0.005	0.001 0.002	0.0005 0.001
1	0.325	1.000	3.078	6.314	12.706	31.821	63.657	127.32	318.31	636.62
2	.289	0.816	1.886	2.920	4.303	6.965	9.925	14.089	22.327	31.598
3	.277	.765	1.638	2.353	3.182	4.541	5.841	7.453	10.214	12.924
4	.271	.741	1.533	2.132	2.776	3.747	4.604	5.598	7.173	8.610
5	0.267	0.727	1.476	2.015	2.571	3.365	4.032	4.773	5.893	6.869
6	.265	.718	1.440	1.943	2.447	3.143	3.707	4.317	5.208	5.959
7	.263	.711	1.415	1.895	2.365	2.998	3.499	4.029	4.785	5.408
8	.262	.706	1.397	1.860	2.306	2.896	3.355	3.833	4.501	5.041
9	.261	.703	1.383	1.833	2.262	2.821	3.250	3.690	4.297	4.781
10	0.260	0.700	1.372	1.812	2.228	2.764	3.169	3.581	4.144	4.587
11	.260	.697	1.363	1.796	2.201	2.718	3.106	3.497	4.025	4.437
12	.259	.695	1.356	1.782	2.179	2.681	3.055	3.428	3.930	4.318
13	.259	.694	1.350	1.771	2.160	2.650	3.012	3.372	3.852	4.221
14	.258	.692	1.345	1.761	2.145	2.624	2.977	3.326	3.787	4.140
15	0.258	0.691	1.341	1.753	2.131	2.602	2.947	3.286	3.733	4.073
16	.258	.690	1.337	1.746	2.120	2.583	2.921	3.252	3.686	4.015
17	.257	.689	1.333	1.740	2.110	2.567	2.898	3.222	3.646	3.965
18	.257	.688	1.330	1.734	2.101	2.552	2.878	3.197	3.610	3.922
19	.257	.688	1.328	1.729	2.093	2.539	2.861	3.174	3.579	3.883
20	0.257	0.687	1.325	1.725	2.086	2.528	2.845	3.153	3.552	3.850
21	.257	.686	1.323	1.721	2.080	2.518	2.831	3.135	3.527	3.819
22	.256	.686	1.321	1.717	2.074	2.508	2.819	3.119	3.505	3.792
23	.256	.685	1.319	1.714	2.069	2.500	2.807	3.104	3.485	3.767
24	.256	.685	1.318	1.711	2.064	2.492	2.797	3.091	3.467	3.745
25	0.256	0.684	1.316	1.708	2.060	2.485	2.787	3.078	3.450	3.725
26	.256	.684	1.315	1.706	2.056	2.479	2.779	3.067	3.435	3.707
27	.256	.684	1.314	1.703	2.052	2.473	2.771	3.057	3.421	3.690
28	.256	.683	1.313	1.701	2.048	2.467	2.763	3.047	3.408	3.674
29	.256	.683	1.311	1.699	2.045	2.462	2.756	3.038	3.396	3.659
30	0.256	0.683	1.310	1.697	2.042	2.457	2.750	3.030	3.385	3.646
40	.255	.681	1.303	1.684	2.021	2.423	2.704	2.971	3.307	3.551
60	.254	.679	1.296	1.671	2.000	2.390	2.660	2.915	3.232	3.460
120	.254	.677	1.289	1.658	1.980	2.358	2.617	2.860	3.160	3.373
∞	.253	.674	1.282	1.645	1.960	2.326	2.576	2.807	3.090	3.291

1 T = area under one tail; 2 T = area under both tails.

For 25 degrees of freedom (d.f.), $P(t > 2.060) = 0.025$ and $P(t < -2.060$ or $t > 2.060) = 0.05$.

Source: Biometrika Tables for Statisticians, Vol. I. Edited by E. S. Pearson and H. O. Hartley, 3rd edition, 1966. Reprinted with the permission of the Biometrika Trustees.

INTRODUCTORY
ECONOMETRICS

WITH APPLICATIONS

Second Edition

THE DRYDEN PRESS SERIES IN ECONOMICS

Aronson
The Electronic Scorecard

Asch and Seneca
Government and the Marketplace,
Second Edition

Baker
**An Introduction to
International Economics**

Baumol and Blinder
Economics: Principles and Policy,
Fifth Edition (Also available in micro
and macro paperbacks)

Baumol, Panzar, and Willig
**Contestable Markets and the Theory
of Industry Structure,** *Revised Edition*

Berch
**The Endless Day: The Political
Economy of Women and Work**

Breit and Elzinga
**The Antitrust Casebook: Milestones
in Economic Regulation,** *Second Edition*

Campbell, Campbell, and Dolan
Money, Banking, and Monetary Policy

Clark and Veseth
Economics: Cost and Choice
(Also available in micro and macro
paperbacks)

Claudon and Olsen
Eco Talk

Clower, Graves, and Sexton
Intermediate Microeconomics

Demmert
**Economics:
Understanding the Market Process**

Dolan and Lindsey
Economics, *Sixth Edition* (Also available
in micro and macro paperbacks)

Eckert and Leftwich
**The Price System and Resource
Allocation,** *Tenth Edition*

Edgmand, Moomaw, and Olson
Economics and Contemporary Issues

Estey
**The Unions: Structure, Development,
and Management,** *Third Edition*

Fort and Lowinger
**Applications and Exercises in
Intermediate Microeconomics**

Friedman
Milton Friedman Speaks

Gardner
Comparative Economic Systems

Glahe
Macroeconomics: Theory and Policy,
Third Edition

Glahe
**Microeconomics: Theory and
Application,** *Second Edition*

Griffin and Steele
Energy Economics and Policy, *Second Edition*

Gwartney and Stroup
Economics: Private and Public Choice,
Sixth Edition (Also available in micro
and macro paperbacks)

Gwartney, Stroup, and Clark
Essentials of Economics, *Second Edition*

Heilbroner and Singer
**The Economic Transformation of
America: 1600 to the Present,**
Second Edition

Hoerneman, Howard, Wilson, and Cole
**CAPER: Computer Assisted
Program for Economic Review**

Hirsch and Rufolo
**Public Finance and Expenditure
in a Federal System**

Hirschey and Pappas
**Fundamentals of Managerial
Economics,** *Fourth Edition*

Hyman
**Public Finance: A Contemporary
Application of Theory to Policy,**
Third Edition

Johnson and Roberts
**Money and Banking: A Market-
Oriented Approach,** *Third Edition*

Kaufman
The Economics of Labor Markets,
Third Edition

Keating and Wilson
**Fundamentals of
Managerial Economics**

Keating and Wilson
Managerial Economics, *Second Edition*

Kidwell and Peterson
**Financial Institutions, Markets,
and Money,** *Fourth Edition*

Klein
Money and the Economy, *Sixth Edition*

Kohn
**Money, Banking, and
Financial Markets**

Kreinin
**International Economics:
A Policy Approach,** *Sixth Edition*

Landsburg
Price Theory and Applications,
Second Edition

Link, Miller, and Bergman
**EconoGraph II: Interactive Software
for Principles of Economics**

Lott and Ray
Econometrics Data Sets

Nicholson
**Intermediate Microeconomics and
Its Application,** *Fifth Edition*

Nicholson
**Microeconomic Theory: Basic
Principles and Extensions,** *Fifth Edition*

Ormiston
Intermediate Microeconomics

Oser and Brue
The Evolution of Economic Thought,
Fourth Edition

Pappas and Hirschey
Managerial Economics, *Sixth Edition*

Puth
American Economic History,
Second Edition

Ragan and Thomas
Principles of Economics (Also
available in micro and macro
paperbacks)

Ramanathan
**Introductory Econometrics with
Applications,** *Second Edition*

Rukstad
**Corporate Decision Making
in the World Economy:
Company Case Studies**

Rukstad
**Macroeconomic Decision Making in
the World Economy: Text and Cases,**
Third Edition

Samuelson and Marks
Managerial Economics

Scarth
**Macroeconomics: An Introduction
to Advanced Methods**

Seidman
Macroeconomics

Smith and Spudeck
**Interest Rates: Principles
and Applications**

Thomas
**Economics: Principles and
Applications** (Also available in micro
and macro paperbacks)

Wachtel
Labor and the Economy, *Second Edition*

Walton and Rockoff
History of the American Economy,
Sixth Edition

Welch and Welch
Economics: Theory and Practice,
Fourth Edition

Yarbrough and Yarbrough
**The World Economy:
Trade and Finance,** *Second Edition*

Zimbalist, Sherman, and Brown
**Comparing Economic Systems:
A Political-Economic Approach,**
Second Edition

INTRODUCTORY ECONOMETRICS

WITH APPLICATIONS

Second Edition

RAMU RAMANATHAN

University of California, San Diego

The Dryden Press
Harcourt Brace Jovanovich College Publishers
Fort Worth   Philadelphia   San Diego   New York   Orlando   Austin   San Antonio
Toronto   Montreal   London   Sydney   Tokyo

To my family: Vimala, Sadhana, Pradeep, and Sridhar

ISBN: 0-15-546489-2

Library of Congress Catalog Card Number: 91-72934

Printed in the United States of America

PREFACE

The response to the first edition of this book has been flattering both in terms of adoptions and in the number of favorable responses from around the world. The revised edition has incorporated many suggestions, but has kept the basic structure the same, namely, (1) practical applications are emphasized without sacrificing theoretical underpinnings, (2) step-by-step procedures for hypothesis testing to improve model specifications are presented, (3) reinforcing the understanding of methods through "hands-on" practice sessions is emphasized, (4) detailed steps are provided for carrying out empirical projects, and (5) an easy-to-use regression package is included in order to enable users to reproduce the empirical examples and applications. Theory, "walk-through" applications, and hands-on empirical practice are better integrated in this edition because all practice computer sessions are now included within the chapters themselves, with references to them in the relevant sections. Also, most of the data sets have been updated and many new data sets have been added.

Changes in Individual Chapters

The changes made in individual chapters are summarized below.

- Calculus topics in Chapter 2 have been moved to the chapter appendix so that the text proper does not require any calculus in this chapter or in later chapters. Probability and statistics sections have been expanded. Practice computer sessions, problems, and exercises have been added.
- Logarithms and exponential functions have been moved from Chapter 2 to the Chapter 3 appendix. *P*-value approach to hypothesis testing has been expanded into a separate section.
- The section on hypothesis testing in Chapter 4 has been expanded considerably.
- In Chapter 6, the sections on piece-wise linear regression and structural change tests have been expanded.
- Wald, Likelihood Ratio, and Lagrange Multiplier tests are illustrated in Chapter 7 with a new application. A discussion of the Hendry/LSE methodology of going from a general to a specific model is now included.

- Chapter 8 (formerly Chapter 11) includes a discussion of White's *Heteroscedasticity Consistent Covariance Matrix Estimator, Multiplicative Heteroscedasticity*, and the *Estimated Generalized Least Squares* procedure, with illustrative examples.
- In Chapter 9 on serial correlation, the Hildreth–Lu and Cochrane–Orcutt procedures are compared with a numerical example. The ARCH test has been moved to this chapter, and a discussion of *random walks* and *unit roots* is included.
- The *Dickey–Fuller test* for unit roots is discussed in Chapter 10, with an empirical example.
- Chapter 11 on forecasting discusses *exponential smoothing, adaptive forecasts, cointegration*, and the *Augmented Dickey–Fuller* test, with empirical examples.
- The probit model is included in Chapter 12, with an empirical example.
- The *Granger causality test* is now included in Chapter 13.
- The Instructor's Manual has been expanded considerably.

Changes in the Computer Program ECSLIB

The program has undergone numerous changes; among the salient ones are the following:

- Ready-made command input files are provided so that all empirical examples can be reproduced with a simple DOS command.
- An extremely easy to use ASCII text editor is now included. It can be used to create data files as well as command input files. This editor can also be accessed from within ECSLIB.
- It is now possible to execute a DOS command without leaving ECSLIB.
- White's *heteroscedasticity consistent covariance matrix estimator* can be obtained with a single command.
- Data sets supplied on the diskette can now be read directly by other regression packages.

Prerequisites

The book requires a knowledge of basic probability and statistics. But because calculus topics have been moved to the appendix of Chapter 2, no calculus prerequisite is required for the text. However, the appendix is written in such a way that a rudimentary understanding can be achieved without a prior calculus course. By providing a comprehensive and self-contained treatment of the relevant topics, Chapter 2 will enable students to obtain a uniform background in probability and statistics. And students with a calculus background will find the appendices useful in obtaining a good theoretical foundation.

Suggested Course of Study

Because colleges differ considerably in the lengths of their terms (quarter or semester) and in their prerequisites (calculus or no calculus), no single outline can serve all econometrics courses. However, Chapters 1 through 9 constitute "core" material that almost all instructors are likely to cover. The remaining chapters present special topics from which selections can be made as time permits. Chapter 14 on how to conduct an empirical project will be useful if students are required to carry out an empirical study.

At the University of California, San Diego, probability and statistics (Chapter 2 of the book) are covered in one quarter and basic econometrics (Chapters 1, 3 through 9, and perhaps 13) is covered in a second quarter. Both courses are required for an economics major. The third quarter of the econometrics sequence is optional and covers the remaining chapters. In this final course, students carry out a complete empirical project. The entire book can usefully be covered in a two-semester or three-quarter sequence.

Many colleges offer a single course (usually a semester long) on probability, statistics, and econometrics, followed by an elective course on advanced topics. In such a case, the instructor might spend four weeks on Chapter 2 and devote the rest of the term to the "core" material in Chapters 3 through 9.

Acknowledgments

In revising this book, I have benefited from the advice of numerous colleagues, correspondents, and students. My colleagues Carrol Foster, Clive Granger, and Hal White, and my son Pradeep have read parts of the new manuscript and offered suggestions for revisions.

Michael Beenstock, Richard Bennett, Richard Bugnics, Thomas Cowing, Fekru Debebe, William Donnelly, Pami Dua, Susan Porter-Hueck, Robert Mayer, David Molina, Jan Ondrich, David Sapsford, and Jeff Wooldridge gave detailed suggestions for improving the text, both in content and in presentation, as well as the ECSLIB package that accompanies the book. Loic Sadoulet, a former student and undergraduate tutor, has been invaluable in critiquing the book from the point of view of students.

Among correspondents whose comments on both the book and the program have helped in this revision, mention should be made of the following; Oyugi Aseto, Assane Djeto, Joseph Earley, Marek Gruszczynski, Hans-Helmut Kotz, Klaus Diter John, Raphael Pardo, Michel Pouchain, Milton Searl, and Paul Wilson.

I am also grateful for the strong support and encouragement from Rick Hammonds, the Economics and Finance Editor at Harcourt Brace Jovanovich.

About the Author

Ramu Ramanathan has an M.A. in Mathematics from the University of Madras, India, an M.Stat. in Statistics from the Indian Statistical Institute, and a Ph.D. in Economics from the University of Minnesota. His areas of interest are applied econometrics, energy economics, economic growth, and international trade. His articles in these areas have appeared in leading journals in the U.S., U.K., Australia, and India. He is the author of *Introduction to the theory of economic growth*, and coauthor of *San Diego: An economic analysis*; *Measuring external effects in solid waste management*; and *Regional load curve models*. He is a senior professor at the University of California, San Diego, where he has been a faculty member for the past 25 years. He is also an Associate Editor of *ENERGY: The International Journal*; President of Quantitative Economic Research (QUERI), a consulting firm; and a member of the University of California Energy Research Group Advisory Committee. During 1983–84, Dr. Ramanathan also served as a member of the Energy Finance Advisory Committee for the San Diego Association of Governments, and played a leading role in its functions.

CONTENTS

PART II BASICS

Chapter 4   **Multiple Regression Models**   158

PART IV   *SOME SPECIAL ISSUES WITH CROSS-SECTION AND TIME SERIES DATA*

Chapter 11   **Forecasting**   472

Chapter 12   **Qualitative and Limited Dependent Variables**   513

PART VI   *PRACTICE*

PART I

BACKGROUND

P art I consists of two chapters that are intended to provide a background for those that follow. The introductory chapter describes what econometrics is all about and gives examples of real-world applications. It goes on to provide a brief description of each of the steps an econometrician takes in carrying out an empirical study. Chapter 2 summarizes the concepts of probability and statistics as used in econometrics. This chapter is written so that those of you who have had a basic statistics course but have no calculus background can still obtain enough knowledge to understand the later material.

CHAPTER 1

Introduction

In simple terms, **econometrics** deals with the application of statistical methods to economics. More broadly, it is concerned with (1) estimating economic relationships, (2) confronting economic theory with facts and testing hypotheses involving economic behavior, and (3) forecasting the behavior of economic variables. In the following sections we illustrate each of these activities with a number of short, real-world examples.

Estimating Economic Relationships

Empirical economics provides numerous examples of attempts to estimate economic relationships from data. A brief list of examples might include the following:

1. Analysts from both the government and the private sector will be interested in estimating the demand/supply of various products and services.
2. A private firm might be interested in estimating the effect of various levels of advertising on sales and profits.
3. Stock market analysts will seek to relate the price of a stock to the characteristics of the company issuing the stock, as well as to the overall state of the economy.
4. Federal and state governments might want to evaluate the impact of monetary and fiscal policies on such important variables as employment or unemployment, income, imports and exports, interest rates, inflation rates, and budget deficits.

5. Local governments will be concerned with the relationship between revenues and the various factors, such as tax rate and population, that determine those revenues.
6. Municipalities might be interested in the impact of a company locating in their area. Of particular interest would be the effects on housing demand, employment levels, sales and property revenues, such public service requirements as schools, sewage treatment facilities, water, electricity, and so on.

Testing Hypotheses

As in any science, a good deal of economics is concerned with **testing hypotheses** about economic behavior. This point can be illustrated by these examples:

1. A fast food chain might want to determine whether its new advertising campaign has been effective in increasing sales.
2. Both government and private analysts should be interested in whether demand is elastic or inelastic with respect to price and income.
3. Virtually any company might want to know whether returns to the scale of operation is increasing or decreasing.
4. Both tobacco companies and medical researchers should be interested in whether the surgeon general's report on smoking and lung cancer (and other respiratory illnesses) have resulted in a significant reduction in cigarette consumption.
5. Macro economists might want to measure the effectiveness of various government policies.
6. A public utilities commission should be interested in whether regulations requiring better insulation of home and buildings have significantly reduced energy consumption.
7. Law enforcement agencies and state legislatures might want to measure the effectiveness of tightening laws against drinking and driving in reducing deaths and injuries attributable to them.

Forecasting

Once variables have been identified and we have measured their apparent effect on the subject of study, we might want to use the estimated relationships to project future values. A few examples of such **forecasting** are as follows:

1. Firms forecast sales, profits, cost of production, and inventory requirements.
2. Utilities project demand for energy so that adequate generating facilities can be built and/or arrangements can be made to buy power from outside.
3. Numerous firms forecast stock market indices and the price of specific stocks.
4. The federal government projects such things as revenues, expenditures, inflation, unemployment, budget and trade deficits.
5. Municipalities routinely forecast local growth in such areas as population; employment; numbers of residential, commercial, and industrial establishments; needs for schools, roads, police, and fire stations, utilities; and so on.

Unlike the natural sciences, where a researcher can often control the experimental environment in a laboratory, economics most frequently deals with nonexperimental data. This constraint means that there will be uncertainty in these three standard investigations; (1) estimated relationships are not precise, (2) conclusions from hypothesis testing are subject to either the error of accepting a false hypothesis or that of rejecting a true hypothesis, and (3) forecasts based on estimated relationships are almost never exactly on target. To reduce the level of uncertainty, an econometrician will usually estimate several different relationships among the variables under study. He or she will then conduct a series of tests to determine which relationships most closely described or predicted the actual behavior of variables of interest.

    This uncertainty makes statistical methodology very important in econometrics. The next chapter presents a summary of the basic statistical concepts needed in this book and should be referred to, as needed, in later chapters. Let us now take a look at the basis for developing an empirical study.

1.2   Basic Ingredients of an Empirical Study

    An investigator conducting an empirical study follows a number of basic steps. They are (1) formulating a model, (2) gathering the data, (3) estimating the model, (4) subjecting the model to hypothesis testing, and (5) interpreting the results. Figure 1.1

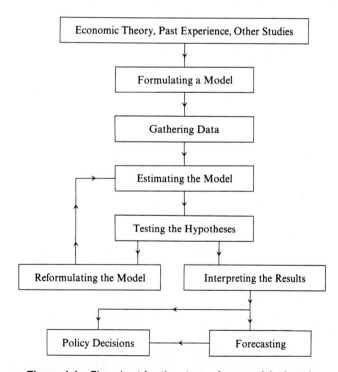

Figure 1.1   Flowchart for the steps of an empirical study

presents these steps in flowchart form. In this section we give a brief description of
each of these activities. Chapter 14 goes into each of these topics in more detail. If an
instructor plans to require an empirical project as part of a course on econometrics,
Chapter 14 should be assigned early.

Formulating a Model

Every analysis of an economic, social, political, or physical system is based on
some underlying logical structure (known as a **model**) that describes the behavior of
the agents in the system, and is the basic framework of analysis. In economics, as in
the physical sciences, this model is set up in the form of equations, which, in this case,
describe the behavior of economic and related variables. The model that an
investigator formulates might consist of a single equation or a system involving
several equations.

Single Equation Models   In a single equation specification, the analyst selects a
single variable (denoted by Y) whose behavior the researcher is interested in
explaining. Y is referred to by a number of names, **dependent variable** most
commonly, but also by *regressand, left-hand side variable*. The investigator then
identifies a number of variables (denoted by Xs) that have **causal effects** on the
dependent variable. These variables are also referred to in a number of ways;
independent variable is the usual term, but they are also called the *exogenous variable,
explanatory variable, regressor, right-hand side variable*. The choice of independent
variables might come from economic theory, past experience, other studies, or from
intuitive judgment. As an example, consider a firm that is interested in determining
its labor requirements. The company's economic analyst might use the basic
microeconomic theory of profit maximization to determine how many persons to
hire. The profit of the firm would depend on the price and quantity of the product it
sells, the number of persons it employs, the wage rate, interest rate, costs of capital
and raw materials, and so on. The principle of profit maximization would lead to a
theoretical relationship between the number of persons (or worker-hours) and the
other variables just listed. In this example, Y would be the number of persons (or
worker-hours) to be employed, and the Xs would be the price of the good, wage and
interest rates, the cost of raw materials, and so on. The goal would be to estimate the
theoretical relation and use it to make policy decisions.

Simultaneous Equation Models   In some econometric studies, the investigator
may be interested in more than one dependent variable and hence formulate several
equations at the same time. These are known as **simultaneous equation models**.
Estimating demand and supply equations is an example of this type of formulation.
Macroeconomic models are another example of simultaneous equation specification. One of the equations might be a consumption function that relates aggregate
consumption to disposable income and the interest rate. Another might be the
investment function, relating investment to disposable income and the interest rate.
There would also be a money demand function, relating money demand to income
and the interest rate. Other equations could be equilibrium conditions that relate
aggregate demand to aggregate supply and money demand to money supply.

Example 1.1

The basic structure of an econometric model will be better understood with a simple example in which the dependent variable (Y) is related to a single independent variable (X). Consider a real estate agent who is interested in relating the sale price of a house to its characteristics, such as the lot size, the living area, the number of bedrooms and bathrooms it has, the types of built-in appliances it has, whether it has a swimming pool, whether it has a view, and so on. In particular, the agent would want to know what the contribution of a specific attribute is toward increasing the value of the property. Although all these characteristics are important in explaining the differences in prices across houses, for purposes of illustration let us consider a single characteristic, say the living area. Suppose PRICE is the sale price of a house and SQFT is the living area in square feet. Assuming for simplicity that the relationship between these two variables is linear, we obtain the equation PRICE = $\alpha + \beta$SQFT, where α is the intercept and β is the slope of the straight line. Suppose we identify two houses with the same living area. In spite of this, their sale prices need not be the same. This might be due to pure random chance or, more likely, due to differences between the two houses in characteristics that were not taken into account by the model (such as the yard size). Thus, the relationship is not likely to be precise but rather subject to errors. To allow for these errors, an **econometric model** would be formulated as follows:

$$\text{PRICE} = \alpha + \beta\text{SQFT} + u \tag{1.1}$$

where u is an unobserved random variable called the **error term** (also known as the *disturbance term,* or *stochastic term*) with certain statistical properties described later. The error term will vary from observation to observation. Equation (1.1) is known as the **linear regression model**, or the **simple linear regression model**. The straight line $\alpha + \beta$SQFT is called the *deterministic* part of the model and the error term u is called the *stochastic* part.

Continuing with the real estate example, suppose we fix SQFT at the five levels 1500, 1750, 2000, 2250, and 2500, enumerate *all the houses in a given locality* that have SQFT at (or very close to) one of these levels, and obtain their sale prices.[1] As pointed out earlier, even if two houses had the same living area, their sale prices might be different. What we are interested in here is measuring how much the variation in price is statistically due to the factor "SQFT." If the pairs of values PRICE and SQFT are plotted on coordinate axes, they form a graph like the one in Figure 1.2. Because larger homes command higher prices, we expect the points in the diagram to exhibit an upward shift as we move to the right on the horizontal axis.

Next we calculate the average price at each of the five levels of SQFT. In Figure 1.2 these points are denoted by ×. The assumption behind equation (1.1), which is of course subject to evaluation, is that these average points lie on the

· · · · · · ·

[1] *In practice, such a complete census of the population of houses would not be done because of the high cost. Instead, a sample would be drawn at random and observations made on it.*

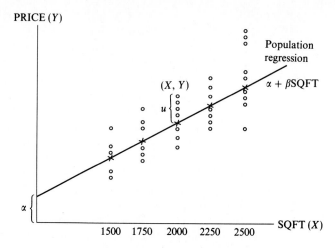

Figure 1.2 A graph of PRICE against SQFT

straight line $\alpha + \beta$SQFT. The deterministic part is thus a "statistical average" relation between the dependent variable and the independent variable(s), *for the entire population* of houses in the locality under study. For this reason, α and β are known as the **population parameters** (or sometimes as the **true parameters**). The "true" average relationship $\alpha + \beta$SQFT (referred to as the **population regression**) is never known but, as will be described in detail in Chapter 3, an "estimated" relationship (known as the **sample regression**) is obtainable from a sample. The unobservable error term u represents the effects of the omitted variables (yard size, age of house, and all the other characteristics that influence the sale price), as well as those of any inherently unpredictable effects.

Since it would be prohibitively expensive to survey all the houses in an area to determine the values of α and β, an investigator would instead obtain a sample of houses at random and use the information obtained for this sample to draw inferences not only about the population values of α and β but also about the adequacy of the linear regression assumption behind equation (1.1). Because the conclusions are based on a sample of houses, they too are subject to errors. It is important to study these errors to find out whether the formulations can be improved and the conclusions strengthened. □

Gathering Data

In order to estimate the econometric model that a researcher specifies, sample data on the dependent and independent variables are needed. If the analyst is interested in explaining the variation of the dependent variable over time, he or she must obtain measurements at different points in time (referred to as **time series data**). For instance, a municipality might want to forecast the demand for housing for five or ten years into the future. This requires identifying the variables that influenced past demand for housing in that municipality, obtaining time series data over several years in the past, and using them in an appropriate model to generate forecasts of future demand. The interval or "periodicity" of the time series will be annual, quarterly, or monthly, depending on whether the municipality wishes to account for changes in annual, quarterly, or monthly demand for housing. The type of data available often dictates the periodicity of the data gathered.

While time series data represent observations for different time periods, **cross-section data** represent measurements *at a given point in time*. For example, a state's department of housing might wish to explain why housing demand varies across municipalities. This objective calls for obtaining observations on the characteristics of various municipalities at a certain period.

Most data are obtained from readily available public or private sources (Chapter 14 has more details on this). Frequently, however, these sources are not adequate for the problem in hand, or such data might simply not be available. In such a case, a special survey is conducted to gather the relevant information. For instance, some years ago several public utility commissions were interested in studying how consumers would respond to time-of-day pricing of electricity. Time-of-day pricing means that the price of electricity varies over different hours of the day, with higher prices during peak periods and lower prices during off-peak hours. In order to obtain the relevant data, utilities selected a number of residential customers and equipped their homes with meters that recorded the usage during every hour of the day. The usage was then monitored for at least a full year so that the response over different seasons could be recorded. Because this type of data collection results in times series data for a cross section of households, it is known as **pooled cross-section and time series data**, or sometimes as *panel data*. Special econometric techniques are needed to handle these types of data.

In the process of obtaining the data, an empirical investigator must consider the fact that the available data may not exactly match the analyst's requirements. As an example, a great deal of economic theory is concerned with the interest rate. Yet there is no such thing as a single interest rate. If the analyst is interested in studying the demand for housing, he or she would use the mortgage rate. If, however, the focus is on capital expenditures for new plants and equipment, the "prime rate" or some other borrowing rate tied to it would be the proper interest rate measure.

Thus, a good deal of judgment as well as care is needed in the data processing stage of an empirical study. An investigator should not only select data appropriate for the problem studied, but should also be aware of the limitations of the data used, because the validity of the conclusion will also depend on the accuracy of the data.

Estimating the Model

After the model has been formulated and the relevant data gathered, a basic task of an investigator is to estimate the unknown parameters of the model. In the preceding example we would obtain estimates of the intercept term α, the slope term β, and the parameters (such as the mean and variance) of the probability distribution of u. The estimated equation may then be used for testing hypothesis and/or for forecasting the values of the dependent variable, given the values of the independent variables. A variety of estimation procedures is available for model estimation. As will be studied later, the nature of the problem under investigation and that of the model specified usually dictate the procedures used.

Testing the Hypotheses

The preliminary estimation of an econometric model does not always give satisfactory results. The formulation of the basic econometric model is typically guided by economic theory, the analyst's understanding of the underlying behavior, and by past experience or studies. These ingredients of a model provide only a general framework for the econometric specification. Consequently, the first results might surprise the investigator because variables that were thought to be important a priori, appear after the fact to be empirically unimportant or they may have effects going in unexpected directions (frequently referred to as "wrong signs"). The economic analyst would therefore subject the model's hypotheses to a variety of tests in order to improve model specification. The goal is to find robust conclusions—that is, conclusions that are not sensitive to model specification. To achieve this objective, one usually has to reformulate the models, and perhaps reestimate them with different techniques. Testing hypotheses is not done just to improve model specification, but also to test the validity of a body of theory.

Interpreting the Results

The final stage of the empirical investigation is to interpret the results. The conclusions might support an economic theory or contradict it, thus requiring a reexamination of the theory. If the results are relevant for making policy decisions, then such decisions will also be made at this stage. Alternatively, the empirical analyst might use the final set of models to forecast one or more dependent variables under different scenarios of the future, and use these results for policy purposes.

- -

SUMMARY

The field of econometrics is concerned with estimating economic relationships, subjecting economic theory to hypothesis testing, and forecasting economic or other variables. An econometrician generally starts with a body of theory, then combines this with intuitive judgment, and/or past experience or studies, to formulate an econometric model. This process involves deciding upon one or more dependent variables and identifying the independent variables that have *causal effects* on them. The economic analyst should also decide whether time series or cross-section data are appropriate. The next step is to gather the relevant data. At this stage, an investigator often finds that compromises will have to be made because the measured data might not match what the theory requires. Once the data have been obtained, the practitioner estimates the parameters of one or more preliminary models. These are then subjected to a variety of tests with a view to identifying possible misspecification and erroneous methodology. Based on these tests, the model or models are reformulated and reestimated until the investigator is satisfied that any conclusions drawn from them are robust. The final stage is interpreting the results and deciding whether they support or refute the body of theory that the econometrician is testing empirically. The final models may also be used for deriving policy implications and/or forecasting the values of the dependent variables under alternative scenarios.

KEY TERMS

Causal effects
Cross-section data
Dependent variable
Econometric model
Econometrics
Error term
Forecasting
Independent variable
Linear regression model
Model

Pooled cross-section and
    time series data
Population parameter
Population regression
Sample regression
Simple linear regression model
Simultaneous equation models
Testing hypotheses
Time series data
True parameter

CHAPTER 2

Summary of Probability and Statistics

■ In this chapter, we summarize many of the basic concepts of probability and statistics that are used in econometrics. An attempt has been made to make the chapter as self-contained as possible, so that it will serve as a useful reference for later chapters. Very few proofs are presented, however. Instead, definitions of key concepts are presented in italics under the heading "Definition," and the results useful in later applications are displayed in bold characters under the heading "Property." Practice problems and computer sessions are included in this chapter. However, the chapter is not intended to serve as a substitute for textbooks on the topics covered, although it should prove a more than adequate guide to the statistical foundations of econometrics. For a complete discussion of the relevant topics, you should refer to the excellent books listed in the bibliography at the end of this chapter. Sections indicated with an asterisk (∗) are more advanced. They may be skipped in an elementary course on econometrics without losing the gist of the subject matter.

2.1   Probability, Random Variables, and Distributions

Events and Sample Spaces

An investigator typically conducts an experiment that might be as simple as tossing a coin or rolling a pair of dice, or as complicated as making a survey of economic agents or conducting an experimental medical treatment program. A possible outcome of an experiment is referred to as an *event*. The outcome "head" in a coin toss experiment, a total of five points in the roll of a pair of dice, the level of income of a household, and the curing of a patient are examples of events. The set of all possible outcomes is called the *sample space*, and its individual elements are called **elementary events** or **sample points**. For example, consider the experiment of throwing a single die. The sample space consists of the six sample points 1, 2, ..., 6. If the occurrence of an event A precludes the occurrence of another event B (that is, they cannot occur together), then A and B are said to be *mutually exclusive* or *disjoint*. For example, if a coin is tossed, the occurrence of a head precludes that of a tail.

If two events A and B occur together, the outcome is denoted as $A \cap B$ (the symbol $\cap$ is called the **intersection** and denotes "and"). $A \cup B$ means A or B or both occurring (the symbol $\cup$ is called **union** and denotes "either or both"). The event that A does not occur is denoted by $\bar{A}$. The following example illustrates these concepts:

A: All economics majors.
B: All female students.
$\bar{B}$: The set of all male students.
$A \cap B$: All female economics majors.
$A \cup B$: Students who are either females, or economics majors, or both.

The **probability** of an event is defined in a number of ways, all of which are useful.

Definition 2.1 (Classical definition)
If events can occur in n mutually exclusive and equally likely ways and if n_A of these outcomes have an attribute A, then the probability of A is n_A/n. This is denoted as $P(A) = n_A/n$.

As an example, consider the experiment of throwing a pair of dice. The sample space consists of the 36 sample points: $(1, 1), (1, 2), \ldots, (6, 6)$, where the first number is the outcome of the first die and the second number is the outcome of the second die. Each is equally likely, and hence the probability of each of these outcomes is $\frac{1}{36}$. Next consider the event A, "total score is 4." This can occur in the three mutually exclusive ways, $(1, 3), (2, 2)$, and $(3, 1)$. Hence $P(A) = \frac{3}{36}$.

Definition 2.2 (Frequency definition)
The probability of an event is the average fraction of times it occurs when an experiment is repeated an infinite number of times. More formally, let n_A be the number of times an event A occurs in n trials of an experiment. Then the probability of A is $P(A) = \lim_{n \to \infty}(n_A/n)$, provided the limit exists.

Thus, if an experiment is repeatedly carried out, then the limiting frequency of an event is taken to be the probability of that event. As it is impractical to conduct any experiment an infinite number of times, the usefulness of this definition is when the number of observations is large. As an illustration, the U.S. Internal Revenue Service has the information about the adjusted gross incomes from all individual (including jointly filed) income tax returns for the entire United States. Suppose we form the income intervals 0–10,000, 10,000–20,000, 20,000–30,000 and so on and calculate the fraction of the tax returns that falls in each income group. The fraction of the returns that falls in the income group 40,000–50,000 can be taken to be the probability that a tax return drawn at random will have income falling in that interval. This concept, known as the **frequency distribution**, is illustrated in Figure 2.1. The horizontal axis represents annual income (in thousands) and the vertical axis gives the percent of returns in each interval. The proportion is plotted against the mid point of the intervals. If the size of the population is sufficiently large and the intervals small enough, we can approximate the frequencies with a smooth curve as shown in the diagram.

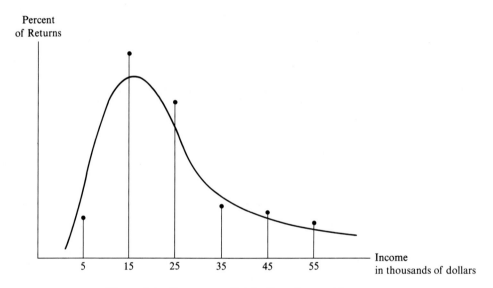

Figure 2.1   Frequency distribution of annual incomes

Try Practice Computer Session 2.1 described at the end of this chapter.

Definition 2.3 (Axiomatic definition)*
The probability of an event A is a real number such that $P(A) \geq 0$ for every event A in the sample space. Also, if $A_1, A_2, \ldots, A_n$ are mutually exclusive events, then $P(A_1$ or A_2 or $\ldots$ or $A_n) = P(A_1) + P(A_2) + \cdots + P(A_n) = \sum_i P(A_i)$, where $\sum_i$ is the summation over the index i. Finally, the sum of the probabilities of all elementary event's is equal to 1.

Consider the dice throwing experiment described above and the event A "total score is 4." A can be represented as $A_1 \cup A_2 \cup A_3$, where A_1 is (1, 3), A_2 is (2, 2), and A_3 is (3, 1). Hence, $P(A) = P(A_1 \cup A_2 \cup A_3) = P(A_1) + P(A_2) + P(A_3) = \frac{1}{36} + \frac{1}{36} + \frac{1}{36} = \frac{3}{36}$, which was the value obtained by the classical definition.

From the axiomatic definition of probability, the following properties of probabilities can be derived.

Property 2.1

a. $0 \le P(A) \le 1$.
b. $P(\bar{A}) = 1 - P(A)$.
c. $P(A \cup B) = P(A) + P(B) - P(A \cap B)$.

Conditional Probability

Conditional probability is the probability of one event occurring *given* that another has already occurred.

Definition 2.4 (Conditional Probability)

Let A and B be two events such that $P(B) > 0$. The conditional probability of A given that B has occurred, denoted by $P(A|B)$, is given by $\dfrac{P(A \cap B)}{P(B)}$.

Example 2.1

A high school has 1000 student drivers of whom 600 attended a driver's training course. A survey of all these drivers was conducted over a one year period to find out how many of them were involved in at least one accident in which they were at fault. The results are tabulated in Table 2.1. What is the probability that a student who took the course was not involved in any accident?

TABLE 2.1 Hypothetical data on driver training and accidents

	Attended course	Did not attend course	Total
Had accidents	30	70	100
No accidents	570	330	900
Total	600	400	1000

Denote by A the event that a student was involved in at least one accident and by T the event that a student took the training course. Then, by the classical definition, $P(A \cap T) = 30/1000 = 0.03$. $P(A \cap \bar{T}) = 70/1000 = 0.07$. $P(\bar{A} \cap T) = 570/1000 = 0.57$. $P(\bar{A} \cap \bar{T}) = 330/1000 = 0.33$. Note that the four probabilities sum to 1. The event T is the union of the disjoint events $(T \cap A)$ and $(T \cap \bar{A})$. Therefore, by the axiomatic approach, $P(T) = P(T \cap A) + P(T \cap \bar{A}) = 0.60$. The conditional probability that a student was not involved in any accident given that he or she had driver training is therefore given by $P(\bar{A} \mid T) = P(\bar{A} \cap T) \div P(T) = 0.57/0.60 = 0.95$. This result could have been obtained directly from the table by noting that out of the 600 students who took the course 570 had no accidents. Therefore the desired probability is $570/600 = 0.95$. However, the set theoretic approach is used here to illustrate its usefulness in other situations where it may not be possible to construct a table.

Practice Problems

2.1 Calculate $P(A)$, $P(\bar{T})$, and $P(A \mid \bar{T})$ in Example 2.1 using the set theoretic approach.

2.2 A rental car company operates between two cities A and B. In city A it has a Fords and b Chevrolets. In city B it has c Fords and d Chevrolets. A customer picks a car at random from city A, drives it to city B, and leaves it there. A second customer then chooses a car at random from city B. What is the probability that it is a Ford?

2.3 With probability 0.7 I set my wrist watch alarm to alert me to get ready for class. If the alarm is set, I am on time to class with probability 0.99. If it is not set, I am on time only 60 percent of the time. What is the probability that I will be on time? Given that I was on time, what is the probability that the alarm was set?

Statistical Independence

Suppose the probability of A given that B has occurred is the same as the probability of A without any condition. In other words, the information that B has occurred does not change the probability of A occurring. Then we say that the two events are statistically independent. The formal definition is in 2.5.

Definition 2.5 (Statistical independence)
Two events A and B for which $P(A) > 0$ and $P(B) > 0$ are said to be **statistically independent** if and only if $P(A \cap B) = P(A) \cdot P(B)$. Equivalently, $P(A \mid B) = P(A)$ and $P(B \mid A) = P(B)$.

In Example 2.1 $P(A \cap T) = 0.03$. $P(A)P(T) = (0.1)(0.60) = 0.06 \neq P(A \cap T)$. Hence driver training and accidents are not independent.

Random Variables

A **random variable** (also known as a *stochastic variable*) is a variable whose value is a real number determined by the outcome of an experiment. Examples include the temperature at a certain time, the number of calls coming through a switchboard in a 5-minute interval, the income of a family, and the inventories of a firm. A random variable is *discrete* if it can take only selected values. The number of defective TV tubes in a lot of 20 and the number of heads in 10 tosses of a coin are examples of discrete random variables. A random variable is *continuous* if it can take any value in a real interval. When measured accurately, the height of a person, the temperature at a particular instant, and the amount of energy consumed in an hour are examples of continuous random variables.

To keep the presentation simple, we illustrate the various concepts using mostly discrete random variables. The propositions extend easily to the case of a continuous random variable.

Density Functions and Distribution Functions

Let X be a random variable and x be a particular value it can take. Then the function $F(x) = P(X \leq x)$—that is, the probability that the random variable X takes a value not exceeding the real number x, for each x in $(-\infty, \infty)$—is called the **distribution function** of the random variable (also known as the *cumulative distribution function* or the *cumulative density function*, or just *cdf*). For a discrete random variable, $f(x) = P(X = x)$. [If $F(x)$ is differentiable, then $f(x) = F'(x)$ is the **probability density function (pdf)** of x.] These statements are summarized in a number of definitions.

Definition 2.6 (Density and Distribution functions)

If X is a random variable and x is a particular value it can assume, then the probability $P(X \leq x)$ is called the cumulative distribution function of X (or just cdf), and is denoted by $F(x)$. If X is a discrete random variable, the function $f(x) = P(X = x)$ is called its probability density function (or just pef). For a discrete random variable $\sum_{i=1}^{n} f(x_i) = 1$, where $x_1, x_2, \ldots, x_n$ are the possible distinct outcomes.

The Binomial Distribution

As an example of a discrete density function, let X be the number of heads in three tosses of a coin. X can take the values 0, 1, 2, or 3. The eight mutually exclusive outcomes, each of which is equally likely, are given by (HHH), (HHT), (HTH), (THH), (HTT), (THT), (TTH), and (TTT). It follows from this that $P(X = 2) = P(\text{HHT}) + P(\text{HTH}) + P(\text{THH}) = \frac{3}{8}$. By proceeding in the same way, we can obtain the probabilities for each possible value of X. Table 2.2 gives the density function $f(x)$ and the distribution function $F(x)$ for the four possible values of X.

The distribution is a member of a family of distributions known as the **binomial distribution**. It arises when there are only two possible outcomes to an experiment, one designated as a "success" and the other as a "failure." Let p be the probability of a success in a given trial. The probability of a failure is $1 - p$. Also assume that the probability of a success is the same for each trial and that the trials are independent. Let X be the number of successes in n independent trials. Then what is $f(x) = P(X = x)$?

TABLE 2.2   Probability and Cumulative Probability Density for the Number of Heads in Three Tosses of a Coin

X	0	1	2	3
$f(x)$	$\frac{1}{8}$	$\frac{3}{8}$	$\frac{3}{8}$	$\frac{1}{8}$
$F(x)$	$\frac{1}{8}$	$\frac{4}{8}$	$\frac{7}{8}$	1

First consider the special case of four trials and denote success by S and failure by F. A single success can occur in one of four ways ($SFFF$, $FSFF$, $FFSF$, $FFFS$). Each of these has the probability $p(1-p)^3$. Therefore, $f(1) = 4p(1-p)^3$. Two successes can occur in six distinct ways ($SSFF$, $SFSF$, $SFFS$, $FSSF$, $FSFS$, $FFSS$). The probability for this is $f(2) = 6p^2(1-p)^2$. Using the *factorial* notation $n! = n(n-1)\cdots 1$ this can also be written as $f(2) = \dfrac{4!}{2!2!}\,p^2(1-p)^2$. By a similar argument, $f(3)$ can be written as $f(3) = \dfrac{4!}{3!1!}\,p^3(1-p)$. The general form of the density function for the binomial distribution is given by (not proved)

$$B(x; n, p) = f(x) = \binom{n}{x}p^x q^{n-x} = \frac{n!}{x!(n-x)!}\,p^x q^{n-x} \qquad x = 0, 1, \ldots, n$$

where $1 - p = q$.

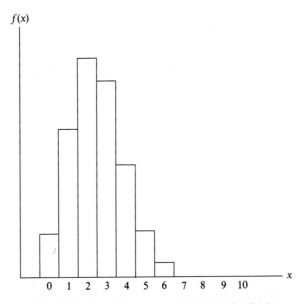

Figure 2.2   Bar diagram for a binomial distribution

Figure 2.2 is a representation of the binomial distribution for $n = 10$ and $p = 0.25$. It is called a **bar diagram** in which the x-axis represents the number of successes and the y-axis represents the probabilities. To give the appearance of continuity, the probability for x is attributed equally to all points in the interval $x - \frac{1}{2}$ to $x + \frac{1}{2}$.

Practice Problems

2.4　The science teacher in a high school gives a test consisting of 20 multiple choice questions with 4 answers to each of them of which only one is correct. One of the students who has been goofing off all semester decides to check off answers at random. What is the probability that he will get half of the questions right? (You need not actually calculate it, just write down the formula.)

2.5　A market research organization wants to test the claim that 60 percent of all residents of a certain area prefer Brand A cola drink to Brand B. It is decided to take a random sample of 18 persons and reject the claim if fewer than 9 of them prefer Brand A. What is the probability that the market research organization will make the error of rejecting the claim even though it is correct? (Use Table A.6 to compute the probability.)

The Normal Distribution

The most widely used continuous distribution is the **normal distribution** (also known as the *Gaussian distribution*). In its simplest form, known as the standard normal distribution (or **standardized normal**), its pdf is

$$f(x) = \frac{1}{\sqrt{2\pi}} e^{-x^2/2} \qquad -\infty < x < \infty$$

The normal density $f(x)$ is symmetric around the origin and is bell-shaped (see Figure 2.3. The cdf for a normal distribution is the shaded area to the left of x in Figure 2.3 $P(a \leq X \leq b)$ is given by the shaded area between a and b.

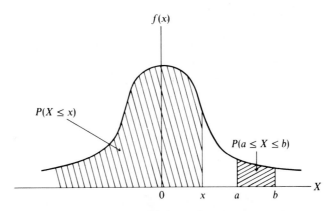

Figure 2.3　Graph of the standard normal density

2.2   Mathematical Expectation, Mean, and Variance

Consider the binomial experiment described earlier in which a coin is tossed three times. Suppose we were paid 3 dollars if the outcome were three heads, 2 dollars if there were two heads, 1 dollar if there was only one head, and none if all three tosses resulted in tails. On average, what would we expect to win per trial of three tosses? We note from Table 2.2. that in eight trials we can expect, *on average*, one event in which all three tosses are heads (resulting in a payoff of 3 dollars), three events with two heads (with a total payoff of 6 dollars, calculated as 2 dollars for each of the three events), and three events with one head (with a total payoff of 3 dollars). We can thus expect a grand total payoff of 12 dollars $(3 + 6 + 3)$ in eight trials, giving an average payoff of $1.50 per trial.

Mathematical Expectation and the Mean of a Distribution

The average value computed in the previous section is called the **expected value of** X (also known as the *mathematical expectation of* X and the *mean of the distribution of* X). It is also known as the *first moment around the origin*. It is denoted by $E(X)$ or by **μ**. $E(X)$ is a weighted average of X, with the weights being the corresponding probabilities. In the general case, suppose a discrete random variable can take the values $x_1, x_2, \ldots, x_n$. $P(X = x_i) = f(x_i)$ is its density function. If the payoff for the outcome $X = x_i$ were x_i dollars, the average payoff would be $x_1 f(x_1) + x_2 f(x_2) + \cdots + x_n f(x_n) = \sum[x_i f(x_i)]$, where $\sum$ denotes the summation over each of the terms, for $i = 1$ to n. We thus have the following general expression for the mean of a discrete distribution:

$$E(X) = \sum_{i=1}^{i=n} [x_i f(x_i)] \tag{2.1}$$

There is no reason why the payoff should be limited to x. It can be any function of x. Suppose the payoff were x^2. The average payoff would then be $\sum[x_i^2 f(x_i)]$. This is called the *second moment of the distribution of* X around the origin. The concept of mathematical expectation can be extended to any function of x. Thus we have the following definition.

Definition 2.7 (Expected Value)

For a discrete random variable, the expected value of the function $g(X)$ is defined as

$$E[g(X)] = \sum[g(x_i)f(x_i)] \tag{2.2}$$

Practice Problems

2.6   Suppose 10,000 one-dollar lottery tickets are sold and there are three prizes, first prize $5,000, second prize $2,000, and third prize $500. What is the expected win?

2.7 A baker has the following PDF for the demand for loaves of bread (in dozens per day).

x	0	1	2	3	4	5	6 or more
$f(x)$	.05	.10	.25	.30	.20	.10	0

What should the average stock be?

We write without proof a number of results involving expectations. It is recommended that these be studied carefully because they will be used frequently in later chapters. [Try and prove them.]

Property 2.2

a. $E(X - \mu) = E(X) - \mu = 0$.
b. If c is a constant or a nonrandom variable, $E(c) = c$.
c. If c is a constant or is nonrandom, $E[cg(X)] = cE[g(X)]$.
d. $E[u(X) + v(X)] = E[u(X)] + E[v(X)]$.

In words, the expected value of the deviation from the mean is zero. The expected value of a constant or a nonrandom variable is itself. The expected value of a constant times a random variable is the constant times the expected value. The expected value of a sum of functions of X is the sum of the expectations.

The Variance of a Random Variable

Let $\mu = E(X)$ be the mean of the distribution of X. A special case of the function $g(X)$, whose expectation was defined in equation (2.2), is of considerable interest. Let $g(X) = (X - \mu)^2$. $X - \mu$ is a measure of how far X deviates from the mean μ. Squaring this magnifies large deviations. The probability-weighted average of these squared deviations (or, more specifically, their expected value) is a measure of the dispersion of the values of X around the mean value μ. It is called the **variance of the distribution** (or the *second moment around the mean*) and is denoted by σ^2 or Var(X). Formally, we have the following definition.

Definition 2.8 (Variance)
The variance of X is defined as

$$\sigma^2 = \text{Var}(X) = E[(X - \mu)^2] = \sum(x_i - \mu)^2 f(x_i) \tag{2.3}$$

The positive square root (σ) of this is called the **standard deviation (s.d.)**. Property 2.3 lists several properties of the variance.

Property 2.3

a. $\sigma^2 = E[X^2 - 2\mu X + \mu^2] = E(X^2) - 2\mu E(X) + \mu^2 = E(X^2) - \mu^2.$
b. It follows from this that if c is a constant or is nonrandom, $\text{Var}(c) = 0.$
c. If a and b are constants or nonrandom, $\text{Var}(a + bX) = b^2\sigma^2.$

As an exercise, compute the mean, variance, and standard deviation for the PDF in Problem 2.7.

It can be shown that the binomial distribution discussed earlier has the mean $\mu = np$ and the variance $\sigma^2 = np(1 - p)$, where n is the number of trials and p is the probability of success of a single trial. The normal distribution, presented in Section 2.1, has mean zero and variance unity. A general normal distribution, with mean μ and variance σ^2, conventionally written as $N(\mu, \sigma^2)$, has the following density function:

$$f(x) = \frac{1}{(\sigma\sqrt{2\pi})} \exp\left[-\frac{(x - \mu)^2}{2\sigma^2}\right] \qquad -\infty < x < \infty \qquad (2.4)$$

where exp stands for the exponential function. If X is distributed normally, it is written as $X \sim N(\mu, \sigma^2)$. Three normal probability distributions are presented in Figure 2.4. Several properties of the normal distribution are listed in Property 2.4.

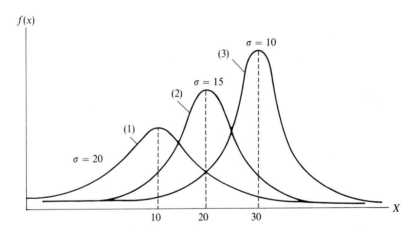

Figure 2.4   Three normal distributions

Property 2.4

The normal distribution, with mean μ and variance σ^2 [written as $N(\mu, \sigma^2)$] has the following properties:

a. It is symmetric around the mean value μ and has a bell shape.
b. The area under a normal curve between $\mu - \sigma$ and $\mu + \sigma$—that is, within 1 standard deviation from the mean—is slightly over $\frac{2}{3}$ (0.6826). About 95 percent of the area lies between 2 standard deviations from the mean—

that is, between $\mu - 2\sigma$ and $\mu + 2\sigma$. Approximately 99.7 percent of the area lies within 3 standard deviations from the mean. Thus, virtually the entire distribution lies between $\mu - 3\sigma$ and $\mu + 3\sigma$.

c. If X has the normal distribution, with mean μ and standard deviation σ, then the "standardized" random variable $Z = (X - \mu)/\sigma$ has the standard normal distribution $N(0, 1)$. Because of this property, the area between the points a and b in $N(\mu, \sigma^2)$ is the same as the area between the *standardized* endpoints $(a - \mu)/\sigma$ and $(b - \mu)/\sigma$. Table A.1 has the areas under the standard normal between the mean zero and various values of Z.

Example 2.2

A manufacturer of tires has found that the life time of a certain kind of tire is a normal random variable with a mean of 30,000 miles and standard deviation 2,000 miles. The company wishes to guarantee it for N miles with a full refund if the tire does not last that long. Suppose it wants to make sure that the probability that a tire will be returned is no more than 0.10 (that is, no more than 10% of the tires sold will be returned). What value of N should be chosen?

Let X be the life of the tire. Then X is distributed as $N(30000, 2000^2)$. We want $P(X \leq N) \leq 0.10$. $P(X \leq N) = P\left(\dfrac{X - \mu}{\sigma} \leq \dfrac{N - \mu}{\sigma} \right) \leq 0.10$. Let $Z = \dfrac{X - \mu}{\sigma}$ be the standard normal. Then $P\left(Z \leq \dfrac{N - \mu}{\sigma} \right) \leq 0.10$. From Table A.1 of the Appendix, we note that $P(0 \leq Z \leq 1.282) = 0.40$, which means that if $\dfrac{N - \mu}{\sigma} \leq -1.282$ then the above inequality will hold. Thus $N \leq \mu - 1.282\sigma = 30000 - (1.282)2000$, that is, $N \leq 27{,}436$ miles. $\qquad\square$

Besides the mean and variance of a distribution, there are other measures that characterize a distribution. These are described below.

Mode of a Distribution

The point(s) for which $f(x)$ is maximum is (are) called the **mode**. It is the most frequently observed value of X. Thus, for example, in Figure 2.2, the mode is 2.

Median, Upper and Lower Quartiles, and Percentiles

A value of x such that $P(X < x) \leq \frac{1}{2}$, and $P(X \leq x) \geq \frac{1}{2}$ is called a **median of the distribution**. If the point is unique, then it is *the* median. Thus the median is the point on either side of which lies 50 percent of the distribution. Instead of $\frac{1}{2}$, we could use any probability between 0 and 1. The point(s) with an area $\frac{1}{4}$ to the left is (are) called the **lower quartiles**, and the point(s) corresponding to $\frac{3}{4}$ are the **upper quartiles**. For any probability p, the values of x for which the area to the right is p are called the **upper pth percentiles** (sometimes also known as **quantiles**). Students who have taken the Scholastic Aptitude Test (SAT) or the Graduate Record Examination (GRE) should be familiar with the percentiles of an empirically observed distribution. Most people would also be familiar with median income, median value of property, and so on. The median is preferred as an "average" measure rather than the arithmetic mean because the latter might distort the picture if extreme values are present. For example, the income of a millionaire averaged with those of persons below 30,000 will result in a large mean.

Coefficient of Variation

The coefficient of variation is defined as the ratio σ/μ, where the numerator is the standard deviation and the denominator is the mean. It is a measure of the dispersion of a distribution *relative to its mean*. We will encounter this concept again in Chapter 14 on carrying out an empirical project.

Skewness and Kurtosis

If a distribution is not symmetric about the mean, then it is called **skewed**. Figure 2.5 gives two kinds of skewness, positive (that is, to the right with a long tail in that direction) and negative (that is, to the left). A commonly used measure of skewness is $\dfrac{[E(X - \mu)^3]}{\sigma^3}$. For a symmetric distribution such as the normal, this is zero.

The peakedness of a distribution is called **kurtosis**. A narrow distribution is called **leptokurtic** (like an Indian tepee) and a flat distribution is called **platykurtic** (like a platypus). These are illustrated in Figure 2.6. One measure of Kurtosis is $\dfrac{E(X - \mu)^4}{\sigma^4} - 3$. It is called **excess kurtosis**. For a normal distribution, kurtosis is 0, for a leptokurtic distribution it is positive and for a platykurtic distribution it is negative. In econometrics, skewness and kurtosis measures are often used to analyze the errors generated when a particular curve is fitted to the data. Practice Computer Session 2.2 illustrates the above measures for a sample data on the grade point averages of 427 students.

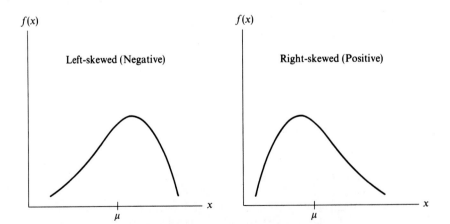

Figure 2.5 Skewness of a distribution

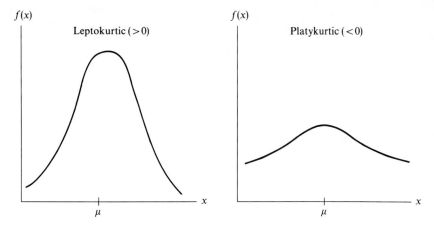

Figure 2.6   Kurtosis of a distribution

2.3   Joint Probability Distributions of Two Random Variables

Probability functions defined over a pair of random variables are known as *joint probability distributions* or as *bivariate distributions*. To keep the presentation simple, our discussion focuses only on discrete random variables. The generalization to the continuous case is quite straightforward, requiring the use of integrals instead of summations. Let X and Y be discrete random variables, and x and y be possible values they can respectively attain. The probability that $X = x$ and $Y = y$ is called the *joint density function* for X and Y and is denoted by $f_{XY}(x, y)$. Thus, $f_{XY}(x, y) = P(X = x, Y = y)$. Because a probability density function is generally represented by $f(\ )$, we use the subscript XY to identify the fact that the random variables in question are X and Y jointly.

As an example, consider the experiment of rolling a pair of dice. Let X be the number of 3s and Y be the number of 5s. There are 36 possible outcomes (6×6), each having a probability of $\frac{1}{36}$. X and Y can each take only the values 0, 1, and 2. It is easy to verify that the joint probabilities are as given in Table 2.3. For instance, the joint event $\{X = 1, Y = 1\}$ can occur only when the outcome is either (3, 5) or (5, 3), each with a probability of $\frac{1}{36}$. Therefore, $f(1, 1) = P(X = 1, Y = 1) = \frac{2}{36}$. Other probabilities are calculated similarly (verify these as a practice problem).

Marginal Densities

The probability density of X by itself is obtained by summing the probabilities over the Y values. Let $f_X(x) = P(X = x)$ be the density function of X alone. To calculate this note that the event $X = x$ can occur only in the three mutually exclusive ways $\{X = x, Y = 0\}$, $\{X = x, Y = 1\}$, and $\{X = x, Y = 2\}$. Therefore, $P(X = x) = P(X = x, Y = 0) + P(X = x, Y = 1) + P(X = x, Y = 2)$. For example, $P(X = 1) = \frac{8}{36} + \frac{2}{36} + 0 = \frac{10}{36}$. This is simply the sum of the probability entries in Table 2.3 that correspond to $X = 1$. We see from this that the numbers in the bottom

TABLE 2.3   Joint Probability Distribution for the Number of 3s (X) and the Number of 5s (Y) When a Pair of Dice is Rolled

X / Y	0	1	2	$f_Y(y)$
0	$\frac{16}{36}$	$\frac{8}{36}$	$\frac{1}{36}$	$\frac{25}{36}$
1	$\frac{8}{36}$	$\frac{2}{36}$	0	$\frac{10}{36}$
2	$\frac{1}{36}$	0	0	$\frac{1}{36}$
$f_X(x)$	$\frac{25}{36}$	$\frac{10}{36}$	$\frac{1}{36}$	1

row of Table 2.3 give $f_X(x)$. Similarly, the numbers in the extreme right-hand side column give $f_Y(y)$. These are called the *marginal density functions*.

Definition 2.9 (Marginal Density)
Let X be a discrete random variable that can take the values $x_1, x_2, \ldots, x_m$; Y be a discrete random variable that can take the values $y_1, y_2, \ldots, y_n$; and let $f_{XY}(x, y)$ be the joint density function. Then the marginal density of X is given by $f_X(x) = \sum_{j=1}^{j=n} f_{XY}(x, y_j)$ and that of Y is given by $f_Y(y) = \sum_{i=1}^{i=m} f_{XY}(x_i, y)$.

Conditional Probability
In the dice example given previously, we can calculate the probability that $Y = 0$ *given the condition* that $X = 1$. This is denoted by $P(Y = 0 \mid X = 1)$ and is obtained by dividing the joint probability $P(Y = 0, X = 1)$ by the marginal probability that $X = 1$ (see Definition 2.4 on conditional probability).

$$P(Y = 0 \mid X = 1) = P(Y = 0, X = 1) \div P(X = 1) = \tfrac{8}{36} \div \tfrac{10}{36} = 0.8$$

Similarly, $P(Y = 1 \mid X = 1) = 0.2$. The reason for dividing by $P(X = 1)$ is that the sum of the conditional probabilities, given $X = 1$, should equal 1. By proceeding similarly, we obtain the **conditional density** of Y given X, which is defined as the ratio of the joint density between X and $Y [f_{XY}(x, y)]$ divided by the marginal density of $X [f_X(x)]$. It is represented by $f_{Y \mid X}(x, y)$, the subscript denoting the fact that Y is conditional on X. It should be noted that the conditional probability will depend on both x and y.

Practice Problem
2.8   Derive the conditional densities of each of these cases separately; (1) Y given $X = 0$, (2) Y given $X = 2$, (3) X given $Y = 0$, (4) X given $Y = 1$, and (5) X given $Y = 2$.

Definition 2.10 (Conditional Density)
The conditional density of Y is defined as

$$f_{Y|X}(x, y) = \frac{f_{XY}(x, y)}{f_X(x)}$$

provided that $f_X(x) \neq 0$. The definition for the conditional density of X given Y is similar.

In the case of discrete random variables we have

$$P(Y = y \mid X = x) = P(Y = y, X = x)/P(X = x)$$

and

$$P(X = x \mid Y = y) = P(Y = y, X = x)/P(Y = y)$$

Conditional distributions and their properties are of a great deal of interest in econometric analyses. As mentioned in Chapter 1, the investigator is interested in the behavior of one or more **dependent variables** (denoted by Y) that are related to a number of **independent variables** (denoted by X). Forecasts of *dependent* variables are generally made *conditional on given values of the independent variables*. In the real estate example, for instance, a realtor would want to obtain a conditional prediction of the price of a house given its characteristics such as the living area, lot size, and so on.

Statistical Independence
The concept of independence introduced the Section 2.1 can be extended to joint probability densities. Suppose the probability that $Y = y$ given $X = x$ is the same as the probability that $Y = y$ for all x and y. In other words, the condition that $X = x$ does not alter the probability values of Y, and hence the conditional density is the same as the marginal density. We then say that X and Y are **statistically independent**. If X and Y are independent, then knowing that one of them has occurred does not affect the probability of occurrence of the other. As an example, let X be the outcome when a coin is tossed and let Y be the outcome when it is tossed a second time. The probability that X is a head is $\frac{1}{2}$. Whether the first toss resulted in a head or a tail, the probability of a head in the second toss is still $\frac{1}{2}$. The two events X and Y are thus statistically independent. Another example of independent random variables is the income of a person and the shoe size.

Definition 2.11 (Statistical Independence)
The random variables X and Y are said to be statistically independent if $f_{XY}(x, y) = f_X(x)f_Y(y)$ for all values of x and y for which $f_{XY}(x, y)$ is defined. Equivalently, X and Y are independent if $f_{X|Y}(x, y) = f_X(x)$ and $f_{Y|X}(x, y) = f_Y(y)$. In the case of a discrete random variable, this condition becomes

$P(X = x, Y = y) = P(X = x)P(Y = y)$. [It follows from this definition that $P(Y = y \mid X = x) = P(Y = y)$ and $P(X = x \mid Y = y) = P(X = x)$.]

Let us examine whether X and Y in Table 2.3 are independent. We have $P(X = 0, Y = 0) = \frac{16}{36}$. For X and Y to be independent, this should be equal to the product of $P(X = 0)$ and $P(Y = 0)$, each of which is $\frac{25}{36}$. We note that the condition for independence is not met and hence X and Y are statistically dependent. From the table we see that the probability that $X = 1$ is $\frac{10}{36}$. However, the probability that $X = 1$, given that $Y = 1$, is 0.2, calculated as $\frac{2}{36}[P(X = 1, Y = 1)]$ divided by $\frac{10}{36}[P(Y = 1)]$. We thus note that the information that Y is 1 (that is, that one of the dice shows a 5) does affect the probability that $X = 1$ (that is, that the other shows a 3).

Mathematical Expectation in a Two-Variable Case

The concept of mathematical expectation is easily extended to bivariate random variables. Given the function $g(X, Y)$ and the joint density function $f(x, y)$, the expected value of $g(X, Y)$ is obtained (again for the discrete case) by multiplying $g(x, y)$ by $f(x, y)$ and summing it over all the possible values of x and y. We thus have the following definition.

Definition 2.12 (Expected Value)

The expected value of $g(X, Y)$ is defined as

$$E[g(X, Y)] = \sum_{X=x} \sum_{Y=y} g(x, y)f(x, y)$$

where the double summation indicates summation over all the possible values of x and y. [The expectation is thus a weighted sum with the joint probability as the weight.]

Let μ_x be the expected value (that is, mean) of the random variable X, and let μ_y be the expected value of the random variable Y. Their variances are defined as in the univariate case:

$$\sigma_x^2 = E[(X - \mu_x)^2] \quad \text{and} \quad \sigma_y^2 = E[(Y - \mu_y)^2] \tag{2.5}$$

 Practice Problem

2.9   For the joint density given in Table 2.3, compute the means $\mu_x = E(X)$, $\mu_y = E(Y)$, and the variances σ_x^2, σ_y^2.

Covariance and Correlation

When we are dealing with two random variables, one of the main items of interest is how closely they are related. The concepts of **covariance** and **correlation** are two ways to measure the "closeness" of two random variables.

Consider the function $g(X, Y) = (X - \mu_x)(Y - \mu_y)$. The expected value of this function is called the **covariance between X and Y** and is denoted by σ_{xy} or by **Cov(X, Y)**.

Definition 2.13 (Covariance)

The covariance between X and Y is defined as

$$
\begin{aligned}
\sigma_{xy} = \text{Cov}(X, Y) &= E[(X - \mu_x)(Y - \mu_y)] \\
&= E[XY - X\mu_y - \mu_x Y + \mu_x \mu_y] \\
&= E(XY) - \mu_y E(X) - \mu_x E(Y) + \mu_x \mu_y \\
&= E(XY) - \mu_x \mu_y
\end{aligned}
\tag{2.6}
$$

The definitions of variance and covariance are the same for both discrete and continuous distributions. Just as variance is a measure of the dispersion of a random variable around its mean, the covariance between two random variables is a measure of the joint association between them. Suppose X and Y are positively related so that Y increases when X increases, as illustrated in Figure 2.7. The circles represent pairs of values of X and Y that are possible outcomes. The dashed lines indicate the means μ_x and μ_y. By translating the axes to the dashed lines with origin at (μ_x, μ_y), we can see that $X_i - \mu_x$ and $Y_i - \mu_y$ are the distances from the new origin, for a typical outcome denoted by the suffix i. It is readily seen from the figure that the points in the first and fourth quadrants will make the product $(X - \mu_x)(Y - \mu_y)$ positive, because the individual terms are either both positive or both negative. In

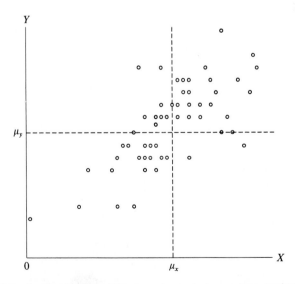

Figure 2.7 An illustration of the covariance between two random variables

contrast, the points in the second and fourth quadrants will make the product negative, because one of the terms is positive and the other is negative. When we compute the covariance measure, which is a weighted sum of these products, the net result is likely to be positive because there are more positive terms than the opposite. Therefore, the covariance is likely to be positive. In the case when X and Y move in opposite directions, $\text{Cov}(X, Y)$ will be negative.

Although the covariance measure is useful in identifying the nature of the association between X and Y, it has a serious problem—namely, the numerical value is very sensitive to the units in which X and Y are measured. If X were a financial variable measured in dollars rather than in thousands of dollars, the covariance measure would go up by a factor of 1000. To avoid this problem, a "normalized" covariance measure is used. This measure is called the **correlation coefficient** between X and Y and is denoted as ρ_{xy}.

Definition 2.14 (Coefficient of Correlation)

The coefficient of correlation between X and Y is defined as

$$\rho_{xy} = \frac{\sigma_{xy}}{\sigma_x \sigma_y} = \frac{\text{Cov}(X, Y)}{[\text{Var}(X)\text{Var}(Y)]^{1/2}} \tag{2.7}$$

If X and Y are positively related, the correlation coefficient will be positive. If X and Y are negatively related, they will move in opposite directions. In this case, the covariance and correlation coefficient will both be negative. It is possible for the correlation coefficient to be zero. In this case, we say that x and y are uncorrelated. It can be shown that $\rho_{xy}^2 \leq 1$ or equivalently that $|\rho_{xy}| \leq 1$. $|\rho_{xy}|$ will be equal to 1 if and only if there is an exact *linear relation* between X and Y of the form $Y - \mu_y = \beta(X - \mu_x)$. If $|\rho_{xy}| = 1$, then X and Y are said to be perfectly correlated. It should be noted that perfect correlation occurs only when X and Y are *exactly linearly related*. Thus, for instance, Y may be of the form $Y = X^2$, which is an exact relation, but the correlation coefficient between X and Y will not be 1. The coefficient of correlation thus measures the extent of linear association between two variables.

If X and Y are independent, $f_{XY}(x, y) = f_X(x)f_Y(y)$. Note from the definition of σ_{xy} that in this case,

$$\sigma_{xy} = \sum_x \sum_y (x - \mu_x)(y - \mu_y)f_X(x)f_Y(y)$$

Because x and y are now separable, we have

$$\sigma_{xy} = \left[\sum_x (x - \mu_x)f_X(x)\right]\left[\sum_y (y - \mu_y)f_Y(y)\right]$$

$$= E(X - \mu_x)E(Y - \mu_y)$$

TABLE 2.4 An Example Showing That Zero Covariance Need Not Imply Independence

X \ Y	6	8	10	$f_X(x)$
1	0.2	0	0.2	0.4
2	0	0.2	0	0.2
3	0.2	0	0.2	0.4
$f_Y(y)$	0.4	0.2	0.4	1

But $E(X - \mu_x) = E(X) - \mu_x = 0$ (see Property 2.2a). Hence $\sigma_{xy} = 0$ and $\rho_{xy} = 0$ if two random variables are independent. In other words, *if X and Y are independent random variables, then they are uncorrelated.*

The converse need not be true (that is, zero correlation need not imply independence), as may be seen from the following counterexample. Let $f_{XY}(x, y)$ be as in Table 2.4.

$$\text{Cov}(X, Y) = E(XY) - E(X)E(Y)$$
$$E(X) = (1 \times 0.4) + (2 \times 0.2) + (3 \times 0.4) = 2$$
$$E(Y) = (6 \times 0.4) + (8 \times 0.2) + (10 \times 0.4) = 8$$
$$E(XY) = (6 \times 1 \times 0.2) + (6 \times 3 \times 0.2) + (8 \times 2 \times 0.2) + (10 \times 1 \times 0.2)$$
$$+ (10 \times 3 \times 0.2) = 16$$

Hence $\text{Cov}(X, Y) = 0$. But X and Y are not independent because $P(X = 2, Y = 6) = 0$, $P(X = 2) = 0.2$, and $P(Y = 6) = 0.4$. Hence the joint probability is not the product of individual probabilities.

 Practice Problems

2.10 For the random variables X and Y with joint probabilities given in Table 2.3, compute $\text{Cov}(X, Y)$ and ρ_{xy}. [Note that you have already computed the means and variances in Problem 2.9.]

2.11 Suppose the random variable X can assume only the values 1, 2, 3, 4, and 5, each with equal probability. Let $Y = X^2$. Compute the coefficient of correlation between X and Y and show that it is not equal to 1, even though X and Y have an exact relationship.

Property 2.5 lists a number of properties involving two random variables.

Property 2.5

a. If a and b are constants, then $\text{Var}(aX + bY) = a^2 \text{Var}(X) + b^2 \text{Var}(Y) + 2ab \text{Cov}(X, Y)$. As a special case of this, $\text{Var}(X + Y) = \text{Var}(X) + \text{Var}(Y) + 2 \text{Cov}(X, Y)$. Also, $\text{Var}(X - Y) = \text{Var}(X) + \text{Var}(Y) - 2 \text{Cov}(X, Y)$.

b. The correlation coefficient ρ_{xy} lies between -1 and $+1$.

c. If X and Y are independent, then $\sigma_{xy} = \text{Cov}(X, Y) = 0 = \rho_{xy}$; that is, X and Y are uncorrelated. It follows from this and (a) that, in this case, $\text{Var}(X + Y) = \text{Var}(X) + \text{Var}(Y)$ and $\text{Var}(X - Y) = \text{Var}(X) + \text{Var}(Y)$.

d. $|\rho_{xy}|$ will be equal to 1 if and only if there is an exact linear relation between X and Y of the form $Y - \mu_y = \beta(X - \mu_x)$.

e. The correlation between X and itself is 1.

f. If $U = a_0 + a_1 X + a_2 Y$ and $V = b_0 + b_1 X + b_2 Y$, then $\rho_{uv} \neq \rho_{xy}$. This means that correlation is not invariant under a linear transformation.

Conditional Mean

In the earlier discussion on conditional probabilities we mentioned that econometric analysis is predominantly concerned with the conditional distribution of dependent variables given the values of the independent variables. The mean of the conditional distribution is of particular interest in econometrics. Given a value of the random variable X, another random variable Y associated with it will have a range of possible values, giving rise to the probability distribution of Y given X. Because every outcome of Y may not be forecastable, we may have to restrict our attention to the average value of Y associated with the given value of X. This average is the **conditional mean of Y given X** (also known as the **regression of Y on X**).

Definition 2.15 (Conditional Mean)
The conditional mean of Y given X (also known as the regression of Y on X) is defined as

$$E(Y \mid X) = \sum_y y f_{Y\mid X}(x, y) \tag{2.8}$$

The conditional mean of Y given X is thus the expected value of Y, calculated using as weights the probability that $Y = y$, given that $X = x$. Because the summation is over all the values of y, $E(Y \mid X)$ is a function of X only.

In Chapter 1, we introduced the simple linear regression model $\text{PRICE} = \alpha + \beta\text{SQFT} + u$ [equation (1.1)] and stated that u is a random variable with certain statistical properties. As can be seen from Figure 1.2, u is the deviation of the actual price from the value $\alpha + \beta\text{SQFT}$. When discussing Figure 1.2, we fixed the value of SQFT at a certain level and plotted the values of PRICE that corresponded to this SQFT. The distribution of PRICE obtained this way is precisely the conditional distribution of PRICE, given the value of SQFT. We also computed the average of the PRICE values for each fixed level of SQFT. This average is the same as the conditional mean or conditional expectation. The conditional expectation of PRICE given SQFT is $E(\text{PRICE}\mid\text{SQFT}) = \alpha + \beta\text{SQFT} + E(u\mid\text{SQFT}) = \alpha + \beta\text{SQFT}$, if $E(u\mid\text{SQFT}) = 0$. Thus, if the stochastic error term u

is such that its conditional mean is zero (which is a reasonable assumption, as can be seen from Figure 1.2), then the deterministic part of the model ($\alpha + \beta$SQFT) is nothing but $E(\text{PRICE} | \text{SQFT})$.

Multivariate Distributions

All the preceding concepts can be extended to more than two random variables. This topic is covered in more detail in the appendix to this chapter (Section 2.A.1). A number of useful results on multivariate distributions that will be needed later on are summarized in Property 2.6. Properties involving the variances of sums of random variables are described in Section 2.A.1.

Property 2.6

> a. If $a_1, a_2, \ldots, a_n$ are constants, then $E[a_1x_1 + a_2x_2 + \cdots + a_nx_n] = a_1E(x_1) + a_2E(x_2) + \cdots + a_nE(x_n)$. Thus, the expectation of a linear combination of terms is the linear combination of the expectations. In summation notation, $E\left[\sum(a_ix_i)\right] = \sum E(a_ix_i) = \sum a_iE(x_i)$.
> b. If each x_i has the same mean so that $E(x_i) = \mu$, we have $E(\sum a_ix_i) = \mu\sum a_i$. In particular, if the a_i's are all equal to $1/n$, we have $E(\sum x_i/n) = E(\bar{x}) = \mu$. Thus, the expected value of the mean of several identically distributed random variables is equal to their common mean.

2.4   The Chi-Square, *t*-, and *F*-distributions

In testing hypotheses on econometric models, four distributions are used predominantly. These are the *normal, chi-square, Student's t-, and Fisher's F-distributions*. The normal distribution and its properties have already been examined. In this section, we discuss the other three distributions.

The Chi-square Distribution

The distribution of the sum of squares of n independent standard normal random variables is called the **chi-square (χ^2) distribution** with n degrees of freedom and is written as χ_n^2. More formally, consider the n random variables $Z_1, Z_2, \ldots, Z_n$, all of which are independently and identically distributed (iid) as the standard normal $N(0, 1)$. Define a new random variable X that is the sum of the squares of the Zs. Thus

$$X = Z_1^2 + Z_2^2 + \cdots + Z_n^2 = \sum Z_i^2$$

The distribution of the random variable X is χ_n^2. Because X is nonnegative, the chi-square distribution is defined only over $0 \leq x < \infty$. The density function of χ_n^2 depends on only one parameter, called the **degrees of freedom** (frequently abbreviated as **d.f.**). The mean of χ_n^2 can be shown to be n. Figure 2.8 presents the graphs of the chi-square densities for a number of selected values of the degrees of freedom. We note that when $n = 1$, the density function is strictly decreasing.

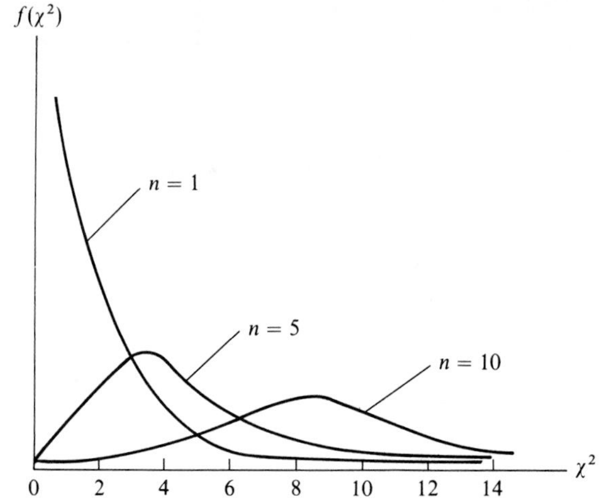

Figure 2.8 Chi-square distribution for d.f. (n) 1, 5, and 10

For higher degrees of freedom, it rises quickly to a maximum but tapers off slowly to the right with a long "tail." A number of properties of the χ^2 distribution are summarized in Property 2.7.

Property 2.7

a. The chi-square distribution has the additive property; namely, if $X \sim \chi_m^2$ and $Y \sim \chi_n^2$ with X and Y independent, then their sum $X + Y \sim \chi_{m+n}^2$. It follows from this that the sum of several independent chi-square random variables is also chi-square.

b. If $x_1, x_2, \ldots, x_n$ are independent and normally distributed random variables with mean μ_i and variance σ_i^2, then the sum of squares $U = \sum (x_i - \mu_i)^2 / \sigma_i^2$ has the chi-square distribution with n d.f. This result follows from the fact that $Z_i = (x_i - \mu_i)/\sigma_i$ has the standard normal distribution and the Zs are independent, thus making their sum of squares χ_n^2. As a special case of this, if $\mu_i = \mu$ and $\sigma_i^2 = \sigma^2$—that is, if the Zs are iid—then $\sum (x_i - \mu)^2 / \sigma^2 \sim \chi_n^2$.

Table A.3 of Appendix A presents the values of χ^2 for which the areas to the right correspond to specified probabilities. Section 2.10 on testing hypotheses illustrates the use of the chi-square distribution.

The Student's *t*-distribution

The distribution of the ratio of a normal variate to the square root of an independent χ_n^2 is called the **Student's *t*-distribution** with n degrees of freedom (and is written as t_n). Suppose $Z \sim N(0, 1)$ and $U \sim \chi_n^2$, with Z and U independent. Define the random variable $t = Z/\sqrt{U/n} = (Z\sqrt{n})/\sqrt{U}$. The distribution of t is the t-distribution.

Table A.2 presents the values of t for which the areas in the tails correspond to specified probabilities. Some of the properties of the t-distribution are listed in Property 2.8.

Property 2.8

> The t-distribution with n d.f. has the following properties:
>
> a. The t-distribution is symmetric around the origin and has a shape similar to that of the normal distribution.
> b. For large n, the t-distribution is approximately distributed as $N(0, 1)$. The approximation is quite good even for $n = 30$.

The *F*-distribution

Another distribution of considerable interest in econometrics is Fisher's **F-distribution**. It is the ratio of two independent chi-squares. Let $U \sim \chi^2_m$ and $V \sim \chi^2_n$ be independent of each other. Then the distribution of $F = (U/m) \div (V/n)$ is called the F-distribution with m and n d.f., and it is written as $F \sim F_{m,n}$. The first number is the degrees of freedom for the numerator and the second number is the degrees of freedom for the denominator. Tables A.4a, A.4b, and A.4c have values of F for several combinations of m, n, and the probabilities 0.01, 0.05, and 0.10. Some of the properties of the F-distribution are listed in Property 2.9.

Practice Computer Session 2.3 gives you practice in calculating probabilities for normal, chi-square, t-, and F-distributions.

Property 2.9

> The F-distribution with m and n d.f. has the following properties:
>
> a. The F-distribution has a shape similar to that of a chi-square.
> b. If the random variable t has the Student's t-distribution with n d.f., then t^2 has the F-distribution with d.f. 1 and n. Thus, $t^2_n \sim F_{1,n}$.

2.5 Random Sampling

A statistical investigation arises out of the need to solve a particular problem. It might be an attempt to rationalize past behavior of agents or to forecast their future behavior. In formulating the problem, it is important to identify the relevant *statistical universe*, or the *population*, which is the totality of elements about which some information is desired. The term *population* is used in a general sense and is not restricted to living things. All the seeds in a storage bin, all the firms in a city, and all the bottles of milk produced by a dairy are examples of populations. Sometimes a population is also referred to as the **parent population**.

An analyst is interested in drawing inferences about several attributes of a population. It would clearly be prohibitively expensive to study every element of a population in order to derive the inferences. The investigator would therefore draw a sample of the elements, make observations on them, and use these observations to draw conclusions about the characteristics of the parent population that the sample represents. This process is known as *sampling*. Several types of sampling are possible: random sampling, judgment sampling, selective sampling, sampling with and without replacement, stratified sampling, and so on. In this book we focus our attention only on **random sampling**, the most common type of sampling.

Definition 2.16 (Random Sampling)

A simple random sample of *n* elements is a sample that has the property that every combination of *n* elements has an equal chance of being the selected sample. A random sample of observations on a random variable X is a set of **independent, identically distributed (iid)** random variables $X_1, X_2, \ldots, X_n$, each of which has the same probability distribution as that of X.

It should be stressed that even though an observation on a random variable is simply a measured attribute, conceptually the observation is itself a random variable. Thus, if we select a person at random and measure his or her height, we obtain a numerical value. However, it is still a random variable because if we select another person at random, we will observe another value. A single observation from this experiment is hence a random variable, even though it has a specific numerical value. As such, it has a probability density function.

An important and useful consequence of obtaining a random sample of observations on a random variable is that the joint density function of the random sample assumes a simple form. To see this, let X be a discrete random variable with the probability density function $f(x)$. Let $x_1, x_2, \ldots, x_n$ be a random sample of observations from this distribution. Then their joint density function is $f(x_1, x_2, \ldots, x_n) = P(X = x_1, X = x_2, \ldots, X = x_n)$. In Definition 2.11 we stated that if two random variables are independent, then their joint density function is the product of the individual density functions. The same result holds for any number of independent random variables. Therefore, the joint probability density of the x's is simply the product of individual probability densities. Hence,

$$f(x_1, x_2, \ldots, x_n) = f(x_1)f(x_2) \cdots f(x_n) = \prod_{i=1}^{i=n} f(x_i) \qquad (2.9)$$

where the symbol $\prod$ is the notation for a product and is similar to the summation symbol $\sum$.

2.6 Sampling Distributions

It was pointed out in Section 2.5 that observations on a random variable are themselves random variables, even though they have specific values. It follows, therefore, that any function of these observations is also a random variable and hence would have its own probability distribution. A function of the observed random variables that does not contain any unknown parameters is called a **sample statistic**. The two most frequently used sample statistics are the **sample mean** (denoted by $\bar{x}$) and the **sample variance** (denoted by s^2):

$$\text{Sample mean:} \quad \bar{x} = (x_1 + x_2 + \cdots + x_n)/n = \frac{1}{n}\sum x_i \qquad (2.10)$$

$$\text{Sample variance:} \quad s^2 = \frac{1}{n-1}(x_1 - \bar{x})^2 + \frac{1}{n-1}(x_2 - \bar{x})^2$$

$$+ \cdots + \frac{1}{n-1}(x_n - \bar{x})^2 \qquad (2.11)$$

$$= \frac{1}{n-1}\sum(x_i - \bar{x})^2$$

The reason for dividing by $n - 1$ rather than by n is given in the next section. The square root of the sample variance is called the **sample standard deviation**. The distinction between a sample statistic and a **population parameter** must be clearly understood. Suppose the random variable X has expected value μ and variance σ^2. These are the population parameters that are fixed and not random. In contrast, however, the sample mean $\bar{x}$ and the sample variance s^2 are random variables. This is because different trials of an experiment will result in different values for the sample mean and variance. Because these sample statistics are random variables, it makes sense to talk about their distributions. If we draw a random sample of size n and compute the sample mean $\bar{x}$, we get a certain value. Repeat this experiment an infinite number of times, each time drawing a random sample of the same size n. We will obtain an infinite number of values for the sample mean. We can then compute the fraction of times these mean values fall in a specified interval. This gives the *probability that the sample mean will lie in that interval* (refer to the frequency definition of probability presented in Section 2.1). By varying this interval, we can obtain the whole range of probabilities, thus generating a probability distribution. This distribution is called the **distribution of the sample mean**. In a similar manner, we can compute the sample variance for each replication of the trial, and use the various values generated this way to obtain the **distribution of the sample variance**. Because the sample mean and variance were for a sample of the specified size n, we would expect their sampling distributions to depend on n as well as on the parameters of the parent distribution from which the sample was drawn.

Sampling from a Normal Population

The sampling distributions of the mean and the sample variance are of considerable interest in econometrics and statistics, especially when the parent population from which the observations are drawn has the normal distribution. Let X be a random variable that has the normal distribution with mean μ and variance σ^2. Thus $X \sim N(\mu, \sigma^2)$. Let us draw a random sample of size n from this population, measure the random variable, and obtain the observations $x_1, x_2, \ldots, x_n$. What are the sampling distributions of $\bar{x}$ and s^2? We note that the sample mean is a linear combination of n random variates. From Property 2.A.1e of Section 2.A.1 we see that this linear combination also has a normal distribution. In particular, $\bar{x}$ also has mean μ and $\text{Var}(\bar{x}) = \sigma^2/n$. We thus have the following property.

Property 2.10

a. If a random sample $x_1, x_2, \ldots, x_n$ is drawn from a normal population with mean μ and variance σ^2, the sample mean $\bar{x}$ is distributed normally with mean μ and variance σ^2/n. Thus, $\bar{x} \sim N(\mu, \sigma^2/n)$. We note from this that the distribution of the sample mean has a smaller dispersion around the mean, and the larger the sample size the smaller the variance.

b. The distribution of $Z = (\bar{x} - \mu)/(\sigma/\sqrt{n}) = \sqrt{n}(\bar{x} - \mu)/\sigma$ is $N(0, 1)$.

The distribution of the sample variance s^2 defined in equation (2.11) is also of considerable interest. Note that $(n - 1)s^2 = \sum(x_i - \bar{x})^2$ is the sum of squares of the deviations of a typical observation from the sample mean. We know that $x_i - \bar{x}$ has the normal distribution because it is a linear combination of the x's, which are normal. In Section 2.4 we saw that the chi-square was defined as the sum of squares of independent normal random variables. In Property 2.7b we stated that $\sum(x_i - \mu)^2/\sigma^2$ is distributed as χ_n^2. Can we infer from this that $\sum(x_i - \bar{x})^2/\sigma^2$ also has the chi-square distribution? The answer is yes, but with a slight modification. Although this sum of squares also has the chi-square distribution, its degrees of freedom is $n - 1$ and not n. By substituting $\bar{x}$ for μ, we "lose a degree of freedom." This is because the deviations $(x_i - \bar{x})$ are not independent, even though the x_i's are. The total deviation $\sum(x_i - \bar{x})$ is always zero, and hence we can designate only $n - 1$ of them independently. The nth one would be determined by the condition that the n deviations must add up to zero. Hence $(n - 1)s^2/\sigma^2$ has the chi-square distribution with d.f. $n - 1$. This and other related properties are summarized in Property 2.11.

Property 2.11

a. If a random sample $x_1, x_2, \ldots, x_n$ is drawn from a normal population with mean μ and variance σ^2, the sample variance $s^2 = \dfrac{1}{n - 1}\sum(x_i - \bar{x})^2$ has the property that $(n - 1)s^2/\sigma^2 = \sum(x_i - \bar{x})^2/\sigma^2 \sim \chi_{n-1}^2$.

b. Because the mean of a χ^2 is its d.f.—that is, $E(\chi_m^2) = m$—$E\left[\dfrac{(n-1)s^2}{\sigma^2}\right] = n - 1$. It follows from this that $E(s^2) = \sigma^2$. We now see the reason for dividing $\sum(x_i - \bar{x})^2$ by $n - 1$. If we had used n instead, the expected value would not have been equal to σ^2.

c. We know from Property 2.10b that $Z = \sqrt{n}(\bar{x} - \mu)/\sigma \sim N(0, 1)$. Also from Property 2.11a, $U = (n - 1)s^2/\sigma^2 \sim \chi_{n-1}^2$. It can be shown that Z is independent of U. We note from the definition of the t-distribution in Section 2.4 that it is derived as the ratio of a standard normal to the square root of a chi-square. Thus, $t = Z/\sqrt{U/(n - 1)}$. Substituting for Z and

U from above and simplifying the terms, we get the result that $t = \sqrt{n}(\bar{x} - \mu)/s \sim t_{n-1}$. Comparing this with Property 2.10b, we note that if σ is replaced by s, the resulting distribution is no longer normal but is a t-distribution.

2.7 Properties of Estimators

We have discussed the particular topics in probability and statistics given so far in order to prepare ourselves for the two basic objectives of any empirical study: the estimation of unknown parameters and the testing of hypotheses. In this and the next two sections we discuss the problem of estimation. Hypothesis testing is covered in Section 2.10.

In an empirical investigation, the analyst very often knows, or can approximate, the general form of the probability distributions of the random variables of interest. The specific values of the population parameters of the distributions are, however, unknown. As mentioned earlier, a complete census of the population is out of the question because of the enormous cost that would involve. The investigator therefore obtains a sample of observations on the variables of interest and uses them to draw inferences about the underlying probability distribution.

As an illustration, suppose we know that the height of a person is approximately normally distributed but we don't know the mean μ of the distribution or its variance σ^2. The problem of estimation is simply one of selecting a sample of people, measuring each person's height, and then using the measurements to obtain estimates of μ and σ^2. The term **estimator** is used to refer to the formula that gives us a numerical value of the parameter of interest. The numerical value itself is referred to as an **estimate**. In this example, an obvious estimator for μ is the sample mean $\bar{x}$. An alternative estimator is to take the heights of the tallest and shortest persons and average them. Which estimator is better? In order to answer this question, we need some criteria for choosing among alternative estimators. Numerous criteria have been developed to judge the "goodness" of an estimator, but we discuss in the following sections only those concepts that are most frequently used in econometrics. Some of them refer to small samples and others are appropriate only for large samples.

Small-Sample Properties of Estimators

The standard notation to denote an unknown parameter is θ and an estimator is denoted by $\hat{\theta}$. It should be emphasized that $\hat{\theta}$ is a function of the observations $x_1, x_2, \ldots, x_n$ and does not depend on any unknown parameters. An estimator is thus a sample statistic. However, because the x's are random variables, so is $\hat{\theta}$.

Unbiasedness Because $\hat{\theta}$ is a random variable, it has a probability distribution with a certain mean, which is $E(\hat{\theta})$. If this mean is the same as the unknown parameter θ, we say that the estimator is **unbiased**. Thus we have the following definition.

Definition 2.17 (Unbiasedness)
An estimator $\hat{\theta}$ is said to be an unbiased estimator of θ if $E(\hat{\theta}) = \theta$. If this equality does not hold, the estimator is said to be biased and the bias is $E(\hat{\theta}) - \theta$.

Although in a given trial $\hat{\theta}$ may not equal θ, if we repeat the trial an infinite number of times and compute $\hat{\theta}$ each time, the average of these values should be θ if the estimator is to be unbiased.

Efficiency While unbiasedness is clearly a desirable characteristic for any estimator to possess, we need additional criteria because it is possible to construct an infinite number of unbiased estimators. In the example of measuring heights, we know that the sample mean $\bar{x}$ is unbiased because $E(\bar{x}) = \mu$. But the alternative estimator, proposed earlier, that averages the height of the tallest person (call it x_{max}) and that of the shortest person (call it x_{min}) is also unbiased. Let $\hat{\theta} = \frac{1}{2}(x_{max} + x_{min})$. Then $E(\hat{\theta}) = \frac{1}{2}[E(x_{max}) + E(x_{min})] = \mu$ and hence $\hat{\theta}$ is also unbiased. It is easy to verify that any weighted average of the x's is an unbiased estimator of μ, provided the weights add up to 1. We therefore need more criteria to distinguish between two unbiased estimators.

We have seen that the variance of a random variable is a measure of its dispersion around the mean. A smaller variance means that, on average, the values of the random variable are closer to the mean than those for another random variable with the same mean but a higher variance. This suggests that we could use the variances of two different unbiased estimators as a means of choosing between the two. The one with the smaller variance is clearly more desirable because, on average, it is closer to the true mean θ. This is the concept of **efficiency**.

Definition 2.18 (Efficiency)
a. Let $\hat{\theta}_1$ and $\hat{\theta}_2$ be two unbiased estimators of the parameter θ. If $\text{Var}(\hat{\theta}_1) < \text{Var}(\hat{\theta}_2)$, then we say that $\hat{\theta}_1$ is more efficient than $\hat{\theta}_2$.
b. The ratio $[\text{Var}(\hat{\theta}_1)]/[\text{Var}(\hat{\theta}_2)]$ is called the relative efficiency.
c. Among all the unbiased estimators of θ, the one with the smallest variance is called the minimum variance unbiased estimator.

Let us apply this to the height example. Let $\hat{\theta}_1$ be the sample mean and $\hat{\theta}_2$ be the mean of the heights of the tallest and shortest persons. From Property 2.10a, $\text{Var}(\hat{\theta}_1) = \sigma^2/n$ and $\text{Var}(\hat{\theta}_2) = \sigma^2/2$. If the sample size is more than two, $\hat{\theta}_1$ has a smaller variance and hence is clearly preferable. Thus, $\hat{\theta}_1$ is more efficient than $\hat{\theta}_2$.

Mean Squared Error   Consider two estimators: One is unbiased and the other, though biased, has a much smaller variance, indicating that, on average, it might be closer to the true mean than the unbiased estimator. In this case, we might be willing to allow some bias in order to gain on the variance side. A measure that permits this trade-off between unbiasedness and variance is the **mean squared error**.

Definition 2.19 (Mean Squared Error)

a. The mean squared error of an estimator $\hat{\theta}$ is defined as $\text{MSE}(\theta) = E[(\hat{\theta} - \theta)^2]$, which is the expected value of the square of the deviation of $\hat{\theta}$ from θ.

b. If $\hat{\theta}_1$ and $\hat{\theta}_2$ are two alternative estimators of θ and $\text{MSE}(\hat{\theta}_1) < \text{MSE}(\hat{\theta}_2)$, then $\hat{\theta}_1$ is said to be mean squared efficient compared to $\hat{\theta}_2$. If they are both unbiased, $\hat{\theta}_1$ is more efficient, as in Definition 2.18a.

c. Among all possible estimators of θ, the one with the smallest mean squared error is called the minimum mean squared error estimator.

It is easy to show that the mean squared error is equal to the sum of the variance and the square of the bias. Thus, if $b(\theta) = E(\hat{\theta}) - \theta$ is the bias in the estimator $\hat{\theta}$, then $\text{MSE} = \text{Var}(\hat{\theta}) + [b(\theta)]^2$. Note that $b(\theta)$ is independent of the x's and is hence fixed and nonrandom.

$$\text{MSE} = E[(\hat{\theta} - \theta)^2] = E[\hat{\theta} - E(\hat{\theta}) + E(\hat{\theta}) - \theta]^2$$
$$= E[\hat{\theta} - E(\hat{\theta}) + b(\theta)]^2 = E[\hat{\theta} - E(\hat{\theta})]^2 + [b(\theta)]^2 + 2b(\theta)E[\hat{\theta} - E(\hat{\theta})]$$

The first term is the variance of $\hat{\theta}$ and the third term is zero because $E(\hat{\theta})$ is nonrandom and hence $E[\hat{\theta} - E(\hat{\theta})] = E(\hat{\theta}) - E(\hat{\theta}) = 0$. The desired result follows immediately.

The concept of mean squared error is more frequently used to choose among alternative forecasts of a random variable (see Chapter 11). Forecasts are often biased—that is, they systematically overestimate or underestimate the variable of interest—but some of them may have a smaller variance. The mean squared error is therefore a useful measure for taking account of both the bias and the variance of a forecast.

Best Linear Unbiased Estimator (BLUE)   We saw earlier that every weighted average of the x's is an unbiased estimator of the mean, provided the weights add up to 1. A general estimator of the form $\hat{\theta} = a_1 x_1 + a_2 x_2 + \cdots + a_n x_n = \sum a_i x_i$ (a_i's being constants or nonrandom variables) is called a **linear estimator** of θ. Among the class of all linear estimators of θ that are also unbiased, the one with the smallest variance is called the **best linear unbiased estimator**, or **BLUE**.

Definition 2.20 (Best Linear Unbiased Estimator)

a. An estimator of the form $\hat{\theta} = a_1 x_1 + a_2 x_2 + \cdots + a_n x_n = \sum a_i x_i$, where the a_i's are constants or other nonrandom variables, is called a linear estimator.

b. Among all linear unbiased estimators, the one with the lowest variance is called the best linear unbiased estimator, or BLUE.

An estimator of θ that has the BLUE property thus satisfies three conditions: (1) It is expressed as a linear sum of the observations; (2) it is unbiased, that is, has expected value equal to θ; and (3) the variance of the estimator is no larger than that of any other estimator satisfying conditions (1) and (2).

Large-Sample Properties of Estimators

All the properties discussed previously are applicable to samples of finite sizes. Sometimes an estimator may not possess one or more of the desirable properties in a small sample, but when the size of the sample is large, many of the desirable properties might hold. It is therefore of interest to study these large-sample, or *asymptotic*, properties. In the following discussions we let the sample size n increase indefinitely. Because an estimator will depend on n, we denote it as $\hat{\theta}_n$.

Asymptotic Unbiasedness   The bias in an estimator is the difference between its expected value and the true parameter θ. This bias might depend on the sample size n. If the bias goes to zero as n increases to infinity, we say that the estimator is *asymptotically unbiased*.

Definition 2.21 (Asymptotic Unbiasedness)

An estimator $\hat{\theta}_n$ is said to be asymptotically unbiased if $\lim_{n\to\infty} E(\hat{\theta}_n) = \theta$, or, equivalently, if $\lim_{n\to\infty} b_n(\theta) = 0$, where $b_n(\theta) = E(\hat{\theta}_n) - \theta$.

Consistency   The most frequently used large-sample property is that of **consistency**. In intuitive terms, consistency means that, as n increases, the estimator $\hat{\theta}_n$ approaches the true value θ. In other words, we draw a random sample of any size from a large population, and compute $\hat{\theta}$. Next we draw one more observation and recompute $\hat{\theta}$ with this extra observation. We repeat this process indefinitely, getting a sequence of estimates for θ. If this sequence converges to θ as n increases to infinity, then $\hat{\theta}$ is a consistent estimator of θ. The formal definition of consistency is given in Definition 2.22.

Definition 2.22 (Consistency)
An estimator $\hat{\theta}_n$ is said to be a consistent estimator of θ if $\lim_{n\to\infty} P(\theta - \epsilon \leq \hat{\theta}_n \leq \theta + \epsilon) = 1$, for all $\epsilon > 0$. This property is expressed as $p \lim(\hat{\theta}_n) = \theta$.

Let us look at this definition more carefully. Consider the fixed (that is, non-random) interval $(\theta - \epsilon, \theta + \epsilon)$, where ϵ is any positive number. Because $\hat{\theta}_n$ is an estimator based on a sample of observations, it is a random variable. We can therefore compute the probability that $\hat{\theta}_n$ lies in the interval defined. If this probability increases to 1 as n increases to infinity *for any* $\epsilon > 0$, we say that $\hat{\theta}_n$ is a *consistent estimator of* θ.

This point is illustrated in Figure 2.9, which graphs the sampling distribution of $\hat{\theta}_n = \bar{x}$ for various values of the sample size n. We note that this distribution becomes more and more "tightly packed" as the sample size increases. In other words, the variance of $\hat{\theta}_n$ approaches zero as the sample size increases. In the limit, the distribution of $\hat{\theta}_n$ collapses to the single point θ.

It should be stressed that the concepts of unbiasedness and consistency are conceptually quite different. Unbiasedness can hold for any sample size, but consistency is strictly a large-sample concept. Figure 2.10 illustrates a biased but consistent estimator.

Does unbiasedness imply consistency? Absolutely not, as is seen from the following trivial counterexample. The first observation x_1 is an unbiased estimator

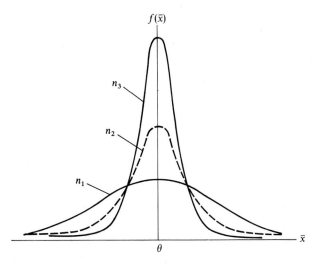

Figure 2.9 Sampling distribution of $\bar{x}$ as the size of the sample increases, $n_3 > n_2 > n_1$

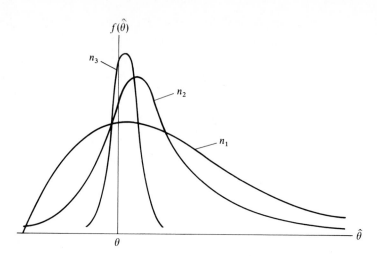

Figure 2.10 Sampling distributions of a biased but consistent estimator, $n_3 > n_2 > n_1$

of the mean θ because $E(x_1) = \theta$. But letting $n \to \infty$ is not going to make x_1 approach θ by any means.

Asymptotic Efficiency* No single estimator can be most efficient (that is, have the smallest variance) for all values of θ. Some are good for certain values of θ and others are more efficient in other ranges of θ. For instance, let $\hat{\theta} = 1.25$, regardless of what the observations are. If the true θ is at or near 1.25, this is a pretty good estimate; but when the true θ is far from 1.25, it is a very poor estimate. When dealing with consistent estimators, however, the range of values of θ for which one estimator is more efficient than another shrinks as the sample size increases. In the limit when $n \to \infty$, the distributions of all consistent estimators collapse to the true parameter θ (recall that the variances go to zero). Preference should therefore be given to those estimators that approach the true θ in the fastest possible way (that is, those whose variances converge to zero the fastest). This is the concept of *asymptotic efficiency* formally defined in Definition 2.23.

Definition 2.23 (Asymptotic Efficiency)
A consistent estimator $\hat{\theta}_1$ is said to be asymptotically efficient if for every other consistent estimator $\hat{\theta}_2$

$$\lim_{n \to \infty} \left[\frac{\text{Var}(\hat{\theta}_2)}{\text{Var}(\hat{\theta}_1)} \right] > 1 \qquad \text{for all } \theta$$

In intuitive terms, a consistent estimator is asymptotically efficient if, for large samples, its variance is smaller than that of any other consistent estimator.

Asymptotic Normality   If the sampling distribution of an estimator approaches the normal distribution as the sample size becomes indefinitely large, we say that the estimator is *asymptotically normal*.

We state without proof two very important large-sample results. These are known as the *law of large numbers* and the *central limit theorem*.

Property 2.12

a. **The law of large numbers:** Let $\bar{Z}$ be the mean of a random sample of values $Z_1, Z_2, \ldots, Z_n$, which are independently and identically distributed. Then $\bar{Z}$ is a consistent estimator of $E(\bar{Z})$. (In simple terms, this means that as n increases, the sample mean of a set of random variables approaches its expected value.) A special case of this arises when $\bar{Z} = \bar{x}$, the sample mean. Because $E(\bar{x}) = \mu$, the population mean, $\bar{x}$ is a consistent estimator of μ. Similarly, $s^2 = \left[\sum(x_i - \bar{x})^2\right]/(n-1)$ converges to σ^2 as n approaches infinity.

b. **The central limit theorem:** Let $x_1, x_2, \ldots, x_n$ be a random sample of observations from the same distribution and let $E(x_i) = \mu$ and $\text{Var}(x_i) = \sigma^2$. Then the sampling distribution of the random variable $Z_n = \sqrt{n}(\bar{x} - \mu)/\sigma$ converges to the standard normal $N(0, 1)$ as n converges to infinity.

The central limit theorem is very powerful because *it holds even when the distribution from which the observations are drawn is not normal.* This means that, if we make sure that the sample size is large, then we can use the random variable Z_n defined above to answer questions about the population from which the observations are drawn, and we need not know the precise distribution from which the observations are drawn.

2.8   Procedures for the Estimation of Parameters

In this section we present two alternative procedures for estimating the unknown parameters of the probability distribution from which the observations $x_1, x_2, \ldots, x_n$ are obtained. In the appendix, Section 2.A.3, two additional advanced methods are described. In the following discussion it is assumed that the investigator knows the nature of the probability distribution but not the values of the parameters.

The Method of Moments

The oldest method of estimating parameters is the **method of moments** devised by Karl Pearson in 1894. If a distribution has k unknown parameters, the procedure is to calculate the first k **sample moments** of the distribution and use them as estimators of the corresponding **population moments**. In Section 2.2, we noted that the **population mean** of the distribution (μ) is also referred to as the *first moment* of the distribution around the origin. It is the weighted average of all possible x's, the weights being the corresponding probabilities. The sample mean ($\bar{x}$) is the arithmetic average of the sample observations $x_1, x_2, \ldots, x_n$. By the method of moments, $\bar{x}$ is taken as an estimator of μ. The variance of a random variable is $\sigma^2 = E[(X - \mu)^2]$ and is known as the *second moment around the mean*. The sample variance (s^2), defined in equation (2.11), is used as an estimator of the **population variance** of the distribution. In most cases, the mean and variance completely characterize a distribution, and hence there is no need to use higher order moments such as the expected value of $(X - \mu)^3$. Because $E(\bar{x}) = \mu$, the sample mean is an unbiased estimator of the population mean. We will see later that the sample mean also possesses several of the other desirable properties described in Section 2.7. It can be shown that $E(s^2) = \sigma^2$ and hence the sample variance s^2 is an unbiased estimator of the population variance σ^2.

The same principle can be applied in estimating the coefficient of correlation between two random variables X and Y (see Definition 2.14). Let $x_1, x_2, \ldots, x_n$ and $y_1, y_2, \ldots, y_n$ be independent random samples of observations (of the same size n) on X and Y, respectively. The population covariance between them is given in Definition 2.13 as $E[(X - \mu_x)(Y - \mu_y)]$, where μ_x and μ_y are the population means of X and Y, respectively. An estimate of this is given by the **sample covariance**

$$s_{xy} = \widehat{\text{Cov}(x, y)} = \frac{1}{n - 1} \sum (x_i - \bar{x})(y_i - \bar{y}) \tag{2.12}$$

If the pairs of values x_i and y_i are plotted, we obtain a graph such as Figure 2.11, in which X and Y are positively related (that is, X and Y generally move in the same direction). Such a plot is known as a *scatter diagram*. Figure 2.7 is similar to this except that in it the points referred to the *population* whereas here they refer to the *sample*. By translating the axes to the dashed lines with origin at ($\bar{x}, \bar{y}$), we can see that $x_i - \bar{x}$ and $y_i - \bar{y}$ are the distances from the mean point ($\bar{x}, \bar{y}$). If the relationship is positive, we would expect most of the points to lie in the first and third quadrants in which the product $(x_i - \bar{x})(y_i - \bar{y})$ will be positive. Because the negative products from the points in the second and fourth quadrants are likely to be dominated by the positive products, we would expect the covariance to be positive. By a similar argument we can see that if the relationship is negative, most of the points will lie in the second and fourth quadrants, giving rise to a negative covariance. This shows that if X and Y are positively related, the covariance and hence the correlation between them will be positive. A negative relation will result in a negative coefficient of correlation. The **sample correlation coefficient** is given by

$$r_{xy} = \frac{s_{xy}}{s_x s_y} = \frac{\sum (x_i - \bar{x})(y_i - \bar{y})}{[\sum (x_i - \bar{x})^2]^{1/2}[\sum (y_i - \bar{y})^2]^{1/2}} \tag{2.13}$$

where s_x and s_y are the sample standard deviations (square roots of the variances) of X and Y, respectively.

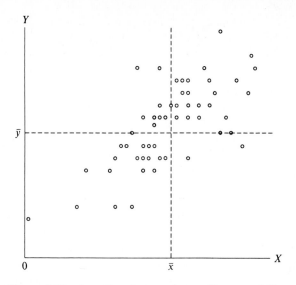

Figure 2.11 A scatter diagram for positive correlation

It was mentioned in Section 2.3 that the correlation coefficient is a measure of a linear relationship between X and Y. Figure 2.12 is a scatter diagram showing the situation when Y is an approximate quadratic function of X. We note that the points are scattered in all four quadrants, and hence the sum $\sum (x_i - \bar{x})(y_i - \bar{y})$ is likely to be small, indicating a low value for r_{xy}. Thus, a low r_{xy} does not mean that X and Y are not closely related, just that they do not have a close *linear* relation.

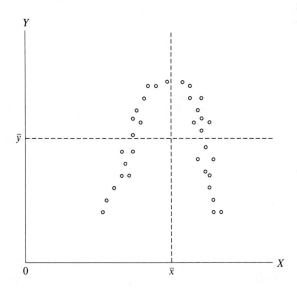

Figure 2.12 A scatter diagram for an approximate quadratic relation

Practice Computer Session 2.4 illustrates the calculation of covariance and correlation between college grade point average and high school grade point average for the data included in the diskette that accompanies the book.

The Method of Least Squares

In econometrics the most commonly used method of estimating parameters is the **method of least squares**. Although it is predominantly used to estimate the parameters of a regression model of the type PRICE $= \alpha + \beta$SQFT $+ u$, encountered in Chapter 1, it is also useful to apply it in the simpler context of estimating the mean of a single random variable X.

Each of the observations x_i is an unbiased estimator of the sample mean μ because $E(x_i) = \mu$. The error in this estimator is $e_i = x_i - \mu$ (that is, $x_i = \mu + e_i$). Consider the sum of the square of this error over the entire sample. That is, let SSE$(\mu) = \sum e_i^2 = \sum(x_i - \mu)^2$. The method of least squares chooses that estimator of μ for which the sample sum of squared errors is a minimum. Squaring the errors accomplishes two things. First, it eliminates the sign of the error. Thus, positive errors and negative errors are treated alike. Second, squaring penalizes large errors because such errors are magnified when squared. The first-order condition for minimizing SSE with respect to μ is given by ∂SSE$/\partial\mu = 0$ (See Appendix Section 2.A.2 on the condition for minimizing a function.) Treating x_i as a constant and differentiating SSE with respect to μ, we have

$$\frac{\partial\text{SSE}}{\partial\mu} = \sum(-2)(x_i - \mu) = (-2)\left[\sum x_i - n\mu\right] = 0$$

Solving this for μ we get the estimator $\hat{\mu} = \bar{x}$. We therefore see that the **least squares estimator** of μ is $\bar{x}$.

In the chapter appendix, Section 2.A.3, two more estimation procedures are discussed; the best linear unbiased estimator (BLUE) and the maximum likelihood estimator (MLE). Interested readers should read that section.

2.9 Interval Estimation

The estimation procedures discussed in the preceding section result in a single estimated value for the unknown parameters of a distribution. These are known as **point estimates**. The sample mean and the sample variance are examples of point estimates. Although point estimates are useful, they are subject to errors. The variance of an estimator measures this uncertainty and gives the precision with which the estimate has been obtained. **Interval estimation** is a way of directly taking account of this uncertainty. Rather than provide a single estimate, interval estimation would provide a range of possible values. For example, instead of saying that the inflation rate next year is expected to be 5.3 percent, we may wish to say that with a certain probability it will lie between 5 percent and 5.5 percent. This is known as a **confidence interval**; it is illustrated below with examples for the mean and variance of the normal distribution.

Confidence Interval for the Mean of a Normal Distribution

Property 2.10a states that if a random variable X is distributed as $N(\mu, \sigma^2)$, then the sample mean $\bar{x}$ is distributed as $N[\mu, (\sigma^2/n)]$. Furthermore, we know from Property 2.11c that the transformed variable $(\bar{x} - \mu)/(s/\sqrt{n})$ has the Student's t-distribution with $n - 1$ d.f. (s is the sample standard deviation). In other words, $t = (\bar{x} - \mu)/(s/\sqrt{n}) \sim t_{n-1}$. Let t^* be the point on this t-distribution such that the area to the right of t^* is 0.025 (that is, $2\frac{1}{2}$ percent). Because the t-distribution is symmetric around zero, it follows that the area to the left of $-t^*$ is also 0.025. Therefore, $P(-t^* \le t \le t^*) = 0.95$. Substituting for t in terms of the sample mean and standard deviation we get the probability statement,

$$P\left[-t^* \le \frac{\bar{x} - \mu}{s/\sqrt{n}} \le t^* \right] = 0.95$$

Multiplying through by $s/\sqrt{n}$ and rearranging terms, we get

$$P[\bar{x} - (s/\sqrt{n})t^* \le \mu \le \bar{x} + (s/\sqrt{n})t^*] = 0.95$$

This means that the true parameter μ lies in the interval $\bar{x} \pm (s/\sqrt{n})t^*$ with probability 0.95. This interval is known as the 95 percent confidence interval for μ. It should be noted that the confidence interval is a random interval because the endpoints $\bar{x} \pm (s/\sqrt{n})t^*$ are themselves random variables. The interpretation of a confidence interval is as follows. If we repeat the experiment of drawing a random sample and computing the confidence interval an infinite number of times, 95 percent of the intervals will include the true mean μ. The choice of the confidence level is at the discretion of the investigator. If very accurate forecasts are not essential, one may settle for a 90 percent confidence interval. It should be noted that as the sample size n increases, the width of the confidence interval becomes smaller. Similarly, as the estimated standard error (s) decreases, the confidence interval decreases in length. In other words, *for a given level of confidence, the higher the sample size or the lower the standard error, the narrower the confidence interval and hence the better the precision of the estimate.*

Example 2.3

Suppose that the average life of a light bulb has been estimated as 450 hours and the estimated standard deviation is 25 hours. Here, $\bar{x} = 450$ and $s = 25$. Let the size of the sample (n) be 25. From the t-table in Appendix A (Table A.2), we see that for 24 d.f. (which is $n - 1$)t^* is 2.064 with an area of 2.5 percent to the right of it. The estimated 95 percent confidence interval is therefore $450 \pm (25/\sqrt{25})2.064$, which gives the range (439.68, 460.32). □

Confidence Interval for the Variance of a Normal Distribution

By proceeding similarly, it is easy to show, using Property 2.11a, that the 95 percent confidence interval for σ^2 is as follows:

$$P\left[\frac{(n-1)s^2}{u_2} \le \sigma^2 \le \frac{(n-1)s^2}{u_1} \right] = 0.95$$

where u_1 and u_2 are obtained from the χ^2_{n-1} distribution such that $P(u \le u_1) = 0.025$ and $P(u \ge u_2) = 0.025$.

Practice Problem

2.12 Using the output from Practice Computer Session 2.4 obtain the 95 percent confidence intervals for the mean and variance for college and high school GPAs.

2.10 Testing Hypotheses

Aside from estimating unknown parameters, testing hypotheses on those parameters is the most important aspect of an empirical investigation. In Chapter 1 we listed a variety of hypotheses that would be of interest. The procedure for hypothesis testing also requires formal concepts and methodologies. This chapter provides a brief review of those topics. Three steps are basic to any hypothesis-testing procedure: (1) Formulate two opposing hypotheses, (2) derive a test statistic and identify its sampling distribution, and (3) derive a decision rule and choose one of the opposing hypotheses.

Null and Alternative Hypotheses

The first step is to formulate two opposing hypotheses: the **null hypothesis** (denoted by H_0) and the **alternative hypothesis** (denoted by H_1). Table 2.5 has examples of null and alternative hypotheses formulated on the mean of a population (μ).

A Statistical Test

A decision rule that selects one of the inferences "accept the null hypothesis" or "reject the null hypothesis" (which amounts to accepting the alternative hypothesis) for every outcome of an experiment is called a **statistical test**. The procedure usually involves first computing a **test statistic** $T(x_1, x_2, \ldots, x_n)$ calculated from the sample of observations. The next step is to derive the sampling distribution of T under the null hypothesis. The final step is to derive a decision rule based on the observed value of T. The range of values of T for which the test procedure recommends rejecting the null hypothesis is called the **critical region**, and the range for which it recommends accepting the null hypothesis is called the **acceptance region**.

Type I and Type II Errors

For any test procedure there are three possible outcomes: (1) A correct decision was made (that is, the procedure accepted a true hypothesis or rejected a false

TABLE 2.5 Null and Alternative Hypotheses

	(a)	(b)	(c)	(d)
H_0	$\mu = \mu_0$	$\mu = \mu_0$	$\mu \le \mu_0$	$\mu \ge \mu_0$
H_1	$\mu = \mu_1$	$\mu \ne \mu_0$	$\mu > \mu_0$	$\mu < \mu_0$

hypothesis), (2) a true hypothesis was rejected, and (3) a false hypothesis was accepted. The error of rejecting H_0 when it is true is called the **type I error**. The error of accepting H_0 when it is false is called the **type II error**. Associated with each of these errors is a probability. These are known as the probabilities of type I and type II errors and are denoted by $P(\text{I})$ and $P(\text{II})$.[1] These concepts are better understood with an example from the legal system that was presented by Kohler (1985). Consider a defendant in a criminal trial. The null hypothesis is that the defendant is "not guilty" and the alternative is that the accused is "guilty." The burden is on the prosecution to prove that the accused is guilty, that is, to convince the jury to reject the null hypothesis. If the jury declares an innocent person "not guilty" or a guilty person "guilty," a correct decision has been made. If an innocent person is found guilty, a type I error has been made because a true hypothesis has been rejected. A type II error occurs when a guilty person is acquitted.

As a second example, suppose a pharmaceutical company claims to have found a cure for a deadly disease. The null hypothesis would be that the drug is not effective in curing the disease, and the burden of proof that it is effective rests with the pharmaceutical company. A type I error would have occurred if an ineffective drug (that is one for which H_0 is true) is accepted as effective (that is, H_0 is rejected). Type II error occurs when a truly effective drug is rejected as ineffective.

Ideally, we would like to keep both $P(\text{I})$ and $P(\text{II})$ as low as possible no matter what the value of an unknown parameter. Unfortunately, an attempt to reduce $P(\text{I})$ automatically increases $P(\text{II})$. For instance, consider the decision rule "always reject H_0," regardless of the observations. This gives $P(\text{II}) = 0$ because we would never accept a false hypothesis. But $P(\text{I}) = 1$ for the values of the parameter for which the hypothesis is really true. Similarly, the rule "always accept H_0" has $P(\text{I}) = 0$ and $P(\text{II}) = 1$.[2] In practice, the trade-off between these errors is not as extreme, but a particular decision rule would be better for some values of the parameter and not for others. *The classical procedure for hypothesis testing is to choose a maximum value for type I error that is acceptable to the investigator, and then derive that decision rule for which type II error is a minimum.* In the criminal trial example, this would mean choosing a decision rule that will find an innocent person guilty no more than a certain percentage of the time (say, 1 percent), and then minimizing the probability that a guilty person will be set free.

In the pharmaceutical example, we would set the probability of approving an ineffective drug to some maximum and minimize the probability of rejecting an effective drug.

The Level of Significance and the Power of a Test

The largest probability of a type I error when H_0 is true is called the **level of significance** (also known as the **size of the test**). In the criminal trial example, this is the maximum probability of convicting an innocent person. The probability of

. . . .

[1] *Sometimes P(I) and P(II) are referred to, respectively, as α and β (which have no connection with the α and β of a regression model).*

[2] *It should be emphasized that although P(I) + P(II) = 1 in these examples, this is generally not the case.*

rejecting a hypothesis when it is false is given by $1 - P(\text{II})$ and is called the **power of a test**. In our example, it is the probability of convicting a guilty person. The standard testing procedure is to find a decision rule for which $P(\text{II})$ is a minimum (or equivalently, the power of the test is a maximum), subject to the restriction that $P(I) \leq \alpha$, where α is a given constant ($0 < \alpha < 1$). Such a test procedure is called a **most powerful test** of size α. The most common levels of significance are 0.01, 0.05, and 0.10.

We now present a few tests of hypotheses frequently used in business and economic decisions. Here we consider only the hypotheses on a normally distributed random variable. The reader should consult one of the references at the end of this chapter for more details on this and other tests.

Testing the Mean of a Normal Distribution

Consider a random variable X which is normally distributed with mean μ and variance σ^2. The most common null hypothesis is of the form $H_0: \mu = \mu_0$. The alternative H_1 might be **one-sided** as in $H_1: \mu > \mu_0$, or **two-sided** as in $H_1: \mu \neq \mu_0$. Each of these cases is now discussed in detail.

A One-Sided Test   In many situations the investigator will have prior knowledge of which side of the two-sided alternative the parameter is likely to be on. For instance, we know that the marginal propensity to consume (the extra consumption per unit extra income) is positive. To test whether the marginal propensity to consume (μ) is zero, the sensible alternative is that $\mu > \mu_0$ ($= 0$ in our example).

By the method of moments, the sample mean $\bar{x}$ is an (unbiased) estimate of μ. If the observed $\bar{x}$ is considerably larger than the μ_0 specified in the null hypothesis, we would suspect that the true μ is most probably larger than μ_0. Thus if $\bar{x} - \mu_0$ is "large" we would reject H_0 that $\mu = \mu_0$. In order to be able to compute probabilities in the distribution of $\bar{x}$ with an unknown σ^2, the actual test statistic used is $t_c = \sqrt{n}(\bar{x} - \mu_0)/s$, where s is the sample standard deviation defined in equation (2.11). The steps involved in the test are summarized in the following list and are illustrated in Figure 2.13.

Procedure for Testing H_0 against H_1

Step 1 $H_0: \mu = \mu_0;$ $H_1: \mu > \mu_0$

Step 2   The test statistic is $t_c = \sqrt{n}(\bar{x} - \mu_0)/s$. Under the null hypothesis, this has the Student's t-distribution with $n - 1$ d.f.

Step 3   In the t-table (Table A.2), look up the entry corresponding to $n - 1$ d.f. and the given level of significance α, and obtain the point $t_{n-1}^*(\alpha)$ such that $P(t > t^*) = \alpha$, the selected level of significance.

Step 4   Reject H_0 if the observed $t_c > t^*$.

In a different situation, if the alternative were $\mu < \mu_0$, the criterion for rejection would be $t_c < -t^*(\alpha)$.

This test is called a **one-sided** test because the alternative is on one side of μ_0 and because the value of t^* is obtained such that the area in one tail of the t-distribution is equal to α (see Figure 2.13). The test is also referred to as a **one-tailed** test.

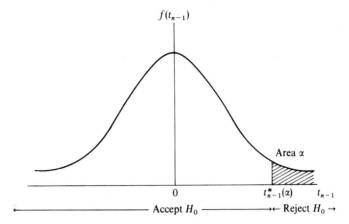

Figure 2.13 One-sided test for $\mu = \mu_0$ against $\mu > \mu_0$ in a normal population

Example 2.4

The label on a carton of light bulbs states that it contains "long-life" bulbs with an average life of 935 hours. An unhappy consumer files a complaint with the Department of Commerce alleging that the claim is false and that the life is considerably less than 935 hours. A Commerce department analyst tested a random sample of 25 light bulbs and found that the average life of the bulbs was 917 hours with a standard deviation of 54 hours. Can the analyst support the company's claim? Assume that the life of a bulb is distributed normally with mean μ and variance σ^2.   □

Step 1   The null and alternate hypotheses are $H_0: \mu = 935$ and $H_1: \mu < 935$.
Step 2 $\bar{x} = 917$, $s = 54$, and $n = 25$. The t-statistic is $t_c = \sqrt{n}(\bar{x} - \mu_0)/s = \sqrt{25}(917 - 935)/54 = -1.67$. Under the null hypothesis, this has a t-distribution with $n - 1 \, (=24)$ degrees of freedom.
Step 3   From the t-table, $t_{24}^{*}(.05) = 1.711$.
Step 4   Because $t_c > -t^*$, we cannot reject the null hypothesis and hence conclude that, *at the 5 percent level of significance, there is no statistical evidence to indicate that the average life is significantly below the company's claim of 935*, even though the observed average is below 935.

A Two-Sided Test   Let H_0 be $\mu = \mu_0$ and H_1 be $\mu \neq \mu_0$. Note that the alternative is a **two-sided alternative**, that is, that μ can be either side of μ_0. Many economic and business decisions might require the formulation of two-sided hypotheses. For instance, a tire manufacturer might want to test whether the average life of a tire is 30,000 miles or not. There may be no a priori information about whether the life will be higher or lower than 30,000. In this case, the procedure is first to obtain a random sample of observations $x_1, x_2, \ldots, x_n$. We stated in Property 2.11c that the sample statistic $t = (\bar{x} - \mu)(s/\sqrt{n})$, where $\bar{x}$ is the sample mean and s is the sample standard deviation defined in equation (2.11), is distributed as t_{n-1}. If the null

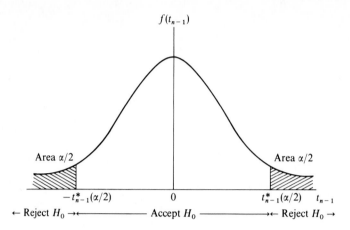

Figure 2.14 Two-tailed test for $\mu = \mu_0$ against $\mu \neq \mu_0$ in a normal population

hypothesis is true, $\mu = \mu_0$. Under this hypothesis, the value of t calculated from the sample is given by $t_c = (\bar{x} - \mu_0)/(s/\sqrt{n}) \sim t_{n-1}$. If the observed sample mean $\bar{x}$ deviates substantially from the null hypothesis $\mu = \mu_0$, the calculated value t_c will be either too large or too small. When this is the case, we reject H_0. From the t-table in Appendix A (Table A.2) obtain $t^*_{n-1}(\alpha/2)$, where t^* is the value in the t-distribution with $n - 1$ d.f. such that $P(t > t^*) = \alpha/2$, and α is the level of significance (usually 0.01 or 0.05 or 0.10). Note that because of the symmetry of the t-distribution around the origin, $P(t < -t^*)$ is also equal to $\alpha/2$. The procedure for testing H_0 against $H_1: \mu \neq \mu_0$ is to reject H_0 if $t_c > t^*$ or $t_c < -t^*$. The steps involved are summarized in the following list and are illustrated in Figure 2.14.

Procedure for Testing H_0 Against H_1

Step 1 $H_0: \mu = \mu_0$ $H_1: \mu \neq \mu_0$

Step 2 The test statistic is $t_c = \sqrt{n}(\bar{x} - \mu_0)/s$. Under the null hypothesis, this has the Student's t-distribution with $n - 1$ d.f.

Step 3 In the t-table (Table A.2), look up the entry corresponding to $n - 1$ d.f. and the given level of significance α, and obtain the point $t^*_{n-1}(\alpha/2)$ such that $P(t > t^*) = \alpha/2$. This gives $P(t < -t^*$ or $t > t^*) = \alpha$, the selected level of significance.

Step 4 Reject H_0 if the observed $t_c > t^*$ or $t_c < -t^*$.

This test is called a **two-sided** (or more commonly a **two-tailed**) **test** because the alternative is on either side of μ_0 and because the value of t^* is obtained such that the area in either tail of the t-distribution is equal to $\alpha/2$ (see Figure 2.14).

Example 2.5

In the light bulb example, suppose the alternative is $\mu \neq 935$. The calculated t-value is still -1.67, and $t^*_{n-1}(\alpha/2) = t^*_{24}(0.025) = 2.064$. Because $t_c > -t^*$, we accept the null hypothesis that $\mu = 935$ and conclude that the average life is not significantly different from 935.   □

Relation Between Hypothesis Testing and Confidence Intervals

There is a close relationship between two-tailed tests and confidence intervals. In the light bulb example, we can calculate the confidence interval for the life of a bulb. From Section 2.9 we note that the confidence interval for μ is $[\bar{x} - (s/\sqrt{n})t^*,$ $\bar{x} + (s/\sqrt{n})t^*]$, which becomes $[917 \pm (54/5)2.064]$ or $(895, 939)$. This is the 95 percent confidence interval for the population mean life of the bulb. We note that this interval includes the value of $\mu_0 = 935$. Hence we accept the null hypothesis. This example shows that the test of hypothesis can be done in another, equivalent way using the confidence interval. The steps are given in the following list:

Step 1 From the test statistic, construct a $1 - \alpha$ confidence interval for the parameter in question (α is the level of significance).

Step 2 Reject the null hypothesis if this confidence interval *does not* include the value of the parameter at the null hypothesis. If the confidence interval includes the value corresponding to H_0, the null hypothesis cannot be rejected.

Relation Between the Sample Size and the Power of a Test*

It is easy to show that, for a given sample standard deviation, the larger the degrees of freedom the greater the power of a test, that is, the smaller the probability of a type II error. For simplicity, we illustrate this point with a numerical example, but it holds in general. Let the alternative hypothesis be $\mu = \mu_1 > \mu_0$, the initial number of degrees of freedom be 24, the sample standard deviation be $s = 25$, and α be 0.05. The critical t^* for this one-sided test is $t_{24}^*(0.025) = 2.064$. The power of the one-tailed test described earlier (for $H_1: \mu > \mu_0$) is the probability of rejecting the hypothesis when it is false (that is, when the alternative is true), which is $P(t > 2.064 \mid \mu = \mu_1)$. This is equivalent to

$$P\left[\frac{\bar{x} - \mu_1}{s/\sqrt{n}} > 2.064\right] = P\left[\frac{\bar{x} - \mu_1}{\sigma/\sqrt{n}} > \frac{2.064s}{\sigma}\right] = P\left[z > \frac{2.064s}{\sigma}\right]$$

where z is the standard normal variate $(\bar{x} - \mu_1)/(\sigma/\sqrt{n})$ (see Property 2.10b). This probability is the area of the standard normal distribution to the right of $2.064(s/\sigma)$. Suppose the degrees of freedom increases to 30 with no change in any of the other values. It will be noted from Table A.2 that t^* decreases to 2.042. The power of the test when the d.f. is 30 is therefore $P[z > (2.042s)/\sigma]$, which must necessarily be larger than $P[z > (2.064s)/\sigma]$. This means that the power of the test increases [that is, $P(\text{II})$ decreases] as the d.f. increases. This result holds for all types of tests.

Testing the Variance of a Normal Population

The null and alternative hypotheses are $H_0: \sigma^2 = \sigma_0^2$ and $H_1: \sigma^2 \neq \sigma_0^2$. From Property 2.11a, we know that $(n - 1)s^2/\sigma^2 = \sum(x_i - \bar{x})^2/\sigma^2 \sim \chi_{n-1}^2$. Compute $u = (n - 1)s^2/\sigma_0^2$ from the sample. Under the null hypothesis, $u \sim \chi_{n-1}^2$. From the

Section 2.9. The data set for this is *data2-2* and the input file is *ps2-4.inp*. The DOS command for execution is similar to those in the first two practice sessions.

2.5 The commands in the file *ps2-5.inp* are useful in obtaining the necessary numbers to perform the test of the hypotheses in Examples 2.6, 2.7, and 2.8. [The data set is *data2-1*.]

EXERCISES*

2.1   Events A and B are equally likely and are independent. The probability of event $A \cap B$ is 0.36. What is the probability of A?

2.2   When a pair of dice is thrown, let the total score be denoted by X. Derive the probability for each of the elementary events.

2.3   You need 18 computer memory chips to install in the "mother board" of a micro-computer. You order 20 memory chips because you know that 10% of all chips are defective. What is the probability that your computer will work?

†2.4   A small commuter airline uses planes with 20 seats. Experience shows that 10% of individuals reserving space in a flight do not show up. If the company takes 23 reservations for each flight, what is the probability that it will be able to accommodate everyone appearing without bumping anyone?

2.5   My wife bought a box of twenty gladiola bulbs from the Greenhouse Nursery. The box states that if fewer than 90% of the bulbs germinate, the manufacturer will refund the price of the entire box. Suppose the probability of germination is only 0.8. What is the probability that my wife will *not* get a refund on her purchase?

†2.6   Consider the discrete random variable X that can take only the values x_1, $x_2, \ldots, x_n$, with the corresponding probabilities $f(x_i)$, $(i = 1, 2, \ldots, n)$. Prove Property 2.2 for this random variable.

2.7   Let X be a discrete random variable with mean μ_x and variance σ_x^2. Define $Z = a + bX$, where a and b are known constants. Show that $\mu_Z = E(Z) = a + b\mu_x$ and $\sigma_Z^2 = V(Z) = b^2\sigma_x^2$.

2.8   In the dice throwing example of Exercise 2.2, compute the mean, variance, and standard deviation of X.

†2.9   Consider the random variable X which can take only the values $1, 2, \ldots, n$. Also assume that each of these outcomes is equally likely (such a distribution is called the *uniform distribution*). Write down the density function $f(x)$ and derive the mean and variance of X.

．　．　．　．　．　．

* Here and throughout the book, exercises indicated by (†) are answered in Appendix C. Those marked by (*) are more difficult and may be skipped at the discretion of the instructor.

2.10 An equipment leasing company rents a tractor for $50 per hour, but the machine tends to break down. In a period of t hours, it breaks downs X times, which costs a *total* of X^2 dollars to repair. X is a random variable with mean and variance both equal to $2t$. Derive the profit function $\pi(X, t)$ and the expected profit as a function of t. What is the optimum number of hours the company should rent out at a stretch in order to maximize expected profit (this part requires the use of derivatives described in Appendix Section 2.A.2)?

†2.11 Suppose that X denotes the annual incomes, in thousands of dollars, and that, for a particular group of people, X is normally distributed with mean 26 and variance 36. A random sample of 25 persons is drawn from the group. What is the probability that the average income is between $17,000 and $33,000?

2.12 The following table shows the joint distribution of two discrete random variables, A and B.

A		10	20	30	40
B	1	.144	.126	.063	.024
	2	.052	.118	.097	.057
	3	.027	.066	.128	.098

Compute the following; (1) unconditional probability that $A = 10$, (2) probability that $A = 10$ given that $B = 3$, (3) conditional expectation of B when $A = 20$, and (4) unconditional expectation of B. Are the two random variables statistically independent? Why or why not?

2.13 Prove properties 2.5a, 2.5c, 2.5e, 2.5f, and 2.6.

†2.14 Let X_1 and X_2 be two random variables, with $\text{Var}(X_i) = \sigma_i^2$ ($i = 1, 2$) and $\text{Cov}(X_1, X_2) = \sigma_{12}$ (their means are unknowns). Now make the transformations $Y = X_1 + X_2$, and $Z = X_1 - X_2$. Derive $\text{Cov}(Y, Z)$ and the condition under which Y and Z will be uncorrelated.

2.15 Let $x_1, x_2, \ldots, x_n$ be a random sample drawn from a population with mean μ and variance σ^2. Let $\bar{x} = \frac{1}{n} \sum_{i=1}^{i=n} x_i$ be the sample mean. Show that $E(\bar{x}) = \mu$ and $\text{Var}(\bar{x}) = \sigma^2/n$. Next let $y = \frac{1}{n} \sum a_i x_i$, where the a_i's are fixed constants. Derive $E(y)$ and $\text{Var}(y)$. What is the condition for $E(y)$ to be equal to μ?

2.16 An insurance company needs to estimate the average amount claimed by its policy holders over one year. A random sample of 81 policy holders reveals that the sample mean claim is $739.98 and the sample standard deviation is $312.70. Compute a 95 percent confidence interval for the average amount claimed. Suppose the insurance company analyst wants to test the hypothesis that the average claim is 800 against the alternative that it is less than 800. Perform this test at the 5 percent level. Be sure to state the assumptions needed to make this a valid test.

†2.17 A stock market analyst wanted to test whether the rate of return of purchasing stock in a certain company exceeded the average return for the market as a whole. In other words, is the average "excess returns" (company's rate of return minus the market average rate of return) positive or negative? We therefore want to test whether the average returns are zero or not. The excess rate of return was computed for 13 periods and the average was 3.1 percent with a standard deviation of 1 percent. Test the hypothesis at the 5 percent level of significance, assuming that excess returns are normally distributed. Derive a 95 percent confidence interval for the average excess returns.

2.18 For a period of 26 weeks, it was found that the sample correlation between the percentage change in the stock market indices in New York and London was 0.370. Test at the 1 percent level, the null hypothesis that the correlation coefficient is zero, against the alternative that is not zero.

†2.19 A sample of 427 college students was drawn and their GPAs measured; X is the college GPA and Y is the high school GPA. We have the following information:

$$\bar{x} = 2.786 \qquad \bar{y} = 3.558$$
$$s_x = 0.541 \qquad s_y = 0.420$$

Test the null hypothesis that there is no difference in the population mean high school and college GPAs against the alternative that they are unequal.

2.20 A random sample of 500 owners of single family homes is drawn from the population of a city. Let the random variable X denote annual household income, in thousands of dollars, and the random variable Y denote the value of the house, also in thousands of dollars. The following information is available:

$$n = 500 \qquad \sum_{1}^{n} x_i = 24{,}838 \qquad \sum_{1}^{n} y_i = 107{,}226$$
$$\sum (x_i - \bar{x})^2 = 66{,}398 \qquad \sum (y_i - \bar{y})^2 = 1{,}398{,}308$$
$$\sum (x_i - \bar{x})(y_i - \bar{y}) = 194{,}293$$

(1) Compute the mean and standard deviation of the value of the houses in this sample. Do the same for household income.
(2) Compute the correlation between income and house value.
(3) Construct a 95 percent confidence interval for the mean value of houses. What assumptions do you have make to do this?
(4) Using a two-tailed test at the 0.01 level, test the hypothesis that the correlation between income and house value is zero.

2.A APPENDIX

Multivariate Distributions, Constrained Optimization, and Advanced Estimation Procedures

This appendix contains topics of an advanced nature that may be skipped in an elementary econometrics course in which the readers are not interested in detailed proofs of propositions. Students in advanced econometrics courses and graduate programs who are interested in formal justifications of the propositions might want to refer to these sections. It is recommended that readers scan through this section quickly but come back to it as needed.

2.A.1 Multivariate Distributions

In this section the concepts discussed in Section 2.3 are extended to more than two random variables. Let $u_1, u_2, \ldots, u_n$ be n random variables. Then their joint probability density function is $f_U(u_1, u_2, \ldots, u_n)$. As before, they are independent if the joint pdf is the product of the individual pdf. Thus we have

$$f_U(u_1, u_2, \ldots, u_n) = f_{U_1}(u_1) \cdot f_{U_2}(u_2) \cdots \cdot f_{U_n}(u_n)$$

In the special case when each of the u's is independently and identically distributed (denoted as iid), we have

$$f_U(u_1, u_2, \ldots, u_n) = f_U(u_1) \cdot f_U(u_2) \cdots \cdot f_U(u_n)$$

where $f_U(u)$ is the common distribution of each of the u's. A number of useful results on multivariate distributions not listed in Property 2.6 are summarized in Property 2.A.1.

Property 2.A.1
a. $\text{Var}\left[\sum(a_i u_i)\right] = \sum_i a_i^2 \text{Var}(u_i) + \sum\sum_{i \neq j} a_i a_j \text{Cov}(u_i, u_j)$, where the a_i's are assumed to be constant or nonrandom.
b. If $u_1, u_2, \ldots, u_n$ are all independent, then every pair of correlations (ρ_{ij}) and covariances will be zero so that $\text{Cov}(u_i, u_j) = 0 = \rho_{ij}$ for all $i \neq j$.
c. It follows from (a) and (b) that when the u's are independent, $\text{Var}\left[\sum(a_i u_i)\right] = \sum a_i^2 \text{Var}(u_i)$, because the covariance terms above will disappear. Thus the variance of the sum of independent random variables is the sum of the variances. In particular, if the variances are the same, so that $\text{Var}(u_i) = \sigma^2$ for each i, then $\text{Var}\left[\sum(a_i u_i)\right] = \sigma^2 \sum a_i^2$.

d. If $u_1, u_2, \ldots, u_n$ are independent random variables such that u_i is normally distributed with mean μ_i and variance σ_i^2—that is, $u_i \sim N(\mu_i, \sigma_i^2)$—then the linear combination of the u's given by $a_1 u_1 + a_2 u_2 + \cdots + a_n u_n$ also has the normal distribution with mean $a_1 \mu_1 + a_2 \mu_2 + \cdots + a_n \mu_n$ and variance $a_1^2 \sigma_1^2 + a_2^2 \sigma_2^2 + \cdots + a_n^2 \sigma_n^2$. In summation notation, $U = \sum (a_i u_i) \sim N[\sum(a_i \mu_i), \sum(a_i^2 \sigma_i^2)]$.

e. If $u_1, u_2, \ldots, u_n$ are independently and identically distributed (iid) as $N(\mu, \sigma^2)$, their mean $\bar{u} = (1/n)\sum u_i$ has the normal distribution with mean μ and variance σ^2/n; that is, $\bar{u} \sim N(\mu, \sigma^2/n)$. Also, $z = \sqrt{n}(\bar{u} - \mu)/\sigma \sim N(0, 1)$.

2.A.2   Maximization and Minimization

Estimation of the unknown parameters of a distribution often involves the maximization or minimization of certain objective functions. For example, in estimating relationships an important objective is to find the "best fit" that somehow minimizes errors. In this section we present the methods of maximization or minimization of objective functions; this is especially useful when the investigator has constraints on the problems under study. The basic principles are first studied for the simple case involving only one variable, with no constraints imposed. These are then extended to many variables and to the case when constraints are present.

Functions, Derivatives, Maxima and Minima

The general relationship between a dependent variable (Y) and an independent variable (X) is expressed in the form of a function denoted by the expression $Y = F(X)$. At the moment, we focus our attention only on functions involving a single variable. We will assume that $F(X)$ is *continuous*; that is, $F(X)$ does not "jump" when X moves only by an infinitesimal amount. A function is said to be *monotonically increasing* if Y increases whenever X increases (see Figure 2.A.1). A supply curve is

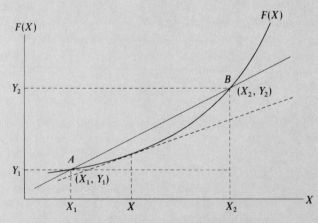

Figure 2.A.1   A monotonic increasing function

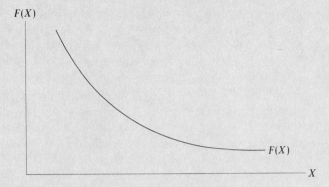

Figure 2.A.2   A monotonic decreasing function

an example of such a function. If Y decreases as X increases, as in Figure 2.A.2, the function is said to be *monotonically decreasing* (a demand curve for example). In Figure 2.A.1, consider the two points A and B whose coordinates are (X_1, Y_1) and (X_2, Y_2). The ratio $(Y_2 - Y_1)/(X_2 - X_1)$ is the *slope* of the straight line connecting A and B that intersects the graph of the function at A and B. The ratio measures the change in Y per unit change in X. It is also denoted by $\Delta Y/\Delta X$, where $\Delta Y = Y_2 - Y_1$ is the change in Y and $\Delta X = X_2 - X_1$ is the change in X. Suppose we make ΔX smaller and smaller so that ultimately A and B coincide at X. Eventually, the straight line AB just touches the graph of $F(X)$. This is the *tangent* of the curve at the point X; the slope of the tangent is called the derivative of Y with respect to X. This is written algebraically as the limit of $\Delta Y/\Delta X$ as ΔX goes to zero, and is denoted either as dY/dX or as $F'(X)$. We thus have the following definition.

Definition 2.A.1
The derivative of Y with respect to X is defined as

$$\frac{dY}{dX} = F'(X) = \lim_{\Delta X \to 0} \frac{\Delta Y}{\Delta X} \qquad \text{provided the limit exists}$$

If the limit exists, $F(X)$ is said to be *differentiable* at X. As an example, suppose X is the total quantity of a good produced by a firm and Y is the total cost of producing it. Then $F(X)$ is the total cost function and the derivative, dY/dX, is the added cost of producing one additional unit, which is known as **marginal cost** in microeconomics. It will be noted from Figures 2.A.1 and 2.A.2 that the derivative $F'(X)$ need not be constant but might depend on the value of X at which it is measured. We can therefore differentiate $F'(X)$ again and get $F''(X) = d^2Y/dX^2$, provided this second derivative exists.

In Figure 2.A.1 the derivative is positive for all X for which $F(X)$ is defined. Similarly, it is always negative in Figure 2.A.2. We readily see that for a monotonic function the derivative always has the same sign. In Figure 2.A.3a we note that $F(X)$ is not monotonic but alternatively rises and falls (unemployment rate is an example). Initially, the slope is positive, then it becomes negative, and again becomes positive. The points A and B have the property that the slope of the tangent is zero. Thus, $F'(X) = 0$ at these points. We note that at A, $F(X)$ attains a local maximum and at B it attains a local minimum. A necessary condition for a *local extremum* (that is, maximum or minimum) is that the first derivative $F'(X)$ should be zero. This condition, known as the *first-order condition*, is not sufficient to identify whether $F(X)$ is at a minimum or maximum. Figure 2.A.3b represents $F'(X)$, and we note that it initially decreases and later increases. The slope of $F'(X)$ is the second derivative $F''(X)$, which is negative at A and positive at B. To distinguish between a minimum and a maximum, we need the *second-order condition* that the second derivative $F''(X)$ should be negative at the point at which the first derivative $F'(X) = 0$, in order for $F(X)$ to attain a maximum. For a minimum, the second-order condition is that $F''(X)$ be positive at the point at which $F'(X) = 0$.

We state without proof a number of useful results on derivatives.

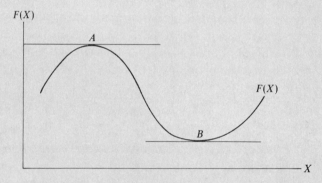

Figure 2.A.3   a. A nonmonotonic function

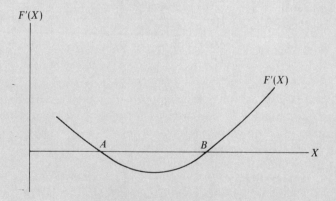

Figure 2.A.3   b. The graph of $F'(X)$

Property 2.A.2

a. The derivative of a constant is zero.
b. The derivative of $F(X) + G(X)$ is the sum of the derivatives $F'(X) + G'(X)$.
c. If a is a constant, the derivative of $aF(X) = aF'(X)$.
d. The derivative of the power function X^m equals mX^{m-1}. As a special case of this, the derivative of $\sqrt{X}$ (that is, $X^{1/2}$) is $1/(2\sqrt{X})$, or $\frac{1}{2}X^{-1/2}$. Similarly, the derivative of $1/X$ (that is, X^{-1}) is $-1/X^2$ (that is, $-X^{-2}$).
e. If $Y = F(Z)$ and $Z = G(X)$, then $\dfrac{dY}{dX} = \dfrac{dY}{dZ}\dfrac{dZ}{dX} = F'G' = F'(Z)G'(X) = F'[G(X)]G'(X)$. [This result is known as the chain rule of differentiation.]

An Application

Suppose a firm is faced with a cost function $C(q)$ (the relationship between total cost and output), where q is the quantity of output produced. Further assume that the firm is in a competitive industry and can sell the output at the fixed market price p per unit. The firm's decision is to choose the quantity of goods to be produced. Its objective is to maximize profits. The total revenue is pq and profit is total revenue minus total cost. The profit function is therefore given by

$$\pi(q) = pq - C(q)$$

As we noted earlier, a condition for maximizing profits is $\pi'(q) = 0 = p - C'(q)$. C' is the derivative of C with respect to q. It is the additional cost of one more unit produced, which as we saw is the *marginal cost*. The condition, therefore, states that in order to maximize profits, a competitive firm should choose the output at which price equals marginal cost. As a specific example, let $C(q) = 10 - 5q + 2q^2$ and the price per unit be 35. Differentiating $C(q)$ with respect to q, the marginal cost function is $C'(q) = -5 + 4q$. Setting this equal to 35 and solving for q, we get $q = 10$. Thus, the profit maximizing output is 10. In the general case when the cost function is quadratic (that is, it depends on the square of q), $C(q) = a + bq + cq^2$ and the marginal cost function is $C'(q) = b + 2cq$. The profit maximizing condition is therefore $p = b + 2cq$. When solved for q, this gives the optimum quantity to produce as $q = (p - b)/2c$. The second-order condition for maximization is $\pi''(q) < 0$. The second derivative of $\pi = -C''(q) = -2c$. For this to be negative, we need the condition that c must be positive. Also, to give a positive output, p must be greater than b. If b is negative, as in the above example, this condition is automatically satisfied because price will always be positive.

Functions of Several Variables

Here we summarize a number of results for a function that depends on several variables. Applications of the multivariate calculus are presented later in this section.

The general form of a function of several variables is $Y = F(X_1, X_2, \ldots, X_n)$. A simple example of this is the generalization of a straight line; $Y = X_1 + 2X_2 + 3X_3 + \cdots + 8X_8$. As before, Y is the dependent variable and the Xs are the independent variables. The change in Y in response to a change in only one of the Xs is of considerable interest. For the moment, consider $X_2, X_3, \ldots, X_n$ as fixed. Treating Y as a function of only X_1, we can measure the change in Y per unit change in X_1. This analogue of the derivative is called the **partial derivative** of Y with respect to X_1, and is written in a number of ways.

Definition 2.A.2

The partial derivative of Y with respect to X_i is defined as

$$\frac{\partial Y}{\partial X_i} = \frac{\partial F}{\partial X_i} = F_i = \lim_{\Delta X_i \to 0} \frac{\Delta Y}{\Delta X_i}$$

Thus, the partial derivative is the response per unit change in one of the independent variables, holding the values of all the other independent variables fixed. In the example we used, $\partial Y / \partial X_8 = 8$.

Example 2.A.1

Let $Y = \beta_1 X_1 + \beta_2 X_2 + \cdots + \beta_n X_n$, where each of the βs is a constant. The partial derivative is then $\partial Y / \partial X_i = \beta_i$. As another example, suppose $Y = aK^2 + bKL + cL^2$ (a, b, and c are constants). The partial derivative of Y with respect to K is $\partial Y / \partial K = 2aK + bL$. This is because the derivative of aK^2 is $2aK$, which gives the first term. The partial derivative of bKL with respect to K is bL because L is treated as fixed. The partial derivative of cL^2 with respect to K is zero because it is independent of K. $\square$

The chain rule of differentiation is applicable here also. Suppose $Y = F(Z)$ and $Z = G(X_1, X_2, \ldots, X_n)$. Then the partial derivative of Y with respect to X_i can be written as

$$\frac{\partial Y}{\partial X_i} = \frac{\partial Y}{\partial Z} \frac{\partial Z}{\partial X_i} = F'(Z) \frac{\partial G}{\partial X_i}$$

Note that this partial derivative would generally depend on all the Xs.

The concepts of maximum and minimum are extended easily to a multivariate function. In order for $F(X_1, X_2, \ldots, X_n)$ to attain a maximum or a minimum, the following conditions have to be met:

$$\frac{\partial F}{\partial X_i} = 0 \qquad \text{for each } i = 1, 2, \ldots, n$$

By setting to zero the partial derivative of F with respect to each X, we get n equations in the n unknowns $X_1, X_2, \ldots, X_n$. Solving these for X_i, we obtain their solutions. When these values are substituted in F, we obtain the maximum or minimum value of Y. Analogous to the second-order condition in a univariate case, there is a similar condition that enables us to distinguish between a maximum point and a minimum point. This condition is very complicated and is not presented here. The reader is referred to the books on mathematics listed at the end of this chapter for more details.

An Application

It is useful to illustrate the preceding concepts with an application. Consider a firm in a competitive industry that faces a fixed commodity price p, a given wage rate w, and a given capital rental rate r. Let $F(K, L)$ be the *production function* that relates the quantity of output produced by the firm to the inputs, capital (K) and labor (L). The firm's objective would be to choose the amounts of labor and capital so as to maximize profits. The profit function $\pi(K, L)$ is given by the value of the output $[pF(K, L)]$ less the cost of capital (Kr) and that of labor (wL).

$$\pi(K, L) = pF(K, L) - rK - wL$$

The two conditions for maximization are $\partial\pi/\partial K = 0$ and $\partial\pi/\partial L = 0$. Taking the partial derivatives of π with respect to K and L and setting them to zero, we get (noting that p, w, and r are fixed)

$$r = p\frac{\partial F}{\partial K} \quad \text{and} \quad w = p\frac{\partial F}{\partial L}$$

$\partial F/\partial K$ is the extra output per unit extra capital input and is called the *marginal product of capital*. Similarly, $\partial F/\partial L$ is the *marginal product of labor*. Also, $p\partial F/\partial L$ and $p\partial F/\partial K$ are the values of the corresponding marginal products. The first-order conditions imply that firms would maximize profits when they choose K and L such that the value of the marginal product of labor equals the wage rate and the value of the marginal product of capital equals the rental rate.

Let us apply this to a specific production function. Let $Y = F(K, L) = K^\alpha L^\beta$, where Y is the quantity of output produced. This is known as the *Cobb–Douglas production function*. The marginal product of capital is

$$\frac{\partial Y}{\partial K} = \alpha K^{\alpha-1}L^\beta = \frac{\alpha K^\alpha L^\beta}{K} = \frac{\alpha Y}{K}$$

Similarly, the marginal product of labor is $\partial F/\partial L = \beta Y/L$. For profit maximization, the first-order conditions are $\alpha Y/K = r/p$ and $\beta Y/L = w/p$. These can be solved for the amounts of labor and capital as $L = \beta Yp/w$ and $K = \alpha Yp/r$.

As a numerical example, let $\alpha = 0.2$, $\beta = 0.6$, $p = 10$, $w = 4$, and $r = 0.1$. From these values, we get $L = \beta Yp/w = 1.5Y$ and $K = \alpha Yp/r = 20Y$. Substituting these in the production function we obtain

$$Y = (20Y)^{0.2}(1.5Y)^{0.6} = 20^{0.2}1.5^{0.6}Y^{0.8} = 2.321992Y^{0.8}$$

Dividing both sides by $Y^{0.8}$, we get $Y^{0.2} = 2.321992$. Solving this, we get the total output Y as 67.5. The *derived demands* for labor and capital are then obtained as $L = \beta Yp/w = 101.25$ and $K = \alpha Yp/r = 1350$.

Optimization Under Constraints

In economics, we frequently encounter the need to maximize or minimize a multivariate function subject to one or more constraints. For instance, let $U(X_1, X_2)$ be the utility a consumer derives from the consumption of two commodities. X_1 is the consumption of the first commodity and X_2 is the consumption of the second commodity. Let p_1 be the price of the first good, p_2 the price of the second good, and Y the consumer's income, all of which are assumed to be fixed. The objective of the consumer is to maximize the utility function subject to the constraint that the total amounts spent on the two commodities $(p_1 X_1 + p_2 X_2)$ be exactly equal to the consumer's income (Y). Thus, the problem reduces to choosing the values of X_1 and X_2 such that $U(X_1, X_2)$ is a maximum, subject to the budget condition that $Y = p_1 X_1 + p_2 X_2$.

As a second example, consider a public utility company that generates electricity and sells it to its customers in a service area. Being a regulated monopoly, it is not permitted to maximize profits. Instead, the public utility commission and the company generate forecasts of the electricity requirements for the next one or two decades and then choose that electricity-generating technology (or combination of technologies) that minimizes the cost of producing the target output. In other words, the firm minimizes the cost of production subject to the constraint that the output must be a fixed quantity.

Both these problems are examples of *constrained optimization*. This topic is usually covered only in third semester calculus courses. An understanding of this is *not* essential to learning the basics of econometrics. We are discussing it here because some of the theoretical proofs presented, in this and later chapter appendices, depend on this section. Readers not interested in those proofs may skip this section entirely without loss of continuity. However, the discussion here is simple enough to be understood even by those who have not had a course on advanced calculus. Also, the student will find the application presented here useful in other courses.

Lagrange's Method of Constrained Optimization

The general problem is to maximize the function $F(X_1, X_2, \ldots, X_n)$ subject to the constraint $G(X_1, X_2, \ldots, X_n) = 0$. First write the *Lagrangian function*

$$H(X_1, X_2, \ldots, X_n, \lambda) = F(X_1, X_2, \ldots, X_n) + \lambda G(X_1, X_2, \ldots, X_n)$$

where λ is called the *Lagrange multiplier* and is a new unknown. It can be shown that the maximization of F subject to the constraint $G = 0$ is equivalent to maximizing the function H with respect to each of the Xs *without any constraint*. The problem has thus been reduced to the earlier form, with a modified function and an additional unknown (λ). Setting the partial derivatives of H with respect to the unknowns to zero, we get the $n + 1$ first-order conditions, $G(X_1, X_2, \ldots, X_n) = 0$ and $\partial G / \partial X_i = 0$, for $i = 1, 2, \ldots, n$. These conditions can be solved, in general, for the $n + 1$ unknowns $X_1, X_2, \ldots, X_n$, and the Lagrange multiplier λ.

Application to the Cost Minimization Problem

In the electricity generation example, the company minimizes the cost function subject to the constraint that a certain target output must be produced. Let Y_0 be the target output. The constraint is then $Y_0 = F(K, L)$, where $F(\ )$ is the production function encountered earlier. K and L are the amounts of capital and labor the utility will use in order to generate the output Y_0. The cost corresponding to this is $Kr + Lw$, where w is the wage rate and r is the capital rental rate, both assumed fixed. The utility's optimization problem is that of choosing K and L so as to minimize $Kr + Lw$ subject to the constraint $Y_0 = F(K, L)$. The Lagrangian function here is

$$H(K, L, \lambda) = Kr + Lw + \lambda[Y_0 - F(K, L)]$$

The first-order conditions are now given by $\partial H/\partial K = \partial H/\partial L = \partial H/\partial \lambda = 0$. These translate to the following three conditions in the unknowns K, L, and λ, which can be solved, in general, for the optimum levels of capital and labor to use:

$$r = \lambda \frac{\partial F}{\partial K}, \qquad w = \lambda \frac{\partial F}{\partial L}, \qquad Y_0 = F(K, L)$$

Extension to Several Constraints

The Lagrange multiplier principle can be applied even when there is more than one constraint. The modification is to add more Lagrange multiplier terms in the Lagrangian function, one for each constraint. Thus, the problem of maximizing $F(X_1, X_2, \ldots, X_n)$ subject to the two constraints $G(X_1, X_2, \ldots, X_n) = 0$ and $Q(X_1, X_2, \ldots, X_n) = 0$ can be solved with the modified Lagrangian function

$$H(X_1, X_2, \ldots, X_n) = F(X_1, X_2, \ldots, X_n) + \lambda G(X_1, X_2, \ldots, X_n)$$
$$+ \mu Q(X_1, X_2, \ldots, X_n)$$

where λ and μ are the Lagrange multipliers corresponding to the two constraints. The first-order conditions for maximization are the following $n + 2$ conditions:

$$G(X_1, X_2, \ldots, X_n) = 0$$
$$Q(X_1, X_2, \ldots, X_n) = 0$$
$$\frac{\partial F}{\partial X_i} + \lambda \frac{\partial G}{\partial X_i} + \mu \frac{\partial Q}{\partial X_i} = 0 \qquad \text{for } i = 1, 2, \ldots, n$$

2.A.3 More on Estimation Procedures

In Section 2.8 we discussed two methods of estimating the unknown parameters of a distribution. In this section we present two other, more advanced methods.

Best Linear Unbiased Estimator (BLUE)

Definition 2.20 stated that a desirable property for an estimator is to be a minimum variance unbiased linear estimator so that it is most efficient (see

Definition 2.18 on efficiency). In this section we derive such an estimator. The sample mean is a weighted average of the observations, with the weight for each observation being $1/n$. Consider another linear combination of the x's $\tilde{\beta} = \sum a_i x_i$, where the a_i's are nonrandom constants. This is called a *linear estimator*. We can ask the question, "Under what condition will $\tilde{\beta}$ be unbiased?" Using Property 2.6a the expected value of $\tilde{\beta}$ is given by $E(\tilde{\beta}) = \sum a_i \mu = \mu \sum a_i$. For this to be equal to μ, we need the condition that $\sum a_i = 1$. Thus, any linear combination of the observations for which the sum of the weights is 1, will be an unbiased estimator of μ. The *best linear unbiased estimator* (also called BLUE) is one for which we choose the weight a_i such that the variance of $\sum a_i x_i$ is the smallest, subject to the condition that $\sum a_i = 1$. From Property 2.A.1c, $\text{Var}(\tilde{\beta}) = \sigma^2 \sum a_i^2$. Therefore, $\tilde{\beta}$ will be BLUE if we choose a_i such that $\sum a_i^2$ is a minimum subject to the constraint that $\sum a_i = 1$. We readily see that this is an application of the Lagrange multiplier principle described in Section 2.A.2. The Lagrangian function is

$$H = \sum a_i^2 + \lambda(1 - \sum a_i)$$

The first-order conditions are $\partial H/\partial a_i = \partial H/\partial \lambda = 0$. We get $\partial H/\partial a_i = 2a_i - \lambda$. Hence, $2a_i = \lambda$ and $\sum a_i = 1$ are the required conditions. Summing $2a_i$ over i, we get $2 \sum a_i = n\lambda$. But $\sum a_i = 1$. Hence, we have $n\lambda = 2$ or $\lambda = 2/n$. Because λ is also equal to $2a_i$, the condition becomes $2a_i = 2/n$, or $a_i = 1/n$. Thus, the BLUE procedure yields the weight $1/n$ to minimize the variance of the linear combination of the x's subject to the condition that it be unbiased. Using this we get $\tilde{\beta} = \sum x_i/n = \bar{x}$. Thus, the sample mean obtained earlier is also BLUE. This means that *the sample mean is most efficient among all unbiased linear combinations of the observations.*

The Principle of Maximum Likelihood

This is another method, proposed by the British statistician R. A. Fisher, for obtaining estimates of unknown parameters from a sample of observations. This method is better explained with an example. Suppose a pharmaceutical company has invented a new drug to combat a disease. The company claims that the cure rate is 90 percent. A chemist from the Food and Drug Administration conducts preliminary tests and disputes that claim, saying that the cure rate is 70 percent. They go to a statistician to resolve the dispute, The statistician's task is to decide whether the cure rate is 70 percent or 90 percent.[3] Because the experiment has only two outcomes (a cure being a "success"), the underlying probability model is the binomial distribution described in Section 2.1. Let p be the probability of a success, that is, that the patient is cured. The statistician's task is to choose between the two alternative estimates for p: 0.9 and 0.7.

To resolve the dispute, the analyst draws a random sample of ten patients (in practice, several thousand observations will be drawn) and finds that eight of them were cured. The question is "Did eight successes out of ten occur when the true

[3] In practice, the question will be posed as one of estimating the cure rate without restricting the choice to just two values. To keep the discussion simple, we assume that a choice is to be made only between 0.9 and 0.7.

probability of success was 0.9 or 0.7?" The *principle of maximum likelihood* is based on the intuitive notion that "an event occurred because it was most likely to." According to this principle, we compute the probability (which is called *likelihood* in the context of estimation) of the observed outcome under the two alternatives under consideration, and choose that alternative for which the probability of observing what we observed is the maximum. The belief is that the observed sample values are more likely to have come from this population than from others. In our example, the probability of observing eight successes out of ten is given by

$$\frac{10!}{8!2!}0.9^8 0.1^2 = 0.1937 \qquad \text{if } p = 0.9$$

$$\frac{10!}{8!2!}0.7^8 0.3^2 = 0.2335 \qquad \text{if } p = 0.7$$

Because the probability is higher for $p = 0.7$, the *maximum likelihood estimate* of the probability of a cure is 0.7 (when the choice is between 0.9 and 0.7).

The general principle of maximum of likelihood uses the following procedure. Let X be the random variable whose probability distribution depends on the unknown parameter θ. The probability density is $f(x, \theta)$. A random sample x_1, $x_2, \ldots, x_n$ of independent observations is drawn. Because the x's are independent, the *joint density* of the sample is the product $f(x_1, \theta) \cdot f(x_2, \theta) \cdot \cdots \cdot f(x_n, \theta)$. This is called the *likelihood function* and is denoted by $L(x, \theta)$.

$$L(x, \theta) = \prod_{i=1}^{n} f(x_i, \theta) = f(x_1, \theta) \cdot f(x_2, \theta) \cdot \cdots \cdot f(x_n, \theta)$$

If the possible values of θ are discrete, the procedure is to evaluate $L(x, \theta)$ for each possible value under consideration and choose the value for which L is the highest. If $L(x, \theta)$ is differentiable, maximize it over the range of permissible values of θ. This gives the first and second-order conditions

$$\frac{dL}{d\theta} = 0 \qquad \text{and} \qquad \frac{d^2L}{d\theta^2} < 0$$

If this principle is applied to the drug-testing example used earlier, the maximum likelihood estimate of the probability is 0.8. Taking the logarithm of both sides of the likelihood function, we have

$$\ln L(x, \theta) = \sum \ln[f(x_i, \theta)]$$

Because logarithm is a *monotonic transformation* (that is, if $x_1 > x_2$, then $\ln x_1 > \ln x_2$), maximizing $L(x, \theta)$ is equivalent to maximizing $\ln L(x, \theta)$. It is often more convenient to maximize this log likelihood function.

Suppose the likelihood function has several unknown parameters θ_i ($i = 1, 2, \ldots, k$) such as, for example, the mean $\mu(\theta_1)$ and variance $\sigma^2(\theta_2)$ of the distribution. Then the maximization is that of $L(x, \theta_1, \theta_2, \ldots, \theta_k)$. The first-order conditions are then $\partial L/\partial \theta_i = 0$ for $i = 1$ to k. The k resulting equations are jointly solved for the θs. In practice, it is often easier to maximize $\ln L$ and use the conditions $\partial \ln L/\partial \theta_i = 0$, to solve for the θs.

Properties of Maximum Likelihood Estimators

Maximum likelihood estimators have a number of desirable properties. These are listed in Property 2.A.3.

Property 2.A.3

Maximum likelihood estimators are

a. consistent
b. asymptotically efficient; that is, for large n, no other consistent estimator has a smaller variance.
c. asymptotically normal; that is, for large n, they closely approximate the normal distribution, even if the distribution from which the observations were drawn was not normal.

Example 2.A.2

Suppose a random variable X has the normal distribution with mean μ and variance σ^2. A random sample of observations $x_1, x_2, \ldots, x_n$ is drawn. What are the maximum likelihood estimators of μ and σ^2? From equation (2.4) we know that the density function for x_i is given by

$$f(x_i, \mu, \sigma^2) = \frac{1}{\sigma\sqrt{2\pi}} e^{-(x_i - \mu)^2/(2\sigma^2)}$$

The likelihood function is therefore given by

$$L(x, \mu, \sigma^2) = \left[\frac{1}{\sigma\sqrt{2\pi}}\right]^n e^{-[\Sigma(x_i - \mu)^2]/(2\sigma^2)}$$

By taking the logarithm of this we get the log likelihood function as

$$\ln L = -n \ln \sigma - n \ln(\sqrt{2\pi}) - \frac{1}{2\sigma^2} \sum(x_i - \mu)^2$$

We note that $\ln L$ depends on μ only through the last term involving the sum of squares of deviations of x_i from the mean μ. Because there is a minus sign in front of that term, maximizing $\ln L$ is equivalent to minimizing $\sum(x_i - \mu)^2$, which is the same as the least squares procedure described earlier. The estimate of μ that minimizes this sum of squares (and hence maximizes the likelihood) is the sample mean $\bar{x}$. Therefore, *the sample mean $\bar{x}$ is the maximum likelihood estimator of μ if X is normally distributed as $N(\mu, \sigma^2)$.*

To get the maximum likelihood estimator of σ^2, partially differentiate $\ln L$ with respect to σ. We get the first-order condition (note that x, n, and μ are treated as constants in this partial differentiation)

$$-\frac{n}{\sigma} - \frac{1}{2} \sum(x_i - \mu)^2(-2\sigma^{-3}) = 0$$

It is easy to verify that the maximum likelihood estimator of σ^2, denoted by $\hat{\sigma}^2$, is given by $\hat{\sigma}^2 = (1/n)\sum(x_i - \bar{x})^2$. In deriving this, we have used the estimate $\bar{x}$ for μ. Comparing this to equation (2.11) we note that the sample variance s^2 and the maximum likelihood estimator $\hat{\sigma}^2$ are different. Because $E(s^2) = \sigma^2$ by Property 2.11b, $E(\hat{\sigma}^2) \neq \sigma^2$. This establishes the result that *the maximum likelihood estimator of a parameter need not be unbiased.* By Property 2.A.3a, however, it is consistent. It is also asymptotically unbiased.   □

2.A.4 Derivation of the Statistic for Testing the Equality of the Means of Two Normal Populations

Because the sample mean from a normally distributed random variable is also normally distributed, and the difference of two normal random variables is also normal, we have

$$\bar{x} - \bar{y} \sim N\left[\mu_x - \mu_y, \sigma^2\left(\frac{1}{m} + \frac{1}{n}\right)\right]$$

We also know from Property 2.4c that subtracting the mean and dividing by the standard deviation yields a standard normal random variable with mean 0 and variance 1. Also, under the null hypothesis, $\mu_x = \mu_y$. Therefore

$$z = \frac{\bar{x} - \bar{y}}{\sigma\left[\dfrac{1}{m} + \dfrac{1}{n}\right]^{1/2}} \sim N(0, 1)$$

We cannot use this in a test because σ is known. It can be estimated from the sample as

$$s^2 = \frac{(m - 1)s_x^2 + (n - 1)s_y^2}{m + n - 2}$$

where

$$s_x^2 = \frac{1}{m - 1}\left[\sum(x_i - \bar{x})^2\right] \quad \text{and} \quad s_y^2 = \frac{1}{n - 1}\left[\sum(y_j - \bar{y})^2\right]$$

are the sample variances of the two scores. If we replace σ by its estimate s, however, the distribution is no longer normal but is Student's t with d.f. $m + n - 2$ (equal to the total sample size minus two because we estimated the two parameters μ_x and μ_y. The test statistic is therefore given by

$$t_c = \frac{\bar{x} - \bar{y}}{s\left[\dfrac{1}{m} + \dfrac{1}{n}\right]^{1/2}} \sim t_{m+n-2}$$

the sale price of the house, on average, by 0.065 thousands of dollars (note that the unit is important), or 65 dollars. More realistically, a 100-square-foot increase in SQFT is expected to increase the average price by \$6500. α is the intercept term and corresponds to the conditional mean of Y when X is zero. When X is zero, there is no house to speak of and hence α can be interpreted as the average price of a vacant lot. If α were 21.1, the average land value of an empty lot would be \$21,100.

In formulating the simple linear relation between PRICE and SQFT, we are ignoring the fact that the price of a house depends on other characteristics as well, such as lot size and number of bathrooms. Thus, we are basically assuming that all these effects are absorbed by the error term u_t, or are indirectly captured by SQFT. The error term is actually a combination of four different effects:

1. It accounts for the effects of variables omitted from the model.
2. It captures the effects of nonlinearities in the relationship between Y and X. Thus, if the true model were $Y_t = \alpha + \beta X_t + \gamma X_t^2 + v_t$ and we assumed that it was as in equation (3.1), then the effect of X_t^2 would be absorbed into u_t.
3. Errors in measuring X and Y are also absorbed by u_t.
4. u_t also includes inherently unpredictable random effects.

Although the model we are examining is very simple and certainly not realistic, the various concepts in econometrics are easily understood with the two-variable regression example. In Chapter 4 we extend the analysis to the case where more than one explanatory variable is included.

Having formulated the model, our next objective is to obtain the "best" estimates for α and β. After that has been established, we examine the reliability of those estimates as well as that of Assumption 3.1, then test hypotheses on them and use the estimated line to obtain conditional forecasts of the price of a house, given X. Before we can achieve these objectives, however, additional assumptions have to be imposed on u_t and X_t. These are now discussed one by one. Table 3.2 has a complete list of assumptions.

TABLE 3.2 Assumptions of the Simple Linear Regression Model

3.1	The regression model is linear in the unknown coefficients α and β; that is, $Y_t = \alpha + \beta X_t + u_t$, for $t = 1, 2, \ldots, T$.
3.2	The error term u_t is a random variable with zero mean; that is, $E(u_t) = 0$.
3.3	Not all of the Xs are the same; at least one of them is different.
3.4	X_t is given and nonrandom, implying that it is uncorrelated with u_t; that is, $\mathrm{Cov}(X_t, u_t) = E(X_t u_t) - E(X_t)E(u_t) = 0$.
3.5	u_t has a constant variance for all t; that is, $\mathrm{Var}(u_t) = E(u_t^2) = \sigma^2$.
3.6	u_t and u_s are independently distributed for all $t \neq s$, so that $\mathrm{Cov}(u_t, u_s) = E(u_t u_s) = 0$.
3.7	u_t is normally distributed so that $u_t \sim N(0, \sigma^2)$, which implies that $Y_t \mid X_t \sim N(\alpha + \beta X_t, \sigma^2)$.

Assumption 3.2 (errors average to zero)
Each u_t is a random variable with $E(u_t) = 0$.

In Figure 3.1 we note that some of the observed points lie above the line $\alpha + \beta X$ and some below. This means that some of the error terms are positive and some are negative. Because $\alpha + \beta X$ is the average line, it seems reasonable to assume that these random errors cancel out, on average, *in the population*. Therefore, the assumption that u_t is a random variable with expected value zero is realistic.

Assumption 3.3 (some of the Xs are different)
Not all the values of X_t are the same. At least one of the values of X_t is different from the others. In other words, the sample variance $\dfrac{1}{T-1}\sum_t (X_t - \bar{X})^2$ is not zero.

This is an important assumption because otherwise the model cannot be estimated, as will be seen formally in Section 3.2. On an intuitive level, if X_t does not vary, it cannot explain why Y_t varies. As an example, suppose Y_t is the consumption expenditure of a household in the tth month, and X_t is household income from wages in the same month. Typically, monthly wages do not vary very much but expenditure varies considerably from month to month. If income does not vary, it cannot explain variations in consumption. This does not mean that income is unimportant as a determinant of consumption. If wages go up in the next year, average consumption would also go up. Figure 3.2 illustrates Assumption 3.3 this graphically. In the house example, suppose information was gathered only about houses with a living area of 1500 square feet. The sample scatter diagram will be as in Figure 3.2. It is clear from the diagram that this information is inadequate for estimating the population regression line $\alpha + \beta X$.

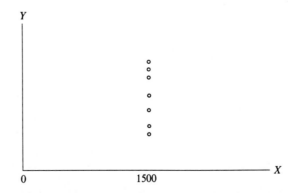

Figure 3.2   An example in which X-values do not vary

Assumption 3.4 (X's are nonrandom)

$E(u_t) = 0$, each X_t is given, and is hence not a random variable, implying that
$\text{Cov}(X_t, u_t) = E(X_t u_t) - E(X_t) E(u_t) = X_t E(u_t) - X_t E(u_t) = 0$.

At this point, the reader should review Section 2.3 on joint probability distributions, with special attention to the sections on statistical independence, mathematical expectation in a two-variable case, covariance and correlation, and conditional mean. The assumption that X_t is given (that is, we look at only conditional properties) means that it can be treated as nonrandom. $E(X_t u_t) = 0$ implies that the population covariance between X_t and u_t is zero. X and u are hence uncorrelated. We will see in Section 3.3 that Assumption 3.4 is crucial to establishing that our methods of estimating α and β have certain desirable properties. On an intuitive level, if X and u are correlated, then as X changes so will u. In this case, the expected value of Y will not be $\alpha + \beta X$. This point is explored more fully in Section 3.3.

Assumption 3.5 (constant error variance)

All the u's are identically distributed with the finite variance σ^2, so that
$\text{Var}(u_t) = E(u_t^2) = \sigma^2$.

Assumption 3.6 (uncorrelated error)

The u's are also independently distributed so that $\text{Cov}(u_t, u_s) = E(u_t u_s) = 0$ for all $t \neq s$.

These assumptions imply that the residuals are independently and identically distributed (iid). We note from Figure 1.2 that for a given X, there is a scatter of Y values that determines a conditional distribution. The errors u_t are the deviations from the conditional mean $\alpha + \beta X_t$. Assumption 3.5 implies that the distribution of u_t has the same variance (σ^2) as that of u_s for a different observation s. Figure 3.3c is an example where the variances are not constant across observations. Assumption 3.5 is relaxed in Chapter 8. Assumption 3.6 (which is relaxed in Chapter 9) implies that u_t and u_s are independent and hence uncorrelated. In particular, successive errors are uncorrelated and are not clustered together. Figure 3.3d is an example where this assumption is violated.

Assumption 3.7 (normality of errors)

Each u_t is distributed as $N(0, \sigma^2)$, which implies that the conditional density of Y given X–that is, $Y|X$–is distributed as $N(\alpha + \beta X, \sigma^2)$.

Thus, the error terms $u_1, u_2, \ldots, u_T$ are assumed to be independently and identically distributed as normal with mean zero and the common variance σ^2. We will see in Section 3.5 that Assumption 3.7 is fundamental to hypothesis testing. Table 3.2 summarizes all the assumptions made so far. Error terms that satisfy Assumptions 3.2 through 3.7 are often referred to as **well-behaved errors**.

Practice Problem

3.1   In each of the four diagrams in Figure 3.3, explain why the model violates the assumption noted below it.

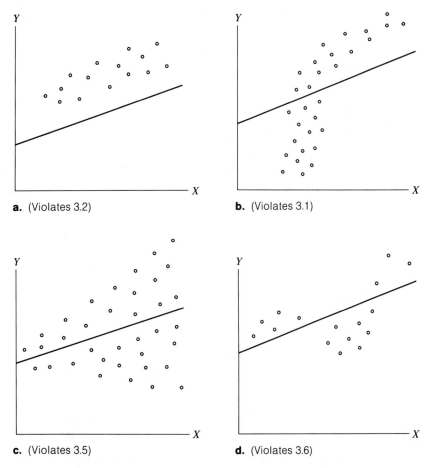

a. (Violates 3.2)   **b.** (Violates 3.1)

c. (Violates 3.5)   **d.** (Violates 3.6)

Figure 3.3   Examples of violations of the assumptions

3.2   Procedures for the Estimation of Parameters

In this section we discuss two different approaches to estimating the unknown parameters. Two other methods are discussed in the chapter appendix.

A Simple Method Based on the Assumptions $E(u_t) = 0 = E(X_t u_t)$[1]

The simple linear regression model has three unknown parameters: α, β, and σ^2. We postpone the problem of estimating σ^2 to Section 3.4. To estimate α and β we need two equations. These can be derived from a number of premises. In the previous section we made several assumptions about the model and the disturbance term u_t. Assumption 3.2 stated that $E(u_t) = 0$, that is, that the errors, u_t average out in the population. In other words, the *population mean of u_t is zero*. Assumption 3.4 stated that $E(X_t u_t) = 0$, that is, that X_t and u_t are uncorrelated, again in the population. Suppose we stipulate that similar conditions be satisfied *in the sample*. More specifically, let $\hat{\alpha}$ (read as "alpha hat") denote the sample estimate of α, and $\hat{\beta}$ denote the estimate of β. Then an estimate of the error term is obtained as $\hat{u}_t = Y_t - \hat{\alpha} - \hat{\beta} X_t$. The term $\hat{u}_t$ is referred to as the **estimated residual**, or simply the **residual**.[2] The sample analogue of the condition $E(u_t) = 0$ is that $(1/T)\sum \hat{u}_t = 0$; that is, the *sample mean of $\hat{u}_t$ is zero*. We thus obtain the following condition:

$$\frac{1}{T}\sum \hat{u}_t = 0 = \frac{1}{T}\sum(Y_t - \hat{\alpha} - \hat{\beta} X_t) = \frac{1}{T}\sum Y_t - \frac{1}{T}(T\hat{\alpha}) - \hat{\beta}\frac{1}{T}\sum X_t \quad (3.2)$$

$(1/T)\sum Y_t$ is the sample mean of Y, denoted by $\bar{Y}$, and $(1/T)\sum X_t$ is the sample mean of X, denoted by $\bar{X}$. We also note that $\sum \hat{\alpha}$ is $T\hat{\alpha}$ because every term has $\hat{\alpha}$ and there are T terms. Using these results in equation (3.2), we get the following equation:

$$\bar{Y} = \hat{\alpha} + \hat{\beta}\bar{X} \quad (3.3)$$

The straight line $\hat{\alpha} + \hat{\beta}X$ is the *estimated* line and is known as the **sample regression line**, or the **fitted straight line**. We see from equation (3.3) that the sample regression line passes through the mean point $(\bar{X}, \bar{Y})$. We will see in Exercise 3.4c that this property need not hold unless the constant term α is present in the model.

The second condition for obtaining $\hat{\alpha}$ and $\hat{\beta}$ is provided by Assumption 3.4, that $E(X_t u_t) = 0$. The sample statistic corresponding to $E(X_t u_t)$ is $(1/T)\sum(X_t\hat{u}_t)$. Setting this to zero we obtain the condition

$$\frac{1}{T}\sum(X_t\hat{u}_t) = \frac{1}{T}\sum[X_t(Y_t - \hat{\alpha} - \hat{\beta} X_t)] = 0 \quad (3.4)$$

Taking the summation term by term, and noting that $\hat{\alpha}$ and $\hat{\beta}$ can be taken out of the summation because they appear for each t, we get (canceling T)

$$\sum(X_t Y_t) - \hat{\alpha}\sum X_t - \hat{\beta}\sum X_t^2 = 0$$

or

$$\sum(X_t Y_t) = \hat{\alpha}\sum X_t + \hat{\beta}\sum X_t^2 \quad (3.5)$$

· · · · · · ·

[1] *It can be shown that this method is a particular variation of the method of moments described in Section 2.8.*

[2] *Some authors and instructors prefer to use a for $\hat{\alpha}$, b for $\hat{\beta}$ and e_t for $\hat{u}_t$. We have adopted the ^ notation conventional in statistical theory because it makes a clear distinction between the true value and an estimated value and also identifies the parameter that is being estimated.*

Equations 3.2 and 3.5 are known as the **normal equations** (no connection with the normal distribution). We postpone the actual solutions for $\hat{\alpha}$ and $\hat{\beta}$ until the next section.

The Method of Least Squares

The method just described, although quite simple to use, is ad hoc and is not based on any optimality principle. In econometrics, the most frequently used estimation procedure is the **method of least squares**. It is also known as **ordinary least squares (OLS)**, as opposed to other types of least squares procedures that will be discussed in later chapters. Denoting the estimates of α and β by $\hat{\alpha}$ and $\hat{\beta}$, the estimated residual is equal to $\hat{u}_t = Y_t - \hat{\alpha} - \hat{\beta}X_t$. The optimality criterion used by the least squares procedure is to minimize the objective function

$$\text{ESS}(\hat{\alpha}, \hat{\beta}) = \sum_{t=1}^{t=T} \hat{u}_t^2 = \sum_{t=1}^{t=T} (Y_t - \hat{\alpha} - \hat{\beta}X_t)^2$$

with respect to the unknown parameters $\hat{\alpha}$ and $\hat{\beta}$. ESS is the sum of squared residuals and the OLS procedure minimizes the sum of squared residuals.

On a more intuitive level, suppose we choose a particular set of values $\hat{\alpha}$ and $\hat{\beta}$, that is, a particular straight line $\hat{\alpha} + \hat{\beta}X$. The deviation of Y_t from this chosen line is given by the estimated residual $\hat{u}_t = Y_t - \hat{\alpha} - \hat{\beta}X_t$, which can be computed from the data. Next square this and sum it over all the observations. The *observed* sum of squares of residuals [denoted as the **error sum of squares (ESS)**] is therefore $\sum \hat{u}_t^2$.[3] Associated with each choice of straight line there is an error sum of squares. The OLS procedure would select those values $\hat{\alpha}$ and $\hat{\beta}$ for which ESS is a minimum.

Squaring accomplishes two things. First, it removes the sign of the error and hence treats positive errors and negative errors alike. Second, squaring has the property of penalizing large errors substantially. As an example, suppose the sample residuals were 1, 2, -1, and -2 for a particular choice of the regression coefficients $\hat{\alpha}$ and $\hat{\beta}$. Compare this with another choice that generates the residuals -1, -1, -1, and 3. The sum of the absolute values of the errors is the same in both cases. Although the second choice has lowered two of the errors from 2 to 1 in absolute value, it also results in a large error, namely 3, which is undesirable. If we obtain ESS for the two cases, we get the value 10 for the first case ($1^2 + 2^2 + 1^2 + 2^2$) and the value $12(1^2 + 1^2 + 1^2 + 3^2)$ for the second case. The least squares method imposes a heavy penalty on the large error and hence would have chosen the first straight line. We will see in Section 3.3 that the procedure of minimizing ESS has other desirable properties as well.

The conditions for minimization are (see Section 2.A.2 on minimizing a function involving two variables)

$$\frac{\partial \text{ESS}}{\partial \hat{\alpha}} = 0 \quad \text{and} \quad \frac{\partial \text{ESS}}{\partial \hat{\beta}} = 0$$

· · · · · · ·

[3] *It is somewhat confusing to call the sum of squared residuals ESS, but this notation is used by many well-known computer programs and comes from the Analysis of Variance literature (see the end of Section 3.6).*

It is shown in Section 3.A.2 of the appendix to this chapter that these two conditions lead to the same normal equations, (3.2) and (3.5). Therefore, the estimates of α and β obtained using the least squares procedure are identical to those obtained by the method of the previous section. The assumptions required by the OLS method are, however, fewer. As we see in Section 3.A.2, the derivation of the normal equations does not need Assumptions 3.2 and 3.4, which the previous method used. All we need are two or more observations and Assumption 3.3. With only one observation, we cannot fit any straight line (or equivalently, an infinite number of straight lines can go through that one point). With two observations, the straight line is unique, and we get a perfect fit; but with more observations several straight lines are possible. The least squares method selects that straight line for which the sum of squares of vertical deviations (in Figure 3.1) is the smallest.

The Method of Maximum Likelihood*

We mention the method of maximum likelihood only in passing. It is described in Section 2.A.3. In Section 3.A.4, the principle is applied to the simple regression model. The method is based on yet another type of optimality criterion, and gives the same estimators as those of the OLS procedures. In simple terms, the maximum likelihood procedure selects those estimates that maximize the probability of the observed sample.

From the preceding discussion we see that three different approaches to the problem of estimating α and β yield exactly the same results. Then why is it necessary to consider all three? The answer is that in later chapters we will find that when some of the assumptions listed in Table 3.2 are relaxed, these procedures, in fact, yield different answers.

Solutions to the Normal Equations

The normal equations are reproduced below for reference.

$$\bar{Y} = \hat{\alpha} + \hat{\beta}\bar{X} \tag{3.3}$$

$$\sum X_t Y_t = \hat{\alpha}\sum X_t + \hat{\beta}\sum X_t^2 \tag{3.5}$$

To solve these for $\hat{\alpha}$ and $\hat{\beta}$ we proceed as follows.

From equation (3.3),

$$\hat{\alpha} = \bar{Y} - \hat{\beta}\bar{X} = \frac{1}{T}\sum Y_t - \hat{\beta}\frac{1}{T}\sum X_t. \tag{3.6}$$

Substitute for $\hat{\alpha}$ from this into (3.5):

$$\sum X_t Y_t = \left[\frac{1}{T}\sum Y_t - \hat{\beta}\frac{1}{T}\sum X_t\right](\sum X_t) + \hat{\beta}\sum X_t^2.$$

Now group the $\hat{\beta}$ terms together:

$$\sum X_t Y_t = \left[\frac{(\sum X_t)(\sum Y_t)}{T}\right] + \hat{\beta}\left[\sum X_t^2 - \frac{(\sum X_t)^2}{T}\right].$$

Solving this for $\hat{\beta}$ we get

$$\hat{\beta} = \frac{\left[\sum X_t Y_t - \dfrac{(\sum X_t)(\sum Y_t)}{T} \right]}{\left[\sum X_t^2 - \dfrac{(\sum X_t)^2}{T} \right]}.$$

Using a simplifying notation, this can be expressed as

$$\hat{\beta} = \frac{S_{xy}}{S_{xx}} \tag{3.7}$$

where

$$S_{xx} = \left[\sum X_t^2 - \frac{(\sum X_t)^2}{T} \right] \tag{3.8}$$

and

$$S_{xy} = \left[\sum X_t Y_t - \frac{(\sum X_t)(\sum Y_t)}{T} \right] \tag{3.9}$$

The notation S_{xx} and S_{xy} can be remembered in a more intuitive way. Define $x_t = X_t - \bar{X}$ and $y_t = Y_t - \bar{Y}$, where the bar denotes the sample mean. Thus the lower case variable denotes the deviation of the upper case variable from its mean. In the Appendix Section 3.A.1, the following results are shown.

$$\sum x_t = 0 = \sum y_t$$

$$S_{xx} = \sum x_t^2 = \sum X_t^2 - \frac{1}{T}(\sum X_t)^2 \tag{3.10}$$

$$S_{xy} = \sum x_t y_t = \sum X_t Y_t - \frac{1}{T}[(\sum X_t)(\sum Y_t)] \tag{3.11}$$

S_{xy} can thus be remembered as the "sum of x_t times y_t." Similarly, S_{xx} is the sum of x_t times x_t, which is the sum of x_t squared.

Equations (3.6) and (3.7) represent the solution to the normal equations [(3.2) and (3.5)] and give us the **sample estimates** $\hat{\alpha}$ and $\hat{\beta}$ for the **population parameters** α and β. Assumption 3.3 is needed because otherwise S_{xx} would be zero and hence equation (3.7) could not be solved for $\hat{\beta}$. In obtaining the OLS estimates of α and β we did not use Assumptions 3.2, 3.4, 3.5, 3.6, and 3.7.

Comparing equations (3.9), (3.11) with equation (2.12), we note that $S_{xy} = (T-1)\widehat{\text{Cov}(X, Y)}$. Similarly, from equations (3.8), (3.10), and (2.11) we see that $S_{xx} = (T-1)\widehat{\text{Var}(X)}$. Therefore, the estimated slope coefficient can also be written as

$$\hat{\beta} = \frac{\widehat{\text{Cov}(X, Y)}}{\widehat{\text{Var}(X)}} \tag{3.7'}$$

In other words, $\hat{\beta}$ can also be expressed as the ratio of the estimated covariance between X and Y, and the estimated variance of X.

Example 3.1

For the data presented in Table 3.1, the estimated simple linear relation is $\hat{Y}_t = 52.351 + 0.13875X_t$. $\hat{Y}_t$ is the estimated or predicted value of price (in thousands of dollars) that corresponds to X_t. The regression coefficient for X_t is the estimated *marginal* effect of living area for an average house. Thus, if the living area is increased by one unit, the estimated average price is expected to go up by 0.13875 thousands of dollars (that is, by \$138.75). More realistically, for each 100-square-foot increase in the area, the estimated price is expected to go up, on average, by \$13,875. The average estimated price of an empty lot (for which $X_t = 0$) is given by \$52,351.   □

Practice Problems

3.2   Copy the two columns of numbers in Table 3.1 onto a ruled sheet of paper. In the first column of the worksheet copy the values for Y_t (PRICE) and in the second column copy the values for X_t (SQFT). Use a calculator and prepare two more columns of numbers. Square each entry in the second column and enter it in the third column (X_t^2). Multiply corresponding entries in the first and second columns and enter the number in the fourth column (X_tY_t). Next, sum each column and verify the following totals:

$$\sum X_t = 26{,}753 \qquad \sum X_t^2 = 55{,}462{,}515$$
$$\sum Y_t = 4{,}444.9 \qquad \sum X_tY_t = 9{,}095{,}985.5$$

To avoid round-off errors be sure to use as many digits as the calculator will allow. Next, compute S_{xy} from equation (3.9) and S_{xx} from equation (3.8). Finally, compute $\hat{\beta}$ from (3.7) and $\hat{\alpha}$ from (3.6) and verify the values presented earlier. [Aren't you glad computers do all the work nowadays?]

3.3   Consider the following equations:
a. $Y_t = \alpha + \beta X_t + u_t$
b. $Y_t = \hat{\alpha} + \hat{\beta} X_t + \hat{u}_t$
c. $Y_t = \hat{\alpha} + \hat{\beta} X_t + u_t$
d. $\hat{Y}_t = \alpha + \beta X_t$
e. $\hat{Y}_t = \alpha + \beta X_t + \hat{u}_t$
f. $\sum u_t = 0$
g. $\sum X_t u_t = 0$
     In equations (f) and (g), the summation is over the sample for $t = 1, 2, \ldots, T$. Carefully explain why equations (a) and (b) are correct but (c), (d), (e), (f), and (g) are incorrect. A diagram would be useful in answering this question.

3.4   You want to estimate the relationship $F = \alpha + \beta W + u$, where F is the fuel consumption (per mile) of a merchant ship and W is the weight of the ship. In estimating the unknown parameters, are cross-section data more appropriate than time series data for a given ship over several years? Explain.

3.3 Properties of Estimators

Although the least squares as well as the other procedures give an estimate of the straight-line relationship that would be the "best fit" for the data, we would like to answer several other questions. For example, what are the statistical properties of $\hat{\alpha}$ and $\hat{\beta}$? What measure of reliability do they have? How can we use them to test hypotheses or generate forecasts? We now take up a discussion of each of these issues. It might be useful at this point to review Section 2.7, which gives a summary of the desirable properties of estimators.

Property 3.1
(*Unbiasedness*)

Under Assumptions 3.2 and 3.4, $[E(u_t) = 0,\ E(X_t u_t) = 0]$, the least squares estimators $\hat{\alpha}$ and $\hat{\beta}$ are unbiased; that is, $E(\hat{\alpha}) = \alpha$ and $E(\hat{\beta}) = \beta$.

Unbiasedness is clearly desirable because it means that, on average, the estimated values will be the true values, even though in a particular sample this may not be so.

PROOF* (Readers not interested in the proof may skip it without loss of continuity.) From equation (3.7), $E(\beta) = E(S_{xy}/S_{xx})$. But by Assumption 3.4 X_t is nonrandom and hence so is S_{xx}. This means that in taking expectations, terms involving X_t can be brought outside the expectations. Therefore, we have $E(\hat{\beta}) = \dfrac{1}{S_{xx}} E(S_{xy})$. In equation (3.9), substitute for Y_t from equation (3.1) and also use $T\alpha$ for $\sum \alpha$.

$$S_{xy} = \sum X_t(\alpha + \beta X_t + u_t) - \left[\frac{(\sum X_t)(T\alpha + \beta \sum X_t + \sum u_t)}{T}\right]$$
$$= \alpha \sum X_t + \beta \sum X_t^2 + \sum X_t u_t - \alpha \sum X_t$$
$$\quad - \beta\left[\frac{(\sum X_t)^2}{T}\right] - \left[\frac{(\sum X_t)(\sum u_t)}{T}\right] \tag{3.12}$$
$$= \beta\left[\sum X_t^2 - \frac{(\sum X_t)^2}{T}\right] + \left[\sum X_t u_t - \frac{(\sum X_t)(\sum u_t)}{T}\right]$$
$$= \beta S_{xx} + S_{xu}$$

where S_{xx} is given by equation (3.8) and

$$S_{xu} = \sum X_t u_t - \frac{(\sum X_t)(\sum u_t)}{T} \tag{3.13}$$
$$= \sum X_t u_t - \bar{X} \sum u_t = \sum (X_t - \bar{X})u_t$$

$\bar{X}$ is the sample mean of X. X_t is nonrandom, $\bar{X}$ appears in every term, and the expectation of a sum of terms is equal to the sum of the expectations. Therefore,

$$E(S_{xu}) = \sum E(X_t u_t) - \bar{X} \sum E(u_t) = \sum X_t E(u_t) - \bar{X} \sum E(u_t) = 0$$

by Assumption 3.2. Hence, $E(S_{xy}) = \beta S_{xx}$, which means that $E(\hat{\beta}) = E(S_{xy})/S_{xx} = \beta$. Thus, $\hat{\beta}$ is an unbiased estimator of β. The proof is similar for $\hat{\alpha}$. It should be pointed out that this proof of unbiasedness crucially depends on Assumption 3.4. If $E(X_t u_t) \neq 0$, $\hat{\beta}$ would be biased. $\qquad\square$

Although unbiasedness is a desirable property, by itself it does not make an estimator "good," and an unbiased estimator is not unique. Consider, for instance, the alternative estimator $\tilde{\beta} = (Y_2 - Y_1)/(X_2 - X_1)$. It will be noted that $\tilde{\beta}$ (read as "beta tilde") is simply the slope of the straight line connecting the first two scatter points (X_1, Y_1) and (X_2, Y_2). It is easy to show that $\tilde{\beta}$ is also unbiased.

$$\tilde{\beta} = \frac{Y_2 - Y_1}{X_2 - X_1} = \frac{(\alpha + \beta X_2 + u_2) - (\alpha + \beta X_1 + u_1)}{X_2 - X_1} = \beta + \frac{u_2 - u_1}{X_2 - X_1}$$

As before, the Xs are nonstochastic and $E(u_2) = E(u_1) = 0$. Therefore $\tilde{\beta}$ is also unbiased. In fact, it is possible to construct an infinite number of such unbiased estimators. Because $\tilde{\beta}$ throws away observations 3 through T, intuitively it cannot be a "good" estimator. In Exercise 3.1, all the observations are used to construct yet another unbiased estimator, but this too is not as desirable as other possible unbiased estimators. We therefore need additional criteria to judge whether an estimator is "good."

A second criterion to consider is that of *consistency*, which is a large sample property defined in Section 2.7.

Property 3.2
(*Consistency*)

The least squares estimators are consistent provided $\text{Cov}(X, u) = E(X_t u_t) = 0$ and $0 < \text{Var}(X) < \infty$.

In intuitive terms, consistency is the property that the estimator converges to the true value as the sample size is increased indefinitely. The estimator $\tilde{\beta}$ presented above is clearly not consistent because increasing the sample size does not affect it.

PROOF* (This proof also may be skipped without loss of continuity.) From equations (3.12) and (3.7)

$$\hat{\beta} = \beta + \frac{S_{xu}/T}{S_{xx}/T} \qquad (3.14)$$

By the law of large numbers S_{xu}/T converges to its expectation, which is $\text{Cov}(X, u)$. Similarly, S_{xx}/T converges to $\text{Var}(X)$. It follows therefore that, as T converges to infinity, $\hat{\beta}$ converges to $\beta + [\text{Cov}(X, u)]/\text{Var}(X)$, which would equal

β if $\text{Cov}(X, u) = 0$—that is, if X and u are uncorrelated. Thus, $\hat{\beta}$ is a consistent estimator of β. □

Although $\hat{\beta}$ is unbiased and consistent, we still need additional criteria because it is possible to construct other unbiased and consistent estimators. Exercise 3.1 has an example of such an estimator. The criterion that we will use next is *efficiency* (defined in Section 2.7). In simple terms, an unbiased estimator is said to be more efficient if it has a smaller variance than another unbiased estimator.

Property 3.3
(*Efficiency, BLUE, and the Gauss–Markov Theorem*)

Under Assumptions 3.2 through 3.6, ordinary least squares estimators are most efficient among unbiased linear estimators. OLS procedure thus yields Best Linear Unbiased Estimates (BLUE).

This result (proved in Section 3.A.3) is known as the Gauss–Markov Theorem, which states that OLS estimators are BLUE; that is, among all linear combinations of the Ys that are unbiased, the OLS estimators of α and β have the smallest variance.

In summary, the ordinary least squares (OLS) procedure of estimating the regression coefficients of a model yields several desirable properties; estimators are (1) unbiased, (2) consistent, and (3) most efficient. Unbiasedness and consistency require the assumptions $E(u_t) = 0$ and $\text{Cov}(X_t, u_t) = 0$. Efficiency and BLUE require, in addition, $\text{Var}(u_t) = \sigma^2$ and $\text{Cov}(u_t, u_s) = 0$, for $t \neq s$.

Practice Problems

3.5 State the assumptions essential for the least squares estimators to be (a) unbiased, (b) consistent, (c) BLUE, and (d) normally distributed. Be sure to explain, in each case, where your assumptions are used.

3.6 Using equation (3.6), show that $\hat{\alpha}$ is unbiased. Clearly state the assumptions needed for this.

3.7 Try Exercises 3.1 through 3.11.

3.4 The Precision of the Estimators

We have just seen that OLS estimates possess a number of nice properties. The next step of the analysis is to obtain numerical measures of the precision of the estimates. We know from the theory of probability that the variance of a random variable is a measure of its dispersion around the mean. The smaller the variance, the closer, on average, individual values are to the mean. Also, when dealing with confidence intervals, we know that the smaller the variance of the random variable, the narrower the confidence interval of a parameter. The variance of an estimator is thus an indicator of the precision of the estimator. It is therefore of considerable interest to compute the variables of $\hat{\alpha}$ and $\hat{\beta}$.

Because $\hat{\alpha}$ and $\hat{\beta}$ depend on the Ys, which in turn depend on the random variables $u_1, u_2, \ldots, u_T$, they are also random variables with associated distributions. The following equations are derived in Section 3.A.5 of the appendix to this chapter.

$$\text{Var}(\hat{\beta}) = \sigma_{\hat{\beta}}^2 = E[(\hat{\beta} - \beta)^2] = \frac{\sigma^2}{S_{xx}} \tag{3.15}$$

$$\text{Var}(\hat{\alpha}) = \sigma_{\hat{\alpha}}^2 = E[(\hat{\alpha} - \alpha)^2] = \frac{\sum X_t^2}{TS_{xx}}\sigma^2 \tag{3.16}$$

$$\text{Cov}(\hat{\alpha}, \hat{\beta}) = \sigma_{\hat{\alpha}\hat{\beta}} = E[(\hat{\alpha} - \alpha)(\hat{\beta} - \beta)] = -\frac{\bar{X}}{S_{xx}}\sigma^2 \tag{3.17}$$

where S_{xx} is defined in equation (3.8) and σ^2 is the variance of the error terms. It should be noted that if S_{xx} increases, these variances and covariance (in absolute value) decrease. This demonstrates that a *higher variation in X and a larger sample size are desirable because they improve the precision with which the parameters are estimated.*

The above expressions are **population variances** and are unknown because σ^2 is unknown. They can, however, be estimated because σ^2 can be estimated from the sample. Note that $\hat{Y}_t = \hat{\alpha} + \hat{\beta}X_t$ is the estimated straight line. Therefore, $\hat{u}_t = Y_t - \hat{\alpha} - \hat{\beta}X_t$ is an estimate of u_t and is called the *estimated residual*. An obvious estimator of σ^2 is $\sum \hat{u}_t^2/T$, but it happens to be biased. An unbiased estimator of σ^2 is given by (see Section 3.A.6 for proof)

$$s^2 = \hat{\sigma}^2 = \frac{\sum \hat{u}_t^2}{T - 2} \tag{3.18}$$

The reason for dividing by $T - 2$ is similar to that given for dividing the chi-square by $T - 1$, which was discussed in Section 2.6. There, $T - 1$ was used because of the condition $\sum(x_i - \bar{x}) = 0$. Here, there are two conditions given by the normal equations (3.2) and (3.5), and hence we use $T - 2$. The square root of the estimated variance is called the **standard error of the residuals** or the **standard error of the regression**. Using this estimate we can obtain estimates of the variances and covariance of $\hat{\alpha}$ and $\hat{\beta}$. The square roots of the variances are called the **standard errors of the regression coefficients** and are denoted by $s_{\hat{\alpha}}$ and $s_{\hat{\beta}}$. The estimated variances and covariance of the estimated regression coefficients are

$$s_{\hat{\beta}}^2 = \frac{\hat{\sigma}^2}{S_{xx}} \tag{3.19}$$

$$s_{\hat{\alpha}}^2 = \frac{\sum X_t^2}{TS_{xx}}\hat{\sigma}^2 \tag{3.20}$$

$$\sigma_{\hat{\alpha}\hat{\beta}} = -\frac{\bar{X}}{S_{xx}}\hat{\sigma}^2 \tag{3.21}$$

To summarize what we have done so far: First, we obtained the estimated regression coefficients $\hat{\alpha}$ and $\hat{\beta}$ using equations (3.6) and (3.7). This gave us an estimated relationship between Y and X. We then calculated the predicted value of Y_t as $\hat{Y}_t = \hat{\alpha} + \hat{\beta}X_t$. From this we obtained the residual $\hat{u}_t$ as $Y_t - \hat{Y}_t$. Then we obtained an estimate of the variance of u_t from equation (3.18). Substituting this in equations (3.15), (3.16), and (3.17), we obtained the variances and covariance of $\hat{\alpha}$ and $\hat{\beta}$. The computationally efficient method of performing these calculations is discussed in Section 3.7.

Example 3.2

The following standard errors are given for the home price example.

standard error of the residuals $= s = \hat{\sigma} = 39.023$

standard error for $\hat{\alpha} = s_{\hat{\alpha}} = 37.285$

standard error for $\hat{\beta} = s_{\hat{\beta}} = 0.01873$

covariance between $\hat{\alpha}$ and $\hat{\beta} = S_{\hat{\alpha}\hat{\beta}} = -0.671$ □

Practice Computer Session 3.1 at the end of this chapter gives instructions to reproduce the above results as well as those in later sections.

3.5 Tests of Hypotheses

As mentioned earlier, testing statistical hypotheses is one of the main tasks of an econometrician. In the regression model (3.1), if β is zero, the predicted value of Y will be independent of X, implying that X has no effect on Y. Thus, the hypothesis $\beta = 0$ is of interest here, and we would strongly hope that it would be rejected. The correlation coefficient (ρ) between the two variables X and Y measures the closeness of association between the two variables. The sample estimate of ρ is given in equation (2.19). If $\rho = 0$, the variables are uncorrelated. Another test of interest is therefore $\rho = 0$. In this section we discuss the procedures for testing hypotheses on α and β only. The test on ρ is undertaken in the next section. We strongly recommend that, before proceeding, readers review Section 2.10 on hypothesis testing.

Hypothesis testing consists of three basic steps: (1) formulating two opposing hypotheses (null and alternative hypotheses), (2) deriving a test statistic and its statistical distribution under the null hypothesis, and (3) deriving a decision rule for rejecting or accepting the null hypothesis. In the home price example the null hypothesis is $H_0: \beta = 0$. Because we would expect β to be positive, a natural alternative hypothesis is $H_1: \beta > 0$. Later we also consider the two-sided alternative $H_1: \beta \neq 0$. In order to carry out this test, $\hat{\beta}$ and its estimated standard error $s_{\hat{\beta}}$ are used to derive a test statistic.

Derivation of a Test Statistic

In this section we show that the test statistic $t_c = (\hat{\beta} - \beta_0)/s_{\hat{\beta}}$ has the Student's t-distribution, under the null hypothesis, with $T - 2$ degrees of freedom (the d.f. is $T - 2$ here because we are estimating two parameters, α and β).

PROOF (Readers not interested in the formal derivation may skip this part.) First, it is possible to show the following property.

Property 3.4

> a. $\hat{\alpha}$ and $\hat{\beta}$ are distributed normally.
> b. $(\sum \hat{u}_t^2)/\sigma^2 = [(T-2)\hat{\sigma}^2]/\sigma^2$ has a chi-square distribution with $T-2$ d.f.
> c. $\hat{\alpha}$ and $\hat{\beta}$ are distributed independently of $\hat{\sigma}^2$.

Property 3.4a follows from the fact that $\hat{\alpha}$ and $\hat{\beta}$ are linear combinations of u_t and that u_t is normally distributed. For the formal proof of Parts b and c, the reader is referred to Hogg and Craig (1978, pp. 296–298). Utilizing these results we have

$$\hat{\alpha} \sim N(\alpha, \sigma_{\hat{\alpha}}^2), \qquad \hat{\beta} \sim N(\beta, \sigma_{\hat{\beta}}^2), \qquad \frac{\sum \hat{u}_t^2}{\sigma^2} \sim \chi_{T-2}^2$$

where $\sigma_{\hat{\alpha}}^2$ and $\sigma_{\hat{\beta}}^2$ are the variances of $\hat{\alpha}$ and $\hat{\beta}$ given by equations (3.15) and (3.16), respectively. By standardizing the distributions of the estimated parameters— that is, subtracting the mean and dividing by the standard deviation—we will get

$$\frac{(\hat{\alpha} - \alpha)}{\sigma_{\hat{\alpha}}} \sim N(0.1), \qquad \frac{(\hat{\beta} - \beta)}{\sigma_{\hat{\beta}}} \sim N(0,1), \qquad \frac{(T-2)\hat{\sigma}^2}{\sigma^2} \sim \chi_{T-2}^2$$

In Section 2.4, the t-distribution was defined as the ratio of a standard normal to the square root of a chi-square independent of it. Applying this to $\hat{\beta}$ and using equations (3.15), (3.18) and (3.19), we obtain

$$t = \frac{(\hat{\beta} - \beta)}{\sigma_{\hat{\beta}}} \div \left[\frac{\hat{\sigma}^2}{\sigma^2}\right]^{1/2} = \frac{\sigma(\hat{\beta} - \beta)}{\hat{\sigma}\sigma_{\hat{\beta}}} = \frac{(\hat{\beta} - \beta)}{s_{\hat{\beta}}} \sim t_{T-2}$$

where

$$s_{\hat{\beta}} = \frac{\hat{\sigma}}{\sqrt{S_{xx}}} = \frac{\hat{\sigma}}{\sigma} \frac{\sigma}{\sqrt{S_{xx}}} = \frac{\hat{\sigma}\sigma_{\hat{\beta}}}{\sigma}$$

The $s_{\hat{\beta}}$ is the estimated standard error of $\hat{\beta}$ given in equation (3.19). $\square$

The above t is the test statistic based on which a decision rule is formulated. The test is known as the *t*-test. The steps for testing the desired hypothesis are given below, separately for two-tailed and one-tailed tests.

Decision Rule

One-Tailed Test

Step 1 $H_0: \beta = \beta_0$ $\qquad$ $H_1: \beta > \beta_0$

Step 2 The test statistic is $t_c = (\hat{\beta} - \beta_0)/s_{\hat{\beta}}$, which can be calculated from the sample. Under the null hypothesis, it has the t-distribution with

$T - 2$ d.f. If the calculated t_c is "large," we would suspect that β is probably not equal to β_0. This leads to the next step.

Step 3 In the t-table inside the front cover of the book, look up the entry for $T - 2$ d.f. and the given level of significance (say a) and find the point $t^*_{T-2}(a)$ such that $P(t > t^*) = a$.

Step 4 Reject H_0 if $t_c > t^*$. If the alternative had been $\beta < \beta_0$, the test criterion would have been to reject H_0 if $t_c < -t^*$.

The above test is illustrated graphically in Figure 3.4 (we are using the symbol a for the level of significance in order to avoid confusion with the intercept term α). If the calculated t-statistic (t_c) falls in the shaded area of the figure (known as the **critical region**), then $t_c > t^*$. In that case the null hypothesis is rejected and we conclude that β is *significantly greater than β_0*.

Example 3.3

In the home price example, $\beta_0 = 0$. Therefore $t_c = \hat{\beta}/s_{\hat{\beta}}$, that is, the test statistic is simply the ratio of the estimated regression coefficient divided by its standard error. This ratio is known as the **t-statistic**. The estimate is $\hat{\beta} = 0.13875$, and from Example 3.2, $s_{\hat{\beta}} = 0.01873$. Therefore, the calculated t-statistic is $t_c = 0.13875/0.01873 = 7.41$. The degrees of freedom are $T - 2 = 14 - 2 = 12$. Let the level of significance (referred to above as a) be 1 percent, that is, $a = 0.01$. From the t-table inside the front cover of this book, $t^*_{12}(0.01) = 2.681$. Because $t_c > t^*$, we reject H_0 and conclude, not surprisingly, that β is **significantly greater than zero** at the 1 percent level of significance. It should be noted that this coefficient is significant even at the 0.05 percent level of significance because $t^*_{12}(0.0005) = 4.318$.

The t-statistic for $\hat{\alpha}$ is given by $t_c = 52.351/37.285 = 1.404$ which is smaller than $t^*_{12}(0.05) = 1.782$. Hence we cannot reject H_0 but instead conclude that α is **statistically not greater than zero** at the 5 percent level. This result on α is troublesome because it will be recalled that $\hat{\alpha}$ is expected to measure the average price of an empty lot (that is, for $X = 0$). The insignificance of $\hat{\alpha}$ points to two

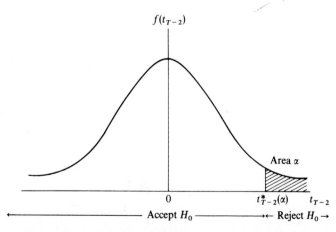

Figure 3.4 One tailed test for $\beta = \beta_0$ against $\beta > \beta_0$

things. First, $X = 0$ is well outside the sample range and hence estimating $\hat{Y}$ when $X = 0$ will not be very reliable (more on this in Section 3.10). Second, as can be readily seen from Figure 3.1, the two variable specification is inadequate for explaining the observed variation in price. It will be seen in Chapter 4 that $\hat{\alpha}$ captures the average effects of omitted variables and nonlinearities, in addition to the own effect when X is zero. The net effect could very well make $\hat{\alpha}$ insignificant. □

The *p*-Value Approach to Hypothesis Testing

The *t*-test can also be carried out in an equivalent way. First calculate the probability that the random variable t is greater than the observed t_c, that is, calculate

$$p\text{-}value = P(t > t_c)$$

This probability (referred to as the **p-value**) is the same as the probability of Type I error—that is, the probability of rejecting a true hypothesis. A high value for this probability implies that the consequences of erroneously rejecting a true H_0 are severe. A low *p*-value implies that the consequences of rejecting a true H_0 erroneously are not very severe (that is, the probability of making a mistake of type I is low) and hence we are "safe" in rejecting H_0. The decision rule is therefore to *accept* H_0 (that is, not reject it) if the *p*-value is too high, say more than 0.10, 0.05, or 0.01. In other words, **if the *p*-value is higher than the specified level of significance (say *a*), we conclude that the regression coefficient is not significantly greater than β_0 at the level *a*. If the *p*-value is less than *a* we reject H_0 and conclude that β is significantly greater than β_0.**

To see the equivalence of the two approaches, we note from Figure 3.5 that if $P(t > t_c)$ is *less than* the level *a*, then the point corresponding to t_c must necessarily be to the *right* of $t^*_{T-2}(a)$. This means that t_c will fall in the rejection region. Similarly, if $P(t > t_c) > a$, then t_c must be to the left of t^* and hence fall into the accep-

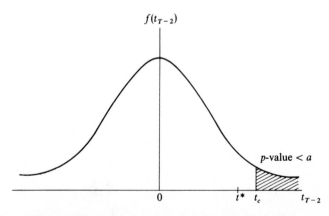

Figure 3.5 *p*-value approach to hypothesis testing

tance region. The modified steps for the *p*-value approach are as follows:

Step 3a Calculate the probability (denoted as *p-value*) that *t* is greater than t_c, that is, compute the area to the right of the *calculated* t_c.

Step 4a Reject H_0 and conclude that the coefficient is significant if the *p*-value is *less than* the given level of significance (*a*).

In summary, β is judged to be significantly greater than β_0 if the *t*-statistic is high or the *p*-value is low, how high or low being determined by the investigator. The traditional method of hypothesis testing requires one to look up tabulated values for the critical *t**. The *p*-value approach, however, requires a computer program that calculates the areas in the tail for any given value of t_c. More and more computer programs are providing these *p*-values (the ECSLIB program used in the empirical applications in this book is an example) and hence this method is not hard to implement.

Example 3.3a

To apply the *p*-value approach to the home price example, we calculate the probability that *t* is greater than the observed value of 7.41 for β. Using ECSLIB this was calculated as a value less than 0.0001 (refer to the output from Practice Computer Session 3.1). This means that, if we reject the null hypothesis, there is a less than 0.01 percent chance of making a mistake of type I, and hence it is "safe" to reject H_0 and conclude that β is significantly greater than zero. For the parameter α, the *p*-value is 0.093, that is, $P(t > 1.404) = 0.093$. Now if $H_0 : \alpha = 0$ is rejected, the probability of making a type I error is 9.3 percent, which is higher than 5 percent. Therefore, we cannot reject H_0 at 5 percent, which means that we conclude, as we did before, that (at the 5 percent level of significance) α is statistically not greater than zero. We see from this that the *p*-value approach is superior because we know the precise level at which a coefficient is significant and can judge whether this level is low enough to justify rejecting H_0. After all, there is nothing sacred about values such as 0.01, 0.05, and 0.10. □

Two-tailed Test

The procedure for a two-sided alternative is quite similar. The steps are as follows:

Step 1 $H_0 : \beta = \beta_0 \qquad H_0 : \beta \neq \beta_0$

Step 2 The test statistic is $t_c = (\hat{\beta} - \beta_0)/s_{\hat{\beta}}$, which is the same as before. Under the null hypothesis, t_c is distributed as t_{T-2}.

Step 3 In the *t*-table inside the front cover, look up the entry for $T - 2$ d.f. and the given level of significance (say *a*) and find the point $t^*_{T-2}(\alpha/2)$ such that $P(t > t^*) = \alpha/2$ (one-half of the level of significance).

Step 3a To use the *p*-value approach, calculate

$$p\text{-}value = P(t > t_c \text{ or } t < -t_c) = 2P(t > t_c)$$

because of the symmetry of the *t*-distribution around the origin.

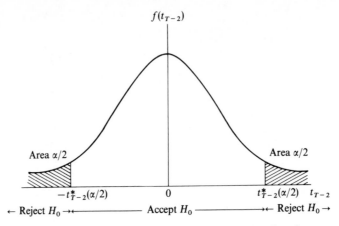

Figure 3.6 Two-tailed test for $\beta = \beta_0$ against $\beta \neq \beta_0$

Step 4   Reject H_0 if $t_c > t^*$ or $t_c < -t^*$ and conclude that β **is significantly different from β_0 at the level a.**

Step 4a   In the case of the p-value approach, reject H_0 if p-value $< a$, the level of significance.

The two-tailed test is illustrated graphically in Figure 3.6. The degrees of freedom here also are $T - 2$. If the calculated t-statistic (t_c) falls in the shaded area in the figure, the null hypothesis is rejected and we conclude that β is significantly different from β_0. A critical value of $t^* = 2$ is often used as a rule of thumb to judge the significance of a t-statistic at 5 percent (for a two-tailed test). This is because t^* is nearly 2 for degrees of freedom over 25.

Example 3.4

The calculated t_c for the home price example is the same as before; that is, it is still 7.41 for $\hat{\beta}$ and 1.404 for $\hat{\alpha}$. From the t-table, $t_{12}^*(0.005) = 3.055$, which means that the area in both tails corresponding to 3.055 is 0.01. Because $t_c > t^*$, for $\hat{\beta}$, we reject H_0 here also and conclude that β is **significantly different from zero** at the 1 percent level of significance. For $\hat{\alpha}$, $t_{12}^*(0.025) = 2.179$ which is greater than t_c. Therefore we cannot reject the null hypothesis here either (note that we are using a 5 percent test for α). From Step 3a, the p-value for $\hat{\alpha} = 2P(t > 1.404) = 0.186$ (note that the p-value corresponding to t_c for the two-sided case is twice that for the one-sided alternative). Because a type I error of 18.6 percent is unacceptably high, we cannot reject $H_0 : \alpha = 0$. It follows that α is not statistically significant but β is.   □

Testing σ^2

Although a test for the significance of the error variance σ^2 is not common, we present it here for completeness. The steps are as follows:

Step 1 $H_0 : \sigma^2 = \sigma_0^2$ $H_1 : \sigma^2 \neq \sigma_0^2$

Step 2 The test statistic here is $Q_c = (T-2)\dfrac{\hat\sigma^2}{\sigma_0^2}$. From Property 3.4b, the distribution of this, under the null hypothesis, is chi-squared with $T-2$ d.f. If Q is "large" we would suspect that σ^2 is probably not equal to σ_0^2.

Step 3 From the chi-square table inside the front cover, look up the value $Q_{T-2}^*(a)$ such that the area to the right is a.

Step 4 Reject H_0 at the level a if $Q_c > Q_{T-2}^*(a)$.

The reason that this test is not common is that, in general, an investigator does not have *a priori* information about which value of σ_0^2 to use in the null hypothesis.

Practice Problems

3.8 For the home price example, test the hypothesis $H_0: \beta = 0.1$ against $H_1: \beta \neq 0.1$ at the levels of significance 0.05 and 0.01.

3.9 Show that if a coefficient is significant at the 1 percent level, it will also be significant at any level higher than that.

3.10 Show that if a coefficient is insignificant at the 10 percent level, it will not be significant at any level lower than that.

3.11 Try the relevant parts of the empirical questions in the exercises.

3.6 Goodness of Fit

It is clear from Figure 3.1 that no straight line will adequately "fit" the data because many of the values predicted by a straight line will be far away from the actual values. To be able to judge whether a particular relationship describes the observed values better than an alternative relationship, it would be desirable to have a numerical measure of **goodness of fit**. In this section, we develop such a measure.

In trying to make predictions about the dependent variable Y if the only information we have is that the observed values of Y came from some probability distribution, then perhaps the best we can do is to estimate the mean and variance using $\bar Y$ and $\hat\sigma_Y^2 = \left[\sum(Y_t - \bar Y)^2\right]/(T-1)$. If we are asked to predict Y, then we simply use the average $\bar Y$ because there is no other information to use. The error in predicting observation t is $Y_t - \bar Y$. Squaring this and summing over all the observations, we obtain a measure of the **total variation** of Y_t from $\bar Y$ as $\sum(Y_t - \bar Y)^2$. This is known as the **total sum of squares** (TSS). The sample standard deviation of Y is a measure of the dispersion of Y_t around its mean $\bar Y$, or equivalently, the dispersion of the error in using $\bar Y$ as a predictor. It is given by $\hat\sigma_Y = \sqrt{\text{TSS}/(T-1)}$.

Suppose we are now told that Y is related to another variable X according to equation (3.1). Then we would expect that a prior knowledge of the value that X takes will help us make a better prediction of Y than simply $\bar Y$. More specifically, if we have the estimates $\hat\alpha$ and $\hat\beta$ and also know that X takes the value X_t, then our estimate of Y_t will be $\hat Y_t = \hat\alpha + \hat\beta X_t$. The error in this estimate is $\hat u_t = Y_t - \hat Y_t$. Squaring this and summing over all the observations, we obtain the **error sum of squares** (ESS), or the **sum of squares of the residuals**, as $\text{ESS} = \sum \hat u_t^2$. The standard error of the residuals is $\hat\sigma = \sqrt{\text{ESS}/(T-2)}$. It measures the dispersion of the error in using $\hat{Y}_t$ as a predictor and is often compared with $\hat{\sigma}_Y$ given above to see how much of a reduction there has been. Because a small ESS is desirable, a large reduction would be ideal. In the example we are using, $\hat{\sigma}_Y = 88.498$ and $\hat{\sigma} = 39.023$, a reduction of more than half the original value.

This method is not satisfactory, however, because the standard errors are very sensitive to the unit in which Y was measured. It would be desirable to have instead a measure of goodness of fit that is not sensitive to the units of measurement. This issue is taken up next.

A measure of the total variation of $\hat{Y}_t$ from $\bar{Y}$ (which is also the mean of $\hat{Y}_t$), for the entire sample, is $\sum(\hat{Y}_t - \bar{Y})^2$. This is known as the **regression sum of squares (RSS)**. In Section 3.A.7 it is shown that

$$\sum(Y_t - \bar{Y})^2 = \sum(\hat{Y}_t - \bar{Y})^2 + \sum \hat{u}_t^2 \qquad (3.22)$$

Thus, TSS = RSS + ESS. We note that $(Y_t - \bar{Y}) = (\hat{Y}_t - \bar{Y}) + \hat{u}_t$. Equation (3.22) states that the same decomposition holds for squares also. Figure 3.7 illustrates this decomposition. If the relationship between X and Y is "close," the scatter points (X_t, Y_t) will lie near the straight line $\hat{\alpha} + \hat{\beta}X$. In other words, ESS will be small and RSS will be large. The ratio

$$\frac{\text{RSS}}{\text{TSS}} = 1 - \frac{\text{ESS}}{\text{TSS}}$$

is called the **coefficient of multiple determination** and is denoted by R^2. The term *multiple* does not apply in the case of simple regression because we use only the one independent variable X. However, because the expression is the same for multiple regression as well, we use the same term here.

$$R^2 = 1 - \frac{\sum \hat{u}_t^2}{\sum(Y_t - \bar{Y})^2} = 1 - \frac{\text{ESS}}{\text{TSS}} = \frac{\text{RSS}}{\text{TSS}} \qquad 0 \leq R^2 \leq 1 \qquad (3.23)$$

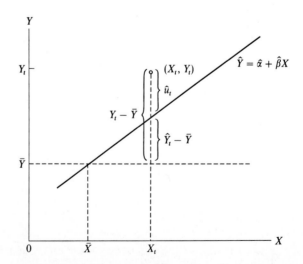

Figure 3.7 The decomposition of the sums of squares

R^2 will clearly lie between 0 and 1. It is unit-free because both the numerator and the denominator have the same units. The closer the observed points are to the estimated straight line, the better the "fit," which means that ESS will be smaller and R^2 will be higher. Thus, R^2 is a measure of the goodness of fit, and a high R^2 is desirable. ESS is also called the **unexplained variation** because $\hat{u}_t$ is the effect of variables other than X_t that are not in the model. RSS is the **explained variation**. Thus, TSS, the total variation in Y, can be broken into two components: (1) RSS, which is that part accounted for by X; and (2) ESS, which is the unaccounted part. A small value of R^2 implies that a lot of the variation in Y has not been explained by X. We may have to look for other variables that exert influence over Y.

Example 3.5

In the home price example, TSS, ESS, and R^2 have the following values (refer to the output from Practice Computer Session 3.1):

$$\text{TSS} = 101{,}815 \qquad \text{ESS} = 18{,}274 \qquad R^2 = 0.821$$

Thus, 82.1 percent of the variation in the price of a house in the sample is explained by the corresponding living area. In Chapter 4 we will find that adding other explanatory variables, such as the number of bedrooms and bathrooms, improves the model fit. $\qquad\qquad\square$

Besides being the proportion of total variation in Y explained by the model, R^2 has another interpretation. It also measures the correlation between the observed value Y_t and the predicted value $\hat{Y}_t(r_{Y_t\hat{Y}_t})$. The reader should refer to a discussion of the population and sample correlation coefficients presented in Sections 2.3 and 2.8. It's shown in Section 3.A.8 that

$$r_{Y\hat{Y}}^2 = \frac{\widehat{\text{Cov}^2(Y_t, \hat{Y}_t)}}{\widehat{\text{Var}(Y_t)}\,\widehat{\text{Var}(\hat{Y}_t)}} = \frac{\text{RSS}}{\text{TSS}} = R^2 \tag{3.24}$$

Thus, the square of the simple correlation between the observed value Y_t and the value $\hat{Y}_t$ predicted by the regression model is the same as R^2 defined in equation (3.23). This result holds even if there are more explanatory variables, *provided the regression has a constant term*. If the regression has no constant term— that is, if $\alpha = 0$—the sum of squares decomposition given above no longer holds (see Exercise 3.4). Instead, we have $\sum Y_t^2 = \sum \hat{Y}_t^2 + \sum \hat{u}_t^2$. The value of R^2 obtained as $1 - (\sum \hat{u}_t^2)/(\sum Y_t^2)$, is not comparable to the R^2 obtained earlier because the denominators are different. For comparison purposes it is preferable to calculate R^2 as in (3.23), even though it may have a negative value.

Test of Goodness of Fit

It is possible to conduct a formal test for the goodness of fit. Let ρ be the population correlation coefficient between X and Y defined in equation (2.7). As seen in equation (2.13), an estimate of ρ^2 is given by $r_{xy}^2 = S_{xy}^2/(S_{xx}S_{yy})$, where S_{xx} and

S_{xy} are defined in equations (3.8) and (3.9) and

$$S_{yy} = \sum Y_t^2 - \left[\frac{(\sum Y_t)^2}{T} \right] = \sum (Y_t - \bar{Y})^2 = \text{TSS} \qquad (3.25)$$

It is shown in Section 3.A.9 that r_{xy}^2 is identical to R^2. In Section 2.10, on testing hypotheses, we presented the method of testing for the hypothesis that X and Y are uncorrelated. The test is known as the **F-test**. The steps for the test are as follows:

Step 1 $H_0: \rho_{xy} = 0$ $H_1: \rho_{xy} \neq 0$

Step 2 The test statistic is $F_c = R^2(T - 2)/(1 - R^2)$. It can also be calculated as $F_c = \text{RSS}(T - 2)/\text{ESS}$. Under the null hypothesis, it has an F-distribution with 1 d.f. for the numerator and $T - 2$ d.f. for the denominator.

Step 3 Look up in the F-table the entry corresponding to 1 d.f. for the numerator and $T - 2$ d.f. for the denominator, for the poiint $F^*_{1, T-2}(a)$ such that the area to the right of F^* is a, the level of significance.

Step 4 Reject the null hypothesis (at the level a) if $F_c > F^*$.

Example 3.6

In the home price example, $R^2 = 0.821$. $F_c = 0.821(14 - 2)/(1 - 0.821) = 54.86$. From Example 3.5, ESS = 18,274, and RSS = TSS − ESS = 83,541. Therefore, F_c could also be calculated using the alternative formula in Step 2: $F_c = 83541(14 - 2)/18274 = 54.86$. The degrees of freedom are 1 for the numerator and 12 for the denominator. For a 5 percent level, $a = 0.05$ and hence $F^*_{1, 12}(0.05) = 4.75$ from Table A.4b. Because $F_c > F^*$, we reject (at the 5 percent level) the null hypothesis that X and Y are uncorrelated. In fact, because $F_c > F^*_{1, 12}(0.01) = 9.33$, the null hypothesis is rejected at the 1 percent level also. Thus, even though the value of R^2 is well below 1, it is significantly different from zero. □

Practice Problem

3.13 Try Exercises 3.10, 3.11, and the goodness of fit parts of empirical questions.

Presentation of Regression Results

The results of a regression analysis are presented in a variety of ways. A very common way is to write the estimated equation with the t-statistics below each regression coefficient, as in the following:

$$\widehat{\text{PRICE}} = 52.351 + 0.13875 \, \text{SQFT}$$
$$\qquad\quad (1.404) \qquad\quad (7.41)$$

$$R^2 = 0.821 \qquad \text{d.f.} = 12 \qquad \hat{\sigma} = 39.023$$

Another form is to have the standard error below a regression coefficient:

$$\widehat{\text{PRICE}} = 52.351 + 0.13875 \, \text{SQFT}$$
$$\qquad\quad (37.29) \qquad\quad (0.019)$$

TABLE 3.3 Analysis of Variance Table

Source	Sum of Squares	d.f.	Mean Square (SS ÷ d.f.)	F
Regression (RSS)	$\sum(\hat{Y}_t - \bar{Y})^2 = 83{,}541$	1	83,541	$\dfrac{\text{RSS}(T-2)}{\text{ESS}} = 54.86$
Error (ESS)	$\sum \hat{u}_t^2 = 18{,}274$	$T - 2 = 12$	1,523	
Total (TSS)	$\sum(Y_t - \bar{Y})^2 = 101{,}815$	$T - 1 = 13$	7,832	

If several alternative models have been estimated, it is more convenient to present the results in a tabular form, as in Table 4.2.

The decomposition of the total sum of squares into its components is often summarized in the form known as the **Analysis of Variance (ANOVA)** table (Table 3.3).

3.7 An Efficient Computational Procedure

The algebraic expressions for $\hat{\alpha}$, $\hat{\beta}$, and associated statistics are cumbersome when actual computations are involved. Here, therefore, we discuss the computational procedure for the simple regression model. In estimating more advanced models, we would rely on computers to make the calculations, but even there, efficient methods of computation must be devised. In the applications in Section 3.9 we present a sample computer output. It should be mentioned that computers and programs differ a great deal in round-off errors. Very large numbers cause round-off errors, especially when the sums of squares are computed. It is a good practice, therefore, to scale numerical values so that the resulting numbers are no longer than a few thousands. For instance, rather than enter population as 324,789, it should be expressed in thousandths and entered as 324.789. Similarly, large financial measures such as the U.S. gross national product should be entered in billionths.

The first step in this procedure is to compute the following sums:

$$\sum X_t, \quad \sum Y_t, \quad \sum X_t^2, \quad \sum Y_t^2, \quad \text{and} \quad \sum X_t Y_t$$

Next compute the following:

$$S_{xx} = \sum X_t^2 - \left[\frac{(\sum X_t)^2}{T}\right]$$

$$S_{yy} = \sum Y_t^2 - \left[\frac{(\sum Y_t)^2}{T}\right]$$

$$S_{xy} = \sum X_t Y_t - \left[\frac{(\sum X_t)(\sum Y_t)}{T}\right]$$

The regression coefficients are then estimated as

$$\hat{\beta} = \frac{S_{xy}}{S_{xx}} \quad \text{and} \quad \hat{\alpha} = \bar{Y} - \hat{\beta}\bar{X}$$

To calculate ESS $= \sum \hat{u}_t^2$, we would ordinarily be tempted to obtain $\hat{Y}_t = \hat{\alpha} + \hat{\beta}X_t$ first, then get $\hat{u}_t = Y_t - \hat{Y}_t$, and finally calculate $\sum \hat{u}_t^2$. There is, however, a computationally more efficient way to obtain ESS. It is shown in Section 3.A.9 that RSS $= \hat{\beta}S_{xy}$. As we have already calculated $\hat{\beta}$ and S_{xy}, RSS is readily computed. From the above and TSS (which is the same as S_{yy}), we can quickly obtain ESS as TSS $-$ RSS, without having to get $\hat{Y}_t$ and $\hat{u}_t$ for each observation. We next get

$$\hat{\sigma}^2 = \frac{\text{ESS}}{T - 2} \quad \text{and} \quad R^2 = 1 - \frac{\text{ESS}}{\text{TSS}}$$

The standard errors of $\hat{\alpha}$ and $\hat{\beta}$ are obtained as follows:

$$s_{\hat{\beta}} = \frac{\hat{\sigma}}{\sqrt{S_{xx}}} \quad \text{and} \quad s_{\hat{\alpha}} = \hat{\sigma}\left[\frac{\sum X_t^2}{TS_{xx}}\right]^{1/2}$$

3.8 Scaling and Units of Measurement

Suppose we had measured PRICE in actual dollars rather than in thousands of dollars. In Table 3.1 the column for PRICE would now have entries such as 199900, 228000, and so on. How would the estimates of the regression coefficients, their standard errors, R^2, and so on be affected by this change in units? This question is examined here for measuring both PRICE and SQFT in different units. First we reproduce the model here.

$$\text{PRICE} = \alpha + \beta\text{SQFT} + u$$

Let PRICE* be price in actual dollars. Then PRICE* = 1000 PRICE. Multiply every term in the equation by 1000 and substitute PRICE* in the left-hand side. We then obtain

$$\text{PRICE*} = 1000\alpha + 1000\,\beta\text{SQFT} + 1000u = \alpha* + \beta*\text{SQFT} + u*$$

If we apply the OLS method to this equation and minimize $\sum(u_t^*)^2$, we would get estimates of $\alpha*$ and $\beta*$. It is readily seen that the new regression coefficients would be equal to the old values multiplied by 1000. Thus, *changing the scale of measurement of the dependent variable in a linear regression model results in the corresponding scaling of each of the regression coefficients*. Because $u* = 1000u$, the residuals and standard errors will also be multiplied by 1000. The sum of squares will be multiplied by a million (1000 squared). It should be noted that the t-statistics, F-statistics, and R^2 will not be affected because they involve ratios in which the scale factor cancels out.

What are the consequences of changing the scale of an *independent variable*? Suppose SQFT was measured in hundreds of square feet rather than in actual square feet, Let SQFT' be square feet in hundreds. Then SQFT = 100SQFT'. Substituting this in the basic model, we get

$$\text{PRICE} = \alpha + \beta 100\text{SQFT}' + u$$

It is evident from this that if we regress PRICE against CONSTANT and SQFT', the only coefficient that will be affected is that of SQFT. If β_2' is the coefficient of SQFT', then $\hat{\beta}_2' = 100\hat{\beta}$. Its standard error will also be multiplied by 100. But all other measures—ESS, the t-statistics, R^2, and F-statistics in particular—will be unaffected. In conclusion, *if the scale of measurement of an independent variable is changed in a linear regression model, its regression coefficient and the corresponding standard errors are affected by the same scale but all other statistics are unchanged.*

There is a particularly good reason to scale values so that the resulting numbers are not large and are similar to those of other variables. This is because large numbers cause round-off errors, especially when sums of squares are computed, which adversely affect the accuracy of results.

To obtain a practical understanding of the consequences of changing units, try Practice Computer Session 3.2 at the end of this chapter.

 Practice Problem

3.12 Suppose you define a new variable $X^* = \text{SQFT} - 1000$ (that is, X^* is the square feet in excess of 1000) and estimate the model PRICE $= a + bX^* + v$. Explain how you can derive $\hat{a}$ and $\hat{b}$ from $\hat{\alpha}$ and $\hat{\beta}$, *without really estimating the new model.*

3.9 Application: Relation between Federal Income Taxes and Adjusted Gross Income

In this section, we present a "walk-through" application in which the two-variable regression model is illustrated. Table 3.4 presents cross-section data on federal income taxes and adjusted gross income for the 50 U.S. states and the District of Columbia for 1987. They are both measured in billions of dollars. An annotated computer printout using the ECSLIB program is shown in Figure 3.8. Items in bold letters are inputs to the program and items in italics are the author's comments on the results. You are encouraged to study the annotations carefully and to use ECSLIB or your own regression program to reproduce the results. Practice Computer Session 3.3 has the instructions to generate the results and to carry out further analysis. The following is the estimated model along with t-statistics in parentheses:

$$\widehat{\text{Tax}} = \underset{(-3.04)}{-0.305} + \underset{(121.7)}{0.14492} \text{ Income}$$

$$R^2 = 0.997 \qquad \text{d.f.} = 49 \qquad F = 14{,}820 \qquad \hat{\sigma} = 0.549$$

TABLE 3.4   Data on Adjusted Gross Income and Taxes by States (1987) in Billions of Dollars

State	Income	Taxes	State	Income	Taxes
1. Maine	12.363	1.556	27. N. Carolina	65.455	8.182
2. New Hampshire	15.125	2.211	28. S. Carolina	31.120	3.678
3. Vermont	5.917	0.762	29. Georgia	66.241	8.760
4. Massachusetts	85.614	12.911	30. Florida	140.279	20.737
5. Rhode Island	11.857	1.625	31. Kentucky	31.245	3.924
6. Connecticut	55.090	9.184	32. Tennessee	46.293	6.203
7. New York	235.395	34.943	33. Alabama	35.491	4.426
8. New Jersey	122.659	18.919	34. Mississippi	18.120	2.094
9. Pennsylvania	131.422	18.200	35. Arkansas	18.303	2.186
10. Ohio	117.267	15.568	36. Louisiana	34.439	4.456
11. Indiana	56.972	7.533	37. Oklahoma	27.519	3.516
12. Illinois	139.482	20.913	38. Texas	164.815	23.936
13. Michigan	106.119	14.633	39. Montana	6.429	0.778
14. Wisconsin	50.642	6.362	40. Idaho	7.810	0.904
15. Minnesota	49.166	6.369	41. Wyoming	4.509	0.605
16. Iowa	26.435	3.359	42. Colorado	36.992	4.885
17. Missouri	52.928	7.218	43. New Mexico	12.700	1.524
18. N. Dakota	5.614	0.707	44. Arizona	36.151	4.615
19. S. Dakota	5.536	0.709	45. Utah	14.379	1.584
20. Nebraska	15.195	1.955	46. Nevada	13.020	1.909
21. Kansas	25.880	3.536	47. Washington	52.165	7.214
22. Delaware	8.241	1.125	48. Oregon	27.523	3.369
23. Maryland	65.238	9.071	49. California	355.447	50.216
24. D.C.	9.058	1.382	50. Alaska	6.927	1.044
25. Virginia	74.654	10.171	51. Hawaii	12.670	1.641
26. W. Virginia	14.483	1.747			

Source: Statistical Abstract of the United States, 1990.

The model fits very well because 99.7 percent of the variation in taxes is explained by income. The F-statistic is extremely high, which also indicates a close relationship. The t-statistics for both $\hat{\alpha}$ and $\hat{\beta}$ are significant at levels below 0.5 percent. The marginal effect of income on taxes is 0.14492. This means that an increase of \$100 in adjusted gross income is expected to increase taxes, on average, by \$14.49.

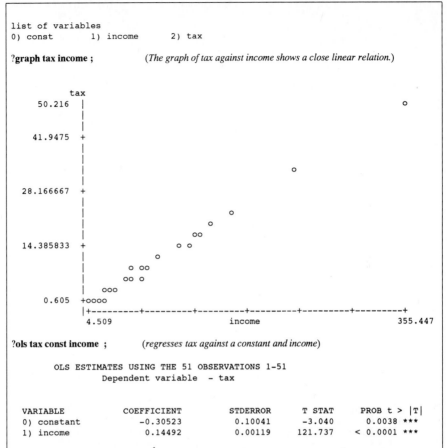

```
list of variables
0) const        1) income       2) tax

?graph tax income ;           (The graph of tax against income shows a close linear relation.)


          tax
   50.216 |                                                         o
          |
          |
  41.9475 +
          |
          |
          |                                             o
          |
28.166667 +
          |
          |                                   o
          |                              o
          |                           oo
14.385833 +                       o  o o
          |                     o
          |              o  oo
          |            oo  o
          |     ooo
    0.605 +oooo
          |+---------+---------+---------+---------+---------+---------+
             4.509                     income                   355.447
```

?ols tax const income ;   *(regresses tax against a constant and income)*

        OLS ESTIMATES USING THE 51 OBSERVATIONS 1-51
              Dependent variable - tax

VARIABLE	COEFFICIENT	STDERROR	T STAT	PROB t > |T|
0) constant	-0.30523	0.10041	-3.040	0.0038 ***
1) income	0.14492	0.00119	121.737	< 0.0001 ***

The estimated income coefficient is $\hat\beta$ = 0.14492 and the estimated constant term is $\hat\alpha$ = - 0.30523. The t-statistic (coefficient divided by stderror) for income is 121.737, which is extremely significant. PROB t > |T| is the area on both tails (for the observed t-value of 121.737) of the t-distribution with 49 (= T - 2) degrees of freedom. This area is referred to as pvalue in the book (for a two-tailed test). The coefficient is significant even at levels below 0.0001. The pvalue of 0.0038 for the constant term implies that the probability of a type I error for a two-tailed test is 0.0038. This means that if we reject the null hypothesis that α = 0, the probability of a type I error is very low and hence we can safely conclude that α = 0. The marginal tax rate is 14.492 percent; that is, for each one hundred dollar increase in income, individuals are expected to pay, on average, \$14.49 in federal taxes. As mentioned in the text, the constant term captures a variety of effects

Figure 3.8 Annotated computer output for the income tax relation

and hence the negative sign is not to be taken seriously. The F-statistic given below is extremely high and is significant at levels below 0.0001, indicating that the fit is very good. The value of R-squared indicates that 99.7 percent of the variation in taxes is explained by the adjusted gross income. The difference between Adjusted and Unadjusted R-squared in the output below is explained in Chapter 4. The Durbin-Watson statistic and the first-order serial correlation coefficient are explained in Chapter 9, which deals with the violation of Assumption 3.6 that the error terms of two observations are uncorrelated. Mean of the dependent variable is $\bar{Y}$. Standard deviation (S.D.) is s_y.

```
Mean of dep. var.          7.55010    S.D. of dep. variable          9.47429
Error Sum of Sq (ESS)     14.79040    Std Err of Resid. (sgmahat)    0.54940
Unadjusted R-squared         0.997    Adjusted R-squared             0.997
F-statistic (1, 49)      14819.906    (Probability F > 14819.906 is < 0.00001)
Durbin-Watson Stat.          1.360    First-order auto corr coeff    0.320
```

?genr ut = uhat ;   (*Copy the estimated residuals internally stored in uhat into ut*)
Generated var. no. 3 (ut)
?genr taxhat = tax - ut ;   (*"fitted" value = observed tax - residuals is saved as taxhat*)
Generated var. no. 4 (taxhat)
?print ut tax taxhat ;   (*Print residuals, observed and predicted tax*)
Varname: ut, period: 1, maxobs: 51, obs range: full 1-51, current 1-51

```
0.06956003   0.32428513   0.20972803   0.80886971   0.21189063   1.50547254
1.13428942   1.44822971  -0.54072284  -1.12135021  -0.41827089   1.00420486
-0.4407584  -0.67191386  -0.45100881  -0.16678406  -0.14720583   0.19863943
0.21194336   0.05814058   0.09064772   0.23592902  -0.07819714   0.37452764
-0.34278384 -0.04667486  -0.99864524  -0.5267442   -0.53455403   0.71270193
-0.29885947 -0.20064755  -0.41219879  -0.22675662  -0.16127737  -0.22974072
-0.16687964  0.35589276   0.1515279    0.07739045   0.25677838  -0.1707269
-0.01127872 -0.31884739  -0.19460296   0.3273462   -0.04063025  -0.31445933
-0.99090112  0.34535669   0.11006894
```

Varname: tax, period: 1, maxobs: 51, obs range: full 1-51, current 1-51

```
1.556   2.211   0.762   12.911   1.625   9.184   34.943   18.919   18.2    15.568
7.533   20.913  14.633   6.362   6.369   3.359    7.218    0.707   0.709    1.955
3.536   1.125   9.071    1.382  10.171   1.747    8.182    3.678   8.76    20.737   3.924
6.203   4.426   2.094    2.186   4.456   3.516   23.936    0.778   0.904    0.605   4.885
1.524   4.615   1.584    1.909   7.214   3.369   50.216    1.044   1.641
```

Varname: taxhat, period: 1, maxobs: 51, obs range: full 1-51, current 1-51

```
1.48643997   1.88671487   0.55227197   12.10213029   1.41310937   7.67852746
33.80871058  17.47077029  18.74072284   16.68935021   7.95127089  19.90879514
15.0737584    7.03391386   6.82000881    3.52578406   7.36520583   0.50836057
0.49705664   1.89685942   3.44535228    0.88907098   9.14919714   1.00747236
10.51378384   1.79367486   9.18064524    4.2047442    9.29455403  20.02429807
4.22285947   6.40364755   4.83819879    2.32075662   2.34727737   4.68574072
3.68287964  23.58010724   0.6264721     0.82660955   0.34822162   5.0557269
1.53527872   4.93384739   1.77860296    1.5816538    7.25463025   3.68345933
51.20690112  0.69864331   1.53093106
```

Figure 3.8   (Continued)

3.10 Confidence Intervals

It was pointed out in Section 2.9 that one way to directly take into account the fact that α and β are estimated with uncertainty is to compute confidence intervals. Thus, for example, rather than say that $\hat{\beta} = 0.139$ we might want to say that with a certain probability, $\hat{\beta}$ will lie between 0.09 and 0.17. From the derivation of the test statistics in Section 3.5,

$$\frac{\hat{\alpha} - \alpha}{s_{\hat{\alpha}}} \sim t_{T-2} \qquad \text{and} \qquad \frac{\hat{\beta} - \beta}{s_{\hat{\beta}}} \sim t_{T-2}$$

Let $t_{T-2}^*(0.025)$ be the point on the t-distribution with $T-2$ d.f. such that $P(t > t^*) = 0.025$. This implies that $P(-t^* \leq t \leq t^*) = 0.95$. Then

$$P\left(-t^* \leq \frac{\hat{\alpha} - \alpha}{s_{\hat{\alpha}}} \leq t^*\right) = 0.95 = P(\hat{\alpha} - t^* s_{\hat{\alpha}} \leq \alpha \leq \hat{\alpha} + t^* s_{\hat{\alpha}})$$

It follows from this that the 95 percent confidence intervals for α and β are, respectively, $\hat{\alpha} \pm t^* s_{\hat{\alpha}}$ and $\hat{\beta} \pm t^* s_{\hat{\beta}}$.

Example 3.7

In the home price example, the standard errors for $\hat{\alpha}$ and $\hat{\beta}$ are $s_{\hat{\alpha}} = 37.285$ and $s_{\hat{\beta}} = 0.18373$. Also, from the t-table, $t_{12}^*(0.025) = 2.179$. The 95 percent confidence intervals are therefore

$$52.351 \pm (2.179 \times 37.285) = (-28.893, 133.595) \qquad \text{for } \alpha$$

$$0.13875 \pm (2.179 \times 0.018373) = (0.099, 0.179) \qquad \text{for } \beta \qquad \square$$

Note that these confidence intervals are quite wide. This is an indication of the poor fit of the simple linear regression model specified here. A better specification of the model should make confidence intervals narrower.

Practice Problem

3.13 Construct confidence intervals for each of the regression coefficients in the empirical questions in the exercises.

3.11 Forecasting

As stated earlier, a common use of the regression model is for forecasting (this topic is discussed more fully in Chapter 11). In the house example, we could ask what the predicted sale price of a home with a living area of 2000 square feet will be. The estimated regression model is $\hat{Y} = 52.351 + 0.13875X$. Thus, when $X = 2000$, the forecast of Y is $52.351 + (2000 \times 0.13875) = 329.851$. Because price is measured in thousands of dollars, this forecast is also in thousands of dollars. Thus, according to the model, the estimated *average* price of a 2000 square feet house is $329,851. It is evident that, in general, if X takes the value X_0, the predicted value of Y_0 is given by $\hat{Y}_0 = \hat{\alpha} + \hat{\beta}X_0$. The conditional mean of the predictor of Y given $X = X_0$ is

$$E(\hat{Y}\,|\,X = X_0) = E(\hat{\alpha}) + X_0 E(\hat{\beta}) = \alpha + \beta X_0 = E(Y\,|\,X = X_0)$$

Thus, $\hat{Y}_0$ is an unbiased conditional predictor of the average sale price given X_0.

Confidence Interval for the Mean Predictor

Because α and β are estimated with imprecision, the predictor $\hat{Y}_0$ is also subject to error. To take account of this, we compute a standard error and confidence interval for the mean predictor. The following is an estimator of the variance of the predictor (see Section 3.A.10 for proof):

$$s_{\hat{Y}_0}^2 = \hat{\sigma}^2 \left[\frac{1}{T} + \frac{(X_0 - \bar{X})^2}{S_{xx}} \right] \tag{3.26}$$

The confidence interval of the mean forecast is given by

$$[\hat{Y}_0 - t^* s_{\hat{Y}_0},\ \hat{Y}_0 + t^* s_{\hat{Y}_0}]$$

where t^* is the critical value of the t-distribution obtained earlier. Note that when X_0 is farther away from the mean $\bar{X}$, $s_{\hat{Y}_0}$ is larger and the corresponding confidence interval is wider. This means that if a forecast is made too far outside the sample range, the reliability of the forecast decreases. If $X_0 = \bar{X}$, then the confidence interval has the smallest length. Figure 3.9 gives an idea of the "confidence band" for various values of X_0.

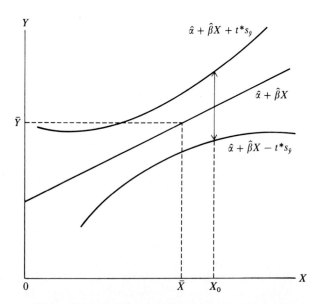

Figure 3.9 Confidence interval band for forecast

Confidence Interval for the Point Forecast

The sample variance given in the previous section is that for predicting the mean. We would also like the variance of the prediction error for the true value Y_0 that corresponds to X_0. This is derived in Appendix Section 3.A.11 as follows:

$$s_{\hat{u}_0}^2 = \mathrm{Var}(\hat{u}_0) = \hat{\sigma}^2 \left[1 + \frac{1}{T} + \frac{(X_0 - \bar{X})^2}{S_{xx}} \right] > s_{\hat{Y}_0}^2 \qquad (3.27)$$

where $\hat{u}_0 = Y_0 - \hat{Y}_0$ is the error in the point forecast. The confidence interval is obtained by using $s_{\hat{u}_0}$ instead of $s_{\hat{Y}_0}$.

Example 3.8

In the home price example, we have $s_{\hat{Y}_0}^2 = 111.555$ and $s_{\hat{u}_0}^2 = 1634.353$ and the corresponding confidence intervals for $X_0 = 2000$ are, respectively, $(307, 353)$ and $(242, 418)$. (See Practice Computer Session 3.4 to reproduce these results.)

Which of these two types of confidence intervals should one choose? Because the main interest is in the forecast error with respect to the true Y_0, equation (3.27) is to be preferred. Note that this confidence interval is much wider than that based on equation (3.26). ☐

Comparison of Forecasts

Economic and business analysts often use more than one model to generate forecasts. A common measure used to compare the forecasting performance of different models is the **mean squared error** (or sometimes its square root, called the **root mean squared error**).

Let Y_t^f be the forecast of the dependent variable for time t, and Y_t be the actual value. The mean squared error is computed as

$$\mathrm{MSE} = \frac{\sum(Y_t^f - Y_t)^2}{T - 2} \qquad \mathrm{RMSE} = \sqrt{\mathrm{MSE}}$$

If two different models are used to predict Y, the one with a smaller MSE is judged to be superior for forecasting purposes.

Practice Problem

3.14   In Exercise 3.28 forecast U.S. population in 1989 and 1990 using both models and compute confidence intervals. How do they compare with the actually known values for 1989 and 1990?

3.12   Causality in a Regression Model

In specifying the model as $Y = \alpha + \beta X + u$, we implicitly assumed that X *causes Y*. Although R^2 measures the goodness of fit, it cannot be used to *identify causality*. In other words, the fact that X and Y are highly correlated does not indicate whether changes in X cause changes in Y or vice versa. Economic theory, the investigator's own knowledge of the underlying behavior, past experience, and so on must suggest

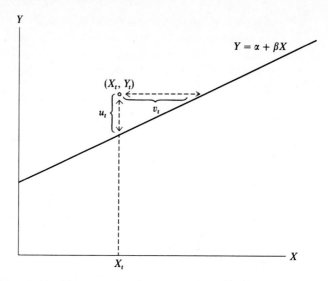

Figure 3.10 Minimizing vertical versus horizontal sums of squares

which way the causation goes. It is however possible to test for the apparent direction of causation (more on this in Chapter 13). The reader is referred to the papers by Granger (1969) and Sims (1972) for details.

As an illustration of the importance of correctly specifying causality, suppose we reversed X and Y and estimated the model

$$X_t = \alpha^* + \beta^* Y_t + v_t \tag{3.1'}$$

Would we get the same fitted straight line as before? The answer, in general, is no, because the least squares procedure applied to equation (3.1) minimizes the sum of squares of vertical deviations from the straight line (see Figure 3.10). In contrast, the reverse straight line minimizes the sum of squares of horizontal deviations v_t. Solving for Y_t in terms of X_t, equation (3.1') can be rewritten as follows:

$$Y_t = -\left(\frac{\alpha^*}{\beta^*}\right) + \left(\frac{1}{\beta^*}\right)X_t - \left(\frac{v_t}{\beta^*}\right) = \alpha' + \beta' X_t + v_t'$$

Minimizing $\sum \hat{u}_t^2$, as was done for equation (3.1), and minimizing $\sum \hat{v}_t^2$ will generally give different answers. More specifically, the estimated value of β' will be different from that of β from equation (3.1).

Example 3.9

The estimated relation when $\sum \hat{u}_t^2$ was minimized was (see Practice Computer Session 3.5)

$$\widehat{\text{PRICE}} = 52.351 + 0.13875 \text{ SQFT}$$

When the causation is reversed and $\sum \hat{v}_t^2$ is minimized, we get

$$\widehat{\text{SQFT}} = 33.385 + 5.91366 \text{ PRICE}$$

Inverting the estimated relation and writing $\widehat{PRICE}$ as a function of SQFT, we have

$$\widehat{PRICE} = -5.645 + 0.169\ SQFT$$

We note that the sign of the constant term is reversed and that the slope term is quite different. □

Under what conditions will the two estimated lines be identical? To answer this, first apply OLS to equation (3.1′); that is, minimize $\sum \hat{v}_t^2$. Reversing X and Y in equation (3.7), we have

$$\hat{\beta}* = \frac{S_{xy}}{S_{yy}} = \frac{1}{\hat{\beta}'}$$

and hence $\hat{\beta}' = S_{yy}/S_{xy}$. The least squares estimator that minimizes $\sum \hat{u}_t^2$ is $\hat{\beta} = S_{xy}/S_{xx}$. For $\hat{\beta}'$ to be equal to $\hat{\beta}$, the condition is

$$\frac{S_{xy}}{S_{xx}} = \frac{S_{yy}}{S_{xy}} \quad \text{or} \quad \frac{S_{xy}^2}{S_{xx}S_{yy}} = 1$$

But the left-hand side of the second equation is r_{xy}^2, the square of the simple correlation between X and Y [defined in equation (2.13)]. Thus, the required condition is that X and Y must be perfectly correlated. Property 2.5d stated that if there is a perfect correlation between two variables, then there must be an exact linear relationship between them. Hence, the fit between X and Y must be perfect in order for us to get the same fitted straight line whether we apply OLS to equation (3.1) or to (3.1′). In general, the correlation between X and Y will not be perfect, and hence we will not get the same straight line. This stresses the importance of specifying the direction of causation appropriately rather than blindly choosing an X and a Y.

The causation can also go both ways, a situation known as **feedback**. The price and quantity of a good are examples of this. Because price and quantity are jointly determined by the interaction of demand and supply, each can influence the other. Similarly, there is feedback between aggregate income and consumption or investment. These situations come under the topic of simultaneous equation models, which are discussed in Chapter 13.

3.13 Nonlinear Relationships

The relationship between the dependent variable Y and the independent variable X has so far been assumed to be linear. The simple linear regression model is also capable, however, of capturing nonlinear relationships between Y and X. In this section we explore only those nonlinear relationships that can be estimated in the framework of the simple linear regression model. More general functional forms are discussed in the next chapter. The present chapter makes extensive use of the logarithmic and exponential functions discussed in Section 3.A.12. It might be useful to review them at this point.

Linear-log Relationship

In a **linear-log model**, the dependent variable is unchanged but the independent variable appears in logarithmic form. Thus

$$Y = \alpha + \beta \ln X + u \tag{3.28}$$

For a positive β, Figure 3.11a graphs the relation as a nonlinear function, while Figure 3.11b graphs it as a linear function with $\ln X$ on the horizontal axis. This relation gives $\Delta Y/\Delta X = \beta/X$. If $\beta > 0$, the marginal increase in Y with respect to an increase in X is a decreasing function of X.

As an example, let Y be the output of wheat and X be the number of acres cultivated. Then $\Delta Y/\Delta X$ is the marginal product of an extra acre cultivated. We hypothesize that the marginal product will decrease as acreage increases. When the acreage is low, we expect that the most fertile land will be cultivated first. As acreage

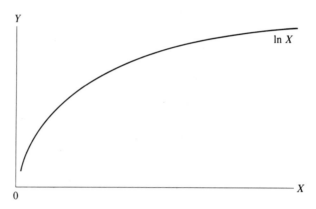

a. A linear-log functional form

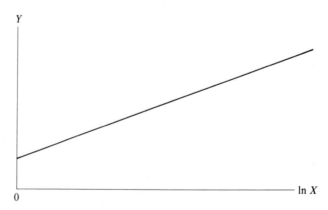

b. A graph of Y against ln X

Figure 3.11

goes up, less fertile areas will be put to use; the additional output from these areas may not be as high as the output from the more fertile lands. This suggests a diminishing marginal product of wheat acreage. A linear-log formulation would enable us to capture this relationship.

Practice Problems

3.15   Derive an expression for the elasticity of Y with respect to X in the linear and linear-log models.

3.16   Graph equation (3.28) when $\beta < 0$ (assume for simplicity that $\alpha = 0$).

As another example, let Y be the price of a house and X be the living area. Consider two houses, one with a living area of 1300 square feet and another with a living area of 3200 square feet. We can expect that the *additional price* a consumer will be willing to pay for 100 *additional square feet* of living area will be higher when $X = 1300$ than when $X = 3200$. This is because the latter house is already quite large, and a buyer might not be induced to pay much extra to increase it further. This means that the marginal effect of SQFT on PRICE can be expected to decrease as SQFT increases. One way to test this is to fit a linear-log model and test $H_0: \beta = 0$ against $H_1: \beta > 0$. This will be recognized as a one-tailed test. The decision rule is to reject H_0 if $t_c > t_{T-2}^{*}(0.05)$. We note from Example 3.A.3 of Section 3.A.12 that in this model the elasticity of Y with respect to X is β/Y. One can calculate the elasticity at the mean as $\beta/\bar{Y}$. If the data are time series, a more interesting elasticity would be the one corresponding to the most recent observation—that is, for $t = T$. This elasticity is β/Y_T.

Example 3.10

We estimated the linear-log model using the home price data in Table 3.1. Following are the results, along with the linear formulation. The values in parentheses are t-statistics. The results can be verified using Practice Computer Session 3.6.

$$\widehat{\text{PRICE}} = \underset{(1.4)}{52.351} + \underset{(7.4)}{0.139}\,\text{SQFT} \qquad R^2 = 0.821$$

$$\widehat{\text{PRICE}} = \underset{(-6.1)}{-1660.811} + \underset{(7.2)}{263.316}\,\ln(\text{SQFT}) \qquad R^2 = 0.814$$

The regression coefficient for ln(SQFT) is highly significant, thus supporting the hypothesis that the marginal effect of the living area decreases as the number of square feet increases. However, the value of R^2 is slightly lower in the linear-log model as compared to the linear model. Therefore, in terms of the goodness of fit between the two models, the linear relationship is to be preferred, although only by a very slight margin. Note that in this model the intercept term does not have the interpretation that it is the price of an empty lot. When SQFT = 0, its logarithm is undefined (or is $-\infty$). Because the range of SQFT in our data set is from 1000 to 3000, it is meaningless to extrapolate to values of SQFT well below 1000 or above 3000.   □

Practice Problem

3.17 Compute the elasticities of PRICE with respect to SQFT for the estimated linear and linear-log models when SQFT is 1500, 2000, and 2500. How do they compare with each other?

Reciprocal Transformation

A functional form frequently used to estimate demand curves is the reciprocal transformation:

$$Y = \alpha + \beta\left(\frac{1}{X}\right) + u$$

Because demand curves are typically downward sloping, we would expect β to be positive. Note that when X becomes large, Y asymptotically approaches α (see Figure 3.12). Moving α up and down one can determine whether the curve intersects the X-axis or not.

 Practice Problem

3.18 Graph the function for $\beta < 0$, $\alpha > 0$.

Log-Linear Relationship (or Semilog model)

Suppose we have a variable P that is growing at approximately a constant rate. More specifically, let $P_t = (1 + g)P_{t-1}$, where g is the fixed growth rate between the time periods $t - 1$ and t. P might be the population and g its rate of growth. By repeated substitution we get $P_t = P_0(1 + g)^t$. Using data on P_t, we wish to estimate the growth rate g. This relationship does not appear in the convenient linear form used in the previous sections. However, it is possible to convert this to the linear form. Taking logarithms of both sides, we obtain $\ln P_t = \ln P_0 + t \ln(1 + g)$. Define $Y_t = \ln P_t$, $X_t = t$, $\alpha = \ln P_0$, and $\beta = \ln(1 + g)$. Then the relation may be rewritten

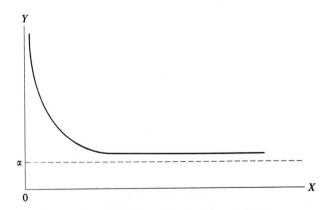

Figure 3.12 A reciprocal relationship

as $Y_t = \alpha + \beta X_t$. Since Y and X may not satisfy the relationship exactly, we add the error term u_t, making the relationship the familiar simple regression model of equation (3.1). The transformed model thus becomes

$$\ln P_t = \alpha + \beta t + u_t \tag{3.29}$$

Exponentiating this we get the original model as

$$P_t = e^{\alpha + \beta t + u_t} \tag{3.30}$$

Equation (3.30) is an exponential relation and is illustrated in Figure 3.13a. It should be noted that the disturbance term in equation (3.30) is multiplicative. Equation (3.29) is linear when the dependent variable is in a logarithmic form. This is illustrated in Figure 3.13b. With $\ln P_t$ on the vertical axis, the formulation becomes a straight line. The first step toward estimating the growth rate (g) is to transform

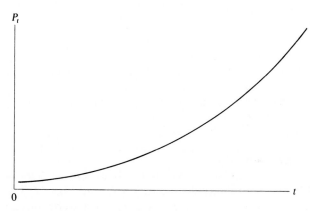

a. An exponential functional form

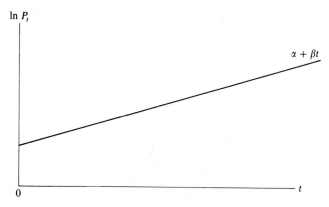

b. A log-linear functional form

Figure 3.13

the observations $P_1, P_2, \ldots, P_T$ using the logarithmic transformation so that we get $Y_t = \ln P_t$. Then we regress Y_t against a constant term and time t. We have

$$\ln P_0 = \hat{\alpha} \qquad \text{and} \qquad \ln(1 + g) = \hat{\beta}$$

Solving for g and P_0, we have

$$\hat{P}_0 = e^{\hat{\alpha}} \qquad \text{and} \qquad \hat{g} = e^{\hat{\beta}} - 1 \tag{3.31}$$

The estimated relationship now becomes $\hat{P}_t = e^{\hat{\alpha} + \hat{\beta}t}$, which can be used for prediction. [However, as will be seen in Chapter 11, because $E(e^{\hat{\alpha}}) \neq e^{\alpha}$, the estimator is biased though consistent.] Any hypothesis on g can be translated (with trivial exceptions) to an equivalent hypothesis on β. Because the transformed dependent variable is in log form, this model is known as the **log-linear model**, or sometimes as the **semilog model**.[1] If the model is written as $\ln P_t = \alpha + \beta X_t + u_t$, β is the marginal effect of X_t on $\ln P_t$ and not on P_t. Differentiating both sides with respect to X_t (see Section 2.A.2 on differentiation), we get

$$\beta = \frac{d(\ln P_t)}{dX_t} = \frac{1}{P_t} \frac{dP_t}{dX_t}$$

The term dP_t/P_t can be interpreted as the *change* in P_t divided by P_t. When multiplied by 100, β gives the *percentage change in P_t per unit change in X_t*. For a calculation of the elasticity of P with respect to X, the reader is referred to Example 3.A.4 in Section 3.A.12.

Example 3.11

The log-linear model is widely used in human capital literature in which theory suggests that the logarithm of earnings or wages be used as the dependent variable. This is then related to the number of years of schooling, the number of years of experience, and so on. Table 3.9 at the end of the chapter has data on the salary (in thousands of dollars) and years since Ph.D. was achieved for a small sample of university professors. The estimated log-linear model and associated statistics (*t*-values in parentheses) are presented below (see Practice Computer Session 3.7 to generate these results and to carry out further analysis with this data set):

$$\widehat{\ln(\text{salary})} = 3.760 + 0.0256 \text{ years}$$
$$\phantom{\widehat{\ln(\text{salary})} = } {\scriptstyle (48.5)} \quad {\scriptstyle (5.7)}$$

$$R^2 = 0.564 \qquad \text{d.f.} = 25 \qquad \hat{\sigma} = 0.197 \qquad F = 32.386$$

The model explains only 56.4 percent of the variation in salaries, which is not surprising because the number of years since Ph.D. is only one of several variables that account for salaries. A number of crucial variables have been omitted from the model, in particular, the extent of published research carried

. . . . . .

---

[1] *The linear-log model is also referred to by some authors as the semilog model, but to avoid confusion we use that terminology only for the log-linear model.*

out by the faculty member (can you identify other omitted variables?). The t- and F-statistics, however, indicate very high significance of the regression coefficients (verify it). The interpretation of the regression coefficient for years (0.0256) is that, between two professors identical in all other respects, the one with one more year since Ph.D. is expected to have, on average, an additional salary of 2.56 percent. □

Double-log Models

In Section 3.A.12, Example 3.A.1, we presented an example of a demand function that has the general form $q = q_0 p^\beta$, where q is the quantity demanded and p is the price. Taking logarithms of both sides and adding an error term, we have the following model known as the **double-log formulation** (because both the dependent and independent variables are in logarithms).

$$\ln q = \ln q_0 + \beta \ln p + u$$

The procedure for estimating this model is to transform p and q using the logarithmic transformation, thus obtaining $Y = \ln q$ and $X = \ln p$. The model then becomes the familiar simple linear regression model. Recall from Section 3.A.12, Example 3.A.1, that β can be interpreted as being the constant elasticity of demand with respect to price (which we would expect to have a negative sign).

Example 3.12

Using the data in Table 3.1, we estimated the double-log model

$$\ln \text{PRICE} = \alpha + \beta \ln \text{SQFT} + u$$

The estimated model and relevant statistics, with t-values in parentheses, is given below (carry out Practice Computer Session 3.6 to reproduce these results):

$$\widehat{\ln(\text{SQFT})} = \underset{(-0.72)}{-0.508} + \underset{(8.79)}{0.82977} \ln(\text{SQFT})$$

$$R^2 = 0.866 \qquad \text{d.f.} = 12 \qquad \hat{\sigma} = 0.103 \qquad F = 77.3$$

Note that the intercept term has a very low t-statistic (in absolute value). The p-value for a two-tailed test is 0.4876. This means that if we reject $H_0: \alpha = 0$ against $H_1: \alpha \neq 0$, there is a 48.76 percent chance of making a Type I error, which is unacceptably high (for a one-sided test the p-value would be half, but even 24.38 percent is too high). Therefore it is not safe to reject H_0. We therefore conclude that α *is not statistically significantly different from zero*. The slope term is highly significant and, because it is positive, supports the hypothesis that as SQFT increases, its marginal effect on PRICE decreases. The elasticity of PRICE with respect to SQFT is 0.83. This implies that a 1 percent increase in SQFT is expected to increase the average price by 0.83 percent. More realistically, a 10 percent increase in SQFT is expected to increase PRICE, on average, by 8.3 percent (which, of course, is less than 10 percent). The value of R^2 for the double-log model is 0.866, whereas it was 0.821 for the linear model. Does this mean that the former model is a better "fit" than the latter? This question is answered in the next section (in the meantime, you may want to think about the answer). □

Practice Problem

3.19   Test the null hypothesis $\beta = 1.0$ against the alternative $\beta < 1.0$. Choose your own level of significance to answer this, but also use your regression program to compute the p-value for the test statistic and use to it to decide whether it is acceptable or not. Clearly state the decision rule that justifies your conclusion.

3.14   Comparison of R^2 Values Between Models

Although economic theory provides a guide to identifying the explanatory variables and sometimes indicating the functional form, the true relationship is unknown. Therefore, econometricians often formulate several alternative models and choose the best among them. The linear and double-log formulations are two frequently used alternatives. It should be emphasized, however, that it is improper to compare the values of R^2 from these two models because the respective dependent variables are different. R^2 in a linear model measures the fraction of variation in Y explained by the independent variables, whereas in a double-log model or in a log-linear model, R^2 measures the fraction of variation in $\ln Y$ explained by the model. Thus, in Example 3.12, 0.866 is the fraction of the variance of $ln(SQFT)$ explained by the double-log model, whereas 0.821 is the fraction of the variance of $SQFT$ explained by the linear model. For proper comparability, the dependent variables must be the same.

There is, however, a heuristic way of comparing the goodness of fit. First we estimate the double-log or log-linear model and compute the predicted values of $\ln Y$. Then we take the antilog (by exponential transformation) to get $\hat{Y}$, the predicted value of Y. Finally, we compute the square of the simple correlation between Y and $\hat{Y}$. This is comparable to the R^2 from a linear model because both these values measure the closeness of the observed Y to the values predicted by the two models. We could also compare the error sum of squares and the variance of the residuals using the relationships

$$\text{ESS} = \sum(Y - \hat{Y})^2 \quad \text{and} \quad \hat{\sigma}^2 = \frac{\text{ESS}}{(T - 2)}$$

It will be readily seen that this is equivalent to comparing the mean squared errors (defined in Section 3.11). However, a caveat should be added to this proposed method. As mentioned in Section 3.13, the predicted value of Y from a model with $\ln Y$ as the dependent variable is biased (more on this in Chapter 11). This should be borne in mind when judging the superiority of a linear model over a log model. The actual mechanics of carrying out such a comparison are described in Practice Computer Session 3.6.

3.15   Empirical Example: Regional Variation in Banking Costs

While developing the least squares estimation procedure, we used the home price example to illustrate each of the steps involved. In this section we present an empirical example of the simple linear regression model, taken from published research. One does not frequently encounter the simple linear model in actual empirical research; almost all economic variables are related to several explanatory variables. Nevertheless, the paper by Bell and Murphy (1969) did use the simple linear formulation. The presentation here is a condensed version of the paper. Interested readers are referred to the original article.

Bell and Murphy (1969) estimated the cost structure of commercial banking firms using data for several SMSAs (Standard Metropolitan Statistical Areas) in the northeastern United States. We discuss here only a small portion of their study, the part relevant to simple regression analysis.

The data are cross sections of 41 SMSAs for the year 1965. In the first stage of the analysis the authors estimated the relationship between the direct processing costs of banks and a number of independent variables: number of demand deposit accounts, rental rate of capital used in the production of demand deposits, wage area index for demand deposits, price of material used in demand deposits, average balance per account, a weighted average of items such as checks processed, transit items, and so on. For the precise definitions of these variables, refer to the cited article. The cost function was estimated using a multiple regression model. The estimated cost function was then used to examine intra-area dispersion in costs— that is, the variation in the cost of production *within* a given SMSA. A question of particular interest was whether large banks with many branches have a cost advantage that works against small banks. Using the characteristics of individual banks within an area in the estimated cost function, the authors obtained average cost measures for all the banks within an SMSA. This was then related to the size of the bank as measured by the number of demand deposit accounts. The model used for this is the following:

$$AC_t = AN_t^{II}U_t$$

where AC_t is the estimated average cost of the tth bank, N_t is the number of demand deposit accounts, and U_t is the multiplicative disturbance term. A and II are unknown parameters to be estimated.

Taking the logarithms of both sides we get

$$\ln AC_t = \ln A + II \ln N_t + \ln U_t = \alpha + \beta \ln N_t + u_t$$

This will be recognized as the double-log model of Section 3.13. Table 3.5 contains estimates of $\ln A$, II, the t-values for II, and the R^2 for each of the SMSAs. Note that very few of the R^2 values are high. The authors point out that only 6 of the 38 t-values are statistically significant, indicating that it is highly probable that $II = 0$ for many SMSAs. The results suggest that scale economies that can be generated by large banks are offset by branching. Thus, small banks can operate as economically as large banks with numerous small branches. The reader is referred to the paper by Bell and Murphy for a more detailed discussion of this question as well as of other aspects of regulation and banking costs.

TABLE 3.5 Relationship between Average Cost and Size of Bank[1]

Standard Metropolitan Statistical Area	Log A	II	t-value for II	R^2	Degrees of Freedom
Fall River	5.2709	−0.2206	−6.5473	0.9772	1
Lawrence−Haverhill	3.2674	0.0206	0.5738	0.0761	4
Brockton	3.3879	−0.0004	−0.0857	0.0037	2
Jersey City	3.3938	0.0001	0.0146	0.0000	7
Rochester	3.3614	0.0044	0.6783	0.0280	16
Springfield	3.3791	−0.0007	−0.0885	0.0008	10
Atlantic City	3.3420	−0.0004	−0.0621	0.0013	3
Worcester	3.3269	0.0052	0.7700	0.0899	6
Bridgeport	3.3438	0.0058	1.3567	0.2691	5
Trenton	3.4079	−0.0024	−0.3720	0.0194	7
Philadelphia	3.2861	0.0070	2.6291*	0.0834	76
Albany	3.3299	0.0071	1.6087	0.1560	14
Syracuse	3.3177	0.0037	0.9602	0.1033	8
Providence	3.2859	0.0163	2.4549*	0.4011	9
York	3.3970	−0.0003	−0.0606	0.0002	21
Utica−Rome	3.3518	0.0014	0.3465	0.0148	8
New Britain	3.7693	−0.0416	−4.3014*	0.8605	3
Binghamton	3.3533	0.0034	0.3906	0.0150	10
New Haven	3.4036	0.0031	0.7108	0.0673	7
New Bedford	2.6014	0.0834	2.3415	0.8457	1
Wilmington	3.3278	0.0046	1.1200	0.0822	14
Pittsfield	3.0082	0.0404	0.5273	0.1221	2
Paterson−Clifton−Passaic	3.3851	−0.0050	−1.5272	0.0721	30
Newark	3.3778	0.0009	0.2893	0.0020	42
Boston	3.3537	0.0028	0.8737	0.0089	85
Scranton	3.4140	−0.0065	−1.0107	0.0567	17
Portland	3.2925	0.0077	4.1706	0.8969	2
Altoona	3.3581	0.0028	0.4226	0.0562	3
Reading	3.3202	0.0032	0.7002	0.0363	13
New York	3.2795	0.0130	4.5137*	0.2114	76
Johnstown	3.4345	−0.0083	−0.9804	0.0459	20
Manchester	4.0215	−0.0799	−4.6693*	0.9160	2
Buffalo	3.1543	0.0237	3.5389*	0.6415	7
Allentown	3.3823	−0.0044	−0.9965*	0.0284	34
Wilkes-Barre−Hazleton	3.3499	−0.0036	−0.5838	0.0160	21
Lancaster	3.2946	−0.0057	−1.0611	0.0487	22
Harrisburg	3.2300	0.0041	0.6194	0.0151	25

[1] Dependent variable is the estimated average cost per demand deposit account.
* t-value statistically different from zero at the 5 percent level.
Source: Bell and Murphy, 1969. Reprinted with permission of the Regional Science Research Institute.

SUMMARY

Even though a simple two-variable linear regression model has been used in this chapter, almost all the basic aspects of carrying out empirical analyses have been covered here. It will be useful to summarize the results derived so far.

The simple linear regression model is $Y_t = \alpha + \beta X_t + u_t, (t = 1, 2, ..., T)$. X_t and Y_t are the tth observations on the independent variable and the dependent variable, respectively, α and β are unknown population parameters to be estimated from the data on X and Y, u_t is an unobserved error term that is a random variable whose properties are stated below. T is the total number of observations. The slope (β) is interpreted as the marginal effect on Y_t of a unit increase in X_t. The intercept (α) is interpreted as the average value of Y when $X = 0$, $\alpha + \beta X_t$ is the conditional mean of Y when $X = X_t$.

The ordinary least squares (OLS) procedure minimizes the sum of squared errors $\sum \hat{u}_t^2$ and obtains estimates (denoted by $\hat{\alpha}$ and $\hat{\beta}$) of the intercept α and the slope β. The only requirement for estimating the parameters by OLS is that T be at least 2 and that at least one of the Xs be different—that is, that not all the Xs be the same.

If u_t is a random variable with mean zero, and X_t is given and nonrandom, then $E(u_t) = 0$ and $E(X_t u_t) = 0$. The sample analogue of these gives the conditions $\sum \hat{u}_t = 0$ and $\sum X_t \hat{u}_t = 0$. The solution to these equations yields the same estimates as the OLS procedure.

Under the assumptions just specified, OLS estimators are unbiased and consistent. Consistency holds even if X_t is random, provided $Cov(X, u) = 0$ and $0 < Var(X) < \infty$—that is, provided that X and u are uncorrelated and X is not constant.

If the u's are independently and identically distributed (iid) with finite variance, $\hat{\alpha}$ and $\hat{\beta}$ are also best linear unbiased estimators (BLUE); that is, among all the unbiased linear combinations of the Ys, $\hat{\alpha}$ and $\hat{\beta}$ have the lowest variance. This result is known as the Gauss–Markov Theorem and means that, besides being unbiased and consistent, OLS estimators are also most efficient. If the u's are iid as $N(0, \sigma^2)$. OLS estimators are also maximum likelihood estimators (MLE).

From $\hat{\alpha}$ and $\hat{\beta}$, the predicted value of Y_t (denoted as $\hat{Y}_t$) is obtained as $\hat{Y}_t = \hat{\alpha} + \hat{\beta} X_t$, and the residual is estimated as $\hat{u}_t = Y_t - \hat{Y}_t$. The standard error of the residuals is an estimator of the standard deviation σ and is given by $\hat{\sigma} = [\sum \hat{u}_t^2/(T - 2)]^{1/2}$. From this, the standard errors of $\hat{\alpha}$ and $\hat{\beta}$ ($s_{\hat{\alpha}}$ and $s_{\hat{\beta}}$) can be derived. The smaller the standard errors, the greater the precision of the estimates of the parameters. A higher variation in X is desirable because this tends to improve the precision of individual estimators.

The steps for testing a one-sided alternative on β are as follows:

Step 1 $H_0: \beta = \beta_0$ $H_1: \beta > \beta_0$

Step 2   The test statistic is $t_c = (\hat{\beta} - \beta_0)/s_{\hat{\beta}}$, where $s_{\hat{\beta}}$ is the estimated standard error for $\hat{\beta}$. Under the null hypothesis, this has the t-distribution with $T - 2$ d.f.

Step 3 Look up in the t-table the entry corresponding to $T - 2$ d.f. and the given level of significance (say a), and find the point $t^*_{T-2}(a)$ such that $P(t > t^*) = a$.

Step 4 Reject H_0 at the level a if $t > t^*$. If the alternative had been $\beta < \beta_0$, rejection would have been when $t_c < -t^*$.

The test can also be carried out in an equivalent way. The modified Steps 3 and 4 are as follows:

Step 3a Calculate the probability (denoted as p-value) that $t > t_c$.

Step 4a Reject H_0 and conclude that the coefficient is significant if the p-value is less than the given level of significance (a).

The steps for a two-sided alternative are as follows:

Step 1 $H_0: \beta = \beta_0$ $H_1: \beta \neq \beta_0$

Step 2 The test statistic is $t_c = (\hat{\beta} - \beta_0)/s_{\hat{\beta}}$. Under the null hypothesis, this has the t-distribution with $T - 2$ d.f.

Step 3 Look up in the t-table the entry corresponding to $T - 2$ d.f. and the level of significance (a) and find the point $t^*_{T-2}(a/2)$ such that $P(t > t^*) = a/2$ (one-half the level of significance).

Step 4 Reject H_0 at the level a if $t_c > t^*$ or $t_c < -t^*$.

The modified steps for the p-value approach are as follows:

Step 3a Calculate p-value $= 2P(t > t_c)$.

Step 4a Reject H_0 if the p-value is less than the preselected level of significance.

A statistic that measures the goodness of fit of a model is given by $R^2 = 1 - (\text{ESS/TSS})$, where $\text{ESS} = \sum \hat{u}_t^2$ and $\text{TSS} = \sum (Y_t - \bar{Y})^2$. R^2 lies between 0 and 1. The higher its value, the better the fit. R^2 has two interpretations: (1) It is the proportion of the total variance in Y that the model explains, and (2) it is the square of the correlation coefficient between the observed value (Y_t) of the dependent variable and the predicted value ($\hat{Y}_t$).

A test for the goodness of fit of the model as a whole can be carried out using the value of R^2. The steps are as follows (ρ_{xy} is the population correlation coefficient between X and Y):

Step 1 $H_0: \rho_{xy} = 0$ $H_1: \rho_{xy} \neq 0$

Step 2 The test statistic is $F_c = R^2(T - 2)/(1 - R^2)$. Under the null hypothesis, it has an F-distribution with d.f. 1 and $T - 2$.

Step 3 Look up in the F-table the entry corresponding to 1 d.f. in the numerator and $T - 2$ d.f. in the denominator, and the given level of significance (say a), and find the point F^* such that $P(F > F^*) = a$.

Step 4 Reject H_0 at the level a if $F_c > F^*$.

The 95 percent confidence interval for β is given by

$$(\hat{\beta} - t^* s_{\hat{\beta}}, \hat{\beta} + t^* s_{\hat{\beta}})$$

The conditional predictor of Y, given that X is X_0, is $Y = \hat{\alpha} + \hat{\beta}X_0$. Its variance (a measure of the reliability of the prediction) increases with the distance of X_0 from the mean $\bar{X}$. Thus, the farther X_0 is from the mean of X, the less reliable is the forecast.

Changing the scale of measurement of the dependent variable results in the corresponding scaling of each of the regression coefficients. The values of R^2 and the t-statistics are, however, unchanged. If the scale of measurement of an independent variable is changed, its regression coefficient and the corresponding standard errors are affected by the same scale, but all other statistics are unchanged.

It is very important to specify correctly the causality in a regression model. The standard assumption is that X causes Y. If X and Y are reversed, however, and the model estimated is $X_t = \alpha^* + \beta^*Y_t + v_t$, the fitted straight line will generally be different from that derived from the model $Y_t = \alpha + \beta X_t + u_t$.

The simple linear regression model can be used to handle nonlinear relationships also, *provided the model is linear in the parameters*. Common alternative functional forms used are: semilog or log-linear model, linear-log relationship, double-log model, and the reciprocal transformation.

It is improper to compare the values of R^2 between models unless they both have the same left-hand side variables. If the dependent variables are different, one can use the alternative models to predict the value of the same variable and then compute the coefficient of correlation between the predicted and observed values of this variable. These are comparable across models. It should be noted, however, that forecasts of the level of the dependent variable generated from a log-linear or double-log model are biased.

KEY TERMS

Analysis of variance (ANOVA)
Best linear unbiased estimator
 (BLUE)
Coefficient of multiple determination
Conditional mean of Y given X
Double-log formulation
Engel curve
Error sum of squares (ESS)
Estimated residual
Explained variation
Feedback
Fitted straight line
F-test
Gauss–Markhov Theorem
Goodness of fit
Instantaneous rate of growth
Linear estimator
Linear-log model

Log-linear model
Marginal effect of X on Y
Mean squared error
Method of least squares
Normal equations
Ordinary least squares (OLS)
Population parameters
Population regression line
Population variances
p-values
Regression sum of squares (RSS)
Residual
Root mean squared error
Sample estimates
Sample regression line
Sample scatter diagram
Semilog model
Significantly different from zero

Simple linear regression model
Standard error of a regression
  coefficient
Standard error of the regression
Standard error of the residuals
Statistically insignificant
Statistically significant
Sum of squares of the residuals (ESS)

Total sum of squares (TSS)
Total variation
t-statistic
t-test
Two-variable regression model
Unexplained variation
Well-behaved errors

REFERENCES

Bell, Frederick W., and Murphy, Neil B. "The Impact of Regulation on Inter- and Intra-regional Variation in Commercial Banking Costs." *J. Regional Science* 9 (1969): 225–238.

Economic Report of the President. Washington, D.C.: U.S. Government Printing Office, 1991.

Gordon, Robert J. "Inflation, Flexible Exchange Rates and the Natural Rate of Unemployment." In *Workers, Jobs, and Inflation*, ed. Martin N. Bailey. Washington, D.C.: Brookings Institution, 1982.

Granger, C. W. J. "Investigating Causal Relations by Econometric Models and Cross-Spectral Models." *Econometrica*, Vol. 37 (1969): 424–438.

Hogg, Robert V., and Craig, Allen T. *Introduction to Mathematical Statistics.* New York: Macmillan, 1978.

Okun, Arthur M. "Potential GNP: Its Measurement and Significance." *Proceedings of the Business and Economic Statistics Section*, American Statistical Association, 1962. Reprinted in Okun's *The Political Economy of Prosperity* (Washington, D.C.: Brookings Institution, 1970).

Perry, George. "Potential Output and Productivity." *Brookings Papers on Economic Activity*, Vol. 8, no. 1 (1977).

Sims, C. A. "Money, Income, and Causality." *American Economic Review*, Vol. 62 (1972): 540–552.

Statistical Abstract of the United States. Washington, D.C.: U.S. Government Printing Office, 1990.

Tatom, John A. "Economic Growth and Unemployment: A Reapprisal of the Conventional View." *Federal Reserve Bank of St. Louis Review* (Oct. 1978).

PRACTICE COMPUTER SESSIONS

This section sketches the steps for duplicating all of the empirical results presented in this chapter. It is quite similar to that in Chapter 2. If you have not carried out the practice sessions in Chapter 2, you should do them before proceeding further. As in Chapter 2, ready-made batch files are set up in the diskette. If you are using a program other than ECSLIB, use the DOS command TYPE to list the lines of the input files (e.g., TYPE PS3−1.INP), and then use them as a guide to reproducing the results. If you plan to use the ECSLIB program, first read

Appendix B, print out the documentation, and carry out the practice session described in the manual.

3.1 Use the following DOS command to execute the ECSLIB commands in the ready-made batch file called *ps3-1.inp* (study this batch command carefully because you will be executing similar ones for other sessions).

$$\text{ecslib data3-1} < \text{ps3-1.inp} > \text{ps3-1.out}$$

(If you do not have a hard disk, add the drive prefix where necessary.) To get a printout, set the printer paper so that the top of the perforation separating pages is just above the ribbon and turn it on. Then use the DOS command

$$\text{lpr ps3-1.out} > \text{prn}$$

to send the output file to the printer. The results are used in the various illustrative examples in this chapter. Appendix B and the help file *ecslib.hlp* printed earlier along with the documentation should be useful in interpreting the output.

3.2 This session should help you understand better the effect of changing units (Section 3.8). The data set is the same (*data3-1*) and the input command file is *ps3-2.inp*.

3.3 To reproduce Figure 3.8 and to carry the application in Section 3.9 further, use data file *data3-4* and input file *ps3-3.inp*.

3.4 Use data file *data3-1* and input file *ps3-4.inp* to verify the confidence interval calculations in Example 3.8.

3.5 Example 3.9 can be verified using the same data file and input file *ps3-5.inp*.

3.6 To reproduce Examples 3.10 and 3.12, use *data3-1* and *ps3-6.inp*.

3.7 To verify the results for Example 3.11, use *data3-9* and *ps3-7.inp*.

EXERCISES

Theoretical Questions

†3.1 Assume that the model is $Y_t = \alpha + \beta X_t + u_t$. Given the T observations $(X_1, Y_1), (X_2, Y_2), \ldots, (X_T, Y_T)$, construct an estimate of β as follows. First connect the first and second points of the scatter diagram and compute the slope of that line. Then connect the first and third points and compute its slope. Proceed similarly and finally connect the first and last points and compute the slope of that line. Finally, average all these slopes and call that $\hat{\beta}$, the estimate of β.

Draw a scatter diagram, give a geometric representation of $\hat{\beta}$, and derive an algebraic expression for it. Next compute the expected value of $\hat{\beta}$. Be sure to state any assumptions you made in computing the expectation. Is the estimate biased or unbiased? Explain. Finally, prove without any derivations why this estimate is inferior to the one we obtained earlier using the OLS procedure. Explain what you mean by "inferior."

3.2 Answer the same questions as in 3.1 when an estimate of β is obtained by the following alternative procedure. Draw a straight line from (X_t, Y_t) to the mean point $(\bar{X}, \bar{Y})$, for each t.

3.3 In the model $Y_t = \alpha + \beta X_t + u_t$, an estimate of β is obtained as follows:

$$\tilde{\beta} = \frac{1}{T-1} \sum_{t=2}^{t=T} \left[\frac{Y_t - Y_{t-1}}{X_t - X_{t-1}} \right]$$

a. Give a geometric interpretation of $\tilde{\beta}$.
b. Show that $\tilde{\beta}$ is unbiased and consistent. Be sure to state the assumptions needed to prove this.
c. Without actually deriving the variance of $\tilde{\beta}$, argue why this estimator is inefficient relative to the OLS estimator of β.

†3.4 Consider the model $Y_t = \beta X_t + u_t$ in which there is no intercept. Some of the following questions depend on the appendix to this chapter and can be omitted in an elementary course.
a. Show that the simple method described in Section 3.2 yields two different estimates for β. The first one is $\tilde{\beta} = \bar{Y}/\bar{X}$, where $\bar{X}$ and $\bar{Y}$ are the sample means. The second one is $\hat{\beta} = (\sum X_t Y_t)/(\sum X_t^2)$.
b. Show that both $\tilde{\beta}$ and $\hat{\beta}$ are unbiased. Be sure to state all the assumptions you make to prove your result.
c. Show that the fitted line $\tilde{Y} = \hat{\beta} X$ will generally *not* go through the average point $(\bar{X}, \bar{Y})$, but that the fitted line $\bar{Y} = \tilde{\beta} X$ will.
*d. By proceeding as in Section 3.A.2 show that $\hat{\beta}$ is the OLS estimator of β.
*e. By proceeding as in Section 3.A.3 show that $\hat{\beta}$ is BLUE.
*f. Using this result explain why the Gauss–Markov Theorem is applicable here, and prove (without any derivations) that $\hat{\beta}$ is superior to $\tilde{\beta}$.

3.5 Suppose the model is as in Exercise 3.4. An estimate of β is derived as follows. In the scatter diagram for X and Y, draw a line from the origin to each of the points $(X_1, Y_1), (X_2, Y_2), \ldots, (X_T, Y_T)$. Then compute the average (β^*) of the slopes of these lines.
a. Write an algebraic expression for β^*.
b. Prove that β^* is an unbiased estimator of β.
c. Without formal derivations, argue why the OLS estimator given in Exercise 3.4d is superior to β^*.

3.6 Suppose you've specified the regression model as $Y_t = \beta X_t + v_t$ and obtained the OLS estimate as $\hat{\beta} = \sum(X_t Y_t)/\sum(X_t^2)$. However, the true model has a constant term so that Y_t is actually given by $\alpha + \beta X_t + u_t$, where u_t has zero expectation. Show that $\hat{\beta}$ is biased. Derive the condition under which $\hat{\beta}$ will be unbiased even though the wrong model was used. What is the intuitive interpretation of the condition you derived?

3.7   In the regression model $Y_t = \alpha + \beta X_t + u_t$, let $\hat{\beta}$ be the OLS estimate of β. Then $\hat{u}_t = Y_t - \hat{\alpha} - \hat{\beta} X_t$ is the residual after removing the effect of $\hat{u}_t X_t$ on Y_t. Show that X_t and $\hat{u}_t$ are uncorrelated, that is, prove that $\text{Cov}(X_t, u_t) = 0$.

†3.8   Instead of expressing the model as $Y_t = \alpha + \beta X_t + u_t$ suppose we had specified it as $X_t = \alpha* + \beta* Y_t + v_t$ and minimized $\sum \hat{v}_t^2$ with respect to $\hat{\alpha}*$ and $\hat{\beta}*$. Denote the estimated line as $X_t = \hat{\alpha}* + \hat{\beta}* Y_t$. Show that this line will, in general, be different from the original estimated line $Y_t = \hat{\alpha} + \hat{\beta} X_t$. Then derive the conditions under which the two straight lines will be identical.

†3.9   State the assumptions essential for each of the following:
a. Estimating α and β by the simple method based on the assumptions $E(u_t) = 0 = E(X_t u_t)$.
b. Estimating α and β by the OLS procedure.
Be sure to explain where in the estimation procedures your assumptions are used.

3.10   Show that the estimated slope coefficient can also be written as

$$\hat{\beta} = \frac{\widehat{\text{Cov}(X, Y)}}{\widehat{\text{Var}(X)}}$$

where $\text{Cov}(X, Y)$ and $\text{Var}(X)$ are the covariance between X and Y and the variance of X respectively. In other words, $\hat{\beta}$ can also be expressed as the ratio of the estimated covariance between X and Y, and the estimated variance of X. [You will need to make use of the properties given in Section 3.A.1.]

3.11   Show that the OLS estimator $\hat{\beta}$ can also be written as $r(s_y/s_x)$, where r is the sample correlation coefficient between X and Y given in equation (2.13), s_x^2 is the sample variance of X given in equation (2.12), and s_y^2 is the sample variance of Y. [*Hint* : Use the relation $\hat{\beta} = \widehat{\text{Cov}(X, Y)}/\widehat{\text{Var}(X)}$ derived in Exercise 3.10.]

†3.12   Consider the regression model $E = \alpha + \beta N + u$, where E is the starting salary (in dollars) of a new employee of a firm and N is the number of years of college attended. There are 50 new employees.
a. What are the intuitive/economic interpretations of α and β?
b. The error term u has all the properties you need but you do not know its distribution, although you do know that it is *not* normally distributed.
   i. List all the properties of the least squares estimates $\hat{\alpha}$ and $\hat{\beta}$ that are still valid. For each property explain briefly why it holds.
   ii. State all the properties of $\hat{\alpha}$ and $\hat{\beta}$ that are no longer valid and any other problems caused by the lack of knowledge. Briefly justify your answer.
c. Suppose E is measured in hundreds of dollars. Describe the effect of this change in units on the estimated regression coefficients and their standard errors, t- and F-statistics, and the value of R^2.

3.13   You are working for a company that produces a number of health and beauty products. The sales manager gives you the company's total annual sales in millions of dollars for 25 years and you are asked to project the sales for the next three years. Formulate a simple regression model that relates sales to a linear time trend, that is, where the independent variable is "time" (t). What would your data table (columns of X_t and Y_t) look like? Write down an expression for the predicted sales in year 28.

3.14 An analyst graphs the observations on a dependent variable (Y_t) against the observations on an independent variable (X_t) and finds it to be the following:

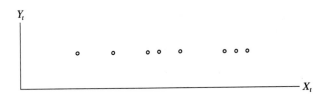

Is the analyst justified in feeling elated thinking he will get a perfect fit with $R^2 = 1$? Why or why not?

3.15 Consider the model given in Exercise 3.4. Let $\hat{Y}_t = \hat{\beta}X_t$ be the predicted value ($\hat{\beta}$ being the OLS estimator derived in Exercise 3.4d) and $\hat{u}_t = Y_t - \hat{Y}_t$ be the error in prediction. Show that $\sum Y_t^2 = \sum \hat{Y}_t^2 + \sum \hat{u}_t^2$. [Note that $\bar{Y}$ is not subtracted as was done in equation (3.22).]

†3.16 For each of the nonlinear models presented in Section 3.13 examine the consequences of changing the scale of units of (a) the dependent variable and (b) the independent variable. How are the coefficients, t-statistics, R^2, and F-values affected?

3.17 An economist wants to estimate the elasticity of Y with respect to X from data on X and Y. She believes that the elasticity is constant for all X and Y. Describe step by step how she may obtain an estimate of the elasticity.

Empirical Questions

The data needed to answer some of these questions are at the end of the exercises.

3.18 The Office of the Registrar of a university campus took a random sample of 427 students and obtained their grade point average in college (COLGPA), high school GPA (HSGPA), verbal Scholastic Aptitude Test scores (VSAT), and the mathematics scores in the SAT (MSAT). Three alternative models were estimated and the results were as follows (values in parentheses are standard errors):

$$\widehat{\text{COLGPA}} = \underset{(0.20463)}{0.92058} + \underset{(0.05712)}{0.52417} \text{ HSGPA} \qquad R^2 = 0.165$$

$$\widehat{\text{COLGPA}} = \underset{(0.14128)}{1.99740} + \underset{(0.00028)}{0.00157} \text{ VSAT} \qquad R^2 = 0.070$$

$$\widehat{\text{COLGPA}} = \underset{(0.15135)}{1.62845} + \underset{(0.00026)}{0.00204} \text{ MSAT} \qquad R^2 = 0.124$$

a. Compute appropriate F-statistics and test each model for goodness of fit using a 1 percent level of significance. Are the models significant overall?

b. Test each regression coefficient (exclude the constant term) for significance at the 1 percent level. Be sure to state the null hypothesis and an appropriate alternative.

c. What do the low values for R^2 indicate? Which is the "best" model and why?

d. Explain why the two-variable model is inadequate. What variables do you think would be important in explaining the variation in COLGPA?

†3.19 A staff member for a political campaign estimated the model $V_t = \alpha + \beta P_t + u_t$, for $t = 1, 2, \ldots, 22$, where V_t is voter turnout in precinct t and P_t is the precinct's population. When the results were being printed out, the printer ribbon became twisted, smudging some of the results. With the information already provided fill in the blanks.

Coefficient	Estimate	Std. error	T-ratio
$\hat{\alpha}$	26.034	____	14.955
$\hat{\beta}$	0.137	0.028	____
ESS = 305.96	$\bar{P} = 54.478$	$s_v^2 = 31.954$	$s_p^2 = 925.91$
$r_{vp} = $ ____	$R^2 = $ ____	$\hat{\sigma}^2 = $ ____	$\bar{V} = $ ____

3.20 Table 3.6 has data for a compact car on the cumulative cost of maintenance (excluding gasoline), the number of miles driven (in thousands), and the number of weeks of ownership.

a. Estimate the following models:

$$\text{cost} = \alpha_1 + \beta_1 \text{ miles} + u$$
$$\text{cost} = \alpha_2 + \beta_2 \text{ weeks} + v$$

b. Do the signs of the estimated coefficients agree with your intuition?

c. Test each regression coefficient for statistical significance. What do you conclude?

d. Which model fits better? Explain.

e. Suppose miles were measured in actual units rather than in thousands. Describe the effects on the estimated regression coefficients and the summary statistics.

3.21 Do companies with large assets usually have a high return on invested capital? More specifically, is there a relationship between return on invested capital and the total assets of a company? Address this question using the data for 26 U.S. companies in the food processing industry presented in Table 3.7. Return is given in percents and assets in millions of dollars (1989). First estimate a simple linear regression with return as the dependent variable. Test each regression coefficient for statistical significance at 10 percent. Also compute p-values and identify the actual levels of significance. Test the

TABLE 3.6 Data on a Toyota Station Wagon

Weeks	Miles	Cost	Weeks	Miles	Cost
5	0.8	11	279	43.7	1182
12	3.0	16	281	44.3	1231
30	4.9	55	313	47.6	1244
40	7.1	66	326	48.9	1257
42	7.6	76	328	49.1	1260
53	10.1	83	329	49.2	1342
66	12.0	135	336.5	50.0	1356
73	12.8	160	338	50.1	1467
79	13.9	163	342.5	50.6	1518
101	18.6	211	344.5	50.8	1557
114	21.1	258	351	51.6	1565
129	23.2	322	366	53.2	1583
150	25.3	374	384	55.7	1609
180	28.7	408	388	56.0	2825
195	30.5	478	402	57.3	2893
196	30.6	489	432	60.2	2918
204	31.4	536	433	60.3	3011
212	32.9	590	436	60.6	3077
224	35.3	604	436	63.0	3095
227	35.3	704	456	63.7	3154
232	36.6	985	463.5	63.9	3162
235	37.0	1021	465	65.1	3217
239	38.1	1030	478	65.8	3274
249	39.5	1096	485	67.7	3320
260	40.7	1114	498.5	72.1	3329
271	43.0	1134	526	72.1	3401
272	43.1	1157	527	73.6	3412
273.5	43.2	1176	538	74.4	3425
276	43.4	1182			

model for overall significance. What do you conclude? Do you think the model should include additional variables? Name a few variables that you think ought to be there, justify your choice, and indicate the direction of their effect on returns (that is, positive or negative).

3.22 Table 3.8 has cross-section data on total 1989 sales and profits (both in

TABLE 3.7 Assets (millions of dollars) and Return (%) on Invested Capital (1989) for 26 U.S. Companies in the Food Processing Industry

Obs	Return	Assets	Obs	Return	Assets
1	20.2	4479	14	15.4	710
2	21.7	3390	15	13.2	865
3	13.4	5262	16	7.3	1325
4	26.2	3174	17	12	1660
5	17.9	4495	18	19.9	482
6	13.4	3125	19	21.1	276
7	20	5403	20	14.2	526
8	14.6	1814	21	14.9	716
9	10	2190	22	10.1	439
10	31.1	499	23	7.7	43
11	8.2	2592	24	17.9	218
12	21.4	714	25	18.9	154
13	13.2	1136	26	22.5	135

Source: *Business Week*, April 13, 1990, page 229.

TABLE 3.8 Total Sales (billions of dollars) and Profits (millions of dollars) for 32 Discount and Fashion Retailing Companies in the United States

Obs	Profits	Sales	Obs	Profits	Sales
1	25.811	1075.9	17	2.651	74.9
2	53.794	1445.8	18	3.254	31.1
3	16.103	802	19	1.258	32.3
4	4.788	321.1	20	1.651	72.3
5	4.648	346.9	21	2.492	51.4
6	9.526	515	22	1.074	61.2
7	7.554	398.1	23	0.384	33.3
8	13.644	410	24	1.627	31.9
9	8.82	329	25	0.809	36.4
10	2.759	112	26	1.23	31
11	2.671	114.9	27	0.458	40.1
12	3.049	148.1	28	0.346	26
13	1.587	97.6	29	0.545	29.1
14	5.269	122.5	30	0.479	22.2
15	2.313	130.3	31	2.18	31.5
16	2.149	86.8	32	3.307	72

Source: *Business Week*, April 13, 1990, page 225.

millions of dollars) for 32 discount and fashion retailing companies in the United States.

a. Estimate the model, $PROFITS_t = \alpha + \beta SALES_t + u_t$.

b. Draw the scatter diagram. Do you expect a good fit? Compute R^2. Is the actual fit good?

c. Estimate the standard error of the residuals and the standard errors of $\hat{\alpha}$ and $\hat{\beta}$.

d. Perform t-tests for the hypotheses $\alpha = 0$ and $\beta = 0$, choosing your own level of significance. In each case state the null and alternative hypotheses, the distribution of the test statistic, and the criterion for acceptance or rejection of the null hypothesis.

e. Suppose profits are measured in dollars instead of millions. Describe the effect of this change in units on regression coefficients, standard errors, t- and F-statistics, and the value of R^2.

f. What other factors do you think the profits of a company depend on?

3.23 Table 3.9 has data on the salary (in thousands of dollars) and years since a Ph.D. was awarded, for a sample of 27 professors of various ranks at a university. Estimate the model $salary = \alpha + \beta\ years + u$. Test the model for overall significance (using your own level of significance). Also test each regression coefficient for significance at the 1 percent level. What does the value of R^2 indicate to you? Graph salary against years and ask yourself whether the model is adequate for explaining the variations in salary levels.

TABLE 3.9 Salary (thousands of dollars) and Years Since Ph.D. for 27 Professors

Obs	Years	Salary	Obs	Years	Salary
1	1	42.2	15	16	87
2	2	42.4	16	19	78
3	4	44.5	17	21	48.3
4	4	45	18	21	60.6
5	5	49.3	19	21	83.5
6	6	43.9	20	21	87
7	6	47.7	21	21	98.6
8	6	49.3	22	22	91.3
9	8	44.6	23	24	70.6
10	12	66.6	24	25	72.4
11	13	73.9	25	26	85.4
12	15	52.9	26	28	55.4
13	15	77.4	27	29	98.3
14	15	78			

TABLE 3.10 Business School Tuition and Average Starting Salary of MBAs (thousands of dollars)

Obs	Tuition	Startpay	Obs	Tuition	Startpay
1	16.65	63.07	11	17.25	73.415
2	16.5	72.475	12	6.153	50.945
3	16.4	78.93	13	16.2	55.99
4	16.67	67.71	14	11.7	63.81
5	14.094	79.135	15	8.175	47.11
6	16.5	56.635	16	16.1	53.93
7	15.836	53.52	17	15.49	55.8
8	16.95	62.165	18	4.277	43.985
9	16.58	56.89	19	7.846	53.84
10	8.51	59.335	20	14.7	45.41

Source: *Business Week*, October 29, 1990, page 54.

Based on your results what recommendations would you give to improve the model specification?

3.24 Business schools that train MBAs vary a great deal in the tuition they charge. As one would suspect, the average starting salary of the graduating MBAs also varies substantially. Is there a relationship between the two? In other words, is the average starting salary higher if the school's tuition is also higher? Table 3.10 has the tuition and average starting salaries (both measured in thousands of dollars) for 20 schools highly ranked by *Business Week*. Estimate the parameters of the model salary $= \alpha + \beta$ tuition $+ u$. Graph salary against tuition and indicate whether you expect a good fit? Compute the value of R^2 and see whether it supports what the graph indicates. What do the results suggest about the appropriateness of the model? Test individual coefficients for significance at the 10 percent level. Compute the *p*-values and indicate the level at which the slope coefficient will be significantly positive. Is this level acceptable? Justify your answers. What other characteristics of business schools do you think ought to be included in the model to make it sufficiently sensible to explain the variation in starting salaries?

3.25 Table 3.11 has annual data from 1948 through 1988 for the population of the United Kingdom (in millions). Generate a variable called TIME that takes the value 1 for 1948, 2 for 1949, and so on up to 39 for 1988. Graph population against TIME and state whether a linear time trend is a good approximation. Estimate the linear time trend POP $= \alpha + \beta$ TIME $+ u$. As before, test the model for overall significance and for the significance of individual coefficients. Evaluate the model's adequacy in explaining the growth in U.K. population.

TABLE 3.11 Population of the United Kingdom (millions)

Year	Population	Year	Population
1948	50.03	1969	55.27
1949	50.32	1970	55.42
1950	50.62	1971	55.61
1951	50.56	1972	55.78
1952	50.72	1973	55.91
1953	50.86	1974	55.92
1954	51.05	1975	55.90
1955	51.20	1976	55.89
1956	51.41	1977	55.85
1957	51.63	1978	55.84
1958	51.84	1979	55.88
1959	52.13	1980	55.95
1960	52.35	1981	56.35
1961	52.81	1982	56.34
1962	53.27	1983	56.38
1963	53.54	1984	56.49
1964	53.85	1985	56.62
1965	54.18	1986	56.76
1966	54.50	1987	56.93
1967	54.80	1988	57.08
1968	55.05		

Source: University of California, San Diego, Social Science Data Base.

3.26 Carry out a parallel analysis for the United States using the data in Table 3.12. Compare the rates of growth of the two countries and indicate which country's population has grown faster since World War II.

3.27 A widely used relationship in consumer theory is the **Engel curve** which relates the expenditure on a particular category to the income of an individual or family. Table 3.13 presents data on total income and expenditures on domestic travel for each of the 50 states of the United States and for the District of Columbia. Both variables are measured in billions of dollars. Do the same kind of analysis that you have been doing in previous exercises, that is, graph the appropriate relationship, estimate a relevant simple linear regression model, and test it for overall and individual coefficients' significance. What are the interpretations of the intercept and slope coefficients?

TABLE 3.12 Population of the United States
(millions)

Year	Population	Year	Population
1948	146.631	1970	205.052
1949	149.188	1971	207.661
1950	152.271	1972	209.896
1951	154.878	1973	211.909
1952	157.553	1974	213.854
1953	160.184	1975	215.973
1954	163.026	1976	218.035
1955	165.931	1977	220.239
1956	168.903	1978	222.585
1957	171.984	1979	225.055
1958	174.882	1980	227.757
1959	177.830	1981	230.138
1960	180.671	1982	232.520
1961	183.691	1983	234.799
1962	186.538	1984	237.001
1963	189.242	1985	239.279
1964	191.889	1986	241.625
1965	194.303	1987	243.942
1966	196.560	1988	246.307
1967	198.712	1989	248.762
1968	200.706	1990	251.394
1969	202.677		

Source: Economic Report of the President, 1991. Table B-31, page 321.

Should other variables be included in the model? If so, indicate what they are and why you think that they should be included.

3.28   Table 3.14 has annual data for the United States on the population (millions) and the gross national product (GNP, in billions of dollars). Estimate the model $GNP = \alpha + \beta\,POP + u$, and compute the associated standard errors, t-statistics, goodness of fit measure, and so on. Graph GNP against POP and indicate whether you expect a good fit for the simple linear regression model. Next generate a time trend (TIME) as you did in Exercise 3.25 and estimate the alternative model $GNP = \alpha^* + \beta^*\,TIME + v$. Which model explains the variations in GNP better?

TABLE 3.13   U.S. Personal Income and Expenditures on Travel (billions of current dollars)

State	Exptrav	Income	State	Exptrav	Income
Alabama	2.042	49.2	Montana	0.728	10.0
Alaska	0.857	9.7	Nebraska	1.359	22.5
Arizona	5.635	48.7	Nevada	8.246	16.5
Arkansas	1.909	27.3	New Hampshire	2.002	19.1
California	35.797	491.4	New Jersey	13.289	155.6
Colorado	5.455	51.6	New Mexico	1.918	17.8
Connecticut	3.108	68.3	New York	17.193	320.0
Delaware	0.725	10.6	N. Carolina	6.742	85.6
D.C.	1.442	12.1	N. Dakota	0.647	8.6
Florida	24.34	187.5	Ohio	7.535	157.6
Georgia	5.709	89.6	Okhlahoma	2.927	41.1
Hawaii	3.301	16.8	Oregon	2.794	37.9
Idaho	1.061	11.8	Pennsylvania	11.673	181.5
Illinois	10.609	189.9	Rhode Island	0.571	15.5
Indiana	3.289	77.3	S. Carolona	4.294	41.4
Iowa	1.996	39.6	S. Dakota	0.626	8.8
Kansas	2.168	37.3	Tennessee	4.565	63.0
Kentucky	2.428	44.7	Texas	15.72	232.3
Louisiana	3.845	51.2	Utah	2.148	19.4
Maine	2.154	16.6	Vermont	1.576	7.8
Maryland	5.322	82.6	Virginia	6.852	97.8
Massachusetts	6.721	112.0	Washington	4.469	71.0
Michigan	8.620	143.2	W. Virginia	1.432	20.9
Minnesota	5.551	67.0	Wisconsin	4.386	70.5
Mississippi	1.331	27.0	Wyoming	0.760	6.3
Missouri	5.291	74.7			

Source: 1990 U.S. Statistical Abstract Tables 409, and 705.

3.29   The sales manager of a company believes that his company's sales (S_t) have been growing according to the model $S_t = S_0(1 + g)^t$. He obtains the following OLS regression results:

$$\widehat{\ln S_t} = 3.6889 + 0.0583t.$$

a. What is his estimate of the growth rate (g)?
b. What is his estimate of S_0?
c. Estimate the company's sales five periods into the future.

TABLE 3.14   U.S. Population (millions) and GNP (billions of dollars)

Year	GNP	Population	Year	GNP	Population
1948	1108.7	146.631	1970	2416.2	205.052
1949	1109.0	149.188	1971	2484.8	207.661
1950	1203.7	152.271	1972	2608.5	209.896
1951	1328.2	154.878	1973	2744.1	211.909
1952	1380.0	157.553	1974	2729.3	213.854
1953	1435.3	160.184	1975	2695.0	215.973
1954	1416.2	163.026	1976	2826.7	218.035
1955	1494.9	165.931	1977	2958.6	220.239
1956	1525.6	168.903	1978	3115.2	222.585
1957	1551.1	171.984	1979	3192.4	225.055
1958	1539.2	174.882	1980	3187.1	227.757
1959	1629.1	177.83	1981	3248.8	230.138
1960	1665.3	180.671	1982	3166.0	232.520
1961	1708.7	183.691	1983	3279.1	234.799
1962	1799.4	186.538	1984	3501.4	237.001
1963	1873.3	189.242	1985	3618.7	239.279
1964	1973.3	191.889	1986	3717.9	241.625
1965	2087.6	194.303	1987	3845.3	243.942
1966	2208.3	196.560	1988	4076.9	246.307
1967	2271.4	198.712	1989	4117.7	248.762
1968	2365.6	200.706	1990	4155.8	251.394
1969	2423.3	202.677			

Source: Economic Report of the President, 1991, Tables B-2 and B-31.

3.30   Table 3.15 has monthly data from January 1983 through May 1990 for a company that produces sealing compounds used in construction. The variables are

Q = Number of gallons of compound shipped in the month

P = price per gallon in dollars

Graph quantity against price and indicate whether you expect a "good fit" between shipments and the price. Next estimate a linear regression model relating quantity to price. Test the model for overall goodness of fit and also test each regression coefficient for significance. In each case, state the null and alternative hypothesis, the test statistic and its distribution, and the decision rule. What do you conclude? Next, repeat the procedure for a double-log model of shipments against price. In this model, test whether the shipments are unitary elastic or not with respect to price. Are they elastic or inelastic?

TABLE 3.15 Data on Sealing Compound Shipments and Price

Period	Quantity	Price	Period	Quantity	Price
1983.01	120	9.9	1985.12	2230	8.86
1983.02	829	8.74	1986.01	4225	8.25
1983.03	1928	5.48	1986.02	1045	13.69
1983.04	930	8.97	1986.03	3475	8.49
1983.05	722	9.49	1986.04	4320	8.32
1983.06	2184	8.45	1986.05	4910	8.29
1983.07	2632	8.75	1986.06	2265	13.48
1983.08	4799	7.35	1986.07	2655	11.21
1983.09	3185	8.58	1986.08	4120	8.24
1983.10	6202	8.73	1986.09	1095	8.26
1983.11	2234	8.67	1986.10	3740	7.76
1983.12	1806	8.56	1986.11	680	8.59
1984.01	1692	8	1986.12	635	9.47
1984.02	1865	7.8	1987.01	305	10.22
1984.03	3587	7.73	1987.02	2250	8.26
1984.04	1975	8.08	1987.03	2515	8.45
1984.05	3619	8.11	1987.04	1205	13.69
1984.06	2560	7.8	1987.05	5765	8.71
1984.07	4135	8.58	1987.06	2675	8.92
1984.08	1648	8.72	1987.07	3455	8.47
1984.09	1555	10.04	1987.08	5930	9
1984.10	1626	8.57	1987.09	2300	8.38
1984.11	2685	8.71	1987.10	2865	8.43
1984.12	627	8.84	1987.11	1165	9.11
1985.01	484	9.2	1987.12	485	12.85
1985.02	781	9.07	1988.01	90	13.35
1985.03	2527	9.36	1988.02	965	14.21
1985.04	2108	8.69	1988.03	2370	8.26
1985.05	3986	9.22	1988.04	2635	8.64
1985.06	1909	8.69	1988.05	4265	8.55
1985.07	2609	8.47	1988.06	740	9.31
1985.08	7723	7.84	1988.07	190	10.72
1985.09	7149	8.34	1988.08	2740	6.97
1985.10	3417	8.07	1988.09	4425	8.76
1985.11	3980	8.18	1988.10	1325	8.35

TABLE 3.15 (*Continued*)

Period	Quantity	Price	Period	Quantity	Price
1988.11	3185	7.37	1989.09	3165	9.56
1988.12	3685	8.17	1989.10	3470	9.01
1989.01	1715	8.25	1989.11	410	8.83
1989.02	1790	8.43	1989.12	1390	10.9
1989.03	2890	8.33	1990.01	1150	6.83
1989.04	2855	9.31	1990.02	1190	10.34
1989.05	3685	9	1990.03	1620	8.6
1989.06	3015	8.14	1990.04	3355	9.54
1989.07	2985	8.6	1990.05	2555	10.63
1989.08	3320	9.03			

Source: Data compiled by Carroll Foster.

3.A   APPENDIX

Miscellaneous Derivations

3.A.1   Certain Useful Results on Summations

A number of simple but useful properties relating to summations are presented in this section.

Property 3.A.1

> If $\bar{X} = \sum_{t=1}^{t=T}(X_t/T)$ is the sample mean, then $\sum_{t=1}^{t=T}(X_t - \bar{X}) = 0$.

PROOF

$$\sum(X_t - \bar{X}) = \left(\sum X_t\right) - \left(\sum \bar{X}\right) = \left(\sum X_t\right) - T\bar{X}$$

because $\bar{X}$ is the same for each t. But, from the definition of $\bar{X}$, $T\bar{X} = \sum X_t$. Therefore, the last two terms cancel each other and hence $\sum(X_t - \bar{X}) = 0$.   □

Property 3.A.2

> $S_{xx} = \sum(X_t - \bar{X})^2 = \sum X_t^2 - T(\bar{X})^2 = \sum X_t^2 - \dfrac{1}{T}\left(\sum X_t\right)^2$.

PROOF

$$\sum(X_t - \bar{X})^2 = \sum[X_t^2 - 2X_t\bar{X} + (\bar{X})^2] = \sum X_t^2 - \sum 2\bar{X}X_t + \sum(\bar{X})^2$$

As before, $\bar{X}$ is the same for each t. Hence, the above $= \sum X_t^2 - 2\bar{X}\sum X_t + T(\bar{X})^2$. Also, $\sum X_t = T\bar{X}$. Therefore the expression becomes $\sum X_t^2 - 2\bar{X}T\bar{X} + T(\bar{X})^2$. Combining the second and third terms, we get the first part of the property. We know that $\bar{X} = (\sum X_t)/T$. Substituting for $\bar{X}$ from this, we get the second part of the property.

Property 3.A.3

> $S_{xy} = \sum(X_t - \bar{X})(Y_t - \bar{Y}) = \sum X_t Y_t - T\bar{X}\bar{Y} = \sum X_t Y_t - [(\sum X_t)(\sum Y_t)/T]$

PROOF

$$\sum (X_t - \bar{X})(Y_t - \bar{Y}) = \sum (X_t Y_t - X_t \bar{Y} - Y_t \bar{X} + \bar{X}\bar{Y})$$
$$= \sum X_t Y_t - \bar{Y}\sum X_t - \bar{X}\sum Y_t + T\bar{X}\bar{Y}$$
$$= \sum X_t Y_t - \bar{Y}T\bar{X} - \bar{X}T\bar{Y} + T\bar{X}\bar{Y}$$
$$= \sum X_t Y_t - T\bar{X}\bar{Y}$$

Substituting $\bar{X} = \left(\sum X_t\right)/T$ and $\bar{Y} = \left(\sum Y_t\right)/T$, we get the second equality. $\quad\square$

Property 3.A.4   If $w_t = \dfrac{X_t - \bar{X}}{S_{xx}}$, then $\sum w_t = 0$, $\sum (w_t X_t) = 1$, and $\sum w_t^2 = 1/S_{xx}$, where S_{xx} is as defined in Property 3.A.2.

PROOF

$$\sum w_t = \sum \left[\frac{X_t - \bar{X}}{S_{xx}}\right] = \frac{\sum (X_t - \bar{X})}{S_{xx}}$$

because S_{xx} is the same for each t and can be taken out of the summation. Also, from Property 3.A.1, $\sum (X_t - \bar{X}) = 0$. Hence $\sum w_t = 0$.

$$\sum w_t X_t = \sum w_t X_t - \bar{X}\sum w_t$$

because we just proved that $\sum w_t = 0$. Taking the $\bar{X}$ inside the second summation and combining terms we get $\sum w_t X_t = \sum w_t (X_t - \bar{X})$. If we substitute for w_t

$$\sum w_t X_t = \sum w_t (X_t - \bar{X}) = \sum \left[\frac{X_t - \bar{X}}{S_{xx}}\right](X_t - \bar{X})$$

Again, S_{xx} can be taken out of the summation; and hence the above expression becomes [noting that S_{xx} is $\sum (X_t - \bar{X})^2$]

$$\sum w_t X_t = \frac{\sum (X_t - \bar{X})(X_t - \bar{X})}{\sum (X_t - \bar{X})^2} = 1$$

Given that $w_t = (X_t - \bar{X})/S_{xx}$, we get

$$\sum w_t^2 = \sum \left[\frac{(X_t - \bar{X})^2}{S_{xx}^2}\right] = \frac{S_{xx}}{S_{xx}^2} = \frac{1}{S_{xx}} = \frac{1}{\sum (X_t - \bar{X})^2} \quad\square$$

3.A.2   Derivation of the Normal Equations by Least Squares

In this section we apply the method of least squares, presented in Section 3.2, and derive the normal equations (3.2) and (3.5). The least squares criterion is to choose those values of $\hat{\alpha}$ and $\hat{\beta}$ that minimize the sum of squared errors:

$$\text{ESS}(\hat{\alpha}, \hat{\beta}) = \sum_{t=1}^{t=T} \hat{u}_t^2 = \sum_{t=1}^{t=T} (Y_t - \hat{\alpha} - \hat{\beta}X_t)^2$$

To minimize ESS with respect to $\hat{\alpha}$ and $\hat{\beta}$, we set the partial derivatives (see Section 2.A.2 on partial derivatives) $\partial \text{ESS}/\partial \hat{\alpha}$ and $\partial \text{ESS}/\partial \hat{\beta}$ to zero and solve the resulting equations. We have

$$\frac{\partial \text{ESS}}{\partial \hat{\alpha}} = \frac{\sum \partial(\hat{u}_t^2)}{\partial \hat{\alpha}} = \sum 2\hat{u}_t \frac{\partial \hat{u}_t}{\partial \hat{\alpha}} = 2\sum (Y_t - \hat{\alpha} - \hat{\beta}X_t)(-1) = 0$$

$$\frac{\partial \text{ESS}}{\partial \hat{\beta}} = \frac{\sum \partial(\hat{u}_t^2)}{\partial \hat{\beta}} = \sum 2\hat{u}_t \frac{\partial \hat{u}_t}{\partial \hat{\beta}} = 2\sum (Y_t - \hat{\alpha} - \hat{\beta}X_t)(-X_t) = 0$$

from which we obtain the following equations:

$$\sum (Y_t - \hat{\alpha} - \hat{\beta}X_t) = 0$$
$$\sum (Y_t - \hat{\alpha} - \hat{\beta}X_t)X_t = 0$$

Taking the summation term by term and noting that $\hat{\alpha}$ and $\hat{\beta}$ can be factored out of summations because they do not depend on t, we get

$$\sum Y_t = T\hat{\alpha} + \hat{\beta}\sum X_t$$
$$\sum Y_t X_t = \hat{\alpha}\sum X_t + \hat{\beta}\sum X_t^2$$

The first equation is equivalent to equation (3.2) and the second equation is the same as equation (3.5).

3.A.3   Best Linear Unbiased Estimator (BLUE) and the Gauss–Markov Theorem

From statistical theory we know that one of the desirable properties for an estimator is to be a minimum various unbiased linear estimator (see Definition 2.19). In other words, among all linear combinations of the dependent variable that are unbiased, we would like to choose the one that has the smallest variance. This is the Best Linear Unbiased Estimator (BLUE) property. In this section we prove the Gauss–Markov Theorem which states that the OLS estimator derived in Section 3.2 also has the BLUE property.

First note that the OLS estimator $\hat{\beta}$ can indeed be expressed as a linear combination of Y_t. To see this we reproduce equation (3.9) below.

$$S_{xy} = \left[\sum X_t Y_t - \frac{(\sum X_t)(\sum Y_t)}{T} \right] \tag{3.9}$$

Noting that $\bar{X} = \sum X_t/T$, this can be expressed as

$$\sum X_t Y_t - \bar{X}\sum Y_t = \sum (X_t - \bar{X})Y_t$$

Because $\hat{\beta} = S_{xy}/S_{xx}$ from equation (3.7), we have

$$\hat{\beta} = \sum \left[\frac{X_t - \bar{X}}{S_{xx}} \right] Y_t$$

which is a linear combination of Y_t with the weight $\left[\dfrac{X_t - \bar{X}}{S_{xx}} \right]$ that depends on X_t.

Now consider a general linear combination of the Ys that takes the form $\tilde{\beta} = \sum a_t Y_t$, where a_t is nonrandom. The best linear unbiased estimator (BLUE) has the two properties: (1) $\tilde{\beta}$ is unbiased and (2) Var($\tilde{\beta}$) is the smallest.

$$\tilde{\beta} = \sum a_t Y_t = \sum a_t(\alpha + \beta X_t + u_t) = \alpha \sum a_t + \beta \sum a_t X_t + \sum a_t u_t$$

Because a_t and X_t are nonstochastic and $E(\sum a_t u_t) = \sum E(a_t u_t) = \sum a_t E(u_t) = 0$, $E(\tilde{\beta}) = \alpha \sum a_t + \beta \sum a_t X_t$. For this to be equal to β for all α and β, $\sum a_t$ must be zero and $\sum a_t X_t$ must be equal to one. Var($\tilde{\beta}$) = Var($\sum a_t u_t$) because the first two terms of $\tilde{\beta}$ can be treated as constant. Since the u's are iid, Var($\tilde{\beta}$) = $\sum a_t^2$ Var(u_t) = $\sigma^2 \sum a_t^2$. By Assumption 3.6, the covariance terms will be zero.

Thus, the problem of obtaining the best linear unbiased estimator reduces to that of choosing a_t such that $\sum a_t^2$ is minimum subject to the two conditions $\sum a_t = 0$ and $\sum a_t X_t = 1$. This is an example of constrained minimization (see Section 2.A.2). By the Lagrange method of minimization subject to restrictions, this is equivalent to minimizing $\sum a_t^2 + \lambda \sum a_t + \mu(\sum a_t X_t - 1)$, where λ and μ are Lagrange multipliers. The first-order condition for minimization is given by partially differentiating the above with respect to a_t, treating all other a's and X_t as constant. This gives the condition,

$$2a_t + \lambda + \mu X_t = 0 \qquad \text{or} \qquad \lambda + \mu X_t = -2a_t$$

Summing each term over t we get

$$T\lambda + \mu \sum X_t = -2 \sum a_t = 0 \qquad \text{(because } \sum a_t = 0\text{)}$$

which can be solved for λ as $\lambda = -\mu \sum X_t/T = -\mu \bar{X}$. Next multiply each term of the first-order condition by X_t and then sum over t. This gives the following equation:

$$\lambda \sum X_t + \mu \sum X_t^2 = -2 \sum a_t X_t = -2 \qquad \text{(because } \sum a_t X_t = 1\text{)}$$

Substitute for λ in this, group the μ terms, and solve for μ and λ. We get (using the relation $\bar{X} = \sum X_t/T$)

$$\mu = \frac{-2}{S_{xx}} \qquad \text{and} \qquad \lambda = \frac{(2\bar{X})}{S_{xx}}$$

where S_{xx} is defined in equation (3.8). Using these to solve for a_t, we obtain

$$a_t = \frac{-\lambda}{2} - \frac{\mu X_t}{2} = \frac{X_t - \bar{X}}{S_{xx}}$$

From this,

$$\tilde{\beta} = \sum a_t Y_t = \sum \left[\frac{X_t - \bar{X}}{S_{xx}} \right] Y_t$$

This is exactly the same as the estimator given earlier in this section. We therefore have the Gauss–Markov Theorem that the OLS estimator is also BLUE.

3.A.4   Maximum Likelihood Estimation

The motivation for the maximum likelihood estimation method is described in detail in Section 2.A.3. The reader should study that section before starting this one. In that section the method was applied to the case in which the mean and variance of a normal distribution were estimated. Here we apply the same technique to the regression problem. Because the maximum likelihood principle requires a knowledge of the distribution in question, we need Assumption 3.7. The steps for deriving a maximum likelihood estimator are straightforward. First, set up the likelihood function relating the joint density function of the observations to the unknown parameters. To maximize this, partially differentiate the logarithm of the likelihood function with respect to each unknown parameter and set it to zero. Then solve the resulting first-order conditions for the maximum likelihood estimators. The density function of u is given by [see equation (2.4)]

$$f(u) = \frac{1}{(\sigma\sqrt{2\pi})} e^{-u^2/2\sigma^2}$$

Because the observations were drawn independently, the likelihood function of u_1, $u_2, \ldots, u_T$ is

$$L(\alpha, \beta, \sigma^2) = f(u_1)f(u_2)\cdot\cdots\cdot f(u_T)$$

$$= \frac{1}{(\sigma\sqrt{2\pi})^T} e^{-\Sigma u_t^2/(2\sigma^2)}$$

$$= \frac{1}{(\sigma\sqrt{2\pi})^T} e^{-\Sigma(Y_t - \alpha - \beta X_t)^2/(2\sigma^2)}$$

It is more convenient to maximize the logarithm of the likelihood function, which is equivalent to maximizing L because the logarithm is a monotonic increasing transformation; that is, if $a > b$, then $\ln(a) > \ln(b)$.

$$\ln L = -T \ln \sigma - T \ln(\sqrt{2\pi}) - \sum \left[\frac{(Y_t - \alpha - \beta X_t)^2}{2\sigma^2} \right]$$

$$= -T \ln \sigma - T \ln(\sqrt{2\pi}) - \frac{\text{SSE}}{2\sigma^2}$$

where $\text{SSE} = \sum(Y_t - \alpha - \beta X_t)^2$. The only place where α and β appear is in SSE. Therefore, maximizing $\ln L$ is equivalent to minimizing SSE (because there is a negative sign before SSE). But minimizing SSE gives the least squares estimators. Therefore, least squares estimators are also MLE provided the u's are iid as $N(0, \sigma^2)$. Because maximum likelihood estimators are consistent and asymptotically efficient, so are the OLS estimators.

To obtain the MLE of σ^2, differentiate $\ln L$ partially with respect to σ and set the result to zero. We would then have

$$\frac{\partial(\ln L)}{\partial \sigma} = -\frac{T}{\sigma} + \frac{\text{SSE}}{\sigma^3} = 0$$

Solving this for σ^2 we get $\sigma^2 = \text{SSE}/T$. But SSE depends on α and β. However, we can use their estimates $\hat{\alpha}$ and $\hat{\beta}$. We therefore get the MLE of the variance of u_t as $\tilde{\sigma}^2 = \sum \hat{u}_t^2 / T$. As stated earlier, this is not unbiased. An unbiased estimate is obtained by dividing $\sum \hat{u}_1^2$ by $T - 2$ and using $\hat{\sigma}^2$ defined in equation (3.18).

3.A.5   Derivation of the Variances of the Estimators

From equation (3.7), $\hat{\beta} = S_{xy}/S_{xx}$. Because X is nonrandom by Assumption 3.3, S_{xx} is also nonrandom and hence $\text{Var}(\hat{\beta}) = \text{Var}(S_{xy})/S_{xx}^2$. From equation (3.12), $S_{xy} = \beta S_{xx} + S_{xu}$, and therefore $\text{Var}(S_{xy}) = \text{Var}(S_{xu})$. We note from equation (3.13) that $S_{xu} = \sum (X_t - \bar{X})u_t$. It is stated in Property 2.A.1c that the variance of a sum of random variables is the sum of the variances provided the covariance terms are zero. By Assumption 3.6, u_t and u_s are uncorrelated for all $t \neq s$ and the covariances are zero. Therefore

$$\text{Var}(S_{xu}) = \text{Var}\left[\sum (X_t - \bar{X})u_t\right] = \sum \text{Var}[(X_t - \bar{X})u_t] = \sum (X_t - \bar{X})^2 \text{Var}(u_t)$$

By Assumption 3.5, $\text{Var}(u_t) = \sigma^2$. Therefore, $\text{Var}(S_{xu}) = \sigma^2 \sum (X_t - \bar{X})^2 = \sigma^2 S_{xx}$. It follows from this that

$$\text{Var}(\hat{\beta}) = \frac{\text{Var}(S_{xy})}{S_{xx}^2} = \frac{\sigma^2 S_{xx}}{S_{xx}^2} = \frac{\sigma^2}{S_{xx}}$$

We have thus derived equation 3.15. The procedure for deriving equations (3.16) and (3.17) is similar and is left as an exercise to the reader.

3.A.6   Unbiased Estimator of the Variance of the Error Term

In equation (3.15), it was stated that $s^2 = \hat{\sigma}^2 = \left(\sum \hat{u}_t^2\right)/(T - 2)$ is an unbiased estimator of σ^2. This is proved here.

$$\hat{u}_t = Y_t - \hat{\alpha} - \hat{\beta}X_t = Y_t - (\bar{Y} - \hat{\beta}\bar{X}) - \hat{\beta}X_t$$

using equation (3.6) for $\hat{\alpha}$. Because Y_t is given by equation (3.1), $\bar{Y} = \alpha + \beta\bar{X} + \bar{u}$, where $\bar{u}$ is $\sum u_t / T$. We therefore have, grouping all the β terms,

$$\hat{u}_t = (\alpha + \beta X_t + u_t) - (\alpha + \beta\bar{X} + \bar{u}) + \hat{\beta}\bar{X} - \hat{\beta}X_t$$
$$= (u_t - \bar{u}) - (\hat{\beta} - \beta)(X_t - \bar{X})$$

The sum of squares of $\hat{u}_t$ is therefore given by

$$\sum \hat{u}_t^2 = \sum (u_t - \bar{u})^2 + (\hat{\beta} - \beta)^2 \sum (X_t - \bar{X})^2 - 2(\hat{\beta} - \beta) \sum (X_t - \bar{X})(u_t - \bar{u})$$
$$= S_{uu} + (\hat{\beta} - \beta)^2 S_{xx} - 2(\hat{\beta} - \beta) S_{xu}$$

using the notation similar to that in equations (3.8) and (3.13). From equation (3.12), $S_{xu} = S_{xy} - \beta S_{xx} = S_{xx}(\hat{\beta} - \beta)$. Substituting this in the above equation and combining the second and third terms we have,

$$\sum \hat{u}_t^2 = S_{uu} - (\hat{\beta} - \beta)^2 S_{xx}$$

To compute the expected value of the error sum of squares, we need $E(S_{uu})$ and $E(\hat{\beta} - \beta)^2$. We note from Property 2.11b that $E(S_{uu}) = (T - 1) \text{Var}(u) = (T - 1)\sigma^2$. Also,

$$E(\hat{\beta} - \beta)^2] = \text{Var}(\hat{\beta}) = \frac{\sigma^2}{S_{xx}}$$

from equation (3.15). Putting all this together, we obtain

$$E(\sum \hat{u}_t^2) = E(S_{uu}) - S_{xx}E[(\hat{\beta} - \beta)^2] = (T - 1)\sigma^2 - \sigma^2 = (T - 2)\sigma^2$$

Dividing through by $T - 2$ we have the desired result that

$$E(\hat{\sigma}^2) = E\left[\frac{\sum \hat{u}_t^2}{T - 2}\right] = \sigma^2$$

Hence, $\hat{\sigma}^2$ is an unbiased estimator of σ^2.

3.A.7   Derivation of Equation 3.22

The total sum of squares can be rewritten as follows:

$$\sum (Y_t - \bar{Y})^2 = \sum (Y_t - \hat{Y}_t + \hat{Y}_t - \bar{Y})^2$$
$$= \sum (Y_t - \hat{Y}_t)^2 + \sum (\hat{Y}_t - \bar{Y})^2 + 2\sum (Y_t - \hat{Y}_t)(\hat{Y}_t - \bar{Y})$$

As $\hat{u}_t = Y_t - \hat{Y}_t$, the first two terms are what we had in equation (3.22). All we need now is to show that $\sum (Y_t - \hat{Y}_t)(\hat{Y}_t - \bar{Y}) = \sum \hat{u}_t(\hat{Y}_t - \bar{Y}) = 0$.

$$\sum \hat{u}_t(\hat{Y}_t - \bar{Y}) = \sum \hat{u}_t(\hat{\alpha} + \hat{\beta}X_t - \bar{Y}) = \hat{\alpha}\sum \hat{u}_t + \hat{\beta}\sum \hat{u}_t X_t - \bar{Y}\sum \hat{u}_t$$

From the first normal equation (3.2), $\sum \hat{u}_t = \sum (Y_t - \hat{\alpha} - \hat{\beta}X_t) = 0$. From equation (3.4), $\sum \hat{u}_t X_t = \sum (Y_t - \hat{\alpha} - \hat{\beta}X_t)X_t = 0$, thus proving the result.

3.A.8   Derivation of Equation 3.24

To derive equation (3.24), we first derive the sample covariance (denoted by $\widehat{\text{Cov}}$) between Y_t and $\hat{Y}_t$. From equation (2.12),

$$\widehat{\text{Cov}(Y_t, \hat{Y}_t)} = \frac{1}{T - 1} \sum (Y_t - \bar{Y})(\hat{Y}_t - \bar{Y})$$

Note that the mean of $\hat{Y}_t$ is also $\bar{Y}$ because $\hat{\alpha} + \hat{\beta}\bar{X} = \bar{Y}$. Also,

$$Y_t - \bar{Y} = (Y_t - \hat{Y}_t) + (\hat{Y}_t - \bar{Y}) = \hat{u}_t + (\hat{Y}_t - \bar{Y})$$

Therefore,

$$\widehat{\text{Cov}(Y_t, \hat{Y}_t)} = \frac{\sum \hat{u}_t(\hat{Y}_t - \bar{Y})}{T - 1} + \frac{\sum(\hat{Y}_t - \bar{Y})^2}{T - 1}$$

It was shown in the previous section that the first term is zero. Hence the covariance between Y_t and $\hat{Y}_t$ is the same as the second term, which is $\text{RSS}/(T - 1)$:

$$\widehat{\text{Cov}(Y_t, \hat{Y}_t)} = \frac{\text{RSS}}{T - 1}$$

We also have

$$\widehat{\text{Var}(Y_t)} = \frac{\text{TSS}}{T - 1} \quad \text{and} \quad \widehat{\text{Var}(\hat{Y}_t)} = \frac{\sum(\hat{Y}_t - \bar{Y})^2}{T - 1} = \frac{\text{RSS}}{T - 1}$$

It will be recalled from equation (2.13) that the square of the simple correlation coefficient between Y_t and $\hat{Y}_t$ is given by

$$r_{Y\hat{Y}}^2 = \frac{\widehat{\text{Cov}^2(Y_t, \hat{Y}_t)}}{\widehat{\text{Var}(Y_t)}\,\widehat{\text{Var}(\hat{Y}_t)}}$$

Substituting for the covariance and variances from the expressions just derived and canceling $T - 1$, we have

$$r_{Y\hat{Y}}^2 = \frac{\text{RSS}^2}{\text{TSS RSS}} = \frac{\text{RSS}}{\text{TSS}} = R^2$$

Thus, the square of the simple correlation between the observed value Y_t and the value $\hat{Y}_t$ predicted by the regression model is the same as R^2 defined in equation (3.23).

3.A.9   Proof That $r_{xy}^2 = R^2$

Here we show that R^2 is also equal to the square of the simple correlation between X and Y. From equation (2.13), $r_{xy}^2 = S_{xy}^2/(S_{xx}S_{yy})$. S_{yy} is the same as the total sum of squares TSS. Also, $\text{RSS} = \sum(\hat{Y}_t - \bar{Y})^2$. Because $\hat{Y}_t = \hat{\alpha} + \hat{\beta}X_t$ and $\bar{Y} = \hat{\alpha} + \hat{\beta}\bar{X}$, we have $\hat{Y}_t - \bar{Y} = \hat{\beta}(X_t - \bar{X})$. Therefore,

$$\text{RSS} = \sum(\hat{Y}_t - \bar{Y})^2 = \hat{\beta}^2 \sum(X_t - \bar{X})^2 = \hat{\beta}^2 S_{xx}$$

From equation (3.7), $\hat{\beta} = S_{xy}/S_{xx}$. Substituting this for one of the $\hat{\beta}$s above, we obtain

$$\text{RSS} = \hat{\beta}\left(\frac{S_{xy}}{S_{xx}}\right)(S_{xx}) = \hat{\beta}S_{xy}$$

Let $Z = \ln Y$ and $W = \ln X$. Then, using the result that $d(\ln Y) = dY/Y$,

$$\frac{dZ}{dW} = \frac{d(\ln Y)}{d(\ln X)} = \frac{dY}{Y} \div \frac{dX}{X} \qquad (3.A.2)$$

$$= \frac{X}{Y} \frac{dY}{dX} = \eta$$

Thus, the *elasticity of Y with respect to X is the same as the derivative of* $\ln Y$ *with respect to* $\ln X$. If Y decreases as X increases, then $dY/dX < 0$ and hence $\eta < 0$. In practical applications, however, only the absolute value ($|\eta|$) is used.

Example 3.A.1

The demand function for a product is often represented as a function of the form $p^{-1/2}$, where p is the price and the exponent could be any number other than $\frac{1}{2}$. The general form commonly used for the demand function is $q = p^\beta$, where q is the quantity demanded and price is p (β is assumed to be a constant). As price increases, we would expect the quantity demanded to decrease. Therefore, β will be negative. To obtain the *price elasticity of demand*, first differentiate q with respect to p to obtain $dq/dp = \beta p^{\beta - 1}$. The price elasticity is obtained by substituting this in equation (3.A.1). We get

$$\eta = \frac{p}{q} \frac{dq}{dp} = \frac{p}{p^\beta} \beta p^{\beta - 1} = \beta$$

We note that in this example the elasticity of demand is a constant for all p and q. However, this need not always be the case, as will be seen in other examples given below. The elasticity could also have been derived using equation (3.A.2). Taking the logarithm of the demand function, we get $\ln q = \beta \ln p$. Because the elasticity is the ratio $d(\ln q)/d(\ln p)$, we have $\eta = \beta$. If the absolute value of β is less than 1, we say that demand is *price inelastic*. If it is greater than 1, it is *price elastic*, and if $\beta = -1$, it is *unitary elastic*. If $\beta = -0.8$, then a doubling of price (that is, a 100 percent increase) will decrease demand by 80 percent.

If we take the logarithm of both sides of the demand function, we get $\ln q = \beta \ln p$. An expression like this is called a **double-log function** because both sides are in logarithms. □

Example 3.A.2

Suppose Y stands for sales tax revenues and X represents total sales. Because sales tax is usually a fixed fraction of total sales, we have the relation $Y = \beta X$, where β is the fixed sales tax rate. Then $dY/dX = \beta$, but the elasticity is not constant because

$$\eta = \frac{X}{Y} \frac{dY}{dX} = \frac{\beta X}{Y}$$

Thus, the elasticity varies according to what the values of X and Y are. □

Example 3.A.3

In certain cases (Section 3.13 has concrete examples of this), the relation between X and Y is of the form $Y = \beta \ln X$. This is known as a **linear-log function**. In this case, $dY/dX = \beta/X$. The elasticity is $(X/Y)(dY/dX) = \beta/Y$. Here the elasticity does not depend on X but on Y only. β has an interesting property here. We note from the above derivation that

$$\beta = X\frac{dY}{dX} = \frac{dY}{(dX/X)} \qquad \text{or} \qquad dY = \beta\frac{dX}{X}$$

The expression dX/X [or $d(\ln X)$], when multiplied by 100, can be interpreted as the *percentage change* in X. And dY is the change in the level of Y. Thus, $\beta/100$ is the change in the level of Y for a 1 percent change in X. As an example, if Y is measured in dollars and $\beta = 1.85$, then a 1 percent increase in X will increase Y by 1.85 dollars. $\square$

Example 3.A.4

Another relation that is often encountered is $\ln Y = \beta X$ (which is equivalent to the exponential function $Y = e^{\beta X}$). Because the left-hand side is a logarithm and the right-hand side is in a linear form, this relation is known as the **log-linear formulation**. This relationship is also sometimes referred to as the **semilog function**. In this example, the elasticity is

$$\eta = \frac{X}{Y}\frac{dY}{dX} = \frac{X}{e^{\beta X}}\beta e^{\beta X} = \beta X$$

Here, the elasticity depends on X only. Differentiating $\ln Y$ with respect to X, we get $\beta = (dY/Y)/dX$ and $dY/Y = \beta dX$, which means that a one unit increase in X will change Y by 100β percent. If, for example, β is 0.85 and X is measured in dollars, a 1 dollar increase in X will increase Y by 85 percent. $\square$

CHAPTER 4

Multiple Regression Models

■ In Chapter 3 we confined ourselves to the simple case of a two-variable regression. We now take up **multiple regression**, which relates a given dependent variable Y to several independent variables, $X_1, X_2, \ldots, X_k$. As before, we start with a linear formulation but extend it to accommodate nonlinearities. The multiple linear regression model has the following general formulation:

$$Y_t = \beta_1 X_{t1} + \beta_2 X_{t2} + \cdots + \beta_k X_{tk} + u_t \tag{4.1}$$

The subscript t refers to the observation number and varies from 1 to T. The assumptions made on the disturbance term u_t are identical to those specified in Chapter 3. In the real estate example used in that chapter, the dependent variable was the price of a single family home. Table 4.1 presents additional data for the 14 sample houses sold. Note that the data for X_1 is simply a column of 1s and corresponds to a constant term. Despite this, X_1 is in the model to allow for an "intercept." Including the constant term, there are k independent variables and hence k unknown regression coefficients to estimate.

The multiple linear model for this example will be as follows:

$$\text{PRICE} = \beta_1 + \beta_2 \text{SQFT} + \beta_3 \text{BEDRMS} + \beta_4 \text{BATHS} + u \tag{4.2}$$

As before, price is measured in thousands of dollars. Besides the square footage of the living area, price is related to the number of bedrooms as well as the number of bathrooms.

The effect of a change in Y_t when only X_{ti} is changed is given by $\Delta Y_t / \Delta X_{ti} = \beta_i$. Hence, the interpretation of the regression coefficient β_i is that, *keeping the values of all the other variables the same*, if X_{ti} is changed by one unit, Y_t is expected to change,

TABLE 4.1 Data for Single Family Houses (Price in thousands of dollars)

t	PRICE (Y)	CONSTANT (X_1)	SQFT (X_2)	BEDRMS (X_3)	BATHS (X_4)
1	199.9	1	1065	3	1.75
2	228	1	1254	3	2
3	235	1	1300	3	2
4	285	1	1577	4	2.5
5	239	1	1600	3	2
6	293	1	1750	4	2
7	285	1	1800	4	2.75
8	365	1	1870	4	2
9	295	1	1935	4	2.5
10	290	1	1948	4	2
11	385	1	2254	4	3
12	505	1	2600	3	2.5
13	425	1	2800	4	3
14	415	1	3000	4	3

on average, by β_i units. Thus, β_4 in equation (4.2) is interpreted as: Between two houses with the same SQFT and BEDRMS, the one with an extra bathroom is expected to sell, on average, for β_4 thousand dollars more. Multiple regression analysis thus enables us to control for a subset of explanatory variables and examine the effect of a selected independent variable.

4.1 Normal Equations

In the case of the multiple regression model, Assumption 3.4 is modified as follows: *Each X is given and nonrandom so that* $\mathrm{Cov}(X_{ti}, u_t) = E(X_{ti}u_t) = 0$ *for each i from* 1 *to k and each t from* 1 *to T.* Thus, *each of the independent variables is assumed to be uncorrelated with the error term.* Under Assumptions 3.2 through 3.7, the four different estimation procedures discussed in Chapter 3 yield the same set of estimates for the βs. The simple method described in Section 3.2 would set the sample mean of the residual $\hat{u}_t$ to zero and also set the sample covariance between X_i and u to zero for the other variables. We therefore get the k normal equations

$$\frac{1}{T}\sum \hat{u}_t = 0$$

$$\frac{1}{T}\sum (X_{ti}\hat{u}_t) = 0 = \sum X_{ti}(Y_t - \hat{\beta}_1 - \hat{\beta}_2 X_{t2} - \cdots - \hat{\beta}_k X_{tk})$$

for $i = 2, 3, \ldots, k$. In the case of the ordinary least squares procedure (OLS), we define the sum of squared errors as

$$\text{ESS} = \sum_{t=1}^{t=T} \hat{u}_t^2 = \sum_{t=1}^{t=T} (Y_t - \hat{\beta}_1 - \hat{\beta}_2 X_{t2} - \cdots - \hat{\beta}_k X_{tk})^2$$

OLS procedure minimizes ESS with respect to $\hat{\beta}_1, \hat{\beta}_2, \ldots, \hat{\beta}_k$. By proceeding as in Section 3.A.2 we can derive the normal equations, which are identical to the above. We thus obtain k equations in the k unknown regression coefficients (the summations are over the index t—that is, over observations):

$$\sum Y_t = T\hat{\beta}_1 + \hat{\beta}_2 \sum X_{t2} + \cdots + \hat{\beta}_k \sum X_{tk}$$
$$\sum Y_t X_{t2} = \hat{\beta}_1 \sum X_{t2} + \hat{\beta}_2 \sum X_{t2}^2 + \cdots + \hat{\beta}_k \sum X_{tk} X_{t2}$$
$$\cdots\cdots\cdots\cdots\cdots\cdots\cdots\cdots\cdots\cdots\cdots\cdots\cdots\cdots\cdots$$
$$\sum Y_t X_{ti} = \hat{\beta}_1 \sum X_{ti} + \hat{\beta}_2 \sum X_{t2} X_{ti} + \cdots + \hat{\beta}_k \sum X_{tk} X_{ti}$$
$$\sum Y_t X_{tk} = \hat{\beta}_1 \sum X_{tk} + \hat{\beta}_2 \sum X_{t2} X_{tk} + \cdots + \hat{\beta}_k \sum X_{tk}^2$$

The k equations can generally be solved uniquely for the βs. Standard computer programs do all the calculations once the data have been entered and the dependent and independent variables specified. Appendix 4.A.1 describes the steps for a three-variable model in which Y is regressed against a constant term, X_2, and X_3.

Properties 3.1 through 3.3 are valid in the case of multiple linear regression also. Thus the OLS estimates are BLUE, unbiased, efficient, and consistent. Residuals and predicted values are obtained from the following relations:

$$\hat{u}_t = Y_t - \hat{\beta}_1 - \hat{\beta}_2 X_{t2} - \cdots - \hat{\beta}_k X_{tk}$$
$$\hat{Y}_t = \hat{\beta}_1 + \hat{\beta}_2 X_{t2} + \cdots + \hat{\beta}_k X_{tk} = Y_t - \hat{u}_t$$

Example 4.1

For the model specified in equation (4.2), the estimated relation is (see Practice Computer Session 4.1)

$$\widehat{\text{PRICE}} = 129.062 + 0.1548\,\text{SQFT} - 21.588\,\text{BEDRMS} - 12.193\,\text{BATHS}$$

We note immediately that the regression coefficients for BEDRMS and BATHS are both negative. One might intuitively feel that adding a bedroom and/or a bathroom should increase the value of the property. However, the regression coefficient has the proper interpretation only when other things are equal. Thus, if we increase the number of bedrooms, *holding SQFT and BATHS constant*, the average price is expected to go down by $21,588. If the same living area is divided up to provide one more bedroom, each room will be much smaller. The data indicate that, on average, buyers value such a division lower and hence would be willing to pay only a smaller price.

A similar argument also applies to BATHS. Holding SQFT and BEDRMS constant, if we add a bathroom, the average price is expected to decrease by $12,193. Again, adding a bathroom but keeping the total number of square feet the same also means having smaller bedrooms. The results reveal buyers' aversion and hence we observe a reduction in the average price. We note from the above arguments that what appeared at first to be unexpected signs (commonly referred to as "wrong signs") had a sensible explanation.

Suppose we add a bedroom and increase the overall number of square feet by 300 (allowing for an additional hallway and other related items). Then BEDRMS will increase by one and SQFT will increase by 300. The change in average price (ΔPRICE) as a result of this combined effect will be

$$\widehat{\Delta\text{PRICE}} = \hat{\beta}_2 \, \Delta\text{SQFT} + \hat{\beta}_3 \, \Delta\text{BEDRMS} = 300\hat{\beta}_2 + \hat{\beta}_3 \qquad \square$$

In the model this amounts to a net increase of \$24,852 in the estimated average price [calculated as $(300 \times 0.1548) - 21.588$, in thousands of dollars], which appears reasonable.

Practice Problems

4.1 Suppose a bedroom and a bathroom are added, with an increase in the living area of 350 square feet. By how much is the average price expected to go up? Is the numerical value believable?

4.2 Forecast the average price of a house with 4 bedrooms, 3 baths, and 2500 square feet of living area. Does the forecast appear reasonable for the data given in Table 4.1?

An unbiased estimator of the residual variance σ^2 is obtained by $s^2 = \hat{\sigma}^2 = \sum \hat{u}_t^2/(T-k)$, where T is the number of observations used in the estimation and k is the number of regression coefficients estimated, including the constant term. The proof of this statement is similar, in principle, to that given in Section 3.A.6 but is much more complicated because there are k normal equations here [see Johnston (1984), pp. 180–181]. In Chapter 3 we divided the error sum of squares by $T - 2$ to get an unbiased estimator of σ^2. Here, the k normal equations impose k constraints, resulting in a "loss" of k degrees of freedom. Hence we divide by $T - k$. Because $\hat{\sigma}^2$ should be nonnegative, T must be larger than k. The procedure for computing standard errors of the $\hat{\beta}$s is similar but the calculations are now much more tedious. Computer programs provide all the statistics needed to estimate the parameters and test hypotheses on them. It can be shown that $\sum \hat{u}_t^2/\sigma^2$ has the chi-square distribution with $T - k$ degrees of freedom [see Johnston (1984), p. 181]. These results are summarized in Property 4.1.

Property 4.1

a. The multiple regression model cannot be estimated unless the number of observations (T) exceeds the number of regression coefficients (k), including the constant term.

b. An unbiased estimator of the error variance (σ^2) is given by

$$s^2 = \hat{\sigma}^2 = \frac{\text{ESS}}{T-k} = \frac{\sum \hat{u}_t^2}{T-k}$$

where ESS is the sum of squares of the residuals.

c. ESS/σ^2 has the chi-square distribution with $T - k$ d.f. Note that this property critically depends on Assumption 3.7 that the error terms u_t are normally distributed as $N(0, \sigma^2)$.

4.2 Standardized Regression and Beta Coefficients*

In equation (4.2), the values of β_2 and β_4 represent the marginal effects of SQFT and BATHS, respectively. Because these two variables measure different effects, the estimated coefficients are not comparable in numerical terms. In order to compare the numerical value of one regression coefficient with that of another, we often need to estimate a modified regression known as the **standardized regression**. This practice is common in the finance literature, in which stock and bond prices are frequently related to market averages and to the characteristics of the firm [see, for example, Brealey and Myers (1981) and Friend, Blume, and Crockett (1970)].

Let $y_t = Y_t - \bar{Y}$ and $x_{ti} = X_{ti} - \bar{X}_i$ (for $i = 2, 3, \ldots, k$) be the deviation of each of the variables from the corresponding mean. Also, let s_y be the sample standard deviation of y, and s_{x_i} be the sample standard deviation of the ith explanatory variable (X_i). Then the standardized regression is defined as

$$y_t^* = \beta_2^* x_{t2}^* + \beta_3^* x_{t3}^* + \cdots + \beta_k^* x_{tk}^* + u_t^* \tag{4.1*}$$

where

$$y_t^* = \frac{Y_t - \bar{Y}}{s_y}, \qquad x_{ti}^* = \frac{X_{ti} - \bar{X}_i}{s_{x_i}},$$

and

$$u_t^* = \frac{u_t - \bar{u}}{s_u}$$

The constant term (X_{t1}) drops out because its mean is also 1. Note that because each variable is transformed to a standardized form by subtracting the mean and dividing by the standard deviation, the transformed variables are unit-free. The regression coefficients β_i^* are known as the **beta coefficients** and are directly comparable to each other in numerical value. A change of 1 standard deviation in the ith independent variable is expected to change the dependent variable by β_i^* standard deviations. The relationship between the original regression coefficients β_i and the beta coefficients β_i^* can be expressed as in Property 4.2.

Property 4.2

If β_i is the regression coefficient for X_i and β_i^* is the corresponding beta coefficient, s_y is the sample standard deviation of the dependent variable Y, and s_{x_i} is the sample standard deviation of the ith independent variable X_i, then $\hat{\beta}_i^* = \hat{\beta}_i s_{x_i}/s_y$.

PROOF* (The proof may be skipped without loss of continuity.) Compute the mean of each term in equation (4.1) and subtract from it. We get

$$Y_t - \bar{Y} = \beta_2(X_{t2} - \bar{X}_2) + \beta_3(X_{t3} - \bar{X}_3) + \cdots + \beta_k(X_{tk} - \bar{X}_k) + (u_t - \bar{u})$$

or

$$y_t = \beta_2 x_{t2} + \beta_3 x_{t3} + \cdots + \beta_k x_{tk} + (u_t - \bar{u}) \qquad (4.1')$$

Equation (4.1') is known as the **model in deviation form**. Next divide each term by s_y. The left-hand side becomes y_t^*. The estimated version of (4.1') is given by setting the unpredictable error term to zero. Dividing each term by s_y and noting that $y_t^* = y_t/s_y$, we obtain the following estimated equation:

$$\hat{y}_t^* = \hat{\beta}_2 \frac{x_{t2}}{s_y} + \hat{\beta}_3 \frac{x_{t3}}{s_y} + \cdots + \hat{\beta}_k \frac{x_{tk}}{s_y} = \hat{\beta}_2 \frac{s_{x_2}}{s_{x_2}} \frac{x_{t2}}{s_y} + \cdots + \hat{\beta}_k \frac{s_{x_k}}{s_{x_k}} \frac{x_{tk}}{s_y}$$

Because $x_{ti}^* = x_{ti}/s_{x_i}$, when we compare this equation with (4.1*), we see that

$$\hat{\beta}_i^* = \frac{\hat{\beta}_i s_{x_i}}{s_y} \qquad \square$$

Example 4.2

For the data in Table 4.1, the estimated standardized regression is (See Practice Computer Session 4.2)

$$\widehat{PRICE}^* = 1.011 \text{ SQFT}^* - 0.121 \text{ BEDRMS}^* - 0.061 \text{ BATHS}^*$$

The interpretation is that, holding BEDRMS and BATHS constants, an increase of one standard deviation from the mean of SQFT is expected to increase the average PRICE by 1.011 standard deviation from its mean. Numerically, SQFT has the biggest impact on the standardized price. $\square$

Practice Problems

4.3 How is the error sum of squares ESS affected by the standardization procedure? In other words, compare the error sums of squares between equations (4.1) and (4.1*).

4.4 In the two-variable regression model $Y_t = \alpha + \beta X_t + u_t$, show that $\hat{\beta}^*$ is the same as the simple correlation coefficient between X and Y. [*Hint*: Use the fact that $\hat{\beta} = \widehat{Cov(X, Y)}/\widehat{Var(X)}$.]

4.3 Goodness of Fit

When measuring goodness of fit, the total sum of squares, regression sum of squares, and error sum of squares have the same form as before, and TSS = RSS + ESS here also (provided the model has a constant term). Thus

$$\text{TSS} = \sum(Y_t - \bar{Y})^2 \qquad \text{RSS} = \sum(\hat{Y}_t - \bar{Y})^2 \qquad \text{ESS} = \sum \hat{u}_t^2$$

The goodness of fit is measured as before by $R^2 = 1 - (\text{ESS}/\text{TSS})$. This way of defining R^2, however, creates a problem. It can be shown that the addition of any variable (whether or not it makes sense in the context) will increase R^2. The algebraic proof of this statement is quite tedious, but we can argue it intuitively. When a new variable is added and ESS minimized, we are minimizing over a larger set of variables and hence the new ESS is likely to be smaller (at least not larger). More specifically, suppose the term $\beta_{k+1} X_{tk+1}$ is added to equation (4.1) and a new model obtained. If the *minimum* sum of squares for this new model is *higher* than that for the old model, then setting β_{k+1} to zero and using the old estimates for the other βs is better, and hence the new estimates could not have minimized ESS. It follows that when a new variable is added, the corresponding R^2 cannot decrease but is likely to increase. This being so, there is always a temptation to add new variables in order to do just that—increase R^2—regardless of the importance of the variables to the problem at hand.

To penalize this kind of "fishing expedition," a different measure of goodness of fit is used more frequently. This measure is called the **adjusted R^2** or **R^2 adjusted for degrees of freedom** (we encountered this in the computer printouts in Chapter 3). To develop this measure, first recall that R^2 measures the fraction of the variance of Y "explained" by the model; equivalently, it is one minus the fraction "unexplained," which is due to the error variance $\text{Var}(u)$. A natural measure, call it $\bar{R}^2$ (R-bar squared), is therefore

$$\bar{R}^2 = 1 - \frac{\widehat{\text{Var}(u)}}{\widehat{\text{Var}(Y)}}$$

We know that an unbiased estimator of $\sigma^2 = \text{Var}(u)$ is given by $\text{ESS}/(T - k)$, and an unbiased estimator of $\text{Var}(Y)$ is given by $\text{TSS}/(T - 1)$. Substituting these in the above equation, we obtain

$$\bar{R}^2 = 1 - \frac{\text{ESS}/(T - k)}{\text{TSS}/(T - 1)} = 1 - \frac{\text{ESS}(T - 1)}{\text{TSS}(T - k)} = 1 - \frac{T - 1}{T - k}(1 - R^2)$$

The addition of a variable leads to a gain in R^2 but also to a loss of one d.f., because we are estimating an extra parameter. The adjusted R^2 is a better measure of goodness of fit because it allows for the trade-off between increased R^2 and decreased d.f. Also note that because $(T - 1)/(T - k)$ is never less than 1, $\bar{R}^2$ will never be higher than R^2. However, while R^2 cannot be negative, $\bar{R}^2$ can be less than zero. For example, when $T = 26$, $k = 6$, and $R^2 = 0.1$, we have $\bar{R}^2 = -0.125$. A negative $\bar{R}^2$ indicates that the model does not describe the data generating process adequately.

Example 4.3

Table 4.2 presents the estimated regression coefficients and associated statistics for four alternative models (Practice Computer Session 4.1 has instructions for reproducing these). Entries below the degrees of freedom (d.f.) are discussed in the next section. Model A is the same as the one presented in Chapter 3. In Model B,

TABLE 4.2 Estimated Models for the Home Price Data[1]

Variable	Model A	Model B	Model C	Model D
CONSTANT	52.351 (1.404)	121.179 (1.511)	129.062 (1.462)	317.493 (13.423)
SQFT	0.13875 (7.407)	0.14831 (6.993)	0.1548 (4.847)	
BEDRMS		−23.911 (−0.970)	−21.588 (−0.799)	
BATHS			−12.193 (−0.282)	
ESS	18,274	16,833	16,700	101,815
R^2	0.821	0.835	0.836	0.000
$\bar{R}^2$	0.806	0.805	0.787	0.000
F	54.861	27.767	16.989	180.189
d.f.	12	11	10	13
SGMASQ	1,523*	1,530	1,670	7,832
AIC	1,737*	1,846	2,112	8,389
FPE	1,740*	1,858	2,147	8,391
HQ	1,722*	1,822	2,077	8,354
SCHWARZ	1,903*	2,117	2,535	8,781
SHIBATA	1,678*	1,718	1,874	8,311
GCV	1,777*	1,948	2,338	8,434
RICE	1,827*	2,104	2,783	8,485

[1] *Values in parentheses are the corresponding t-statistics, that is, coefficient divided by its standard error. An asterisk denotes the model that is "best" for the criterion.*

BEDRMS has been added, and in Model C both BEDRMS and BATHS have been added. Model D has no explanatory variables, just a constant term. It will be used in Section 4.5. It is clear from Table 4.2 that, as more variables are added, the residual sum of squares steadily decreases and R^2 increases. $\bar{R}^2$, however, decreases as more variables are added. This means that the gain in R^2 is more than offset by the loss in degrees of freedom, resulting in a net loss in the "goodness of fit." Model D has a zero value for R^2 because its ESS and TSS are the same. This is not surprising because there is nothing in the model that explains the variation in PRICE. It is included here because of its usefulness in testing hypotheses (covered in Section 4.5). □

In Model A, SQFT explains 80.6 percent of the variation in home prices. When all three variables are included, however, the model explains 78.7 percent of the variation in prices, which is reasonable for a cross-section study. If additional variables had been included, the model's explanatory power would have been higher. For instance, information on the lot size, the number and type of built-in appliances, and so on are possible variables to include. As such information was not available in the sample data, however, we could not include more variables. In Chapter 6 we discuss the effect of a swimming pool on the price.

Practice Problems

4.5   Show that $\bar{R}^2$ and $\hat{\sigma}^2$ move inversely to each other; that is, if $\bar{R}^2$ goes up, then $\hat{\sigma}^2$ must necessarily decrease. (Thus, choosing a model that has a higher $\bar{R}^2$ is equivalent to choosing one that has a lower $\hat{\sigma}^2$).

4.6   Compare the values of ESS and R^2 between equations (4.1) and (4.1*).

Computing R^2 and $\bar{R}^2$ When There Is No Constant Term

The sum of squares decomposition TSS = RSS + ESS is valid only if the model has a constant term. If the model has no constant term, the appropriate decomposition can be shown to be $\sum Y_t^2 = \sum \hat{Y}_t^2 + \sum \hat{u}_t^2$. Note that the mean $\bar{Y}$ is not subtracted here. Some computer programs calculate R^2 as $1 - (\text{ESS}/\sum Y_t^2)$ when the intercept term is absent. It should be pointed out, however, that the value computed this way is not comparable to the value computed with TSS because the denominators are different between the two models. If the goal is to compare the models with and without constant terms, in terms of their goodness of fit, the formula for R^2 should not be model-dependent. It would be better to use $1 - (\text{ESS}/\text{TSS})$ in both cases so that R^2 could be compared. If R^2 is computed using TSS in the denominator, it is possible for it to be negative when the constant term is absent from the model. Such a negative value indicates that the model might be poorly specified.

We argued earlier that $\bar{R}^2 = 1 - [\widehat{\text{Var}(\hat{u})}/\widehat{\text{Var}(Y)}]$ is a better measure of the variation in Y explained by the model. This suggests the formula

$$\bar{R}^2 = 1 - \frac{\text{ESS} \div (T - k)}{\text{TSS} \div (T - 1)}$$

in all cases.

Because computer programs differ in the manner in which R^2 and $\bar{R}^2$ values are calculated, in the absence of the constant term, it is recommended that the reader test whatever program is being used and identify whether the measures are comparable across models. Investigators often exclude the constant term if it is insignificant in order to improve the statistical significance of the remaining variables. Unless there is a strong theoretical reason for omitting a constant term (the standardized model of the previous section did not have a constant term), the practice is discouraged because it may lead to model misspecification (more on this in Section 4.7.).

4.4   General Criteria for Model Selection

We showed earlier that by increasing the number of variables in a model, the residual sum of squares $\sum \hat{u}_t^2$ will decrease and R^2 will increase, but at the cost of a loss in degrees of freedom. $\bar{R}^2$ and the standard error of the residuals,

$[\text{ESS}/(T - k)]^{1/2}$, take account of the trade-off between the reduction in ESS and the loss of degrees of freedom. These are the most commonly used criteria for model comparison.

In general, simpler models are recommended for two technical reasons. First, the inclusion of too many variables makes the relative precision of individual coefficients worse. This point will be explored in detail in Chapter 5. Second, the resulting loss of degrees of freedom would reduce the power of tests performed on the coefficients. Thus, the probability of accepting a false hypothesis (type II error) increases as the degrees of freedom decreases. It is therefore desirable to develop criteria that penalize larger models but do not go to the extreme of always choosing a simpler model.

In recent years several criteria for choosing among models have been proposed. All of these take the form of the residual sum of squares (ESS) multiplied by a penalty factor that depends on the complexity of the model. A more complex model will reduce ESS but raise the penalty. The criteria thus provide other types of trade-offs between goodness of fit and model complexity. A model with a lower value of a criterion statistic is judged to be preferable. In this section we present a brief summary of penalty factors without going into the technical motivation for each. For a more detailed summary, along with some applications, the reader should refer to the paper by Engle and Brown (1985).

Akaike (1970, 1974) developed two procedures, one known as the **finite prediction error (FPE)** and the other known as the **Akaike information criterion (AIC)**. Hannan and Quinn (1979) suggest another procedure (which will be referred to as the **HQ criterion**). Other criteria include those by Schwarz (1978), Shibata (1981), and Rice (1984), and a **generalized cross validation (GCV)** method developed by Craven and Wahba (1979) and used by Engle, Granger, Rice, and Weiss (1986). Each of these statistics is based on some optimality property, details of which will be found in the papers cited (note that the papers require a knowledge of linear algebra). Table 4.3 summarizes the various criteria (T is the number of observations and k is the number of parameters estimated).

There is no need to include $\bar{R}^2$ in the criteria because $\bar{R}^2$ and SGMASQ ($\hat{\sigma}^2$) are inversely related, and hence a lower SGMASQ automatically implies a higher value for $\bar{R}^2$.

TABLE 4.3 Model Selection Criteria

SGMASQ:	$\left(\dfrac{\text{ESS}}{T}\right)\left[1 - \left(\dfrac{k}{T}\right)\right]^{-1}$	HQ:	$\left(\dfrac{\text{ESS}}{T}\right)(\ln T)^{2k/T}$
AIC:	$\left(\dfrac{\text{ESS}}{T}\right)e^{(2k/T)}$	RICE:	$\left(\dfrac{\text{ESS}}{T}\right)\left[1 - \left(\dfrac{2k}{T}\right)\right]^{-1}$
FPE:	$\left(\dfrac{\text{ESS}}{T}\right)\dfrac{T + k}{T - k}$	SCHWARZ:	$\left(\dfrac{\text{ESS}}{T}\right)T^{k/T}$
GCV:	$\left(\dfrac{\text{ESS}}{T}\right)\left[1 - \left(\dfrac{k}{T}\right)\right]^{-2}$	SHIBATA:	$\left(\dfrac{\text{ESS}}{T}\right)\dfrac{T + 2k}{T}$

Ideally, we would like a model to have lower values for all these statistics, as compared to an alternative model. Although it is possible to rank some of these criteria for a given ESS, T, and k, this ordering is meaningless because models differ in both ESS and k. In the appendix, Section 4.A.2, certain special cases have been examined more closely. In these special cases some of the criteria might become redundant—that is, a model found to be superior under one criterion will also be superior under a different criterion. In general, however, it is possible to find a model superior under one criterion and inferior under another. For example, the Schwarz criterion penalizes model complexity more heavily than do other measures and hence might give a different conclusion. A model that outperforms another in several of these criteria might be preferred.

The special cases in which some of the criteria become redundant are listed in Property 4.3. For proof, see appendix Section 4.A.2.

Property 4.3*

a. If SGMASQ decreases (that is, $\bar{R}^2$ increases) when one or more variables are dropped, then GCV and RICE will also decrease, making these criteria redundant.

b. Suppose the value of AIC decreases when some variables are dropped. Then the value of SCHWARZ will also decrease provided there are at least 8 observations. Similarly, the value of HQ will decrease provided there are at least 16 observations.

c. Suppose the value of RICE increases when some variables are dropped. Then SHIBATA will also increase.

Example 4.4

For the home price data, Table 4.2 has the eight model selection statistics for each of the three models. All the criteria prefer the simplest model, in which the only explanatory variable is SQFT. This means that the reduction in ESS due to a more complex model is not enough to offset the penalty factor associated with it. This result should not really surprise us. The living area is determined by the number of bedrooms and bathrooms in the house. Model A therefore indirectly accounts for BEDRMS and BATHS. Hence, we should not expect Models B and C to be so much better as to lower ESS sufficiently. □

Practice Problem

4.7 Is Property 4.3 applicable in Example 4.4? Which criteria, if any, are redundant?

4.5 Testing Hypotheses

In this section we discuss three types of hypothesis testing: (1) testing the statistical significance of individual coefficients, (2) testing several regression coefficients jointly, and (3) testing a linear combination of regression coefficients.

Testing Individual Coefficients

As in Chapter 3, the test of hypothesis on a single regression coefficient is carried out with a t-test. The properties that each $\hat{\beta}_i$ has a normal distribution and that ESS/σ^2 has a chi-square distribution extend to the multivariate case also. The only modification is that ESS/σ^2 is distributed as chi-square with $T - k$ d.f. The steps for carrying out tests on an individual coefficient are as follows:

One-tailed Test

Step 1 $H_0: \beta = \beta_0$ $\qquad$ $H_1: \beta > \beta_0$

Step 2 Construct the t-statistic $t_c = (\hat{\beta} - \beta_0)/s_{\hat{\beta}}$, where $\hat{\beta}$ is the estimate and $s_{\hat{\beta}}$ is its standard error. If $\beta_0 = 0$, this t-value reduces to the ratio of the regression coefficient to its standard error. Under H_0, it has a t-distribution with $T - k$ d.f.

Step 3 Look up in the t-table the entry corresponding to $T - k$ d.f. and find the point $t^*_{T-k}(a)$ such that the area to the right of it is equal to the level of significance (a).

Step 4 Reject the null hypothesis if $t_c > t^*$. If the alternative had been $H_1: \beta < \beta_0$, H_0 would have been rejected if $t_c < -t^*$.

To use the p-value approach, compute p-value $= P(t > t_c)$ and reject H_0 if the p-value is less than the level of significance.

Example 4.5

Let us apply this to Models B and C in Table 4.2. Model B has 11 d.f. $(14 - 3)$ and Model C has 10 d.f. From Table A.2, $t^*_{11}(0.05) = 1.796$ and $t^*_{10}(0.05) = 1.812$ for a 5 percent test. Thus, for a regression coefficient to be significantly different from zero, the t-statistics given in Table 4.2 must be greater than 1.796 for Model B and greater than 1.812 for Model C. We note that in every model the regression coefficient for SQFT is significant, whereas all the other regression coefficients are insignificant. This means that in those cases we accept the null hypothesis that the corresponding coefficient is zero.

Would a level of significance other than 5 percent have rejected the null hypothesis? After all, there is nothing special about 5 percent. If the actual level of significance were slightly higher, we might still be willing to reject the null hypothesis. We note from Table A.2 that for a 10 percent level, $t^*_{10}(0.1) = 1.372$. The t-statistic for BEDRMS in Model C is -0.799, which is greater than -1.372. Therefore, we conclude that BEDRMS is insignificant in Model C, at the level of significance 10 percent. BEDRMS is not significant in Model B even at the 10 percent level. $\qquad\square$

Using the ECSLIB program we computed the p-values for the coefficients of BEDRMS and BATHS (see Practice Computer Session 4.1). They range from 0.175 to 0.39, implying that, if we reject the null hypothesis that these coefficients are zero, there is a 17.5 to 39 percent chance of making a mistake of Type I. As these are unacceptably high, we do not reject H_0 but instead conclude that the coefficients are not significantly different from zero.

Two-Tailed Test

Step 1 $H_0: \beta = \beta_0$ $H_1: \beta \neq \beta_0$

Step 2 Construct the same t-statistic $t_c = (\hat{\beta} - \beta_0)/s_{\hat{\beta}}$, where $\hat{\beta}$ is the estimate and $s_{\hat{\beta}}$ is its standard error. Under H_0, it has a t-distribution with $T - k$ d.f.

Step 3 Look up in the t-table A.2 the entry corresponding to $T - k$ d.f. and find $t^*_{T-k}(a/2)$ such that the area to the right of it is one-half the level of significance.

Step 4 Reject the null hypothesis if $t_c > t^*$ or $t_c < -t^*$.

To use the p-value approach, compute p-value $= P(t < -t_c \text{ or } t > t_c) = 2P(t > t_c)$ and reject H_0 if the p-value is less than the level of significance.

Example 4.6

Let us apply the two-tailed test to Models B and C. In Model B the d.f. is 11 and hence $t^*_{11}(0.025)$ is 2.201 for a 5 percent level of significance. In Model C, $t^*_{10}(0.025) = 2.228$. Thus, for a regression coefficient to be significantly different from zero at the 5 percent level, the t-statistics given in Table 4.2 must be greater than 2.201 in absolute value for Model B and greater than 2.228 in absolute value for Model C. We note that in every model the regression coefficient for SQFT is significant, whereas all the other regression coefficients are insignificant. This means that in those cases we accept the null hypothesis that the corresponding coefficient is zero.

Would a level of significance other than 5 percent have rejected the null hypothesis? The p-values are now twice those obtained earlier (that is, 0.35 to 0.78). As these are unacceptably high, the conclusion is that the observed nonzero values for these regression coefficients are due only to random sampling errors. Thus, given the value of SQFT, the variables BEDRMS and BATHS do not significantly affect the price of a home. This result confirms the earlier one in which Model A was judged superior according to all eight criteria.   □

Practice Problems

4.8 Compare the value of t-statistics beween equations (4.1) and (4.1*).

4.9 Using your regression program, estimate Models B and C and verify the results in Table 4.2.

It is possible to establish the following property [see Haitovsky (1969)].

Property 4.4

If the absolute value of the t-statistic of a regression coefficient is less than 1, then dropping it from the model will increase the adjusted R^2. Similarly, dropping a variable whose t-statistic is greater than 1 (in absolute value) will reduce $\bar{R}^2$. (This suggests that, in addition to the critical t-value, we can use a t-value of 1 as a guide in determining whether a variable is a candidate to be dropped.)

Testing Several Coefficients Jointly

The t-test on individual coefficients is for the significance of particular coefficients. It is also possible to test the **joint significance** of several regression coefficients. For example, consider the following models:

(U) $\text{PRICE} = \beta_1 + \beta_2 \text{SQFT} + \beta_3 \text{BEDROOMS} + \beta_4 \text{BATHS} + \mu$

(R) $\text{PRICE} = \gamma_1 + \gamma_2 \text{SQFT} + \nu$

Model U (which is Model C in Table 4.2) is called the **unrestricted model** and Model R (which is Model A in Table 4.2) is called the **restricted model**. This is because β_3 and β_4 are restricted to be zero in Model R. It is possible to test the joint hypothesis $\beta_3 = \beta_4 = 0$ against the alternative that at least one of them is nonzero. The test for this joint hypothesis is known as the **Wald test** [Wald (1943)]. The procedure is as follows.

General Wald Test   Let the restricted and unrestricted models be (omitting the t-subscript):

(U) $Y = \beta_1 + \beta_2 X_2 + \cdots + \beta_m X_m + \beta_{m+1} X_{m+1} + \cdots + \beta_k X_k + u$

(R) $Y = \beta_1 + \beta_2 X_2 + \cdots + \beta_m X_m + \nu$

Although Model U appears different, it is identical to equation (4.1). Model R is obtained by omitting several variables from Model U, namely, $X_{m+1}, X_{m+2}, \ldots, X_k$. Note that (U) contains k unknown regression coefficients and (R) contains m unknown regression coefficients. Thus Model R has $k - m$ fewer parameters. The question we will presently address is whether the $k - m$ excluded variables have a significant *joint* effect on Y.

Suppose these omitted variables have no significant effect on Y. Then the error sum of squares of Model R (ESS_R) will not be very different from the error sum of squares of Model U (ESS_U). In other words, their difference $\text{ESS}_R - \text{ESS}_U$ will be small. But how small is small? We know that ESS is sensitive to the units of measurement, and hence it can be made large or small by simply changing the scale. "Small" or "large" is determined by comparing the above difference to ESS_U, the error sum of squares of the full unrestricted model. Thus $\text{ESS}_R - \text{ESS}_U$ is compared to ESS_U. If the former is "small" relative to the latter, we conclude that omitting $X_{m+1}, X_{m+2}, \ldots, X_k$ has not changed ESS sufficiently to believe that their coefficients are significant.

We know that sums of squares have a chi-square distribution (see Section 2.4). Thus, ESS_U/σ^2 is a chi-square with $T - k$ d.f. (T observations minus k parameters in Model U). It can be shown that, because of the additive property of chi-square (Property 2.7a), $(\text{ESS}_R - \text{ESS}_U)/\sigma^2$ is also chi-square with d.f. equal to the number of variables omitted in (R). In Section 2.4 we saw that the ratio of two independent chi-squares has an F-distribution that has two parameters: a d.f. for the numerator of the ratio and a d.f. for the denominator. The test statistic is based on this F-ratio.

The formal steps for the Wald test are as follows:

Step 1 The null hypothesis is $H_0: \beta_{m+1} = \beta_{m+2} = \cdots = \beta_k = 0$. The alternative hypothesis is H_1: at least one of the βs is nonzero. The null hypothesis has thus $k - m$ restrictions.

Step 2 Compute the error sums of squares ESS_U and ESS_R for the unrestricted and restricted models, respectively. We know from Property 4.1c that ESS_U/σ^2 has the chi-square distribution with d.f. $DF_U = T - k$ (that is, T observations minus k coefficients estimated). Similarly, ESS_R/σ^2 has the chi-square distribution with d.f. $DF_R = T - m$. It can be shown that they are independent and, by the additive property of chi-square, their difference $(ESS_R - ESS_U)/\sigma^2$ is also chi-square with d.f. equal to the difference in d.f., that is, $DF_R - DF_U$. Note that $DF_R - DF_U$ is also $k - m$ which is the number of restrictions in the null hypothesis (that is, the number of excluded variables). In Section 2.4, we defined the F-distribution as the ratio of two independent chi-square random variables. This gives the test statistic

$$F_c = \frac{(ESS_R - ESS_U) \div (DF_R - DF_U)}{ESS_U \div DF_U}$$

$$= \frac{(\text{difference in error sum of squares} \div \text{difference in d.f.})}{(\text{error sum of squares of Model U} \div \text{d.f. of Model U})} \quad (4.3)$$

Division by the degrees of freedom gives the sum of squares per degree of freedom. Under the null hypothesis, F_c has the F-distribution with m d.f. for the numerator and $T - k$ d.f. for the denominator.

Step 3 From the entry in the F-table that corresponds to the d.f. m for the numerator, $T - k$ for the denominator, and the given level of significance (call it a), obtain $F^*_{m,\,T-k}(a)$ such that the area to the right of F^* is a.

Step 4 The null hypothesis is rejected at the level a if $F_c > F^*$.

For the p-value approach, compute p-value $= P(F > F_c)$ and reject the null hypothesis if p-value is *less than* the level of significance.

Example 4.7

In our real estate example, $H_0: \beta_3 = \beta_4 = 0$, and H_1: at least one of the β's is nonzero. Thus, Model U is the same as Model C in Table 4.2, and Model R is Model A. The number of restrictions is therefore 2. Also, $ESS_R = 18,274$ and $ESS_U = 16,700$ (see Table 4.2). The degrees of freedom for Model U is 10. Hence, the calculated F-statistic is

$$F_c = \frac{(18,274 - 16,700)/2}{16,700/10} = 0.471$$

From the F-table (Table A.4b), $F^*_{2,10}(0.05) = 4.1$. Because F_c is not greater than F^*, we cannot reject the null hypothesis, and hence conclude that β_3 and β_4 are indeed insignificant at the 5 percent level. Even if the level were 10 percent (see Table A.4c), $F^*_{2,10}(0.1) = 2.92 > F_c$. This means that in terms of the significance of the independent variables, the simpler Model A is better. A similar test could have been used to compare Models B and A, but it is unnecessary because the difference between these two models is in only one variable, namely, BEDRMS. In this case, the F-distribution will have only 1 d.f. in the numerator. When this happens, the value of F is simply the square of the t-statistic for BEDRMS. It is easy to verify this. Model B is now unrestricted and hence

$$F_c = \frac{(18{,}274 - 16{,}833)/1}{16{,}833/11} = 0.941$$

whose square root is 0.97, which is the same as the t-statistic in Table 4.2. Thus, the *Wald test need be performed only when there are two or more zero regression coefficients in the null hypotheses.*

The p-value for this example is $P(F > 0.471) = 0.64$. Because a 64 percent chance of rejecting a true H_0 (that the coefficients for BEDRMS and BATHS are zero) is unacceptably high, we do not reject H_0 but instead conclude that the coefficients are statistically insignificantly different from zero.

We see from Table 4.2 that the constant term is not significant in any of the models (except Model D). Nevertheless, it is not wise to drop the constant term from the model. This is because the constant term indirectly captures the average effects of omitted variables (this point is discussed more fully in Section 4.7). Hence, dropping the constant term might result in a serious model misspecification. ☐

Special Wald Test for Overall Goodness of Fit As a special case of the Wald test, consider the following two models:

(U) $Y = \beta_1 + \beta_2 X_2 + \cdots + \beta_k X_k + u$

(SR) $Y = \beta_1 + w$

Model U is the multiple regression model in equation (4.1), with X_1 being the constant term. In Model SR (super restricted), all but the constant term have been omitted; that is, we have imposed the $k - 1$ restrictions $\beta_2 = \beta_3 = \cdots = \beta_k = 0$. This hypothesis will test the statement "None of the coefficients in the model (excluding the constant term) is statistically significant." A Wald test can be performed for this hypothesis. If the hypothesis is not rejected, we conclude that none of the included variables can jointly explain the variation in Y. This means that we have a poor model and must reformulate it. ESS_U is the error sum of squares for the full model.

To get ESS_{SR}, we first minimize $\sum w^2 = \sum (Y_t - \beta_1)^2$ with respect to β_1. It is easy to verify that $\hat{\beta}_1 = \bar{Y}$ (see Section 2.9 for proof). Hence, we have $ESS_{SR} = \sum (Y_t - \bar{Y})^2$, which is the same as the total sum of squares (TSS_U) of Model U (it is also the total sum of squares for Model SR). The F-statistic now becomes

$$F_c = \frac{(TSS_U - ESS_U)/(k-1)}{ESS_U/(T-k)} = \frac{RSS_U/(k-1)}{ESS_U/(T-k)} = \frac{R^2/(k-1)}{(1-R^2)/(T-k)} \qquad (4.4)$$

which can be computed from the unadjusted R^2 of the full model. Almost all regression programs provide this F-statistic as part of the summary statistics for a model. The first task should be to make sure that this F-test is rejected [that is, that $F_c > F^*_{k-1, T-k}(a)$]. If it is not, we have a model in which none of the independent variables explains the variations in the dependent variable, and hence the model has to be reformulated.

As stated earlier, RSS measures the variation in the predicted value $\hat{Y}_t$, and ESS measures the variation in the error term. The F-statistic tests the equality of the two variances (see Section 2.10 on the test for equality of two variances) using the ratio of two chi-square statistics.

Example 4.8

Table 4.2 provides the Wald F-statistic, given in equation (4.4), for the home price example. For Model C, $k = 4$, and hence $k - 1 = 3$ and $T - k = 14 - 4 = 10$. The degrees of freedom for the F-statistic are therefore 3 for the numerator and 10 for the denominator. From the F-table, A.4b, the critical value for a 5 percent test is $F^*_{3,10}(0.05) = 3.71$. Because the F-value in Table 4.2 is 16.989 for Model C, we reject the null hypothesis that all the regression coefficients except the constant term are zero. Thus, at least one of the other regression coefficients is significantly different from zero. From the t-test for the coefficient for SQFT, we already know that this is the case. It is easy to verify that $F^*_{2,11}(0.05) = 3.98$ for Model B and $F^*_{1,12}(0.05) = 4.75$ for Model A, and hence all the models reject the null hypothesis that none of the explanatory variables is significant.

We note that the F-statistics for Models B and C are much lower than that for Model A. This is because the differences in R^2 are fairly small, whereas the ratio $(T - 1)/(T - k)$ increases substantially as k increases. We thus see from equation (4.4) that this can account for the large difference in F. In general, however, the differences in F across models are unimportant. Only the result of the Wald test is of interest. $\square$

Practice Problem

4.10 In Table 4.2, Model D is the super restricted model that regresses PRICE against only a constant term. Compare this model with Model C as the unrestricted model, and verify the Wald F-value reported in Table 4.2 for Model C. Next do the same for Models A and B. Finally, explain why $R^2 = \bar{R}^2 = 0$ for Model D.

The difference between the two types of F-tests should be carefully noted. *The formula given in equation (4.4) is not applicable when only a few variables have been omitted. It is applicable only when the restricted model has just a constant term.* The F-statistic printed by computer programs tests the overall goodness of fit, whereas the F-statistic calculated from equation (4.3) tests whether a subset of the coefficients is significantly different from zero.

Computing the F-statistic When the Model Has No Constant Term In Section 4.3 we discussed the differences in R^2 measures between two models, one with a constant term and the other without, and argued that the same formula should be used in both cases to compare their relative goodness of fit. When computing the F-ratio, however, the formula will be different. To see why this is so, consider the following two models:

$$\text{(A)} \qquad Y = \beta_2 X_2 + \beta_3 X_3 + \cdots + \beta_k X_k + u$$

$$\text{(B)} \qquad Y = w$$

where the constant term $X_1(=1)$ has been eliminated. Note that the unrestricted Model A has only $k - 1$ parameters now (which means the degrees of freedom is $T - k + 1$) and the restricted Model B has none (with d.f. T). To test for the overall fit of the model, the null hypothesis is again $H_0: \beta_2 = \beta_3 = \cdots = \beta_k = 0$ and the alternative is the same as before. The Wald test is applicable here also and the appropriate formula is equation (4.3). Let $\text{ESS}_A = \sum \hat{u}_t^2$ be the error sum of squares of Model A. In Model B, the error sum of squares will be $\text{ESS}_B = \sum Y_t^2$. The value of F is therefore given by

$$F_c = \frac{(\text{ESS}_B - \text{ESS}_A)/(k - 1)}{\text{ESS}_A/(T - k + 1)} = \frac{(\sum Y_t^2 - \sum \hat{u}_t^2)/(k - 1)}{\text{ESS}_A/(T - k + 1)} = \frac{\sum \hat{Y}_t^2/(k - 1)}{\text{ESS}_A/(T - k + 1)}$$

$$(4.4a)$$

because of the decomposition $\sum Y_t^2 = \sum \hat{Y}_t^2 + \sum \hat{u}_t^2$ in the absence of a constant. Under the null hypothesis, this has an F-distribution with $k - 1$ and $T - k + 1$ d.f. The criterion for acceptance/rejection of H_0 is similar. The F-statistic presented for Model D tests the hypothesis that the constant term is zero. Because only one coefficient will be omitted here, the F-value is the square of the t-statistic. Therefore, $F = 180 \cdot 189$ even though $R^2 = 0$. Note that the formula just given for testing the overall goodness of fit is quite different from that in equation (4.4).

Testing a Linear Combination of Coefficients

Very often we encounter hypotheses that are stated in terms of linear combinations of regression coefficients. As an illustration, consider the following aggregate consumption function:

$$C_t = \beta_1 + \beta_2 W_t + \beta_3 P_t + u_t$$

where C is the aggregate consumption expenditures in the United States, W is the total wage bill, and P is all other income, most of which will be profits and other returns on capital. β_2 is the marginal propensity to consume out of wage income, and β_3 is the marginal propensity to consume out of other income. The hypothesis $\beta_2 = \beta_3$ implies that an *extra* dollar of wage income and an *extra* dollar of other income both contribute the same *extra* amount to average consumption. The t-tests on individual coefficients are no longer applicable because the hypothesis is a linear combination of two regression coefficients. The hypothesis $H_0: \beta_2 = \beta_3$ versus $H_1: \beta_2 \neq \beta_3$ can be tested in three different ways, all of which will lead to the same conclusion.

In later sections we will encounter other types of linear combinations such as $\beta_2 + \beta_3 = 1$, or $\beta_2 + \beta_3 = 0$. We now develop the procedures for testing such linear combinations of regression coefficents. This is done in the context of the following (unrestricted) model with two independent variables (X_2 and X_3).

$$\text{(U)} \qquad Y_t = \beta_1 + \beta_2 X_{t2} + \beta_3 X_{t3} + u_t \tag{4.5}$$

Method 1 (Wald test)

Step 1 Using the restriction, solve for one of the coefficients in terms of the others and substitute that in the unrestricted model to obtain the restricted model. Thus, to test $\beta_2 = \beta_3$, substitute for β_3 in equation (4.5) and obtain the following:

$$\text{(R)} \qquad \begin{aligned} Y_t &= \beta_1 + \beta_2 X_{t2} + \beta_3 X_{t3} + u_t \\ &= \beta_1 + \beta_2 (X_{t2} + X_{t3}) + u_t \end{aligned} \tag{4.6}$$

Rewrite the restricted model by grouping terms appropriately. In our case we would generate the new variable $Z_t = X_{t2} + X_{t3}$ and write the model as

$$\text{(R)} \qquad Y_t = \beta_1 + \beta_2 Z_{t2} + u_t$$

Step 2 Estimate the restricted and unrestricted models and obtain the error sums of squares ESS_R and ESS_U.

Step 3 Compute the Wald F-statistic, using equation (4.3), and d.f. for the numerator and denominator.

Step 4 From the F-table obtain the point F^* such that the area to the right is equal to the level of significance. Alternatively, compute p-value $= P(F > F_c)$.

Step 5 Reject H_0 if $F_c > F_c^*$ or if p-value is less than the level of significance.

Practice Problem
4.11 Derive the restricted models for the tests $\beta_2 + \beta_3 = 1$ and $\beta_2 + \beta_3 = 0$.

Example 4.9

Table 4.10 at the end of this chapter shows annual data for the United States for the period 1948–1989 (which gives $T = 42$). The definitions for the variables are as follows:

CONS(C_t)   Real consumption expenditures in billions of 1982 dollars

GNP(Y_t)   Real gross national product in billions of 1982 dollars

WAGES   Total compensation of employees (wages, salaries, and supplements) in billions of current dollars

PRDEFL   Implicit price deflator for consumption, 1982 = 100 (this is a price index for consumption goods)

The model we will be estimating is the following consumption function presented earlier.

$$\text{(U)} \qquad C_t = \beta_1 + \beta_2 W_t + \beta_3 P_t + u_t \tag{4.5}$$

where the variables are as defined earlier. Before estimating the model we have to perform some transformations of the data to get all financial variables in "real" terms (that is, in constant dollars adjusted for inflation).

Consumption is already in real terms. To get the wage bill in real terms (W_t), we divide WAGES by PRDEFL and multiply by 100. Total profits and other income from capital are then obtained as GNP minus real wage bill.

$$W_t = \frac{100 \text{ WAGES}_t}{\text{PRDEFL}_t} \qquad P_t = Y_t - W_t$$

In equation (4.5) impose the restriction $\beta_2 = \beta_3$. We get

$$\text{(R)} \qquad C_t = \beta_1 + \beta_2 W_t + \beta_2 P_t + u_t = \beta_1 + \beta_2(W_t + P_t) + u_t$$
$$= \beta_1 + \beta_2 Y_t + u_t \qquad (4.6)$$

where $Y_t = W_t + P_t$ is aggregate income. Equation (4.5) is the unrestricted model (with $T - 3$ d.f.) and equation (4.6) is the restricted model. We can therefore compute the Wald F-statistic given in equation (4.3) (with $k - m = 1$ because there is only one restriction). Thus

$$F_c = \frac{(\text{ESS}_R - \text{ESS}_U)/1}{\text{ESS}_U/(T - 3)}$$

will be tested against $F^*_{1, T-3}(0.05)$ and the null hypothesis rejected if $F_c > F^*$.

Applying this to the aggregate consumption data, we have the estimated equations (4.5) and (4.6). (See Practice Computer Session 4.3.)

$$\hat{C}_t = -107.23 + 0.74 W_t + 0.56 P_t \quad \text{ESS}_U = 52,968$$
$$\hat{C}_t = -141.59 + 0.68 Y_t \quad \text{ESS}_R = 54,156$$
$$F_c = \frac{(54,156 - 52,968)/1}{52,968/39} = 0.875$$

From Table A.4b, $F^*_{1,39}(0.05) = 4.09$. Because $F_c < F^*$, we accept the null hypothesis and conclude that the marginal propensities to consume out of wages and profits are not significantly different from each other at the 5 percent level. Thus, although their numerical values are quite different, statistically the difference is due to random chance. □

Method 2 (Indirect t-test)

In the second method, the model is transformed in a different way and an indirect t-test carried out. The steps are as follows:

Step 1 Define a new parameter, call it δ, which takes the value zero when the null hypothesis is true. Thus, when H_0 is $\beta_2 = \beta_3$, we would define $\delta = \beta_2 - \beta_3$, and when $\beta_2 + \beta_3 = 1$ is the null hypothesis, $\delta = \beta_2 + \beta_3 - 1$.

Step 2 Express one of the parameters in terms of δ and the remaining parameters, substitute for it in the model, and group terms appropriately.

Step 3 Carry out a t-test on $\hat{\delta}$, the estimate of δ.

Example 4.10

In the consumption function case, $\delta = \beta_2 - \beta_3$. The null hypothesis now becomes $H_0: \delta = 0$ versus $H_1: \delta \neq 0$. Also, $\beta_3 = \beta_2 - \delta$. Substituting this in the model we get

$$C_t = \beta_1 + \beta_2 W_t + (\beta_2 - \delta)P_t + u_t$$
$$= \beta_1 + \beta_2(W_t + P_t) - \delta P_t + u_t$$

Because $Y_t = W_t + P_t$, this model becomes

$$C_t = \beta_1 + \beta_2 Y_t - \delta P_t + u_t \qquad (4.7)$$

which is conceptually equivalent to equation (4.5). Now regress C against a constant, Y, and against P, and use the t-statistic for δ to test the desired hypothesis. In this case the test reduces to the standard t-test but on a modified model. [As a practice problem, apply the technique to $\beta_2 + \beta_3 = 1$.]

For our data, the estimated equation (4.7) is (see Practice Computer Session 4.3)

$$\hat{C}_t = \underset{(-2.7)}{-107.23} + \underset{(10.9)}{0.74 Y_t} - \underset{(-0.9)}{0.18 P_t}$$

The values in parentheses are the corresponding t-statistics. For $\hat{\delta}$ the t-value is -0.9 which is numerically lower than $t_{39}^*(0.025) = 2.023$. Hence the null hypothesis is accepted here also.

In this particular example a caveat should be added. We will see in Chapters 9 and 13 that this model violates Assumption 3.4 that the error terms be uncorrelated with Y and Assumption 3.6 that the error terms of different observations be uncorrelated. This casts doubt on the hypothesis testing. Nevertheless, the approach is still sound; that is, the procedure is to incorporate the hypothesis into the model and reformulate it. A test procedure is then carried out on the model. ☐

Method 3 (Direct *t*-test)

The last method applies a t-test directly and does not require the estimation of another regression.

Step 1 As in Method 2, define a new parameter, call it δ, which takes the value zero when the null hypothesis is true. Thus, when H_0 is $\beta_2 = \beta_3$, we would define $\delta = \beta_2 - \beta_3$, and when $\beta_2 + \beta_3 = 1$ is the null hypothesis, $\delta = \beta_2 + \beta_3 - 1$.

Step 2 Derive the statistical distribution of δ directly and use it to construct a t-statistic.

Step 3 Carry out a t-test on $\hat{\delta}$, the estimate of δ, using this directly computed statistic.

The above test is illustrated here only for the example we have been using, namely, $H_0: \beta_2 = \beta_3$. [As a practice problem, apply this method to the hypothesis $\beta_2 + \beta_3 = 1$.].

Because the OLS estimators are linear combinations of the dependent variable and hence that of the normally distributed error terms, we know that

$$\hat{\beta}_2 \sim N(\beta_2, \sigma_{\hat{\beta}_2}^2) \qquad \hat{\beta}_3 \sim N(\beta_3, \sigma_{\hat{\beta}_3}^2)$$

Furthermore, a linear combination of normal variates is also normal. Hence,

$$\hat{\beta}_2 - \hat{\beta}_3 \sim N[\beta_2 - \beta_3, \text{Var}(\hat{\beta}_2 - \hat{\beta}_3)]$$

From Property 2.5a, the variance of $\hat{\beta}_2 - \hat{\beta}_3$ is given by $\text{Var}(\hat{\beta}_2) + \text{Var}(\hat{\beta}_3) - 2\,\text{Cov}(\beta_2, \beta_3)$. Converting the above to a standard normal distribution (by subtracting the mean and dividing by the standard deviation), we have

$$\frac{\hat{\beta}_2 - \hat{\beta}_3 - (\beta_2 - \beta_3)}{[\text{Var}(\hat{\beta}_2) + \text{Var}(\hat{\beta}_3) - 2\,\text{Cov}(\hat{\beta}_2, \hat{\beta}_3)]^{1/2}} \sim N(0, 1)$$

Under the null hypothesis, $H_0: \beta_2 - \beta_3 = 0$. Also, we do not know the variances and covariance exactly, but they can be estimated (most computer packages provide them as an option). If we substitute estimates of these variances and covariance, the above statistic is not distributed as $N(0, 1)$, but its statistical distribution is t_{T-k} ($T - 3$ in our example). Thus, the same t-test can be applied on the t-statistic computed from the above expression with appropriate estimates substituted. The calculated t-statistic is

$$t_c = \frac{\hat{\beta}_2 - \hat{\beta}_3}{[\widehat{\text{Var}}(\hat{\beta}_2) + \widehat{\text{Var}}(\hat{\beta}_3) - 2\,\widehat{\text{Cov}}(\hat{\beta}_2, \hat{\beta}_3)]^{1/2}}$$

because $\beta_2 = \beta_3$ under the null hypothesis. For a 5 percent level of significance, H_0 is rejected in favor of $H_1: \beta_2 - \beta_3 > 0$ if the computed t_c exceeds $t^*_{T-k}(0.05)$. For a two-sided alternative, $H_1: \beta_2 \neq \beta_3$, obtain $t^*_{T-k}(0.025)$ and reject H_0 if $t_c > t^*$ or $t_c < -t^*$. Because this method involves several auxiliary calculations, one of the other methods is recommended over Method 3.

Example 4.11

As an illustration, we consider equation (4.5), which was estimated using the data in Table 4.10. The estimated equation with the variances and covariance is the following (See Practice Computer Session 4.3):

$$\hat{C}_t = -107.226 + 0.743W_t + 0.561P_t$$
$$\bar{R}^2 = 0.998 \qquad \text{d.f.} = 39 \qquad \text{ESS} = 52968$$
$$\widehat{\text{Var}\,\hat{\beta}_2} = (0.0683)^2 \qquad \widehat{\text{Var}\,\hat{\beta}_3} = (0.127)^2 \qquad \widehat{\text{Cov}(\hat{\beta}_2, \hat{\beta}_3)} = -0.009$$

The t-statistic is given by

$$t_c = \frac{0.743 - 0.561}{[(0.0683)^2 + (0.127)^2 - 2(-0.009)]^{1/2}} = 0.925$$

Because $t^*_{39}(0.025)$, which is 2.023, is much higher than this, we accept the null hypothesis that the marginal propensities to consume out of wages and other income are equal. This result holds whether the alternative is one-sided or two-sided. □

We see that all three methods yield the same conclusion. Of the three methods presented, Method 2 is the easiest to implement because it does not require an auxiliary computation but can be used to test the desired hypothesis with a direct t-test on a slightly modified model. The Wald test discussed in Method 1 is, however, applicable in more general cases.

4.6   More on Functional Forms

The Double-log Model

In Section 3.13 we presented an example of the double-log model in which the dependent and independent variables entered the regression equation in logarithmic form. The double-log formulation is applicable more generally. For instance, in Section 2.A.2 we introduced the **Cobb-Douglas production function**, which has the following general form:

$$Q_t = cK_t^\alpha L_t^\beta$$

where Q is the output, L is the amount of labor used in worker-hours, K is capital in machine-hours, and c, α, and β are unknown parameters. Taking logarithms of both sides and adding an error term, we get the following econometric formulation ($\beta_1 = \ln c$):

$$\ln Q_t = \beta_1 + \alpha \ln K_t + \beta \ln L_t + u_t$$

In Example 3.A.1, it was shown that α and β can be interpreted as the elasticities. We thus have (denoting changes by Δ)

$$\alpha = \frac{K}{Q} \frac{\Delta Q}{\Delta K} = \frac{\Delta(\ln Q)}{\Delta(\ln K)}$$

$100\Delta(\ln Q) = 100\Delta Q/Q$ is the percentage change in Q. Therefore, α is the percentage change in Q divided by the percentage change in K. This is the **elasticity of output with respect to capital**. In a similar manner, β is the **elasticity of output with respect to labor**. Thus, the regression coefficients in a double-log model are simply the respective elasticities. Note that because of this property, the numerical values of the coefficients for different independent variables are directly comparable as in the case of beta coefficients.

We can derive another interesting result for this model. Suppose the quantities of capital and labor inputs are doubled. Then the output is

$$Q_1 = c(2K)^\alpha(2L)^\beta = 2^{\alpha+\beta}Q$$

If $\alpha + \beta = 1$, $Q_1 = 2Q$. Thus, the output would also be doubled if $\alpha + \beta = 1$. This is the well-known condition for **constant returns to scale**. If the estimated elasticities are such that $\hat\alpha + \hat\beta > 1$, they indicate **increasing returns to scale**, and $\hat\alpha + \hat\beta < 1$ indicates **decreasing returns to scale**. A formal test for constant returns to scale would be of interest. The null hypothesis is $H_0: \alpha + \beta = 1$ and the alternative is $H_1: \alpha + \beta \neq 1$. In Section 4.5 we developed three tests for hypotheses involving linear combinations of regression coefficients. To apply Method 2, define $\beta_2 = \alpha + \beta - 1$. Solving this for β, we get $\beta = \beta_2 + 1 - \alpha$. Substituting this in the model we get

$$\ln Q_t = \beta_1 + \alpha \ln K_t + (\beta_2 + 1 - \alpha) \ln L_t + u_t$$
$$= \beta_1 + \alpha(\ln K_t - \ln L_t) + (\beta_2 + 1) \ln L_t + u_t$$

Defining $Y_t = \ln Q_t$, $X_{t1} = \ln K_t - \ln L_t$, $X_{t2} = \ln L_t$, and $\beta_3 = \beta_2 + 1$, the model becomes

$$Y_t = \beta_1 + \alpha X_{t1} + \beta_3 X_{t2} + u_t$$

The null hypothesis is $1 = \alpha + \beta = \alpha + \beta_2 + 1 - \alpha = \beta_3$. Therefore, the null and alternative hypotheses become $H_0: \beta_3 = 1$ and $H_1: \beta_3 \neq 1$. First we transform the data and create the variables Y, X_1, and X_2. Next we regress Y against a constant term, X_1, and X_2. β is estimated as $\hat{\beta}_3 - \hat{\alpha}$. To test for constant returns to scale, we use a t-test with $T - 3$ d.f. and test the hypothesis that $\beta_3 = 1$. [$t_c = (\hat{\beta} - 1)/s_{\hat{\beta}}$, where $s_{\hat{\beta}}$ is the standard error of $\hat{\beta}$.]

Practice Problems

4.12 Describe step by step how the same test may be performed using methods 1 and 3 described in Section 4.5.

4.13 Assume that constant returns to scale holds; that is, $\alpha + \beta = 1$. Under this assumption, describe how the Cobb-Douglas production function can be estimated.

4.14 Changes in technology often "shift" production relations; that is, with the same amount of inputs, one can get more output because of technical progress. A Cobb-Douglas production function that incorporates this is given by $Y_t = cK_t^\alpha L_t^\beta e^{\lambda t}$, where λ is known as the **technical change coefficient**. Describe how one can estimate λ (along with α and β) with data on Y_t, K_t, and L_t.

Polynomial Curve Fitting

Very often investigators use a polynomial to relate a dependent variable to an independent variable. This model would be

$$Y = \beta_1 + \beta_2 X + \beta_3 X^2 + \beta_4 X^3 + \cdots + \beta_k X^k + u$$

The estimation procedure consists of creating new variables X^2, X^3, and so on through transformations and then regressing Y against a constant term, X, and against these transformed variables. The degree of the polynomial (k) is constrained by the number of observations. If $k = 3$, we have a cubic relation; and if $k = 2$, we have a quadratic formulation. Quadratic formulations are frequently used to fit U-shaped cost functions and other nonlinear relations. A cubic curve is often fitted to approximate the shape in Figure 4.1 (see the section on the logit model). In general, polynomials of orders greater than 2 should be avoided. One of the reasons for this is the fact that each polynomial term means the loss of an extra degree of freedom. As was mentioned in Chapter 3, a loss of degrees of freedom means a reduction in

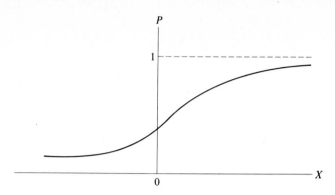

Figure 4.1 Graph of the logistic curve

the precision of the parameter estimates and a reduction in the power of tests. Also, we will see in Chapter 5 that the possible high correlation between X, X^2, and X^3 makes individual coefficients less efficient.

 Practice Problem

4.15 Using the home price data, estimate the following quadratic relation between price and square feet:

$$\text{PRICE} = \beta_1 + \beta_2\text{SQFT} + \beta_3\text{SQFT}^2 + \mu$$

What is the economic interpretation of the hypothesis $\beta_3 = 0$? Test this hypothesis against the alternative $H_1: \beta_3 < 0$. What do you conclude about the marginal effect of SQFT on PRICE? Compare this model, in terms of the selection criteria, with the linear-log model estimated in Example 3.10 (see Practice Computer Session 4.4).

4.16 Estimate the model $\text{PRICE} = \beta_1 + \beta_2 \ln \text{SQFT} + \beta_3\text{BATHS} + u$, and compare the results with those in Table 4.2 and those in Problem 4.15.

Interaction Terms

The marginal effect of one explanatory variable may sometimes depend on another variable. To illustrate, Klein and Morgan (1951) proposed a hypothesis regarding the interaction of income and assets in determining consumption patterns. They argued that the marginal propensity to consume will also depend on assets—a wealthier person is likely to have a different marginal propensity to consume out of income. To capture this, let $C = \alpha + \beta Y + u$. The hypothesis is that β depends on assets. A simple way to allow for this is to assume that $\beta = \beta_1 + \beta_2 A$. Substituting this in the consumption function, we get $C = \alpha + (\beta_1 + \beta_2 A)Y + u$. This reduces to the model $C = \alpha + \beta_1 Y + \beta_2(AY) + u$. The term AY is known as the **interaction term** because it captures the interaction between the income and asset effects. For estimation purposes, we create a new variable Z, which is equal to the product of Y and A, and then regress C against a constant, against Y, and against Z. If β_2 is statistically significant, there is evidence of an interaction between income and assets.

As a second example, consider the relationship $E_t = \alpha + \beta T_t + u$, where E_t is the number of kilowatt-hours of electricity consumption and T_t is the temperature at time t. If this model is estimated for the summer season, we would expect β to be positive because, as the temperature rises in the summer, there will be a greater demand for air conditioning and hence electricity consumption will rise. We may hypothesize, however, that the marginal effect of T on E might depend on the price of electricity (P_t). If electricity is expensive, consumers might postpone turning on the air conditioner and/or switch it off sooner. One way to test for this effect is to assume that $\beta = \beta_0 + \beta_1 P_t$. We are thus assuming that the marginal effect of temperature on electricity consumption depends on price. Substituting this in the relation, we get

$$E_t = \alpha + (\beta_0 + \beta_1 P_t)T_t + u_t$$
$$= \alpha + \beta_0 T_t + \beta_1 (P_t T_t) + u_t$$

To estimate the parameters, we generate $Z_t = P_t T_t$ and regress E against a constant, T, and Z. The significance of β_1 is evidence of an interaction effect between temperature and price.

Lags in Behavior

The effects of economic and other variables are rarely instantaneous; it takes some time for consumers, producers, and other economic agents to respond. Macroeconomic theory tells us that the equilibrium gross national product (Y) is determined by a number of exogenous variables, in particular, by government expenditure (G), taxes (T), money supply (M), exports (X), and so on. Because the equilibrium effect is felt only after the passage of some time, econometric models using time series data are often formulated with lags in behavior. An example of such a model is the following:

$$Y_t = \beta_1 + \beta_2 G_t + \beta_3 G_{t-1} + \beta_4 M_t + \beta_5 M_{t-1}$$
$$+ \beta_6 T_t + \beta_7 T_{t-1} + \beta_8 X_t + \beta_9 X_{t-1} + u_t$$

The estimation procedure here is quite straightforward. We simply create the lagged variables G_{t-1}, M_{t-1}, T_{t-1}, and X_{t-1}, and regress Y_t against these variables, *using observations 2 through T.* Because G_{t-1} and the others are not defined for $t = 1$, we lose the first observation in the estimation. A number of problems arise in this model, however, because the independent variables are correlated with each other and also because degrees of freedom are lost when higher lags are added. These issues are discussed in detail in Chapter 10.

Lags in behavior might also take the form of lags in the dependent variable. The model might thus take the form

$$Y_t = \beta_1 + \beta_2 Y_{t-1} + \beta_3 X_t + u_t$$

As an example, let Y_t be the consumption expenditure at time t and X_t be the income. Because consumers tend to maintain the standard of living they are accustomed to, we might expect their present consumption to be closely related to their previous consumption. Thus, Y_t can be expected to depend on Y_{t-1} also.

The Logit Model*

In some cases the dependent variable may take values only between 0 and 1. For instance, we may relate the fraction of people who voted for a particular president to its determinants. Alternatively, we may relate the fraction of people who bought cars in a certain period to its determinants. If an ordinary regression model is used in such cases, there is no assurance that the predicted value will lie between 0 and 1. To make sure that such a situation does not arise, the following functional form (known as the **logistic curve**) is commonly adopted:

$$\ln\left[\frac{P}{1-P}\right] = \alpha + \beta X + u$$

where P is the value of the dependent variable between 0 and 1. This model is more commonly known as the **logit model**. Solving this equation for P (by first exponentiating both sides) we get

$$P = \frac{1}{1 + e^{-(\alpha + \beta X + u)}}$$

It is easy to see that if $\beta > 0$, then P takes the value 0 when $X = -\infty$, and 1 when $X = \infty$. Thus, P can never be outside the range [0, 1]. The logistic curve has the shape presented in Figure 4.1. Such a curve is also used to fit growth patterns. For example, the sales of a new product (such as compact disk players) might initially grow fast and then taper off. The logit model is estimated by regressing $\ln[P/(1-P)]$ against a constant and X. Models of this type are explored more fully in Chapter 12.

The Box-Cox Transformation*

Consider the following model, which uses a transformation known as the **Box-Cox transformation** [see Box and Cox (1964)]:

$$\frac{Y^\lambda - 1}{\lambda} = \alpha + \beta \frac{X^\lambda - 1}{\lambda} + u$$

It can be shown that when $\lambda = 0$ this model reduces to the double-log form $\ln Y = \alpha + \beta \ln X + u$. For $\lambda = 1$, we get the linear case $Y - 1 = \alpha + \beta(X - 1) + u$ or $Y = \alpha^* + \beta X + u$, where $\alpha^* = \alpha - \beta + 1$. For other values of λ we get a non-linear model that can be estimated by the maximum likelihood procedure using a nonlinear optimization program. If the range of values of λ is known a priori (say -1 to $+1$), we can choose a value of λ aand form new variables $Y^* = (Y^\lambda - 1)/\lambda$ and $X^* = (X^\lambda - 1)/\lambda$. Then we regress Y^* against X^* and the constant term and obtain the error sum of squares. We repeat this procedure for different values of λ and choose the one for which the error sum of squares is the smallest. This *search procedure* can be carried out using a linear regression program and does not require a nonlinear regression program. An extension to this approach is to use $X^* = (X^\mu - 1)/\mu$, search over both λ and μ (from -1 to $+1$), and choose that combination for which ESS is a minimum.

Nonlinearity in Parameters*

We have seen a variety of ways in which nonlinearities in variables can easily be handled in the linear regression context as long as the variables can be suitably transformed so that we obtain a model that is linear in the unknown regression coefficients. There are situations, however, in which this may not be possible. The Box-Cox function is an example of such a situation in which the relationship is nonlinear in parameters and cannot be transformed into a linear form except for the special cases discussed. Another example is the *constant elasticity of substitution* (*CES*) production function, which has the following form:

$$Q = \gamma[\delta K^{-\rho} + (1 - \delta)L^{-\rho}]^{-v/\rho}e^{u_t}$$
$$(\gamma > 0, 0 < \delta < 1, v > 0, \rho \geq -1)$$

γ, δ, v, and ρ are the unknown parameters that appear nonlinearly. They can be estimated only by the maximum likelihood procedure or by nonlinear least squares methods. In this case, however, Kmenta (1986, p. 515) has provided the following quadratic approximation:

$$\ln Q = \ln \gamma + \gamma\delta \ln K + v(1 - \delta) \ln L - \tfrac{1}{2}\rho v\delta(1 - \delta)[\ln K - \ln L]^2 + u$$
$$= \beta_1 + \beta_2 \ln K + \beta_3 \ln L + \beta_4(\ln K - \ln L)^2 + u$$

The estimates of the original parameters of the CES production function can be obtained from estimates of the βs.

Although it is easy to transform variables and include them in the regression model, indiscriminate use of transformations should be avoided. It is wise to look for some theoretical basis for the transformation and to keep the model as simple as possible.

4.7 Specification Errors

The true relationships among economic variables are never known and therefore we can expect errors in the specification of econometric models. In the real estate example (Table 4.2), for instance, we have seen that SQFT is an important determinant of PRICE. If we had excluded this variable from the specification, we would have omitted a variable that truly belonged in the model. On the other hand, suppose the true specification had been Model A but we retained the variables BEDRMS and BATHS even though they were insignificant. This too would have been an error because we would have included variables that did not belong in the model. In this section we examine the theoretical consequences of these two types of specification errors—namely, (1) the omission of a variable that belongs in the model and (2) the inclusion of an irrelevant variable. Thus, only the deterministic part of a model is addressed here. Misspecifications, which are also possible in the error structure, are discussed in later chapters.

Omission of an Important Variable

We first consider a case in which a variable that belongs in the model is omitted. Suppose the *true* model is

$$Y_t = \beta_1 + \beta_2 X_{t2} + \beta_3 X_{t3} + u_t$$

but we estimate the model

$$Y_t = \beta_1 + \beta_2 X_{t2} + v_t$$

In other words, the true value of β_3 is nonzero but we assume that it is zero, and hence omit variable X_3 from the specification. The error terms of the true model are assumed to satisfy Assumptions 3.2 through 3.7. The consequences of this type of misspecification are summarized in the following property.

Property 4.5

> a. If an independent variable whose true regression coefficient is nonzero is excluded from a model, the estimated values of all the other regression coefficients will be biased unless the excluded variable is uncorrelated with every included variable.
> b. Even if this condition is met, the estimated constant term is generally biased and hence forecasts will also be biased.
> c. The estimated variance of the regression coefficient of an included variable will generally be biased, and hence tests of hypotheses are invalid.

We see from Property 4.5 that the consequences of omitting an important variable are very serious. Estimates and forecasts are biased and tests of hypotheses are no longer valid. The cause of the bias is fairly easy to see. Comparing the two models we see that $v_t = \beta_3 X_{t3} + u_t$. The expected value of the error term in the erroneous model is $E(v_t) = \beta_3 X_{t3} \neq 0$. Therefore, v_t violates Assumption 3.2. More seriously, the covariance between X_{t2} and v_t is given by (see Section 2.3 on covariances):

$$\text{Cov}(X_{t2}, v_t) = \text{Cov}(X_{t2}, \beta_3 X_{t3} + u_t) = \beta_3 \text{Cov}(X_{t2}, X_{t3}) + \text{Cov}(X_{t2}, u_t)$$
$$= \beta_2 \text{Cov}(X_{t2}, X_{t3})$$

because X_2 and u are uncorrelated. Therefore, unless the covariance between X_2 and X_3 is zero—that is, unless X_2 and X_3 are uncorrelated—the covariance between X_2 and v will not be zero, thus violating Assumption 3.4 also. The properties of unbiasedness and consistency depend on these two assumptions. It follows, therefore, that $\hat{\beta}_2$ will not be unbiased or consistent. Appendix Section 4.A.3 has a more rigorous proof of Properties 4.5a and 4.5b, and has derived the bias due to the omission of a relevant variable. It is also shown there that the $\hat{\beta}$s capture part of the effects of the omitted variable X_3. One may therefore find that the numerical value of an estimate is very different from what one might expect beforehand. If several independent variables have been omitted from the model, the condition for unbiasedness and consistency is that *every omitted independent variable must be uncorrelated with every included variable.*

Example 4.12

It is useful to give an empirical illustration of the specification bias due to the omission of important variables. Table 4.11 at the end of the chapter has annual data on housing starts in the United States for the period 1963–1985. An estimated relation between housing starts (in thousands), GNP (in billions of 1982 dollars), and the mortgage rate (in percent) is as follows (see Practice Computer Session 4.5 for details):

Model A: $\widehat{\text{HOUSING}} = 687.898 + 0.905\text{GNP} - 169.658\text{INTRATE}$
$$\underset{(1.80)}{} \qquad \underset{(3.64)}{} \qquad \underset{(-3.87)}{}$$

$$\bar{R}^2 = 0.375 \qquad F(2, 20) = 7.609 \qquad \text{d.f.} = 20$$

From basic demand theory, we would expect the demand for housing to rise as income rises. On the other hand, if the mortgage rate increases, the cost of owning a house rises, and hence the demand for housing will decline. We note that the signs of the estimated coefficients agree with our prior intuition. We also see from the t-statistics in parentheses that GNP and INTRATE are very significant. $\bar{R}^2$, however, is not very high for time series data. Suppose we had omitted the important variable INTRATE. The estimated model would be as follows:

Model B: $\widehat{\text{HOUSING}} = 1442.209 + 0.058\text{GNP}$
$$\underset{(3.39)}{} \qquad \underset{(0.38)}{}$$

$$\bar{R}^2 = -0.04 \qquad F(1, 21) = 0.144 \qquad \text{d.f.} = 21$$

The change in the results is dramatic. First of all, $\bar{R}^2$ has now become negative, indicating a poor fit. This is reinforced by the F-statistic, which is low and insignificant. The t-statistic for GNP is insignificant, indicating that GNP has a negligible effect on housing starts. Finally, the estimated value of the GNP coefficient is dramatically altered. These results are totally unacceptable and are a consequence of the omission of the mortgage rate, which is an important determinant of housing demand.[1]   □

Practice Problem

4.17*   In a simple linear model, suppose you had erroneously omitted the constant term; that is, suppose the true model was $Y_t = \alpha + \beta X_t + u_t$, but you estimated it as $Y_t = \beta X_t + v_t$. The least squares estimated would be $\hat{\beta} = [\sum(X_t Y_t)]/[\sum(X_t^2)]$. Show that this is biased. Derive the condition under

· · · · · · ·

[1] *The caveat mentioned in Example 4.10 (Section 4.5) is applicable here also.*

which $\hat{\beta}$ would be unbiased even though the wrong model was used. What is the intuitive interpretation of the condition you derived?

[In this and similar exercises at the end of this chapter, proceed as follows: (1) Use the *estimated model* and derive an algebraic expression for the parameter estimate; (2) substitute for Y_t from the *true model* in terms of X_t, u_t, and the parameters of the true model (we use the true model because Y_t is determined by that and not by the wrong model); (3) compute the expected value of the estimator; and (4) compare the expected value with the true value and check for unbiasedness and, if necessary, derive the conditions for unbiasedness.]

The Dangers of Omitting a Constant Term   We saw above that $\hat{\beta}_1$ and $\hat{\beta}_2$ capture part of the effect of the omitted variable X_3. It was therefore useful to have included the constant term in the model. If the constant term had been omitted, then the regression line would have been forced through the origin, which might be a serious misspecification. We note from the scatter diagram in Figure 3.1 that to constrain the regression line to go through the origin would mean a biased estimate for the slope and larger errors. The conclusion from this discussion is, again, that the constant term should always be retained unless there is a strong theoretical reason not to do so (in Chapter 8 we will encounter a case where theory dictates that the constant term be absent).

Inclusion of an Irrelevant Variable

Suppose that the *true* model is

$$Y_t = \beta_1 + \beta_2 X_{t2} + u_t$$

but we erroneously include the variable X_3 so that we estimate the model

$$Y_t = \beta_1 + \beta_2 X_{t2} + \beta_3 X_{t3} + v_t$$

As before, the true residual u_t is assumed to satisfy Assumptions 3.2 through 3.7 of Chapter 3. What are the consequences of this kind of misspecification? Is the estimator of β_2 biased? Is it still BLUE? Are the tests of hypotheses valid? The answers to these questions are summarized in the following property.

Property 4.6

a. If an independent variable whose true regression coefficient is zero (that is, the variable is redundant) is included in the model, the estimated values of all the other regression coefficients will still be unbiased and consistent.

b. Their variance, however, will be higher than that without the irrelevant variable, and hence the coefficients will be inefficient.

c. Because the estimated variances of the regression coefficients are unbiased, tests of hypotheses are still valid.

The consequences of including an irrelevant variable are thus less serious as compared to omitting an important variable.

PROOF* It is shown in Section 4.A.4 that

$$E(\hat{\beta}_2) = \beta_2 \quad \text{and} \quad E(\hat{\beta}_3) = 0$$

Therefore, $\hat{\beta}_2$ is unbiased, and the expectation of β_3 is zero. Consistency also holds. These results generalize to a multiple regression model with many explanatory variables. Thus, the inclusion of irrelevant variables does not bias the estimates of the remaining coefficients. Because estimators are unbiased and consistent, so are forecasts based on them.

The next step is to compute the variance of $\hat{\beta}_2$ in order to examine the efficiency property. We have, from Section 4.A.4,

$$\text{Var}(\hat{\beta}_2) = \frac{\sigma^2}{S_{22}(1 - r^2)}$$

where r^2 is the square of the simple correlation [see equation (2.13)] between X_2 and X_3, defined as $r^2 = S_{23}^2/(S_{22} S_{33})$. Let us compare this with the variance of the OLS estimator (call it β_2^*) that would have been obtained had the true model been used. From Chapter 3 equations (3.7) and (3.15),

$$\beta_2^* = \frac{S_{y2}}{S_{22}} \quad \text{and} \quad \text{Var}(\beta_2^*) = \frac{\sigma^2}{S_{22}}$$

The relative efficiency (refer to Definition 2.18b) of $\hat{\beta}_2$ with respect to β_2^* is

$$\frac{\text{Var}(\hat{\beta}_2)}{\text{Var}(\beta_2^*)} = \frac{1}{1 - r^2} \geq 1$$

It is therefore clear that the estimator of β_2 using the wrong model is inefficient unless $r^2 = 0$—that is, unless X_2 and X_3 are uncorrelated. Because of this inefficiency, t-statistics tend to be lower, and hence we may erroneously conclude that variables are statistically insignificant when, in fact, they are actually significant. It can be shown [see Johnston (1984), p. 262] that the estimator of the variance of $\hat{\beta}_2$ is unbiased and hence tests of hypotheses are still valid. □

Example 4.13

Table 4.11 has data for population (POP) and the unemployment rate (UNEMP) also. Population is measured in millions and unemployment is a percentage rate. We can expect that the higher the population, the more the number of housing units started. Unemployment rate is a reasonable measure for the business cycle. When unemployment is high, consumers are likely to postpone the purchase of a house. It therefore seems reasonable to add POP and UNEMP as explanatory variables. The modified model is as follows (with t-values in parentheses):

Model C: $\overline{\text{HOUSING}} = 5087.434 + 1.756\text{GNP} - 174.692\text{INTRATE}$
$\phantom{Model C: \overline{HOUSING} = 5087.434}{\scriptstyle(0.5)}{\scriptstyle(0.8)}{\scriptstyle(-2.9)}$

$- 33.434\text{POP} + 79.720\text{UNEMP}$
${\scriptstyle(-0.4)}{\scriptstyle(0.7)}$

$\bar{R}^2 = 0.328 \qquad F(4, 18) = 3.681 \qquad \text{d.f.} = 18$

Comparing this to Model A we note many significant differences. GNP, which was originally significant, is now insignificant. The t-statistic for INTRATE has also declined although it still remains significant. This is exactly what the theoretical analysis predicted. Property 4.6b stated that the variances of the coefficients are likely to be larger, which implies that t-statistics are likely to be smaller. The t-statistics for POP and UNEMP are very low, indicating that these variables are probably not important as *additional* determinants of housing, given that GNP and INTRATE measure the size of the economy and the business cycle. In fact, we can perform a Wald test for omitting POP and UNEMP. Treating Model C as the unrestricted model and Model A as the restricted model, the Wald F-statistic [see equation (4.3)] is given by

$$F_c = \frac{(ESS_A - ESS_C) \div (d.f._A - d.f._C)}{ESS_C \div d.f._C}$$

$$= \frac{(1491140 - 1444274)/2}{1444274/18}$$

$$= 0.292$$

The observed F_c is very small and is insignificant even at the 25 percent level (the p-value is 0.75). Thus, the Wald test would not reject the null hypothesis that the regression coefficients for POP and UNEMP are zero. We also note that the signs for POP and UNEMP are opposite to what we expected. However, in view of the insignificance of these coefficients, their signs are irrelevant and can be attributed to chance. □

Practice Problem

4.18 Instead of adding both POP and UNEMP, as was done here, add to Model A only the unemployment rate (call this Model D). Compare the results with those of Model A. Are the results very different?

Comparing the theoretical consequences of adding an irrelevant variable with those of omitting an important variable, we observe a trade-off. The former specification error causes estimators to be inefficient, though unbiased. The latter type of error causes bias in estimates and hypothesis tests. Since the true relationships are never known, we face the dilemma of choosing the most appropriate formulation. An investigator who puts more emphasis on unbiasedness, consistency, and reliability of tests would rather keep an irrelevant variable than face the consequences of omitting a crucial variable. On the other hand, if a researcher cannot tolerate inefficient estimators, deleting the offending variable(s) would be preferable. Economic theory and an understanding of the underlying behavior can often help out in the dilemma. The model selection criteria discussed earlier can help as well. In Chapter 7 we will see that tests for specification will also help. All this involves a lot of judgment. Blind adherence to mechanical criteria is to be avoided at all costs.

Saving Behavior in India

In a study of the saving behavior of households in India, Ramanathan (1969) examined in detail the nature of the effects on saving of income and net worth and their interactions. This was done for several socioeconomic subgroups. The data were cross-section for 503 households in New Delhi.

It is well known from economic theory and empirical investigations that income and net worth are two of the most important determinants of saving. One might hypothesize that the marginal propensity to save is an increasing function of income. At low income levels, most of the income will be spent on necessities and hence not much of an extra dollar earned is likely to be saved. At higher income levels, however, we expect that a greater fraction of extra income will be saved. This means that the higher the level of income, the higher the marginal propensity to save. Under this hypothesis, the saving relation may be written as

$$S = \alpha_1 + \alpha_2 Y + \alpha_3 Y^2 + \text{other factors}$$

or

$$S = \beta_1 + \beta_2 \ln Y + \text{other factors}$$

where S is the level of saving and Y is income, both measured in rupees. We expect α_3 and β_2 to be positive, because then $\Delta S/\Delta Y$ will increase with income (Δ represents change).

The relevance of wealth to consumption and saving is also well recognized [see Klein and Morgan (1951)]. In Section 4.6 we discussed the interaction between income and wealth. Low income groups, with pressing needs for funds, will exhibit a negative relation between saving and net worth, and high income groups, a positive relation. This suggests the following alternative formulations:

$$\frac{\Delta S}{\Delta W} = \alpha_4 + \alpha_5 Y \qquad \text{or} \qquad \frac{\Delta S}{\Delta W} = \beta_3 + \beta_4 \ln Y$$

We expect α_4 and β_4 to be negative and the other two coefficients to be positive. The saving relations that will generate these partial effects are

$$S = \alpha_4 W + \alpha_5 WY + \text{other factors}$$
$$S = \beta_3 W + \beta_4 W \ln Y + \text{other factors}$$

Combining these with the earlier ones, we get the following alternative models (note that it is possible to mix linear and nonlinear forms):

Model A: $\quad S = \alpha_1 + a_2 Y + \alpha_3 Y^2 + \alpha_4 W + \alpha_5 WY + u_1$

Model B: $\quad S = \beta_1 + \beta_2 \ln Y + \beta_3 W + \beta_4 W \ln Y + u_2$

The estimated saving relations for the entire sample of households are as follows, with t-statistics in parentheses:

$$\hat{S} = -51.5 - 0.047Y + 0.000022Y^2 - 0.019W + 0.00000056WY$$
$$\quad\quad (-1.9)\quad (-0.9)\quad\quad\quad (3.0)\quad\quad\quad (-1.8)\quad\quad\quad (0.4)$$

$$\bar{R}^2 = 0.05 \quad\quad \text{d.f.} = 498 \quad\quad F = 6.55$$

$$\hat{S} = 123.6 - 37.0 \ln Y - 0.156W + 0.0187W \ln Y$$
$$\quad\quad (1.4)\quad (-2.0)\quad\quad (-2.6)\quad\quad (0.6)$$

$$\bar{R}^2 = 0.04 \quad\quad \text{d.f.} = 499 \quad\quad F = 6.93$$

We note that the value of $\bar{R}^2$ is extremely low in both cases. This means that only a very small fraction of the variation in saving is captured by the specified models. If the households are separated by occupation groups, however, the goodness of fit improves. Table 4.4 presents the values of $\bar{R}^2$ for different occupation groups and shows a much better fit. In general, Model A has higher values for $\bar{R}^2$ than Model B.

When $\bar{R}^2$ values are so low, we might wonder whether the entire model isn't questionable. This can be checked for Model A with the joint hypotheses $\alpha_2 = \alpha_3 = \alpha_4 = \alpha_5 = 0$. The Wald F-statistic for this hypothesis is 6.55, which, under the null hypothesis, has the F-distribution with 4 and 498 d.f. At the 1 percent level of significance, $F^*_{4,498}(0.01)$ is 3.32, which is below the observed F. We therefore reject the null hypothesis and conclude that at least one of the individual regression coefficients is significantly different from zero.

This conclusion is reinforced when we look at the t-statistics for individual coefficients. For a two-tailed 5 percent test, $t^*_{498}(0.025) = 1.96$. We note that in Model A only the Y^2 term is significant at the 5 percent level. In Model B the terms $\ln Y$ and W are significant at this level. In Model A, the t-statistic for the interaction term is very low, indicating no support for the hypothesis that the marginal propensity to save out of income interacts with wealth. If this variable is dropped

TABLE 4.4 Values of $\bar{R}^2$ for Different Occupation Groups

Occupation Group	Model A	Model B	T^*
All households	0.05	0.04	503
Self-employed businessperson	0.28	0.33	92
Manager, executive	0.07	0.05	87
Professional	0.18	0.16	48
Clerical, sales	0.33	0.34	132
Service, unskilled	0.48	0.45	39
Self-employed artisan	0.63	0.55	39

* T is the number of observations in the subgroup.
Source: Ramanathan (1969). Reprinted with the permission of the American Statistical Association.

and the model reestimated, we get

$$S = -50.32 - 0.056Y + 0.000024Y^2 - 0.015W$$
$$\quad\quad (-1.9) \quad (-1.3) \quad\quad (4.3) \quad\quad (-2.2)$$

$$\bar{R}^2 = 0.05 \quad\quad \text{d.f.} = 499 \quad\quad F = 8.75$$

Although the income term is, strictly speaking, insignificant, it has been retained by the author in order to avoid the misspecification of omitting an important variable such as income. The marginal propensity to save out of income is $-0.056 + 0.000048Y$. We note that when incomes rises, the marginal propensity to save also rises, thus adding support to the hypothesis specified earlier.

Ramanathan also estimated these models separately for a number of socioeconomic groups. Households were classified by occupation, employment status, age of head of household, home ownership, and education of head of household, and the models were estimated for each group. For results on these regressions, the reader is referred to the original paper.

Practice Problem

4.19   The regression coefficient for Y^2 is 0.000024, which appears to be very small. Yet the t-statistic shows that it is statistically significant. Explain this apparent contradiction.

Net Migration Rates and the Quality of Life

Liu (1975) has examined the relationships between the variations in net migration rates among states and a number of explanatory variables, including the "quality of life." The data are cross-section over the 50 states, and the basic model used is the following:

$$\text{MIGRATE} = f(\text{QOL, Y, E, IS, ES, AP, ED, HW})$$

where

MIGRATE = net migration rate between 1960 and 1970

QOL = index of the quality of life

Y = index of state income as a ratio to U.S. income

E = ratio of state employment to U.S. employment

IS = index of individual status

ES = index of economic status

AP = index of agricultural production

ED = index of educational development

HW = index of health and welfare provision

Based on criteria developed by President Eisenhower's Commission of National Goals, Liu constructed each of the indices listed above. QOL is an arithmetic

The econometric model using all the explanatory variables is as follows:

$$\text{WLFP} = \beta_1 + \beta_2\text{YF} + \beta_3\text{YM} + \beta_4\text{EDUC} + \beta_5\text{UE} + \beta_6\text{MR} + \beta_7\text{DR}$$
$$+ \beta_8\text{URB} + \beta_9\text{WH} + u$$

Before actually estimating the model it will be useful to discuss the signs of the regression coefficients that one might expect. This discussion is drawn on "economic theory" as opposed to "econometric theory." The reader is referred to the papers by O'Neill (1981), Kelley and Da Silva (1980), and King (1978) for details on some of the theories.

YF: Since this is a measure of money offerings to female workers, we would expect this to have a positive effect on WLFP. In other words, the higher the wage, the more the participation by women. However, we should also bear in mind that labor theory says that the "income effect" on labor is negative; that is, as income rises, workers desire more leisure (less work). At the prevailing wages, the latter effect is likely to be smaller; and hence, on balance, we would expect a positive sign. This could be tested with a quadratic term in YF.

YM: As husbands earn more, their wives need not work as much. Hence, we might expect this coefficient to be negative. It is also possible that because many women are well qualified, higher male incomes might induce more females to seek such jobs. However, this would affect the type of job and probably not whether more women would join the labor force.

EDUC: More education implies more (as well as more desirable) job opportunities available to women. Thus, we would expect this coefficient to be positive.

UE: Unemployment rate has both negative and positive effects. The "discouraged worker hypothesis" states that a higher unemployment rate might be an indication to women (and minorities) that searches for employment may be futile. This might induce them to drop out of the labor force, which would give a negative sign. There is also a positive effect. If a husband loses his job, the wife might enter the labor force to compensate for the loss in earnings. If this effect is not very strong, the negative sign will prevail.

MR: If a woman is married, she tends to have fewer opportunities to work (especially when there are children), and perhaps a reduced desire or need to work. Thus, a higher marriage rate is likely to reduce WLFP.

DR: We would expect a positive sign for this because, when the divorce rate is high, more women are likely to enter the labor force to support themselves.

URB: In urban areas employment opportunities are more diverse than in rural areas. One might therefore expect that states having a larger fraction of the population living in urban areas might have a higher women's participation rate. On the other hand, rural women tend to help out by feeding livestock and poultry and doing other farm chores. Thus, they will already be part of the labor force. This means that if a state has more rural areas (that is, less URB), then women's labor force participation may be higher, resulting in a negative sign. The net effect can be determined only empirically.

WH: There is no clear sign one might expect for this beforehand. If nonwhite women are relatively unskilled and seek employment as maids and housekeepers, we would expect a negative sign for this coefficient because the higher WH, the fewer the number of nonwhites. Also, if white women are relatively affluent, they may not enter the labor force. This also would yield a negative sign. If these assumptions are false, the result will be a positive sign or zero.

The estimated model is as follows (the t-statistics are in parentheses): (Practice Computer Session 4.6 provides the instructions needed to reproduce all the results of this section.)

Model A

$$\widehat{\text{WLFP}} = \underset{(4.22)}{50.881} + \underset{(3.64)}{0.0045\text{YF}} - \underset{(-0.02)}{0.00001\text{YM}} + \underset{(3.99)}{0.2779\text{EDUC}} - \underset{(-3.71)}{1.1191\text{UE}}$$

$$- \underset{(-1.33)}{0.2243\text{MR}} + \underset{(1.17)}{0.2268\text{DR}} - \underset{(-2.11)}{0.0691\text{URB}} - \underset{(-3.54)}{0.1284\text{WH}}$$

$$\bar{R}^2 = 0.681 \qquad F(8, 41) = 14.066 \qquad ESS = 222.0523$$

It is clear from the F-statistic that we strongly reject the null hypothesis that all the regression coefficients except the constant term are zero. Also, $t_{41}^*(0.025) = 2.02$ at the 5 percent level of significance. Comparing this with the t-statistics presented above, we note that YM, MR, and DR are *individually insignificant*. Could they be *jointly significant*? To answer this we need to perform the Wald F-test presented in equation (4.3). This requires our estimating the restricted model in which these three variables are absent. The resulting equation is as follows:

Model B

$$\widehat{\text{WLFP}} = \underset{(8.70)}{37.454} + \underset{(6.27)}{0.0050\text{YF}} + \underset{(4.87)}{0.2446\ \text{EDUC}} - \underset{(-3.91)}{1.0440\text{UE}}$$

$$- \underset{(-1.84)}{0.0497\text{URB}} - \underset{(-3.51)}{0.1216\text{WH}}$$

$$\bar{R}^2 = 0.684 \qquad F(5, 44) = 22.23 \qquad ESS = 235.8151$$

The F-statistic for testing $H_0: \beta_2 = \beta_5 = \beta_6 = 0$, against H_1: at least one of them is nonzero is given by

$$F_c = \frac{(235.8151 - 222.0523)/3}{(222.0523/41)} = 0.847$$

It is easy to verify that such a low F-statistic cannot reject the null hypothesis, even at the 25 percent level of significance. This suggests that we accept the null hypothesis that the coefficients for YM, MR, and DR are zero—that is, that we accept that these variables do not significantly affect the labor force participation rate of women. Thus, although the signs of their regression coefficients agreed with our prior intuition, the observed values are perhaps nonzero due to sampling reasons only.

However, in view of the discussion in Section 4.7 regarding the dangers of omitting relevant variables, we should be a little more cautious and not rush to drop the three variables simultaneously. Because YM had an extremely low t-value omitting it does not seem to be serious. It was pointed out in Property 4.4 that a *t*-value of 1 is a useful cutoff in deciding whether a variable is a candidate for elimination. Table 4.6 presents several alternative models and their associated statistics, including the model selection criteria discussed in Section 4.4.

According to $\bar{R}^2$, the best model is Model C, although the differences in $\bar{R}^2$ are trivial. In terms of the model selection criteria, however, Model B is the best. This latter conclusion is somewhat overstated because Property 4.3b is applicable here. AIC decreases when MR and DR are eliminated from Model C. Because the number of observations exceeds 16, both SCHWARZ and HQ become redundant. Even so, Model B would still be judged the best. In Model C the marriage and divorce rates are significant only at the 15 to 20 percent levels of significance. In Model B the urban population variable is not significant at the 5 percent level but is significant at

TABLE 4.6 Results for Several Alternative Models

Variable	Model A	Model B	Model C	Model D	Model E
CONSTANT	50.881 (4.22)	37.454 (8.70)	50.995 (4.89)	45.199 (4.73)	36.484 (8.32)
YF	0.005 (3.64)	0.005 (6.27)	0.005 (5.15)	0.005 (5.54)	0.004 (5.87)
YM	−0.00001 (−0.02)				
EDUC	0.278 (3.99)	0.245 (4.87)	0.277 (4.86)	0.269 (4.71)	0.227 (4.49)
UE	−1.119 (−3.71)	−1.044 (−3.91)	−1.122 (−4.16)	−1.080 (−4.00)	−1.048 (−3.83)
MR	−0.224 (−1.33)		−0.226 (−1.47)	−0.121 (−0.91)	
DR	0.227 (1.17)		0.228 (1.33)		
URB	−0.069 (−2.11)	−0.050 (−1.84)	−0.069 (−2.30)	−0.061 (−2.05)	
WH	−0.128 (−3.54)	−0.122 (−3.51)	−0.129 (−3.66)	−0.128 (−3.62)	−0.113 (−3.21)
$\bar{R}^2$	0.681	0.684	0.688*	0.683	0.667
SGMASQ	5.416	5.359	5.287*	5.381	5.645
AIC	6.365	5.996*	6.116	6.123	6.206
FPE	6.391	6.003*	6.133	6.134	6.210
HQ	7.257	6.543	6.872	6.780	6.674
SHWARZ	8.980	7.542*	8.305	8.002	7.513
SHIBATA	6.040	5.848*	5.862	5.924	6.097
GCV	6.605	6.090*	6.294	6.257	6.273
RICE	6.939	6.206*	6.531	6.427	6.351

Note: An asterisk denotes the best model for that criterion.

the 7 percent level. Should this variable be dropped? We note from Model E that if URB is dropped, all the criteria statistics worsen. Also, there is nothing rigid about 5 percent being the level of significance. An investigator can use his or her own judgment in deciding whether a higher level is acceptable. Finally, we had theoretical reasons for believing that URB was important. It is therefore recommended that this variable be kept in the regression because it has a high, though not quite significant, t-statistic. Keeping it in the model would reduce any omitted variable bias. Thus, Model B would be our choice as the final model.

Note from this analysis that a considerable amount of judgment is involved in model selection. Although we should use the estimates and test results as guides, we should not rely blindly on empirical estimates.

The signs of all the regression coefficients in the final Model B agree with this discussion. The value of the coefficient for YF is quite robust across models. The positive sign for YF indicates that the "backward-bending supply curve effect" on labor—namely, that as wages increase workers prefer more leisure and less participation in the labor force—is not strong. Other things being equal, a \$100 increase in women's earnings is expected to increase their participation rate, on average, by one-half percent. Although the results have not been presented, we included a quadratic term for YF to test whether there is a nonlinearity in YF that indicates backward-bending supply effects. The statistics were only worse, indicating that nonlinearities may not be present.

The negative sign for URB means that the diversity of employment opportunities for women in urban areas is not strong enough to offset the fact that women in rural areas work on the farm and hence are part of the labor force. The magnitude of the coefficient is, however, not very large. A 1 percent increase in URB is likely to reduce average WLFP by only 0.05 percent.

The negative sign for UE supports the "discouraged worker hypothesis," which states that when the unemployment rate is high, those seeking employment might get discouraged and drop out of the labor force. The magnitude of the coefficient is quite high. A 1 percent increase in UE means an expected 1 percent decrease in WLFP, on average.

The value of $\bar{R}^2$ indicates that only about 68 percent of the variation across states in labor force participation is explained by Model B. Thus, we may have omitted some variables that would improve the explanatory power. However, it is quite typical for cross-section data to yield low R^2, as was seen in Ramanathan's study on saving behavior. Because many time series data generally grow over time, models based on them tend to give relatively good fits. This can be seen from the value of $\bar{R}^2$ (0.998) for the consumption function presented in Example 4.11. With additional data, we might have been able to provide a better explanation of women's labor force participation rates. Possible variables to be included in the regression are:

1. Measures of family size, birth rates, and number of children under a "threshold" age; these would tend to reduce the opportunities for women to work.
2. A variable measuring college-educated women.

3. Age distribution of women.
4. Welfare payments to single women with children; this could dictate whether women work or choose to remain at home (the availability of day care will have the same effect).
5. Measures to capture regional differences; farm states and industrial states may have different behavioral patterns.

SUMMARY

In the multiple linear regression model, the dependent variable (Y) is regressed against the k independent variables $X_1, X_2, \ldots, X_k$. X_1 is generally set to 1 so that a constant intercept term can be included. As before, the OLS procedure minimizes the error sum of squares $\sum \hat{u}_t^2$ and gives k normal equations. These equations can generally be solved uniquely for the coefficients, provided the number of observations is larger than k.

An unbiased estimator of the error variance (σ^2) is given by $s^2 = \hat{\sigma}^2 = (\sum \hat{u}_t^2)/(T - k)$. Under the assumption that the error terms u_t are independently and identically distributed as $N(0, \sigma^2)$, the statistic $[(T - k)\hat{\sigma}^2]/\sigma^2$ has a chi-square distribution with $T - k$ d.f.

If each variable in a model is expressed in standardized form by subtracting the mean and dividing by the standard deviation, the resulting model is known as the *standardized regression*, and the regression coefficients are known as the *beta coefficients*. This formulation is frequently used in the finance literature.

The goodness of fit is measured in one of two equivalent ways. From the estimated equation, the residual is measured as $\hat{u}_t = Y_t - \hat{\beta}_1 - \hat{\beta}_2 X_2 - \cdots - \hat{\beta}_k X_k$. The error sum of squares (ESS) is $\sum \hat{u}_t^2$ and the total sum of squares (TSS) is $\sum (Y_t - \bar{Y})^2$. The standard error of the regression given by $\hat{\sigma} = [\text{ESS}/(T - k)]^{1/2}$ can be compared with $\hat{\sigma}_Y = [\text{TSS}/(T - 1)]^{1/2}$ to see how much of a reduction there is. A unit-free measure is given by the *adjusted R-squared* (denoted by $\bar{R}^2$), which can be computed as

$$\bar{R}^2 = 1 - \frac{\text{ESS}(T - 1)}{\text{TSS}(T - k)} = 1 - \frac{T - 1}{T - k}(1 - R^2)$$

$\bar{R}^2$ can be interpreted as the variation in Y_t explained by the model. Unlike R^2, which is $1 - (\text{ESS}/\text{TSS})$, $\bar{R}^2$ takes account of the trade-off between a gain in R^2 due to an added variable and a loss in the degrees of freedom.

In this chapter we also discussed eight different criteria for choosing among competing models. A simpler model is preferable because (1) the inclusion of too many variables makes the relative precision of individual coefficients worse (as will be seen in detail in the next chapter), and (2) adding variables means a loss of degrees of freedom, which makes the power of a test worse. The model selection criteria take the form of the error sum of squares multiplied by a penalty factor that depends on the complexity of the model. A model is judged to be superior if it has lower values for the criteria statistics in a majority of the specifications. However, in certain special cases one or more of the criteria may become redundant.

To test whether an individual coefficient (β) is significantly different from zero, we first compute the t-statistic (t_c), which is the ratio of the estimated coefficient to its estimated standard error. If $t_c > t^*_{T-k}(a/2)$ or $t_c < -t^*_{T-k}(a/2)$, where t^* is the point on the t-distribution with $T - k$ d.f. such that the probability that $t > t^*$ is equal to one-half of the level of significance a, the null hypothesis $H_0: \beta = 0$ is rejected in favor of the alternative $H_1: \beta \neq 0$. If the alternative is one-sided, we obtain t^* such that the area to the right of it is equal to the level of significance. Then we reject H_0 in favor of $\beta > 0$ if $t_c > t^*$ or in favor of $\beta < 0$ if $t_c < -t^*$.

To test whether a subset of regression coefficients is zero, a joint F-test, known as the *Wald test*, is carried out. More specifically, to test $H_0: \beta_{m+1} = \beta_{m+2} = \cdots = \beta_k = 0$ against the alternative that at least one of them is nonzero, we first estimate the unrestricted model (U):

$$\text{(U)} \qquad Y = \beta_1 + \beta_2 X_2 + \cdots + \beta_m X_m + \beta_{m+1} X_{m+1} + \cdots + \beta_k X_k + u$$

Next we omit the last $k - m$ variables and estimate the restricted model (R):

$$\text{(R)} \qquad Y = \beta_1 + \beta_2 X_2 + \cdots + \beta_m X_m + v$$

Then we compute the Wald F-statistic

$$F_c = \frac{(\text{ESS}_R - \text{ESS}_U)/(k - m)}{\text{ESS}_U/(T - k)}$$

The null hypothesis is rejected if $F_c > F^*_{k-m, T-k}(a)$, where F^* is that point on the F-distribution with $k - m$ and $T - k$ degrees of freedom such that the probability that $F > F^*$ is a (for example 0.05 or 0.01). The Wald test need not be performed if only one regression coefficient is omitted from the model. This is because a t-test on the corresponding coefficient is equivalent.

Testing a linear combination of regression coefficients may be done in three equivalent ways. A t-statistic on the linear combination of estimates has $T - k$ d.f. and can be used in a t-test similar to that on an individual regression coefficient. Alternatively, the linear combination may be incorporated into the model and a t-or F-test performed.

Confidence intervals for individual coefficients are similar to those derived in Chapter 3. Confidence interval of the forecast $\hat{Y} = \hat{\beta}_1 + \hat{\beta}_2 X_2 + \cdots + \hat{\beta}_k X_k$ is, however, much more complicated and will not be covered in this book.

Quadratic and higher powers of independent variables, or lags in variables, are easily accommodated in a regression model provided the *unknown regression coefficients appear linearly*. One simply makes the suitable transformation of the data and incorporates them in the model. The marginal effect of one variable can be made to depend on another explanatory variable through interaction terms. Some models cannot be converted to a form that is linear in parameters. In such cases, the estimation procedure consists of nonlinear least squares or maximum likelihood methods.

Indiscriminate transformation of data and "data mining" to find the "best fit" should be avoided because they often lead to the substantiation of any hypothesis one might think of, however contradictory such substantiations might be. Mechanical criteria should not be applied blindly without regard to theory or some understanding of the underlying behavior.

The consequences of including an irrelavant variable (that is, one for which the true regression coefficient is zero) are as follows:

1. Estimated regression coefficients using the wrong model and forecasts based on these estimates are unbiased and consistent.
2. The estimates are inefficient and are not BLUE because the estimator based on the true model is BLUE.
3. Tests of hypotheses are still valid because the estimated variances are also unbiased. However, the power of tests is reduced. In other words, the probability of accepting a false hypothesis (type II error) is higher when the wrong model is used.

The consequences of omitting a variable that ought to belong in a model are as follows:

1. Estimated regression coefficients, using the incorrect model, and forecasts based on these estimates, are biased and inconsistent.
2. Estimated variances are also biased and therefore tests of hypotheses are no longer valid.

Comparing the theoretical consequences of adding an irrelevant variable with those of omitting an important variable, we observe a trade-off. The former specification error causes estimators to be inefficient, though unbiased. The latter type of error causes bias in estimates and hypothesis tests. Since the true relationships are never known, we face the dilemma of choosing the most appropriate formulation. An investigator who puts more emphasis on unbiasedness, consistency, and reliability of tests would rather keep an irrelevant variable than face the consequences of omitting a crucial variable. On the other hand, if a researcher cannot tolerate inefficient estimators, deleting the offending variable(s) would be preferable. Economic theory and an understanding of the underlying behavior can often help in the dilemma. The model selection criteria discussed earlier can also help. Tests for specification (Chapter 7) will help as well.

Because the constant term captures the average effects of omitted variables, it is not wise, in general, to omit the constant term from the specification, even if it is very significant and/or has an unexpected sign.

KEY TERMS

Adjusted R^2

Akaike information criterion (AIC)

Beta coefficient

Box–Cox transformation

Cobb–Douglas production function

Constant returns to scale

Decreasing returns to scale
Elasticity of output with respect to
  capital
Elasticity of output with respect to
  labor
Finite prediction error (FPE)
Generalized cross validation (GCV)
HQ criterion
Increasing returns to scale
Interaction term
Joint significance

Logistic curve
Logit model
Model in deviation form
Multiple regression
Restricted model
R^2 adjusted for degrees of freedom
Standardized regression
Technical change coefficient
Unrestricted model
Wald test

REFERENCES

Some of the following references require a knowledge of linear algebra.

Akaike, H. "Statistical Predictor Identification." *Annals Instit. Stat. Math.*, Vol. 22 (1970): 203–217.

———. "A New Look at Statistical Model Identification." *IEEE Trans. Auto. Control*, Vol. 19 (1974): 716–723.

Box, G. E. P., and Cox, D. R. "An Analysis of Transformations." *J. Royal Stat. Society*, Series. B (1964).

Brealey, Richard, and Myers, Stewart. *Principles of Corporate Finance.* New York: McGraw-Hill, 1981.

Craven, P., and Wahba, G. "Smoothing Noisy Data with Spline Functions." *Num. Math.*, Vol. 13 (1979): 377–403.

Economic Report of the President. Washington, D. C.: U. S. Government Printing Office, 1986, 1987.

Engle, R. F., and Brown, Scott. "Model Selection for Forecasting." *J. Computation in Statistics* (1985).

Engle, R. F., Granger, C. W., Rice, J., and Weiss, A. "Semi-parametric Estimates of the Relation Between Weather and Electricity Sales." *J. Amer. Stat. Assoc.* 81 (June 1986).

Friend, Irwin; Blume, Marshall; and Crockett, Jean. *Mutual Fund and Other Institutional Investors: A New Perspective.* New York: McGraw-Hill, 1970.

Haitovsky, Y. "A Note on the Maximization of $\bar{R}^2$." *American Statistician* (February 1969): 20–21.

Hannan, E. J., and Quinn, B. "The Determination of the Order of an Autoregression." *J. Royal Stat. Society*, Series B, Vol. 41 (1979): 190–195.

Heien, Dale. "The Cost of the U. S. Dairy Price Support Program: 1949–74." *Review of Economics and Statistics* 59 (*February* 1977): 1–8.

Johnston, J. *Econometric Methods.* New York: McGraw-Hill, 1984.

Kelley, A. C., and Da Silva, L. M. "The Choice of Family Size and the Compatibility of Female Work Force Participation in the Low-income Setting." *Revue Economique* (November 1980): 1081–1103.

King, A. G. "Industrial Structure, the Flexibility of Working Hours, and Women's Labor Force Participation." *Rev. Econ. Stat.* (August 1978): 399–407.

Klein, L. R., and Morgan, J. N. "Results of Alternative Statistical Treatment of Sample Survey Data." *J. Amer. Stat. Assoc.*, Vol. 47 (December 1951).

Kmenta, Jan. *Elements of Econometrics.* New York: Macmillan, 1986.

Liu, Ben-chieh. "Differential Net Migration Rates and the Quality of Life." *Review of Economics and Statistics* LVII (August 1975): 329–337.

O'Neil, June. "A Time-Series Analysis of Women's Labor Force Participation." *Amer. Econ. Assoc.*, *Papers and Proceedings*, (May 1981): 76–80.

Ramanathan, R., "An Econometric Exploration of Indian Saving Behavior." *J. Amer. Stat. Assoc.*, Vol. 64 (March 1969): 90–101.

Rice, J. "Bandwidth Choice for Nonparametric Kernel Regression." *Annals of Stat.*, Vol. 12 (1984): 1215–1230.

Schwarz, G. "Estimating the Dimension of a Model." *Annals of Stat.*, Vol. 6 (1978).

Shibata, R. "An Optimal Selection of Regression Variables." *Biometrika*, Vol. 68 (1981).

Wald, A. "Tests of Statistical Hypotheses Concerning Several Parameters When the Number of Observations Is Large." *Transactions of the Amer. Math. Society*, Vol. 54 (1943).

PRACTICE COMPUTER SESSIONS

The procedure for running the ready made batch files, included in the program diskette, and printing the output file is the same as that used in the Chapter 3 practice sessions.

4.1 The commands for reproducing the results in Table 4.2 are in *ps4-1.inp* and the data file used is *data4-1*.

4.2 The results of Section 4.2 on standardized regression, as well as those needed to answer Practice Problems 4.3, 4.6, and 4.8, can be obtained (again using *data4-1*) with the batch file *ps4-2.inp*.

4.3 The file *ps4−3.inp* has the commands needed to verify Examples 4.9, 4.10, and 4.11 of Section 4.5. The data file for this is *data4-10*.

4.4 Practice problems 4.15 and 4.16 in Section 4.6 also use the data file *data4-1*, and the commands needed are in the file *ps4-4.inp*.

4.5 Examples 4.12 and 4.13 in Section 4.7 can be verified using the commands in *ps4-5.inp* along with the data in *data4-11*.

4.6 The results presented in Table 4.6 for the application in Section 4.9 can be obtained with the data file *data4-12* and the command file *ps4-6.inp*.

4.7   To estimate the models in Table 4.7 of Exercise 4.7 use the data in *data4-13* and the commands in *ps4-7.inp*.

4.8   The commands in *ps4-8.inp* will be useful (along with the data in *data4-14*) in verifying the results in Table 4.8 of Exercise 4.9.

EXERCISES

Theoretical Questions

4.1   In the model $Y_t = \beta_1 + \beta_2 X_{t1} + \beta_3 X_{t2} + u_t$, suppose it is known that $\beta_2 = 1$. Describe how you would obtain the best estimates for β_1 and β_3 when β_2 is known to be 1.

†4.2   Let C be total consumption expenditures of a family, Y its income, and N the size of the family. Formulate an econometric model that incorporates the following assumptions: (a) the marginal propensity to consume decreases as income increases, and (b) the marginal effect of family size on consumption decreases as N increases (because of economies of scale in cooking, rents, and so on). Describe how you would test the hypotheses implicit in these statements.

4.3   Consider the following model for electricity consumption:

$$\ln E_t = \beta_1 + \beta_2 \ln Y_t + \beta_3 \ln P_t + u_t$$

where E is per capita electricity consumption in kilowatt-hours, Y is per capita income, and P is the price of electricity, at time t. Suppose we believe that the price elasticity of electricity is not constant but is continuously changing over time. Thus $\beta_3 = f(t)$.
   a. Assume a simple form for $f(t)$ and formulate an econometric model that will enable you to test this belief.
   b. Describe in detail (including which regressions to run, test statistics to compute, and so on) how you will test the relevant hypotheses.

4.4   For each of the following models, derive the elasticities of Y with respect to X:

$$\ln Y = \alpha + \beta X + \text{error}$$
$$Y = \alpha + \beta X + \gamma \ln X + \text{error}$$
$$Y = \alpha + \beta X + \gamma X^2 + \text{error}$$
$$Y = \alpha + \beta X + \gamma X Z + \text{error}$$
$$Y = \alpha + \beta/X + \text{error}$$

4.5   In a two-variable regression model, suppose you unnecessarily included a constant term. In other words, the true model is $Y_t = \beta X_t + u_t$, whereas you estimated the model $Y_t = \alpha + \beta X_t + v_t$. Derive the expected value of the OLS estimator of β. Is the estimator biased or not? If yes, state the condition(s) under which it might become unbiased.

†4.6 Suppose you did not have data on an independent variable X_t but used a proxy variable Z_t instead. For instance, you wanted to use the wage rate in the service industry but could only get the wage rate in the manufacturing industry. Examine the consequence of this kind of specification error. More specifically, let the true model be $Y_t = \beta X_t + u_t$, but assume you used the model $Y_t = \beta Z_t + v_t$ instead. Under what conditions will the OLS estimate of β be (a) unbiased and (b) consistent?

Empirical Questions

4.7 Table 4.7 presents the estimated coefficients and related statistics for a number of alternative models on poverty rates. Table 4.13 presents 1980

TABLE 4.7 Estimated Models for Poverty Rate Data

Variable	Model A	Model B	Model C	Model D
CONST	27.955 (1.83)	27.851 (3.21)	25.924 (9.07)	27.646 (10.28)
URB	0.0238 (2.09)	0.0238 (2.19)	0.0235 (2.20)	0.0206 (1.93)
FAMSIZE	−0.4576 (−0.20)	−0.4667 (−0.24)		
EDUC1	−0.0018 (−0.01)			
EDUC2	−0.1632 (−0.82)	−0.1617 (−2.58)	−0.1517 (−3.29)	−0.1594 (−3.43)
EDUC3	0.1458 (1.72)	0.1453 (2.23)	0.1425 (2.25)	0.1298 (2.03)
UNEMP	0.1112 (1.55)	0.1113 (1.58)	0.1118 (1.61)	
MEDINC	−0.5392 (−4.00)	−0.5393 (−4.06)	−0.5496 (−4.42)	−0.5364 (−4.26)
$\bar{R}^2$	0.570	0.578	0.586	0.574
F	11.795	14.036	17.144	20.183
ESS	133.952	133.953	134.098	140.755
SGMASQ	2.679	2.627	2.579	2.656
AIC	3.043	2.940	2.843	2.883
FPE	3.049	2.944	2.846	2.885
HQ	3.399	3.239	3.090	3.090
SCHWARZ	4.043	3.770	3.519	3.444
SHIBATA	2.947	2.867	2.790	2.845
GCV	3.108	2.987	2.876	2.906
RICE	3.189	3.044	2.915	2.932

Values in parentheses are the t-statistics.

census data for 58 California counties relating the poverty rate to several of its determinants. The dependent variable is the poverty rate.

a. Explain why each of the variables might belong in the model. What signs would you expect a priori for each of the variables in Model A? Do the observed signs agree with your intuition? If not, do you have a rationalization for the unexpected sign?

b. In each model, apply the Wald test to test the joint significance of the variables in the model. Be sure to state the null and alternative hypotheses in each case and the degrees of freedom for the F-statistic. What do you conclude about the models?

c. Apply the t-test to each of the regression coefficients in each of the models (be sure to indicate the degrees of freedom) and test whether the regression coefficients are significant. Be sure to state the null and alternative hypotheses.

d. Consider Model A as the unrestricted model and Model C as the restricted model. Use these two models to perform a relevant test. State the null and alternative hypotheses, the appropriate test statistic, its distribution under the null hypothesis and its degrees of freedom. Based on your test, would you recommend that certain variables be dropped from Model A? If yes, what are they and why? If not, why not?

e. Which of the four models do you consider the best? Explain your reasons.

f. In Model D, suppose you want to test the hypothesis that the sum of the regression coefficients for EDUC2 and EDUC3 is zero. For each of the three methods described in the chapter, show how you will carry out a test for this hypothesis. More specifically, state what regressions, if any, you would run; what statistic you would compute; its distribution under the null hypothesis, including the degrees of freedom; and the criteria for accepting/rejecting the hypothesis.

g. Are there any missing variables? Justify your answer.

4.8   In a study of early retirements, the following equations were estimated using 1980 census data for 44 States (values in parentheses are t-statistics):

$$\widehat{RETRD} = -3.930 + 1.627\ HLTH - 0.0005\ MSSEC + 0.0005\ MPUBAS$$
$$\text{(A)}\qquad {\scriptstyle(-0.4)\qquad (5.4)\qquad\qquad (-0.26)\qquad\qquad\qquad (0.28)}$$
$$+ 0.549\ UNEMP + 0.153\ DEP + 0.077\ RACE$$
$${\scriptstyle(2.2)\qquad\qquad (1.6)\qquad\qquad (2.3)}$$

$$\bar{R}^2 = 0.654 \qquad \hat{\sigma} = 2.175 \qquad ESS = 175.088$$

$$\widehat{RETRD} = -5.093 + 1.596\ HLTH + 0.557\ UNEMP + 0.153\ DEP$$
$$\text{(B)}\qquad {\scriptstyle(-1.6)\qquad (6.5)\qquad\qquad (2.3)\qquad\qquad (1.8)}$$
$$+ 0.083\ RACE$$
$${\scriptstyle(3.5)}$$

$$\bar{R}^2 = 0.671 \qquad \hat{\sigma} = 2.121 \qquad ESS = 175.524$$

where

   RETRD = retired men who are between the ages of 16 and 65

HLTH = percent of people between 16 and 64 years who are prevented from working due to disability

MSSEC = mean social security income ($)

MPUBAS = mean public assistance income ($)

UNEMP = unemployment rate (in percent)

DEP = percent of households that represent married couples with children under 18

RACE = percent of men who are nonwhite

Test both models for overall significance (you have enough information to answer the question). Also test each regression coefficient (except the constant term) for significance at the 5 percent and 10 percent levels. Next test the hypothesis that the coefficients for MSSEC and MPUBAS are both jointly insignificant. State your null and alternative hypotheses, test statistic, distribution and d.f., and the criterion to accept or reject the null. What do you conclude? State the signs you would expect for the coefficients in Model B and whether the actual signs agree with your intuition. Finally, comment on the adequacy of the model.

†4.9   Table 4.8 has the estimated results for a number of models on deaths due to heart disease. Table 4.14 presents data on the death rates due to coronary heart disease in the United States, along with those for a number of other variables it may be related to. The data are annual for the period 1947–1980.

a. Explain why each of the independent variables might affect the death rate due to coronary heart disease. What signs would you expect a priori for each of the regression coefficients? Do the observed signs agree with your intuition? If not, do you have an alternative explanation for the unexpected sign?

b. Would you say that the fit is good? What do the values of F in Table 4.8 mean? Formally test a relevant hypothesis. Be sure to state the null and alternative hypotheses, the degrees of freedom for the F-statistic, and the criterion for rejecting or accepting the hypothesis. What do you conclude?

c. Test each of the regression coefficients for statistical significance. Based on your test, would you recommend that any of the variables be dropped?

d. Perform relevant Wald F-tests for excluding variables. State the null and alternative hypotheses, and the degrees of freedom. What do you conclude?

e. Which of the models is the best? Explain your reasons.

f. Identify any variables that belong in the model but have been omitted.

4.10   A study of 40 top television markets was carried out in 1979–80 and data gathered on a number of variables regarding the demand for cable TV, which was fairly new then. The dependent variable was SUB, the number of sub-

TABLE 4.8 Estimated Models for Heart Disease Data

Variables	Model A	Model B	Model C
CONST	226.002 (1.54)	247.004 (1.94)	139.678 (1.79)
CAL	−69.983 (−0.89)	−77.762 (−1.06)	
CIG	10.116 (2.00)	10.640 (2.32)	10.706 (2.33)
UNEMP	−0.613 (−0.39)		
EDFAT	2.810 (1.68)	2.733 (2.40)	3.380 (3.50)
MEAT	0.112 (0.46)		
SPIRITS	21.716 (2.57)	23.650 (3.11)	26.749 (3.80)
BEER	−3.467 (−2.67)	−3.849 (−4.27)	−4.132 (−4.79)
WINE	−4.562 (−0.28)		
$\bar{R}^2$	0.645	0.674	0.672
F	8.508	14.633	17.932
ESS	1980	2040	2122
SGMASQ	79.212	72.868	73.184
AIC	98.895	85.407	83.766
FPE	100.180	85.727	83.946
HQ	113.504	93.624	90.430
SCHWARZ	148.130	111.809	104.846
SHIBATA	89.079	81.188	80.780
GCV	107.728	88.482	85.801
RICE	123.769	92.741	88.430

Values in parentheses are t-statistics.

scribers (in thousands) in each market, and the independent variables were as follows:

HOME = number of homes passed by each system (in thousands)

INST = installation fee ($)

SVC = monthly service charge ($)

TV = number of signals carried by each cable system

AGE = age of the system in years

$$\text{AIR} = \text{number of TV signals received with good signals without cable}$$

$$Y = \text{per capita income in the area}$$

The estimated model with all the variables is given below with *standard errors* (not *t*-statistics) in parentheses:

$$\widehat{\text{SUB}} = -6.808 + 0.406 \text{ HOME} - 0.526 \text{ INST} + 2.039 \text{ SVC}$$
$$\phantom{\widehat{\text{SUB}} = } (26.7) \quad\;\; (0.035) \qquad\quad (0.476) \qquad\quad (2.127)$$

$$+ 0.757 \text{ TV} + 1.194 \text{ AGE} - 5.111 \text{ AIR} + 0.0017 \text{ Y}$$
$$(0.688) \qquad\;\; (0.503) \qquad\;\; (1.518) \qquad\;\; (0.00347)$$

$$\text{ESS} = 4{,}923.914 \qquad \text{TSS} = 43{,}865.001$$

Compute $\hat{\sigma}^2$, R^2, and $\bar{R}^2$ and use them to test the model for overall significance. State your null hypothesis and the alternative and describe how you obtain the test statistic, its distribution, d.f., and the test criterion. Also test each regression coefficient (except the constant term) for significance at the 10 percent level. Based on your results, would you recommend that some of the variables be dropped from the specification. If yes, explain what and why. A second model was also estimated and the results are as follows (values in parentheses are now *t*-statistics):

$$\widehat{\text{SUB}} = 12.869 + 0.412 \text{ HOME} + 1.140 \text{ AGE} - 3.462 \text{ AIR}$$
$$\phantom{\widehat{\text{SUB}} = } (2.00) \qquad (13.29) \qquad\qquad (2.78) \qquad\;\; (-3.34)$$

$$\text{ESS} = 5{,}595.615$$

Compute R^2 and $\bar{R}^2$ and compare them with the previous models. Use the two models to test a relevant hypothesis that use both model estimates. Again, state your null hypothesis and the alternative and describe how you obtain the test statistic, its distribution, d.f., and the test criterion. Also test each regression coefficient (except the constant term) for significance at the 10 percent level. What do you conclude? Do the signs of the regression coefficients agree with your prior intuition? Explain.

4.11 Using your multiple regression program, enter the data in Tables 4.13 and 4.14 (at end of section) and estimate your own alternative models, including any nonlinear terms that might make sense. Do you find any of them to be superior to the ones presented?

4.12 A labor economist wished to examine the effects of schooling and experience on earnings. Using cross-section data, she obtained the following relationships:

$$\widehat{\ln E} = 7.71 + 0.094S + 0.023N - 0.000325N^2$$
$$\phantom{\widehat{\ln E} = } (0.113) \quad\; (0.005) \quad\; (0.009) \qquad (0.000187)$$

$$R^2 = 0.337 \qquad T = 60$$

where $\ln E$ is the natural logarithm of earnings, S is the number of years of schooling, and N is the number of years of experience. R^2 is unadjusted and the values in parentheses are standard errors.

a. Test the hypothesis (state the null and alternate hypotheses) "Schooling has no effect on earnings." What do you conclude?

b. Test the hypothesis (state the null and alternate hypotheses) "Neither schooling nor experience has any effect on earnings." (You have all the information needed to perform this test.)

c. Describe how you would test the hypothesis "Experience has no effect on earnings." More specifically, state the null and alternative hypotheses; describe what additional regression(s), if any, you would run; write an expression for the test statistic; state its distribution, degrees of freedom, and the acceptance/rejection criterion.

d. Write down or derive the expressions for the elasticity of earnings with respect to (i) schooling, and (ii) experience. What additional information, if any, do you need to compute these elasticities?

4.13 Using the data in Table 4.11 and your regression program, generate the following new variables:

$$LH = \ln(HOUSING) \qquad LP = \ln(POP)$$
$$LG = \ln(GNP) \qquad LU = \ln(UNEMP)$$
$$LR = \ln(INTRATE)$$

a. Verify the results in Table 4.9 (LH is the dependent variable).

b. Which of the three models is the "best"? Explain what you mean by "best."

c. In Model A test the joint hypothesis (at the 5 percent level) that the coefficients for LP, LG, LU, and LR are all zero. State the null and alternative hypotheses, the test statistic, its distribution under the null hypothesis, and the criterion for acceptance/rejection. What do you conclude from the test?

d. Test each regression coefficient in Model A (except the constant term) for significance at the 5 percent level. Based on your results, would you recommend that some of the variables be omitted? If yes, what and why?

e. In Model A, test the joint hypothesis that the coefficients for LP and LU are zero. Based on your result would you recommend that these variables be omitted? Explain why or why not.

4.14 As part of a study on industrial employment in San Diego, the following equation was estimated using annual data for 22 years (value of $\bar{R}^2$ was 0.996).

Model A: $\widehat{\ln EMP_t} = -3.89 + 0.51 \ln INCM_t - 0.25 \ln WAGE_t$
$\qquad\qquad\qquad\quad (-0.56) \quad (2.3) \qquad\qquad (-1.7)$
$\qquad\qquad\qquad + 0.62 \ln GOVTEXP_t$
$\qquad\qquad\qquad\quad (5.8)$

where EMP is total employment, INCM is total income, WAGE is the average hourly wage rate, and GOVTEXP is the total expenditure of all local governments.

TABLE 4.9 Estimated Double-log Models for Housing Data

Variable	Model A	Model B	Model C
CONSTANT	4.607 (0.21)	−4.968 (−1.51)	−4.759 (−1.45)
LG	2.914 (1.23)	1.904 (3.86)	1.873 (3.79)
LP	−3.349 (−0.44)		
LU	0.319 (0.95)	0.198 (1.08)	
LR	−1.313 (−3.17)	−1.405 (−4.01)	−1.229 (−3.96)
ESS	0.533	0.538	0.571
R^2	0.479	0.474	0.442
$\bar{R}^2$	0.363	0.391	0.386
F	4.140	5.699	7.907
d.f.	18	19	20
SGMASQ	0.0296	0.0283	0.0286
AIC	0.0358	0.0331	0.0322
FPE	0.0360	0.0333	0.0323
GCV	0.0378	0.0343	0.0328
HQ	0.0381	0.0348	0.0335
RICE	0.0410	0.0359	0.0336
SCHWARZ	0.0458	0.0404	0.0374
SHIBATA	0.0332	0.0315	0.0313

Values in parentheses are the corresponding t-statistics—that is, the coefficient divided by its standard error.

a. Do the signs of the coefficients (excluding the constant term) agree with intuition? Explain. (*t*-statistics are in parentheses.)
b. Test each of the regression coefficients for significance at 1, 5, and 10 percent levels.
c. Suppose you had formulated the following alternative model (Model B):

$$\ln \text{EMP} = \alpha_0 + \alpha_1 \ln \text{POP} + \alpha_2 \ln \text{PERCAPINCM} + \alpha_3 \ln \text{WAGE} + \alpha_4 \ln \text{GOVTEXP} + \text{error}$$

and imposed the restriction $\alpha_1 = \alpha_2$ ahead of time. POP is San Diego population and PERCAPINCM = INCM/POP. Show how you would use Model A's estimates and estimate Model B without rerunning. In other words, write the estimates for α_1, α_2, α_3, and α_4.

d. Because the *t*-statistic is low for WAGE, someone suggests that WAGE be eliminated. If you follow the suggestion, what kind of specification error would you be making? What are the consequences of that for unbiasedness and consistency of estimates and forecasts? Explain.

4.15 The Planning Department of a city estimates the following relationship:

$$\widehat{\log H_t} = 1.12 + 1.14 \log Y_t + 0.96 \log P_t$$
$$\quad\quad (0.8) \quad (10.7) \quad\quad\quad (1.5)$$
$$\bar{R}^2 = 0.98 \quad\quad T = 27$$

where H_t is the total number, at time t, of single family dwellings; Y_t is aggregate income in constant dollars (that is, corrected for inflation); and P_t is the city's population. The values in parentheses are *t*-statistics.
a. Test each of the regression coefficients for significance at 1, 5, and 10 percent levels. Which are significant and at what levels?
b. City Councilman A says, "This model is misspecified because per capita income (Y_t/P_t) should be used *instead of* Y_t." Councilman B says, "Because the model is in double-log form, it doesn't matter whether you use Y_t or (Y_t/P_t) in its place. The models are *essentially identical*." Which of the councilmen is correct and why? If A is correct, what can you say about the bias, hypothesis tests, and so on? If B is correct, show how the regression coefficients of Councilman A's alternative model can be obtained from those above, *without rerunning the regression*.
c. Councilman C says, "The model is misspecified because other variables which belong are omitted." List at least two important variables that ought to be there. Carefully examine the implications of this misspecification on (i) bias of estimates and forecasts and (ii) validity of tests of hypothesis.

4.16 The monthly salary (WAGE), age (AGE), number of years of education beyond the eighth grade (EDUC), and the number of years of experience (EXPER) were obtained for 49 persons in a certain office. The estimated relation between WAGE and the characteristics of a person is as follows (with *t*-statistics in parentheses):

$$\widehat{WAGE} = 632.244 + 142.510EDUC + 43.225EXPER - 1.913AGE$$
$$\quad\quad (1.493) \quad\quad (4.088) \quad\quad\quad (3.022) \quad\quad\quad (-0.22)$$

a. The value of $\bar{R}^2$ is 0.277. Using this information, test the model for overall significance. (*Note*: you have all the information you need to perform the test.)
b. Test the coefficients for EDUC and EXPER for statistical significance at the 1 percent level and AGE for significance at the 10 percent level.
c. Can you rationalize the negative sign for AGE?
d. One would expect the AGE effect to be nonlinear because at a young age we would expect the wages to go up, reach a peak during middle age, and decrease at an older age. Describe carefully how you would test this hypothesis.

4.17 In Exercise 3.18 of Chapter 3, the grade point average (COLGPA) of 427 college students was related separately to their high school GPA (HSGPA), the verbal score (VSAT) in the Scholastic Aptitude Test, and their mathematics score (MSAT) in the same test. When all the variables are included, the estimated model is as follows (standard errors—not t-values—are in parentheses):

$$\widehat{COLGPA} = 0.423 + 0.398 \text{ HSGPA} + 0.00074 \text{ VSAT} + 0.001 \text{ MSAT}$$
$$\quad\quad (0.220) \quad (0.061) \quad\quad\quad\quad (0.00028) \quad\quad\quad (0.0003)$$

$$R^2 = 0.220 \quad\quad T = 427$$

a. In view of the low R^2, we might suspect that the model is inadequate. Test the model for overall goodness of fit. Be sure to state the null and alternative hypotheses, the test statistic, its distribution, and the criterion for acceptance/rejection.

b. Test each regression coefficient (exclude the constant) for significance at the 1 percent level against the alternative that the coefficient is positive. What do you conclude?

c. Suppose a student took a special course to improve his SAT scores and increased the verbal and math scores by 100 points each. On average, how much of an increase in college GPA could one expect from this?

d. Describe step by step how you would use *each* of the methods in Section 4.5 on testing a linear combination of coefficients to test the hypothesis "The marginal effect of verbal SAT scores on COLGPA is the same as the marginal effect of math SAT scores."

e. Should other variables be added to the model? If yes, what are they? If these new variables did belong in the model, what can you say about the statistical properties (unbiasedness, consistency, BLUE, and validity of tests) of the above estimates?

f. The same model was estimated in double-log form and the results are as follows (standard errors in parentheses):

$$\widehat{LCOLGPA} = -1.753 + 0.511\text{LHSGPA} + 0.129\text{LVSAT} + 0.207\text{LMSAY}$$
$$\quad\quad (0.378) \quad (0.082) \quad\quad\quad (0.051) \quad\quad\quad (0.062)$$

$$R^2 = 0.202 \quad\quad T = 427$$

A staff member at the Registrar's office says, "The double-log model is inferior in goodness of fit and hence should be discarded." Is the staff member's claim right? Explain.

g. Suppose you want to test the hypothesis "The verbal and math SAT score elasticities are equal." Describe how each of the methods in Section 4.5 on testing a linear combination of coefficients would be used to test this hypothesis.

4.18 Table 4.15 has the data used in Exercise 4.10. First verify the results in that exercise. Then estimate the double-log version of Model A. As before, test it for overall significance as well as that of individual regression coefficients.

Which variables would you recommend be omitted from the model and why? Omit these (one at a time) and estimate the new model. Interpret the results of the "final" model you obtain by this exercise. What signs would you expect for the regression coefficients? Do the actual coefficients agree with your intuition? If not, can you rationalize the difference?

4.19 Table 4.16 has the data used in Exercise 4.8. Using this data set, carry out an analysis similar to the one in Exercise 4.18.

TABLE 4.10 Annual Data on Consumption, GNP, Wage Bill, and Prices

Year	CONS	GNP	WAGES	PRDEFL
1948	681.8	1108.7	142.1	25.7
1949	695.4	1109.0	142.0	25.6
1950	733.2	1203.7	155.4	26.2
1951	748.7	1328.2	181.6	27.8
1952	771.4	1380.0	196.3	28.4
1953	802.5	1435.3	210.4	29.0
1954	822.7	1416.2	209.4	29.1
1955	873.8	1494.9	225.9	29.5
1956	899.8	1525.6	244.7	30.1
1957	919.7	1551.1	257.8	31.0
1958	932.9	1539.2	259.8	31.6
1959	979.4	1629.1	281.2	32.3
1960	1005.1	1665.3	296.7	32.9
1961	1025.2	1708.7	305.6	33.3
1962	1069.0	1799.4	327.4	33.9
1963	1108.4	1873.3	345.5	34.4
1964	1170.6	1973.3	371.0	35.0
1965	1236.4	2087.6	399.8	35.6
1966	1298.9	2208.3	443.0	36.7
1967	1337.7	2271.4	475.5	37.6
1968	1405.9	2365.6	524.7	39.3
1969	1456.7	2423.3	578.4	41.0
1970	1492.0	2416.2	618.3	42.9
1971	1538.8	2484.8	659.4	44.9
1972	1621.9	2608.5	726.2	46.7
1973	1689.6	2744.1	812.8	49.6

(continued)

TABLE 4.10 (Continued)

Year	CONS	GNP	WAGES	PRDEFL
1974	1674.0	2729.3	891.3	54.8
1975	1711.9	2695.0	948.7	59.2
1976	1803.9	2826.7	1057.9	62.6
1977	1883.8	2958.6	1176.6	66.7
1978	1961.0	3115.2	1329.2	71.6
1979	2004.4	3192.4	1491.4	76.2
1980	2000.4	3187.1	1638.2	86.6
1981	2024.2	3248.8	1807.4	94.6
1982	2050.7	3166.0	1907.0	100.0
1983	2146	3279.1	2020.7	103.9
1984	2249.3	3501.4	2213.9	107.7
1985	2354.8	3618.7	2367.5	110.9
1986	2446.4	3717.9	2511.4	113.8
1987	2513.7	3853.7	2690	117.4
1988	2598.4	4024.4	2907.6	121.3
1989	2668.5	4142.6	3145.4	126.3

Source: Economic Report of the President, 1990. Tables C-2, C-3, and C-24.

TABLE 4.11 Data on the Determinants of Housing Starts

t	HOUSING	POP	GNP	UNEMP	INTRATE
1963	1634.9	189.242	1873.3	5.5	5.89
1964	1561.0	191.889	1973.3	5.0	5.82
1965	1509.7	194.303	2087.6	4.4	5.81
1966	1195.8	196.560	2208.3	3.7	6.25
1967	1321.9	198.712	2271.4	3.7	6.46
1968	1545.4	200.706	2365.6	3.5	6.97
1969	1499.5	202.677	2423.3	3.4	7.80
1970	1469.0	205.052	2416.2	4.8	8.45
1971	2084.5	207.661	2484.8	5.8	7.74
1972	2378.5	209.896	2608.5	5.5	7.60
1973	2057.5	211.909	2744.1	4.8	7.96
1974	1352.5	213.854	2729.3	5.5	8.92
1975	1171.4	215.973	2695.0	8.3	9.00
1976	1547.6	218.035	2826.7	7.6	9.00

TABLE 4.11 (Continued)

t	HOUSING	POP	GNP	UNEMP	INTRATE
1977	2001.7	220.239	2958.6	6.9	9.02
1978	2036.1	222.585	3115.2	6.0	9.56
1979	1760.0	225.055	3192.4	5.8	10.78
1980	1312.6	227.757	3187.1	7.0	12.66
1981	1100.3	230.138	3248.8	7.5	14.70
1982	1072.1	232.520	3166.0	9.5	15.14
1983	1712.5	234.799	3279.1	9.5	12.57
1984	1755.8	237.019	3489.9	7.4	12.38
1985	1745.0	239.283	3585.2	7.1	11.55

Source: Economic Report of the President, 1987, Tables B-50, B-30, B-2, B-35, and B-68.

TABLE 4.12 Determinants of Women's Labor Force Participation Rates

WLFP: Participation Rate (%) of All Women over 16

45.4	59.7	47.8	44.6	52.6	55.3	53.6	51.6	45.8
52.3	57.8	49.0	51.6	50.4	50.1	51.0	43.8	44.2
47.9	54.6	52.9	48.8	54.0	46.2	49.3	49.0	51.3
60.1	54.5	50.6	46.5	48.2	53.9	47.3	48.0	48.0
50.2	45.7	52.4	52.9	49.3	48.9	51.0	49.5	51.8
52.4	50.6	36.5	52.7	51.6				

YF: Median Earnings (in Dollars) by Females

2922	4956	3187	2569	3915	3494	3681	3433	3379
3299	4082	2662	3825	3303	3096	3427	3060	2446
2939	4402	3795	3550	3215	2366	3348	2545	3101
4295	3421	3855	2991	4246	3602	2478	3367	2977
3143	3375	3556	3022	2500	3246	3214	2899	3194
3554	3173	2893	3218	2791				

YM: Median Earnings (in Dollars) by Males

7420	13446	8770	6272	9750	9817	10103	10329	7619
7200	9489	8389	10322	9847	9223	8747	6932	7553
7364	10803	9421	10364	9005	5842	8149	8161	9045
9636	8785	10362	7485	9763	6975	8012	10003	7716
8920	9256	8737	7373	7170	6817	8542	9535	7443
9176	10070	7989	9346	9420				

(continued)

TABLE 4.12 (Continued)

EDUC:	Percent of Female High School Graduates over 24 Years of Age							
53.5	78.1	69.7	52.5	71.8	76.5	67.3	66.9	61.6
53.7	66.5	69.2	62.4	63.2	71.1	69.8	51.3	53
67.7	66.4	69.7	67.3	70.9	50.6	60.8	71.8	71.7
73	69.6	62.9	63	62.6	53.4	66.4	65.7	61
74.6	60.5	56.1	53	67.8	50.7	59.7	77.7	69.6
61.9	75.6	49.8	68.3	73.7				

UE:	Unemployment Rate (%)							
7.1	9.2	5.1	6.2	6.2	4.8	5.1	8	6
5.1	7.7	5.7	5.5	6.4	4.1	3.4	5.6	6.7
7.2	5.6	6.1	7.8	4.2	5.8	4.5	5.1	3.2
5.1	3.1	6.9	6.6	7.1	4.8	3.7	5.9	3.4
6.8	6.9	6.6	5	3.5	5.8	4.5	4.3	5.1
4.7	6.8	6.7	4.5	2.8				

MR:	Marriage Rate (%) of Women at Least 16 Years of Age							
56.4	61.9	58.5	59.6	53	57.2	53.9	54	56.3
61.3	57.3	64.2	53.6	58.1	59.2	59.8	59.1	54.6
56.9	52.6	49.5	55.2	57	54.8	56.6	61	58.9
57	56.7	53.2	58.4	49.2	56.5	60.9	56.3	58.5
60.6	53.8	51.3	55.2	59.5	57.3	58.6	62.4	54.4
55.9	58.1	59.7	56.8	65.2				

DR:	Divorce Rate (%)							
7	8.6	8.2	9.3	6.1	6	4.5	5.3	7.9
6.5	5.5	7.1	4.6	7.7	3.9	5.4	4.5	3.8
5.6	4.1	3	4.8	3.7	5.6	5.7	6.5	4
16.8	5.9	3.2	8	3.7	4.9	3.2	5.5	7.9
7	3.4	3.9	4.7	3.9	6.8	6.9	6.9	4.6
4.5	6.9	5.3	3.6	7.8				

URB:	Percent of Urban Population in State							
58.4	48.4	79.6	50	90.9	78.5	77.4	72.2	80.5
60.3	83.1	54.1	83	64.9	57.2	66.1	52.3	66.1
50.8	76.6	84.6	73.8	66.4	44.5	70.1	53.4	61.5
80.9	56.4	88.9	69.8	88.9	45	44.3	75.8	68
67.1	71.5	87.1	47.6	44.6	58.7	79.7	80.4	32.2
63.1	72.6	39	65.9	60.5				

TABLE 4.12 (*Continued*)

WH: Percent of Females over 16 Years Who Are White								
74	78.5	85.9	83.9	79.3	90	91.6	83.6	86
73.4	33	96.6	82.7	91.8	97.9	92.8	92.6	70.5
99.1	76.2	94.4	86.1	97.3	66.4	89.1	95.1	95.7
88.9	99	84.9	78.4	80.9	77.2	96.8	89.4	87.5
95.6	90.4	95.7	70.2	96.2	84.3	81.1	91.7	99.2
80.1	92.1	96	95.2	95.6				

Source: Data compiled by Katherine McGregor from 1980 census publications.

TABLE 4.13 Data on Poverty Rates in California Counties

POVRATE: Percentage of Families with Income Below Poverty Level								
18.1	8.7	7.5	9.5	7.5	8.8	6.1	11.4	6.7
11.4	10.5	9.4	12.7	7.3	10.2	12.4	11.2	7.1
10.5	12.4	4.9	9.6	9.5	11.8	11.8	6.4	8.9
6.0	6.5	5.2	7.0	8.2	8.8	8.9	10.8	9.1
8.4	10.3	10.8	8.0	4.5	6.7	5.3	8.2	8.8
9.3	9.6	8.1	7.1	10.0	9.0	11.0	9.1	13.2
9.2	6.1	9.1	14.4					

URB: Percentage of Urban Population								
98.9	0	0	70.9	0	31.9	97.0	32.5	42.5
78.3	41.3	56.4	69.8	18.6	82	66.3	23.8	30.1
98.9	47.7	93.3	0	31.6	62.3	35.1	45.8	77.4
80.8	13	99.7	50.4	25.7	82.4	96	45.9	90.1
93.2	100	82.3	75.9	98.2	90.8	97.7	81.4	54.8
0	29.3	94.2	66	80.9	67	36.6	23.5	62.4
9.6	94.6	81.9	71.4					

FAMSIZE: Average Number of Members Per Family								
3.15	3.2	2.87	2.93	2.88	3.18	3.16	3.07	3
3.33	3.2	3.06	3.73	3.01	3.28	3.45	2.76	3.14
3.34	3.31	3	2.86	3.04	3.4	2.99	3.01	3.33
3.03	2.93	3.27	3.12	2.99	3.15	3.11	3.57	3.26
3.16	3.11	3.2	2.95	3.13	3.16	3.29	3.07	3.06
2.9	3.03	3.25	3.04	3.24	3.23	3.06	3.03	3.4
2.93	3.42	3.14	3.22					

(*continued*)

TABLE 4.13 (Continued)

EDUC1: Percentage of the Population 25 Years or Older That
Completed Only 8 Years of Education

12	5.7	9.5	13.3	10.1	21.6	8.5	16.2	7.5
22.5	19.1	10.9	35.1	10.6	21.3	26.5	16.3	11.2
16.9	24.8	4.3	10.4	11.3	25.5	14	3.7	18.4
12	7.8	9.3	10.8	8.7	15.3	10.6	28.3	13.2
10.7	15.8	21.5	11.2	8.7	11	10.5	12.7	10
10.8	12.1	10.6	10.7	21.8	17.9	13.9	9.7	28.7
9.7	13.3	15.4	18.8					

EDUC2: Percentage of the Population 25 Years or Older That
Graduated from High School

76	86.1	76.8	71.6	76.3	64.6	81.7	67.1	81.2
63.7	63	76.4	50.9	74.2	62.1	58.7	66.4	73.1
69.8	60.1	89.9	73.7	76.4	60.4	72.3	88.2	71
75.4	82	80.4	77.4	78.4	68.9	78	56.5	71
78	74	62.6	76.8	81.6	79.1	79.5	77.8	75.6
78.1	75.6	76.8	77.6	62	67.7	69.5	74.5	55.8
77.3	75.9	73.5	63.8					

EDUC3: Percentage of the Population 25 Years or Older That
Completed Four Years of College

22.3	32.4	12.6	16.9	13.8	12.3	25.5	10	17.4
15.5	9.3	18	9.6	12.1	11.8	10.1	10.1	11.9
18.4	10.7	38.3	15.4	17.6	10.5	12.3	22.7	19.6
17.8	17.9	22.6	16.7	14.5	12.7	19.2	10.6	13.1
20.9	28.2	11.5	18.9	25.4	24.6	26.3	23.4	12.4
17.9	14	13.7	19.2	11.7	14.4	9	13.6	10.1
13.7	18.1	27	9.3					

UNEMP: Unemployment Rate Among Persons 16 Years or Older

10.8	6.9	7.2	10.5	9.6	8.2	5.8	15.5	9.5
8.9	12.2	7.8	9.6	6	7.7	8.8	10.1	13.6
6	10.2	11.5	3.9	8.3	11	7.5	6.5	9.1
5.5	9.5	4.1	16.9	9	6.8	9	13.5	7.4
7	6.1	10.2	6.9	13.8	3.5	5.8	4.5	7.9
11.9	13.5	8.7	7	12.7	13.4	11.7	17.6	8.6
12.5	5.4	9.3	16.6					

TABLE 4.13 (Continued)

MEDINC: Median Family Income in Thousands of Dollars								
22.863	17.24	18.065	16.301	17.909	17.842	26.513	15.911	20.182
18.399	16.65	18.479	16.659	18.366	18.78	16.164	13.522	17.563
21.135	17.327	29.721	15.833	17.695	16.563	15.617	20.215	20.005
22.426	18.842	25.919	21.662	17.227	18.682	20.949	18.937	20.039
20.306	20.911	19.12	18.198	27.279	21.63	26.662	20.734	17.024
18.221	16.686	21.606	21.269	18.656	18.545	15.849	16.11	16.172
16.907	23.612	20.495	13.751					

Source: Data compiled by Susan Wong.

TABLE 4.14 Data on Deaths Due to Coronary Heart Disease

CHD: Death Rate (Per Million Population) Due to Coronary Heart Disease in the U.S. During Each of the Years 1947–1980								
321.2	322.7	349.1	355.5	355.8	356.4	360.2	347.5	355.8
350.5	369.1	367.9	363.4	369	362.6	370.3	375.4	365.8
367.4	371.2	364.5	372.6	366	362	361.5	361.2	360.8
349.2	336.2	337.2	332.3	334.3	333.1	336		

CAL: Per Capita Consumption of Calcium Per Day (in Grams)								
1.06	1.02	1.02	1.03	1.03	1.04	1.03	1.03	1.04
1.03	1.03	1.02	1.03	0.99	0.99	0.98	0.96	0.96
0.94	0.95	0.95	0.93	0.94	0.93	0.94	0.94	0.95
0.92	0.92	0.95	0.94	0.93	0.9	0.91		

UNEMP: Percent of Civilian Labor Force Unemployed								
3.9	3.8	5.9	5.3	3.3	3.1	2.9	5.6	4.4
4.2	4.3	6.8	5.5	5.6	6.7	5.6	5.7	5.2
4.5	3.8	3.8	3.6	3.5	4.9	5.9	5.6	4.9
5.6	8.5	7.7	7.1	6.1	5.8	7.1		

CIG: Per Capita Consumption of Cigarettes Measured in Pounds of Tobacco, Using 339 Cigarettes Per Pound of Tobacco								
9.16	9.35	9.33	9.36	9.98	10.41	10.46	9.73	9.48
9.34	9.2	9.45	9.45	9.65	9.85	9.68	9.7	9.2
9.45	9.27	9.12	8.65	8.2	7.78	7.7	7.95	7.94
7.8	7.75	7.44	7.07	7	6.75	7.06		

(continued)

TABLE 4.14 (Continued)

	EDFAT:	Per Capita Intake of Edible Fats and Oil, Measured in Pounds (Includes Lard, Margarine, and Butter)						
42	42.6	42.6	45.9	42.1	44.1	44.1	45.4	45.9
45.3	44.4	45.3	46.2	45.4	45.2	45.7	46.1	47.3
48.5	49.6	49.2	51	51.5	53.3	52.2	54.2	54.4
53.5	53.4	56.1	54.4	56	55.8	56.5		

	MEAT:	Per Capita Intake of Meat in Pounds (Includes Beef, Veal, Pork, Lamb, and Mutton)						
155.3	145.5	144.6	144.6	138	146	155.3	154.7	162.8
166.7	159.1	151.6	159.5	161.4	161	163.1	169.3	174.8
166.7	170.5	177.5	182.7	181.1	186.3	191.8	189	175.7
188	182.4	194.8	193	182.7	177.8	180.2		

	SPIRITS:	Per Capita Consumption of Distilled Spirits in Gallons						
1.28	1.06	1.02	1.02	1.23	1	1.1	1.12	1.07
1.13	1.17	1.12	1.14	1.2	1.19	1.23	1.25	1.28
1.35	1.43	2.29	2.37	2.48	2.61	2.63	2.84	2.81
2.9	2.85	2.36	2.03	2.88	2.7	2.9		

	BEER:	Per Capita Consumption of Malted Liquor in Gallons						
18.08	18.58	18.05	17.41	16.97	16.94	16.71	16.68	16.13
16.04	15.54	15.22	15.28	15.53	15.04	15.26	15.17	15.74
16.19	16.21	26.27	25.88	26.42	28.35	28.38	29.43	29.68
31	31.46	31.58	32.07	32.9	34	34.9		

	WINE:	Per Capita Consumption of Wine in Gallons						
0.77	0.79	0.85	0.93	0.87	0.85	0.9	0.86	0.89
0.89	0.89	0.89	0.89	0.9	0.91	0.91	0.92	0.95
0.95	0.98	1.46	1.51	1.59	1.7	1.92	2.16	2.31
2.26	2.28	2.29	2.36	2.59	2.6	2.65		

Entries in a row are for consecutive time periods.
Source: Data compiled by Jennifer Whisenand.

TABLE 4.15 Data on Cable Television Market

SUB	HOME	INST	SVC	TV	AGE	AIR	Y
105	350	14.95	10	16	11.83	13	9839
90	255.631	15	7.5	15	11.42	11	10606
14	31	15	7	11	7.33	9	10455
11.7	34.84	10	7	22	6.92	10	8958
46	153.434	25	10	20	26	12	11741
11.217	26.621	15	7.66	18	8.83	8	9378
12	18	15	7.5	12	13.08	8	10433
6.428	9.324	15	7	17	5.58	7	10167
20.1	32	10	5.6	10	12.42	8	9218
8.5	28	15	6.5	6	4.92	6	10519
1.6	8	17.5	7.5	8	4.08	6	10025
1.1	5	15	8.95	9	4.25	9	9714
4.355	15.204	10	7	7	10.67	7	9294
78.91	97.889	24.95	9.49	12	17.58	7	9784
19.6	93	20	7.5	9	8.08	7	8173
1	3	9.95	10	13	0.17	6	8967
1.65	2.6	25	7.55	6	13.25	5	10133
13.4	18.284	15.5	6.3	11	12.67	5	9361
18.708	55	15	7	16	5.25	6	9085
1.352	1.7	20	5.6	6	15	6	10067
170	270	15	8.75	15	17	5	8908
15.388	46.54	15	8.73	9	6.83	6	9632
6.555	20.417	5.95	5.95	10	5.67	6	8995
40	120	25	6.5	10	7	5	7787
19.9	46.39	15	7.5	9	11.25	7	8890
2.45	14.5	9.95	6.25	6	2.92	4	8041
3.762	9.5	20	6.5	6	2.17	5	8605
24.882	81.98	18	7.5	8	7.08	4	8639
21.187	39.7	20	6	9	12.17	4	8781
3.487	4.113	10	6.85	11	13.08	4	8551
3	8	10	7.95	9	0.17	6	9306
42.1	99.75	9.95	5.73	8	7.67	5	8346
20.35	33.379	15	7.5	8	10.33	4	8803
23.15	35.5	17.5	6.5	8	12.25	5	8942

(continued)

TABLE 4.15 (*Continued*)

SUB	HOME	INST	SVC	TV	AGE	AIR	Y
9.866	34.775	15	8.25	11	2	4	8591
42.608	64.84	10	6	11	13.08	6	9163
10.371	30.556	20	7.5	8	1	6	7683
5.164	16.5	14.95	6.95	8	4	5	7924
31.15	70.515	9.95	7	10	4.67	4	8454
18.35	42.04	20	7	6	3	4	8429

Source: Data compiled by David Andersen,

TABLE 4.16 Data on Early Retirement and Its Determinants

RETRD	HLTH	MSSEC	MPUBAS	UNEMP	DEP	RACE
14.9	6.2	3678	1875	7.7	32.6	26.6
15.6	1.6	3465	2541	9.5	38.9	21.6
13.8	4.5	4399	2313	5.8	29.9	17.1
16.7	7.6	3684	1854	6.8	31.7	16.7
11.3	4.3	4187	3003	6.6	27.6	23.2
5.7	2.8	3943	2322	4.9	30.9	10.8
9.6	3	4392	3045	4.9	29.9	9.5
12.3	3.8	4210	2402	6.6	30.8	17.5
13	5.1	3715	2988	6.5	12.6	72.8
15	5.2	4395	2390	4.9	23.9	15.9
11.3	2.6	3964	3079	4.5	35.2	64
9.7	3.5	4082	2194	7.9	36.2	4.4
7.9	3.7	4225	2058	7.5	33.3	8.5
7	3.2	4059	2504	5.2	32.7	2.7
7.1	3.3	4109	2316	4	31.2	8.4
18.2	7.1	3809	2212	8.9	34.5	7.6
15.8	5.4	3618	2176	5.8	33.3	29.8
13.8	5.1	3905	2083	7.8	33	1
13.4	3.9	4052	2462	5.8	30.6	24.3
9.8	3.6	4118	2680	4.8	28.4	6.1
8.5	2.6	4006	2493	5.5	33.5	3.3
17.3	6.9	3449	1984	7.2	32.8	34.9
10.8	4.4	4013	2002	6.8	30.2	11.3

TABLE 4.16 (Continued)

RETRD	HLTH	MSSEC	MPUBAS	UNEMP	DEP	RACE
10.5	3.1	4007	2219	8.7	33.7	5.8
5.4	2.5	3933	2400	3.6	32.6	4.8
9	2.9	4050	2330	6.2	27.1	11.9
7.5	3.3	4025	2190	4.7	32.7	1.1
14.8	4.4	3854	2225	7.1	34.7	24.9
11.9	5.4	3628	2054	5.6	31.8	23.7
6.6	2.3	3815	2139	5.6	35.6	4.2
12.1	5.5	3867	2336	4.4	31.4	13.8
11.4	4.1	4225	2474	8.5	28.9	5.3
12.3	4.8	4350	2630	7.8	29.9	9.7
6.3	4.6	4203	2629	7.3	28.4	5.1
12.5	5.4	3636	1934	6.2	34	30.2
7	2.5	3811	2181	5.4	33.6	7.3
14.2	6.2	3750	1874	7.4	31.8	15.8
6	2.7	4219	2541	5.4	42.6	5.3
10.6	4.2	4061	2541	6.3	32.5	0.8
16.1	4.6	3818	2198	4.7	31.5	20.3
6.7	3.7	4180	2672	7.6	29.6	8.2
18.7	7.5	4185	2337	8.8	33.8	3.6
8.3	2.9	4322	2834	6.7	33.1	5.5
7.7	2.1	3931	2196	4.3	36.5	4.7

Source: Data compiled by David Andersen.

4.A APPENDIX

Miscellaneous Derivations

A three-variable regression model relates the dependent variable Y to a constant term and to the two independent variables X_2 and X_3. The formal model is

$$Y_t = \beta_1 + \beta_2 X_{t2} + \beta_3 X_{t3} + u_t \tag{4.A.1}$$

Taking the mean of each term in the model we have

$$\bar{Y} = \beta_1 + \beta_2 \bar{X}_2 + \beta_3 \bar{X}_3 + \bar{u} \tag{4.A.2}$$

Subtracting this from (4.A.1), we obtain the *model in deviation form* as

$$y_t = \beta_2 x_{t2} + \beta_3 x_{t3} + e_t \tag{4.A.3}$$

where $y_t = Y_t - \bar{Y}$, $x_{t2} = X_{t2} - \bar{X}_2$, $x_{t3} = X_{t3} - \bar{X}_3$, and $e_t = u_t - \bar{u}$. The lowercase letters indicate that the variables are deviations from the respective means. The advantage in expressing the model in deviation form is that there are only two parameters (β_2 and β_3) to estimate. If $\hat{\beta}_1$, $\hat{\beta}_2$, and $\hat{\beta}_3$ are the estimates of the regression coefficients, $\hat{\beta}_1$ is estimated as

$$\hat{\beta}_1 = \bar{Y} - \hat{\beta}_2 \bar{X}_2 - \hat{\beta}_3 \bar{X}_3$$

An estimate of the residual term is

$$\hat{u}_t = Y_t - \hat{\beta}_1 - \hat{\beta}_2 X_{t2} - \hat{\beta}_3 X_{t3}$$

The OLS procedure minimizes the error sum of squares $\text{ESS} = \sum \hat{u}_t^2$ with respect to $\hat{\beta}_1$, $\hat{\beta}_2$, and $\hat{\beta}_3$. This is equivalent to (not proven) minimizing $\sum \hat{e}_t^2 = \sum (y_t - \hat{\beta}_2 x_{t2} - \hat{\beta}_3 x_{t3})^2$. Setting to zero the partial derivatives of this with respect to $\hat{\beta}_2$ and $\hat{\beta}_3$, it is easy to verify that the conditions are

$$\sum x_{t2} \hat{e}_t = 0 = \sum x_{t2}(y_t - \hat{\beta}_2 x_{t2} - \hat{\beta}_3 x_{t3})$$
$$\sum x_{t3} \hat{e}_t = 0 \sum x_{t3}(y_t - \hat{\beta}_2 x_{t2} - \hat{\beta}_3 x_{t3})$$

This gives the following two normal equations (ignoring the t-subscript).

$$\hat{\beta}_2 \sum x_2^2 + \hat{\beta}_3 \sum x_2 x_3 = \sum y x_2 \tag{4.A.4}$$
$$\hat{\beta}_2 \sum x_2 x_3 + \hat{\beta}_3 \sum x_3^2 = \sum y x_3 \tag{4.A.5}$$

Using a simplifying notation, this can be rewritten as follows:

$$\hat{\beta}_2 S_{22} + \hat{\beta}_3 S_{23} = S_{y2} \tag{4.A.6}$$
$$\hat{\beta}_2 S_{23} + \hat{\beta}_3 S_{33} = S_{y3} \tag{4.A.7}$$

where

$$S_{22} = \sum x_{t2}^2 = \sum (X_{t2} - \bar{X}_2)^2 \qquad (4.A.8)$$

$$S_{23} = \sum x_{t2}x_{t3} = \sum (X_{t2} - \bar{X}_2)(X_{t3} - \bar{X}_3) \qquad (4.A.9)$$

$$S_{33} = \sum x_{t3}^2 = \sum (X_{t3} - \bar{X}_3)^2 \qquad (4.A.10)$$

$$S_{y2} = \sum y_t x_{t2} = \sum (Y_t - \bar{Y})(X_{t2} - \bar{X}_2) \qquad (4.A.11)$$

$$S_{y3} = \sum y_t x_{t3} = \sum (Y_t - \bar{Y})(X_{t3} - \bar{X}_3) \qquad (4.A.12)$$

The solutions to (4.A.6) and (4.A.7) are

$$\hat{\beta}_2 = (S_{y2}S_{33} - S_{y3}S_{23})/\Delta \qquad (4.A.13)$$

$$\hat{\beta}_3 = (S_{y3}S_{22} - S_{y2}S_{23})/\Delta \qquad (4.A.14)$$

where

$$\Delta = S_{22}S_{33} - S_{23}^2 \qquad (4.A.15)$$

The computation of the variance of the $\hat{\beta}$s is postponed to Appendix 5.A.

4.A.2 More on Model Selection Criteria

In this section we explore special cases in which one or more of the model selection criteria presented in Section 4.4 become superfluous. After an initial model has been estimated, an investigator typically drops one or more variables that are very insignificant. This might increase or decrease $\bar{R}^2$. If it increases $\bar{R}^2$, then we can show that GCV and RICE will both go down. In other words, a model with fewer parameters selected based on $\bar{R}^2$ would also be superior under the other two criteria. This assertion need not be true if $\bar{R}^2$ decreases.

Property 4.A.1

> If SGMASQ decreases (that is, $\bar{R}^2$ increases) when one or more variables are dropped, then GCV and RICE will also decrease, making these criteria redundant.

PROOF Define $\lambda = \text{ESS}/T$ and $\mu = k/T$, where T is the number of observations, k is the number of coefficients estimated (including the constant term) and ESS is the sum of squares of the estimated residuals. Let λ_1, μ_1 denote the values for the initial regression and λ_2, μ_2 be the values for the second regression, in which some variables have been dropped.

$$\text{Given:} \quad \mu_2 < \mu_1 \quad \text{and} \quad \text{SGMASQ}_2 < \text{SGMASQ}_1$$

Because $\text{SGMASQ} = \lambda/(1 - \mu)$ (see Table 4.3), it follows that $\lambda_2/(1 - \mu_2) < \lambda_1/(1 - \mu_1)$. Also, $\text{GCV} = \text{SGMASQ}/(1 - \mu)$. Hence,

$$\text{GCV}_2 = \text{SGMASQ}_2 \frac{1}{1 - \mu_2} < \text{SGMASQ}_1 \frac{1}{1 - \mu_2}$$

Since SGMASQ $= (1 - \mu)$ GCV, we have

$$\text{GCV}_2 < \text{GCV}_1 \frac{1 - \mu_1}{1 - \mu_2} < \text{GCV}_1 \qquad \text{because } \mu_2 < \mu_1.$$

Similarly, RICE $= \text{SGMASQ}(1 - \mu)/(1 - 2\mu)$ and hence,

$$\text{RICE}_2 = \text{SGMASQ}_2 \frac{1 - \mu_2}{1 - 2\mu_2} < \text{SGMASQ}_1 \frac{1 - \mu_2}{1 - 2\mu_2}$$

Because SGMASQ $= \text{RICE}(1 - 2\mu)/(1 - \mu)$,

$$\text{RICE}_2 < \text{RICE}_1 \left(\frac{1 - 2\mu_1}{1 - \mu_1} \frac{1 - \mu_2}{1 - 2\mu_2} \right)$$

RICE is defined only if $T > 2k$ and hence $1 - 2\mu > 0$. It can be shown that the expression in parentheses is less than 1. The condition for that is

$$(1 - 2\mu_1)(1 - \mu_2) < (1 - 2\mu_2)(1 - \mu_1)$$
$$1 - \mu_2 - 2\mu_1 + 2\mu_1\mu_2 < 1 - \mu_1 - 2\mu_2 + 2\mu_1\mu_2$$

Because $\mu_2 < \mu_1$, we readily see that the condition is satisfied. Hence, $\text{RICE}_2 < \text{RICE}_1$. It follows from this that both GCV and RICE are redundant because any model with fewer parameters superior due to SGMASQ or $\bar{R}^2$ will automatically be superior under GCV and RICE. This need not be the case if $\bar{R}^2$ decreases when variables are dropped. □

Practice Problem

4.A.1   Show that GCV and RICE are superfluous also when $\bar{R}^2$ decreases when variables are added.

Note from Table 4.3 that AIC, HQ, and SCHWARZ are closely related. We will presently show that in some circumstances AIC makes the other two redundant.

Property 4.A.2   Suppose the value of AIC decreases when some variables are dropped. Then the value of SCHWARZ will also decrease provided there are at least 8 observations. Similarly, the value of HQ will decrease provided there are at least 16 observations.

PROOF   Taking the logarithms of AIC, HQ, and SCHWARZ and using the same notation as before, we have the following relations:

$$\ln \text{AIC} = \ln \lambda + 2\mu$$
$$\ln \text{SCHWARZ} = \ln \lambda + \mu \ln T$$
$$\ln \text{HQ} = \ln \lambda + 2\mu \ln(\ln T)$$
$$\ln \text{SCHWARZ} = \ln \text{AIC} - 2\mu + \mu \ln T = \ln \text{AIC} + \mu(\ln T - 2)$$

Because $AIC_2 < AIC_1$,

$$\ln SCHWARZ_2 = \ln AIC_2 + \mu_2(\ln T - 2) < \ln AIC_1 + \mu_2(\ln T - 2)$$

Substituting for AIC_1 in terms of $SCHWARZ_1$, we have

$$\ln SCHWARZ_2 < \ln SCHWARZ_1 + (\mu_2 - \mu_1)(\ln T - 2)$$

When variables are dropped, $\mu_2 < \mu_1$. If $\ln T > 2$, the second term will be negative, making $\ln SCHWARZ_2$ smaller than $\ln SCHWARZ_1$. The required condition is therefore $\ln T > 2$; that is, $T > e^2$. If $T \geq 8$, this condition will be satisfied. The proof for HQ is similar and is as follows:

$$\ln HQ = \ln AIC - 2\mu + 2\mu \ln(\ln T) = \ln AIC + 2\mu[\ln(\ln T) - 1]$$

As before, $AIC_2 < AIC_1$ and hence

$$\ln HQ_2 < \ln AIC_1 + 2\mu_2[\ln(\ln T) - 1]$$

This means that

$$\ln HQ_2 < \ln HQ_1 + 2(\mu_2 - \mu_1)[\ln(\ln T) - 1]$$

Because $\mu_2 < \mu_1$, the required condition for $\ln HQ_2$ to be less than $\ln HQ_1$ is that $\ln(\ln T) > 1$; that is, that $T > e^e$. If $T \geq 16$, this condition is satisfied. $\square$

 Practice Problem

4.A.2   Show that if variables are added and AIC increases, SCHWARZ is redundant if $T \geq 8$ and HQ is redundant if $T \geq 16$.

Property 4.A.3

> Suppose the value of RICE increases when some variables are dropped. Then SHIBATA will also increase.

PROOF

$$SHIBATA = \lambda(1 + 2\mu) = RICE(1 - 4\mu^2)$$

Therefore,

$$SHIBATA_2 = RICE_2(1 - 4\mu_2^2) > RICE_1(1 - 4\mu_2^2)$$

because $RICE_2 > RICE_1$. Also, $RICE = SHIBATA/(1 - 4\mu^2)$. Hence,

$$SHIBATA_2 > SHIBATA_1 \frac{1 - 4\mu_2^2}{1 - 4\mu_1^2} > SHIBATA_1$$

provided $(1 - 4\mu_2^2) > (1 - 4\mu_1^2)$. It is readily seen that this condition is satisfied because $\mu_2 < \mu_1$. Therefore SHIBATA also increases. $\square$

 Practice Problem

4.A.3   Show that if RICE drops when variables are added, then so will SHIBATA.

4.A.3 Bias Due to the Omission of a Relevant Variable

The true and the estimated models are

$$\text{True model:} \qquad Y_t = \beta_1 + \beta_2 X_{t2} + \beta_3 X_{t3} + u_t$$

$$\text{Estimated model:} \qquad Y_t = \beta_1 + \beta_2 X_{t2} + v_t$$

OLS estimates of the parameters of the estimated model are given by [see equations (3.3) and (3.7)]:

$$\hat{\beta}_2 = S_{y2}/S_{22} \qquad \text{and} \qquad \hat{\beta}_1 = \bar{Y} - \hat{\beta}_2 \bar{X}_2 \qquad (4.A.16)$$

where S_{y2} and S_{22} are defined in equations (4.A.11) and (4.A.8). The expected value of $\hat{\beta}_2$ is given by $E(S_{y2})/S_{22}$, because S_{22} is nonrandom:

$$S_{y2} = \sum (Y_t - \bar{Y})(X_{t2} - \bar{X}_2) = \sum Y_t (X_{t2} - \bar{X}_2) - \sum \bar{Y}(X_{t2} - \bar{X}_2)$$
$$= \sum Y_t (X_{t2} - \bar{X}_2)$$

because $\bar{Y}$ can be taken out of the summation and $\sum (X_{t2} - \bar{X}_2) = 0$ by Property 3.A.3. Substitute for Y_t from the true model (because that is the true process by which Y_t is generated):

$$S_{y2} = \sum (X_{t2} - \bar{X}_2)(\beta_1 + \beta_2 X_{t2} + \beta_3 X_{t3} + u_t)$$
$$= 0 + \beta_2 \sum (X_{t2} - \bar{X}_2)X_{t2} + \beta_3 \sum (X_{t2} - \bar{X}_2)X_{t3} + \sum (X_{t2} - \bar{X}_2)u_t$$

The first term is zero because of Property 3.A.3. The second term is

$$\sum (X_{t2} - \bar{X}_2)X_{t2} = \sum (X_{t2} - \bar{X}_2)(X_{t2} - \bar{X}_2 + \bar{X}_2)$$
$$= \sum (X_{t2} - \bar{X}_2)^2 + \bar{X}_2 \sum (X_{t2} - \bar{X}_2) = \sum (X_{t2} - \bar{X}_2)^2$$

because the second term is zero. By proceeding similarly,

$$\sum (X_{t2} - \bar{X}_2)X_{t3} = \sum (X_{t2} - \bar{X}_2)(X_{t3} - \bar{X}_3)$$

Using these results we get

$$S_{y2} = \beta_2 \sum (X_{t2} - \bar{X}_2)^2 + \beta_3 \sum (X_{t2} - \bar{X}_2)(X_{t3} - \bar{X}_3) + \sum (X_{t2} - \bar{X}_2)u_t$$
$$= \beta_2 S_{22} + \beta_3 S_{23} + S_{u2}$$

where the notation for the S-terms is similar to the ones given in equations (4.A.8) through (4.A.12). Because X_2 and X_3 are nonrandom and uncorrelated with u, and $E(u) = 0$, then

$$E(S_{y2}) = \beta_2 S_{22} + \beta_3 S_{23} + E(S_{u2}) = \beta_2 S_{22} + \beta_3 S_{23}$$

It follows from this that

$$E(\hat{\beta}_2) = \beta_2 + \beta_3 \left[\frac{S_{23}}{S_{22}} \right]$$

Because $\beta_3 \neq 0$, $\hat{\beta}_2$ will be biased unless $S_{23} = 0$—that is, unless X_2 and X_3 are uncorrelated. This proves Property 4.5a for the models used here. The omitted variable bias is given by $\beta_3(S_{23}/S_{22})$. The direction of the bias depends on whether

β_2 is positive and whether X_2 and X_3 are positively or negatively correlated. As the sample size increases indefinitely, $\hat{\beta}_2$ will not converge to β_2 (if $S_{23} \neq 0$) and hence the estimator is not consistent.

From equation (4.A.16), $\hat{\beta}_1 = \bar{Y} - \hat{\beta}_2 \bar{X}_2$, and hence $E(\hat{\beta}_1) = E(\bar{Y}) - \bar{X}_2 E(\hat{\beta}_2)$. Because $\bar{Y} = \beta_1 + \beta_2 \bar{X}_2 + \beta_3 \bar{X}_3 + \bar{u}$, $E(\bar{Y}) = \beta_1 + \beta_2 \bar{X}_2 + \beta_3 \bar{X}_3$. Substituting for this and for the expectation of β_2, we get,

$$E(\hat{\beta}_1) = \beta_1 + \beta_2 \bar{X}_2 + \beta_3 \bar{X}_3 - \bar{X}_2 \left(\beta_2 + \beta_3 \frac{S_{23}}{S_{22}} \right)$$

$$= \beta_1 + \beta_3 \left(\bar{X}_3 - \bar{X}_2 \frac{S_{23}}{S_{22}} \right)$$

We note from this that the necessary and sufficient condition for $\hat{\beta}_1$ to be unbiased is that $[\bar{X}_3 - \bar{X}_2(S_{23}/S_{22})] = 0$. X_2 and X_3 being uncorrelated is not sufficient to guarantee the unbiasedness of the estimate of the intercept term. In addition, the mean of X_3 must be zero. From the expected values of $\hat{\beta}_1$ and $\hat{\beta}_2$ we note that they capture part of the effects of the omitted variable X_3. This point is significant and should be emphasized. Because of this result, one may find that the numerical value of a regression coefficient is quite different from any prior notions we may have about the magnitude. This indicates that the coefficient in question represents not only the effect of the corresponding variable, but also that of an omitted variable that is correlated with the included variable.

Kmenta (1986, p. 394) has shown that even if $S_{23} = 0$, the estimated variance of $\hat{\beta}_2(s_{\hat{\beta}_2}^2)$ is positively biased; that is, $E[s_{\hat{\beta}_2}^2] = \text{Var}(\hat{\beta}_2) + Q$, where Q is nonnegative. Therefore, the usual tests of hypotheses are no longer valid. The consequences of omitting a relevant variable are therefore quite serious.

4.A.4   Proof of Property 4.6

The estimated model is

$$Y_t = \beta_1 + \beta_2 X_{t2} + \beta_3 X_{t3} + v_t$$

From equations (4.A.13) and (4.A.14)—repeated here along with (4.A.15)—the OLS estimates for β_2 and β_3 are

$$\hat{\beta}_2 = (S_{y2} S_{33} - S_{y3} S_{23})/\Delta \qquad (4.A.13)$$

$$\hat{\beta}_3 = (S_{y3} S_{22} - S_{y2} S_{23})/\Delta \qquad (4.A.14)$$

where

$$\Delta = S_{22} S_{33} - S_{23}^2 \qquad (4.A.15)$$

To check whether $\hat{\beta}_2$ is unbiased or not, we first need the *true* expectations of S_{y2} and S_{y3}. The true model is (in deviation form)

$$y_t = \beta_2 x_{t2} + u_t - \bar{u}$$

Substituting for y_t from the true model into S_{y2} we have

$$S_{y2} = \sum y_t x_{t2} = \sum x_{t2}(\beta_2 x_{t2} + u_t - \bar{u}) = \beta_2 S_{22} + S_{u2}$$
$$E(S_{y2}) = \beta_2 S_{22}$$

because x_{t2} is nonrandom or given and $E(S_{u2}) = 0$. The true specification must be used because y_t is generated by it and not by the estimated equation. In a similar manner,

$$S_{y3} = \sum y_t x_{t3} = \sum x_{t3}(\beta_2 x_{t2} + u_t - \bar{u}) = \beta_2 S_{23} + S_{u3}$$
$$E(S_{y3}) = \beta_2 S_{23}$$

Taking the expectations of equations (4.A.13) and (4.A.14) and substituting for $E(S_{y2})$ and $E(S_{y3})$, we obtain

$$E(\hat{\beta}_2) = [S_{33}\beta_2 S_{22} - S_{23}\beta_2 S_{23}]/\Delta = \beta_2$$
$$E(\hat{\beta}_3) = [S_{22}\beta_2 S_{23} - S_{23}\beta_2 S_{22}]/\Delta = 0$$

Therefore, $\hat{\beta}_2$ is unbiased and the expectation of $\hat{\beta}_3$ is zero, which is the result in Property 4.6a. From the law of large numbers, consistency is easy to establish.

Derivation of the Variance of $\hat{\beta}_2$

The next step is to compute the variance of $\hat{\beta}_2$. We have

$$\text{Var}(S_{y2}) = \text{Var}(\beta_2 S_{22} + S_{u2}) = \text{Var}(S_{u2}) = \sigma^2 S_{22}$$
$$\text{Var}(S_{y3}) = \text{Var}(\beta_2 S_{23} + S_{u3}) = \text{Var}(S_{u3}) = \sigma^2 S_{33}$$
$$\text{Cov}(S_{y2}, S_{y3}) = \text{Cov}(\beta_2 S_{22} + S_{u2}, \beta_2 S_{23} + S_{u3}) = \sigma^2 S_{23}$$

In deriving these, we have made use of the fact that S_{22} and S_{33} can be treated as nonrandom. Using Property 2.7a, we get

$$\text{Var}(\hat{\beta}_2) = [S_{33}^2 \text{Var}(S_{y2}) + S_{23}^2 \text{Var}(S_{y3}) - 2S_{33}S_{23}\text{Cov}(S_{y2}, S_{y3})]/\Delta^2$$
$$= \sigma^2[S_{33}^2 S_{22} + S_{23}^2 S_{33} - 2S_{33}S_{23}S_{23}]/\Delta^2$$
$$= \frac{\sigma^2 S_{33}}{S_{22}S_{33} - S_{23}^2} = \frac{\sigma^2}{S_{22} - (S_{23}^2/S_{33})}$$

Using the fact that r^2, the square of the simple correlation between x_2 and x_3 is defined as $r^2 = S_{23}^2/(S_{22}S_{33})$, the preceding equation can be reduced to

$$\text{Var}(\hat{\beta}_2) = \frac{\sigma^2}{S_{22}(1 - r^2)}$$

thus providing an expression for the variance of $\hat{\beta}_2$.

CHAPTER 5

Multicollinearity

■ There are several consequences of adding new variables to a model, some of which have been pointed out already. First, the residual sum of squares decreases, or equivalently, unadjusted R^2 goes up. However, we lose degrees of freedom because we have to estimate additional parameters. The smaller the degrees of freedom, the lesser the power of a test—that is, the greater the probability of accepting a false hypothesis. There is yet another, potentially serious consequence of adding too many variables to a model. If a model has several variables, it is likely that some of the explanatory variables will be approximately linearly related. This property, known as **multicollinearity**, can drastically alter the results from one model to another, thus making it more difficult to interpret results. We saw several examples of this in Chapter 4. This chapter examines multicollinearity and its consequences in detail. Before presenting a theoretical analysis, it will be useful to examine a few instances of multicollinearity.

5.1 Examples of Multicollinearity

We present two examples in which the addition of apparently sensible variables drastically alters the results. First, we reexamine the housing starts example used in Section 4.7, which relates the number of new housing units started to several aggregate variables; in the second example, we relate the cumulative expenditure for maintaining a car to its age and number of miles driven.

Example 5.1

Let $HOUSING_t$ be the number of housing units (in thousands) started in the United States in the year t, POP_t be the U.S. population in millions, GNP_t be the U.S. gross national product in billions of 1982 dollars, and $INTRATE_t$ be the new home mortgage rate in percent. Using the data in Table 4.11, the following three models were estimated; the results are presented in Table 5.1 (see Practice Computer Session 5.1).

Model A: $HOUSING_t = \alpha_0 + \alpha_1 INTRATE_t + \alpha_2 POP_t + u_{1t}$

Model B: $HOUSING_t = \beta_0 + \beta_1 INTRATE_t + \beta_2 GNP_t + u_{2t}$

Model C: $HOUSING_t = \gamma_0 + \gamma_1 INTRATE_t + \gamma_2 POP_t + \gamma_3 GNP_t + u_{3t}$

We would expect the number of housing units to be influenced both by the size of the population and the level of income. Yet in Model C, which has both these variables, the t-statistics are low and insignificant. When POP or GNP is entered alone, however, the corresponding coefficient is very highly significant. A Wald F-test on excluding POP and GNP from Model C yields an F-statistic of 6.42, which is significant even at 1 percent, indicating that they are jointly significant although individually insignificant. There is thus an apparent contradiction in conclusion. A second result is that the coefficients for POP and GNP in Model C are very different from those in Models A and B. The INTRATE coefficient, however, is less volatile. Although a priori we thought that both population and income belong in the model, the results indicate that when they are present together, drastic changes occur. This is due to the fact that population, gross national product, and interest rate are very highly correlated. The pairwise correlation coefficients for GNP, POP, and INTRATE are

$$r(GNP, POP) = 0.99 \qquad r(GNP, INTRATE) = 0.88$$

$$r(POP, INTRATE) = 0.91$$

TABLE 5.1 Estimates of Housing Starts Relations

Variables	Model A	Model B	Model C
CONSTANT	−3812.93 (−2.40)	687.90 (1.80)	−1315.75 (−0.27)
INTRATE	−198.40 (−3.87)	−169.66 (−3.87)	−184.751 (−3.18)
POP	33.82 (3.61)		14.90 (0.41)
GNP		0.91 (3.64)	0.52 (0.54)
d.f.	20	20	19
$\bar{R}^2$	0.371	0.375	0.348
MSE*	75,029	74,557	77,801

* MSE is mean squared forecast errors ($= \hat{\sigma}^2$).

Thus there is an almost perfect linear relationship between GNP and POP, and a near perfect relationship with INTRATE also. As will be shown later, the observed changes in regression coefficients and t-statistics are a direct result of these high correlations. It should be emphasized that a high correlation between the dependent variable and a given independent variable not only does not cause any problem but is in fact highly desirable. It is the close linear relationships among *independent variables* that can affect model results. □

Example 5.2

Let E_t be the cumulative expenditure at time t on the maintenance (excluding gasoline) for a given automobile, MILES$_t$ be the cumulative mileage in thousands of miles, and, WEEKS$_t$ be its age in weeks since the original purchase. Consider the following three alternative models:

Model A: $E_t = \alpha_0 + \alpha_1 \text{WEEKS}_t + u_{1t}$

Model B: $E_t = \beta_0 + \beta_1 \text{MILES}_t + u_{2t}$

Model C: $E_t = \gamma_0 + \gamma_1 \text{WEEKS}_t + \gamma_2 \text{MILES}_t + u_{3t}$

A car that is driven more will have a greater maintenance expense. Similarly, the older the car the greater the cost of maintaining it. Also, between two cars of the same age, the one with the higher mileage is likely to have the larger maintenance expenditure. We would therefore expect α_1, β_1, γ_1, and γ_2 to be positive. Table 5.2 presents the estimated coefficients and their t-statistics (in parentheses) for the three models, based on actual data for a 1971 Toyota Mark II·station wagon. The data are presented in Table 3.6 (See Practice Computer Session 5.2 for verifying these results.).

It is interesting to note that even though the coefficient for MILES is positive in Model B, it is significantly negative in Model C. Thus, there has been a drastic reversal of the sign. The coefficient for WEEKS has also changed substantially. Second, the t-statistics for WEEKS and MILES are much lower in Model C. Here

TABLE 5.2   Estimated Models of Auto Expenditure

Variables	Model A	Model B	Model C
CONSTANT	−626.24 (−5.98)	−796.07 (−5.91)	7.29 (0.06)
WEEKS	7.35 (22.16)		27.58 (9.58)
MILES		53.45 (18.27)	−151.15 (−7.06)
d.f.	55	55	54
$\bar{R}^2$	0.897	0.856	0.946
MSE*	135,861	190,941	72,010

* MSE is mean squared forecast errors $(=\hat{\sigma}^2)$.

also the reason for the significant change in results is the high correlation between two explanatory variables, in this case WEEKS and MILES, whose correlation coefficient is 0.996.   □

We see from these two examples that high correlation among explanatory variables can make regression coefficients insignificant and/or reverse their signs. Multicollinearity is not limited to just two independent variables. It can, and often does, occur among many independent variables that have an approximate linear relationship.

5.2   Exact Multicollinearity

If two or more independent variables have a linear relationship between or among them, we have **exact** (or **perfect**) **multicollinearity**. In this case there is no unique solution to the normal equations derived from the least squares principle. This point is illustrated with a model with two independent variables, X_2 and X_3, plus the constant. The model is

$$y_t = \beta_1 x_{t2} + \beta_2 x_{t3} + v_t \tag{5.1}$$

in which the constant term is eliminated by expressing each variable as a deviation from its mean (see Section 4.A.1). The corresponding normal equations are as follows (ignoring the t-subscript):

$$\hat{\beta}_2 \sum x_2^2 + \hat{\beta}_3 \sum x_2 x_3 = \sum y x_2 \tag{5.2}$$

$$\hat{\beta}_2 \sum x_2 x_3 + \hat{\beta}_3 \sum x_3^2 = \sum y x_3 \tag{5.3}$$

Let us first consider the simplest case of exact multicollinearity, where $x_3 = 2x_2$. Although one might wonder why an investigator would include x_3 in the model if this is so, Exercise 5.2 presents a case in which this situation might arise inadvertently. Substituting for x_3 in equation (5.3), we get

$$\hat{\beta}_2 \sum x_2(2x_2) + \hat{\beta}_3 \sum x_3(2x_2) = \sum y(2x_2)$$

We readily see that, if we cancel the common factor 2, this equation becomes the same as equation (5.2). Thus the two normal equations are not independent of each other but rather reduce to the same one. A single equation is not enough to obtain a unique solution to the two unknowns $\hat{\beta}_2$ and $\hat{\beta}_3$. Hence, it is not possible to estimate the regression coefficients in the case of exact multicollinearity.

More generally, suppose that x_2 and x_3 were exactly multicollinear with the linear relation $x_3 = ax_2 + b$. Then equation (5.3) could be rewritten as

$$\hat{\beta}_2 \sum x_2 x_3 + \hat{\beta}_3 \sum x_3 x_3 = \sum y x_3$$

or

$$\hat{\beta}_2 \sum x_2(ax_2 + b) + \hat{\beta}_3 \sum x_3(ax_2 + b) = \sum y(ax_2 + b)$$

or

$$a\hat{\beta}_2 \sum x_2^2 + b\hat{\beta}_2 \sum x_2 + a\hat{\beta}_3 \sum x_2 x_3 + b\hat{\beta}_3 \sum x_3 = a \sum y x_2 + b \sum y$$

Because x_1, x_2, and y are deviations from their means, we have, from Property 3.A.1, $\sum x_2 = \sum x_3 = \sum y = 0$. Therefore the preceding equation reduces (after cancelling a) to

$$\hat{\beta}_2 \sum x_2^2 + \hat{\beta}_3 \sum x_2 x_3 = \sum y x_2$$

This is the same as the first normal equation (5.2). In a multiple regression model, if some of the independent variables can be expressed as linear combinations of other independent variables, then the corresponding regression coefficients cannot be estimated. It may, however, be possible for linear combinations of parameters to be estimable.

If an investigator accidentally regresses a model that has exact multicollinearity, most regression programs give an error message of the form "matrix singular" or "exact collinearity encountered." When this happens, one or more of the variables should be dropped from the model. The most frequent case, however, is the situation where a close (but not exact) linear relationship exists. The consequences of this are examined next.

Practice Problem

5.1   Complete Exercises 5.1 and 5.2.

5.3   Near Multicollinearity

Consequences of Ignoring Multicollinearity

Using the notation of Section 4.A.1, the normal equations (5.2) and (5.3) can be solved for the βs as [see equations (4.A.6) through (4.A.15)]

$$\hat{\beta}_2 = \frac{S_{y2}S_{33} - S_{y3}S_{23}}{\Delta} \tag{5.4}$$

$$\hat{\beta}_3 = \frac{S_{y3}S_{22} - S_{y2}S_{23}}{\Delta} \tag{5.5}$$

where

$$\Delta = S_{22}S_{33} - S_{23}^2$$

The following equations have been derived in Appendix 5.A.

$$E(S_{y2}) = \beta_2 S_{22} + \beta_3 S_{23} \tag{5.6}$$

$$E(S_{y3}) = \beta_2 S_{23} + \beta_3 S_{33} \tag{5.7}$$

$$\text{Var}(\hat{\beta}_2) = \frac{\sigma^2 S_{33}}{\Delta} \tag{5.8}$$

$$\text{Var}(\hat{\beta}_3) = \frac{\sigma^2 S_{22}}{\Delta} \tag{5.9}$$

$$\text{Cov}(\hat{\beta}_2, \hat{\beta}_3) = \frac{-\sigma^2 S_{23}}{\Delta} \tag{5.10}$$

Let r be the correlation coefficient between X_1 and X_2 (see equation 2.13). Then by definition, $r^2 = S_{23}^2/(S_{22}S_{33})$. Therefore,

$$\Delta = S_{22}S_{33}(1 - r^2)$$

Using this in the previous equations, we get

$$\text{Var}(\hat{\beta}_2) = \frac{\sigma^2}{S_{22}(1 - r^2)} \tag{5.11}$$

$$\text{Var}(\hat{\beta}_3) = \frac{\sigma^2}{S_{33}(1 - r^2)} \tag{5.12}$$

$$\text{Cov}(\hat{\beta}_2, \hat{\beta}_3) = \frac{-\sigma^2 r}{\sqrt{S_{22}S_{33}}(1 - r^2)} \tag{5.13}$$

Suppose r^2 is very close to 1; that is, r is near ± 1 (**near multicollinearity**). It is evident from equations (5.11) and (5.12) that the variances, and hence the standard errors, of $\hat{\beta}_2$ and $\hat{\beta}_3$ will be very large when r^2 is close to 1. A large variance means a poor precision and a low t-statistic, which results in insignificance. This explains why, in the first example, we found that when both population and GNP were included, their coefficients became insignificant. Second, we see from equation (5.13) that the covariance between the regression coefficients will be huge, in absolute value, if r is close to $+1$ or -1. If the estimates are correlated, each coefficient is capturing part of the effect of the other variable and hence it is difficult to obtain the *separate* effects of X_2 and X_3 on Y. In other words, we cannot hold X_3 constant and increase X_2 alone, because X_3, being correlated with X_2, will also change as a result.

In a model with several variables, the chances of multicollinearity are greater, and therefore interpretation of the results could be more difficult. Polynomial curve fitting could create near multicollinearity problems because terms such as X, X^2, and X^3 are highly correlated. This might result in the insignificance of many of the coefficients, whereas a fit with one of them alone (or with a nonlinear function such as $\ln X$) might produce a significant coefficient.

The danger of multicollinearity is a strong argument against the indiscriminate use of explanatory variables. The importance of theory in formulating models should once again be emphasized. It generally pays to keep a model as simple as possible, at least to start with. With the help of the model selection criteria discussed in Chapter 4, and certain test procedures described in Chapter 7, one can effectively improve the model in a systematic way. Sometimes, however, there may be strong theoretical reasons for including a variable even if multicollinearity might make its coefficient insignificant. This was the case with the wealth variable in the saving behavior application in Section 4.8. The importance of wealth as a determinant of consumption suggests that both variables should be retained in the model even if there is multicollinearity.

Unbiasedness and Other Properties   A natural question that arises is whether multicollinearity invalidates the Gauss–Markhov Theorem, which says that OLS produces best linear unbiased estimators (BLUE). We see from the statement of the Gauss–Markhov Theorem (see Section 3.2) that Assumptions 3.1 through 3.6 are required to prove the theorem. A high correlation among explanatory variables does not violate any of these assumptions. Therefore the OLS estimators are still BLUE. Also, high collinearity has no impact on Assumption 3.7. Therefore, the distribution of the t-statistic is also not affected. By proceeding as we did in Section 3.A.3, we can show that the OLS estimators are still maximum likelihood and are hence consistent. Forecasts are still unbiased and confidence intervals are valid. None of the previous results are therefore affected by multicollinearity. Although the standard errors and t-statistics of regression coefficients are numerically affected, tests based on them are still valid.

While multicollinearity affects individual regression coefficients, its effect on forecasts are often less drastic and may even be beneficial. For example, in Table 5.1 the sample period mean squared error (MSE) of forecasts is presented for each model. Note that, while coefficients vary a great deal across models, MSE does not undergo such a drastic change. The MSE values are also presented in Table 5.2. It is interesting to note that Model C, in which the coefficient for MILES is the reverse of that of Model B, performs considerably better in terms of MSE than either of the other two models. Thus, in this case, the presence of multicollinearity actually helps the forecast performance.

The results of this discussion are summarized in Property 5.1.

Property 5.1

The consequences of ignoring multicollinearity are as follows:

a. If two or more explanatory variables in a multiple regression model are exactly linearly related, then the model cannot be estimated.
b. If some explanatory variables are nearly linearly related, then OLS estimators (and hence forecasts based on them) are still BLUE and MLE and hence are unbiased, efficient, and consistent.
c. The effect of near multicollinearity among explanatory variables is to increase the standard errors of the regression coefficients and reduce the t-statistics, thus making coefficients less significant (and possibly even insignificant). The tests of hypotheses are, however, valid.
d. The covariance between the regression coefficients of a pair of highly correlated variables will be very high, in absolute value, thus making it difficult to interpret individual coefficients.
e. Multicollinearity may not affect the forecasting performance of a model and may possibly even improve it.

Absence of Multicollinearity   For completeness, let us consider the other extreme case, for which $r = 0$—that is, the case for which X_2 and X_3 are uncorrelated (**absence of multicollinearity**) as opposed to perfectly correlated. In this case, $S_{23} = 0$ and hence the two normal equations become

$$S_{22}\hat{\beta}_2 = S_{y2} \quad \text{and} \quad S_{33}\hat{\beta}_2 = S_{y3}$$

It will be recognized that these are the same as the normal equations when Y is regressed *separately* against X_2 and X_3. It is hence evident that when $S_{23} = 0$, the value of $\hat{\beta}_2$, obtained from having both X_2 and X_3 in the model, is *identical* to the value obtained when Y is regressed against a constant term and just X_2. A similar result holds for $\hat{\beta}_3$. The covariance between the two regression coefficients is zero, indicating that the partial effect is entirely due to the variable included and not due to any indirect effect from another included variable. Ideally, we would like r to be close to zero, but in practice this is often not so.

Identifying Multicollinearity

We see from Property 5.1 that multicollinearity is really a problem with the data and not the model per se. In a practical situation, multicollinearity often shows up in a number of ways:

High R^2 with low values for t-statistics: As we see in Exercise 5.3, it is possible to find a situation in which every regression coefficient is insignificant (that is, has low *t*-values), but the Wald *F*-statistic is very highly significant. Similarly, the Wald *F*-value for a group of coefficients may be significant even though individual *t*-values are not.

High values for correlation coefficients: Pairwise correlations among explanatory variables might be high. It is generally a good practice to obtain the correlations between every pair of variables in a regression model and check for high values among explanatory variables. Note that a high correlation coefficient between the dependent variable and an independent variable is not a sign of multicollinearity. In fact such a correlation is highly desired.

Regression coefficients sensitive to specification: Although a high correlation between pairs of independent variables is a sufficient condition for multicollinearity, the converse need not be true. In other words, multicollinearity may be present even though the correlation between two explanatory variables does not appear to be high. This is because three or more variables may be nearly linear. Yet, pairwise correlations may not be high. Kmenta (1986, p. 434) has an example in which three variables are exactly linearly related, but the correlations between any pair of them is no higher than 0.5. In such situations the real evidence of multicollinearity is the observation that regression coefficients are drastically altered (even possibly reversing signs, as in the second example in Section 5.1) when variables are added or dropped.

Formal tests for multicollinearity: Farrar and Glauber (1967) have proposed a group of tests to identify the severity of multicollinearity. The tests consist of a chi-square test, an *F*-test, and a *t*-test. The chi-square test is to identify whether multicollinearity is generally present. This is followed by an *F*-test, to find which variables are causing the multicollinearity; and finally by the *t*-test, to discover the nature of the multicollinearity. These tests are formulated in terms of concepts that involve a knowledge of linear algebra. Interested readers with a background in matrix algebra may want to read their paper.

Belsley, Kuh, and Welsch (1980, Ch. 3) suggest a two-step procedure for testing multicollinearity. The first step is to compute a "condition number" for the matrix of data values. Serious collinearity problems are indicated if this number is over 30. In the second step a "variance decomposition" measure is used. Their method also requires an understanding of linear algebra and is beyond the scope of this book.

These procedures are mentioned only in passing and are quite controversial. Because multicollinearity is a problem with the data and not with a model itself, many econometricians argue that formal tests are either meaningless or not fruitful [see Maddala (1977), p. 186].

Solutions

There is no single solution that will eliminate multicollinearity altogether. A great deal of judgment is required in handling the problem. If an analyst is less interested in interpreting individual coefficients but more interested in forecasting, multicollinearity may not be a serious concern. One can simply ignore it without any dire consequences. Similarly, even with high correlations among independent variables if the regression coefficients are significant and have meaningful signs and magnitudes, one need not be too concerned about multicollinearity. If a coefficient is significant even in the presence of multicollinearity, then that is clearly a robust result.

Eliminating Variables   Because multicollinearity is caused by close relationships among explanatory variables, the surest way to eliminate or reduce the effects of multicollinearity is to drop one or more of the variables from a model. This procedure often improves the standard errors of the remaining coefficients and may make formerly insignificant variables significant, since the elimination of a variable reduces any multicollinearity caused by it. This point is illustrated by Model C of Table 5.1. Eliminating POP, which had the lowest t-statistic (excluding the constant term, which should never be eliminated because it captures the average effects of omitted variables), makes GNP significant, and improves the t-values of the other two coefficients.

Very often investigators include too many variables in a model for fear of otherwise encountering the omitted-variable bias described in Section 4.7. In such a case, the elimination of variables with low t-statistics would generally improve the significance of the remaining variables. What essentially happens in this situation is that the remaining variables are able to capture the effects of the omitted variables with which they are closely associated. There is a danger, however, in dropping too many variabes from the model specification, precisely because that would lead to bias in the estimates. It is generally a good practice to consider the theoretical importance of retaining an insignificant variable if its t-statistic is at least 1 in absolute value.

Using Extraneous Information   The method of using extraneous information is often used in studies on the estimation of demand functions. Time series data on income and the price of a commodity often exhibit a high correlation, which makes estimating the income and price elasticities of demand difficult. A solution to this problem is to estimate the income elasticity from cross-section studies and then use that information in the time series model to estimate the price elasticity. The price elasticity cannot be estimated from the cross-section data because, although consumers differ considerably in income levels, they face basically the same price. Hence there is no variation in price, which is essential for the successful estimation of the price elasticity (refer to the discussion on Assumption 3.3 in Chapter 3). A serious problem with this approach is that the cross-section income elasticity and the time series income elasticity may be measuring entirely different things. This point has been argued by Meyer and Kuh (1957).

Increasing the Sample Size   The procedure of increasing the sample size is sometimes recommended on the ground that such an increase improves the precision of an estimator and hence reduces the adverse effects of multicollinearity. It will be noted from equations (5.11) and (5.12) that, if the sample size increases, then S_{22} and S_{33} will also increase. If the value of r^2, including the new sample, goes down or remains approximately the same, then the variances of $\hat{\beta}_2$ and $\hat{\beta}_3$ will indeed decrease and counteract the effects of multicollinearity. If, however, r^2 goes up substantially, then there may be no benefit to adding to the sample size. Furthermore, an investigator typically collects all the data available (subject to budget and time constraints) and hence adding data may not be feasible as a practical matter.

Other Remedies   A number of methods have been suggested in the literature, most of which are ad hoc, and there is not much agreement among econometricians about their usefulness. Two of these techniques are ridge regression and principal component analysis. They will not be discussed here because they require linear algebra and mathematical statistics beyond the scope of this book. For those with such a background, an excellent treatment of multicollinearity will be found in Judge, Griffiths, Hill, and Lee (1980).

5.4   Applications

Automobile Maintenance Expenditure

It was pointed out that one of the effects of multicollinearity is to change the regression coefficients substantially. If, however, the near linear relationship among the independent variables is taken into account, the differences are not likely to be so large. For example, in the Toyota example, if MILES is regressed against a constant and WEEKS, we get (see Practice Computer Session 5.2).

$$\widehat{\text{MILES}} = 4.191 + 0.134\text{WEEKS}$$
$$\quad\quad\quad (8.74) \quad\;\; (88.11)$$

The t-statistics in parentheses are very highly significant, and the value of $\bar{R}^2$ is 0.993, indicating a near perfect fit. If this relationship is substituted in Model C of Table 5.2, we obtain:

$$\hat{E} = 7.29 + 27.58\text{WEEKS} - 151.15(4.191 + 0.134\text{WEEKS})$$
$$= -626.18 + 7.33\text{WEEKS}$$

which is very close to the values in Model A. Thus, even though Model C appears to be quite different from Model A, when the relationship between the two independent variables MILES and WEEKS is explicitly taken into account, the two models are very close. In practice, however, it is unrealistic to obtain all possible relationships and use them. The solution in such a case is to identify *redundant* variables and delete them from the model.

More on Housing Starts

Table 4.11 contains data on the unemployment rate. We argued before that the unemployment rate is a good index of the business cycle. If the rate is high, utility-maximizing consumers will postpone decisions to purchase houses, and hence the unemployment rate can be expected to have a negative effect on housing demand. A double-log model (for which regression coefficients are elasticities) was estimated, and the results, along with t-statistics in parentheses, are as follows (see Practice Computer Session 5.4 to verify these):

$$\widehat{\text{LH}} = \underset{(0.2)}{4.607} + \underset{(1.2)}{2.914\text{LG}} - \underset{(-0.4)}{3.349\text{LP}} + \underset{(1.0)}{0.319\text{LU}} - \underset{(-3.2)}{1.313\text{LR}}$$

$$\bar{R}^2 = 0.363 \qquad \text{ESS} = 0.53263 \qquad \hat{\sigma}^2 = 0.0296 \qquad \text{d.f.} = 18$$

where LH is the natural logarithm of total new housing units, LG is the logarithm of GNP, LP is the logarithm of population, LU is the logarithm of the unemployment rate, and LR is the logarithm of new home mortgage rates. It should be noted that the $\bar{R}^2$ here is not comparable to those in Table 5.1 because, in this model, the dependent variable is in logarithms whereas in the earlier specification it was linear.

Is there evidence of multicollinearity here? The first thing to note are several unexpected signs. The elasticity for population is negative whereas that for unemployment is positive, both of which are counterintuitive. Second, only interest rate elasticity is significantly different from zero. All the other elasticities have low t-values. As we have prior knowledge that many of the explanatory variables move together, we should suspect the presence of multicollinearity here. To confirm this, we obtain the correlation coefficients for all the independent variables:

LP	LG	LU	LR	
1.000	0.988	0.778	0.946	LP
	1.000	0.691	0.918	LG
		1.000	0.768	LU
			1.000	LR

We find that all the pairwise correlations are high and some of them are near perfect. This is a classic case of multicollinearity. These high correlations indicate that some of the variables might be redundant and hence could be eliminated. The two candidates for elimination are LP and LU, which are insignificant and have unexpected signs. The reestimated model is

$$\widehat{LH} = -4.760 + 1.873LG - 1.229LR$$
$$\underset{(-1.4)}{} \quad \underset{(3.8)}{} \quad \underset{(-4.0)}{}$$

$$\bar{R}^2 = 0.386 \qquad ESS = 0.57105 \qquad \hat{\sigma}^2 = 0.0286 \qquad \text{d.f.} = 20$$

Both LG and LR are now very significant. The Wald F-statistic for omitting LP and LU is given by

$$F_c = \frac{(0.57105 - 0.53263)/2}{0.53263/18} = 0.649$$

It is easy to verify that such a low F is insignificant even at the 10 percent level of significance. Thus, the Wald test accepts the null hypothesis that the regression coefficients for LP and LU are zero.

Have we been successful in eliminating multicollinearity? The answer is no because LG and LR have a correlation of 0.918, which is near perfect. Multicollinearity is therefore still present, but its harmful effect in the form of low t-values has been eliminated. We note that the mean squared forecast errors ($\hat{\sigma}^2$) are almost unchanged. Thus, the forecasting ability of the two models is essentially the same. The regression coefficients, however, are more significant. It is interesting to note that the mortgage interest rate effect is very elastic (that is, is greater than 1 in numerical value) and is practically the same in both models. A 10 percent increase in mortgage rates is expected to reduce housing starts by 12 to 13 percent on average.

 ## Practice Problems
5.2 Rather than drop both LP and LU simultaneously, use your regression program to eliminate only LP and reestimate the model. Does LU become significant now? Should it also be dropped? Is the interest elasticity still robust?

SUMMARY

If there exists an exact linear relationship between two or more explanatory variables, the variables are said to be *exactly multicollinear*. In such a situation the regression coefficients corresponding to these independent variables cannot be uniquely estimated.

If several explanatory variables are nearly multicollinear, OLS estimates are still unbiased, consistent, and BLUE. Therefore, forecasts are also unbiased and consistent. Furthermore, all the tests of hypotheses are valid.

The effect of near multicollinearity is to increase the standard errors of the regression coefficients and lower their t-statistics. This tends to make the coefficients less significant than they would be if multicollinearity were absent. One should therefore be cautious in drawing inferences and not jump to the conclusion that every insignificant variable should be omitted.

If several variables are nearly multicollinear, the covariance between any pair of the regression coefficients is high, indicating that each coefficient is capturing part of the effect of another variable. It is possible to have signs reversed when a new variable is added or deleted. This makes interpretation of an individual regression coefficient more difficult. The partial effect of a single variable is hence hard to measure.

A "kitchen sink" specification, in which every conceivable independent variable is included, is not desirable because multicollinearity might make several or all of them insignificant. It is often more prudent to start with a basic model and perform tests for the inclusion of other variables. Chapter 7 discusses how this can be done in a systematic way.

If a pair of independent variables is uncorrelated, then the regression coefficient of each of them is the same whether or not the other variable is included in the model.

Multicollinearity can be identified by examining the pattern of correlation among explanatory variables. Since time series variables tend to grow together, models based on them are more subject to multicollinearity problems than are cross-section models. If deleting one or more independent variables drastically alters results, multicollinearity is surely the cause.

There is no single solution that will eliminate multicollinearity. If the focus is on forecasting, multicollinearity can frequently be ignored because forecasting ability is often not much affected. If similar variables are present in the model, eliminating redundant ones is recommended. Possible candidates are those with very low t-values. One should, however, bear in mind the omitted-variable bias caused by eliminating important variables. Theory should be used to decide whether a variable should be kept in spite of seeming multicollinearity problems.

Increasing the sample size is also recommended provided the new data has the same or lesser collinearity than the original one. Other remedies such as ridge regression and principal component analysis may be used, but these are ad hoc procedures and there is no consensus among econometricians about their usefulness.

KEY TERMS

Absence of multicollinearity   Near multicollinearity
Exact multicollinearity   Perfect multicollinearity
Multicollinearity

REFERENCES

Belsley, D. A.; Kuh, E.; and Welsch, R. E. *Regression Diagnostics, Identifying Influential Data and Sources of Collinearity.* New York: Wiley, 1980.

Farrar, D. E., and Glauber, R. R. "Multicollinearity in Regression Analysis: The Problem Revisited." *Review of Economics and Statistics* (February 1967).

Judge, George G.; Griffiths, William E.; Hill, R. Carter; and Lee, Tsoung-Chao. *The Theory and Practice of Econometrics.* New York: Wiley, 1985.

Kmenta, Jan. *Elements of Econometrics.* New York: McGraw-Hill, 1986.

Maddala, G. S. *Econometrics.* New York: McGraw-Hill, 1977.

Meyer, John, and Kuh, Edwin. "How Extraneous Are Extraneous Estimates?" *Review of Economics and Statistics* (November 1957).

PRACTICE COMPUTER SESSIONS

5.1 To verify Example 5.1 and Table 5.1, use the data file *data4-11* and the command input file *ps5-1.inp.*

5.2 Commands for Example 5.2 and Table 5.2 are in *ps5-2.inp* and the corresponding data file is *data3-6.*

5.3 The first application in Section 5.4 also uses the data file *data3-6* but the single command in *ps5-3.inp.*

5.4 The second application in Section 5.4 uses *data4-11* and the input file *ps5-4.inp.*

EXERCISES

5.1 Suppose that the exact relation between X_2 and X_3 is of the form $x_2 + x_3 = 1$. Show, by proceeding as in Section 5.2, that the second normal equation reduces to the first.

5.2 Suppose you regress Y against X and X^2 in a double-log formulation; that is, you regress ln Y against $X_1 = \ln X$ and $X_2 = \ln(X^2)$. Show that here also the second normal equation degenerates into the first one, thus making it impossible to solve for the regression coefficients.

†5.3 Using 15 years of annual data, planners in San Diego County estimated the following model for water consumption:

$$\widehat{\text{SDWATER}} = -326.9 + 0.305\text{SDHOUSE} + 0.363\text{SDPOP}$$
$$\underset{(-1.7)}{} \quad \underset{(0.9)}{} \quad \underset{(1.4)}{}$$
$$-0.005\text{SDPCY} - 17.87\text{PRWATR} - 1.123\text{SDRAIN}$$
$$\underset{(-0.6)}{} \quad \underset{(-1.2)}{} \quad \underset{(-0.8)}{}$$
$$n = 15 \quad \bar{R}^2 = 0.93 \quad F = 38.9$$

SDWATR = total water consumption (million cubic meters)

SDHOUSE = total number of housing units (thousands)

SDPOP = total population (thousands)

SDPCY = per capita income (dollars)

PRWATR = price of water (dollars/100 cubic meters)

SDRAIN = rainfall in inches

The values in parentheses are t-statistics.

a. Based on economic theory and/or intuition, what signs would you expect for the regression coefficients (exclude the constant) and why? Do the observed signs agree with your intuition?

b. Every t-statistic is insignificant, but the F-statistic is significant (verify this statement). State the reason(s) for this paradoxical result.

c. Would you say the estimates are (i) biased, (ii) inefficient, (iii) inconsistent? Carefully justify your answers.

d. You are asked to formulate a model that explains not total water consumption but *consumption per household*, in terms of average family size and other relevant variables. Using the data described, develop a model that would be appropriate.

5.4 Using Example 5.1, estimate the relation between the U.S. gross national product and population as GNP = $\alpha + \beta$ POP + error. Substitute this in Model C of Table 5.1 and compare the results with those in Model A. Would you consider the modified Model C to be close to Model A?

5.5 For each of the following statements, indicate whether it is justified and explain your reasons:

a. "Because multicollinearity lowers t-statistics, all the insignificant regression coefficients should be dropped from the model because they are redundant."

b. "Multicollinearity raises the standard errors of regression coefficients and hence t- and F-tests are invalid."

5.6 In Exercise 4.17 on grade point, would you expect multicollinearity (MC) among the variables? If so, which variables do you think might cause MC problems? What are the consequences of ignoring MC? In particular are estimates and forecasts biased, inefficient, inconsistent, not BLUE? Explain.

5.7 In Exercise 4.15 the correlation between Y and P was 0.92. What does this convey about the estimated relationship? Specifically, examine the implications on bias of estimates, confidence intervals, validity of tests of hypotheses, and so on.

5.8 In Exercise 4.9 one might expect multicollinearity to be severe. Describe how one can find out whether this is the case. If it is a problem, discuss the various solutions possible. Which would you recommend most, and why?

5.9 "If there is multicollinearity among independent variables, then a variable that appears significant may not indeed be so." Is this statement valid?

Derivation of Equations (5.6)
Through (5.10)

$$S_{y2} = \sum yx_2 = \sum x_2(\beta_2 x_2 + \beta_3 x_3 + v_t) \qquad (5.A.1)$$
$$= \beta_2 S_{22} + \beta_3 S_{23} + S_{v2}$$

using equation (5.1). Because $E(v) = 0$ and the x's are nonrandom, $E(S_{v2}) = E(\sum vx_2) = \sum x_2 E(v) = 0$. Therefore, $E(S_{y2}) = \beta_2 S_{22} + \beta_3 S_{23}$, thus proving equation (5.6). The proof for equation (5.7) is very similar. From (5.A.1) and Property 2.5c, $\mathrm{Var}(S_{y2}) = \mathrm{Var}(S_{v2})$. From Property 2.A.1c,

$$\mathrm{Var}(S_{y2}) = \sum x_2^2 \, \mathrm{Var}(v) = \sigma^2 \sum x_2^2 = \sigma^2 S_{22}$$
$$\mathrm{Var}(S_{y3}) = \sum x_3^2 \, \mathrm{Var}(v) = \sigma^2 \sum x_3^2 = \sigma^2 S_{33}$$
$$\mathrm{Cov}(S_{y2}, S_{y3}) = \sum x_2 x_3 \, \mathrm{Var}(v) = \sigma^2 S_{23}$$

Also, from Property 2.7a,

$$\mathrm{Var}(\hat{\beta}_2) = \frac{1}{\Delta^2} [S_{33}^2 \, \mathrm{Var}(S_{y2}) + S_{23}^2 \, \mathrm{Var}(S_{y3}) - 2S_{33}S_{23} \, \mathrm{Cov}(S_{y2}, S_{y3})]$$

$$= \frac{\sigma^2}{\Delta^2} [S_{33}^2 S_{22} + S_{23}^2 S_{33} - 2S_{33}S_{23}S_{23}]$$

$$= \frac{\sigma^2}{\Delta^2} [S_{33}^2 S_{22} - S_{23}^2 S_{33}] = \frac{\sigma^2}{\Delta^2} S_{33}[S_{33}S_{22} - S_{23}^2] = \frac{\sigma^2 S_{33}}{\Delta}$$

thus proving (5.8). The procedures for (5.9) and (5.10) are similar.

Practice Problem

5.3 Verify equations (5.7), (5.9), and (5.10).

PART III

EXTENSIONS

PART III presents a number of extensions to the basic models studied so far. Chapter 6 discusses how nonquantitative variables such as gender, race, season, affiliation to a political party, and so on, can be handled in a regression context by means of binary (or more commonly, dummy) variables. A variety of examples are provided to illustrate the use of dummy variables, especially in testing whether a relationship might have changed over time. Chapter 7 deals with the usefulness of hypothesis testing as an aid to improving the specification of econometric models. The recently introduced Lagrange Multiplier (LM) tests are discussed in considerable detail, with several applications. Although the term "Lagrange multiplier" might give the impression that an understanding of advanced calculus is essential, this is not the case. The techniques are as intuitive as the widely used Wald test discussed in Chapter 4, and are no more difficult to learn and apply than conventional tests. The payoff of this added coverage, however, is that you will come away with an easy understanding of one of the most powerful, flexible, and frequently used methods for hypothesis testing.

CHAPTER 6

Qualitative (or Dummy) Independent Variables

■ All the variables we have encountered so far have been **quantitative** in nature; that is, they have numerically measurable attributes. The behavior of economic variables may, however, also depend on **qualitative** factors such as the gender of a person, educational status, season, public or private, and so on. As a specific example, consider the following simple regression model (for simplicity, the t-subscript has been omitted):

$$Y = \alpha + \beta X + u \tag{6.1}$$

Let Y be the welfare budget of a state legislature and X be its total revenue. Suppose we are told that between two legislatures with the same total revenues, the one controlled by Democrats will allocate more money for welfare programs. How can we capture the effect of the qualitative variable "political party"? As a second example, let Y be the consumption of energy in a given day and X be the average temperature. When temperature rises in the summer, we would expect energy consumption to go up. Hence the slope coefficient β is likely to be positive. In the winter, however, as temperature rises from, say, 20 degrees to 40 degrees, there is less need for heating, and the consumption is likely to decrease as temperature increases. This suggests that β might be negative in the winter. Thus, the nature of the relationship between energy consumption and temperature can be expected to depend on the qualitative variable "season." In this chapter we study the procedures for taking account of qualitative variables in estimation and hypothesis testing. We confine our attention to qualitative independent variables only. Chapter 12 discusses the case in which the dependent variable is qualitative.

6.1 The Effect of Qualitative Variables on the Intercept Term

Qualitative Variable with Two Categories

To start with, we consider the simplest case, that in which only the intercept term α is affected by a single qualitative variable that has two categories. The procedure is to define **binary variables**, or—more commonly—**dummy variables**, which are numerical, and use them in the econometric formulation. In the welfare budget example, we define the dummy variable D as follows:

$$D = \begin{cases} 1 & \text{if the legislature has a Democratic majority} \\ 0 & \text{otherwise} \end{cases} \qquad (6.2)$$

Thus, there are two categories, "Democrats" and "non-Democrats." The dummy variable D assigns the value 1 to one of the categories (the choice is arbitrary) and 0 to the other. The assumption that the intercept α is different for these two categories is specified as $\alpha = \alpha_0 + \alpha_1 D$. If the legislature is controlled by Republicans, $D = 0$ and hence $\alpha = \alpha_0$. If by Democrats, $\alpha = \alpha_0 + \alpha_1$. Thus, α_1 measures the *difference in the intercept due to a change in party*. Substituting for α, we get the econometric model

$$Y = \alpha_0 + \alpha_1 D + \beta X + u \qquad (6.3)$$

The data column for D will have only the values 1 or 0. For states controlled by Democrats, D will assume the value 1 and for other states it will be 0. α_0, α_1 and β are estimated by regressing Y against a constant, against D, and against X. The estimated relationships for the two parties are

Non-Democrats: $\qquad \hat{Y} = \hat{\alpha}_0 + \hat{\beta} X \qquad (6.4)$

Democrats: $\qquad \hat{Y} = (\hat{\alpha}_0 + \hat{\alpha}_1) + \hat{\beta} X \qquad (6.5)$

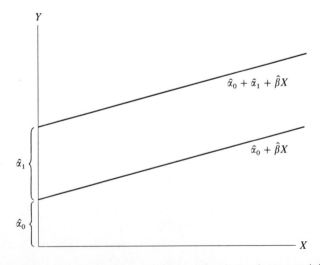

Figure 6.1 An example of an intercept shift using a dummy variable

The category for which the dummy variable assumes a 0 value is called the **control group** and the above process is often referred to as "normalizing on the control group." Figure 6.1 graphs these relationships when the α's and β are positive. We notice that the estimated straight lines are parallel to each other. This is because we have assumed that both the groups have the same β. This assumption is relaxed in the next section.

A natural hypothesis to test is that "there is no difference in the relationships between parties." Comparing equations (6.4) and (6.5) we see that the relationships will be the same if $\alpha_1 = 0$. Thus, we have $H_0: \alpha_1 = 0$ and $H_1: \alpha_1 > 0$ or $\alpha_1 \neq 0$. The appropriate test is the t-test on $\hat{\alpha}_1$, which has $T - 3$ d.f. If a Democrat-controlled legislature did indeed allocate more to welfare programs, we would observe a positive value for $\hat{\alpha}_1$.

Practice Problems

6.1 Suppose the dummy variable had been defined as $D^* = 1$ for non-Democrats and 0 for others. What changes would you expect in the estimated model? In particular, explain how the estimated coefficients of your new model can be derived from those of (6.3), *without rerunning the regression*. Would the standard errors, t-values, R^2, and F-statistic be affected? If so, in what way?

6.2 Suppose D were 1 for Democrats and 2 for Republicans. In what way would the results change?

Example 6.1

Table 6.1 has additional data on the 14 single-family houses, all of which are dummy variables. POOL takes the value 1 if a house has a swimming pool, 0 otherwise. Similarly, FAMROOM stands for the presence of a family room, and FIREPL represents the presence of a fireplace. One might expect that a house that has these characteristics might command a higher price than a similar house without these amenities. Table 6.2 has the estimated coefficients and related statistics for a number of models, including Model A which we estimated earlier (the results can be duplicated with the help of Practice Computer Session 6.1). □

Comparing Model A with Model E, which has all the new variables, we note that $\bar{R}^2$ has increased from 0.806 to 0.890, but that four of the model selection criteria have worsened. RICE is undefined because it requires that the number of observations be greater than twice the number of coefficients estimated, which is not the case here. The t-statistic for POOL is 2.411, which is significant at levels below 1 percent. The regression coefficients for BEDRMS, BATHS, FAMROOM, and FIREPL are, however, insignificant even at levels well above 25 percent (verify it). In Model F these insignificant variables have been eliminated and the model reestimated. Using Model E as the unrestricted model and Model F as the restricted model, we can perform a Wald F-test to test the null hypothesis that the regression coefficients for BEDRMS, BATHS, FAMROOM, and FIREPL are zero. The

TABLE 6.1 Data on Single-Family Homes

PRICE (x 000)	SQFT	BEDRMS	BATHS	POOL	FAMROOM	FIREPL
199.9	1065	3	1.75	1	0	0
228	1254	3	2	0	0	0
235	1300	3	2	1	1	1
285	1577	4	2.5	0	1	1
239	1600	3	2	0	1	1
293	1750	4	2	0	0	1
285	1800	4	2.75	0	1	1
365	1870	4	2	1	1	1
295	1935	4	2.5	0	1	1
290	1948	4	2	0	1	1
385	2254	4	3	1	1	1
505	2600	3	2.5	1	1	1
425	2800	4	3	0	1	1
415	3000	4	3	0	1	1

computed F-statistic is

$$F_c = \frac{(9455 - 9010) \div 4}{9010 \div 7} = 0.086$$

which has the F-distribution with 4 and 7 d.f. It is readily seen that F_c is not significant even at levels above 0.25. We therefore conclude that the corresponding regression coefficients are not jointly significant.

If these variables are omitted, we see that the t-statistics for SQFT and POOL are much higher. Also, $\bar{R}^2$ rises to 0.89. Thus, elimination of the insignificant variables has improved the overall performance of the model. It should be emphasized that the conclusion is not that the omitted variables are unimportant, only that *holding* SQFT and POOL *unchanged*, the inclusion of BEDRMS, BATHS, FAMROOM, and FIREPL does not add to the explanatory power of the model. At least some of the effects of the excluded variables are captured by the variables already in the model. In Model F the coefficient for POOL is 52.790 which implies that between two houses with the same square feet of living area, the one with a pool is expected to sell, on average, for $52,790 more than a house without a pool. Considering the cost of installing a pool, this value appears excessively high. A possible explanation is that, along with a swimming pool, these houses might also contain a jacuzzi, a decked patio, or other such features. Thus, the dummy variable POOL might really be a proxy for many other improvements.

TABLE 6.2 Effect of Dummy Variables on Home Price*

Variable	Model A	Model E	Model F
CONSTANT	52.351 (1.404)	39.057 (0.436)	22.673 (0.768)
SQFT	0.13875 (7.407)	0.14655 (4.869)	0.1444 (10.118)
BEDRMS		−7.046 (−0.245)	
BATHS		−0.264 (−0.006)	
POOL		53.196 (2.411)	52.790 (3.203)
FAMROOM		−21.345 (−0.498)	
FIREPL		26.188 (0.486)	
$\bar{R}^2$	0.806	0.836	0.890
ESS	18,274	9,010	9,455
d.f.	12	7	11
SGMASQ	1,523	1,287	860*
AIC	1,737	1,749	1,037*
FPE	1,740	1,931	1,044*
HQ	1,722	1,698	1,024*
SCHWARZ	1,903	2,408	1,189*
SHIBATA	1,678	1,287	965*
GCV	1,777	2,574	1,094*
RICE	1,827	undefined	1,182*

* Models B, C, and D are in Table 4.2. Values in parentheses are corresponding *t*-statistics. An asterisk denotes the model that is "best" for that criterion.

Practice Problem

6.3 In Section 3.13, we argued that the marginal effect of SQFT on PRICE might decrease as SQFT increases. This suggested using ln(SQFT) instead of SQFT. Using your regression program, reestimate Models A, E, and F in Table 6.2 using ln(SQFT) instead of SQFT. Are the results superior? Next try including SQFT also. Do the results improve or worsen? Derive an expression for the *marginal* effect of SQFT on PRICE. (Practice Computer Session 6.2 will be useful in carrying this out.)

Example 6.2

Sommers and Quinton (1982) carried out a study of the pay and performance in major league baseball, in which dummy variables were used to account for qualitative variables such as National League teams, pennant winning teams, whether a stadium is older or newer, and so on. Before discussing their results, it would be useful to present some background.

The baseball industry is characterized by *monopsony* (or *oligopsony*), in which team owners exercise some degree of control over players' salaries. Until 1975, a baseball player's unsigned contract could be perpetually renewed by the owners. In that year, however, labor arbitrator Peter Seitz ruled that players could seek employment with different owners after playing one year without a signed agreement. Because players could now seek a competitive bidding for their services, we might expect that their wages would be closer to the respective marginal revenue product (the extra revenue per extra hour or labor). More specifically, let R be the total team revenue. Then net profits are $\pi = R - wL - rK$, where L is labor in worker-hours, K represents all other inputs, w is the wage rate, and r is the rental rate. A profit-maximizing team owner would set $\Delta\pi/\Delta L$ to zero, which gives the condition $\Delta R/\Delta L = w$. The left-hand side is the marginal revenue product. Thus, for profits to be maximized, wages should equal the marginal revenue product.

Sommers and Quinton estimated the contribution of a number of individual players toward the marginal revenue, and compared this estimate to the players' salaries as free agents. The following two equations were estimated separately using cross-section observations for 50 teams in a number of SMSAs (Standard Metropolitan Statistical Areas), for the years 1976 and 1977:

$$\widehat{PCTWIN} = 188.45 + 256.33TSA^* + 80.87TSW^* - 55.33XPAN$$
$$\scriptstyle (1.97) \qquad (2.90) \qquad\qquad (2.85) \qquad\qquad (-2.62)$$
$$+ 51.34CONT - 72.07OUT$$
$$\scriptstyle (4.09) \qquad\quad (-6.14)$$
$$R^2 = 0.892 \qquad d.f. = 44$$

$$\widehat{REVENUE} = -2,297,500 + (22,736 - 2095SMSA + 415SMSA^2)PCTWIN$$
$$\scriptstyle (-1.12) \qquad (4.54) \qquad (-1.65) \qquad\qquad (3.22)$$
$$- 313,700STD + 4,298,900XPAN - 3,750,200TWOTM$$
$$\scriptstyle (-0.45) \qquad\qquad (2.70) \qquad\qquad (-3.74)$$
$$- 2513BBPCT$$
$$\scriptstyle (-0.08)$$
$$R^2 = 0.704 \qquad d.f. = 42$$

where

PCTWIN = 1000 times the ratio of games won to games played

REVENUE = home attendance times average ticket price plus estimated concession income plus revenue from broadcasting rights

TSA* = team slugging average (total bases divided by total at bats) as a ratio to the average for the relevant division of the league

TSW^* = team strikeout-to-walk ratio (strikeouts divided by walks) to similar ratio for league

XPAN = 1 if the team is an expansion club, 0 otherwise

CONT = 1 for pennant or divisional winners, 0 for others

OUT = 1 for teams that were 20 or more games out of first place at the end of the season, 0 for others

SMSA = the population of the SMSA

STD = 1 if the stadium is older, 0 otherwise

TWOTM = 1 if the team shares a home SMSA with another team

BBPCT = percentage of black players in the team

To allow for an interaction between PCTWIN and the size of the SMSA in the revenue function, the authors assumed that ΔREVENUE/ΔPCTWIN is a quadratic function of SMSA. Because the focus in this example is only on the dummy variables, we do not interpret any of the other results. Sommers and Quinton used these estimated equations to calculate the marginal revenue products of 14 players and compared them with the corresponding salaries. Their conclusion was that, contrary to popular opinion, the ball players were grossly underpaid.

In the PCTWIN equation all the dummy variables were significant. Expansion clubs finished, on average, 55 points lower. Out of first place teams had 72 fewer points, on average. In the REVENUE equation STD was not significant, indicating that it did not matter whether a stadium was older or newer. The significance of TWOTM and its negative value indicate, not surprisingly, that having a second team in the same city is detrimental to revenue.   □

Qualitative Variable with Many Categories

The number of possible categories in a qualitative variable might be more than two. For example, let Y be the savings of a household and X be its income. We would expect the relationship between savings and income to be different for different age groups. For a given income, a young household might spend more, on average, than one headed by a middle-age person. This is because the latter might save more for educating the children and for retirement. A retired family is likely to spend more, on average, because the need to save for the future is reduced. If we have the exact age of the head of a household, this can be entered in a model as a quantitative variable. If, however, only the age group is known (for example, whether the head belongs to the age group under 25, 25 to 55, or over 55), how do we account for the qualitative variable "age group of the head of household"? The procedure here is to choose one of the groups as the control group and define dummy variables for the other two groups. More specifically, we define

$$A_1 = \begin{cases} 1 & \text{if the head of the household is 25 to 55} \\ 0 & \text{otherwise} \end{cases} \tag{6.6}$$

$$A_2 = \begin{cases} 1 & \text{if the head of the household is over 55} \\ 0 & \text{otherwise} \end{cases} \tag{6.7}$$

The control group (that is, the one for which both A_1 and A_2 are zero) is all the households for which the head is under 25 years of age. To allow for α to be different for the different groups, we assume that $\alpha = \alpha_0 + \alpha_1 A_1 + \alpha_2 A_2$. Substituting this into equation (6.1) we get

$$Y = \alpha_0 + \alpha_1 A_1 + \alpha_2 A_2 + \beta X + u \tag{6.8}$$

For a young household, $A_1 = A_2 = 0$, For the middle-age group, $A_1 = 1$ and $A_2 = 0$. For the oldest age group, $A_1 = 0$ and $A_2 = 1$. The estimated models for the three groups are as follows:

$$\text{Age} < 25: \qquad \hat{Y} = \hat{\alpha}_0 + \hat{\beta}X \tag{6.9}$$

$$\text{Age } 25\text{--}55: \qquad \hat{Y} = (\hat{\alpha}_0 + \hat{\alpha}_1) + \hat{\beta}X \tag{6.10}$$

$$\text{Age} > 55: \qquad \hat{Y} = (\hat{\alpha}_0 + \hat{\alpha}_2) + \hat{\beta}X \tag{6.11}$$

$\hat{\alpha}_1$ is an estimate of the difference in intercept between a young and a middle-age household. $\hat{\alpha}_2$ is an estimate of the difference between a young and an old household. Thus, *the intercept shifters are the deviations from the control group.* The graph for the estimated lines will be parallel to each other.

There is a special reason for not defining a third dummy variable A_3 that takes the value 1 for a young household and 0 for others. If we had assumed that $\alpha = \alpha_0 + \alpha_1 A_1 + \alpha_2 A_2 + \alpha_3 A_3$, we would have exact multicollinearity because $A_1 + A_2 + A_3$ is always equal to 1, which is the constant term (see Table 6.3). This is known as the **dummy variable trap**. To avoid this problem, *the number of dummy variables is always one less than the number of categories.* Thus, if we wanted to capture seasonal differences between electricity consumption and temperature, we would define three dummy variables (because there are four seasons). To capture monthly differences, we need 11 dummy variables.

Several hypotheses are of interest here. To test the hypothesis that the senior age group behaves like the young household, we simply carry out a t-test on $\hat{\alpha}_2$. To test the hypothesis that "there is no difference in the savings function due to age," the hypothesis is H_0: $\alpha_1 = \alpha_2 = 0$ and the alternative is H_1: at least one of the coefficients is nonzero. This hypothesis is tested using the Wald test described in Section 4.5. The unrestricted model will be equation (6.8) and the restricted model is $Y = \alpha_0 + \beta X + u$. The Wald F, derived from the respective sums of squares, will have d.f. 2 and $T - 4$. The hypothesis that "there is no difference in behavior between the middle and the old age groups" implies that $\alpha_1 = \alpha_2$. This can be tested using the three methods described in Section 4.5. To apply the Wald test, impose this condition on equation (6.8). We ge the restricted model

$$\begin{aligned} Y &= \alpha_0 + \alpha_1 A_1 + \alpha_1 A_2 + \beta X + u \\ &= \alpha_0 + \alpha_1(A_1 + A_2) + \beta X + u \end{aligned} \tag{6.12}$$

The procedure for estimating the restricted model is to create a new variable $Z = A_1 + A_2$ and regress Y against a constant, Z, and X. A Wald test is then carried out between this and equation (6.8) by comparing the sums of squares of the estimated residuals. The F-statistic will now have d.f. 1 and $T - 4$.

 Practice Problems

6.4   Suppose we had used the third dummy variable A_3 defined above and formulated the model as $Y = \beta_1 A_1 + \beta_2 A_2 + \beta_3 A_3 + \beta X + u$, *without a constant term*. Show that there is no problem here with exact multicollinearity. Describe how estimates of the αs can be obtained from estimates of the βs. [Because the constant term captures the mean effects of omitted variables, it is essential to retain it in the specification; hence this type of formulation should be avoided.]

6.5   Choose a different age group as the control, say the oldest, and reformulate the model. How are the estimates of the new model related to those in equation (6.8)? More specifically, derive the estimates of your new model from those for equation (6.8). Describe how the tests of hypotheses specified may be conducted in this new formulation.

Several Qualitative Variables

The dummy variable analysis is easily extended to the case in which there are several qualitative variables, some of which may have more than one category. To illustrate, consider the savings function described earlier in which Y is household savings and X is household income. One can hypothesize that besides the age of the head, other factors such as home ownership, education level, occupation status, and so on are also important determinants of household savings. Suppose, for instance, we have information that the household head has a postgraduate degree, a bachelor's degree only, or a high school education. Further, suppose that we know that the occupation of the head is one of the following categories: managerial or executive, skilled worker, unskilled worker, clerical, self-employed businessperson or professional. Also, the exact age of head is unknown; we know only which age group he or she belongs to. How do we incorporate these variables into the analysis? The procedure is to define as many dummy variables as needed and enter them all in the model. The unrestricted model would be as follows:

$$Y = \beta_0 + \beta_1 A_1 + \beta_2 A_2 + \beta_3 H + \beta_4 E_1 + \beta_5 E_2 + \beta_6 O_1 \\ + \beta_7 O_2 + \beta_8 O_3 + \beta_9 O_4 + \beta_{10} X + u \tag{6.13}$$

where

$$A_1 = \begin{cases} 1 & \text{if the age of head is between 25 and 55} \\ 0 & \text{otherwise} \end{cases}$$

$$A_2 = \begin{cases} 1 & \text{if the age of head is over 55} \\ 0 & \text{otherwise} \end{cases}$$

TABLE 6.3   Sample Data Values with Several Qualitative Variables

t	Y	const	X	A_1	A_2	H	E_1	E_2	O_1	O_2	O_3	O_4
1	Y_1	1	X_1	1	0	1	1	0	0	1	0	0
2	Y_2	1	X_2	1	0	0	0	0	0	0	0	1
3	Y_3	1	X_3	0	0	0	0	1	0	0	0	0
4	Y_4	1	X_4	0	1	0	1	0	0	0	1	0
5	Y_5	1	X_5	0	1	0	1	0	0	1	0	0

$$H = \begin{cases} 1 & \text{if the household owns the house} \\ 0 & \text{otherwise} \end{cases}$$

$$E_1 = \begin{cases} 1 & \text{if the household head has a postgraduate degree} \\ 0 & \text{otherwise} \end{cases}$$

$$E_2 = \begin{cases} 1 & \text{if the household head has a bachelor's degree only} \\ 0 & \text{otherwise} \end{cases}$$

$$O_1 = \begin{cases} 1 & \text{if the household head is a manager} \\ 0 & \text{otherwise} \end{cases}$$

$$O_2 = \begin{cases} 1 & \text{if the household head is a skilled worker} \\ 0 & \text{otherwise} \end{cases}$$

$$O_3 = \begin{cases} 1 & \text{if the household head is a clerical worker} \\ 0 & \text{otherwise} \end{cases}$$

$$O_4 = \begin{cases} 1 & \text{if the household head is self-employed} \\ 0 & \text{otherwise} \end{cases}$$

It should be noted that the control groups are: age of head under 25, unskilled workers, and households whose head had a high school education only. An example of a data matrix is given in Table 6.3. The estimation of the parameters is done by regressing Y against a constant term, A_1, A_2, H, E_1, E_2, O_1, O_2, O_3, O_4, and X (additional quantitative variables are easily added if the model calls for them). Home-ownership status is tested with a t-test on $\hat{\beta}_3$ (with $T - 11$ d.f.). Educational status is tested with a Wald test under the null hypothesis that $\beta_4 = \beta_5 = 0$. The unrestricted model is equation (6.13), and the restricted model is the one obtained by omitting E_1 and E_2 from (6.13). The degrees of freedom for the F-statistic would be 2 and $T - 11$. Similarly, to test whether occupational status matters in explaining variations in savings, the Wald test is used for the null hypothesis that $\beta_6 = \beta_7 = \beta_8 = \beta_9 = 0$. Many other tests are possible; these are left as exercises for the reader.

Practice Problems

6.6   Write the estimated relation for a middle-age household that owns the home and whose head has a B.A. degree and works as a clerical worker.

6.7   Describe, step by step, how each of the following tests of hypotheses is carried out: (a) "The saving behavior of clerical workers is the same as those of skilled workers," and (b) "Occupational status has no significant effect on saving behavior." More specifically, describe the regression(s) to run, the test statistics to compute, the distribution of the statistics under the null hypothesis (including the degrees of freedom), and the criterion for acceptance or rejection of the null hypothesis.

Example 6.3

The principles described above are used here to relate the monthly wages of an employee to a number of employee characteristics. Table 6.9 at the end of the chapter has the complete data for a sample of 49 employees at a particular institution. The explanatory variables include the number of years of education (EDUC) beyond the eighth grade when the person was hired, the number of years of experience (EXPER) at the particular institution, and the age of the person (AGE). Also included are dummy variables for gender, race, and job type (e.g., clerical, maintenance, or craft). The categories are male (GENDER = 1), white (RACE = 1), clerical worker (CLERICAL = 1), maintenance worker (MAINT = 1), and craft worker (CRAFTS = 1). The control groups are female, nonwhite, and professional, and we have zero values for these dummy variables. Labor economic theory of wage determination suggests that the dependent variable should be expressed in logarithms.[1] The basic model (call it Model A) has no dummy variables.

$$(A) \qquad \ln(\text{WAGE}) = \alpha + \beta \, \text{EDUC} + \gamma \, \text{EXPER} + \delta \, \text{AGE} + u$$

Suppose we hypothesize that α is not the same for all employees but differs according to gender, race, and occupational status (the case when β, γ, and δ might also depend on these variables is examined in Section 6.2). To test this, assume that

$$\alpha = \alpha_0 + \alpha_1 \, \text{GENDER} + \alpha_2 \, \text{RACE} + \alpha_3 \, \text{CLERICAL}$$
$$+ \, \alpha_4 \, \text{MAINT} + \alpha_5 \, \text{CRAFTS}$$

and test the hypothesis that $\alpha_1 = \alpha_2 = \cdots = \alpha_5 = 0$.

Substituting for α in Model A we obtain Model B, the unrestricted model that relates $\ln(\text{WAGE})$ to a number of quantitative as well as dummy variables.

$$\begin{aligned} \ln(\text{WAGE}) = \alpha_0 &+ \alpha_1 \, \text{GENDER} + \alpha_2 \, \text{RACE} + \alpha_3 \, \text{CLERICAL} \\ (B) \qquad &+ \alpha_4 \, \text{MAINT} + \alpha_5 \, \text{CRAFTS} + \beta \, \text{EDUC} \\ &+ \gamma \, \text{EXPER} + \delta \, \text{AGE} + u \end{aligned}$$

∎ ∎ ∎ ∎ ∎ ∎

---

[1] *The rationale is as follows: suppose the return to an extra year of schooling is r. Then $w_1 = (1 + r)w_0$, where w is wages. For 2 years of schooling $w_2 = (1 + r)^2 w_0$ and so on. For s years we have $w_s = (1 + r)^s w_0$. Taking logarithms, we have $\ln(w_s) = s \ln(1 + r) + \ln(w_0) = \alpha + \beta s$. We thus obtain a log-linear relation between wages and years of schooling.*

This is the log-linear model, discussed in Section 3.13, in which the marginal effects are measured as percentage change in WAGE (after multiplying by 100). Thus, for two employees with identical characteristics, except that one is male (with GENDER $= 1$) and the other female, we would expect, on average, a difference of $100 \, \alpha_1$ percent in their respective monthly wages.

The estimated coefficients, their t-statistics, and model selection statistics are presented in Table 6.4 for four different formulations (see Practice Computer Session 6.3 for reproducing those results). The value of $\bar{R}^2$ for the basic model (A) is 0.283, which is very unimpressive even for a cross-section study. This model is an average of all categories of employees and is likely to be different for various

TABLE 6.4 Estimated Models for Wage Determination

Variable	Model A	Model B	Model C	Model D
CONSTANT	6.836 (33.6)	7.471 (47.5)	7.380 (60.6)	7.507 (89.53)
EDUC	0.065 (3.85)	0.017 (1.27)	0.018 (1.42)	
EXPER	0.023 (3.30)	0.017 (3.63)	0.016 (3.57)	0.014 (3.32)
AGE	0.00039 (0.10)	−0.002 (−0.92)		
GENDER		0.243 (3.36)	0.228 (3.24)	0.247 (3.53)
RACE		0.111 (1.81)	0.101 (1.68)	0.129 (2.25)
CLERICAL		−0.462 (−5.71)	−0.464 (−5.75)	−0.490 (−6.16)
MAINT		−0.527 (−5.59)	−0.521 (−5.55)	−0.576 (−6.64)
CRAFTS		−0.343 (−4.12)	−0.327 (−4.03)	−0.358 (−4.51)
$\bar{R}^2$	0.283	0.718	0.719*	0.712
ESS	3.157	1.105*	1.128	1.184
$\hat{\sigma}^2$	0.07015	0.02762	0.02751*	0.02819
AIC	0.07585	0.03256	0.03191*	0.03215
FPE	0.07587	0.03269	0.03200*	0.03221
HQ	0.08042	0.03714	0.03588	0.03562*
SCHWARZ	0.08851	0.04608	0.04346	0.04212*
SHIBATA	0.07494	0.03083	0.03054*	0.03106
GCV	0.07638	0.03384	0.03288*	0.03288*
RICE	0.07699	0.03564	0.03418	0.03382*

An asterisk indicates the "best" model for that criterion. The values in parentheses are t-statistics.

skill levels as well as for gender and race. It is therefore sensible to include the dummy variables that take those into account, as is done in Model B. We immediately note that there is a remarkable increase in $\bar{R}^2$ from 0.283 to 0.718. Thus, allowing for differences due to occupational status, gender, and race improves the model performance substantially. However, some of the regression coefficients are insignificant, in particular, those for EDUC and AGE. In Model C, AGE is omitted and in Model D EDUC is also excluded. The model selection statistics prefer Model C over the other models, although Model D is a close second. In Model C, the regression coefficient for EDUC is significant only at the 16.2 percent level (as indicated by the *p*-value obtained in Practice Computer Session 6.3). However, we do not omit this variable because EDUC is a theoretically important variable and it is safer to keep it, even if the estimates might be less efficient, in order to avoid the omitted variable bias problem discussed in Chapter 4. We therefore use Model C for the final interpretation. □

Interpretation of the Results   The variables included in the final model explain 71.9 percent of the variation in logarithm of WAGE, which is quite high for a cross-section study. An additional year of experience is expected to result in an increase of 1.6 percent in average monthly salary. Other things being equal, an additional year of education results in an average increase of 1.8 percent in salary. Holding other variables constant, a male worker is expected to earn, on average, 22.8 percent more in salary than a female worker with similar characteristics. This differential is very high and might lead one to the interpretation that there is gender discrimination in the salary structure. Being white results in a lesser difference in average salary (10.1 percent). All the occupational status coefficients have negative signs—not surprising because the control group contains professionals who would be expected to earn considerably more than clerical, maintenance, or craft workers.

The model, although informative, has some limitations which are discussed in Section 6.2.

Analysis of Variance Models*

It is possible for all the independent variables in a model to be binary. Such models are known as **analysis of variance (ANOVA) models**. They are very common in agricultural economics, market research, sociology, and psychology. In this section we introduce ANOVA models only briefly. For more details, refer to a book on statistics or experimental designs.

Consider an agricultural experiment in which the investigator plans to study the average yield per acre due to three types of hybrid seeds treated with four different doses of fertilizer. The designer of the experiment divides a large area of land into a number of plots and plants, at random, various combinations of seeds and doses. The observed yield in each plot is then related to the corresponding type of seed and the dose of fertilizer. An experimental designer would formulate the model as follows:

$$Y_{ijk} = \mu + a_j + b_k + \epsilon_{ijk}$$

where Y_{ijk} is the observed yield in the ith plot using the jth seed ($j = 1, 2, 3$) and kth dose of fertilizer ($k = 1, 2, 3, 4$), μ is the "grand mean," a_j is the "seed effect," and b_k is the "fertilizer effect." ϵ_{ijk} is an unobservable random error term. Thus, the average yield is composed of an overall effect common to all plots, which is modified by the type of seed and fertilizer dosage in a particular plot. Because a_j and b_k are deviations from the overall mean, we have the conditions $\sum a_j = \sum b_k = 0$. Due to these constraints, the eight parameters (μ, three a's, and four b's) reduce, in effect, to only six. This model is written as follows for selected combinations:

$$Y_{i12} = \mu + a_1 + b_2 + \epsilon_{i12}$$
$$Y_{i34} = \mu + a_3 + b_4 + \epsilon_{i34}$$

The same model can be formulated with only dummy variables. For the seed varieties, define two dummy variables: $S_1 = 1$ if the first seed variety is chosen. 0 otherwise; $S_2 = 1$ if the second seed variety is chosen, 0 otherwise. Similarly, define three dummy variables for the fertilizer doses; $D_1 = 1$ when the first dose is used. $D_2 = 1$ for the second dose, and $D_3 = 1$ for the third dose. Note that the control group is the third variety of seed and the fourth dose. The econometric formulation is

$$Y = \alpha_0 + \alpha_1 S_1 + \alpha_2 S_2 + \beta_1 D_1 + \beta_2 D_2 + \beta_3 D_3 + u$$

Here also there are six unknown parameters to estimate. For the two combinations listed above, the model becomes

$$Y = \alpha_0 + \alpha_1 + \beta_2 + u \qquad (S_1 = D_2 = 1, S_2 = D_1 = D_3 = 0)$$
$$Y = \alpha_0 + u \qquad (S_1 = S_2 = D_1 = D_2 = D_3 = 0)$$

In comparing the two approaches we note that $\alpha_0 + \alpha_1 + \beta_2 = \mu + a_1 + b_2$ and $\alpha_0 = \mu + a_3 + b_4$. It is possible to show that there is one-to-one correspondence between the econometric model and the experimental design model. The hypothesis that there is no difference among the seeds can be translated as $a_1 = a_2 = a_3 = 0$, or equivalently as $\alpha_1 = \alpha_2 = 0$. Similarly, the hypothesis that there is no difference in yield due to fertilizer dose can be tested by either $b_1 = b_2 = b_3 = b_4 = 0$ or $\beta_1 = \beta_2 = \beta_3 = 0$.

 Practice Problem

6.8 Write all the relations between a's, b's and α's, β's; solve for each a and each b in terms of the α's and β's; and show how the experimental design formulation can be derived from the econometric formulation.

6.2 The Effect of Qualitative Variables on the Slope Term

Shifts in the Slope Term Only

In this section we allow for the possibility that β might be different for different qualitative variables (such models are known as **analysis of covariance models**). For instance, in the welfare budget example, how can we test the hypothesis that

β is different between states controlled by Democrats and those controlled by Republicans? We first assume that the intercept α is unchanged. (This is relaxed in the next section.) The procedure is analogous to the case in which the intercept shifted between categories. Let $\beta = \beta_0 + \beta_1 D$, where $D = 1$ for Democrats and 0 for all others. Equation (6.1) now becomes

$$Y = \alpha + (\beta_0 + \beta_1 D)X + u$$
$$= \alpha + \beta_0 X + \beta_1 (DX) + u \qquad (6.14)$$

$\beta_1 DX$ represents the interaction term described in Section 4.6. To estimate the model, we multiply the dummy variable by X and create a new variable $Z = DX$. Then we regress Y against a constant term, X, and Z. The estimated relations are as follows (they are graphed in Figure 6.2, under the assumption that α and the βs are all positive):

Non-Democrats: $\qquad \hat{Y} = \hat{\alpha} + \hat{\beta}_0 X \qquad\qquad\qquad$ (6.15)

Democrats: $\qquad\quad\; \hat{Y} = \hat{\alpha} + (\hat{\beta}_0 + \hat{\beta}_1)X \qquad\quad$ (6.16)

Because the intercept is assumed to be the same, the straight lines start from the same point but have different slopes. If a legislature controlled by Republicans receives an extra dollar in revenue, it is expected to allocate an average of $\hat{\beta}_0$ dollars more on welfare programs. Similarly, legislatures dominated by Democrats are expected to allocate an average of $\hat{\beta}_0 + \hat{\beta}_1$ dollars of each extra dollar revenue to welfare programs. Thus, $\hat{\beta}_1$ measures the difference in the estimated slopes.

The procedure for hypothesis testing is also similar to the previous case, in which only the intercept was shifted. A t-test on $\hat{\beta}_1$ (d.f. $T - 3$) will test that there is no difference in the slopes.

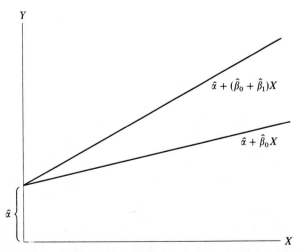

Figure 6.2 An example of a slope shift using a dummy variable

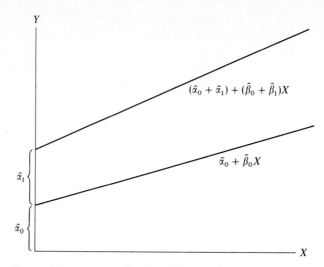

Figure 6.3 An example of a shift in the intercept and slope

Shifts in Both the Intercept and Slope Terms

Allowing for shifts in both the intercept and the slope is a straightforward procedure. We simply let $\alpha = \alpha_0 + \alpha_1 D$ and $\beta = \beta_0 + \beta_1 D$. Substituting this into equation (6.1) we get the unrestricted model as

$$
\begin{aligned}
Y &= \alpha_0 + \alpha_1 D + (\beta_0 + \beta_1 D)X + u \\
&= \alpha_0 + \alpha_1 D + \beta_0 X + \beta_1(DX) + u
\end{aligned}
\tag{6.17}
$$

Regress Y against a constant, D, X, and the interaction term DX. The estimated relations for the two political parties are

$$
\text{Democrat:} \qquad \hat{Y} = (\hat{\alpha}_0 + \hat{\alpha}_1) + (\hat{\beta}_0 + \hat{\beta}_1)X \tag{6.18}
$$

$$
\text{Non-Democrat:} \qquad \hat{Y} = \hat{\alpha}_0 + \hat{\beta}_0 X \tag{6.19}
$$

Figure 6.3 graphs these relationships when all the αs and βs are positive. To test the hypothesis that there is no difference in the entire relationship, we have $H_0\colon \alpha_1 = \beta_1 = 0$. The test is the Wald F-test with equation (6.17) as the unrestricted model and $Y = \alpha_0 + \beta_0 X + u$ as the restricted model. The F-statistic will have 2 and $T - 4$ d.f.

It is possible to separate the states into Democratic-controlled and the rest, and run separate regressions for each of the two groups. The major disadvantage of this approach is that the number of observations in each group will be much smaller and hence the precision of the estimates will be lower compared to pooling the sample.

Example 6.4

The use of the analysis of covariance is illustrated here with the help of the model for the determination of wage presented in Example 6.3. In that example, the final model related the logarithm of wages to EDUC, EXPER, GENDER, RACE, CLERICAL, MAINT, and CRAFTS. We thus had

(C) $\quad \ln(\text{WAGE}) = \alpha_0 + \alpha_1 \text{ GENDER} + \alpha_2 \text{ RACE} + \alpha_3 \text{ CLERICAL}$
$\qquad + \alpha_4 \text{ MAINT} + \alpha_5 \text{ CRAFTS} + \beta \text{ EDUC}$
$\qquad + \gamma \text{ EXPER} + u$

We use the above model as the starting point here. Suppose we want to test whether the *marginal* effects of EDUC and EXPER depend on GENDER and RACE (for simplicity we ignore the other dummy variables). We would then allow the "slope" coefficients β and γ to depend on these dummy variables. For instance, we would assume that

$$\beta = \beta_0 + \beta_1 \text{ GENDER} + \beta_2 \text{ RACE} \quad \text{and} \quad \gamma = \gamma_0 + \gamma_1 \text{ GENDER} + \gamma_2 \text{ RACE}$$

Substituting for β and γ into Model C we obtain

(E)
$\quad \ln(\text{WAGE}) = \alpha_0 + \alpha_1 \text{ GENDER} + \alpha_2 \text{ RACE} + \alpha_3 \text{ CLERICAL}$
$\qquad + \alpha_4 \text{ MAINT} + \alpha_5 \text{ CRAFTS}$
$\qquad + \text{EDUC} (\beta_0 + \beta_1 \text{ GENDER} + \beta_2 \text{ RACE})$
$\qquad + \text{EXPER} (\gamma_0 + \gamma_1 \text{ GENDER} + \gamma_2 \text{ RACE}) + u$

Note that the model contains several interaction terms. Define EDC_GEN = EDUC∗GENDER, EDU_RACE = EDUC∗RACE, EXP_GEN = EXPER∗GENDER, and EXP_RACE = EXPER∗RACE. Table 6.5 has an annotated partial computer output that illustrates the steps for carrying out the analysis (Practice Computer Session 6.4 has complete details). Model E is the unrestricted model including the interaction terms mentioned above (Model D is in Table 6.4). We note that the coefficients for several variables have p-values in excess of 0.50 (EDUC, EXPER, GENDER, RACE, and EXP_RACE). As these are unacceptably high, they are candidates for exclusion. It can be noted from the second page of the printout that the Wald F-statistic for exclusion is 0.1964 with a p-value of 0.961949, which is too high, leading us to accept the hypothesis that all these coefficients are zero. This supports the earlier conclusion that these variables might be omitted from the model specification. A good reason to exclude them is to reduce any multicollinearity introduced by their inclusion. We saw in Chapter 5 that if "redundant" variables are retained in the model, estimates are less efficient, although they are unbiased. In Model F, which has omitted these variables, the regression coefficient for ED_GEN has the high p-value of 0.356. If this variable is also omitted, we obtain Model G in which all the remaining variables have extremely significant coefficients. Also, the model selection statistics have the lowest values indicating that Model G has the "best" overall fit.

Interpretation of the Results The adjusted R^2 has risen slightly from 0.719 for Model C to 0.759 for Model G. Not surprisingly, the dummy variables for occupational status (CLERICAL, MAINT, and CRAFTS) are still highly

is adequate and on whether the model is an accurate and complete description of what the sample data represent. For instance, we have not allowed the slope coefficients to depend on occupational status. A complete analysis would allow for shifts in both the intercept and slope terms due to all the qualitative variables. The next chapter addresses this issue from a different approach. In the meantime, you are encouraged to use the data supplied here and carry out a full analysis (see Practice Computer Session 6.5) □

6.3 Piecewise Linear Regression*

The dummy variable approach is useful in modeling a nonlinear relationship that can be approximated with several linear relationships, known as **piecewise linear relationships**. As an example, consider the U.S. income tax, which is progressive; that is, higher income households pay a larger proportion of an extra dollar earned than lower income households. In other words, the marginal tax rate increases with income. Suppose there is no tax for households with adjusted gross income of $15,000 or less, a low marginal tax for those with incomes between $15,000 and $40,000, a medium marginal tax for adjusted incomes between $40,000 and $100,000, and a higher tax rate for households with incomes in excess of $100,000. The relation between income tax paid (Y) and adjusted gross income (X) will be piecewise linear, as in Figure 6.4a. To estimate the tax function in the various ranges we define appropriate dummy variables. Because there are three income segments two dummy variables are needed:

$$D_1 = \begin{cases} 1 & \text{if adjusted gross income is in the range \$40,000–\$100,000} \\ 0 & \text{otherwise} \end{cases}$$

$$D_2 = \begin{cases} 1 & \text{if adjusted gross income is above \$100,000} \\ 0 & \text{otherwise} \end{cases}$$

Next, assume that $Y = \alpha + \beta X + u$, with $\alpha = \alpha_0 + \alpha_1 D_1 + \alpha_2 D_2$ and $\beta = \beta_0 + \beta_1 D_1 + \beta_2 D_2$. The complete unrestricted model then becomes

$$\begin{aligned} Y &= \alpha_0 + \alpha_1 D_1 + \alpha_2 D_2 + (\beta_0 + \beta_1 D_1 + \beta_2 D_2)X + u \\ &= \alpha_0 + \alpha_1 D_1 + \alpha_2 D_2 + \beta_0 X + \beta_1 D_1 X + \beta_2 D_2 X + u \end{aligned} \qquad (6.20)$$

To estimate this model, we simply create new variables $Z_1 = D_1 X$ and $Z_2 = D_2 X$, and regress Y against a constant, D_1, D_2, X, Z_1, and Z_2. The estimated relations in the three income ranges are as follows:

$$\$15,000–\$40,000: \qquad \hat{Y} = \hat{\alpha}_0 + \hat{\beta}_0 X \qquad (6.21)$$

$$\$40,000–\$100,000: \qquad \hat{Y} = (\hat{\alpha}_0 + \hat{\alpha}_1) + (\hat{\beta}_0 + \hat{\beta}_1)X \qquad (6.22)$$

$$\text{over } \$100,000 \qquad \hat{Y} = (\hat{\alpha}_0 + \hat{\alpha}_2) + (\hat{\beta}_0 + \hat{\beta}_2)X \qquad (6.23)$$

The problem with this approach, however, is that (6.21) and (6.22) need not meet at $X = 40$ (see Figure 6.4b), and (6.22) and (6.23) need not meet at $X = 100$. To keep the discussion general, let us call the value of X at which the first kink occurs

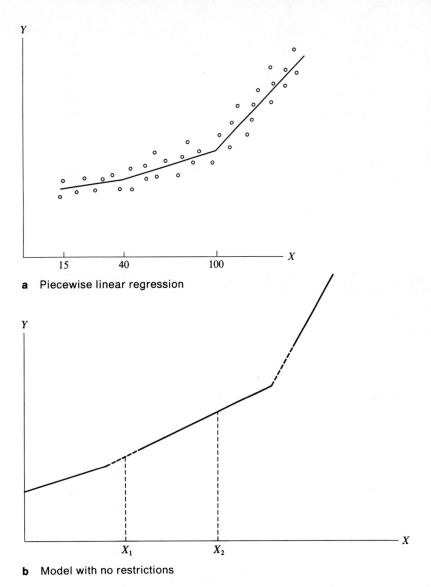

a Piecewise linear regression

b Model with no restrictions

Figure 6.4

X_1, and the one at which the second kink occurs X_2. For the first kink we need the condition

$$\hat{\alpha}_0 + \hat{\beta}_0 X_1 = \hat{\alpha}_0 + \hat{\alpha}_1 + (\hat{\beta}_0 + \hat{\beta}_1)X_1$$

Cancelling common terms, this reduces to $\hat{\alpha}_1 + \hat{\beta}_1 X_1 = 0$. It is easy to verify that the condition for the second kink is $\hat{\alpha}_2 + \hat{\beta}_2 X_2 = 0$. To impose these conditions, we solve for $\hat{\alpha}_1$ and $\hat{\alpha}_2$ and substitute in equation (6.20). The model then becomes

$$Y = \alpha_0 - \beta_1 X_1 D_1 - \beta_2 X_2 D_2 + \beta_0 X + \beta_1 D_1 X + \beta_2 D_2 X + u$$
$$= \alpha_0 + \beta_0 X + \beta_1 D_1 (X - X_1) + \beta_2 D_2 (X - X_2) + u \qquad (6.24)$$

Next define the new variables $Z_1^* = D_1(X - X_1)$, and $Z_2^* = D_2(X - X_2)$. The procedure now is to regress Y against a constant, X, Z_1^*, and Z_2^*.

Practice Problem

6.9 Define the dummy variable $D_4 = 1$ if adjusted gross income exceeds $40,000, and 0 otherwise. Next use D_4 *instead of* D_1 and reformulate equation (6.20). Carefully describe how the parameters of your model can be obtained from those of equation (6.20) *without rerunning any regressions*.

6.4 Estimating Seasonal Effects

Another example of the use of dummy variables occurs in estimating seasonal effects of independent variables. Consider the relationship $E = \alpha + \beta T + u$, presented earlier, between electricity consumption and temperature. In the summer, as the temperature rises, demand for air conditioning pushes electricity consumption up. Thus, we would expect β to have a positive sign, giving a positive relationship between E and T. In the winter, however, as temperature rises (from, say, 20 degrees to 40 degrees), the demand for heating a house becomes lower, and hence we would expect β to be negative in the winter, giving a negative relation between E and T. How can we capture the effect on E of the qualitative variable "season," which has four classes: fall, winter, spring, and summer? This is accomplished by defining three dummy variables known as **seasonal dummies**. As explained earlier, we do not define four dummy variables in order to avoid perfect collinearity. The fall season is used here as the control period:

$$D_1 = \begin{cases} 1 & \text{if the season is winter} \\ 0 & \text{otherwise} \end{cases}$$

$$D_2 = \begin{cases} 1 & \text{if the season is spring} \\ 0 & \text{otherwise} \end{cases}$$

$$D_3 = \begin{cases} 1 & \text{if the season is summer} \\ 0 & \text{otherwise} \end{cases}$$

Now let $\alpha = \alpha_0 + \alpha_1 D_1 + \alpha_2 D_2 + \alpha_3 D_3$ and $\beta = \beta_0 + \beta_1 D_1 + \beta_2 D_2 + \beta_3 D_3$. The fully general specification is obtained by substituting these into the relationship between E and T:

$$E = \alpha_0 + \alpha_1 D_1 + \alpha_2 D_2 + \alpha_3 D_3 + \beta_0 T$$
$$+ \beta_1 D_1 T + \beta_2 D_2 T + \beta_3 D_3 T + u \qquad (6.25)$$

The estimated models for each of the seasons are as follows:

$$\text{Fall:} \qquad \hat{E} = \hat{\alpha}_0 + \hat{\beta}_0 T$$

$$\text{Winter:} \qquad \hat{E} = (\hat{\alpha}_0 + \hat{\alpha}_1) + (\hat{\beta}_0 + \hat{\beta}_1)T$$

$$\text{Spring:} \qquad \hat{E} = (\hat{\alpha}_0 + \hat{\alpha}_2) + (\hat{\beta}_0 + \hat{\beta}_2)T$$

$$\text{Summer:} \qquad \hat{E} = (\hat{\alpha}_0 + \hat{\alpha}_3) + (\hat{\beta}_0 + \hat{\beta}_3)T$$

α_1 is the deviation of the winter intercept term from that of the fall quarter and β_1 is the deviation of the winter slope term from that of fall. A variety of tests can be performed on these models. For instance, a plausible hypothesis is that there is no difference in the relationships between the fall and spring seasons. Comparing the equations for the fall and spring, the hypothesis implies that $\alpha_2 = \beta_2 = 0$. This is tested with a Wald test in which equation (6.25) is the unrestricted model and the restricted model is

$$E = \alpha_0 + \alpha_1 D_1 + \alpha_3 D_3 + \beta_0 T + \beta_1 D_1 T + \beta_3 D_3 T + u \qquad (6.26)$$

Some investigators prefer to retain seasonal dummies in the model even if a few of them are insignificant. It is not clear that this is desirable, however, since redundant dummy variables might unnecessarily reduce the precision of the other parameters. If certain periods are found to be alike (say the fall and spring), one might consolidate them into one season by defining a dummy $D = 1$ for fall or spring and 0 elsewhere. To test the hypothesis that all the seasons have the same relation, the conditions are $\alpha_1 = \alpha_2 = \alpha_3 = \beta_1 = \beta_2 = \beta_3 = 0$. The unrestricted model will be (6.25) and the restricted model will be $E = \alpha_0 + \beta T + u$. The degrees of freedom for the Wald F-statistics are 6 for the numerator and the number of observations minus 8 for the denominator (explain why). We would expect to reject this hypothesis because we argued earlier that the relationship between E and T will be positive in the summer and negative in the winter.

Practice Problem

6.10   Redo the previous analysis using the spring quarter, instead of the fall, as the control.

Instead of defining three dummy variables, suppose we had defined a single variable as follows:

$$D = \begin{cases} 1 & \text{if the season is fall} \\ 2 & \text{if the season is winter} \\ 3 & \text{if the season is spring} \\ 4 & \text{if the season is summer} \end{cases}$$

Next assume that $\alpha = \alpha_0 D$ and $\beta = \beta_0 D$. The model now becomes

$$E = \alpha_0 D + \beta_0 D T + u \qquad (6.27)$$

and the estimated relations now become

Fall:	$\hat{E} = \hat{\alpha}_0 + \hat{\beta}_0 T$
Winter:	$\hat{E} = 2\hat{\alpha}_0 + 2\hat{\beta}_0 T$
Spring:	$\hat{E} = 3\hat{\alpha}_0 + 3\hat{\beta}_0 T$
Summer:	$\hat{E} = 4\hat{\alpha}_0 + 4\hat{\beta}_0 T$

How does this alternative compare with the three-dummy approach we adopted earlier? Note that although the equations for the fall are identical, the others are very different. In particular, comparing fall with winter we see that the difference in intercept between these seasons is α_0. There is no reason why this difference should equal the fall intercept. In fact, the difference in intercept between any two successive seasons is α_0. We are thus assuming that the shift in intercept is the same across all successive seasons. Similarly, the difference in the slopes beween any two successive seasons is always β_0. This assumption is too restrictive and is not likely to hold in general. Therefore, the alternative approach will lead to serious model misspecification and should be abandoned in favor of the general approach with three dummy variables presented earlier.

6.5 Testing for Structural Change Using Dummy Variables

The relationship between the dependent and independent variables may undergo a **structural change**; that is, the relationship might have changed from one period to another. For example, suppose C is the consumption of gasoline in the United States in a given period, and the independent variables are price (P) and income (Y). There have been three periods since 1970 when gasoline prices increased drastically, causing possible changes in the behavioral pattern of gasoline consumption. The first started in 1974 soon after the OPEC (Organization of Petroleum Exporting Countries) cartel started to control world oil prices. The second was in 1979, soon after the revolution in Iran. The last one occurred in 1990 when Iraq invaded Kuwait. It is reasonable to expect the price and income elasticities of gasoline consumption to be different in the four periods divided by these years. The statistical test for structural change is known as the **Chow-test** [after Gregory Chow (1960), who first popularized it]. This section presents two approaches to testing for structural change. The first one consists of dividing the sample into two or more groups, estimating the model separately for each period and with all the sample pooled, and then constructing an F-statistic with which to perform the test. In the second approach, we use dummy variables.

Test Based on Splitting the Sample

Suppose we want to test whether there has been a structural change at time $t = T_1$. The procedure is to divide the sample of T observations into two groups—group 1 consisting of the first T_1 observations and group 2 consisting of the remaining $T_2 = T - T_1$ observations. Estimate the model (with k regression coefficients) separately for each of the two sample groups and compute the sum of squared residuals ESS_1 and ESS_2. The unrestricted sum of squares is therefore given by $ESS_U = ESS_1 + ESS_2$. When divided by σ^2 this will have a chi-square distribution with d.f. $T_1 - k + T_2 - k = T - 2k$, because estimation of the model separately implies that each equation has k regression coefficients. Next assume that the regression coefficients are the same before and after period T_1. Estimate the model again but with the pooled sample, and obtain ESS_R. The appropriate test statistic is now

$$F_c = \frac{(ESS_R - ESS_1 - ESS_2) \div k}{(ESS_1 + ESS_2) \div (T - 2k)}$$

The test procedure is to reject the null hypothesis that there is no structural change if F_c exceeds $F^*_{k, T-2k}$, the point on the F-distribution with k and $T - 2k$ d.f. such that the area to the right is equal to the level of significance.

Test Based on Dummy Variables

The test can also be conducted using the dummy variable technique developed in this chapter [see Franklin Fisher (1970) for more on this approach]. This method is illustrated here for the gasoline consumption example described above (for the 1974 and 1979 shifts only).

Let the basic model be

$$\ln C = \alpha + \beta \ln P + \gamma \ln Y + u \tag{6.28}$$

This is a double-log model in which β is the price elasticity and γ is the income elasticity. We define two dummy variables as follows (1974.1 refers to the first quarter of 1974; other quarters are indicated in the same way):

$$D_1 = \begin{cases} 1 & \text{for the period 1974.1 onward} \\ 0 & \text{otherwise.} \end{cases}$$

$$D_2 = \begin{cases} 1 & \text{for the period 1979.1 onward} \\ 0 & \text{otherwise} \end{cases}$$

Note that for all the periods from 1979.1, both D_1 and D_2 are 1. To test whether the structures for the three periods (prior to 1974.1, 1974.1 through 1978.4, and 1979.1 onward) are different, the specification must assume the following:

$$\alpha = \alpha_0 + \alpha_1 D_1 + \alpha_2 D_2 \qquad \beta = \beta_0 + \beta_1 D_1 + \beta_2 D_2 \qquad \gamma = \gamma_0 + \gamma_1 D_1 + \gamma_2 D_2$$

Substituting these into equation (6.28), we get the unrestricted model

$$\begin{aligned} \ln C &= \alpha_0 + \alpha_1 D_1 + \alpha_2 D_2 + (\beta_0 + \beta_1 D_1 + \beta_2 D_2) \ln P \\ &\quad + (\gamma_0 + \gamma_1 D_1 + \gamma_2 D_2) \ln Y + u \\ &= \alpha_0 + \alpha_1 D_1 + \alpha_2 D_2 + \beta_0 \ln P + \beta_1 (D_1 \ln P) + \cdots + u \end{aligned}$$

To estimate this, we first create new variables $Z_1 = D_1 \ln P$, $Z_2 = D_2 \ln P$, $Z_3 = D_1 \ln Y$, and $Z_4 = D_2 \ln Y$. Next we regress $\ln C$ against a constant, D_1, D_2, $\ln P$,

$Z_1, Z_2, \ln Y, Z_3$, and Z_4. The estimated models are

Prior to 1974.1: $\qquad \widehat{\ln C} = \hat{\alpha}_0 + \hat{\beta}_0 \ln P + \hat{\gamma}_0 \ln Y$

1974.1–1978.4: $\qquad \widehat{\ln C} = \hat{\alpha}_0 + \hat{\alpha}_1 + (\hat{\beta}_0 + \hat{\beta}_1) \ln P + (\hat{\gamma}_0 + \hat{\gamma}_1) \ln Y$

1979.1 onward: $\qquad \widehat{\ln C} = \hat{\alpha}_0 + \hat{\alpha}_1 + \hat{\alpha}_2 + (\hat{\beta}_0 + \hat{\beta}_1 + \hat{\beta}_2) \ln P$
$$+ (\hat{\gamma}_0 + \hat{\gamma}_1 + \hat{\gamma}_2) \ln Y$$

By comparing these relations, we can test a variety of hypotheses. For instance, the hypothesis $\alpha_1 = \alpha_2 = \beta_1 = \beta_2 = \gamma_1 = \gamma_2 = 0$ indicates that there is no structural change whatsoever. A t-test on β_2 will test whether the price elasticity is the same between 1974.1 – 1978.4 and 1979.1 onward. Many other hypotheses are left as exercises.

The dummy variable approach has an advantage over splitting the sample; namely, we can test, if we so desire, just a few of the regression coefficients for structural change rather than the entire relation as the latter method would do.

We see from the unrestricted model for $\ln C$ that if the intercept as well as all the slope coefficients are allowed to be different across seasons, the number of interaction terms, and hence the number of regression coefficients to be estimated, could be large. This would result in the loss of several degrees of freedom and a reduction in the power of tests. A researcher is therefore well advised to guard against the proliferation of dummy variables thus leading one to "data mining." A useful approach would be to formulate a basic model without dummy variables and then use the model specification tests described in Chapter 7 to test whether additional dummy variables and interaction terms should be included in the model.

Practice Problems

6.11 Describe how to test the hypothesis that the income elasticity is unchanged in all the three periods.

6.12 Describe how to test the hypothesis that the intercept is the same for all the periods.

6.13 Suppose the dummy variable D_3, defined here, is used instead of D_1:

$$D_3 = \begin{cases} 1 & \text{for the period 1974.1–1978.4} \\ 0 & \text{otherwise} \end{cases}$$

Redo the preceding analysis under this assumption. What is the relation between the coefficients obtained this way and those obtained earlier?

6.6 Testing the Equality of Coefficients Across Equations

Many situations arise in which there is a need to test hypotheses on regression coefficients over different relationships. As an illustration, let MS_i be the starting salary of the ith new male employee of a particular firm and MX_i be the number of years of prior experience ($i = 1, 2, \ldots, m$). Assuming for simplicity that the male employees are similar in other respects such as age, education, and so on, the relation between starting salary and prior experience is as follows:

$$\text{Male:} \quad \text{MS}_i = a_0 + a_1 \text{MX}_i + u_i \qquad (i = 1, 2, \ldots, m)$$

A similar model can be specified for female employees. Let FS_j be the starting salary of the jth new female employee of the firm and FX_j be the number of years of prior experience ($j = 1, 2, \ldots, n$). The model for females is

$$\text{Female:} \quad \text{FS}_j = b_0 + b_1 \text{FX}_j + v_j \qquad (j = 1, 2, \ldots, n)$$

a_0 and b_0 are the expected mean salaries for employees with no prior experience (that is, $\text{MX} = \text{FX} = 0$). A natural hypothesis to test is $a_0 = b_0$; that is, there is no gender difference in the intercepts. a_1 and b_1 measure the expected mean *extra* starting salary for one *extra* year of experience; that is, they are the marginal effects of experience. The hypothesis $a_1 = b_1$ means that the marginal effects are the same, on average, for both males and females. The joint hypothesis $a_0 = b_0$ and $a_1 = b_1$ means that the relationships are identical for the two groups. How can we test these hypotheses that are across different equations?

Here again, dummy variables are useful. We assume that the variances of the error terms u_i and v_j are the same. Otherwise, the problem is complicated and beyond the scope of this book. Define $D = 1$ if the employee is a male and 0 if female. Pool the two samples to get $m + n$ observations on salaries. Call the "stacked" values of salaries $S_t(t = 1, 2, \ldots, m + n)$; that is, the first m observations of the data column for S will be the same as those for the m male employees, and the last n observations of the data column for S will be the same as those for the n female employees (see Table 6.6). Let X_t denote a similarly stacked set of values of experience. If the relation between starting salary and experience is the same across genders, then $a_0 = b_0(= \alpha, \text{ say})$ and $a_1 = b_1(= \beta, \text{ say})$. In this case, the restricted model becomes

$$S_t = \alpha + \beta X_t + u_t \qquad (t = 1, 2, \ldots, m + n)$$

TABLE 6.6 Pooled Data for Males and Females

t	S_t	X_t	D_t
1	MS_1	MX_1	1
2	MS_2	MX_2	1
m	MS_m	MX_m	1
$m + 1$	FS_1	FX_1	0
$m + 2$	FS_2	FX_2	0
$m + n$	FS_n	FX_n	0

To test whether α and β are different for males and females, we would first assume that $\alpha = \alpha_0 + \alpha_1 D$ and $\beta = \beta_0 + \beta_1 D$, and formulate the unrestricted model as

$$S_t = \alpha_0 + \alpha_1 D_t + \beta_0 X_t + \beta_1(D_t X_t) + u_t$$

It will be readily seen that the estimated models for the two groups are

$$\text{Females:} \quad \hat{S}_t = \hat{\alpha}_0 + \hat{\beta}_0 X_t$$
$$\text{Males:} \quad \hat{S}_t = (\hat{\alpha}_0 + \hat{\alpha}_1) + (\hat{\beta}_0 + \hat{\beta}_1) X_t$$

$\hat{\alpha}_1$ and $\hat{\beta}_1$ measure the differential in salary between males and females. The joint hypothesis $\alpha_1 = \beta_1 = 0$ means that the relationships are identical between the two groups. This is tested with the familiar Wald test for a subset of coefficients. The separate hypotheses $\alpha_1 = 0$ or $\beta_1 = 0$ are tested using a straightforward t-test. There are other, equivalent ways of testing the various hypotheses presented here, but the dummy variable approach is easy to use and is recommended because pooling the samples increases the degrees of freedom and hence improves the precision of estimates and increases the power of tests of hypotheses.

Practice Problem

6.14   Try Exercise 6.7.

6.7   Empirical Example: Motor Carrier Deregulation

Blair, Kaserman, and McClave (1986) carried out a study of the effect of deregulation on the price structure of intrastate trucking services in Florida. The deregulation went into effect on July 1, 1980, and the authors' data comprise over 27,000 observations, covering ten trucking firms and four time periods, one before deregulation. The authors assumed that the supply of trucking services to an individual shipper is infinitely price elastic at the market rate. The dependent variable was ln(PTM), where PTM is the price of the shipment per ton-mile in 1980 dollars. The quantitative independent variables were the following: ln(WT), where WT is the midpoint of the various weight classes; PD is the price of diesel fuel in 1980 cents per gallon; and ln(DIST), where DIST is the number of miles the shipment traveled. The study also included a number of dummy variables: ORIGJ is 1 when the shipment originated from Jacksonville, ORIGM is 1 if the shipment originated from Miami, CLASSi ($i = 1, 2, 3, 4$) denotes five different shipment classification, and DEREG is 1 in the postderegulation period.

The basic model estimated is as follows, with t-statistics in parentheses:

$$\widehat{\ln(\text{PTM})} = 10.1805 + 0.0305\text{ORIGJ} + 0.0254\text{ORIGM} - 0.1590\text{LN(WT)}$$
$$\phantom{\widehat{\ln(\text{PTM})} =} (327.44) \quad\quad (6.31) \quad\quad\quad (5.28) \quad\quad\quad\quad (-133.74)$$

$$- 0.6398\text{LN(DIST)} + 0.2800\text{CLASS1} + 0.5871\text{CLASS2}$$
$$ (-196.00) \quad\quad\quad\quad (16.21) \quad\quad\quad\quad (97.22)$$

$$+ 0.9086\text{CLASS3} + 1.0923\text{CLASS4} + 0.0030\text{PD} - 0.1581\text{DEREG}$$
$$ (150.45) \quad\quad\quad\quad (175.82) \quad\quad\quad (10.42) \quad\quad (-35.08)$$

$$R^2 = 0.79$$

The regression coefficient of primary interest is that for DEREG. This coefficient is both negative and significant at the 1 percent level, indicating that the hypothesis that deregulation resulted in a significant reduction in trucking rates is supported. Other things being equal, the deregulation of intrastate trucking in Florida resulted in an average rate reduction of nearly 15 percent. The remaining variables are also statistically significant at the 1 percent level and have the correct signs for the coefficients.

The authors also tested for the interaction between the dummy variables and a number of quantitative variables, as well as among the dummy variables themselves, but with mixed results. Details may be found in their paper.

6.8 Application: The Demand for a Sealant Used in Construction

A particular company makes a sealing compound used in concrete work for construction and road building. It believed that a competitor spread a rumor about the quality of the company's product causing a loss of sales and profits during the period July 1986 through October 1988. The company filed a lawsuit against the competitor and claimed damages. An expert witness on behalf of the company with a sense of humor calls the company Cement Overcoat, Inc. (COI) and himself Rodney Random, so as to protect the confidentiality of the details of the trial.

Figure 6.5 is a graph showing the quantity (in gallons) of the sealant sold by COI in each month from January 1983 through May 1990. Three interesting patterns

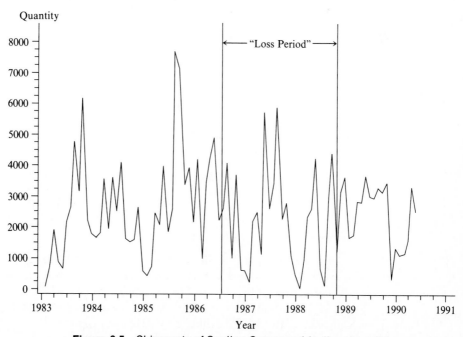

Figure 6.5 Shipments of Sealing Compound (gallons/month)

emerge from the graph. First, there is seasonality in the quantity and, as can be expected, January sales are typically low and sales during August–September are generally high. Second, the sales average appears to have decreased in the "loss" period (July 1986–October 1988) and decreased further in the postloss period. Finally, the height of the summer sales peak has steadily diminished from period to period. Thus, there is some *prima facie* support for the contention that sales were lower during the loss period. In fact, the losses may have continued beyond the litigation period.

Rodney Random obtained data on a number of variables that are likely to affect monthly shipments. Table 6.13 (at the end of the chapter) has monthly data for the following variables for the period January 1983 through May 1990:

Q = shipments of sealing compound used in construction, in gallons/month

P = price per gallon, in dollars

HS = housing starts, in thousands

SHC = index of street and highway construction

OC = overall index of public and private construction

L = 1 for July 1986 through October 1988, when company presumably suffered losses

PL = 1 from November 1988 onward, the post loss period

Random did a thorough analysis of the data set, including carrying out many of the testing procedures described in Chapters 7, 8, and 9. Here we present a modified portion of the analysis that illustrates the usefulness of dummy variables. The starting point is the basic model presented below:

(A) $Q = \beta_1 + \beta_2 P + \beta_3 HS + \beta_4 SHC + \beta_5 OC + \beta_6 L + \beta_7 PL + u$

It will be noted that the terms L and PL are dummy variables that shift the "intercept." The first period is the control and β_6, β_7 measure the deviation of the constant term from the base period (note that L is defined as 1 only for the loss period). OLS estimates of the coefficients are given below along with p-values in parentheses (Practice Computer Session 6.7 has all the details for using the ECSLIB program to reproduce the results of this section):

$$\hat{Q} = -2065 - 301.670P + 14.423HS + 0.629SHC$$
$$\quad\;\; (0.27) \quad\; (0.003) \qquad (0.047) \qquad\quad (0.124)$$
$$+\; 33.677OC - 1075.203L - 733.934PL$$
$$\quad (0.010) \qquad\quad (0.023) \qquad\quad (0.223)$$

$$\bar{R}^2 = 0.354 \qquad \text{d.f.} = 82 \qquad \hat{\sigma} = 1258$$

The signs for the regression coefficients for L and PL are negative indicating that, on average, sales in the latter two periods were below those in the first period, even after correcting for the effects of other explanatory variables such as housing starts, state highway construction, and overall construction. However, the p-value for the coefficient of PL is 0.223, which is unacceptably high. Note that the p-value for the coefficient of L is only 0.023, indicating that average sales were significantly lower in the "loss" period as compared to the first period. However, the model explains only 35.4 percent of the variation in monthly shipments and could use some improvement in specification.

It was noted from Figure 6.5 that there is a seasonal pattern is shipment data. This suggests incorporating dummy variables to capture seasonal effects. Accordingly, 11 dummies were defined, one each for February through December (January was omitted in order to avoid the "dummy variable trap"). These were then added to Model A and a new model (B) was estimated. Because there are numerous terms, the result is not presented here, but it can be obtained using Practice Computer Session 6.7. It was found that the coefficient for L is still significantly negative, but the coefficient for PL, although still negative, was significant only at the 48 percent level. Many of the dummy variables were, however, even more insignificant. We could omit these variables and reestimate the model to see if the significance of the remaining variables would improve. Instead of doing that, we have adopted an approach that directly addresses the loss issue.

The preliminary analysis indicates that there might have been a significant loss in sales during the second period, and perhaps even during the last period. The proper way to obtain a measure of possible sales loss is to exclude the data for the loss and postloss periods. Including them would affect the estimates, thus begging the question we are trying to answer. The procedure adopted estimates the model using the 42 observations for the period 1983.01–1986.06. We can then generate forecasts for the loss and postloss periods and compare them with the actual known values. If the predicted shipments are systematically higher than actual shipments, there is strong evidence of a change in structure and significant losses.

The procedure just described was applied to the first period data and a third model (C) was estimated using the explanatory variables constant term, P, HS, SHC, OC, and the 11 monthly dummies, but *excluding* L and PL which are both zero for the first period. As before, the regression coefficients for many of the dummy variables were insignificant, as was that for housing starts (HS). In order to improve the precision of the remaining coefficients, these variables were omitted and the model reestimated. The estimates for the "final" model (D) are given below with the *p*-values in parentheses:

$$\hat{Q} = \underset{(0.34)}{-1915} - \underset{(0.096)}{1157 \text{dummy6}} - \underset{(0.002)}{499.986P} + \underset{(0.0004)}{1.896 \text{SHC}} + \underset{(0.0006)}{51.928 \text{OC}}$$

$$\bar{R}^2 = 0.513 \qquad \text{d.f.} = 37 \qquad \hat{\sigma} = 1202$$

The coefficient for the June dummy variable was significant at the 9.6 percent level, but all other coefficients (excluding the constant term) were significant at levels below 1 percent. The adjusted R^2 has increased substantially from 0.354, but even the newer model explains only half the variation in shipments. This might be because monthly data are usually volatile (that is, vary a great deal) and are difficult to model.

Model D was next used to forecast shipments for the periods 1986.07–1988.10 and 1988.11–1990.05. Figure 6.6 shows graphs of both the predicted and actual

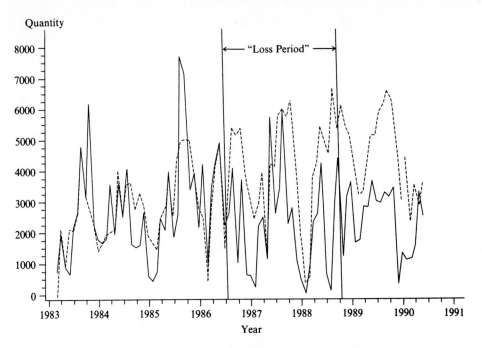

Figure 6.6 Acutal and Forecast Shipments of Sealing Compound
(Actual is in solid lines and forecast is in broken lines)

shipments for the entire 89 months. (Practice Computer Session 6.7 computes the numerical values.) Note that during the first period before the alleged rumor about COI, the model tracks the actual values well, except for a few extreme values. This is not very surprising because OLS gives the lowest error sum of squares and has errors that average to zero. In contrast, however, the forecasts for the "loss" period are systematically above those of the actual values. For the postloss period, the difference is more pronounced. This is the strongest evidence that the structure has indeed changed to the detriment of COI's sales and profits. In fact, the losses continued during the postloss period. Measures of the net loss in sales and revenues have been obtained as follows ($\sum$ refers to the net sum of the losses):

$$\text{Sales} = \sum(\hat{Q}_t - Q_t) = 54,209 + 38,467 = 92,676$$
$$\text{Revenues} = \sum P_t(\hat{Q}_t - Q_t) = 481,575 + 335,597 = 817,172$$

Rodney Random submitted his estimates of losses (different from those above partly because the litigation was in reference to the middle period only) in a detailed report. When the case went to trial, the defendants were so overwhelmed by the strength of Rodney's analysis that all damages to COI were settled out of court and he never had a chance to testify. This caused Rodney a great deal of disappointment because he would have been paid $250 an hour for his testimony.

This example demonstrates how useful dummy variables can be in appropriately modeling real behavior.

SUMMARY

In this chapter we have seen how *qualitative* independent variables such as the gender, educational or occupational status, season, public or private, and so on can be handled in an econometric formulation. The method is very straightforward. First we choose one of the categories of the qualitative variable as *control* (the choice is arbitrary). Then we define *dummy variables* (variables that take only the value 1 or 0) for each of the other categories, *the number of dummy variables being one less than the number of categories* (in order to avoid perfect collinearity among the dummy variables). In a model of the form $Y = a + bX + u$, if the constant term (a) is to be different for the different categories, then we assume the following:

$$a = \alpha_0 + \alpha_1 D_1 + \alpha_2 D_2 + \cdots + \alpha_{m-1} D_{m-1}$$

where m is the number of categories for the dummy variables, and $D_1, D_2, \ldots, D_{m-1}$ are the dummy variables. D_1 will take the value 1 for observations that belong to category 1 and 0 for all other observations. The other Ds are defined similarly. To shift the slope (b) for the different categories, we assume that

$$b = \beta_0 + \beta_1 D_1 + \beta_2 D_2 + \cdots + \beta_{m-1} D_{m-1}$$

To estimate the αs and the βs, we generate the interaction variables $Z_1 = D_1 X$, $Z_2 = D_2 X, \ldots, Z_{m-1} = D_{m-1} X$, where X is a quantitative independent variable. Then we regress Y against a constant term, $D_1, D_2, \ldots, D_{m-1}, X, Z_1, Z_2, \ldots, Z_{m-1}$. The coefficients for the Ds are the $\hat{\alpha}$s and those for the Zs are the $\hat{\beta}$s. Note that the number of coefficients estimated is $2m$ and hence the degrees of freedom are $T - 2m$. This means that unless the number of observations is at least $2m$, the model with the full interaction terms cannot be estimated. If the number of categories is large, the dummy variable and interaction terms can easily proliferate. The problem becomes worse if there are more quantitative variables in the model whose coefficients are to be shifted. In Chapter 7 we describe a procedure for systematically including these dummy variables and interactions.

KEY TERMS

Analysis of covariance model
Analysis of variance (ANOVA) model
Binary variables
Chow-test
Control group
Dummy variables
Dummy variable trap
Piecewise linear relationship
Qualitative variables
Quantitative variables
Seasonal dummies
Structural change

REFERENCES

Blair, Roger D.; Kaserman, David L.; and McClave, James T. "Motor Carrier Deregulation: The Florida Experiment." *Review of Econ. Statistics* (February 1986): 159–164.

Chow, Gregory C. "Tests of Equality Between Sets of Coefficients in Two Linear Regressions," *Econometrica* (1960).

Fisher, Franklin M. "Tests on Equality Between Sets of Coefficients in Two Linear Regressions: An Expository Note." *Econometrica* (1970).

Grether, D. M., and Mieszkowski, P. "Determinants of Real Estate Values." *J. Urban Economics*, Vol. 1 (1974).

Kain, J. K., and Quigley, J. M. "Measuring the Value of Housing Quality." *J. Amer. Stat. Assoc.*, Vol. 65 (June 1970).

Patel, Raman; Sikula, Andrew; and McKenna, John. "The Mobility of the Business Professor—Why?" *Collegiate News and Views*. Vol. 37 (Fall 1983).

Ridker, R. G., and Henning, J. A. "The Determinants of Residential Property Values with Special Reference to Air Pollution." *Review of Econ. Statistics* (May 1967).

Schmalensee, R.; Ramanathan, R.; Ramm, W.; and Smallwood, D. *Measuring External Effects of Solid Waste Management*. U.S. Environment Protection Agency, EPA-600/5-7-010 (March 1975).

Sommers, Paul M., and Quinton, Noel. "Pay and Performance in Major League Baseball: The Case of the First Family of Free Agents." *J. Human Resources* (1982): 426–436.

PRACTICE COMPUTER SESSIONS

6.1 Using the data file *data6-1* and the commands in *ps6-1.inp*, the results in Table 6.2 can be duplicated.

6.2 Practice Problem 6.3 uses the same data file and needs the commands in *ps6-2.inp*. You are encouraged, however, to carry the analysis further. First copy the input file using the command *copy ps6-2.inp inp1*. Next execute ECSLIB interactively using the DOS command *ecslib*, choosing the option 0 and the data file *data6-1*. When the ? prompt appears, type *run inp1* to execute the commands in *inp1*. Look at the *p*-values of the regression coefficients, decide on variables to omit, and use the *omit* command to delete variables one at a time (you can learn more about *omit* with the command *help omit*). Continue this process until you have a model in which all variables are significant (at least one *). Finally *quit* ECSLIB, rename *inpfile* as *inp2* (*ren inpfile inp2*), and use the batch command

$$ecslib \ data6\text{-}1 \ < inp2 \ > ps6\text{-}2.out$$

to obtain the output. You can then use the *lpr* command to print the output file. Evaluate the results and choose the "best" model. Explain what you mean by "best." Interpret the results of the final model.

6.3 Example 6.3 uses data file *data6-9* and the commands in *ps6-3.inp*.

6.4 The commands in *ps6-4.inp* along with the data file *data6-9* will enable you to reproduce the results in Example 6.4 and Table 6.5.

6.5 The analysis in Example 6.4 can be carried further using nonlinear terms and other types of interactions for the same data set (*data6-9*). The procedure is similar to that in Practice Computer Session 6.2. Use the input file *ps6 − 5.inp* as a starting point.

6.6 Use the data file *data6-11* and the commands in *ps6-6.inp* to verify the results in Table 6.8 and the Wald *F*-statistic printed by the *omit* command.

6.7 The results of the application Section 6.8 can be duplicated with the data file *data6*-13 and the input command file *ps6-7.inp*.

6.8 The file *data6-a* in the data diskette has the information necessary to carry out an empirical analysis for Exercise 6.4. Use that data set with ECSLIB or any other regression package and carry out the estimation.

EXERCISES

6.1 Consider the consumption function $C_t = \alpha + \beta Y_t + u_t$, where C is aggregate consumption expenditures in the United States and Y_t is disposable income, both in constant dollars. Suppose you have annual data from 1930 onward till 1987. Because the World War II years were different, you wish to exclude that data. Furthermore, the postwar consumption function is likely to be different from the prewar function. Describe how you would go about testing for this.

6.2 The relationships between the monthly expenditure on housing (E) and household income (Y) for three age groups are as follows:

$$\text{Age less than 30:} \quad E = \alpha_1 + \beta_1 Y + u_1$$
$$\text{Age 31 to 55:} \quad E = \alpha_2 + \beta_2 Y + u_2$$
$$\text{Age 56 or over:} \quad E = \alpha_3 + \beta_3 Y + u_3$$

a. What is the economic interpretation of the hypothesis $\beta_1 = \beta_2 = \beta_3$?
b. Describe step by step how the dummy variable approach could be used to test the hypothesis in part a.

6.3 Consider the following relation between employee earnings and their determinants estimated in Example 6.3 using the data in Table 6.9 (at the end of the chapter):

$$\ln(\text{WAGE}) = \alpha + \beta \text{EDUC} + \gamma \text{EXPER} + \delta \text{AGE} + u$$

Modify Practice Computer Session 6.4 and generate all the interactions between a quantitative variable and the dummy variables; for example, AGE_RACE will be AGE multiplied by RACE, and so on. Then estimate the complete "kitchen sink" model (that is, one which contains all the basic variables plus all the interactions). Practice Computer Session 6.5 has the initial steps for this. Next estimate appropriate restricted models that will enable you to carry out each of the following tests, and perform the actual tests. Be sure to indicate the null and alternative hypotheses, the regressions to run, the statistics to compute, their distributions, and the criteria for acceptance or rejection of the hypotheses:

  i. Between two employees with no education beyond the eighth grade, the salary is the same regardless of gender or race.

  ii. The marginal effect of experience is the same for white females and nonwhite males.

  iii. The relation $\ln(\text{WAGE}) = \alpha + \beta\text{EDUC} + \gamma\text{EXP} + \delta\text{AGE} + u$ is the same for white females and nonwhite males.

†6.4 Using data for 427 students, the following basic model (call it Model A) was estimated:

$$\text{COLGPA} = \alpha + \beta\text{HSGPA} + \gamma\text{VSAT} + \delta\text{MSAT} + u$$

where COLGPA and HSGPA are grade point averages at college and in high school, respectively; and VSAT and MSAT are verbal and math scores in the Scholastic Aptitude Test (SAT). A number of other student characteristics were also measured: whether the student lived on campus; whether the student graduated from a public or nonpublic high school; and the student's major in five categories of science, social science, humanities, arts, and undeclared. Describe step by step how you will test each of the following hypotheses. More specifically:

a. Formulate another econometric model (call it Model B) that will enable you to test the hypothesis (clearly define any additional variables you use).

b. State the null and alternative hypotheses in that model.

c. Describe what regression(s) should be run and how the test statistic is derived.

d. Describe the criterion for acceptance or rejection of the null hypothesis. The regression coefficient α is the same whether the student graduated from a public or nonpublic school, whether the student resided on or off campus, and regardless of the student's major.

e. See Practice Computer Session 6.8 for actually carrying out the estimations.

6.5 You are studying the determinants of commercial television market shares. The basic specification is

$$\text{SHARE}_t = \alpha + \beta\text{NSTAT}_t + \gamma\text{CABLE}_t + \delta\text{INCOME}_t + u$$

where SHARE is the market share (in %) of the tth station, NSTAT is the number of competing television stations in the same area, CABLE is the percent of households in the area wired for cable television, and INCOME is per capita income of the locality served by the station.

a. Explain why we can expect the following signs for the marginal effects:

$$\frac{\partial\text{SHARE}}{\partial\text{NSTAT}} < 0, \qquad \frac{\partial\text{SHARE}}{\partial\text{CABLE}} < 0, \qquad \text{and} \qquad \frac{\partial\text{SHARE}}{\partial\text{INCOME}} = 0.$$

b. Describe step by step how you would test the hypothesis that
    i. α will depend on whether or not the tth station is VHF, *and* whether or not it is a network affiliate (ABC, CBS, NBC).
    ii. the *entire relation* will depend on the two qualitative variables listed in hypothesis i.

6.6   Consider the women's labor force participation rate application of Chapter 4, which used cross-section data for states. The final model was

$$\text{WLFP} = a + b\text{YF} + c\text{EDUC} + d\text{UE} + e\text{URB} + f\text{WH} + u$$

where WLFP is the women's rate of participation in the labor force, YF is the median income of females, EDUC is percent of female high school graduates over 24 years of age, UE is the unemployment rate, URB is the percent of urban population in the state, and WH is the percent of females over 16 who are white. Suppose it is believed that there is a geographic difference in this relationship—in other words, that the model will be different for western states as compared to eastern states. In particular, let there be six geographic regions: northwest, southwest, north central, south central, northeast, and southeast. What model(s) would you estimate in order to test for geographic differences in the relation? Describe how you will state the formal hypotheses, compute the test statistic, and decide on criteria to accept or reject the hypotheses.

6.7   The expenditure on clothing (EXP) for a family depends on household income (Y) as well as size of the family (N). A number of households were surveyed separately in urban and rural areas and the following models formulated (the subscript u refers to an urban household and r to a rural household):

$$\text{EXP}_{ui} = \alpha_0 + \alpha_1 Y_{ui} + \alpha_2 N_{ui} + \text{error} \quad (i = 1, 2, \ldots, m)$$
$$\text{EXP}_{rj} = \beta_0 + \beta_1 Y_{rj} + \beta_2 N_{rj} + \text{error} \quad (j = 1, 2, \ldots, n)$$

Describe the economic interpretation of each of the following hypotheses and explain how you would go about testing them:
a. $\alpha_0 = \beta_0$
b. $\alpha_1 = \beta_1$
c. $\alpha_2 = \beta_2$
d. The entire relation is different between urban and rural households.

6.8   Table 6.7 has four models relating the college grade point average (COLGPA) of 427 students to their high school grade point average (HSGPA) and to their verbal and math scores in the Scholastic Aptitude Test (VSAT and MSAT). A number of dummy variables are also included: DCAM = 1 if the student lived on campus, DPUB = 1 if the student graduated from a public high school, and several dummy variables for major categories—science (DSCI), social science (DSOC), humanities (DHUM), and arts (DARTS). The control group is the undeclared students. [*Note*: The entries in parentheses are standard errors.]

TABLE 6.7 Estimated Models for the Grade Point Average Data

Variable	Model A	Model B	Model C	Model D
CONSTANT	0.367 (0.224)	0.368 (0.224)	0.423 (0.220)	0.422 (0.221)
HSGPA	0.406 (0.063)	0.414 (0.062)	0.398 (0.061)	0.389 (0.062)
VSAT	0.00073 (0.00029)	0.00068 (0.00029)	0.00074 (0.00028)	0.00079 (0.00029)
MSAT	0.0011 (0.0003)	0.0011 (0.0003)	0.0010 (0.0003)	0.0010 (0.0003)
DSCI	−0.027 (0.057)	−0.026 (0.057)		
DSOC	0.056 (0.073)	0.054 (0.073)		
DHUM	−0.0041 (0.142)	−0.0068 (0.141)		
DARTS	0.229 (0.189)	0.243 (0.188)		
DCAM	−0.041 (0.052)			−0.040 (0.052)
DPUB	0.029 (0.063)			0.033 (0.063)
ESS	96.204	96.421	97.164	96.932
$\bar{R}^2$	0.211	0.213	0.215	0.213

Values in parentheses are the corresponding standard errors.

a. In the relevant models test whether there is any difference due to the student's living on campus or off campus. State the null and alternative hypotheses, the test statistic and its distribution, and the test criterion.

b. In the relevant models test whether there is any difference due to the student's having graduated from a public or other type of school. State the null and alternative hypotheses, the test statistic and its distribution, and the test criterion.

c. In Model A test whether the dummy variables for majors are *jointly significant* at the 10 percent level. Be sure to state the null and alternative hypotheses, the test statistic and its distribution, and the test criterion. Perform the same test with Model B as the unrestricted model. Do you get the same result?

d. In Model A test the hypothesis that none of the dummy variables has nonzero regression coefficients.

6.9 Consider the following model proposed by Patel, Sikula, and McKenna (1983) of the mobility of the business professor:

$$AVGYR = \alpha + \beta PAPERS + \gamma AGE + u$$

where AVGYR is the mobility index defined as the average number of years employed in the institution, PAPERS is the number of papers published, and AGE is the age of the professor in years. Information is also available about the rank of the professor (assistant, associate, or full professor), whether opportunity for promotion is good, whether opportunity for jobs for spouse is good, and whether the professor is happy with the administration.

a. Develop a model that will enable you to test whether α is the same for professors of all ranks and all the other qualitative characteristics listed. Then describe how you will perform the test "α is the same for all ranks, promotion opportunities, and so on."

b. Now do the same for the entire relation (that is, α, β, and γ).

6.10   A labor economist wanted to estimate the relationship between earnings (E), number of years of experience (N), and education. Because he had no detailed data on education, he divided the sample into three groups based on education and then estimated three separate models:

    (A)   high school or below education: $\ln(E) = \alpha_0 + \alpha_1 N + u$

    (B)   a bachelor's degree only: $\ln(E) = \beta_0 + \beta_1 N + v$

    (C)   a postgraduate degree: $\ln(E) = \gamma_0 + \gamma_1 N + w$

u, v, and w are "well-behaved" random error terms that have equal variances. An econometrician argues that he would get more efficient estimates of the regression coefficients by pooling all the data and formulating a single model that would also take into account the educational level of the person in the sample.

a. Formulate a single econometric model (both deterministic and error parts) that will enable you to measure the relationship among earnings, experience, and education. Explain clearly how you arrived at the formulation.

b. Explain why your model will give more efficient estimates than the ones the labor economist would have estimated.

c. Suppose you want to test the hypothesis that there are no significant differences in the relationships for groups B and C. Describe the regression(s) you will run; state the null and alternative hypotheses; write an expression for a test statistic; state its statistical distribution under the null hypothesis, including degrees of freedom; and indicate the criterion for rejecting the null hypothesis.

6.11   Table 6.10 (at the end of the chapter) has data on air quality in 30 standard metropolitan statistical areas (SMSAs) in the United States, along with several variables that can contribute to air pollution. The cross-sectional data refer to the period 1970–1972 for different variables. SMSAs are integrated economic and social units having 5000 or more inhabitants. Most of them are counties or larger areas.

a. Carefully explain why each of the possible independent variables might affect air quality [refer to the paper by Ridker and Henning (1967) before answering this question]. Indicate the sign you would expect for the regression coefficients. If a particular variable is not relevant, state so.

b. Formulate a basic model with air quality as the dependent variable and a selected list of independent variables (exclude the binary variables at this point). Justify your choice. Using a regression program estimate this model.

c. Do your data have any multicollinearity problems? If yes, are your results affected by them?

d. Describe how the dummy variables might affect the relationship you specified in part b. Formulate a new model and estimate it. Perform appropriate tests to compare the two models. What do you conclude?

e. After choosing the final model, interpret your results.

f. Identify missing variables that would help better explain the variance in air quality across SMSAs.

6.12 Table 6.11 (at the end of the chapter) has detailed data on 59 single family houses in the La Jolla and University City communities of San Diego. La Jolla is a coastal community and is well known for its beautiful coves and beaches. It is also a resort city and is considered a prestigious locale to live in. University City is located about 5 to 10 miles inland. Because of their proximity to the ocean and the other reasons mentioned, La Jolla homes tend to be more expensive. Note from Table 6.11 that a number of variables are binary and take only the values 0 and 1.

Use the data in Table 6.11 and first create the new variable LSQFT = log(SQFT). Then estimate the following basic model:

$$\text{PRICE} = \alpha + \beta\text{SQFT} + \gamma\text{LSQFT} + \delta\text{YARD} + u$$

Do you have a "good" fit? Are the regression coefficients (ignore the constant term) significant? In this model derive the marginal effect of SQFT on PRICE and interpret the results. Next estimate a general model that includes other characteristics of the homes. In this unrestricted model, are some variables candidates to be omitted? Why? Exclude these variables, reestimate the model, and perform a Wald F-test to see if the omitted variables are jointly significant. Repeat this process until you have the "best" model. Explain what you mean by best. Choose your final model and interpret the results.

6.13 Table 6.8 presents estimates and related statistics for three models of automobile prices. Table 6.12 has data on the list price of 106 new 1983 American-made cars and characteristics of cars. Only 2-door and 5-door sedans and hatchbacks are included. The data are from the *1983 Wards Automotive Yearbook*.

a. Perform a Wald test with Model A as the unrestricted model and each of Models B and C as the restricted model. State the null and alternative hypotheses. [Note: ESS can be obtained from the table.]

b. According to the model selection criteria, which is the "best" model? Interpret the results for this model, especially those for the dummy variables. Do you find any counterintuitive signs? Do you have any explanation for them? Are the numerical values of the regression coefficients sensible? If not, do you have any explanation for them?

c. Using your regression program estimate other variations and interpret the results.

TABLE 6.8 Determinants of the List Price of an Automobile

Variables	Model A	Model B	Model C
CONSTANT	28.821 (4.36)	22.957 (5.50)	24.568 (6.19)
WEIGHT	0.303 (3.04)	0.260 (3.61)	0.326 (6.93)
WBASE	−0.073 (−1.40)	−0.068 (−1.79)	−0.084 (−2.30)
LENGTH	−0.009 (−0.30)		
WIDTH	−0.043 (−0.55)		
HEIGHT	−0.326 (−3.12)	−0.288 (−3.24)	−0.309 (−3.54)
LITERS	0.283 (1.16)	0.265 (1.22)	
CARB	−1.027 (−4.13)	−1.017 (−4.37)	−1.051 (−4.54)
TRANS	1.361 (3.25)	1.326 (3.93)	1.381 (4.12)
CRUZ	5.912 (9.67)	5.791 (12.71)	5.705 (12.64)
TILT	2.550 (2.57)	1.989 (3.70)	1.963 (3.65)
DEFOG	−0.727 (−0.63)		
FOURDOOR	−0.264 (−0.54)		
HATCH	0.146 (0.57)		
DIESEL	−0.135 (−0.39)		
$\bar{R}^2$	0.919	0.922	0.922
$\hat{\sigma}^2$	1.275	1.219	1.225
AIC	1.453	1.322	1.317
FPE	1.456	1.323	1.318
HQ	1.693	1.449	1.429
SCHWARZ	2.118	1.658	1.610
SHIBATA	1.405	1.305	1.304
GCV	1.485	1.332	1.325
RICE	1.527	1.344	1.334

TABLE 6.9 Data on Wages and Other Employee Characteristics

WAGE: Wage Rate Per Month for Staff Employees								
1345	2435	1715	1461	1639	1345	1602	1144	1566
1496	1234	1345	1345	3389	1839	981	1345	1566
1187	1345	1345	2167	1402	2115	2218	3575	1972
1234	1926	2165	2365	1345	1839	2613	2533	1602
1839	2218	1529	1461	3307	3833	1839	1461	1433
2115	1839	1288	1288					

EDUC: Years of Education Beyond Eighth Grade When Hired								
6	4	6	6	9	5	7	4	6
4	4	6	5	9	4	4	9	5
6	7	9	4	11	4	8	11	4
4	5	6	6	9	4	5	11	8
9	7	4	1	9	11	4	6	9
6	4	4	6					

EXPER: Number of Years at the Institution								
2	18	4	4	3	8	6	3	23
15	9	3	14	16	20	5	10	4
1	10	2	17	2	15	11	1	1
2	9	15	12	5	14	14	3	5
18	1	10	10	22	3	14	5	3
15	13	9	4					

AGE: Age of Employee								
38	52	45	58	30	43	30	33	51
37	45	55	57	36	60	35	34	28
25	43	42	47	46	52	64	39	39
40	53	59	35	45	37	37	43	32
40	49	43	31	45	31	55	30	28
60	32	58	29					

GENDER = 1 If Employee is Male								
0 If Female								
0	1	1	1	1	0	0	0	1
1	0	0	0	1	1	1	0	0
0	0	0	1	1	1	1	1	1
0	1	0	0	0	0	1	1	0
0	1	0	1	1	1	1	0	1
0	1	1	0					

TABLE 6.9 (*Continued*)

| | | RACE = 1 | If Employee is White | | | | | |
| | | 0 | Otherwise | | | | | |

1	1	1	1	0	1	1	0	0
1	0	1	1	1	1	0	1	0
1	1	1	0	1	0	1	1	1
1	0	1	0	1	0	1	1	1
1	1	0	0	1	1	0	1	0
0	0	0	0					

| | CLERICAL = 1 | If Employee Is a Clerk | | | | | | |
| | 0 | Otherwise | | | | | | |

1	0	0	1	0	1	1	0	0
0	1	1	1	0	0	0	1	1
1	1	1	0	1	0	0	0	0
1	0	0	0	1	0	0	0	1
0	0	1	0	0	0	0	1	0
0	0	0	0					

| | MAINT = 1 | If Employee Is a Maintenance Worker | | | | | | |
| | 0 | Otherwise | | | | | | |

0	0	1	0	0	0	0	1	1
1	0	0	0	0	1	1	0	0
0	0	0	1	0	0	0	0	0
0	1	0	0	0	0	0	0	0
0	0	0	0	0	0	1	0	0
0	1	1	0					

	CRAFTS = 1	If Employee Is a Craftsperson						
	0	Otherwise						
	(Control Group is Professional Employee)							

0	1	0	0	1	0	0	0	0
0	0	0	0	0	0	0	0	0
0	0	0	0	0	1	1	0	1
0	0	0	0	0	0	1	0	0
1	0	0	1	1	0	0	0	1
0	0	0	1					

Source: Data compiled by Susan Wong.

TABLE 6.10 Data on Air Quality and Its Determinants

AIRQUAL: Weight of Suspended Particular Matter

104	85	127	145	84	135	88	118	74
104	64	75	131	129	84	165	80	59
110	120	118	120	120	59	74	124	69
118	129	129						

POPLN: SMSA Population in Thousands

1420	1390	3375	6979	1556	1228	1985	1110	609
7032	1268	1046	11529	4818	1009	2401	1358	3110
679	721	2071	739	372	1065	1857	1404	817
827	539	693						

VALADD: Value Added by Industrial Manufacturers in 1972
(in Thousands of Dollars)

2734.4	2479.2	4845	19733.8	4093.6	1849.8	4179.4	2525.3	1899.2
15257.1	1219	992.9	15120.8	9189.9	1596.9	4157.3	1185.2	3817.7
1686.2	1322	3476.2	1123.8	1151.6	2896.3	5608.6	3700	1395.5
3022.8	1515.4	1878.9						

RAIN: Rainfall in Inches

12.63	47.14	42.77	33.18	34.55	14.81	45.94	39.25	42.36
12.63	59.76	53.9	42.37	42.48	37.18	36.14	12.63	18.69
35.35	35.08	43.05	68.13	35.35	18.69	42.36	29.51	42.92
41.32	31.22	30.95						

COAST = 1 For SMSAs on the Coast
0 Otherwise

1	1	1	0	1	0	1	0	1
1	1	1	1	1	1	1	1	1
0	1	1	1	0	1	1	0	1
0	0	0						

DENSITY: Population Per Square Mile of Area

1815.86	804.86	1907.86	1876.08	340.93	335.52	315.78	360.39	12957.5
1728.19	620.96	529.62	5397.47	1356.04	276.44	787.47	318.63	1255.04
750.28	325.36	916.78	271.59	645.83	819.23	2649.07	9642.86	1105.55
910.79	379.58	455.92						

TABLE 6.10   (*Continued*)

MEDINCM: Median Per Capita Income

4397	5667	15817	32698	6250	4705	7165	4472	2658
33885	5160	3738	59460	19224	3944	9281	5012	15710
2509	2627	8019	2425	1364	4155	8947	5952	4146
3207	853	853						

POVERTY: 100 Times the Percentage of Families with Income Less Than Poverty Level

1939	933	379	961	1791	346	1791	589	478
1939	1305	952	1665	1271	197	1271	1939	1939
1145	1665	392	876	1145	1939	478	285	177
589	853	853						

ELECTR: Electricity Consumed by Industrial Manufacturers

5.2	8.7	14.4	100.7	9.4	9	169.8	9.9	9.4
60	3.4	32.1	32.5	73.3	11.4	98.6	1.7	40.2
17.9	6.9	27.4	24.5	14.4	7	25.1	16.5	4.3
15.3	5.2	19.3						

FUELOIL: Thousands of Barrels of Fuel Oil Consumed in Industrial Manufacturing

175.5	400.1	4079.8	7260.1	60.6	609.4	1843.8	424.8	2535.2
855.9	498.7	72.4	4542.1	19122.9	1434.5	2985.1	39.9	659.9
374	75.4	7679.1	819.7	451.1	18.4	7298.4	692.2	1402.3
225.1	177.3	297.8						

INDESTAB: Number of Industrial Establishments with 20 or More Employees

839	840	1867	5753	1498	596	1064	508	742
5916	937	344	9466	3161	669	981	363	1480
388	305	878	380	221	559	1748	1027	437
465	479	453						

Source: Data compiled by Susan Wong.

TABLE 6.11 Data on Sale Price and Characteristics of Homes

PRICE: Sale Price in Thousands of Dollars								
143	228	280	540	172.686	250	275	345	425
245	210	250	295	302	292.5	340	546	305
590	365	370	362	155	150	225	270	312.5
330	345	114	120	121.5	140.75	134	146	141
145	140	155	200	119.7	126	135	150	177.5
178	195	217.5	110	132.5	145	210	120	132
136.5	195	148	177.5	208				

AGE: Age of House in Years								
32	32	38	20	25	22	22	4	24
15	35	18	10	8	7	8	35	60
8	9	12	8	30	30	35	1	2
3	20	13	12	21	12	10	13	18
13	20	22	19	10	12	15	19	14
7	3	2	12	13	13	3	12	13
20	3	20	14	4				

AIRCON = 1 If House Has Central Air Conditioning 0 Otherwise								
0	0	0	0	0	0	0	0	0
0	0	0	0	1	0	0	0	0
0	0	0	0	0	0	0	0	0
0	0	0	0	0	0	0	0	0
0	0	0	0	0	0	0	0	0
0	0	1	0	0	0	0	0	0
0	0	0	0	0				

BATHS: Number of Bathrooms								
1	1	2	2.5	1.75	2	2	2.5	2.5
2.75	2	2.5	2.5	2.5	2.5	2.5	3	4
2.5	2.5	3.5	2.5	1	1	2	3	2
3.5	2.5	1.75	1.75	2	1.75	2.5	1.75	2
2.5	2	2	2	2	2	1.75	2.5	3
1.75	2.5	2	1.75	2	1.75	2.5	2	1.75
1.75	3	2	5	4				

TABLE 6.11 (*Continued*)

				BEDRMS: Number of Bedrooms				
2	2	2	2	3	3	3	3	3
4	4	4	4	4	4	4	4	5
5	5	5	5	3	3	3	3	3
3	3	3	3	3	3	3	3	3
3	3	3	3	4	4	4	4	4
4	4	2	3	3	3	3	4	4
4	4	3	5	4				

				COND: Condition of House from 1 (Poor) to 6 (Excellent)				
5	2	5	5	3	5	5	5	5
5	4	5	5	5	6	5	5	5
5	5	5	5	5	3	4	6	5
5	5	5	3	5	5	5	5	5
5	4	5	5	4	5	5	5	3
5	5	5	3	5	5	5	5	5
5	5	6	5	5				

				CORNER = 1 If the House Is a Corner Lot 0 Otherwise				
0	0	1	0	0	0	0	1	0
0	0	0	0	0	0	0	0	0
0	1	0	0	0	0	1	0	0
0	0	0	0	0	0	0	0	0
0	0	0	0	0	0	0	0	0
0	0	0	0	0	0	0	0	0
1	0	0	0	1				

				CULD = 1 If House Is in a Cul-de-sac 0 Otherwise				
0	0	0	0	0	0	0	0	0
0	0	0	0	1	0	0	0	0
0	0	0	0	0	0	0	0	0
0	0	1	0	0	0	0	0	0
0	0	0	0	0	0	1	0	1
0	0	0	0	0	0	0	0	0
0	0	0	0	0				

(*continued*)

TABLE 6.11 (Continued)

DISH = 1   If House Has a Built-in Dishwasher
       0   Otherwise

1	0	1	1	1	1	1	1	1
1	1	1	1	1	1	1	1	1
1	1	1	1	0	0	0	1	1
1	1	1	1	1	1	1	1	1
1	1	1	0	1	1	0	1	1
1	1	1	1	1	1	1	1	1
1	1	1	1	1				

FENCE = 1   If House Has a Fence
        0   Otherwise

1	1	1	1	1	1	1	1	0
1	1	1	1	1	0	1	1	1
1	1	1	1	1	1	1	1	0
1	1	1	1	1	1	1	1	1
1	1	1	1	1	1	1	1	1
1	1	1	1	1	1	1	1	1
1	1	1	1	1				

FIREPL: Number of Fireplaces

2	1	1	1	0	1	1	2	1
1	1	1	1	1	1	2	2	2
2	1	1	1	1	1	0	1	2
1	1	0	1	1	1	1	1	1
1	1	1	2	1	1	1	1	1
1	2	1	0	1	1	2	0	1
1	2	1	1	2				

FLOORS: Number of Floors

1	1	1	1	1	1	1	1	1
1	2	1	1	1	2	2	2	1
1	1	1	1	1	1	1	2	1
2	1	1	1	1	1	2	1	1
2	1	1	1	1	1	1	2	2
1	2	1	1	1	1	2	1	1
1	2	1	2	2				

TABLE 6.11 (*Continued*)

GARAGE: Number of Car Spaces in Garage

1	1	2	1	0	2	2	1	2
2	1	2	3	3	3	2	2	1
2	3	3	3	1	2	1	2	2
2	2	2	2	2	2	2	2	2
2	2	2	2	2	2	2	2	1
2	2	2	2	2	2	3	2	2
2	1	2	2	3				

IRREG = 1   If Lot Is Irregular in Shape
0   Otherwise

0	0	1	1	0	1	0	0	0
0	0	1	1	1	0	0	1	0
0	0	0	1	0	0	0	0	0
1	0	0	0	0	1	0	0	1
0	1	0	0	0	1	0	0	0
1	0	1	1	1	0	0	0	1
1	0	0	0	0				

LAJOLLA = 1   If House Is in La Jolla
0   Otherwise

1	1	1	1	1	1	1	1	1
1	1	1	1	1	1	1	1	1
1	1	1	1	1	1	1	1	1
1	1	0	0	0	0	0	0	0
0	0	0	0	0	0	0	0	0
0	0	0	0	0	0	0	0	0
0	0	0	0	0				

LNDRY = 1   Has Laundry Area
0   Otherwise

0	0	1	1	1	1	1	1	1
1	1	1	1	1	1	1	1	1
1	1	1	1	1	1	1	0	1
1	1	1	1	1	1	1	1	1
1	1	1	1	1	1	1	1	1
1	1	1	1	1	1	1	1	1
1	1	1	1	1				

(*continued*)

TABLE 6.11 *(Continued)*

LOTSIZE:	Size of the Lot in Square Feet							
4356	6000	9450	4914	10000	11590	10454	8005	39204
9583	8250	8547	10920	9100	19602	5177	9720	10500
20473	13068	21780	10875	3750	9000	3825	7000	21344
11484	14463	5130	6600	6300	4900	5346	9345	7728
6412	7519	11761	9500	6400	6400	4248	9638	6500
11160	12477	7380	3380	6324	6825	6970	7700	14904
8772	5724	10890	6500	8276				

PATIO:	Number of Patios							
1	1	1	1	1	1	2	2	2
1	1	1	1	1	1	1	1	1
1	1	1	1	0	1	1	0	1
2	1	1	0	1	1	1	1	1
1	1	1	1	1	1	1	1	1
1	0	1	1	1	1	1	1	1
1	1	1	1	1				

POOL = 1	If the House Has a Swimming Pool							
0	Otherwise							
0	0	0	1	0	0	0	0	0
0	1	0	0	0	0	1	0	0
1	0	0	0	0	0	0	1	1
0	0	0	1	0	0	0	0	0
1	0	1	0	0	0	0	0	0
0	0	1	0	0	0	1	0	1
0	0	1	0	0				

ROOMS:	Number of Rooms Excluding Bedrooms and Baths							
2	2	3	2	3	1	2	3	4
3	4	4	3	4	4	4	3	5
5	4	5	4	2	2	2	1	1
5	4	1	2	2	2	3	2	4
4	2	2	2	3	3	2	4	4
3	4	2	2	2	3	4	3	3
3	3	2	4	4				

TABLE 6.11 (*Continued*)

		SPRINK = 1		If There Is Sprinkler System				
		0	Otherwise					
0	0	1	1	1	1	1	1	0
1	0	1	1	1	1	1	1	0
1	1	1	1	0	0	1	1	1
1	1	0	0	0	1	1	1	1
1	1	1	1	1	0	1	1	0
1	1	1	1	0	0	1	0	0
1	1	1	0	1				

		SQFT:	Living Area in Square Feet					
950	965	1800	1200	1900	1500	1900	2524	2500
2475	1914	2519	2530	2100	2300	2600	2618	2800
3775	2785	3200	2650	1007	1115	1200	2100	2184
3000	2400	1250	1464	1300	1640	1641	1650	1900
1650	1500	1500	2000	1584	1583	1600	2050	3000
1925	2278	2048	1450	1700	1600	2540	1584	1584
1800	2268	1364	3000	2536				

		VIEW = 1		If the House Has a View				
		0	Otherwise					
0	1	1	1	0	0	0	1	1
0	1	1	1	1	1	1	0	1
1	1	0	1	0	0	0	1	1
1	1	1	1	0	0	0	1	0
0	0	1	1	0	0	0	1	0
1	0	1	0	1	1	0	0	0
0	1	1	0	0				

TABLE 6.12 Data on List Price and Characteristics of Automobiles

PRICE: List Price in Thousands of Dollars

5.287	5.623	6.973	6.258	6.919	6.369	6.703	7.158	7.308
8.45	10.75	8.473	8.623	8.498	9.277	21.8	5.872	6.075
7.39	7.867	7.564	7.312	7.457	8.813	10.81	8.813	8.983
13.986	9.313	9.112	7.464	8.046	9.117	9.306	9.806	9.364
9.517	10.833	9.559	10.259	13.62	15.752	7.328	7.536	8.088
9.255	9.416	9.514	10.27	9.869	15.738	15.97	16.441	19.182
19.344	21.44	12.215	5.947	6.154	6.749	9.702	6.523	8.203
9.629	10.574	6.059	6.266	7.678	7.721	7.53	6.84	6.943
9.953	8.319	11.198	17.447	20.753	21.241	21.509	5.841	6.379
6.718	6.577	8.249	8.154	8.79	9.341	9.58	18.688	5.841
6.379	6.718	8.014	8.49	8.841	9.011	9.369	6.29	7.25
7.99	5.595	6.27	5.995	6.724	7.697	9.162		

WEIGHT: Weight of Car in Hundreds of Pounds

20.88	21.48	23.13	23.84	24.4	24.03	24.63	24.71	25.26
28.83	31.77	27.1	27.3	31.99	34.9	31.17	20.58	21.22
23.53	24.13	24.12	24.73	25.31	28.58	31.94	25.99	27.17
30.21	32.57	33.35	24.18	24.95	26.81	27.14	28.79	32.48
32.98	36.2	35.85	39.16	38.31	37.23	23.85	24.25	25.62
26.83	27.12	32.45	32.6	36.2	37.08	39.35	39.93	47.65
37.48	38.44	26.39	20.32	20.94	21.56	29.69	27.05	28.69
30.76	37.48	20.32	20.94	20.69	21.79	27.7	27	27.5
30.99	28.76	38.26	40.62	40.04	41.05	35.58	21.75	22.22
23.23	23.23	33.21	24.64	24.9	25.23	34.67	40.19	21.75
22.22	23.17	24.65	25.42	25.64	34.01	33.21	18.83	19.2
19.9	19.45	19.8	28.13	29.06	30.33	32.64		

WBASE: Wheel Base in Inches

94.3	97.3	97.3	101.2	101.2	101.2	104.9	104.9	104.9
101	101	104.9	104.9	108.1	116	96.2	94.3	97.3
101.2	101.2	101.2	104.9	104.9	101	101	104.8	104.8
104.8	108.1	108.1	101.2	104.9	104.9	104.9	104.9	108.1
108.1	108.1	115.9	115.9	119	114	101.2	101.2	104.9
104.9	104.9	108.1	108.1	115.9	114	121.5	121.5	144.5
114	114	101.2	94.2	94.2	94.2	100.4	105.5	105.5
103.5	114.3	94.2	94.2	94.2	94.2	100.4	105.5	105.5
103.8	105.5	114.3	117.3	114.3	117.3	108.6	99.1	96.6
100.1	100.1	112.7	100.1	100.1	103.1	112.7	112.7	99.1
96.6	100.1	100.1	100.1	103.1	112.7	112.7	94.5	94.5
94.5	97.8	97.8	96	108	97.2	109.3		

TABLE 6.12 *(Continued)*

LENGTH: Length of Car in Inches

161.9	164.9	164.9	170.9	173.5	172.4	176.7	176.7	176.7
187.8	187.8	188.3	188.3	192.7	212.2	176.5	161.9	164.9
173.6	173.6	175.9	182.1	183.1	189.8	189.8	188.7	188.7
188.7	198.6	201.9	176.2	182.8	188.4	188.4	188.4	200
200.4	200.4	218.1	218.1	221.1	206.1	173.6	175.9	181.1
189.1	189.1	200.6	200.6	218.4	206.6	221	221	244.3
204.5	204.8	173.1	163.9	163.9	170.3	179.1	195.5	196.5
197.6	211	163.9	163.9	163.9	170.3	179.1	195.5	195.5
197.6	196.5	214	219	216	219	201.2	164.8	174
176	176	205.7	179.6	179.6	187.2	210.1	213.3	164.8
174	176	181.2	179.8	185.6	209.5	205.7	155.3	155.3
155.3	163.8	163.8	167	185	164.6	183.2		

WIDTH: Width of Car in Inches

61.8	61.8	61.8	66	66	66.3	68.3	68.3	68.3
72.8	72.8	69.3	69.3	72.3	75.3	71	61.8	61.8
68.6	68.6	68.6	69.1	69.1	72	72	68.2	68.2
68.2	71.3	72.1	65	69.8	69.5	69.5	69.5	71.6
71.9	71.9	76.3	76.3	76.3	71.4	68.6	68.6	68.9
66.8	66.8	71.6	71.5	76.2	71.5	76.5	76.5	76.5
71.5	71.5	66.5	65.9	65.9	65.9	69.1	71	71
71.1	77.5	65.9	65.9	65.9	65.9	69.1	71	71
71.1	71	77.5	78.1	78.1	78.1	73.6	65.8	66.7
68.6	68.6	74.2	68.5	68.5	68.3	72.7	72.7	65.8
66.7	68.6	68.5	68.5	68.3	72.7	74.2	63.4	63.4
63.4	65	65	72	71.1	72.9	72.3		

HEIGHT: Height in Inches

52.9	52.9	52.9	52	51.9	53.9	53.1	53.9	53.9
50	50	53.7	53.7	55.7	56.4	46.7	52.9	52.9
53.5	51.9	54.8	53.5	53.5	49.8	49.8	54.8	54.8
54.8	55.8	54.7	53.7	53.7	54.1	54.1	54.1	54.9
55.9	55.9	56.7	56.7	57.2	54.6	53.5	54.8	53.7
53.6	53.6	54.5	55.4	56	53.7	54.6	55.6	56.9
54.3	54.3	52	53.3	53.3	50.5	51.9	52.9	53.6
53.2	55.3	53.3	53.3	53.3	50.5	51.9	51.7	52.9
53.4	53.6	55.2	55.9	55.2	56.1	54.8	53.1	50.8
52.7	52.7	55.3	52.5	52.3	52.9	53.2	53.2	53.1
50.8	52.3	52.5	52.9	52.9	53.2	55.3	53.2	52.9
53.2	54.5	54.5	51.6	50.8	55	54.4		

(continued)

TABLE 6.12 *(Continued)*

LITERS: Engine Displacement in Liters

1.6	1.6	1.8	2	2	2	2.5	2.5	2.8
2.5	5	2.5	2.5	3.8	3.8	5.7	1.6	1.6
1.8	1.8	1.8	2.5	2.5	2.5	5	2.5	2.5
2.8	3.8	3.8	2	2.5	2.5	2.5	4.3	3.8
3.8	5.7	3.8	5.7	4.1	4.1	2	2	2.5
2.5	2.5	3.8	3.8	3.8	4.1	4.1	4.1	6
4.1	4.1	2	1.6	1.6	1.6	5	2.3	2.3
3.8	5	1.6	1.6	1.6	1.6	2.3	2.3	2.3
3.8	2.3	5	5	5	5	5	1.6	1.6
2.2	2.2	3.7	2.2	1	2.2	3.7	5.2	1.6
1.6	2.2	2.2	2.2	2.2	3.7	3.7	1.7	1.6
1.8	1.4	1.4	4.2	4.2	2.5	2.5		

CARB = 1   For Carburetor
0   Otherwise for Fuel Injection

1	1	0	0	0	0	0	0	1
0	1	0	0	1	1	0	1	1
0	0	0	0	0	0	1	0	0
1	1	1	0	0	0	0	0	1
1	0	1	0	1	1	0	0	0
0	0	1	1	1	1	0	0	0
0	0	0	1	1	1	1	1	1
1	0	1	1	0	1	1	1	1
1	1	0	0	0	0	0	1	1
1	1	1	1	0	1	1	0	1
1	1	1	1	1	1	1	1	0
0	0	0	1	1	1	1		

TRANS = 1   For Automatic Transmission

0	0	0	0	0	0	0	0	0
0	0	1	1	1	1	1	0	0
0	0	0	0	0	0	0	1	1
1	1	0	0	0	1	1	1	1
1	1	1	1	1	1	0	0	0
1	1	1	1	1	1	1	1	1
1	1	0	0	0	0	0	0	0
1	1	0	0	0	0	0	0	0
1	0	1	1	1	1	1	0	0
0	0	1	0	0	1	1	1	0
0	0	0	0	1	1	1	0	0
0	0	0	0	0	0	0		

TABLE 6.12 *(Continued)*

CRUZ = 1   For Cruise Control

0	0	0	0	0	0	0	0	0
0	0	0	0	0	0	1	0	0
0	0	0	0	0	0	0	0	0
1	0	0	0	0	0	0	0	0
0	0	0	0	1	1	0	0	0
0	0	0	0	0	0	1	1	1
1	1	1	0	0	0	0	0	0
0	0	0	0	0	0	0	0	0
0	0	0	1	1	1	1	0	0
0	0	0	1	1	1	1	0	0
0	0	0	0	0	0	0	1	0
0	0	0	0	0	0	0	0	0
0	0	0	0	0	0	0		

TILT = 1   For Tilt Steering Wheel or Adjustable Steering Column

0	0	0	0	0	0	0	0	0
0	0	0	0	0	0	0	0	0
0	0	0	0	0	0	0	0	0
1	0	0	0	0	0	0	0	0
0	0	0	0	0	1	0	0	0
0	0	0	0	0	1	0	0	0
0	0	0	0	0	0	0	0	0
0	0	0	0	0	0	0	0	0
0	0	0	0	1	1	1	0	0
0	0	0	0	0	0	0	1	0
0	0	0	0	0	0	0	0	0
0.	0	0	0	0	0	0		

DEFOG = 1   For Rear Window Defroster

0	0	0	0	0	0	0	0	0
0	0	0	0	0	0	1	0	0
0	0	0	0	0	0	0	0	0
1	0	0	0	0	0	0	0	0
0	0	0	0	0	1	0	0	0
0	0	0	0	0	0	0	0	0
0	0	0	0	0	0	0	0	0
0	0	0	0	0	0	0	0	0
0	0	0	0	1	1	1	0	0
0	0	0	0	0	0	1	0	
0	0	0	0	0	0	0	0	0
0	0	0	0	0	0	0		

(continued)

TABLE 6.12 (Continued)

FOURDOOR = 1 For Four-Door Model

0	0	0	0	0	0	0	0	0
0	0	0	0	0	0	0	0	0
0	0	0	0	0	0	0	0	0
1	0	0	0	0	0	0	0	0
0	0	0	0	0	0	0	0	0
0	0	0	0	0	0	0	0	0
0	0	1	0	0	0	0	0	0
0	0	0	0	0	0	1	0	0
0	0	0	0	1	0	0	1	0
0	0	0	0	0	0	0	1	1
1	0	0	0	0	0	0		

HATCH = 1 For a Hatchback

0	1	1	0	0	1	0	1	0
0	0	0	1	1	1	0	0	1
0	0	1	0	1	0	0	0	0
1	1	0	1	1	0	1	1	0
1	1	1	1	1	0	0	1	1
0	1	0	1	1	0	0	1	1
0	1	1	0	1	0	0	1	1
0	1	0	1	0	0	0	0	1
0	1	1	1	0	1	1	1	0
1	0	1	0	0	1	0	0	1
0	1	0	1	1	0	1	0	1
0	0	1	0	1	0	1		

DIESEL = 1 If Car Has a Diesel Engine

1	1	1	0	1	0	0	1	1
1	1	0	0	0	0	1	1	1
0	1	0	0	1	1	1	0	0
0	0	0	0	0	0	0	0	0
0	0	0	0	0	0	0	0	0
0	0	0	0	0	0	0	0	0
0	0	0	1	1	1	1	0	0
0	0	1	1	1	1	1	0	0
0	0	0	0	0	0	0	1	1
0	0	0	0	0	0	0	0	1
1	0	0	0	0	0	0	1	1
1	0	0	1	0	1	0		

Source: Data compiled by Susan Wong.

TABLE 6.13   Data on the Determinants of the Shipments of Sealing Compound

PERIOD	Q	P	HS	SHC	OC	L	PL
1983.01	120	9.9	91.3	473.3	110	0	0
1983.02	829	8.74	96.3	403.1	107	0	0
1983.03	1928	5.48	134.6	466.6	114	0	0
1983.04	930	8.97	135.8	642.2	119	0	0
1983.05	722	9.49	174.9	949	135	0	0
1983.06	2184	8.45	173.2	1250.9	135	0	0
1983.07	2632	8.75	161.6	1303.8	123	0	0
1983.08	4799	7.35	176.8	1686.6	136	0	0
1983.09	3185	8.58	154.9	1517	126	0	0
1983.10	6202	8.73	159.3	1344.7	124	0	0
1983.11	2234	8.67	136	1040.1	125	0	0
1983.12	1806	8.56	108.3	639.3	124	0	0
1984.01	1692	8	109.1	452.1	131	0	0
1984.02	1865	7.8	130	452.8	134	0	0
1984.03	3587	7.73	137.5	525.1	132	0	0
1984.04	1975	8.08	172.7	732.4	130	0	0
1984.05	3619	8.11	180.7	1034.8	155	0	0
1984.06	2560	7.8	184	1305.1	139	0	0
1984.07	4135	8.58	162.1	1476	135	0	0
1984.08	1648	8.72	147.4	1563.5	134	0	0
1984.09	1555	10.04	148.5	1459.2	134	0	0
1984.10	1626	8.57	152.3	1345.8	134	0	0
1984.11	2685	8.71	126.2	1052.4	138	0	0
1984.12	627	8.84	98.9	624.7	137	0	0
1985.01	484	9.2	105.4	498.5	141	0	0
1985.02	781	9.07	95.4	439.6	137	0	0
1985.03	2527	9.36	145	549.1	155	0	0
1985.04	2108	8.69	175.8	767.7	146	0	0
1985.05	3986	9.22	170.2	1170.8	153	0	0
1985.06	1909	8.69	163.2	1370.9	143	0	0
1985.07	2609	8.47	160.7	1421	151	0	0
1985.08	7723	7.84	160.7	1548.2	152	0	0
1985.09	7149	8.34	147.7	1480.9	160	0	0
1985.10	3417	8.07	173	1426.2	159	0	0

(continued)

TABLE 6.13 (Continued)

PERIOD	Q	P	HS	SHC	OC	L	PL
1985.11	3980	8.18	124.1	1067.6	153	0	0
1985.12	2230	8.86	120.5	703.8	151	0	0
1986.01	4225	8.25	115.6	562.3	145	0	0
1986.02	1045	13.69	107.2	499.7	161	0	0
1986.03	3475	8.49	151	587.9	152	0	0
1986.04	4320	8.32	188.2	898.8	164	0	0
1986.05	4910	8.29	186.6	1261.5	162	0	0
1986.06	2265	13.48	183.6	1505.3	163	0	0
1986.07	2655	11.21	172	1542	159	1	0
1986.08	4120	8.24	163.8	1633.5	160	1	0
1986.09	1095	8.26	154	1579.5	158	1	0
1986.10	3740	7.76	154.8	1543.1	159	1	0
1986.11	680	8.59	115.6	1019.8	158	1	0
1986.12	635	9.47	113	735.3	162	1	0
1987.01	305	10.22	105.1	590.9	162	1	0
1987.02	2250	8.26	102.8	534.4	153	1	0
1987.03	2515	8.45	141.2	682.2	169	1	0
1987.04	1205	13.69	159.3	897.6	159	1	0
1987.05	5765	8.71	158	1217	158	1	0
1987.06	2675	8.92	162.9	1530.1	169	1	0
1987.07	3455	8.47	152.4	1685.3	168	1	0
1987.08	5930	9	143.6	1774.3	174	1	0
1987.09	2300	8.38	152	1852.2	161	1	0
1987.10	2865	8.43	139.1	1780.1	173	1	0
1987.11	1165	9.11	118.8	1295.1	162	1	0
1987.12	485	12.85	85.4	884.8	167	1	0
1988.01	90	13.35	78.2	554	153	1	0
1988.02	965	14.21	90.2	544.6	166	1	0
1988.03	2370	8.26	128.8	713.1	164	1	0
1988.04	2635	8.64	153.2	1115.9	161	1	0
1988.05	4265	8.55	140.2	1498.8	168	1	0
1988.06	740	9.31	150.2	1828	176	1	0
1988.07	190	10.72	137	1752.5	164	1	0
1988.08	2740	6.97	136.8	1740.6	169	1	0
1988.09	4425	8.76	131.1	1643.9	164	1	0
1988.10	1325	8.35	135.1	1780.6	170	1	0

TABLE 6.13 (*Continued*)

PERIOD	Q	P	HS	SHC	OC	L	PL
1988.11	3185	7.37	113	1364.9	163	0	1
1988.12	3685	8.17	94.2	984	178	0	1
1989.01	1715	8.25	100.1	703.1	172	0	1
1989.02	1790	8.43	85.8	545.8	160	0	1
1989.03	2890	8.33	117.8	642.2	158	0	1
1989.04	2855	9.31	129.4	994.3	175	0	1
1989.05	3685	9	131.7	1529.7	167	0	1
1989.06	3015	8.14	143.2	1765.7	172	0	1
1989.07	2985	8.6	134.7	1697.1	171	0	1
1989.08	3320	9.03	122.4	1978.8	169	0	1
1989.09	3165	9.56	109.3	1898.9	186	0	1
1989.10	3470	9.01	130.1	1730.7	180	0	1
1989.11	410	8.83	96.6	1397.3	167	0	1
1989.12	1390	10.9	75	973.9	166	0	1
1990.01	1150	6.83	99.2	769	160	0	1
1990.02	1190	10.34	86.9	734.9	156	0	1
1990.03	1620	8.6	108.5	783.2	160	0	1
1990.04	3355	9.54	119	1021.2	148	0	1
1990.05	2555	10.63	120.7	1468.4	156	0	1

CHAPTER 7

Testing for Model Specification

■ We have repeatedly stated that the formulation of a satisfactory econometric model is crucial to any conclusions drawn from it. In the previous chapters we have discussed a variety of criteria for judging whether a model is "good." The initial formulation of a model is based on economic theory, an investigator's own knowledge of the underlying behavior, other similar studies, and so on. The analyst might also have some general idea of possible nonlinear effects as well as interactions among variables. Because there is no unique way of characterizing the relationship between the dependent variable and the explanatory variables, a researcher often formulates alternative models and then puts them through a number of diagnostic tests.

In judging the acceptability of an econometric model, the signs of the estimated regression coefficients are important, and it is essential that the investigator have some prior notion of what to expect, at least for the key variables. Suppose, for instance, we are estimating a demand relation and find that the estimated price elasticity is positive. This is a clear sign of possible misspecification either in the deterministic part or in the error structure (or both), and/or faulty econometric methodology. The magnitude of the estimated coefficient is also important. In Section 6.1 we estimated the marginal effect of a swimming pool on the price of a house as $53,196. Because the cost of a swimming pool is considerably less than this, we should look for reasons why the estimate is so high. We argued that the variable POOL might really be a proxy for a number of yard improvements that are related to a pool (such as jacuzzi, deck, patio, and other pavement). Although $\bar{R}^2$ is a useful measure of the goodness of fit, overreliance on this measure is not fruitful. Cross-section studies generally have low $\bar{R}^2$ compared to time series studies, in which most variables exhibit trends and there are high correlations among them. While low $\bar{R}^2$ signals possible omitted variables, choosing models by maximizing $\bar{R}^2$ is not recommended.

In Chapter 4 we recommended eight model selection criteria as useful measures in judging whether one model is "better" than another. Another criterion often used in judging a model is its ability to predict the dependent variable. If forecasting is an important goal of an econometrician, then it is essential that the models' forecasting ability be carefully evaluated (more on this in Chapter 11).

The Data Generation Process (DGP) and the Hendry/LSE Approach

If, in Example 6.4, we allowed the intercept as well as all the slope coefficients to vary according to the various employment characteristics, we would obtain the most general model relating wages to experience; education; age; a variety of characteristics such as gender, race, and occupational status; and all the interactions and nonlinearities. We can estimate this complete model and perform Wald F-tests to see if certain subsets of variables should be omitted. When testing for structural change we could also specify a model with different structures for different time periods and then test for a common structure between two periods. This approach, starting from a very general model and using hypothesis tests to reduce the parametrization, is strongly advocated by Hendry (1985) and many econometricians at the London School of Economics [see also Hendry and Richards (1982, 1983), Gilbert (1986, 1989)]. Their approach has been referred to as the **Hendry/LSE approach**. Although Hendry's emphasis was on time series modeling, the principle is equally applicable to cross-section data. The basic idea, in Hendry's terminology, is that there is a **Data Generation Process (DGP)** underlying the values of economic variables, and that an investigator's job is to approximate it using economic theory, intuition, and experience, and by putting the model through a number of diagnostic tests to see if either model or methodology can be improved.

One of the criticisms levied against the Hendry/LSE methodology is that, because a researcher is usually not sure what the most general specification ought to be, it might amount to indiscriminate "data mining." The various nonlinear and interaction terms might introduce strong multicollinearity, making it difficult to interpret individual regression coefficients. For example, in the motor carrier deregulation example presented in Chapter 6, the logarithm of the price per ton mile of a shipment of cargo was related to the logarithm of the number of miles traveled, the midpoint of a weight class, the price of diesel, and a number of dummy variables (whether the shipment originated at Jacksonville, Miami, or elsewhere in Florida; five different shipment classifications; ten different trucking firms; and four different periods that the data spanned). If the interaction of every dummy variable with every quantitative variable were included, the model would have numerous regressors, many of which would likely be multicollinear. This might cause several of the estimates of the coefficients of the unrestricted model to be insignificant, and also make the interpretation of individual terms difficult and weaken the powers of tests. It is useful, therefore, to have some systematic procedure for testing a model's specification.

There are a number of formal approaches to hypothesis testing, the most common of which are the **Lagrange multiplier (LM) test**, the **likelihood ratio (LR) test**, and the Wald test. In previous chapters the Wald test has been used extensively. The present chapter focuses on the LM test as an alternative means of testing for model specification. The LR test is discussed in the appendix. In all these approaches, two models are formulated, a *restricted model* and an *unrestricted model*. The restricted model is obtained by imposing linear or nonlinear constraints on its parameters, and corresponds to the null hypothesis. The unrestricted model is the alternative. In Chapters 4 and 6 we used the Wald approach to test hypotheses between the unrestricted model and a restricted one in which some of the variables were omitted. This was illustrated in several cross-section and time series applications. The Wald test starts with the alternative (the unrestricted model) and asks whether the null (restricted model) should be preferred. The likelihood ratio test is a direct comparison of the two hypotheses. The Lagrange multiplier principle starts at the null and asks whether a movement toward the alternative is preferred. In other words, the LM procedure specifies a simpler and more parsimonious model and asks whether it pays to add new variables. Thus, we start with a basic formulation and test for the addition of new variables rather than start with the full specification and test whether some of the variables should be omitted. The LM method is quite general and can be applied to other situations, as will be described in later sections and chapters. Both the general to the simple and the simple to the general are useful approaches, and it is recommended that both methods be used to obtain more robust conclusions.

The LM test has been discussed in a number of papers: Aitcheson and Silvey (1958), Silvey (1959), Berndt and Savin (1977), Godfrey (1978), Buse (1982), and Engle (1982, 1984), all of which require a knowledge of linear algebra. In this chapter we present a simplified summary of the test and illustrate its usefulness with several applications. Some theoretical results are summarized in the chapter appendix, along with an explanation of the terms *Lagrange multiplier* and *likelihood ratio*. A geometrical comparison of the three approaches is also made in the appendix and illustrated with simple examples. In the chapter itself we specify the steps required to carry out the LM test and apply them to actual data. Although the LM test is a large-sample test, it has been found to be useful even if the number of observations is only 30. The Wald test is applicable to small samples also. The likelihood ratio test sometimes leads to small-sample tests. These points are discussed in more detail in the appendix.

Hypotheses implied by the omission of variables are special cases of **nested hypotheses**. In a nested formulation, the restricted model is a subset of the unrestricted model. **Nonnested hypotheses** compare totally different models in which one cannot be derived as a subset of another. For instance, omitting some variables and adding others will result in nonnested models. In this book we confine our attention to nested hypotheses only. Readers interested in nonnested hypothesis testing are referred to the papers by Davidson and MacKinnon (1981, 1982) and MacKinnon (1983) but are cautioned that they require a knowledge of linear algebra.

7.1 Lagrange Multiplier Test for Adding Variables

The LM test procedure is easily understood in the case in which the economic or business analyst wants to know whether additional variables should be included in the model (for example, whether dummy variables should be included to shift intercept and slope terms). Consider the following restricted and unrestricted models:

(R) $\quad Y = \beta_1 + \beta_2 X_2 + \beta_3 X_3 + \cdots + \beta_m X_m + u$

(U) $\quad Y = \beta_1 + \beta_2 X_2 + \cdots + \beta_m X_m + \beta_{m+1} X_{m+1} + \cdots + \beta_k X_k + v$

In Model U, the $k - m$ new variables $X_{m+1}, X_{m+2}, \ldots, X_k$ (dummy variables, for example) have been added. The null hypothesis of interest is that the regression coefficients for these added variables is zero. The steps for the LM test are as follows:

Step 1 $H_0: \beta_{m+1} = \beta_{m+2} = \cdots = \beta_k = 0$
            H_1: at least one of these βs is nonzero.

Step 2   Estimate the restricted model R.

Step 3   Obtain the estimated residuals from this model as

$$\hat{u}_R = Y - \hat{\beta}_1 - \hat{\beta}_2 X_2 - \hat{\beta}_3 X_3 - \cdots - \hat{\beta}_m X_m$$

Suppose the "true" specification had been Model U; in this case, the variables $X_{m+1}, X_{m+2}, \ldots, X_k$ should have been included. Their effect would be captured by the residual $\hat{u}_R$. Thus, $\hat{u}_R$ should be related to these omitted variables. In other words, if we regress $\hat{u}_R$ against these variables, we should get a good fit, which is an indicator that at least some of the variables $X_{m+1}, X_{m+2}, \ldots, X_k$ should have been included in the model. This argument leads to the next step.

Step 4   Regress $\hat{u}_R$ against a constant and all the Xs, *including the ones in the restricted model*—that is, against all the variables in the unrestricted model. We will henceforth refer to this second regression as the *auxiliary regression*. Engle (1982) has shown that, for large samples, the sample size (T) multiplied by the unadjusted R^2 for this auxiliary regression has the chi-square distribution with degrees of freedom equal to the *number of restrictions in the null hypothesis*. Thus, in our case, $TR^2 \sim \chi^2_{k-m}$. The reason for including the original variables in the auxiliary regression is to make the test statistic have the convenient form it has. If $TR^2 > \chi^{*2}_{k-m}(a)$, the point on χ^2_{k-m} such that the area to its right is a, the level of significance, we would reject the null hypothesis that the new regression coefficients are all zero. In other words, we would conclude that at least some of the new variables should have been included in the model. The t-values of individual coefficients can give a clue as to which of these omitted variables might be included.

Example 7.1

Let us apply this test to the wage determination example used in the previous chapter (see Example 6.3). Table 7.1 presents an annotated computer output using the ECSLIB program. Practice Computer Session 7.1 can be used to reproduce the results presented here. As in Chapters 3 and 6, inputs to the program are indicated in bold characters and annotated comments in italics. As before, the basic model (designated as R) relates ln(WAGE) to a constant term, EDUC, EXPER, and AGE. The question posed here is whether the dummy variables GENDER, RACE, CLERICAL, MAINT, and CRAFTS have additional power to explain the variation in WAGE. In other words, should these variables be added? To answer this, we regress the residuals from the basic model against all the variables in the unrestricted model (that is, we estimate the auxiliary regression), and perform a TR^2 test. We note from Table 7.1 that R^2 for the auxiliary regression is 0.650 and hence $TR^2 = 31.85$. Under the null hypothesis that the regression coefficients for the dummy variables are all zero, TR^2 should have a chi-square distribution with 5 d.f. From the chi-square table, we see that the critical value for χ_5^2 for the level 0.001 is 20.515, which is considerably smaller than TR^2. Therefore, the observed value of TR^2 is significant even at the 0.1 percent level. Thus, at least one of the added variables can be expected to have a significant effect on WAGE. From the t-values for the dummy variables in the auxiliary regression (the other t-statistics are irrelevant), we note that all of them are significant at levels below 8 percent and hence are strong candidates to be included in the model. The LM test has thus identified potential candidate variables to be added to the basic specification. The rest of the analysis follows the steps carried out in Example 6.3. □

7.2 LM Test for Nonlinearities and Interactions

The principle behind the Lagrange multiplier test makes it also applicable as a **nonlinearity test**—that is, applicable for testing for the presence of nonlinearities in the model, including interaction effects. Consider the simple model $Y = \alpha + \beta X + \gamma Z + u$. Suppose we want to test whether the model should have included nonlinear terms such as X^2 and Z^2 as well as the interaction term XZ. We can decide this by using the LM test as follows. Estimate the model by OLS and calculate the residuals as $\hat{u} = Y - \hat{\alpha} - \hat{\beta}X - \hat{\gamma}Z$. If the terms X^2, Z^2, and XZ should have been present, then their effect would be captured by $\hat{u}$. This suggests that we regress the residual $\hat{u}$ against a constant, X, Z, X^2, Z^2, and XZ. TR^2 from this auxiliary regression is asymptotically distributed as χ_3^2 (because three new variables have been

TABLE 7.2

```
?genr EDUC
Generated va
?genr ED_G
Generated va
?genr ED_R
Generated va
?genr LWAG
Generated va
?list

List of va
  0) const
  5) GENDE
 10) EDUCS

?ols LWAGE


          OL




  VARIABLE

  0) const
  2) EDUC
  3) EXPER
  4) AGE

Unadjusted

?genr DFR =
Generated var
?genr ut = uh
Generated var
?ols ut const I
 ED_GEN EI
(This is the au
terms to the sp
```

hypothes
would re
regressio
model. W
further in
rule of t
coefficien
variables
conservat

TABLE 7.1 Annotated Output for the LM Test for Adding Variables

```
List of variables
  0) const    1) WAGE    2) EDUC    3) EXPER    4) AGE
  5) GENDER   6) RACE    7) CLERICAL 8) MAINT   9) CRAFTS
```

?genr LWAGE = ln(WAGE)   *(Compute logarithm of WAGE)*
Generated var. no. 10 (LWAGE)
?ols LWAGE const EDUC EXPER AGE ;   *(Step 2: Estimate Basic Model R)*

```
          OLS ESTIMATES USING THE 49 OBSERVATIONS 1-49
                    Dependent variable  - LWAGE
```

VARIABLE	COEFFICIENT	STDERROR	T STAT	PROB t > |T|
0) constant	6.83596	0.20343	33.603	< 0.0001 ***
2) EDUC	0.06455	0.01675	3.854	0.0004 ***
3) EXPER	0.02270	0.00687	3.303	0.0019 ***
4) AGE	3.91786e-04	4.03304e-03	0.097	0.9230

Unadjusted R-squared   0.328   Adjusted R-squared   0.283

?genr ut = uhat   *(Step 3: save the residuals)*
Generated var. no. 11 (ut)
?ols ut const EDUC EXPER AGE GENDER RACE CLERICAL MAINT CRAFTS ;
(This the auxiliary regression in Step 4 in which the OLS residuals are regressed against all the variables in the unrestricted model U. The regression coefficients and t-statistics for the original variables in Model R should be ignored here. Note that all the added variables have significant regression coefficients. These are therefore strong candidates for inclusion in the model.)

```
          OLS ESTIMATES USING THE 49 OBSERVATIONS 1-49
                    Dependent variable  - ut
```

VARIABLE	COEFFICIENT	STDERROR	T STAT	PROB t > |T|
0) constant	0.63494	0.15716	4.040	0.0002 ***
2) EDUC	-0.04792	0.01309	-3.661	0.0007 ***
3) EXPER	-0.00533	0.00478	-1.114	0.2718
4) AGE	-0.00288	0.00271	-1.060	0.2954
5) GENDER	0.24349	0.07247	3.360	0.0017 ***
6) RACE	0.11092	0.06128	1.810	0.0778 *
7) CLERICAL	-0.46151	0.08081	-5.711	< 0.0001 ***
8) MAINT	-0.52706	0.09431	-5.588	< 0.0001 ***
9) CRAFTS	-0.34299	0.08318	-4.123	0.0002 ***

Unadjusted R-squared   0.650   Adjusted R-squared   0.580
?genr trsq = $nobs*$rsq   *(Compute TRsquare test statistic)*
Generated var. no. 12 (trsq)
?pvalue 3 5 trsq   *(Compute the pvalue for TRsquare)*
For Chi-square (5), area to the right of 31.849830 is < 0.00001

added). If T

ficients for Z

nonlinearity

stant, X, Z,

test just the

have added

of nonlinear

oretical cons

Example 7

Here we ϵ

and 7.1 a

of the for

In Exa

various c

Suppo

level of e

We can t

are possi

presentat

model.

If we

model wi

ln(WA

Table

multiplie

are signi

results a

generate

regressio

33.849 w

TABLE 7.3 Annotated Output for the LM Test for the Application

```
?square EDUC EXPER AGE  ;                                    (Square the variables)
Created sq_EDUC = EDUC squared  as var no. 10
Created sq_EXPER = EXPER squared  as var no. 11
Created sq_AGE = AGE squared  as var no. 12
?genr ED_GEN=EDUC*GENDER                                    (Generate interaction terms)
Generated var. no. 13 (ED_GEN)
?genr ED_RACE=EDUC*RACE
Generated var. no. 14 (ED_RACE)
?genr ED_CLER=EDUC*CLERICAL
Generated var. no. 15 (ED_CLER)
?genr ED_MAINT=EDUC*MAINT
Generated var. no. 16 (ED_MAINT)
?genr ED_CRAFT=EDUC*CRAFTS
Generated var. no. 17 (ED_CRAFT)
?genr AGE_GEN=AGE*GENDER
Generated var. no. 18 (AGE_GEN)
?genr AGE_RACE=AGE*RACE
Generated var. no. 19 (AGE_RACE)
?genr AGE_CLER=AGE*CLERICAL
Generated var. no. 20 (AGE_CLER)
?genr AGE_MAIN=AGE*MAINT
Generated var. no. 21 (AGE_MAIN)
?genr AGE_CRFT=AGE*CRAFTS
Generated var. no. 22 (AGE_CRFT)
?genr EXP_GEN=EXPER*GENDER
Generated var. no. 23 (EXP_GEN)
?genr EXP_RACE=EXPER*RACE
Generated var. no. 24 (EXP_RACE)
?genr EXP_CLER=EXPER*CLERICAL
Generated var. no. 25 (EXP_CLER)
?genr EXP_MAIN=EXPER*MAINT
Generated var. no. 26 (EXP_MAIN)
?genr EXP_CRFT=EXPER*CRAFTS
Generated var. no. 27 (EXP_CRFT)
?genr LWAGE = ln(WAGE)                                      (Generate logarithm of WAGE)
Generated var. no. 28 (LWAGE)
?list                                                        (List the variables)
period: 1, maxobs: 49, obs range: full 1-49, current 1-49

List of variables
  0) const      1) WAGE       2) EDUC       3) EXPER      4) AGE
  5) GENDER     6) RACE       7) CLERICAL   8) MAINT      9) CRAFTS
 10) sq_EDUC   11) sq_EXPER  12) sq_AGE    13) ED_GEN    14) ED_RACE
 15) ED_CLER   16) ED_MAINT  17) ED_CRAFT  18) AGE_GEN   19) AGE_RACE
 20) AGE_CLER  21) AGE_MAIN  22) AGE_CRFT  23) EXP_GEN   24) EXP_RACE
 25) EXP_CLER  26) EXP_MAIN  27) EXP_CRFT  28) LWAGE
```

TABLE 7.3 *(Continued)*

?ols LWAGE const EDUC EXPER AGE ;   *(Basic Model A)*
```
        OLS ESTIMATES USING THE 49 OBSERVATIONS 1-49
               Dependent variable - LWAGE


    VARIABLE          COEFFICIENT        STDERROR      T STAT     PROB t > |T|

 0) constant          6.83596            0.20343       33.603     < 0.0001 ***
 2) EDUC              0.06455            0.01675        3.854     0.0004 ***
 3) EXPER             0.02270            0.00687        3.303     0.0019 ***
 4) AGE              3.91786e-04         4.03304e-03     0.097     0.9230

Unadjusted R-squared      0.328     Adjusted R-squared           0.283
```

?genr DFR = $df   *(Retrieve degrees of freedom)*
Generated var. no. 29 (DFR)
?genr ut = uhat   *(Save residuals)*
Generated var. no. 30 (ut)
?ols ut const EDUC EXPER AGE GENDER RACE CLERICAL MAINT CRAFTS sq_EDUC
sq_EXPER sq_AGE ED_GEN ED_RACE ED_CLER ED_MAINT ED_CRAFT AGE_GEN
AGE_RACE AGE_CLER AGE_MAIN AGE_CRFT EXP_GEN EXP_RACE EXP_CLER EXP_MAIN
EXP_CRFT ;
[This is the auxiliary regression in which the alternative model has all the nonlinear terms as well as all the interaction terms (products of quantitative and dummy variables). Such a specification is often referred to as the "kitchen sink" model.]

```
           OLS ESTIMATES USING THE 49 OBSERVATIONS 1-49
                  Dependent variable - ut


     VARIABLE          COEFFICIENT        STDERROR      T STAT     PROB t > |T|

  0) constant         -0.88013           1.00287       -0.878     0.3896
  2) EDUC              0.26265           0.13989        1.878     0.0738 *
  3) EXPER             0.02594           0.03544        0.732     0.4719
  4) AGE               0.01184           0.02899        0.408     0.6869
  5) GENDER            0.40913           0.44992        0.909     0.3730
  6) RACE             -0.36392           0.44755       -0.813     0.4248
  7) CLERICAL          0.36774           0.73743        0.499     0.6230
  8) MAINT            -0.24081           0.91539       -0.263     0.7949
  9) CRAFTS            0.10860           0.77179        0.141     0.8894
 10) sq_EDUC          -0.02219           0.01088       -2.038     0.0537 *
 11) sq_EXPER        -8.05344e-04        1.14279e-03    -0.705     0.4884
 12) sq_AGE          -2.37950e-04        3.14818e-04    -0.756     0.4578
```

(continued)

TABLE 7.3 *(Continued)*

VARIABLE	COEFFICIENT	STDERROR	T STAT	PROB t > |T|
13) ED_GEN	0.06995	0.04710	1.485	0.1516
14) ED_RACE	0.03682	0.05596	0.658	0.5174
15) ED_CLER	-0.07611	0.05061	-1.504	0.1468
16) ED_MAINT	-0.20945	0.13046	-1.605	0.1226
17) ED_CRAFT	-0.12452	0.06820	-1.826	0.0815 *
18) AGE_GEN	-0.01507	0.00984	-1.533	0.1396
19) AGE_RACE	0.01043	0.00999	1.044	0.3080
20) AGE_CLER	-0.00409	0.00961	-0.426	0.6745
21) AGE_MAIN	0.02550	0.01213	2.102	0.0472 **
22) AGE_CRFT	0.01145	0.01182	0.968	0.3433
23) EXP_GEN	-0.00475	0.01776	-0.268	0.7915
24) EXP_RACE	-0.02286	0.02464	-0.928	0.3636
25) EXP_CLER	-0.00771	0.02057	-0.375	0.7113
26) EXP_MAIN	-0.00185	0.02723	-0.068	0.9465
27) EXP_CRFT	0.01837	0.01884	0.975	0.3401

Unadjusted R-squared	0.818	Adjusted R-squared	0.603

?genr DFU = $df   *(Retrieve d.f. of unrestricted model)*
Generated var. no. 31 (DFU)
?genr NR = DFR - DFU   *(Compute number of restrictions)*
Generated var. no. 32 (NR)
?genr trsq = $nobs*$rsq   *(Compute TRsquare statistic)*
Generated var. no. 33 (trsq)
?pvalue 3 NR trsq   *(Compute pvalue)*
For Chi-square (23), area to the right of 40.078742 is 0.015060

we can expect a great deal of multicollinearity among the explanatory variables which may have caused some of the coefficients to be insignificant. A conservative rule of thumb is to select those variables for which the *p*-values of the coefficients are less than 0.5 (other researchers may prefer some other rule). According to this we would include GENDER, RACE, sq_EDUC, sq_EXPER, sq_AGE, ED_GEN, ED_CLER, ED_MAINT, ED_CRAFT, AGE_GEN, AGE_RACE, AGE_MAIN, AGE_CRFT, EXP_RACE, and EXP_CRFT in the model. Such a model was estimated and the results are summarized in Table 7.4 under the label Model 1.

We note that several coefficients have very low *t*-statistics, suggesting insignificance. These were omitted a few at a time until a model was obtained that had all coefficients significant at 10 percent or lower levels. The results are shown under Model 2 in the table. Finally, Model 3 is the "kitchen sink" specification which includes all the quadratic and interaction terms. As one would suspect, Model 3 suffers seriously from multicollinearity problems, which often tend to make coefficients insignificant. In terms of the model selection statistics and the significance of the regression coefficients, Model 2 is clearly superior and is chosen as the final model for interpretation.

The Hendry/LSE approach would take Model 3 and eliminate insignificant variables selectively until an "acceptable" model was obtained. The LM test

TABLE 7.4 Selected Model Results for the Application

Variable	Model 1	Model 2	Model 3
CONSTANT	6.25809 (11.879)	6.69328 (36.624)	5.95582 (5.939)
EDUC	0.29236 (3.347)	0.22078 (3.618)	0.32721 (2.339)
EXPER	0.04514 (2.095)	0.01794 (4.287)	0.04864 (1.372)
AGE	0.00465 (0.219)		0.01223 (0.422)
GENDER	0.18628 (0.671)		0.40913 (0.909)
RACE	0.00089 (0.004)		−0.36392 (−0.813)
CLERICAL			0.36774 (0.499)
MAINT			−0.24081 (−0.263)
CRAFTS			0.10860 (0.141)
sq_EDUC	−0.01792 (−2.874)	−0.01109 (−2.506)	−0.02219 (−2.038)
sq_EXPER	−0.00085 (−1.098)		−0.00081 (−0.705)
sq_AGE	−0.00015 (−0.633)	−0.00007 (−2.184)	−0.00024 (−0.756)
ED_GEN	0.06650 (2.191)	0.02960 (2.943)	0.06995 (1.485)
ED_RACE			0.03682 (0.658)
ED_CLER	−0.06110 (−5.843)	−0.06169 (−6.525)	−0.07611 (−1.504)
ED_MAINT	−0.22790 (−3.523)	−0.13896 (−3.119)	−0.20945 (−1.605)
ED_CRAFT	−0.11688 (−3.857)	−0.10726 (−5.504)	−0.12452 (−1.826)
AGE_GEN	−0.01081 (−1.492)		−0.01507 (−1.533)
AGE_RACE	0.00721 (1.127)		0.01043 (1.044)
AGE_CLER			−0.00409 (−0.426)
AGE_MAIN	0.02066 (2.554)	0.00758 (1.700)	0.02550 (2.102)
AGE_CRFT	0.01059 (1.945)	0.01152 (3.649)	0.01145 (0.968)

(continued)

TABLE 7.4 *(Continued)*

Variable	Model 1	Model 2	Model 3
EXP_GEN			−0.00475 (−0.268)
EXP_RACE	−0.02525 (−1.881)		−0.02286 (−0.928)
EXP_CLER			−0.00771 (−0.375)
EXP_MAIN			−0.00185 (−0.068)
EXP_CRFT	0.02402 (2.058)		0.01837 (0.975)
ESS	0.61473	0.78302	0.574710
$\bar{R}^2$	0.790	0.789	0.733
d.f.	30	38	22
SGMASQ	0.020491*	0.020606	0.026123
AIC	0.027245	0.025036*	0.035307
FPE	0.028437	0.025231*	0.040518
HQ	0.035988	0.029413*	0.052436
SCHWARZ	0.056738	0.038283*	0.100135
SHIBATA	0.022275*	0.023155	0.024655
GCV	0.033469	0.026571*	0.058184
RICE	0.055885	0.029001*	undefined

An asterisk denotes the model that is "best" for that criterion. Values in parentheses are t-statistics.

approach started with the basic specification and used the auxiliary regression to select variables to be added to the basic specification. Both approaches are sound and it is recommended that an investigator attempt the analysis both ways so that robust conclusions may be arrived at.

Interpretation of Results The variables included in the model explain 79 percent of the variation in the logarithm of WAGE. For a cross-section study this is quite good. We now examine the marginal effects of each determinant separately.

Education: The number of years of schooling (beyond the eighth grade) is important in explaining wages. It exhibits significant nonlinearity and it interacts significantly with gender and occupational status. The partial effect is

$$\Delta \ln(\text{WAGE})/\Delta \text{EDUC} = 0.221 - 0.022\text{EDUC} + 0.030\text{GENDER}$$
$$- 0.062\text{CLERICAL} - 0.139\text{MAINT} - 0.107\text{CRAFT}$$

It is interesting to note that the marginal effect of schooling decreases with the number of years of education. In other words, the *additional* wages for one *additional* year of education is lower, on average, for a person with an already high level of education as compared to another person with less education. There is thus "diminishing" returns to education. With male and female employees who are similar in other characteristics, a male employee is expected to earn an average of 3 percent more than a female employee. The type of job interacts significantly with education. As compared to professsional employees (the control group), one more year of education means 6.2 percent less in wages for clerical workers, 13.9 percent less for maintenance employees, and 10.7 percent less for craft workers.

Experience: Not surprisingly, the number of years of experience in a given job has a positive effect on wages. There was, however, no significant diminishing returns nor any interaction with the dummy variables. An extra year of experience means an average increase in earnings of only 1.8 percent.

Age: The age of an employee had significant diminishing returns, indicating that, other things being equal, an older employee commands a lower average wage. The marginal effect is

$$\Delta \ln(WAGE)/\Delta AGE = -0.00014AGE + 0.00758MAINT + 0.01152CRAFT$$

The age effect is somewhat offset for maintenance and crafts employees but not for others.

Gender: In Example 6.4, in which a simpler version of the model was used, we found that there was a significant reduction in salary for a female employee as compared to a male employee with similar job attributes. Here the partial effect of gender depends on the amount of education and is given by 0.03 EDUC. The positive sign means that a significant gender differential does exist (with comparable male employees earning, on average, a higher salary) and that the gap increases with education. Thus well-educated women had disproportionately lower average salaries than men with similar characteristics. For instance, when EDUC is 4, that is, when an employee has completed high school, males earn an average of 12 percent more than similar females. With a college education (EDUC = 8), the differential becomes 24 percent, which is unaccountably high.

Race: None of the race variables were significant, indicating no significant wage differential along racial lines.

Type of Job: The sample employees belonged to four differential occupational categories. The control group was professionals, and the others were clerical, maintenance, and craft workers. The partial effects for each of the noncontrol groups are

Clerical:	-0.062 EDUC
Maintenance:	-0.139 EDUC $+ 0.008$ AGE
Crafts:	-0.107 EDUC $+ 0.012$ AGE

As was pointed out earlier, job type and education interacted very strongly. Age has significant positive effects for maintenance and craft workers but not for the others.

■ ■

SUMMARY

Three approaches are most commonly used in *nested hypothesis testing*—that is, in hypotheses in which the restricted model is a subset of the more general unrestricted model. They are the *Wald test, the likelihood ratio* (LR) *test*, and the *Lagrange multiplier* (LM) *test*. The Wald approach (also referred to as the Hendry/LSE approach) formulates a model with many independent variables and then asks whether some should be eliminated. The LM test involves formulating a basic model and then asking whether other variables should be included. Both use judgment and both are useful depending on the context. The LR test treats the two models equally.

Although asymptotically (that is, for large samples) the three tests are equivalent, the LM test has been found to be useful in more general contexts. It is also useful in testing for dummy variable shifts, nonlinear effects, and for the presence of interaction terms. The LM test requires three basic steps: (1) Regress the dependent variable against a list of basic independent variables including the constant; (2) obtain the residuals from the OLS procedure carried out in Step (1); and (3) regress the residuals against all the Xs in Step (1), as well as against new variables (m in number), which might include dummy variables, nonlinear terms, or cross-products (squares and interactions) of the independent variables.

If the product of the sample size (T) and the unadjusted R^2 from this auxiliary regression (that is, TR^2) exceeds $\chi_m^2(a)$, the point on the chi-square distribution with m degrees of freedom, to the right of which there is an area a (the level of significance), then the null hypothesis that the m added variables all have zero coefficients is rejected. If the hypothesis is rejected, the t-values in Step (3) will help to identify the variables that could be added to the basic model. Even if the TR^2 test fails to reject the null hypothesis of zero coefficients, the t-statistics of the auxiliary regression might suggest that some variables ought to be included. These variables could then be added to the basic model for a new set of estimates. We will see in later chapters that the principles of the LM test procedure are applicable in more general contexts.

KEY TERMS

Data generation process (DGP)	LSE approach
Hendry approach	Nested hypotheses
Lagrange multiplier (LM) test	Nonlinearity test
Likelihood ratio (LR) test	Nonnested hypotheses

REFERENCES

Several of the following references require a background in linear algebra.

Aitcheson, J., and Silvey, S. D. "Maximum Likelihood Estimation of Parameters Subject to Restraints." *Annals of Math. Stat.*, Vol. 29 (1958).

Berndt, E. R., and Savin, N. E. "Conflict Among Criteria for Testing Hypotheses in the Multivariate Regression Model." *Econometrica* (July 1977): 1263–1278.

Buse, A. "The Likelihood Ratio, Wald, and Lagrange Multiplier Test: An Expository Note." *The American Statistician* (August 1982): 153–157.

Davidson, R., and MacKinnon, J. G. "Several Tests for Model Specification in the Presence of Alternative Hypotheses." *Econometrica* (1981): 781–793.

———. "Some Non-nested Hypothesis Tests and Relations Among Them." *Review of Econ. Stud.* (1982): 551–565.

Engle, R. F. "A General Approach to Lagrangian Multiplier Diagnostics." *Annals of Econometrics*, Vol. 20 (1982): 83–104.

———. "Wald, Likelihood-Ratio and Lagrangian Multiplier Tests in Econometrics," *Handbook of Econometrics*, ed. Z. Griliches and M. D. Intriligator. New York: North-Holland, 1984.

Gilbert, C. L. "Professor Hendry's Econometric Methodology," *Oxford Bulletin of Economics and Statistics*, Vol. 48 (1986): 283–307.

Gilbert, C. L. "LSE and the British Approach to Time Series Econometrics," *Oxford Economic Papers*, Vol. 41 (1989): 108–128.

Godfrey, L. G. "Testing for Multiplicative Heteroscedasticity." *J. Econometrics*, Vol. 8 (1978).

Hendry, D., and Richards, J. F. "On the Formulation of Empirical Models in Dynamic Econometrics," *J. Econometrics*, Vol. 20 (1982): 3–33.

Hendry, D., and Richards, J. F. "The Econometric Analysis of Economic Time Series," *International Statistical Review*, Vol. 51 (1983): 111–163.

Hendry, D. "Econometric Methodology," paper presented to the Econometric Society Fifth World Congress, MIT (1985).

Johnston, J. *Econometric Methods.* New York: McGraw-Hill, 1984.

MacKinnon, J. G. "Model Specification Tests Against Non-nested Alternatives." *Econometric Reviews* (1983): 85–157.

Mood, A. M.; Graybill, F. A.; and Boes, D. C. *Introduction to the Theory of Statistics.* New York: McGraw-Hill, 1974.

Ramanathan, Ramu. "A Note on the Lagrange Multiplier Test and Model Selection Criteria." Discussion paper No. 1986–19, UCSD Economics Department.

Silvey, D. S. "The Lagrange Multiplier Test." *Annals of Math. Stat.* (1959).

PRACTICE COMPUTER SESSIONS

All the practice sessions in this chapter use the data set *data6-9*.

7.1 To reproduce Example 7.1, use the ECSLIB commands in *ps7-1.inp*.

7.2 For Example 7.2, use the ECSLIB commands in *ps7-2.inp*

7.3 For the application in Section 7.3, the commands in *ps7-3.inp* will be very useful.

EXERCISES

7.1 Use the data in Table 6.1 and first estimate the basic model

$$\text{PRICE} = \alpha + \beta\text{SQFT} + u$$

Then use the LM test approach to test for the addition of the remaining variables and interactions. Then estimate the appropriate models.

7.2 Using the data in Table 6.11 estimate the basic model in Exercise 6.12. Next use the LM test approach to add new variables (define any created by transformations). Contrast this with the results of Exercise 6.12 using the Hendry/LSE approach.

7.3 Redo the application in Section 7.3 using a double-log framework.

†7.4 Let S be the annual savings of a household and Y be its annual income. A basic savings function is $S = a + bY + u$. You also know whether the household owns its home, and what the occupational status of the head is (managerial, clerical, skilled worker, unskilled worker, or self-employed businessperson). Describe how you would use the LM test approach to test whether the above savings function depends on these additional characteristics.

7.5 Describe how you would use the LM test procedure to test for the structural change studied in Section 6.5.

7.6 Let E_t be energy consumption at time t and T_t be the temperature at that time. Consider the relation $E_t = a + bT_t + u_t$ examined in Section 6.4. The effect of temperature on energy consumption is likely to depend on the time of day. For instance, a $30°$ temperature at 2 P.M. will have a different impact than the same temperature at 2 A.M. Thus, this relationship might have a "time-of-day" effect. Describe how you will use the LM test to examine whether the relationship differs according to the time of day.

†7.7 How will you use the LM approach to test the hypotheses stated in Exercise 6.4 of the previous chapter?

7.8 Apply the LM test procedure to Exercise 6.5 and explain how you will test the hypotheses stated in Exercise 6.5b.

7.9 Carry out Exercise 6.6 using the LM test.

7.10 Consider the motor carrier deregulation empirical example of Section 6.7. If you had access to that data set, describe how you would use the LM test procedure to test whether the basic model that related $\ln(\text{PTM})$ to a constant, $\ln(\text{WT})$, PD, and $\ln(\text{DIST})$ is different according to the various dummy variables used by the authors.

7.A APPENDIX

More Details on LR, Wald, and LM Tests

This appendix provides theoretical details about the Wald, likelihood ratio, and Lagrange multiplier tests. Before reading this section, however, it is essential that you read Section 2.A.3 on the maximum likelihood principle and Section 3.A.4 on its application to the simple linear regression model. Although these three test procedures are applicable in general situations, we restrict our attention here to the regression context and, in particular, to a model of the following type:

$$y_t = \alpha x_{t1} + \beta x_{t2} + u_t \qquad (7.A.1)$$

The lowercase letters are used to denote the deviations of the variables from the corresponding means. As was seen in Section 4.A.1, the advantage of this approach is that it eliminates the constant term. Under the assumption that the u's are normally distributed with mean zero and variance σ^2, the logarithm of the likelihood function for the set of observations $y_1, y_2, \ldots, y_T$ and the two unknown parameters α and β can be written as follows (the procedure is analogous to the one in Section 3.A.4):

$$\ln L = -T \ln \sigma - T \ln(\sqrt{2\pi}) - \frac{\sum (y_t - \alpha x_{t1} - \beta x_{t2})^2}{2\sigma^2} \qquad (7.A.2)$$

The null hypothesis we examine is of the form $\beta = \beta_0$, and the alternative is $\beta \neq \beta_0$. This is equivalent to asking the question whether the variable x_2 belongs in the model or not. Each of the test procedures is discussed separately and a geometric comparison of the methods is made. See the papers by Buse (1982) and Engle (1982) for more details on the three tests.

7.A.1 Likelihood Ratio Test

In statistics, the classical test procedure is based on the *likelihood ratio* which, in simple terms, is defined as the ratio of the maximum value of the likelihood function under the null hypothesis divided by its maximum value when no restrictions are imposed. More specifically, let $\hat{\alpha}$ and $\hat{\beta}$ be the maximum likelihood estimators of the two parameters. The likelihood function evaluated at these values is denoted by $L(\hat{\alpha}, \hat{\beta})$, ignoring σ^2. Let $\tilde{\alpha}$ be the maximum likelihood estimator of α under the null hypothesis $\beta = \beta_0$. The corresponding likelihood function is $L(\tilde{\alpha}, \beta_0)$. The likelihood ratio is defined as

$$\lambda = \frac{L(\tilde{\alpha}, \beta_0)}{L(\hat{\alpha}, \hat{\beta})}$$

Because the denominator is based on the unrestricted model, its value cannot be smaller than that of the numerator. Therefore $0 \leq \lambda \leq 1$. If the hypothesis were true, we would intuitively expect λ to be close to 1. If λ is far from 1, the likelihood ratio under the null is very different from that under the unrestricted model, which is the alternative. This suggests that we should reject the null hypothesis if λ is too small. The LR test is formulated as one of rejecting the null if $\lambda \leq K$, where K is determined by the condition that, under the null hypothesis, the probability that $0 \leq \lambda \leq K$ is equal to the level of significance (a), that is, $P(0 \leq \lambda \leq K \mid \beta = \beta_0) = a$.

In a number of cases, the critical region $\lambda \leq K$ can be translated into another form involving a well-known sample statistic such as the t-statistic or an F. In these situations, the LR test reduces to a t-, F-, or χ^2 test. For examples of these cases the reader is referred to Mood, Graybill, and Boes (1974). The various tests presented in Chapter 2 can be derived from this likelihood ratio principle. When λ cannot be conveniently transformed into another statistic whose distribution is known, a large-sample test is often used. It can be shown that, for large sample sizes, the statistic

$$\text{LR} = -2 \ln \lambda = 2 \ln L(\hat{\alpha}, \hat{\beta}) - 2 \ln L(\tilde{\alpha}, \beta_0) \qquad (7.A.3)$$

has a chi-square distribution with degrees of freedom equal to the number of restrictions, which is 1 in our example. The idea behind this test can be represented geometrically. In Figure 7.1 the log of the likelihood function is graphed when there is only a single parameter in the model; that is, α and x_1 are assumed to be absent from the specification. The graph is below the axis because the log of the

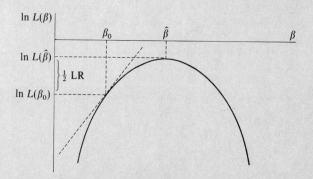

Figure 7.1   Geometric illustration of Wald, LR, and LM tests

likelihood (which is a probability density less than 1) is negative. The point $\hat{\beta}$ corresponds to the case when the likelihood is maximum and β_0 corresponds to the null hypothesis. The LR test is based on the vertical difference, which is the same as one-half LR. If the vertical distance is large, the null hypothesis is rejected.

Example 7.A.1

The Likelihood Ratio test principle is illustrated with the help of a distribution that has only one unknown parameter. Consider the random variable Y that has only two outcomes, one labeled "success" and the other labeled "failure." Assign the value 1 to success and the value 0 to failure. Also let the probability of a success be θ. The density function is therefore $f(Y = 1) = \theta$ and $f(Y = 0) = 1 - \theta$. There is a convenient representation of this, namely, $f(y) = \theta^y(1 - \theta)^{1-y}$. It is readily verified that if $y = 1$, $f(y)$ reduces to θ, and when $y = 0$, $f(y)$ becomes $1 - \theta$. A random variable with this distribution is known as the **Bernoulli Distribution** and is the basis for the Binomial distribution introduced in Chapter 2. Suppose we draw a random sample of size T from the Bernoulli distribution and denote the outcomes as $y_1, y_2, \ldots, y_T$ where y_i takes the value 1 or 0. We use this distribution to illustrate how the Wald, Likelihood Ratio, and Lagrange multiplier test statistics are derived. The likelihood function for the above sample is given by

$$L(y, \theta) = f(y_1)f(y_2) \cdots f(y_T) = \theta^{\Sigma y_i}(1 - \theta)^{T - \Sigma y_i} \qquad (7.A.4)$$

The log-likelihood is

$$\ln L = \left(\sum y_i\right) \ln \theta + \left(T - \sum y_i\right) \ln(1 - \theta) \qquad (7.A.5)$$

To maximize $\ln L$ without any restrictions, we need the condition

$$\frac{\partial \ln L}{\partial \theta} = 0 = \frac{\sum y_i}{\theta} - \frac{T - \sum y_i}{1 - \theta} = \frac{\sum y_i - T\theta}{\theta(1 - \theta)} \qquad (7.A.6)$$

which can be solved for θ as $\hat{\theta} = \bar{y}$, the sample mean. The log-likelihood corresponding to this solution is given by

$$T\bar{y} \ln (\bar{y}) + T(1 - \bar{y}) \ln (1 - \bar{y})$$

Under the null hypothesis $\theta = \theta_0$ the log-likelihood becomes

$$T\bar{y} \ln (\theta_0) + T(1 - \bar{y}) \ln (1 - \theta_0)$$

Substituting these in equation (7.A.3) we get the LR test statistic as

$$LR = 2T\bar{y} \ln \left[\frac{\bar{y}}{\theta_0}\right] + 2T(1 - \bar{y}) \ln \left[\frac{1 - \bar{y}}{1 - \theta_0}\right]$$

For large samples this has a chi-square distribution with 1 d.f. We would reject the null hypothesis that $\theta = \theta_0$ if $LR > K$ where K is the point on χ_1^2 such that the area to the right of K is the level of significance.

7.A.2   The Wald Test

The Wald test uses a horizontal difference instead of a vertical difference. Specifically, the squared horizontal distance $(\hat{\beta} - \beta_0)^2$, weighted by a function of the form $I(\hat{\beta})$, is used:

$$W = (\hat{\beta} - \beta_0)^2 I(\hat{\beta}) \tag{7.A.7}$$

where

$$I(\beta) = -E\left[\frac{\partial^2 \ln L}{\partial \beta^2}\right] \tag{7.A.8}$$

is the expected value of the second derivative of the log-likelihood function with respect to β. It is a measure of the curvature of the log-likelihood function. The I function divided by T is known as the *information matrix*. The computational procedure for this test can be carried out by estimating a restricted model and an unrestricted model, as was done in Chapter 4, and constructing an F-statistic. The formal proof of this requires linear algebra [see Johnston (1984), pp. 187–189).

Example 7.A.2

In the case of the Bernoulli distribution used in Example 7.A.1, the information $I(\theta)$ can be shown to be $\dfrac{T}{\theta(1 - \theta)}$. The Wald test statistic given in equation (7.A.7) reduces to (substituting $\bar{y}$ for θ)

$$W = \frac{T(\bar{y} - \theta_0)^2}{\bar{y}(1 - \bar{y})}$$

As in the LR test case, this has a chi-square distribution for large sample. The null hypothesis will be rejected if W exceeds the critical value K derived in Example 7.A.1.

7.A.3   The Lagrange Multiplier Test

The LM test is based on the Lagrange multiplier technique for constrained optimization presented in Chapter 2. The restricted model is derived by imposing the condition that β is equal to β_0. This suggests that we maximize the logarithm of the likelihood function with respect to α and β, *subject to the restriction $\beta = \beta_0$.* As we see from Section 2.A.2, this is equivalent to maximizing $\ln L(\alpha, \beta) - \mu(\beta - \beta_0)$, where μ is the Lagrange multiplier. The first-order conditions for maximization are

$$\frac{\partial \ln L}{\partial \alpha} = 0 \quad \text{and} \quad \frac{\partial \ln L}{\partial \beta} = \mu$$

If the null hypothesis $\beta = \beta_0$ is true, the restricted maximum likelihood estimators will be near the unrestricted estimates. We note that if the Lagrange multiplier μ is zero, then the equations give the maximum likelihood estimators. Hence, the Lagrange multiplier can be interpreted as being the "shadow price" of the constraint $\beta = \beta_0$. If the price is high, the constraint should be rejected as being inconsistent with the data. That is the motivation behind the LM test. The LM test is based on the partial derivative $(\partial \ln L)/\partial \beta$, which is known as the *score function* and is denoted by $S(\beta)$. Engle (1982) has formally derived the test statistic for a multiple regression model and shown that the test can be performed by running an auxiliary regression on the estimated residuals of the restricted model. The steps for this are in Section 7.1. The LM test statistic is of the form

$$LM = S^2(\beta_0)I(\beta_0)^{-1} \qquad (7.A.9)$$

We readily see from Figure 7.1 that the score function, which is the partial derivative of the log likelihood, is the slope of the graph at the point β_0. The alternative hypothesis corresponds to $S(\beta) = 0$; that is, the slope is close to zero. Thus, the Wald test is based on the horizontal distance between $\hat{\beta}$ and β_0 in the graph, the LR test is based on the vertical distance, and the LM test is based on the slope of the curve at β_0. Each is a reasonable measure of the distance between the null and alternative hypotheses. Engle (1982) and Buse (1982) have shown independently that when the log-likelihood function is a quadratic [as is the case in equation (7.A.2)], all three test procedures give the same result. For a general linear model, there is an inequality among the three test criteria. This is given by

$$W \geq LR \geq LM$$

It follows that whenever the LM test rejects the null hypothesis of zero coefficients, so will the others. Similarly, whenever the Wald test fails to reject the the null, other tests will too. Computationally, the LR rest is the most cumbersome, unless it can be converted to a t-, F-, or χ^2 test. The other two tests are straightforward, as is seen in the text.

Example 7.A.3

In the case of the Bernoulli distribution, the Score function is obtained from equation (7.A.4) as $S(\theta) = \dfrac{\sum y_i - T\theta}{\theta(1 - \theta)}$ from which the LM test is derived.

$$LM = \left[\frac{\sum y_i - T\theta_0}{\theta_0(1 - \theta_0)} \right]^2 \frac{\theta_0(1 - \theta_0)}{T} = \frac{T(\bar{y} - \theta_0)^2}{\theta_0(1 - \theta_0)}$$

As before, the null hypothesis would be rejected if LM is greater than the critical value K. It should be noted that in all the cases the test statistic depends on the sample mean $\bar{y}$. Using the distribution of $\bar{y}$, one can derive a direct test based on it which is applicable to all sample sizes, thus avoiding the use of a limiting chi-square distribution.

SOME SPECIAL ISSUES WITH CROSS-SECTION AND TIME SERIES DATA

Part IV is devoted to a discussion of a variety of issues that arise when an investigator analyzes cross-section and time series data. Chapter 8 deals with heteroscedasticity, a phenomenon that arises when the variance of an error term is not the same across observations. Chapter 9 is concerned with serial correlation (also known as autocorrelation), a phenomenon that occurs when the error term from one observation is correlated with that from another. Serial correlation is a common occurrence in time series data. These chapters begin by exploring the consequences of ignoring heteroscedasticity or autocorrelation and then introduce procedures for testing for the presence of these "problems."

They go on to provide alternative approaches for estimating the parameters of a model. Concepts developed in these chapters are explained with the help of several examples and applications.

CHAPTER 8

Heteroscedasticity

■ In deriving ordinary least squares (OLS) estimates as well as the maximum likelihood estimates (MLE), we made the assumption that the residuals u_t were identically distributed with mean zero and equal variance σ^2 (refer to Assumption 3.5 of Chapter 3). This assumption of equal variance is known as **homoscedasticity** (which means equal scatter). The variance σ^2 is a measure of dispersion of the residuals u_t around their mean zero. Equivalently, it is a measure of dispersion of the observed value of the dependent variable (Y) around the regression line $\beta_1 + \beta_2 X_2 + \cdots + \beta_k X_k$. Homoscedasticity means that the dispersion is the same across all observations.

In many situations commonly encountered with cross-section data, however, this assumption might be false. Suppose, for example, we survey a random sample of households and obtain information about each household's total consumption expenditure and its income in a given year. Households with a low income do not have much flexibility in spending. Most of the income will go for basic necessities such as food, shelter, clothing, and transportation. Therefore, consumption patterns among such low-income households may not vary very much. On the other hand, rich families have a great deal of flexibility in spending. Some might be large consumers; others might be large savers and investors in real estate, the stock market, and so on. This implies that actual consumption might be quite different from average consumption. In other words, it is very likely that higher income households have a larger dispersion around mean consumption than lower income households. In such a case, the scatter diagram between consumption and income would indicate sample points closer to the regression line for low-income households but widely scattered points for high-income households (see Figure 8.1). Such a situation is called **heteroscedasticity** (which means unequal scatter).

Consumption

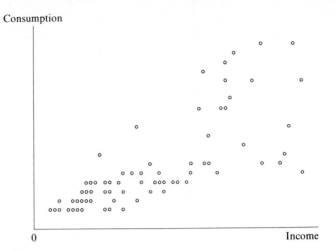

0   Income

Figure 8.1   An example of heteroscedasticity

As a second example, consider a random sample of cities for which we relate the prevalence of crime to the amount of resources available to the city to combat crime. We might expect that the scatter of observed points might be more widely dispersed for large cities as compared to smaller cities. Here again the assumption of constant residual variance might be violated.

In this chapter, we relax the assumption that the residual variance is constant and assume heteroscedasticity. More formally, we modify Assumption 3.5 as follows:

Assumption 3.5a
u_t is a random variable with $E(u_t) = 0$ and $\text{Var}(u_t) = E(u_t^2) = \sigma_t^2$, for $t = 1, 2, \ldots, T$.

Thus, each observation has a different error variance. All the other assumptions on the stochastic disturbance terms will be maintained. Suppose we ignore the heteroscedasticity and use the OLS procedure to estimate the parameters. What are their properties? Are they biased, inefficient, or inconsistent? Are the statistical tests still valid? Is there a procedure that will explicitly take account of heteroscedasticity and give better estimates? These issues are now addressed one by one.

8.1   Consequences of Ignoring Heteroscedasticity

We first study the implications of using the OLS procedure to estimate the regression coefficients in the presence of heteroscedasticity. The model is

$$Y_t = \beta_1 + \beta_2 X_{t2} + \cdots + \beta_k X_{tk} + u_t \tag{8.1}$$

where $\text{Var}(u_t) = \sigma_t^2$ for $t = 1, 2, \ldots, T$. The only change is that the error variances are different for different values of t and are unknown.

Effect on the Properties of the Estimators

The proofs of Properties 3.1 and 3.2 (which state that the OLS estimates are unbiased and consistent) depend only on Assumptions 3.2 and 3.4 (that u_t has zero mean and is uncorrelated with X_t) and not on Assumptions 3.5 or 3.5a. Therefore, the properties of unbiasedness and consistency are not violated by ignoring heteroscedasticity and using OLS to estimate α and β. However, while proving the Gauss-Markhov Theorem (Property 3.3), we used the assumption that $\text{Var}(u_t) = \sigma^2$ in order to minimize the variance of a linear combination of the Ys. Because that assumption is no longer true, it is not possible to assert that the OLS estimate is also more efficient. This means that the OLS estimate is now inefficient. It is possible to find an alternative unbiased linear estimate that has a lower variance than the OLS estimate.

Effect on the Tests of Hypotheses

It can be shown that the estimated variances and covariances of the OLS estimates of the β_is are biased and inconsistent when heteroscedasticity is present but ignored [see Kmenta (1986), pp. 276–279]. Therefore, the tests of hypotheses are no longer valid.

Effect on Forecasting

We just argued that OLS estimates are still unbiased. It follows from this that forecasts based on these estimates will also be unbiased. But because the estimates are inefficient, forecasts will also be inefficient. In other words, the reliability of those forecasts (as measured by their variances) will be inferior to an alternative estimator that is more efficient.

The results obtained in this section are summarized in Property 8.1.

Property 8.1

If heteroscedasticity among the stochastic disturbance terms in a regression model is ignored and the OLS procedure is used to estimate the parameters, then the following properties hold:

a. The estimates and forecasts based on them will still be unbiased and consistent.
b. The OLS estimates are no longer BLUE and will be inefficient. Forecasts will also be inefficient.
c. The estimated variances and covariances of the regression coefficients will be biased and inconsistent, and hence tests of hypotheses are invalid.

8.2 Testing for Heteroscedasticity

Because we know that heteroscedasticity invalidates test results, it would be desirable to test formally whether heteroscedasticity is present. In this section we present the three most commonly used tests for heteroscedasticity.

Goldfeld–Quandt Test

The test proposed by Goldfeld and Quandt (1965) is based on the notion that if the error variances are equal across observations (that is, if they are homoscedastic), then the variance for one part of the sample will be the same as the variance for another part of the sample. One can therefore test for the equality of error variances using the F-test described in Section 2.10. The test becomes a ratio of two sample variances. The sample of observations is divided into three parts, and the middle observations are discarded. The model is then estimated for each of the other two sets of observations and the residual variances computed. Next an F-test is used to test for the equality of these variances. The formal steps for the **Goldfeld–Quandt test** are as follows:

Step 1 Identify a variable (say Z) to which the error variance σ_t^2 is related. Suppose, for instance, that σ_t^2 is suspected of being positively related to Z_t. Arrange the data set according to increasing values of Z_t (Z_t could be one of the Xs in the regression, such as income or population).

Step 2 Divide the sample of T observations into the first T_1 and the last T_2, thus omitting the middle observations $T_1 + 1$ through $T - T_2$. The number of observations to be omitted is arbitrary and is usually between one-sixth and one-third. Note that T_1 and T_2 must be greater than the number of coefficients to be estimated.

Step 3 Estimate separate regressions for observations 1 through T_1 and $T - T_2 + 1$ through T.

Step 4 Obtain the error sum of squares as follows:

$$\text{ESS}_1 = \sum_{t=1}^{t=T_1} \hat{u}_t^2 \quad \text{and} \quad \text{ESS}_2 = \sum_{t=T-T_2+1}^{t=T} \hat{u}_t^2$$

From Property 4.1c we know that ESS/σ^2 has the chi-square distribution. From Section 2.4, the ratio of two independent chi-squares is an F-distribution. This suggests the next step.

Step 5 Compute

$$F_c = \frac{\hat{\sigma}_2^2}{\hat{\sigma}_1^2} = \frac{\text{ESS}_2/(T_2 - k)}{\text{ESS}_1/(T_1 - k)}$$

where k is the number of regression coefficients including the constant term. Under the null hypothesis of homoscedasticity, the computed F_c has an F-distribution with d.f. $T_2 - k$ and $T_1 - k$. If $F_c > F^*$, the point on the F-distribution such that the area to the right is 5 percent, then reject the null hypothesis of homoscedasticity and conclude that heteroscedasticity is present. [*Note*: if $F_c < 1$, then use $1/F_c$. This is because the alternative hypothesis is usually $\sigma_2^2 > \sigma_1^2$.]

Example 8.1

Table 8.1 presents data for the 50 states and the District of Columbia for the following variables (all data are for the year 1987):

TABLE 8.1   U.S. Population (in millions), Personal Income (in billions of dollars) and Expenditures on Travel (in billions of dollars) for 1987

State	Pop.	Exptrav.	Income	State	Pop.	Exptrav.	Income
Wyoming	0.490	0.760	6.3	Arizona	3.400	5.635	48.7
Alaska	0.524	0.857	9.7	S. Carolina	3.426	4.294	41.4
Vermont	0.547	1.576	7.8	Kentucky	3.723	2.428	44.7
D.C.	0.621	1.442	12.1	Alabama	4.084	2.042	49.2
Delaware	0.648	0.725	10.6	Minnesota	4.244	5.551	67.0
N. Dakota	0.671	0.647	8.6	Louisiana	4.448	3.845	51.2
S. Dakota	0.709	0.626	8.8	Maryland	4.536	5.322	82.6
Montana	0.809	0.728	10.0	Washington	4.542	4.469	71.0
Rhode Island	0.986	0.571	15.5	Wisconsin	4.807	4.386	70.5
Idaho	1.000	1.061	11.8	Tennessee	4.855	4.565	63.0
Nevada	1.006	8.246	16.5	Missouri	5.107	5.291	74.7
New Hampshire	1.056	2.002	19.1	Indiana	5.530	3.289	77.3
Hawaii	1.082	3.301	16.8	Massachusetts	5.856	6.721	112.0
Maine	1.186	2.154	16.6	Virginia	5.914	6.852	97.8
New Mexico	1.496	1.918	17.8	Georgia	6.227	5.709	89.6
Nebraska	1.594	1.359	22.5	N. Carolina	6.409	6.742	85.6
Utah	1.680	2.148	19.4	New Jersey	7.674	13.289	155.6
W. Virginia	1.898	1.432	20.9	Michigan	9.205	8.620	143.2
Arkansas	2.388	1.909	27.3	Ohio	10.816	7.535	157.6
Kansas	2.475	2.168	37.3	Illinois	11.584	10.609	189.9
Mississippi	2.624	1.331	27.0	Pennsylvania	11.942	11.673	181.5
Oregon	2.723	2.794	37.9	Florida	12.022	24.340	187.5
Iowa	2.823	1.996	39.6	Texas	16.781	15.720	232.3
Connecticut	3.212	3.108	68.3	New York	17.835	17.193	320.0
Oklahoma	3.259	2.927	41.1	California	27.653	35.797	491.4
Colorado	3.293	5.455	51.6				

Source: 1990 *U.S. Statistical Abstract*, Tables 409 and 705.

POP = population in millions

INCOME = personal income in current dollars (billions)

EXPTRAV = expenditures on domestic travel (billions of dollars)

The basic model is $EXPTRAV_t = \alpha + \beta INCOME_t + u_t$. We might expect that the error variances are heteroscedastic and increase with population. In other words, states with larger populations are likely to have greater variations in the expenditure on travel. To use the Goldfeld–Quandt test for this hypothesis, the observations are first arranged by population. This is already done in Table 8.1. The 51 sample observations were then divided into three equal parts, 1 to 17, 18 to 34, and 35 to 51. The middle observations were discarded, and the model estimated for the first and last sets. The estimated error variances are $\hat{\sigma}_1^2 = 3.025$ and $\hat{\sigma}_2^2 = 12.657$. (Practice Computer Session 8.1 has details on all the tests discussed in this section.) This gives the F-statistic as 4.18. Under the null hypothesis, this has the F-distribution with d.f. 15 and 15. $F_{15,15}^*(0.01) = 3.52$. The null hypothesis of homoscedasticity is therefore rejected at the 1 percent level. We thus conclude that there is significant heteroscedasticity. □

Breusch–Pagan Test

The **Breusch–Pagan test** [Breusch and Pagan (1979)] is based on the Lagrange multiplier test principle described in Chapter 7. Suppose the error variance σ_t^2 is not constant but is related to a number of variables $Z_1, Z_2, \ldots, Z_p$ (some or all of which might be the Xs in the model). More specifically, let the model be

$$Y_t = \beta_1 + \beta_2 X_{t2} + \beta_3 X_{t3} + \cdots + \beta_k X_{tk} + u_t \tag{8.2}$$

$$\sigma_t^2 = \alpha_0 + \alpha_1 Z_{t1} + \alpha_2 Z_{t2} + \cdots + \alpha_p Z_{tp} \tag{8.3}$$

where $\sigma_t^2 = \text{Var}(u_t)$. If $\alpha_1 = \alpha_2 = \cdots = \alpha_p = 0$, then the variance is a constant, indicating homoscedasticity. Thus, it is reasonable to construct a test for the hypothesis $H_0: \alpha_1 = \alpha_2 = \cdots = \alpha_p = 0$. This is the idea behind the Breusch–Pagan test. The LM test consists of running an auxiliary regression and using it to construct a test statistic. The formal steps are as follows:

Step 1 Estimate equation (8.2) by OLS and compute

$$\hat{u}_t = Y_t - \hat{\beta}_1 - \hat{\beta}_2 X_{t2} - \cdots - \hat{\beta}_k X_{tk} \quad \text{and} \quad \hat{\sigma}^2 = \frac{\sum \hat{u}_t^2}{T}$$

Step 2 $\hat{u}_t^2$ is an estimate of the error variance σ_t^2. If equation (8.3) were valid, one would expect $\hat{u}_t^2$ to be related to the Zs. This suggests the auxiliary regression

$$\frac{\hat{u}_t^2}{\hat{\sigma}^2} = \alpha_0 + \alpha_1 Z_{t1} + \alpha_2 Z_{t2} + \cdots + \alpha_p Z_{tp} + v_t \tag{8.4}$$

Step 3 Breusch and Pagan showed that for large samples, under the null hypothesis $H_0: \alpha_1 = \alpha_2 = \cdots = \alpha_p = 0$, one-half of the regression sum of squares (see Section 4.3 on regression sum of squares), RSS/2, of equation (8.4) has the chi-square distribution with p d.f. The test criterion is therefore to reject H_0 if RSS/2 $> \chi_p^2(0.05)$.

Example 8.2

The Breusch–Pagan test was applied to the expenditure travel example presented earlier. The model was estimated for the full sample and the residual saved as $\hat{u}_t = \text{EXPTRAV}_t - \hat{\alpha} - \hat{\beta}\text{INCOME}_t$. The auxiliary regression in Step 2 was next run with $Z_t = \text{POP}_t^2$; that is, the assumption is that σ_t varies with the population (or, equivalently, that the error variance varies with the square of the population). The test statistic is $RSS/2 = 10.5$. Under the null hypothesis of homoscedasticity, this has the chi-square distribution with 1 d.f. $\chi_1^2(0.01) = 6.635$. The Breusch–Pagan test also rejects homoscedasticity at the 1 percent level of significance.

White's Test

The Breusch–Pagan test has been shown to be sensitive to any violation of the normality assumption. Also, the previous tests require a prior knowledge of what might be causing the heteroscedasticity. White (1980) has proposed a direct test for heteroscedasticity that is very closely related to the Breusch–Pagan test but does not assume any prior knowledge of the heteroscedasticity. **White's test** is also a large sample LM test with a particular choice for the Zs, but it does not depend on the normality assumption. The steps for carrying out White's test for heteroscedasticity are described for the following model. The extension for more general models is straightforward.

$$Y_t = \beta_1 + \beta_2 X_{t2} + \beta_3 X_{t3} + u_t \tag{8.5}$$

$$\sigma_t^2 = \alpha_0 + \alpha_1 X_{t2} + \alpha_2 X_{t3} + \alpha_3 X_{t2}^2 + \alpha_4 X_{t3}^2 + \alpha_5 X_{t2}X_{t3} + v_t \tag{8.6}$$

Step 1   Estimate (8.5) by the OLS procedure and obtain $\hat{\beta}_1$, $\hat{\beta}_2$, and $\hat{\beta}_3$.

Step 2   Compute the residual $\hat{u}_t = Y_t - \hat{\beta}_1 - \hat{\beta}_2 X_{t2} - \hat{\beta}_3 X_{t3}$, and square it.

Step 3   Regress the squared residual $\hat{u}_t^2$ against a constant, X_{t2}, X_{t3}, X_{t2}^2, X_{t3}^2, and $X_{t2}X_{t3}$. This is the auxiliary regression corresponding to (8.6).

Step 4   Compute the statistic TR^2, where T is the size of the sample and R^2 is the *unadjusted* R-squared from the auxiliary regression of Step 3.

Step 5   Reject the null hypothesis that $\alpha_1 = \alpha_2 = \alpha_3 = \alpha_4 = \alpha_5 = 0$ if $TR^2 > \chi_5^2$ (0.05), the upper 5 percent point on the chi-square distribution with 5 d.f.

Although the test is a large-sample test, it has been found useful in samples of 30 or more. If the null hypothesis is not rejected, equation (8.6) becomes $\sigma_t^2 = \alpha_0$, which implies that the residuals are homoscedastic. White's test is readily generalized for the multiple regression case with several regressors. In this case, for Step 1, we regress Y against a constant (which must be present) and as many regressors as needed. Then we obtain the residuals from this model and square them to get $\hat{u}_t^2$. We regress the squared residuals against all the variables in the first step, plus the squares of all the independent variables plus the cross products of every pair of regressors. Finally, we compute the TR^2 statistic and reject homoscedasticity if $TR^2 > \chi^2(0.05)$ with degrees of freedom equal to the number of regression coefficients in the *auxiliary regression* with $\hat{u}_t^2$ as the dependent variable, *excluding the constant*. Note that this degrees of freedom is different from that when the LM test is used to test for omitted variables.

Care must be taken in carrying out Step 3, especially if some of the explanatory variables are dummy variables. If X_{t2} is a dummy variable, then X_{t2}^2 is identical to X_{t2} and hence should not be included separately, as otherwise there will be exact multicollinearity and the auxiliary regression cannot be run. Second, if equation (8.5) has several explanatory variables, Step 3 will involve a large number of variables (because of square and cross-product terms). It is then possible for the number of variables in the auxiliary regression to exceed the number of observations, making it impossible to carry out Step 3. If such a situation arises, the investigator will have to exclude some of the variables in this step. Possible candidates are the linear terms X_{t2}, X_{t3}, and so on, but the quadratic and interaction terms should be kept. Perhaps some interaction terms may be excluded. In the general case, with k explanatory variables, *including the constant term*, the auxiliary regression will have $k(k + 1)/2$ terms. The number of observations must be larger than that, and hence $T > k(k + 1)/2$ is a necessary condition.

Example 8.3

We apply White's test to the same example of expenditure on domestic travel. As in the Breusch–Pagan test, the first step is to regress EXPTRAV on a constant and INCOME. The auxiliary regression consists of regressing $\hat{u}_t^2$ against a constant, INCOME, and $INCOME^2$. R^2 for this auxiliary regression is 0.105 and hence $TR^2 = 5.36$. Under the null hypothesis of homoscedasticity, this has a chi-square distribution with 2 d.f. Because the 5 percent critical χ_2^2 is 5.991, White's test does not reject homoscedasticity at 5%. The p-value for 5.36 is 0.068, which means that the test rejects the null hypothesis at 7 percent. □

8.3 Estimation Procedures

If the assumption of homoscedasticity is rejected, we face the problem of trying to find alternative estimation procedures that are superior to ordinary least squares. In this section we discuss a number of approaches to estimation.

Heteroscedasticity Consistent Covariance Matrix (HCCM) Estimation

In Property 8.1 it was mentioned that the estimated variances of the OLS estimates are biased and inconsistent and hence statistical inferences will no longer be valid. If, however, consistent estimates can be obtained for the variances of the estimates, then valid inferences are possible *for large samples*. White (1980) has proposed a method of obtaining consistent estimates of the variances and covariances of the OLS estimates, which he called the **Heteroscedasticity consistent covariance matrix (HCCM) estimator**. Messer and White (1984) showed how a HCCM estimator may be obtained using conventional regression packages. This has been extended by MacKinnon and White (1985) who studied three different ways of obtaining HCCM estimates. They conclude from sampling experiments that the estimator with the best small sample properties is based on what statisticians refer to as the **jackknife** [Effron (1982)]. In simple terms, a jackknife estimator would first estimate a model T times, each time dropping one observation. This generates a series of estimates whose variability is exploited in constructing the jackknife estimator as an average of individual variances and covariances.

Example 8.4

For the expenditure on travel example we have been using, both OLS and HCCM estimates of the standard errors were obtained using the ECSLIB program (see Practice Computer Session 8.2 for the necessary steps). The results are given below, with the OLS standard errors in parentheses and the HCCM standard errors in brackets. It should be emphasized that the HCCM procedure provides consistent estimates of the variances of the estimators, but the estimates of the regression coefficients and the R^2 measures will be unchanged ($\bar{R}^2 = 0.871$).

$$\widehat{\text{EXPTRAV}} = 0.41556 + 0.06743 \text{ INCOME}$$
$$\begin{array}{cc} (0.422) & (0.0037) \\ [0.377] & [0.0067] \end{array}$$

The HCCM standard error for the income coefficient is higher than that obtained by OLS, but the comparison is really not proper because OLS estimates are inconsistent and hence not reliable. □

Generalized (or Weighted) Least Squares

In equation (8.5) we divide every term by σ_t, the standard deviation of u_t. We then obtain the modified model

$$\frac{Y_t}{\sigma_t} = \beta_1 \frac{1}{\sigma_t} + \beta_2 \frac{X_{t2}}{\sigma_t} + \beta_3 \frac{X_{t3}}{\sigma_t} + \frac{u_t}{\sigma_t}$$

or

$$Y_t^* = \beta_1 \frac{1}{\sigma_t} + \beta_2 X_{t2}^* + \beta_3 X_{t3}^* + u_t^* \qquad (8.7)$$

where the asterisks denote corresponding variables divided by σ_t. We have

$$\text{Var}(u_t^*) = \text{Var}\left(\frac{u_t}{\sigma_t}\right) = \frac{\text{Var}(u_t)}{\sigma_t^2} = 1$$

Thus, equation (8.7) satisfies all the conditions required for OLS estimates to possess desirable properties. Hence, estimates obtained by regressing Y_t^* against $(1/\sigma_t)$, X_{t2}^*, and X_{t3}^* (with no constant term) will be BLUE. The procedure just described is a special case of a more general method called **generalized least squares (GLS)**. Although the GLS procedure appears straightforward, the practical problem is that σ_t is unknown and hence we cannot estimate equation (8.7) without additional assumptions.

The GLS procedure applied to the case of heteroscedasticity is also the same as **weighted least squares (WLS)**. Define $w_t = 1/\sigma_t$ and note that (8.7) can be rewritten as follows:

$$w_t Y_t = \beta_1 w_t + \beta_2(w_t X_{t2}) + \beta_3(w_t X_{t3}) + (w_t u_t) \qquad (8.8)$$

Comparing (8.7) and (8.8) we readily see that minimizing the sum of squares of u_t^* is equivalent to minimizing the weighted sum of squares of residuals:

$$\sum(w_t u_t)^2 = \sum(w_t Y_t - \beta_1 w_t - \beta_2 w_t X_{t2} - \beta_3 w_t X_{t3})^2 \qquad (8.9)$$

Thus, each observation on each variable (including the constant term) is given the weight w_t, which is inversely proportional to the standard deviation of u_t. This means that observations for which σ_t is large are given less weight in the WLS procedure. It is easy to verify (see Exercise 8.1) that the resulting estimates are identical to those obtained by applying OLS to equation (8.7). It is possible to show that the weighted least squares estimates are also maximum likelihood (see Exercise 8.2) in the case of normal errors.

Multiplicative Heteroscedasticity with Known Proportional Factor

First consider the simple case in which the structure of the heteroscedasticity is known to have a particular form. In the model in equation (8.5) suppose the heteroscedasticity is such that the residual standard deviation σ_t is proportional to Z_t, which is known. More specifically, suppose equation (8.6) is as follows:

$$\text{Var}(u_t) = \sigma_t^2 = \sigma^2 Z_t^2 \quad \text{or equivalently} \quad \sigma_t = \sigma Z_t \quad (8.10)$$

where the values of Z_t are known for all t. In other words, the residual standard deviation is proportional to some known variable Z_t, the constant of proportionality being σ (unknown). This is known as **multiplicative heteroscedasticity**. In the consumption expenditure example given earlier, Z_t will be household income, and in the crime example, Z_t will be the city's population. Except for this modification, u_t is thought to satisfy all the other assumptions for applying OLS. Dividing every term in equation (8.5) by Z_t,

$$\frac{Y_t}{Z_t} = \beta_1 \frac{1}{Z_t} + \beta_2 \frac{X_{t2}}{Z_t} + \beta_3 \frac{X_{t3}}{Z_t} + \frac{u_t}{Z_t}$$

or

$$Y_t^* = \beta_1 \frac{1}{Z_t} + \beta_2 X_{t2}^* + \beta_3 X_{t3}^* + u_t^* \quad (8.11)$$

where the asterisks denote corresponding variables divided by Z_t. We have

$$\text{Var}(u_t^*) = \text{Var}\left(\frac{u_t}{Z_t}\right) = \frac{\text{Var}(u_t)}{Z_t^2} = \sigma^2$$

Thus, equation (8.11) satisfies all the conditions required for OLS estimates to have desirable properties. Hence estimates obtained by regressing Y_t^* against $(1/Z_t)$, X_{t2}^*, and X_{t3}^* will be BLUE (when $\sigma_t^2 = \sigma^2 Z_t^2$). This is the same as WLS with $w_t = 1/Z_t$. Note that equation (8.11) does not have a constant term, *unless either X_{t2} or X_{t3} is identical to Z_t*. Because the GLS estimates are BLUE, OLS estimates of (8.5) will be inefficient.

Example 8.5

In Section 8.2 we found that, for the travel expenditure example, the assumption that the error variance is related to the state population had solid support from two of the methods of testing for heteroscedasticity. We apply the weighted least squares method to a slightly modified model:

$$\text{EXPTRAV}_t = \alpha + \beta \text{INCOME}_t + u_t$$

$$\sigma_t = \sigma \text{POP}_t \quad \text{or equivalently} \quad \text{Var}(u_t) = \sigma^2 \text{POP}_t^2$$

The assumption that the standard deviation σ_t is proportional to the population is equivalent to assuming that the variance is proportional to the square of the population. Dividing each term by POP_t we get

$$\frac{EXPTRAV_t}{POP_t} = \alpha\left(\frac{1}{POP_t}\right) + \beta\left(\frac{INCOME}{POP_t}\right) + \frac{u_t}{POP_t} \tag{8.12}$$

It is easy to verify that the error term in equation (8.12) has a constant variance because of the assumption that $\sigma_t = \sigma POP_t$. We can therefore apply OLS to equation (8.12). Note that the new dependent variable is simply the per capita expenditure on travel. Similarly, the new independent variables are per capita income and the reciprocal of population, *with no constant term*. We thus see that formulating the model in per capita terms captures any inherent heteroscedasticity caused by the size of the population. If population has a role in a model, it is generally a good practice to express the model in per capita terms. The estimated model is as follows, with t-statistics in parentheses and adjusted R^2 for the transformed model (see Practice Computer Session 8.3):

$$\left(\frac{EXPTRAV}{POP}\right) = \underset{(2.2)}{0.581}\left(\frac{1}{POP}\right) + \underset{(5.0)}{0.069}\left(\frac{INCOME}{POP}\right)$$

$$\bar{R}^2 = 0.126 \qquad F = 44.391$$

Although $\bar{R}^2$ appears low, it refers to the transformed model and not to the original specification in levels. The F-statistic, however, is significant at the 1 percent level. Both t-statistics are also significant at levels below 4 percent. □

Dependent Variable Heteroscedasticity

Another case in which the standard deviation of the error term (σ_t) is assumed to be proportional to some quantity is **Dependent Variable Heteroscedasticity**. For example, Prais and Houthakker (1955) have assumed that the standard deviation (σ_t) is proportional to the mean of the dependent variable (Y_t), so that

$$Y_t = \beta_1 + \beta_2 X_{t2} + \cdots + \beta_k X_{tk} + u_t$$
$$\sigma_t = kE(Y_t) = k(\beta_1 + \beta_2 X_{t2} + \cdots + \beta_k X_{tk})$$

where k is an unknown constant of proportionality. The procedure for estimating the model is as follows:

Step 1 Estimate the regression model and obtain the $\hat{\beta}$ values.

Step 2 Substitute this into the equation for σ_t and obtain

$$\hat{\sigma}_t = \hat{Y}_t = \hat{\beta}_1 + \hat{\beta}_2 X_{t2} + \cdots + \hat{\beta}_k X_{tk}$$

Step 3 Estimate the original model by weighted least squares using the weights $w_t = 1/\hat{Y}_t$, which is equivalent to estimating the following transformed model by OLS:

$$\frac{Y_t}{\hat{Y}_t} = \beta_1 \frac{1}{\hat{Y}_t} + \beta_2 \frac{X_{t2}}{\hat{Y}_t} + \cdots + \beta_k \frac{X_{tk}}{\hat{Y}_t} + \frac{u_t}{\hat{Y}_t}$$

Note that this equation does not have a constant term. Although the procedure is quite straightforward and can be easily implemented in any regression package the estimates are not asymptotically efficient [as was shown by Amemiya (1973) and Harvey (1981)], and hence the procedure is not recommended.

Estimated Generalized Lease Squares (ESLS)

The generalized least squares procedure discussed earlier consists of dividing each variable (including the constant term) by σ_t (the standard deviation of the error term) and then applying ordinary least squares to the resulting transformed model. As the structure of the heteroscedasticity is generally unknown (that is, σ_t is unknown), a researcher must first obtain estimates of σ_t by some means and then use the weighted least squares procedure. This method is known as **Estimated Generalized Least Squares (EGLS)**. The actual procedure for estimating σ_t has, however, varied widely in practice. In this section we present two of the more commonly used techniques. For more details see Kmenta (1986) and Judge et al. (1985).

σ_t^2 a Linear Function of Independent Variables

In carrying out the White's test for heteroscedasticity, we assumed that the variance of the error term is a linear function of a number of independent variables, in particular, squares and cross-products of the variables in the regression models [see equation (8.6)]. This suggests the following EGLS procedure, illustrated here for the model in equations (8.5) and (8.6) but more generally applicable.

Step 1 Estimate equation (8.5) by the OLS procedure and obtain the $\hat{\beta}$ values.
Step 2 Compute the residuals $\hat{u}_t$ and their squares $\hat{u}_t^2$.
Step 3 Estimate the auxiliary equation by regressing $\hat{u}_t^2$ against a constant, X_{t2}, X_{t3}, X_{t2}^2, X_{t3}^2, and $X_{t2}X_{t3}$.
Step 4 Use the estimates of the auxiliary regression and obtain the predicted variance

$$\hat{\sigma}_t^2 = \hat{\alpha}_0 + \hat{\alpha}_1 X_{t2} + \cdots + \hat{\alpha}_5 X_{t2}X_{t3}$$

It turns out that the above estimate of σ_t^2 is not asymptotically efficient and hence a modified estimate is obtained.
Step 5 Regress $\hat{u}_t^2/\hat{\sigma}_t^2$ against each of the variables in Step 3, divided by $\hat{\sigma}_t^2$. Use these estimates in equation (8.6) and get the second-round predictions as $\tilde{\sigma}_t^2$. (See below for some practical difficulties in carrying out this step.)
Step 6 Set the weight w_t to $1/\tilde{\sigma}_t$, which is the reciprocal of the positive square root of $\tilde{\sigma}_t^2$, and use weighted least squares. More specifically, multiply each variable in equation (8.5), including the constant, by w_t and regress $(w_t Y_t)$ against w_t, $(w_t X_{t2})$, and $(w_t X_{t3})$.

The WLS estimates obtained in this way are consistent and so are the estimated variances and covariances of the estimates. Also, the estimates are asymptotically likely to be more efficient than OLS estimators. However, the procedure may fail in practice for a number of reasons. First, as pointed out in White's test, there may be exact collinearity among the independent variables in the auxiliary equation (8.6), due for instance to dummy variables or interaction terms. This is easily overcome, however, by omitting those variables that cause the exact collinearity. A more difficult problem is that there is no guarantee that the predicted variances in Steps 4 and 5 will be positive for all t. If any of them is exactly zero, then the corresponding weight is undefined. If any of them is negative, we cannot take the square root. If any of this happens, we can try regressing $\hat{u}_t$ against just the quadratic terms and exclude the interaction terms. This might yield positive values for $\tilde{\sigma}_t^2$. Alternatively, we might set the weights for such observations to zero and thus effectively exclude them from the estimation procedure.

Example 8.6

It would be useful to apply the method just described to the problem of estimating the relation between expenditure on travel and income. We have seen that the Goldfeld–Quandt test, the Breusch–Pagan test, and the White's test reject homoscedasticity at the 5 percent level of significance. Table 8.2 is an annotated computer output for the heteroscedasticity estimation. See Practice Computer Session 8.4 for details. Note that several of the error variances predicted by the auxiliary regression in Step 3 are negative and are hence unacceptable. As an alternative approach, $\hat{u}_t^2$ was regressed against a constant and the square of income. Note again from Table 8.2 that all the predicted variances ($\hat{\sigma}_t^2$) are positive. However, as mentioned in Step 4, these estimates are inefficient and hence we proceed to Step 5. The predicted variances ($\tilde{\sigma}_t^2$) are in Table 8.2, and we see that they are all positive. The next step is to construct the weight w_t, which is the reciprocal of the square root of the predicted variance (that is, $1/\tilde{\sigma}_t$). For example, for the first observation, $\tilde{\sigma}^2$ is 1.8171782, which gives a weight of 0.741824. We then estimate the weighted model corresponding to equation (8.9). The estimate of the income coefficient has not changed much between OLS and WLS, but that of the constant term has changed considerably. The standard error for the income coefficient is worse compared to OLS, but because the OLS estimates of standard errors are inconsistent, the comparison is not very meaningful. □

Log σ_t^2 a Linear Function of Independent Variables

As we saw in Example 8.6, some of the error variances predicted by the auxiliary regression might be negative and are therefore unacceptable. An alternative procedure that guarantees that the predicted variances are always positive is to use the logarithm of the squared residuals in the auxiliary regression. This is equivalent to

TABLE 8.2 Annotated Partial Computer Output for Example 8.6

```
List of variables
    0) const        1) pop        2) exptrav    3) income
?ols exptrav const income ;                           (Step1: Estimate Model by OLS)

            OLS ESTIMATES USING THE 51 OBSERVATIONS 1-51
                    Dependent variable  - exptrav


    VARIABLE            COEFFICIENT        STDERROR      T STAT    PROB t > |T|

    0) constant          0.41556          0.42232       0.984      0.3300
    3) income            0.06743          0.00367      18.380    < 0.0001 ***

Unadjusted R-squared        0.873     Adjusted R-squared            0.871

?genr usq = uhat*uhat                          (Step 2: Compute the square of residuals)
Generated var. no. 4 (usq)
?genr incmsq = income*income                                        (Square income)
Generated var. no. 5 (incmsq)
?ols usq const income incmsq ;                    (Step 3: Estimate auxiliary regression)

            OLS ESTIMATES USING THE 51 OBSERVATIONS 1-51
                    Dependent variable  - usq


    VARIABLE            COEFFICIENT        STDERROR      T STAT    PROB t > |T|

    0) constant         -2.68901          4.23816      -0.634      0.5288
    3) income            0.15210          0.07318       2.079      0.0430 **
    5) incmsq          -2.56652e-04     1.76147e-04    -1.457      0.1516

Unadjusted R-squared        0.105     Adjusted R-squared            0.068

?genr usqhat1 = usq - uhat                           (Step 4: Predict error variances)
Generated var. no. 6 (usqhat1)
?print usqhat1 ;                          (Note that some of the variances are negative)
Varname: usqhat1, period: 1, maxobs: 51, obs range: full 1-51, current 1-51

-1.74093457 -1.23774154 -1.51820619 -0.88611906 -1.10553663 -1.39988996
-1.37036223 -1.19362704 -0.39304839 -0.92991018 -0.24915688 0.1225588
-0.20608952 -0.23479596 -0.0628653 0.60341282 0.16522578 0.37786773
1.27216374 2.62741031 1.23071329 2.70709279 2.93185633 6.50246983
3.12894517 4.47622885 4.10977854 3.16822434 3.59724624 4.17326761
6.34987667 4.42594064 8.12374061 6.81662224 6.75872818 5.87491824
7.24104987 7.53509235 11.12724115 9.73196662 8.87910284 8.45054711
14.76453968 13.8293722 14.90798156 16.94022568 16.46324186 16.80764038
18.79505023 19.70322078 10.08028672
```

specifying a multiplicative heteroscedasticity. The procedure is as follows:

Step 1   Estimate equation (8.5) by OLS.

Step 2   Compute the residuals $\hat{u}_t$ and their squares $\hat{u}_t^2$.

Step 3   Regress $\ln(\hat{u}_t^2)$ against a constant, X_{t2}, X_{t3}, X_{t2}^2, X_{t3}^2, and $X_{t2}X_{t3}$.

Step 4   From the predicted variances $\ln(\hat{u}_t^2)$ we get $\hat{\sigma}_t^2$ by an exponential

TABLE 8.2   *(Continued)*

?**ols usq const incmsq ;**   *(Alternative estimation with only incomesq)*

```
        OLS ESTIMATES USING THE 51 OBSERVATIONS 1-51
              Dependent variable  - usq


    VARIABLE          COEFFICIENT         STDERROR     T STAT    PROB t > |T|

  0) constant            4.08502          2.79977       1.459      0.1509
  5) incmsq         7.98119e-05       7.17827e-05       1.112      0.2716

Unadjusted R-squared         0.025    Adjusted R-squared            0.005
```

?**genr usqhat2 = usq - uhat**   *(Predict error variances again)*
Generated var. no. 7 (usqhat2)
?**print usqhat2 ;**   *(Now all the variances are positive)*
Varname: usqhat2, period: 1, maxobs: 51, obs range: full 1-51, current 1-51

```
4.08819215 4.09253392 4.08988017 4.09670968 4.09399208 4.0909273
4.09120505 4.09300561 4.10419922 4.09613742 4.10675321 4.1141406
4.10755053 4.10701738 4.11031202 4.12542919 4.11506242 4.11988705
4.14450743 4.19606592 4.14320729 4.19966703 4.21018225 4.45733818
4.21984348 4.2975284 4.27431351 4.22181883 4.24449579 4.27822031
4.44330006 4.29424654 4.62956189 4.48735623 4.48170954 4.40179787
4.53038203 4.5619237 5.08618496 4.84841252 4.72576716 4.66983498
6.0173792 5.72166651 6.06737337 6.96320216 6.71420817 6.89091172
8.39193743 12.25776356 23.35752134
```

?**genr wt1 = 1/usqhat2**   *(Compute weights for Step 5)*
Generated var. no. 8 (wt1)
?print wt1 ;
Varname: wt1, period: 1, maxobs: 51, obs range: full 1-51, current 1-51
```
0.2446069 0.24434739 0.24450594 0.24409833 0.24426037 0.24444336
0.24442676 0.24431924 0.24365289 0.24413243 0.24350136 0.24306413
0.2434541 0.2434857 0.24329053 0.24239902 0.24300968 0.2427251
0.2412832 0.23831847 0.24135891 0.23811412 0.23751941 0.22434914
0.23697561 0.23269189 0.2339557 0.23686474 0.23559924 0.23374205
0.22505795 0.23286972 0.21600316 0.22284837 0.22312914 0.2271799
0.22073194 0.21920577 0.19661102 0.20625308 0.21160585 0.21414033
0.16618531 0.17477425 0.16481597 0.14361209 0.14893789 0.14511868
0.11916199 0.08158095 0.04281276
```

(continued)

transformation (that is, by taking the antilog). Because the exponential transformaton gives only positive values, we are assured that the estimated variances are positive.

Step 5   Obtain EGLS estimates using $w_t = 1/\hat{\sigma}_t$ as the weight.

Estimates obtained this way also yield consistent estimates for the standard errors. Like the previous procedure, this method might also fail if any of the

TABLE 8.2 *(Continued)*

```
?wls wt1 usq const incmsq ;                            (Step 5: Estimate modified model)


          WEIGHTED LEAST SQUARES ESTIMATES USING THE 51 OBSERVATIONS 1-51
          Dependent variable  - usq,    Variable used as weight - wt1


    VARIABLE          COEFFICIENT          STDERROR        T STAT      PROB t > |T|

    0) constant          1.80451          1.99320          0.905        0.3697
    5) incmsq        3.19155e-04      1.63358e-04          1.954        0.0565 *
```

?genr usqhat3 = coeff(0) + (incmsq * coeff(5))   *(Compute predicted variances again)*
Generated var. no. 9 (usqhat3)
?print usqhat3 ;   *(Predicted variances are again positive)*
Varname: usqhat3, period: 1, maxobs: 51, obs range: full 1-51, current 1-51

1.81717832 1.83454034 1.82392844 1.85123851 1.8403713 1.82811575
1.82922641 1.83642654 1.88118799 1.84895017 1.89140095 1.92094191
1.8945893 1.89245735 1.90563205 1.96608315 1.92462814 1.94392105
2.0423739 2.24854785 2.03717487 2.26294812 2.30499675 3.29333278
2.34363043 2.65427969 2.56144715 2.35152951 2.44221095 2.57706978
3.23719666 2.64115605 3.9820272 3.41337007 3.39078987 3.0712362
3.58542319 3.71155314 5.80798801 4.857175 4.36673631 4.14307268
9.53168115 8.34917457 9.73159967 13.31387216 12.31818599 13.02479457
19.02715035 34.48595548 78.87206772

?genr wt2 = 1/(sqrt(usqhat3))   *(Step 6: Compute final weights)*
Generated var. no. 10 (wt2)
?print wt2 ;
Varname: wt2, period: 1, maxobs: 51, obs range: full 1-51, current 1-51

0.74182459 0.73830595 0.74045062 0.73496864 0.73713541 0.73960213
0.73937756 0.73792669 0.72909463 0.73542332 0.72712353 0.72151088
0.72651144 0.72692056 0.72440339 0.71317984 0.72081959 0.7172337
0.69973303 0.6668819 0.70062535 0.66475667 0.65866539 0.55103881
0.65321393 0.61379968 0.62482342 0.65211589 0.63989455 0.62292665
0.55579605 0.61532275 0.5011271 0.54126296 0.54306218 0.57061527
0.52811656 0.51906549 0.41494176 0.4537411 0.4785436 0.4912909
0.32390321 0.34608138 0.32055893 0.27406136 0.28492242 0.27708598
0.229252 0.17028597 0.1126

residuals is exactly zero, because then $\ln(\hat{u}_t^2)$ is undefined. In practice, however, this is not likely to occur. If $\hat{u}_t^2$ is close to zero, then the weight w_t will be large. Thus observations that are predicted with a great deal of precision will be given large weights.

Example 8.7

The above procedure was also applied to the travel expenditure example. Table 8.3 has an annotated partial computer output (Practice Computer Ses-

TABLE 8.2 *(Continued)*

```
?wls wt2 exptrav const income ;                          (Obtain EGSLS estimates)

          WEIGHTED LEAST SQUARES ESTIMATES USING THE 51 OBSERVATIONS 1-51
          Dependent variable  - exptrav,  Variable used as weight - wt2


   VARIABLE          COEFFICIENT        STDERROR      T STAT     PROB t > |T|

   0) constant         0.63744          0.32593       1.956       0.0562 *
   3) income           0.06313          0.00598      10.551      < 0.0001 ***

STATISTICS BASED ON RESIDUALS FOR THE WEIGHTED MODEL

R-squared is suppressed because it is not meaningful.  F-statistic tests the
hypothesis that each coefficient (including the constant term) is zero.

Error Sum of Sq (ESS)      49.08363    Std Err of Resid. (sgmahat)     1.00085
F-statistic (2, 49)        141.599     Probability F > 141.599 is < 0.00001

STATISTICS BASED ON RESIDUALS FOR THE ORIGINAL MODEL

R-squared is computed as the square of the corr. between observed and
predicted dep. var.

Mean of dep. var.          5.39525     S.D. of dep. variable           6.43512
Error Sum of Sq (ESS)    270.09634     Std Err of Resid. (sgmahat)     2.34780
Unadjusted R-squared         0.873     Adjusted R-squared                0.871

MODEL SELECTION STATISTICS

SGMASQ       5.51217     AIC       5.728103     FPE       5.728334
HQ           5.896351    SCHWARZ   6.178913     SHIBATA   5.71138
GCV          5.737157    RICE      5.746731
```

sion 8.5 has the steps to reproduce these results). It will be noted that the regression coefficients and the standard errors are quite similar to those obtained by the method in Example 8.6.

8.4 Application: Women's Labor Force Participation

Here we revisit the labor force participation application of Chapter 4, carry out White's test for heteroscedasticity (because it is more general and more direct than any other test, and does not require prior knowledge of the form of heteroscedasticity), and use the WLS procedure to obtain more efficient EGLS estimates of the parameters. Practice Computer Session 8.6 has the instructions to reproduce the results of this section. As the first step in White's test we start with the final Model B in Table 4.6.

$$\text{WLFP}_t = \alpha_0 + \alpha_1 \text{YF}_t + \alpha_2 \text{EDUC}_t + \alpha_3 \text{UE}_t + \alpha_4 \text{URB}_t + \alpha_5 \text{WH}_t + u_t \quad (8.13)$$

TABLE 8.3 Annotated Partial Computer Output for Example 8.7

```
List of variables
  0) const       1) pop       2) exptrav     3) income

?ols exptrav const income ;                    (Step 1: Estimate model by OLS)

        OLS ESTIMATES USING THE 51 OBSERVATIONS 1-51
               Dependent variable  - exptrav


   VARIABLE        COEFFICIENT      STDERROR      T STAT    PROB t > |T|

   0) constant        0.41556       0.42232       0.984      0.3300
   3) income          0.06743       0.00367      18.380     < 0.0001 ***

Unadjusted R-squared      0.873    Adjusted R-squared          0.871

?genr lnusq = ln(uhat*uhat)              (Step 2: Generate log of squared residuals)
Generated var. no. 4 (lnusq)
?genr incmsq = income*income                           (Square income)
Generated var. no. 5 (incmsq)
?ols lnusq const income incmsq ;               (Auxiliary regression for lnusq)

        OLS ESTIMATES USING THE 51 OBSERVATIONS 1-51
               Dependent variable  - lnusq


   VARIABLE        COEFFICIENT       STDERROR       T STAT    PROB t > |T|

   0) constant       -2.09863        0.48982       -4.284    < 0.0001 ***
   3) income          0.02290        0.00846        2.707     0.0094 ***
   5) incmsq      -3.02830e-05    2.03581e-05       -1.488     0.1434

Unadjusted R-squared      0.223    Adjusted R-squared          0.190

?genr usqhat = exp(lnusq - uhat)          (Step 3: Antilog of predicted variances)
Generated var. no. 6 (usqhat)
?print usqhat ;
Varname: usqhat, period: 1, maxobs: 51, obs range: full 1-51, current 1-51

0.14148026 0.15268201 0.14632979 0.16105118 0.1557746 0.14897552
0.14964349 0.15370683 0.17359501 0.1599835 0.17744337 0.18779985
0.17861231 0.17783227 0.18255752 0.20213548 0.18902809 0.19527489
0.22398916 0.27616257 0.2225657 0.27960017 0.28953992 0.50857638
0.29855992 0.36866829 0.34803701 0.30039245 0.32119249 0.35152267
0.4962986 0.36576255 0.66094732 0.53488057 0.52992648 0.46005358
0.57273982 0.60063773 1.08957753 0.86147601 0.74802729 0.69720523
2.07655648 1.74893839 2.13300697 3.18086567 2.88437105 3.09452157
4.88328552 8.38920313 6.29440552
```

The next step is to get the residual and square it (to get $\hat{u}_t^2$). Then we run an auxiliary regression with $\hat{u}_t^2$ as the dependent variable, the independent variables being a constant, YF, EDUC, UE, URB, WH, their squares such as YF^2, and all the cross-product terms such as YF multiplied by EDUC. This regression will have 21 coefficients to be estimated including the constant term. For White's test the only

TABLE 8.3   *(Continued)*

```
?genr wt = 1/(sqrt(usqhat))                        (Compute weights for EGLS)
Generated var. no. 7 (wt)

?wls wt exptrav const income ;                       (Obtain EGSLS estimates)

        WEIGHTED LEAST SQUARES ESTIMATES USING THE 51 OBSERVATIONS 1-51
        Dependent variable  - exptrav,   Variable used as weight - wt


   VARIABLE          COEFFICIENT        STDERROR       T STAT    PROB t > |T|

   0) constant        0.66803          0.29912        2.233     0.0301  **
   3) income          0.06291          0.00671        9.373     < 0.0001 ***

STATISTICS BASED ON RESIDUALS FOR THE WEIGHTED MODEL

R-squared is suppressed because it is not meaningful. F-statistic tests the
hypothesis that each coefficient (including the constant term) is zero.

Error Sum of Sq (ESS)     406.55730    Std Err of Resid. (sgmahat)     2.88047
F-statistic (2, 49)        111.903     Probability F > 111.903 is < 0.00001
Durbin-Watson Stat.          1.795     First-order auto corr coeff       0.099

STATISTICS BASED ON RESIDUALS FOR THE ORIGINAL MODEL

R-squared is computed as the square of the corr. between observed and
predicted dep. var.

Mean of dep. var.          5.39525     S.D. of dep. variable           6.43512
Error Sum of Sq (ESS)    270.72760     Std Err of Resid. (sgmahat)     2.35054
Unadjusted R-squared         0.873     Adjusted R-squared                0.871

MODEL SELECTION STATISTICS

SGMASQ      5.525053     AIC        5.741491     FPE       5.741722
HQ          5.910132     SCHWARZ    6.193354     SHIBATA   5.724728
GCV         5.750565     RICE       5.760162
```

value we are interested in is that of R^2, which is 0.669. This gives the TR^2 statistics as 33.45, which, under the null hypothesis of homoscedasticity, has a chi-square distribution with 20 d.f. Because this exceeds $\chi^2_{20}(0.05) = 31.41$, we reject homoscedasticity at the 5 percent level.

As we have no prior information about what might have caused the heteroscedasticity, we use the EGLS procedure described earlier. This requires utilizing the estimated auxiliary regression to predict the value of the left-hand side of equation (8.6)—that is, the value of σ_t^2. The 50 predicted values are printed in Table 8.4. It is evident that some of the predicted values (12 out of 50) are negative. Because they represent variances, the negative values are not acceptable. Therefore, we use the alternative procedure described earlier. This consists of regressing the logarithm of $\hat{u}_t^2$ against the variables in the auxiliary regression, predicting $\ln(\hat{u}_t^2)$ and then taking the antilog to get $\tilde{\sigma}_t^2$. Table 8.4 has these predicted error variances,

TABLE 8.4   Predicted Variances and Weights for Heteroscedasticity

Predicted Variances Using $\hat{u}_t^2$ as the Dependent Variable				
0.264598	−0.415319	3.372925	7.954698	3.952265
4.663114	3.700826	1.821783	4.031014	−1.205742
1.145377	−0.862540	4.321866	5.901517	−2.844753
4.806342	14.954063	−1.871110	9.726571	6.766723
7.411338	3.671387	−1.875999	4.455954	1.869758
−1.068033	2.460566	8.364320	0.259744	9.528454
−0.932910	8.507314	7.229769	−0.466124	2.354906
2.343030	−2.343966	11.863565	32.635249	3.501842
0.904617	7.607253	2.152063	8.575059	3.220348
3.818344	−2.653606	36.526652	−0.955099	6.665122
Predicted Variances Using ln $\hat{u}_t^2$ as the Dependent Variable				
0.522558	0.063884	2.512735	1.519796	1.243531
2.217344	4.440255	0.767244	1.999477	1.384570
0.100094	0.809981	2.016157	4.128529	0.737825
1.859681	6.169304	0.156215	1.744587	3.803726
7.993611	1.432283	1.947799	0.735759	2.632881
0.413512	1.000010	4.568106	0.670193	1.984466
0.644091	1.715607	5.581551	0.342140	3.068639
1.933176	0.932853	5.352246	11.266595	2.086994
0.280122	2.599969	1.204218	4.435622	0.065082
2.501393	0.814072	26.262591	2.338251	0.887401

which are all positive. The next step is to construct the weight that is the reciprocal of the square root of the value of $\tilde{\sigma}_t^2$. For example, the weight for the first observation will be $1/\sqrt{0.522558}$, which is 1.383352.

The next step is to multiply each variable and observation by this weight. In other words, compute $WLFP_t^* = w_t WLFP_t$, $YF_t^* = w_t YF_t$, $EDUC^* = w_t EDUC$, $UE^* = w_t UE_t$, $URB_t^* = w_t URB_t$, and $WH^* = w_t WH_t$. Then estimate the model

$$WLFP_t^* = \alpha_0 w_t + \alpha_1 YF_t^* + \alpha_2 EDUC_t^* + \alpha_3 UE_t^* + \alpha_4 URB_t^* + \alpha_5 WH_t^* + u^*$$
(8.4)

with no constant term. These EGLS estimates are presented in Table 8.4 along with their t-statistics. The theory just presented shows that EGLS estimates are asymptotically more efficient than OLS estimates and hence should have lower standard errors, which means higher t-statistics. Although it is reassuring to note that the EGLS estimates in Table 8.5 have consistently higher t-statistics than OLS estimates, because the latter estimates are inefficient, the comparison is strictly not valid. A similar comparison of the model selection statistics is also not valid.

TABLE 8.5 Estimates Using OLS and EGLS

Variables	OLS Method		EGLS Method	
	Coeff	t-stat	Coeff	t-stat
CONSTANT	37.454	8.699	38.850	17.946
YF	0.0050	6.268	0.0046	10.960
EDUC	0.2446	4.872	0.2415	7.055
UE	−1.0440	−3.912	−0.9083	−6.237
URB	−0.0497	−1.844	−0.0606	−5.006
WH	−0.1216	−3.514	−0.1213	−9.175

· ·

SUMMARY

If the variance of the residuals in a linear regression model is the same across all observations, we have *homoscedasticity*. If, on the other hand, the variance is different across the sample, the errors are said to be *heteroscedastic*. If we ignore the presence of heteroscedasticity and apply the OLS procedure, some of the properties of the estimators are altered. OLS estimates are still unbiased and consistent. Forecasts based on them are also unbiased and consistent. Estimates and forecasts, however, are inefficient and hence are no longer BLUE. Because the estimated variances and covariances of the estimates are biased and inconsistent, tests of hypotheses are not valid anymore.

The presence of heteroscedasticity is tested by a number of tests. The *Goldfeld–Quandt test* consists of (1) identifying a variable that might be causing the heteroscedasticity, (2) arranging the observations in increasing order of that variable, (3) estimating the model for the first T_1, and last T_2 observations (T_1 and T_2 being about a third of T), and (4) using an F-test on the ratio of the estimated error variances $\hat{\sigma}_1^2$ and $\hat{\sigma}_2^2$.

The *Breusch–Pagan test* uses all the observations. First estimate the model by OLS and compute the residuals $\hat{u}_t$. Square them and calculate $\hat{\sigma}_t^2 = \sum \hat{u}_t^2/T$. Next regress $\hat{u}_t^2/\hat{\sigma}_t^2$ against a constant and one or more variable (Zs) that might be causing the heteroscedasticity (some of the Zs may be the same as the Xs in the model). One-half of the regression sum of squares (RSS/2) of this auxiliary regression has a chi-square distribution with p d.f. under the null hypothesis of homoscedasticity (p is the number of coefficients in the auxiliary regression *excluding the constant*). If RSS/2 exceeds the critical chi-square value, homoscedasticity is rejected.

White's test is very similar to the Breusch–Pagan test but is more direct and requires no prior knowledge of the form of the heteroscedasticity. First estimate the model by OLS and compute the residuals. Square the residuals and regress them against all the variables in the model plus all the squares and cross products of the variables. Next compute TR^2 from this auxiliary regression. Under the null hypothesis of homoscedasticity, TR^2 has the chi-square distribution with degrees of freedom equal to the number of parameters in the auxiliary regression, *excluding the constant*. If TR^2 exceeds the critical value from this chi-square distribution, we conclude that the residuals are heteroscedastic.

If heteroscedasticity is found, one can use *generalized least squares* (GLS) which are also *weighted least squares* (WLS) to obtain consistent and asymptotically efficient estimates of the parameters. The procedure is to define a weight w_t for each observation equal to the inverse of the standard deviation (that is $1/\sigma_t$) of the tth residual. Because this standard deviation is unknown, we must either assume that it is proportional to some known variable or use the model to estimate σ_t. The general procedure is to use an auxiliary regression similar to that in White's test and predict its dependent variable $(\tilde{u}_t^2)$, which is an estimate of the residual variance. If any of these values is negative, the estimates are not acceptable, and an alternative procedure should be used that guarantees that the predicted variances are positive. The modified procedure is to regress $\ln(\hat{u}_t^2)$ against the variables in White's test and obtain the predicted value. The antilog of this will always be positive and can be used as $\tilde{u}_t^2$. Next set w_t equal to $1/\tilde{u}_t$. Then multiply the dependent variable and each independent variable, *including the constant term* (which must be present in the model), by the corresponding w_t. Finally, regress the transformed dependent variable against all the transformed independent variables. This final regression may not have a constant term. The estimates obtained from this transformed model are known as *estimated generalized least squares* (EGLS) estimates and are asymptotically more efficient than OLS estimates.

KEY TERMS

Breusch–Pagan test	Dependent variable heteroscedasticity
Estimated GLS (EGLS)	Generalized least squares (GLS)
Goldfeld–Quandt test	Heteroscedasticity
Heteroscedasticity consistent	Homoscedasticity
covariance matrix (HCCM)	Jackknife
estimator	Multiplicative heteroscedasticity
Weighted least squares (WLS)	White's test

REFERENCES

Amemiya, T. "Regression Analysis When the Variance of the Dependent Variable Is Proportional to the Squares of Its Expectation." *J. American Statistical Association*, Vol. 68 (December 1973): 928–934.

Amemiya, T. "A Note on a Heteroscedastic Model." *J. Econometrics*, Vol. 6 (November 1977): 365–370.

Breusch, T. S., and Pagan, A. R. "A Simple Test for Heteroscedasticity and Random Coefficient Variation." *Econometrica*, Vol. 47 (September 1979): 1287–1294.

Efron, B. *The Jackknife, the Bootstrap, and Other Resampling Plans.* Philadelphia: Society for Industrial and Applied Mathematics, 1982.

Engle, R. F. "Autoregressive Conditional Heteroscedasticity with Estimates of

Variance of United Kingdom Inflation." *Econometrica*, Vol. 50 (July 1982): 987–1007.

Goldfeld, S. M., and Quandt, R. E. "Some Tests for Homoscedasticity." *J. Amer. Stat. Assoc.*, Vol. 60 (June 1965): 539–547.

Goldfeld, S. M., and Quandt, R. E., *Nonlinear Methods in Econometrics*. Amsterdam: North-Holland, 1972.

Harvey, A. C. *The Econometric Analysis of Time Series*. New York: Wiley, 1981.

Harvey, A. C. "Estimating Regression Models with Multiplicative Heteroscedasticity." *Econometrica*, Vol. 44 (May 1976): 461–466.

Judge, George C., *et al. The Theory and Practice of Econometrics*. New York: Wiley, 1985.

Kmenta, J. *Elements of Econometrics*. New York: Macmillan, 1986.

MacKinnon, J. G., and White, H. "Some Heteroscedasticity-Consistent Covariance Matrix Estimators with Improved Finite Sample Properties." *J. Econometrics*, Vol. 29 (March 1985): 305–325.

Messer, K., and White, H. "A Note on Computing the Heteroscedasticity Consistent Covariance Matrix Using Instrumental Variable Techniques." *Oxford Bulletin of Economics and Statistics*, Vol. 46 (May 1984): 181–184.

Prais, S. J., and Houthakker, H. S. *The Analysis of Family Budgets*. Cambridge: Cambridge University Press, 1955.

Statistical Abstract of the United States. Washington, D.C.: U.S. Department of Commerce, 1990.

White, H. "A Heteroscedasticity-Consistent Covariance Matrix and a Direct Test for Heteroscedasticity." *Econometrica*, Vol. 48 (May 1980): 817–838.

PRACTICE COMPUTER SESSIONS

The first five computer sessions use the data in Table 8.1 (data file name is *data8-1*).

8.1 The command input file *ps8-1.inp* can be used to reproduce Examples 8.1, 8.2, and 8.3, namely, Goldfeld–Quandt, Breusch–Pagan, and White is tests.

8.2 The commands for the OLS and Heteroscedasticity consistent covariance matrix estimates in Example 8.4 are in *ps8-2.inp*.

8.3 Example 8.5 uses the commands in *ps8-3.inp*.

8.4 The commands in *ps8-4.inp* will be useful to reproduce the results in Example 8.6.

8.5 To reproduce the results of Example 8.7 use the command file *ps8-5.inp*.

8.6 The "walk-through" application in Section 8.4 uses the data file in Table 4.8 (*data4-12*) and the commands in *ps8-6.inp*. To override the default limits, use the command *ecslib -v50 data4-12 < ps8-6.inp > ps8-6.out*.

EXERCISES

†8.1*   Consider the model

$$Y_t = \beta_1 + \beta_2 X_{t2} + \beta_3 X_{t3} + u_t$$
$$\mathrm{Var}(u_t) = \sigma_t^2 = \sigma^2 Z_t^2$$

where data are available on Y, X_1, X_2, and Z. The weighted least squares procedure consists of minimizing

$$\mathrm{ESS} = \sum(w_t u_t)^2 = \sum(w_t Y_t - \beta_1 w_t - \beta_2 w_t X_{t2} - \beta_3 w_t X_{t2})^2$$

with respect to the βs, where w_t is known.
   a. Partially differentiate ESS with respect to β_1, β_2, and β_3, and write down the normal equations (w_t is nonrandom).
   b. Derive the normal equations for equation (8.11).
   c. Substitute $w_t = 1/Z_t$ in the normal equations obtained in part a and show that they are identical to those derived in part b.

8.2*   In the model given in Exercise 8.1, let the residual u_t be distributed normally as $N(0, \sigma_t^2)$.
   a. Show that the log-likelihood functions is given by (refer to Section 3.A.4 of Chapter 3)

$$\ln L = -T \ln \sigma - T \ln(\sqrt{2\pi}) - \sum \left[\frac{(Y_t - \beta_1 - \beta_2 X_{t2} - \beta_3 X_{t3})^2}{2\sigma_t^2} \right]$$

   b. When $\sigma_t^2 = \sigma^2 Z_t^2$, show that the maximum likelihood estimates of the βs are identical to the weighted least squares estimates of Exercise 8.1.

†8.3   Consider the model $Y_t = \beta X_t + u_t$ with $E(u_t) = 0$ and $\sigma_t^2 = \sigma^2 X_t^2$. An estimator of β is constructed as follows. Join each point (X_t, Y_t) to the origin, for $t = 1, 2, \ldots, T$. Next measure the slope of each of those lines and calculate the average of these slopes over the T observations. Call this estimator $\tilde{\beta}$.
   a. Write an algebraic expression for $\tilde{\beta}$ in terms of X_t, Y_t, and the sample size T.
   b. Derive the expected value of $\tilde{\beta}$ and show that it is unbiased.
   c. Derive the weighted least squares estimate of β and show that it is identical to $\tilde{\beta}$. Is it BLUE? Without any explicit derivations, compare the efficiency of $\tilde{\beta}$ relative to the OLS estimate of β.

8.4   Suppose it is known that the error variance is proportional to Z_t. Describe how you would obtain WLS estimates in this case.

8.5   Perform all the tests for heteroscedasticity on the time series applications of Chapter 5. If the test is rejected, use EGLS to estimate the parameters. How do they compare with the OLS estimates obtained earlier?

8.6   In Example 8.6 regress $\ln(\hat{u}_t^2)$ against a constant, INCOME, and INCOME^2. Use this alternative auxiliary regression to predict $\hat{\sigma}_t^2$. Use these to create appropriate weights for EGLS. How does your EGLS estimate compare to those obtained in Example 8.6?

8.7   Exercise 4.7 of Chapter 4 related the poverty rate in 58 California counties to a number of determinants. Perform a White's test on this model and, if necessary, reestimate the model using WLS and compare the results with those obtained earlier.

8.8   In the real estate example of Exercise 6.12 the price of a house was related to a number of characteristics of the house. Suppose we hypothesize that the error variance depends on the square of the living area. Starting with your final model of Exercise 6.12, describe how the hypothesis may be tested using the Goldfeld–Quandt, Breusch–Pagan, and White's tests. Suppose you find significant heteroscedasticity but ignore it. What are the properties of your OLS estimates? How will you go about obtaining "better" estimates (explain what you mean by "better")? The steps you describe should be specific to the model and not be just repetitions of the steps in the book.

8.9   In Exercise 6.11 of Chapter 6, the air quality of 30 SMSAs was related to a number of determinants. Test that model for heteroscedasticity and, if necessary, reestimate it using the WLS procedure. Carefully describe each of your steps.

8.10   In Exercise 6.13 of Chapter 6, the list price of a number of cars was related to the characteristics of cars. Test the model for heteroscedasticity and, if necessary, reestimate it using the WLS procedure. Carefully describe each of your steps.

†8.11 Consider the model $S_t = \alpha + \beta Y_t + \gamma A_t + u_t$, where S is the sales of a firm in the tth state, Y is total income in the state, and A is the amount of money spent by the company advertising in that state ($t = 1, 2, \ldots, 50$).

   a. You suspect that the random error term u_t is heteroscedastic with a standard deviation σ_t that depends on the size of the population P_t. Describe step by step how you will go about testing for this. Be sure to state (i) the null and alternative hypotheses, (ii) the regression(s) you will run, (iii) the test statistic you will compute and its distribution (including the degrees of freedom), and (iv) the criterion for acceptance or rejection of the null hypothesis.

   b. Suppose you find that there is heteroscedasticity but ignore it and use OLS to estimate the model. Are your estimates (i) unbiased, (ii) consistent, (iii) efficient? Carefully justify your answer.

   c. Assume that $\sigma_t = \sigma P_t$. Describe step by step how you will obtain estimates that are BLUE (define the term). State any theorem that enables you to justify the claim that your estimates are BLUE.

9.1 Serial Correlation of the First Order

Initially we consider the simplest case of serial correlation called the **first-order serial correlation**. Although we use the simple linear regression model to examine the issues, all the results generalize to the multiple regression case also. If serial correlation is present, then $\text{Cov}(u_t, u_s) \neq 0$ for $t \neq s$; that is, the error for the period t is correlated with the error for the period s. The assumption of first-order autocorrelation is formally stated as follows.

Assumption 9.1

$$Y_t = \alpha + \beta X_t + u_t \tag{9.1}$$

$$u_t = \rho u_{t-1} + \epsilon_t \qquad -1 < \rho < 1 \tag{9.2}$$

The error u_t is thus related to the previous period's error (u_{t-1}), a new error term (ϵ_t), and a new parameter ρ. p must be less than 1 in absolute value; otherwise explosive behavior is possible. Because ρ is the coefficient of the error term lagged one period, it is called the **first-order autocorrelation coefficient**. The process described by equation (9.2) is called the **first-order autoregressive process** [more commonly known as **AR(1)**]. Later in this chapter (Section 9.5) we consider higher order autoregressive processes. The new errors ϵ_t are assumed to satisfy the following conditions.

Assumption 9.2
The errors ϵ_t are independently and identically distributed with zero mean and constant variance so that $E(\epsilon_t) = 0$, $E(\epsilon_t^2) = \sigma_\epsilon^2 < \infty$, and $E(\epsilon_t \epsilon_{t-s}) = 0$ for $s \neq 0$.

The new error terms are thus assumed to have the same properties that the OLS procedure assumed u_t to have. In the time series literature, a series obeying Assumption 9.2 is known as a **white noise series** with zero mean. Because u_t depends on u_{t-1}, we can expect them to be correlated. Note that u_t does not depend directly on u_{t-2}; however, it does do so indirectly through u_{t-1} because u_{t-1} depends on u_{t-2}. Thus, u_t is correlated with all past errors. If the covariance is positive, there is said to be a *positive autocorrelation*, and when the covariance is negative we have *negative autocorrelation*.

9.2 Consequences of Ignoring Serial Correlation

Effect on Properties of Estimates
In Chapter 3 we proved that under Assumptions 3.2 and 3.4 (that is, that u_t has zero mean and is uncorrelated with X_t), the OLS estimates are unbiased and

consistent. Since the proof of these properties did not depend on Assumption 3.6, which is violated by the presence of autocorrelation, *OLS estimates (and forecasts based on them) are unbiased and consistent even if the error terms are serially correlated*. The problem is with the efficiency of the estimates. In the proof of the Gauss–Markov Theorem that established efficiency (Section 3.A.3), one of the steps involved minimization of the variance of the linear combination $\sum a_t u_t$.

$$\text{Var}\left(\sum a_t u_t\right) = \sum a_t^2 \sigma^2 + \sum_{t \neq s} \sum a_t a_s \text{Cov}(u_t, u_s) \qquad (9.3)$$

where the double summation is over all t and s that are different. If $\text{Cov}(u_t, u_s) \neq 0$, the second term on the right-hand side will not vanish. Therefore, minimizing $\sum a_t^2 \sigma^2$ (which gives OLS normal equations) is not equivalent to minimizing equation (9.3). For this reason, the best linear unbiased estimator (BLUE) that minimizes (9.3) will not be the same as the OLS estimator. In other words, OLS estimates are not BLUE and are hence *inefficient*. Thus, the consequences of ignoring autocorrelation are the same as those of ignoring heteroscedasticity, namely, the *estimates and forecasts are unbiased and consistent, but are inefficient*.

We can also show that if the serial correlation in u_t is positive and the independent variable X_t grows over time (which is often the case), then the estimated residual variance $(\hat{\sigma}^2)$ will be an underestimate and the value of R^2 will be an overestimate. In other words, the goodness of fit will be exaggerated and the estimated standard errors will be smaller than the true standard errors. These points are illustrated in Figure 9.2, a typical scatter diagram, with the help of the simple regression model. The heavy line is the "true" regression line $\alpha + \beta X$. Suppose there is positive autocorrelation; that is, the covariance between two successive stochastic disturbance terms is positive. Further suppose that the first scatter point (X_1, Y_1) is above the true line. This means that u_1 will be positive. Because u_2 and u_1 are

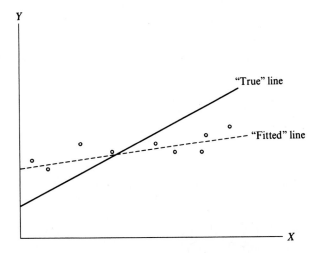

Figure 9.2 Underestimation of the residual variance

positively correlated, u_2 is likely to be positive, putting (X_2, Y_2) also above the line. Hence, the first few scatter points are likely to be above the true regression line. Suppose one of the scatter points happens to be below the true line because of the random nature of the u's. Then the next few points are also likely to be below the true line.

Because the least squares procedure minimizes the sum of squared deviations, the "fitted" line will look like the dashed line. The *true* variance of the residuals is given by the deviation of (X_t, Y_t) from the true line, which is clearly larger than the *estimated* residual variance, which is calculated from deviations around the fitted line. Hence *the computed error sum of squares (ESS) will be smaller than the true value, and R^2 will be larger than the true value.*

In the general case, the variances of the regression coefficients will be biased. For a detailed analysis of the nature of the bias the reader is referred to Section 8.3 of Kmenta's book (1986).

Effect on Tests of Hypotheses

We just argued that in the common case in which serial correlation is positive and the independent variable is growing over time, estimated standard errors will be smaller than the true ones, and hence the former will be underestimates. This means that the t-statistics will be overestimates, and hence a regression coefficient that appears to be significant may not really be so. The estimated variances of the parameters will be biased and inconsistent. Therefore, the t- and F-tests are no longer valid.

Effect on Forecasting

Although the forecasts will be unbiased (because the estimates are unbiased), they will be inefficient with larger variances. By explicitly taking into account the serial correlation among residuals, it is possible to generate better forecasts than those generated by the OLS procedure. This is demonstrated for the AR(1) error structure specified in equation (9.2).

Suppose we ignore equation (9.2) and obtain the OLS estimates of $\hat{\alpha}$ and $\hat{\beta}$. We saw in Section 3.11 that the OLS prediction would be $\hat{Y}_t = \hat{\alpha} + \hat{\beta}X_t$. Because u_t is random, it could not be predicted; and hence we set it equal to its mean value, which is zero. In the case of the first-order serial correlation, however, u_t is predictable from equation (9.2), provided ρ can be estimated (call it $\hat{\rho}$). We have $\hat{u}_t = \hat{\rho}\hat{u}_{t-1}$. At time t, the residual for the previous period ($\hat{u}_{t-1}$) is known. Therefore, the AR(1) prediction will be

$$\tilde{Y}_t = \hat{\alpha} + \hat{\beta}X_t + \hat{\rho}\hat{u}_{t-1} = \hat{\alpha} + \hat{\beta}X_t + \hat{\rho}(Y_{t-1} - \hat{\alpha} - \hat{\beta}X_{t-1}) \qquad (9.4)$$

making use of the fact that $\hat{u}_{t-1} = Y_{t-1} - \hat{\alpha} - \hat{\beta}X_{t-1}$. Equation (9.4) uses the presence of serial correlation to generate the prediction; thus, $\tilde{Y}_t$ will be more efficient than that obtained by the OLS procedure. The procedure for estimating ρ is described in Section 9.4.

The results obtained in this section are summarized in Property 9.1.

Property 9.1

If serial correlation among the stochastic disturbance terms in a regression model is ignored and the OLS procedure is used to estimate the parameters, then the following properties hold:

a. The estimates and forecasts based on them will still be unbiased and consistent.

b. The OLS estimates are no longer BLUE and will be inefficient. Forecasts will also be inefficient.

c. The estimated variances of the regression coefficients will be biased, and hence tests of hypotheses are invalid. If the serial correlation is positive and the independent variable X_t is growing over time, then the standard errors will be underestimates of the true values. This means that the computed R^2 will be an overestimate, indicating a better fit than actually exists. Also, the t-statistics in such a case will tend to appear more significant than they actually are.

9.3 Testing for First-Order Serial Correlation

In this section, we confine ourselves to testing first-order autocorrelation. The procedure is generalized in Section 9.5 to the case of higher orders. In conjunction with formally testing for serial correlation, it is useful to identify autocorrelation through other means. A useful device is the residual plot.

The Residual Plot

The **residual plot** is simply a graph of the estimated residuals $\hat{u}_t$ against time (t). An example of the residual plot is given in Figure 9.3. The plot represents the estimated residuals of Model C in Table 5.2, which related the cumulative expenditure on the maintenance (excluding gasoline) of a Toyota station wagon to the cumulative miles driven and the age of the car. In Figure 9.3 we observe a clear tendency for successive residuals to cluster on one side of the zero line or the other. This is a graphical indication of the presence of serial correlation. If $\hat{u}_t$ were independent, this clustering would not be likely to happen. As the first step toward identifying the presence of serial correlation, it is a good practice to plot $\hat{u}_t$ against t and look for the clustering effect.

The Durbin–Watson Test

Although the residual plot is a useful graphical device for identifying the presence of serial correlation, formal tests for autocorrelation are essential. In this section we present the most common test for first-order serial correlation, namely, the **Durbin–Watson (DW) test** [Durbin and Watson (1950, 1951)]. A test based on the Lagrange multiplier approach discussed in Chapter 7 is presented in the next section.

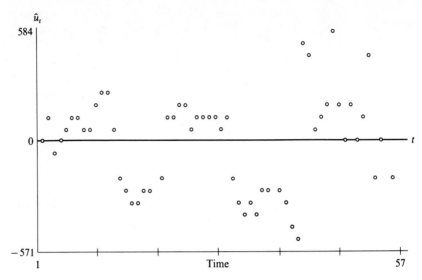

Figure 9.3 Residual plot for Toyota maintenance expenditure

The steps for carrying out the Durbin–Watson test for AR(1) are described for the following multiple regression model:

$$Y_t = \beta_1 + \beta_2 X_{t2} + \beta_3 X_{t3} + \cdots + \beta_k X_{tk} + u_t \tag{9.5}$$

$$u_t = \rho u_{t-1} + \epsilon_t$$

Step 1 Estimate the model by ordinary least squares and compute the residuals $\hat{u}_t$ as $Y_t - \hat{\beta}_1 - \hat{\beta}_2 X_2 - \hat{\beta}_3 X_3 - \cdots - \hat{\beta}_k X_k$.

Step 2 Compute the Durbin–Watson statistic

$$d = \frac{\sum\limits_{t=2}^{t=T} (\hat{u}_t - \hat{u}_{t-1})^2}{\sum\limits_{t=1}^{t=T} \hat{u}_t^2} \tag{9.6}$$

The exact distribution of d depends on ρ which is unknown, as well as the observations on the X's. Durbin and Watson showed that the distribution of d is bounded by two limiting distributions. These are used to construct critical regions for the Durbin–Watson test.

Step 3a To test $H_0: \rho = 0$ against $\rho > 0$ (one-tailed test), look up in Table A.5b, Appendix A, the critical values for the Durbin–Watson statistic, and write the numbers d_L and d_U. Note that the table gives k', which is the number of regression coefficients estimated, *excluding the constant*. Reject H_0 if $d \leq d_L$. If $d \geq d_U$, we cannot reject H_0. If $d_L < d < d_U$, the test is inconclusive.

Step 3b To test for negative serial correlation (that is, for $H_1: \rho < 0$), use $4 - d$. This is done when d is greater than 2. If $4 - d \leq d_L$, we conclude that there is significant negative autocorrelation. If $4 - d \geq d_U$, we conclude that there is no negative autocorrelation. The test is inconclusive if $d_L < 4 - d < d_U$.

Step 3c If the alternative is $H_1: \rho \neq 0$, we have a two-tailed test. Refer to Table A.5a and obtain d_L and d_U. Reject H_0 if $d \leq d_L$ or $d \geq 4 - d_L$, and accept it if $d_U \leq d \leq 4 - d_U$. The inconclusive ranges are $(d_L < d < d_U)$ and $(4 - d_U < d < 4 - d_L)$.

The inconclusiveness of the DW test arises from the fact that there is no exact small-sample distribution for the DW statistic d. Durbin and Watson tabulated the critical values for the limiting distributions of d, for different values of the sample size T and the number of coefficients k', *not counting the constant term*. When the test is inconclusive, one might try the Lagrange multiplier test described next. Alternatively, other functional forms or estimation procedures could be tried.

From the estimated residuals we can obtain an estimate of the first-order serial correlation coefficient as

$$\hat{\rho} = \frac{\sum\limits_{t=2}^{t=T} \hat{u}_t \hat{u}_{t-1}}{\sum\limits_{t=1}^{t=T} \hat{u}_t^2} \tag{9.7}$$

This estimate is approximately equal to the one obtained by regressing $\hat{u}_t$ against $\hat{u}_{t-1}$ *without a constant term*. It is shown in Appendix 9.A that the DW statistic d is approximately equal to $2(1 - \hat{\rho})$. Thus,

$$d \approx 2(1 - \hat{\rho}) \tag{9.6a}$$

Because ρ can range from -1 to $+1$, the range for d is 0 to 4. When ρ is 0, d is 2. Thus, a DW statistic of nearly 2 means there is no first-order serial correlation. A strong positive autocorrelation means ρ is close to $+1$. This indicates low values of d. Similarly, values of d close to 4 indicate a strong negative serial correlation; that is, ρ is close to -1.

The various possible situations are described in the following diagram. The null hypothesis is $H_0: \rho = 0$.

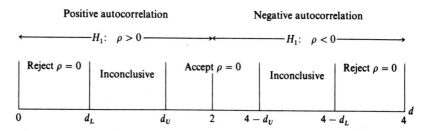

The DW test is invalid if some of the Xs are lags of the dependent variable—that is, if they are of the form $Y_{t-1}, Y_{t-2}, \ldots$. Problems created by such lagged variables are examined in Chapter 10.

Example 9.1

For the Toyota example for which the residual plot is presented in Figure 9.3, the DW statistic is $d = 0.802$. (See Practice Computer Session 9.1.) The number of observations is 57 and $k' = 2$. For a one-tailed test the critical lower and upper bounds are (from Table A.5b), $d_L = 1.50$ and $d_U = 1.645$. Because $d < d_L$, we reject the null hypothesis that $\rho = 0$. For a two-tailed test the critical values are obtained from Table A.5a as $d_L = 1.425$ and $d_U = 1.565$. This test is also rejected at the 5 percent level. We therefore conclude that there is significant first-order serial correlation in the residuals at the 5 percent level. ☐

Example 9.2

As a second example, consider Model C in Table 4.8, which relates the death rates due to coronary heart disease to per capita consumption of cigarettes, per capita intake of edible fats and oil, per capita consumption of distilled spirits, and per capita consumption of beer. In this example, we have $T = 34$, $k' = 4$, $d = 1.485$, $d_L = 1.12$ and $d_U = 1.63$, for a two-tailed test. (See Practice Computer Session 9.2.) Because d is between d_L and d_U, we have an inconclusive test. We can easily see that the same is true for a one-tailed test. Some computer programs (for example, SHAZAM) calculate the exact p-value based on the user's observations. However, the Lagrange Multiplier test discussed next is preferable. ☐

Practice Problem

9.1 In Example 5.1 of Chapter 5 we related housing starts to variables such as GNP and interest rate and used time series data to estimate several different models. Use the Durbin–Watson test on those models to test for first order serial correlation (both one-tailed and two-tailed tests). Be sure to state the null and alternative hypotheses and the criterion for acceptance or rejection of the null. Based on your results, what do you conclude about the properties of the OLS estimates obtained in Chapter 5?

The Lagrange Multiplier Test

The LM test described in Chapter 7 is useful in identifying serial correlation not only of the first order but of higher orders as well. Here we confine ourselves to the first-order case. The general case is taken up in Section 9.5. The steps for carrying out the LM test are as follows:

Step 1 This step is identical to Step 1 of the DW test; that is, estimate equation (9.5) by OLS and compute its residuals.

Step 2 Regress $\hat{u}_t$ against a constant, $X_{t2}, \ldots, X_{tk}$, and $\hat{u}_{t-1}$, using the $T - 1$ observations 2 through T. This is similar to the auxiliary regression in Step 4 of Section 7.1. Next compute $(T - 1)R^2$ from this auxiliary regression. T-1 is used because the effective number of observations is $T - 1$.

Step 3 Reject the null hypothesis of zero autocorrelation in favor of the alternative that $\rho \neq 0$ if $(T - 1)R^2 > \chi_1^2(0.05)$ the value of χ_1^2 in the chi-square distribution with 1 d.f. such that the area to the right of it is 0.05.

If there were serial correlation in the residuals, we would expect $\hat{u}_t$ to be related to $\hat{u}_{t-1}$. This is the motivation behind the auxiliary regression in which $\hat{u}_{t-1}$ is included along with all the independent variables in the model. Note that the LM test does not have the inconclusiveness of the DW test. In practice, the investigator should apply both tests to reinforce the conclusions. If the two tests give contradictory results, there is no certain way to choose between them. However, an alternative formulation of the model may resolve the difficulty.

Example 9.3

In the Toyota maintenance example, the DW test was conclusive in rejecting the null hypothesis of no serial correlation. To carry out the LM test, we regress the estimated residuals $\hat{u}_t$ against MILES, WEEKS, and $\hat{u}_{t-1}$. Practice Computer Session 9.3 has details on the steps for carrying this out. The estimated auxiliary regression is as follows (values in parentheses are t-statistics):

$$\hat{u}_t = -54.460 - \underset{(-0.8)}{2.031}\text{WEEKS} + \underset{(0.8)}{14.889}\text{MILES} + \underset{(5.5)}{0.614}\hat{u}_{t-1}$$
$$\underset{(-0.5)}{}$$

$$R^2 = 0.365 \qquad T = 57 \qquad (T-1)R^2 = 20.44$$

The number of observations used is 56 because $\hat{u}_{t-1}$ is defined only for the period 2–57, and hence we lose the first observation $(T-1)R^2 = 20.44$ and $\chi_1^2(0.01) = 6.6349$. The null hypothesis is therefore also rejected by the LM test.

☐

Example 9.4

In the heart disease example, the auxiliary regression is the following (see Practice Computer Session 9.4):

$$\hat{u}_t = \underset{(1.4)}{113.628} - \underset{(-1.1)}{4.675}\text{CIG} - \underset{(-1.6)}{1.579}\text{EDFAT} + \underset{(0.1)}{0.361}\text{SPIRITS}$$
$$+ \underset{(0.3)}{0.207}\text{BEER} + \underset{(1.4)}{0.259}\hat{u}_{t-1}$$

$$R^2 = 0.137 \qquad T = 34 \qquad (T-1)R^2 = 4.521$$

The critical chi-square is $\chi_1^2(0.05) = 3.841$, which is less than $(T-1)R^2$. Also, the p-value for 4.521 was 0.033. The LM test thus rejects the null hypothesis of zero autocorrelation, whereas the DW test was inconclusive.

☐

Practice Problem

9.2   Redo Practice Problem 9.1 using the LM test approach.

9.4   Treatment of Serial Correlation

No estimation procedure can guarantee the elimination of serial correlation, because the nature of the autocorrelation is generally unknown. In some cases, however, a change in the functional form of the model might eliminate apparent

Subtracting the second equation from the first we get

$$g = \ln(Y_t) - \ln(Y_{t-1})$$

Thus, the difference in the logarithms is the growth rate. The estimated relation for the farm population was

$$gfarmpop_t = \underset{(-6.8)}{-0.066} + \underset{(1.91)}{0.00083t} \qquad d = 1.955$$
$$\bar{R}^2 = 0.070$$

It should be noted that, because the dependent variable is different from the two previous regressions, the values of $\bar{R}^2$ are not comparable. The DW statistic is very close to 2 and it is readily verified that there is no evidence of first-order autocorrelation. Thus, an appropriate modification of the functional form has eliminated apparent serial correlation. Does this mean that the third formulation is the "best"? The answer depends on what "best" means. A researcher interested in forecasting farm population will base judgment on the model's ability to forecast it. This issue is addressed more systematically in Chapter 11. ☐

Estimation Procedures

When modified functional forms do not eliminate autocorrelation, several estimation procedures are available that will produce more efficient estimates than those obtained by the OLS procedure. These are discussed next. It should be pointed out that these methods need to be applied only for time series data. With cross-section data one can rearrange the observations in any manner and get a DW statistic that is acceptable. This suggests, however, that the DW test is meaningless for cross-section data. Because time series data cannot be rearranged, an investigator needs to be concerned about possible serial correlation.

Cochrane–Orcutt Iterative Procedure

The **Cochrane–Orcutt (CORC) iterative procedure** [Cochrane and Orcutt (1949)] requires the transformation of the regression model (9.5) to a form in which the OLS procedure is applicable. Rewriting equation (9.5) for the period $t - 1$ we get

$$Y_{t-1} = \beta_1 + \beta_2 X_{(t-1)2} + \beta_3 X_{(t-1)3} + \cdots + \beta_k X_{(t-1)k} + u_{t-1} \qquad (9.5')$$

Multiplying (9.5') term by term by ρ and subtracting from (9.5) we obtain

$$Y_t - \rho Y_{t-1} = \beta_1(1 - \rho) + \beta_2[X_{t2} - \rho X_{(t-1)2}] + \beta_3[X_{t3} - \rho X_{(t-1)3}]$$
$$+ \cdots + \beta_k[X_{tk} - \rho X_{(t-1)k}] + \epsilon_t$$

where we have used the fact that $u_t = \rho u_{t-1} + \epsilon_t$. This equation can be rewritten as follows:

$$Y_t^* = \beta_1^* + \beta_2 X_{t2}^* + \beta_3 X_{t3}^* + \cdots + \beta_k X_{tk}^* + \epsilon_t \qquad (9.8)$$

where

$$Y_t^* = Y_t - \rho Y_{t-1}, \qquad \beta_1^* = \beta_1(1 - \rho), \qquad \text{and} \qquad X_{ti}^* = X_{ti} - \rho X_{(t-1)i}, \qquad \text{for}$$
$$t = 2, 3, \ldots, T \qquad \text{and} \qquad i = 2, \ldots, k$$

The transformation that generates the variables Y^* and the X^*s is known as **quasi-differencing**, or **generalized differencing**. β_1^* is just the new constant term. Note that the error term in equation (9.8) satisfies all the properties needed for applying the least squares procedure. If ρ were known, we could apply OLS to (9.8) and obtain estimates that are BLUE. However, ρ is unknown and has to be estimated from the sample. The steps for carrying out the Cochrane–Orcutt procedure are as follows:

Step 1 Estimate equation (9.5) by OLS and compute its residual $\hat{u}_t$.

Step 2 Estimate the first-order serial correlation coefficient ($\hat{\rho}$) from equation (9.7).

Step 3 Transform the variables as follows:

$$Y_t^* = Y_t - \hat{\rho}Y_{t-1}, \qquad X_{t2}^* = X_{t2} - \hat{\rho}X_{(t-1)2}, \text{ and so on}$$

Note that the starred variables are defined only for $t = 2\text{-}T$ because of the presence of the term involving $t - 1$.

Step 4 Regress Y_t^* against a constant $X_{t2}^*, X_{t3}^*, \ldots, X_{tk}^*$ and get OLS estimates of the transformed equation (9.8).

Step 5 Use these estimates for the βs in (9.5) and obtain a new set of estimates of $\hat{u}_t$. Then go back and repeat Step 2 with these new values until the following stopping rule applies.

Step 6 This iterative procedure can be stopped when the estimates of ρ from two successive iterations differ by no more than some preselected value, such as 0.001. The final $\hat{\rho}$ is then used to get the CORC estimates from equation (9.8).

Because the constant term is also multiplied by $1 - \hat{\rho}$, $\hat{\beta}_1$ is obtained as $\hat{\beta}_1^*/(1 - \hat{\rho})$, where $\hat{\beta}_1^*$ is the estimated constant term in the *transformed equation* (9.8). Most standard regression programs carry out all the steps of this procedure with simple commands, thus relieving the user of the drudgery of the iteration process. Some programs report the estimated constant term of the *original model* (that is, $\hat{\beta}_1$) so the user need not (and should not) divide by $(1 - \hat{\rho})$. The user is also cautioned about identifying what the reported R^2, error sum of squares, and so on represent. If they relate to equation (9.8), the values are not comparable to the corresponding OLS estimates because the left-hand sides of equations (9.5) and (9.8) are quite different. Similarly, the reported Durbin–Watson statistic often refers to the residuals of (9.8) and not to those of (9.5). A DW test on this would test for a *second-order serial correlation* for $\hat{u}_t$ [because the underlying model will be AR(1) on ϵ_t].

The Cochrane–Orcutt procedure can be shown to converge to the maximum likelihood estimates, which we know are consistent and asymptotically efficient. The iterative procedure generally converges quickly and does not require more than three to six iterations. It should be noted that the number of observations used in estimating (9.8) is only $T - 1$ because we lose the first observation. With k parameters, the degrees of freedom are $T - k - 1$. Hypothesis testing can be done in the usual way. It is possible to preserve the first observation by using the following transformation just for $t = 1$ (the justification for this step is provided in Appendix 9.A):

$$Y_1^* = Y_1(1 - \rho^2)^{1/2} \quad \text{and} \quad X_{1i}^* = X_{1i}(1 - \rho^2)^{1/2} \quad \text{for } i = 1 \text{ to } k$$

Example 9.6

The heart disease example presented in Model C of Table 4.8 was found to have significant autocorrelation (according to the LM test), and hence we reestimated the model by CORC. The estimated equation given below was obtained using the ECSLIB program, which ignores the first observation (see Practice Computer Session 9.6). Because programs differ in the criterion for convergence, answers might differ somewhat from program to program. The difference, however, should not be large

$$\widehat{CHD} = 341.023 + 2.903CIG + 0.373EDFAT + 12.045SPIRITS - 2.206BEER$$
$$\phantom{\widehat{CHD} = } (4.2) \quad\quad (0.6) \quad\quad\quad (0.4) \quad\quad\quad\quad (1.83) \quad\quad\quad\quad (-2.5)$$

The values in parentheses are t-statistics. The number of iterations required is 12 and the final $\hat{\rho}$ is 0.613. Comparing this with the results in Table 4.8 we note that all the coefficients and the t-values are quite different, which is not surprising because the t-tests in Table 4.8 are invalid. We can perform a DW test on the estimated ϵs from the transformed model (9.8) to check whether the ϵs exhibit first-order autocorrelation. The DW d for the equation was 2.232. From Table A.5a we have (for $T = 33$ and $k' = 4$) $d_L = 1.10$ and $d_U = 1.63$. Because $4 - d = 1.771 > d_U$, we conclude that there is no serial correlation in the ϵs. □

Hildreth–Lu Search Procedure

A frequently used alternative to the Cochrane–Orcutt procedure is the **Hildredth–Lu (HILU) search procedure** [Hildreth and Lu (1960)], which has the following steps:

Step 1 Choose a value of ρ (say ρ_1). Using this value, transform the variables and estimate equation (9.8) by OLS.

Step 2 From these estimates, derive $\hat{\epsilon}_t$ from equation (9.8) and the error sum of squares associated with it. Call it $ESS_\epsilon(\rho_1)$. Next choose a different ρ (ρ_2) and repeat Steps 1 and 2.

Step 3 By varying ρ from -1 to $+1$ in some systematic way (say, at steps of length 0.05 or 0.01), we can get a series of values of $ESS_\epsilon(\rho)$. Choose that ρ for which ESS_ϵ is a minimum. This is the final ρ that globally minimizes the error sum of squares of the transformed model. Equation (9.8) is then estimated with this final ρ as the optimum solution.

Example 9.7

In the original Hildreth–Lu paper there are nearly two dozen examples of estimation by the HILU procedure. We reproduce one of them here. Table 9.2

TABLE 9.2 Demand for Ice Cream and Its Determinants

t	DEMAND	PRICE	INCOME	TEMP
1	0.386	0.270	78	41
2	0.374	0.282	79	56
3	0.393	0.277	81	63
4	0.425	0.280	80	68
5	0.406	0.272	76	69
6	0.344	0.262	78	65
7	0.327	0.275	82	61
8	0.288	0.267	79	47
9	0.269	0.265	76	32
10	0.256	0.277	79	24
11	0.286	0.282	82	28
12	0.298	0.270	85	26
13	0.329	0.272	86	32
14	0.318	0.287	83	40
15	0.381	0.277	84	55
16	0.381	0.287	82	63
17	0.470	0.280	80	72
18	0.443	0.277	78	72
19	0.386	0.277	84	67
20	0.342	0.277	86	60
21	0.319	0.292	85	44
22	0.307	0.287	87	40
23	0.284	0.277	94	32
24	0.326	0.285	92	27
25	0.309	0.282	95	28
26	0.359	0.265	96	33
27	0.376	0.265	94	41
28	0.416	0.265	96	52
29	0.437	0.268	91	64
30	0.548	0.260	90	71

Source: Hildreth and Lu (1960), p. 73. Reprinted with the permission of the Michigan State University.

has data on the demand for ice cream. The observations refer to four-week periods from March 18, 1951, to July 11, 1953. The variable definitions are as follows:

DEMAND = Per capita consumption of ice cream in pints

PRICE = Price per pint in dollars

INCOME = Weekly family income in dollars

TEMP = Mean temperature in Fahrenheit

TABLE 9.3 Hildreth-Lu Estimates of the Demand for Ice Cream

ρ	CONST.	PRICE	INCOME	TEMP	ESS
1.0	.64927	−.9358	−.00197	.00272	.025823
.9	.64166	−.9824	−.00149	.02284	.027317
.8	.53264	−1.0064	−.00044	.00303	.026854
.7	.41572	−1.0001	.00075	.00321	.026470
.6	.30779	−.9728	.00182	.00336	.026022
.5	.22084	−.9342	.00264	.00348	.025622
.42	.16779	−.9004	.00311	.00354	.025459
.41	.16229	−.8967	.00316	.00355	.025452
.4	.15653	−.8916	.00321	.00356	.025453
.39	.15136	−.8876	.00325	.00357	.025454
.3	.11148	−.8502	.00357	.00361	.025674
.2	.08025	−.8101	.00379	.00364	.026395
.1	.05903	−.7733	.00392	.00364	.027666
0	.04406	−.7378	.00398	.00364	.029521
−.1	.03387	−.7058	.00400	.00363	.031964
−.2	.02680	−.6766	.00400	.00362	.034995
−.3	.02210	−.6505	.00398	.00360	.038612
−.4	.01895	−.6270	.00395	.00359	.042810
−.5	.01695	−.6060	.00392	.00357	.047585
−.6	.01580	−.5872	.00388	.00355	.052933
−.7	.01538	−.5707	.00384	.00354	.058846
−.8	.01544	−.5560	.00380	.00352	.065324
−.9	.01587	−.5432	.00376	.00350	.072361
−1.0	.01651	−.5315	.00372	.00349	.079958

Source: Hildreth and Lu (1960), Table 19, p. 36. Reprinted with the permission of the Michigan State University.

Table 9.3 has the estimated regression coefficients and the error sum of squares of equation (9.8) for each step of the search procedure. The row corresponding to $\rho = 0$ represents the OLS estimates (using observations 2 through 30). The HILU procedure minimizes $ESS(\epsilon)$ when $\rho = 0.41$. Note that OLS and HILU estimates differ considerably.

The CORC procedure was also applied to these data. It took only two rounds of iterations for convergence. The final $\hat{\rho}$ was 0.40083, and the CORC estimates and t-statistics are as follows (see Practice Computer Session 9.7 to reproduce this):

$$\widehat{DEMAND} = 0.157 - 0.892PRICE + 0.0032INCOME$$
$$\quad\quad\quad\quad\; {\scriptstyle (0.5)} \quad\quad {\scriptstyle (-1.1)} \quad\quad\quad\quad\quad {\scriptstyle (2.07)}$$
$$+ \; 0.00356TEMP$$
$$\quad {\scriptstyle (6.42)}$$

These estimates are quite close to the HILU estimates. The DW statistic for equation (9.8) is 1.55. With $T = 29$ and $k' = 3$, we have $d_L = 1.10$ and $d_U = 1.54$ for a two-tailed test. It is evident that the DW test does not reject the null hypothesis of zero serial correlation of the residuals of equation (9.8). In other words, we conclude that there is no autocorrelation.   □

Practice Problem

9.3   Use the data in Table 9.2 to estimate a double-log model using OLS. The double-log model will give income, price, and temperature elasticities. Perform a DW test on the residuals. Is there evidence of first-order autocorrelation? If there is, use the CORC and HILU procedures and compare the estimates.

A Comparison of the Two Procedures

The HILU procedure basically searches for the value of ρ between -1 and $+1$ that minimizes the sum of squares of the residuals of equation (9.8). If the step intervals are small, the procedure involves running a large number of regressions; hence, compared to the CORC procedure, the HILU method is computer intensive. On the other hand, the CORC procedure iterates to a local minimum of $ESS(\rho)$ and might miss the global minimum if there is more than one local minimum. This observation is illustrated in Figure 9.5 which has local minima at the points A and B. The points indicated by circles correspond to the HILU steps. It is quite possible that the CORC technique will iterate to the local minimum at A, thus completely missing the global minimum at B. Note that the HILU approach would choose the point corresponding to $\hat{\rho}_H$ and miss the true global minimum, but only slightly. Hildreth and Lu experimented with nearly two dozen data sets and found no multiple minima, which might indicate that they are perhaps not common. A hybrid procedure would be to search at broad steps, such as 0.1 which requires 19 regressions (excluding the end points -1 and $+1$). Choose the ρ that has the smallest ESS in this first pass as the starting point of a CORC procedure and iterate to a final solution. Thus, in Figure 9.5, HILU will choose $\hat{\rho}_H$ in the first pass, and CORC will then iterate to the global minimum at B.

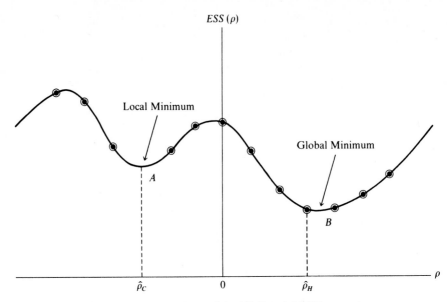

Figure 9.5 A comparison of the HILU and CORC procedures

Most well-known computer programs offer both the iterative procedure and the search procedure; it is wise to use them both to make sure that CORC has not missed the global minimum; better yet, use the hybrid method.

Example 9.8

We now provide an example in which the CORC and HILU estimates are indeed different (Practice Computer Session 9.8 has the details to reproduce this example). Consider the following model estimated in Chapter 4 using the data in Table 4.10.

$$C_t = \beta_1 + \beta_2 W_t + \beta_3 P_t + u_t$$

where C_t is aggregate consumption expenditures, W_t is the total wage bill, and P_t is total profits, all measured in real terms in billions of dollars for the United States for the period 1948–1989.

The Durbin–Watson statistic for first-order autocorrelation is 0.479, which indicates strong serial correlation. The CORC method starts with the estimated ρ (0.719) obtained from the OLS residuals and performs eight iterations to yield the final value of 0.797 (in the ECSLIB program convergence stops when successive $\hat{\rho}$ values do not differ by 0.001). The HILU method uses the hybrid procedure recommended above and initially searches from -0.9 to $+0.9$ in steps of 0.1 and also at -0.99 and 0.99. In this first pass, ESS is minimum at 0.99. The program then uses this as the starting point and does one CORC iteration to yield the final $\hat{\rho}$ as 0.9907, which is considerably different from the final value of 0.797 obtained by CORC. Figures 9.6a and 9.6b explain why the two proce-

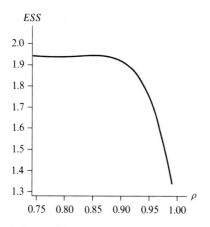

Figure 9.6a Plot of ESS versus ρ for 0.75–1.0

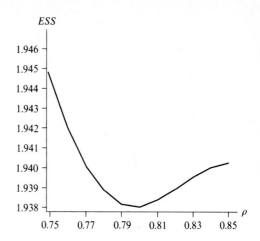

Figure 9.6b Plot of ESS versus ρ for 0.75–0.85

dures give such different $\hat{\rho}$ values. In Figure 9.6a ESS is plotted against ρ for the range 0.75 to 1.0, and Figure 9.6b graphs ESS only for the interval 0.75 to 0.85 in order to produce better resolution. It will be noted that CORC starts at 0.72 and converges to the local minimum at 0.80, whereas the hybrid HILU–CORC method has accurately selected 0.99 as the minimum. It is thus evident from this example that the mixed HILU–CORC approach is likely to be superior to using either singly because it exploits the comparative advantage of each method. □

9.5 Higher Order Serial Correlation

As mentioned earlier, the nature of the error structure is generally unknown. The investigator must therefore formulate as general a model as possible for the error and let the data discriminate between alternative formulations. The principles explained in the previous sections are applicable to serial correlations of higher order. In this section we discuss the procedures for testing for higher order auto-correlation and for estimating model parameters when the disturbance terms follow a general order serial correlation. The general specification of a model with autoregressive error terms is as follows:

$$Y_t = \beta_1 + \beta_2 X_{t2} + \beta_3 X_{t3} + \cdots + \beta_k X_k + u_t \tag{9.9}$$

$$u_t = \rho_1 u_{t-1} + \rho_2 u_{t-2} + \rho_3 u_{t-3} + \cdots + \rho_p u_{t-p} + \epsilon_t \tag{9.10}$$

Equation (9.10) is known as the **pth-order autoregressive process** of the residuals, or **AR(p)**. If we had quarterly data, we might expect that a fourth-order autore-gressive model would be appropriate. Similarly, monthly data are likely to exhibit a twelfth-order autocorrelation and hourly data might have a 24th-order serial correlation. We would therefore need measures to identify a general order autoregressive error structure as well as estimation procedures that take account of such higher orders.

Lagrange Multiplier Test of Higher Order Autocorrelation

The LM test described in Section 9.2 to test for first-order serial correlation can easily be extended to higher orders. The motivation for the procedure will be apparent if we combine equations (9.9) and (9.10) as follows:

$$Y_t = \beta_1 + \beta_2 X_{t2} + \cdots + \beta_k X_{tk} + \rho_1 u_{t-1} + \rho_2 u_{t-2} + \cdots + \rho_p u_{t-p} + \epsilon_t$$

The null hypothesis is that each of the ρs is zero (that is, $\rho_1 = \rho_2 = \cdots = \rho_p = 0$) against the alternative that at least one of them is not zero. The null hypothesis is very similar to the one we carried out in Chapter 7 for testing the addition of new variables. In this case, the new variables are $u_{t-1}, u_{t-2}, \ldots, u_{t-k}$, which can be estimated by $\hat{u}_{t-1}, \hat{u}_{t-2}, \ldots, \hat{u}_{t-p}$. The steps for the LM test are as follows:

Step 1 Estimate equation (9.9) by OLS and obtain the residuals $\hat{u}_t$.

Step 2 Regress $\hat{u}_t$ against all the independent variables in equation (9.9) plus $\hat{u}_{t-1}, \hat{u}_{t-2}, \ldots, \hat{u}_{t-p}$. The effective number of observations used in this auxiliary regressions is $T - p$ because $t - p$ is defined only for the period $p + 1$ to T.

Step 3 Compute $(T - p)R^2$ from the auxiliary regression run in Step 2. If it exceeds $\chi^2_p(0.05)$, the value of the chi-square distribution with p degrees of freedom such that the area to the right is 0.05, then reject H_0: $\rho_1 = \rho_2 = \cdots = \rho_p = 0$ in favor of H_1: *at least one of the ρ's is significantly different from zero.*

Although the test procedure itself is straightforward, the investigator has to decide a priori the order p for the autoregressive model given by equation (9.10). The periodicity of the data (quarterly, monthly, weekly, or whatever) will often suggest the size of p. It was pointed out in Step 2 that the sample size effectively becomes $T - p$. Furthermore, the auxiliary regression has p autoregressive coefficients plus k coefficients for the $k - 1$ explanatory variables and the constant term. Therefore, $T - p$ must be at least $p + k$ (as otherwise we will have negative degrees of freedom), which means that T must be at least $k + 2p$ before the auxiliary regression can even be estimated. If the size of the sample is not adequate, we might drop some of the autoregressive terms. For example, with monthly data, we might formulate lags for $t = 1, 2, 3,$ and 12 and set the other autoregressive coefficients to zero. The application in Section 9.8 presents an example of testing for higher order autocorrelation.

Estimating a Model with General Order Autoregressive Errors

If the LM test rejects the null hypothesis of no serial correlation, we must estimate efficiently the parameters of equation (9.9) and (9.10). The pth-order generalization of equation (9.8) is

$$
\begin{aligned}
Y_t &- \rho_1 Y_{t-1} - \rho_2 Y_{t-2} - \rho_3 Y_{t-3} - \cdots - \rho_p Y_{t-p} \\
&= \beta_1 (1 - \rho_1 - \rho_2 - \cdots - \rho_p) \\
&\quad + \beta_2 [X_{t2} - \rho_1 X_{(t-1)2} - \cdots - \rho_p X_{(t-p)2}] \\
&\quad + \cdots + \beta_k [X_{tk} - \rho_1 X_{(t-1)k} - \cdots - \rho_p X_{(t-p)k}] + \epsilon_t
\end{aligned}
\tag{9.11}
$$

The Cochrane–Orcutt algorithm in this general context alternates between equations (9.10) and (9.11) and is conceptually no more difficult than the case of first-order serial correlation. In fact, standard regression programs are capable of carrying out the necessary steps although they will be time-consuming because of the iterative process.

Step 1 Estimate equation (9.9) by OLS and save the residuals $\hat{u}_t$.

Step 2 Next regress $\hat{u}_t$ against $\hat{u}_{t-1}, \hat{u}_{t-2}, \ldots, \hat{u}_{t-p}$ (with no constant term) to obtain the estimates $\hat{\rho}_1, \hat{\rho}_2$, and so on of the parameters in equation (9.10). Here also only $T - p$ observations are used.

Step 3 Using these estimates, transform the dependent and independent variables to get the new variables in equation (9.11).

Step 4 Estimate the transformed model (9.11) and obtain the second round estimates of the βs.

Step 5 From the new estimates of the βs, compute a revised estimate of the residual $\hat{u}_t$ using equation (9.9). Then go back to Step 2 and iterate until some criterion is satisfied. For example, the error sum of squares of equation (9.11) can be computed and the iteration terminated when its value changes by less than 0.1 percent or some other value. Alternatively, the iteration could continue until the value of the logarithm of the likelihood function for equation (9.11) does not change by more than some preset percentage level.

The final ρs obtained in Step 5 can then be used to make one last transformation of the data to estimate (9.11). At convergence, the estimates of both the βs and the ρs are maximum likelihood. The standard errors and t-statistics obtained from equation (9.11) are consistent and asymptotically efficient unless some of the Xs contain lagged dependent variables (that is, terms such as Y_{t-1}, Y_{t-2}, and so on). Problems created by such lagged dependent variables are examined in Chapter 10. The preceding method is illustrated in the application in Section 9.8.

Forecasts and Goodness of Fit in AR Models

Equation (9.4) presents an expression for the prediction of Y_t that takes explicit account of the first-order serial correlation in u_t. The corresponding expression for the general AR model is

$$
\hat{Y}_t = \hat{\beta}_1 + \hat{\beta}_2 X_{t2} + \cdots + \hat{\beta}_k X_{tk} + \hat{\rho}_1 \hat{u}_{t-1} + \hat{\rho}_2 \hat{u}_{t-2} + \cdots + \hat{\rho}_p \hat{u}_{t-p}
\tag{9.12}
$$

At time t, all the lagged $\hat{u}$ terms are estimable and hence the forecast of Y_t obtained this way will be more efficient than the OLS prediction that ignores the $\hat{u}$ terms (assuming, of course, that the specified model and error process are correct). Also, it should be noted that the value of R^2 computed for equation (9.11) measures the variation in the transformed dependent variable and not the variation in Y. It would be more appropriate to compute R^2 as the square of the correlation between the actual Y_t and the predicted $\hat{Y}_t$ obtained from equation (9.12).

Unit Roots and the Random Walk Model

In the case of first-order autoregressive errors, we assumed that the AR(1) coefficient ρ in the equation $u_t = \rho u_{t-1} + \epsilon_t$ was between -1 and $+1$. This was to avoid explosive behavior in the error term. In some situations, ρ may be equal to 1, and the error term becomes $u_t = u_{t-1} + \epsilon_t$. This model is called a **random walk model**. It is easily verified that the variance of u_t goes to infinity as t goes to infinity. This situation is called the **unit root** problem. The problem, however, is easily solved by noting that if $\rho = 1$, then the first difference specification

$$Y_t - Y_{t-1} = \beta_2(X_{t2} - X_{t-1,2}) + \cdots + \beta_k(X_{tk} - X_{t-1,k}) + \epsilon_t$$

has well-behaved errors and hence OLS estimates of this equation are BLUE. In the case of a general-order serial correlation, the unit root problem occurs when the sum of ρs is equal to 1. The procedure here is to solve for the last lag in terms of the others and substitute for it in the model. For example, in the case of a fourth-order lag, suppose $\rho_1 + \rho_2 + \rho_3 + \rho_4 = 1$. Then the left-hand side of equation (9.11) becomes

$$(Y_t - Y_{t-4}) - \rho_1(Y_{t-1} - Y_{t-4}) - \rho_2(Y_{t-2} - Y_{t-4}) - \rho_3(Y_{t-3} - Y_{t-4})$$

The right-hand side variables will undergo a similar transformation and a modified version of equation (9.11) can be estimated.

It is possible to carry out a formal test for a unit root. The procedure for doing it is described in the next chapter.

9.6 Engle's ARCH Test

The types of serial correlation discussed so far refer only to the error term u_t. Thus in AR(p) we postulated that u_t depends linearly on the p past errors $u_{t-1}, u_{t-2}, \ldots,$ u_{t-p}. There is another type of serial correlation that is often encountered in time series data, especially when forecasts are generated. Some forecasters have observed that the variance of prediction errors is not a constant but differs from period to period. For instance, when the Federal Reserve Board switched to controlling money growth rather than the interest rate, as was done before, interest rates became quite volatile (that is, they began to vary a great deal around the mean). Forecast errors associated with interest rate predictions were thus heteroscedastic. Although a mere "structural change" in the variance may have been expected, it was found instead that the variance has been changing steadily. A similar heteroscedasticity was observed when exchange rate policy switched from fixed exchange rates to flexible exchange rates. In the latter case, exchange rates fluctuated a great deal, making their forecast variances larger. In monetary theory and the theory of finance, financial asset portfolios are functions of the expected means and variances of the rates of returns. Increased volatility of security prices or rates of return are often indicators that the variances are not constant over time. Engle (1982) introduced a new approach to modeling heteroscedasticity in a time series context. He called it the **ARCH (autoregressive conditional heteroscedasticity) model**. The process by which the variances are generated is assumed to be as follows:

$$\sigma_t^2 = \alpha_0 + \alpha_1 \sigma_{t-1}^2 + \cdots + \alpha_p \sigma_{t-p}^2 + v_t \tag{9.13}$$

Equation (9.13) is known as the pth order ARCH process. The term *autoregressive* is applicable because the error variance at time t is assumed to depend on previous error variances. Also, the variance at time t is conditional on those in previous periods and hence the term *conditional heteroscedasticity*. The **ARCH test** is on the null hypothesis H_0: $\alpha_1 = \alpha_2 = \cdots = \alpha_p = 0$. The steps for the test are as follows:

Step 1 Estimate equation (9.9) by OLS.
Step 2 Compute the residual $\hat{u}_t = Y_t - \hat{\beta}_1 - \hat{\beta}_2 X_{t2} - \hat{\beta}_3 X_{t3} - \cdots - \hat{\beta}_k X_{tk}$, square it, and generate $\hat{u}_{t-1}^2, \hat{u}_{t-2}^2, \ldots, \hat{u}_{t-p}^2$.
Step 3 Regress $\hat{u}_t^2$ against a constant, $\hat{u}_{t-1}^2, \hat{u}_{t-2}^2, \ldots,$ and $\hat{u}_{t-p}^2$. This is the auxiliary regression, which uses $T - p$ observations.
Step 4 From the R^2 of the auxiliary regression, compute $(T - p)R^2$. Under the null hypothesis H_0, $(T - p)R^2$ has the chi-square distribution with p d.f. Reject H_0 if $(T - p)R^2 > \chi_p^2(0.05)$, the point on χ_p^2 with a 5 percent area to the right of it.

Example 9.9

When Engle introduced the ARCH model, he applied it to a model of the inflation rate in Britain. The model he used is the following:

$$\dot{p}_t = \beta_1 \dot{p}_{t-1} + \beta_2 \dot{p}_{t-4} + \beta_3 \dot{p}_{t-5} + \beta_4(p_{t-1} - w_{t-1}) + \beta_5 + u_t$$

where

$\dot{p}_t =$ the first difference of the logarithm of consumer price index (P_t)—that is, $\ln P_t - \ln P_{t-1}$, the instantaneous rate of change in P_t.

$P_t = \ln P_t$

$w_t = \ln W_t$, W_t being the index of wage rates

The data were quarterly for the period 1958.2 through 1977.2. Engle first tested the model for sixth-order serial correlation in the residuals and found that there was no evidence of serial correlation. He next performed an ARCH test for first and fourth orders. The first-order ARCH effect was not significant, but the chi-square statistic for fourth-order ARCH was 15.2. Because $\chi_4^2(0.01) = 13.277$, the fourth-order ARCH model is significant. Since quarterly data were used, finding a fourth-order ARCH effect is not surprising. There was, however, no fourth-order serial correlation effect in the residuals themselves, just their variances.

□

9.7 Empirical Example: Yields on Taxable and Tax-exempt Debt

Heaton (1986) has studied the effects of relative yields for taxable U.S. government securities and tax-exempt municipal bonds, on the profits of banks. In an earlier study, Fama (1977) argued that the yield on tax-exempt securities should equal 1 minus the tax rate times the yield on taxable securities. More formally,

$$r_e = r_{ne}(1 - \tau)$$

where r_e is the return on tax-exempt securities, r_{ne} is the return on securities that are not exempt from taxes, and τ is the tax rate. If r_e were higher than the right-hand side in the equation, a corporation (or an individual) could make arbitrage profits by purchasing tax-exempt debt and retiring taxable securities. An alternative argument proposed by Trzcinka (1982) is that the relative returns of taxable and nontaxable securities reflect risk premiums.

Heaton used both hypotheses to formulate a model relating profits to the relative yields. He computed the "implied tax rate" (ITR) that gives zero arbitrage profits. In other words, ITR is the rate τ that satisfies the above equation. The values are presented in Table 9.4 for six different maturity periods. We see that ITR is different from the corporate rate, indicating the presence of additional risk. Based on a utility-maximizing framework, Heaton derived the following econometric relationship between expected profits and the ratio of ITR to the actual tax rate (refer to the original paper for details on the theory):

$$P_{t+1} = \beta_0 + \beta_1\left[\frac{ITR_t}{\tau_{t+1}}\right] + \beta_2\left[\frac{ITR_t}{\tau_{t+1}}\right]^2 + u_t$$

This equation was estimated for each maturity period using annual data for FDIC-insured banks for the period 1951–1980. The data are in Table 9.5. Heaton found that estimates based on the OLS procedure indicated the presence of autocorrelation, with $\hat{\rho}$ varying from 0.1 to 0.4. He then used the Cochrane–Orcutt procedure to reestimate the model. Table 9.6 presents the CORC estimates, which can be seen to be significant mostly at the 1 percent level. Adjusted R^2 was quite high and ranged from about 80 percent to about 72 percent. Shorter maturity periods had better fits than longer periods. The DW statistics in Table 9.5 are for the transformed equations. For $T = 29$ and $k' = 2$, $d_L = 1.17$ and $d_U = 1.45$. All the values of d are larger than d_U, indicating that the transformed residuals do not exhibit serial correlation of the first order. The empirical results support Heaton's contention that the incorporation of more realistic assumptions about the tax law can yield better predictability of the profit structure.

TABLE 9.4   Tax Rates Implied by Yields on Prime Municipal Bonds and
U.S. Government Securities

Year	1-Year Rates	2-Year Rates	5-Year Rates	10-Year Rates	20-Year Rates	30-Year Rates	Top Federal Corporate Tax Rate
1951	43.5	44.7	42.9	43.5	40.1	38.8	52.0
1952	47.1	48.8	47.4	41.8	35.2	30.3	52.0
1953	37.5	40.5	38.5	34.1	21.6	20.2	52.0
1954	47.9	45.5	50.0	47.2	32.9	27.4	52.0
1955	41.0	42.2	39.5	33.3	23.5	19.8	52.0
1956	41.2	37.3	32.9	26.9	21.8	17.7	52.0
1957	42.2	39.8	34.1	27.2	20.1	17.1	52.0
1958	45.8	45.1	37.7	31.4	23.9	20.5	52.0
1959	42.4	41.5	36.6	28.0	20.8	16.3	52.0
1960	49.4	46.3	43.8	37.4	30.9	26.4	52.0
1961	55.2	52.6	45.8	36.0	27.8	23.9	52.0
1962	52.5	51.4	46.7	40.4	30.9	26.9	52.0
1963	51.8	49.9	45.7	39.8	31.5	27.4	52.0
1964	49.3	47.4	42.3	37.9	32.5	28.3	48.0
1965	47.7	44.8	40.5	37.9	33.3	28.9	48.0
1966	38.8	38.7	37.3	33.0	29.3	26.9	48.0
1967	41.1	39.3	36.1	32.9	28.6	25.3	48.0
1968	44.0	41.6	36.5	32.2	27.0	23.7	58.0
1969	41.0	38.6	35.2	29.4	22.3	18.5	53.0
1970	44.5	43.8	41.0	33.1	19.5	15.6	48.0
1971	45.7	45.3	43.1	33.7	18.7	14.0	48.0
1972	46.8	46.2	41.8	36.3	19.0	14.6	48.0
1973	51.2	47.4	44.2	41.3	36.1	33.7	48.0
1974	50.6	47.9	46.3	40.8	38.8	37.0	48.0
1975	44.4	44.3	39.5	30.3	25.3	23.3	48.0
1976	48.7	47.7	43.6	37.3	29.1	25.7	48.0
1977	52.6	50.6	45.4	42.5	34.0	30.8	48.0
1978	53.1	51.0	47.6	45.1	39.4	36.6	48.0
1979	53.5	50.9	47.6	46.5	41.0	38.5	46.0
1980	53.1	51.3	48.6	44.8	36.5	33.5	46.0

Source: Heaton (1986), Table 1. Reprinted with the permission of the Ohio State University Press.

TABLE 9.5 Earnings Data of FDIC-Insured Banks

Year	Aggregate Operating Earnings Before Tax (millions of dollars)	Number of Banks	Average Bank Profits (thousands of dollars)
1951	$ 1,690	13,455	$ 125.60
1952	1,900	13,439	141.38
1953	2,110	13,432	157.09
1954	2,140	13,323	160.62
1955	2,420	13,237	182.82
1956	2,770	13,218	209.56
1957	2,930	13,165	222.56
1958	2,890	13,124	220.21
1959	3,410	13,114	260.03
1960	3,790	13,126	288.74
1961	3,630	13,115	276.78
1962	3,630	13,124	276.59
1963	3,790	13,291	285.16
1964	4,130	13,493	306.08
1965	4,330	13,547	319.63
1966	4,950	13,541	365.56
1967	5,230	13,517	386.92
1968	6,120	13,488	453.74
1969	6,730	13,473	499.52
1970	7,130	13,511	527.72
1971	6,710	13,612	492.95
1972	7,250	13,733	527.93
1973	8,710	13,976	623.21
1974	9,250	14,228	650.13
1975	8,980	14,384	624.30
1976	9,910	14,411	687.67
1977	11,570	14,412	802.80
1978	15,100	14,391	1,049.27
1979	17,890	14,364	1,245.47
1980	19,500	14,435	1,350.88

Source: Heaton (1986). Table 2. Reprinted with the permission of the Ohio State University Press.

TABLE 9.6 Regression Results of Heaton's Model

Maturity of Debt	β_0	β_1	β_2	Adj R^2	Durbin–Watson	F-statistic	ρ
One-Year	6.92 (4.44)**	−15.61 (−4.66)**	9.16 (5.15)**	80.4%	1.87	39.36**	0.655
Two-Year	8.79 (5.82)**	−20.47 (−6.07)**	12.25 (6.57)**	83.2	1.96	47.46**	0.552
Five-Year	5.70 (3.86)**	−14.30 (−3.95)**	9.43 (4.29)**	72.8	2.36	26.01**	0.578
Ten-Year	3.02 (3.73)**	−8.26 (−3.74)**	6.32 (4.29)**	75.3	2.32	29.49**	0.692
Twenty-Year	1.74 (3.38)**	−5.59 (−3.11)**	5.54 (3.71)**	74.1	1.55	27.67**	0.702
Thirty-Year	0.86 (2.95)**	−2.88 (−2.23)*	4.00 (3.02)**	72.9	1.66	26.13**	0.723

Note: Estimation performed with Cochrane–Orcutt procedure, t-statistics in parentheses.
* *Significant at 5 percent level.*
** *Significant at 1 percent level.*
Source: Heaton (1986), Table 3. Reprinted with the permission of the Ohio State University Press.

9.8 Application: Demand for Electricity

The application selected to examine the various issues discussed in this chapter uses quarterly data to model the consumption of electricity by residential customers served by the San Diego Gas and Electric Company. The variable we are interested in explaining is the electricity consumption [measured in kilowatt-hours (kwh)] per residential customer. We are particularly interested in estimating the income and price elasticities of demand for electricity, and then studying whether there were any structural changes.

Table 9.10 (at the end of this chapter) presents quarterly data on the following variables from the second quarter of 1972.2 through the fourth quarter of 1990:

RESKWH = Electricity sales to residential customers
(millions of kilowatt-hours)

NOCUST = Number of residential customers (thousands)

PRICE = Average price for the single-family rate tariff (cents/kwh)

CPI = San Diego consumer price index (1982–1984 = 100)

INCOME = San Diego County total personal income, quarterly rates
(millions of current dollars)

CDD = Cooling degree days (explained below)

HDD = Heating degree days

POP = San Diego county population (in thousands)

The data have to be transformed suitably before being used in an econometric formulation. Because we are interested in income and price elasticities of demand, the double-log model is appropriate here. The dependent variable (denoted by LKWH) will therefore be the logarithm of the kwh sales per residential customer. We thus have,

$$LKWH = \ln(RESKWH/NOCUST)$$

Determinants of the Demand for Electricity

One of the major determinants of the demand for any product is income. Because consumption is measured in per customer terms, income should be measured as per capita. Furthermore, the measurement must be in "real" terms to adjust for inflation effects. Thus, the relevant income variable is per capita in constant dollars. Table 9.10 has total personal income in current dollars. Per capita income in current terms is thus INCOME/POP. To convert this to real terms we need to divide by the price index CPI/100. This will measure per capita income in constant dollars for the base period (1982–1984 in our case). The relevant variable is therefore

$$LY = \ln\left(\frac{100 * INCOME}{CPI * POP}\right)$$

Another important determinant of demand is the price of the good in question. Thus, the price of electricity is important. There is no single price of electricity, even for residential customers. Price gradually increases depending on actual consumption. One can argue whether the marginal cost or the average cost of electricity should be used as an explanatory variable. We, however, will not discuss those issues here. The reader is referred to an excellent survey by Lester Taylor (1975). Here we use the average price for the single family rate tariff which is representative for residential customers. The price is measured in cents per kwh in current terms. As price should also be measured in real terms, it should be divided by CPI/100. The price variable is thus

$$LPRICE = \ln(100 * PRICE/CPI)$$

Perhaps the most important determinant of electricity consumption is the weather. When it is cold in the winter, consumers turn on the heat, and on hot summer days they turn on the air conditioner or a fan. We would therefore expect that the temperature significantly influences the consumption pattern. Because the data are for a three-month period, we need a realistic way of capturing the temperature effect. A common method used by almost all utilities around the country is to compute what are known as *degree days*. In the summer, this will be *cooling degree days* (*CDD*), and in the winter it is *heating degree days* (*HDD*). These variables are defined as follows:

$$CDD = \sum_{d=1}^{d=D} \max\left[\frac{MAXTEMP_d + MINTEMP_d}{2} - 65, 0\right]$$

$$HDD = \sum_{d=1}^{d=D} \max\left[65 - \frac{MAXTEMP_d + MINTEMP_d}{2}, 0\right]$$

where D is the number of days in the quarter, MAXTEMP is the maximum temperature, and MINTEMP is the minimum temperature for day d.

Although the formula appears complex, it is easy to explain in simple terms. First we compute the average temperature in a day as the mean of the maximum and minimum air temperatures. If this average is exactly 65° Fahrenheit, it is assumed that the customer does not turn on either the heater or the air conditioner. In the summer, if this mean temperature exceeds 65 by a substantial amount, consumers will use the air conditioner. The extent of this excess temperature is measured as the average minus 65. When this is summed over each of the days in the quarter, we get the cooling degree days. If the average is below 65 in the summer, no action is taken, and hence the CDD term for the day is zero. The principle for computing HDD in the winter is similar. If the average temperature is above 65 in the winter, consumers will be happy to turn off the heater, and the contribution to HDD is nil. When the average is below 65, the difference between 65 and the average is the contribution of the day's weather to the HDD term. Adding the heating degree day for each day of the quarter we get total HDD.

Note from Table 9.10 that for some quarters HDD and CDD are close to zero. This means that the contribution to these variables was almost zero for every day of the particular quarter. Because of this, we should not take the logarithms of HDD and CDD, and hence they must enter the model linearly.

The Basic Model

The basic model specification is given by the following equation:

$$LKWH = \beta_1 + \beta_2 LY + \beta_3 LELP + \beta_4 CDD + \beta_5 HDD + u_t \qquad (9.14)$$

The higher the income, the greater the demand for a "normal" good. β_2 can therefore be expected to be positive. When the price of electricity goes up, its demand will go down. Hence, β_3 can be expected to be negative. An increase in CDD implies more days for which average temperature exceeded 65 degrees. We can expect this to increase the demand for air conditioning, and hence β_4 will be positive. Similarly, if HDD rises, the demand for heating will rise, and hence β_5 will also be positive. The expected signs for the βs (except β_1) are as follows:

$$\beta_2 > 0, \qquad \beta_3 < 0, \qquad \beta_4 > 0, \qquad \beta_5 > 0$$

We have used the 75 observations in Table 9.10 to transform the raw data into the variables specified in equation (9.14). Applying the OLS procedure, the estimated model is given by (Practice Computer Session 9.9 has the details to reproduce all the empirical results in this application)

$$\widehat{LKWH} = 0.188 + 0.128LY - 0.087LPRICE + 0.0002455CDD + 0.0003579HDD$$
$$\quad\;\; (0.6) \quad\;\; (0.7) \qquad\;\; (-2.5) \qquad\qquad (6.8) \qquad\qquad\quad (11.2)$$

$$\bar{R}^2 = 0.664 \qquad \text{d.f.} = 70 \qquad \text{DW } d = 1.162$$

The values in parentheses are t-statistics, but if there is serial correlation, these values (and that of $\bar{R}^2$) are meaningless.

Testing for Serial Correlation

From Table A.5a of Appendix A, we note that for $T = 75$ and $k' = 4$ (the constant term is not counted here), the bounds for the Durbin–Watson statistic are $d_L = 1.45$ and $d_U = 1.67$ for a two-tailed test at the 5 percent level of significance. The computed d is below d_L and hence there is evidence of significant first-order autocorrelation. However, because the data are quarterly, a fourth-order serial correlation would be more appropriate. Thus the error specification would be

$$u_t = \rho_1 u_{t-1} + \rho_2 u_{t-2} + \rho_3 u_{t-3} + \rho_4 u_{t-4} + \epsilon_t$$

The null hypothesis is that $\rho_1 = \rho_2 = \rho_3 = \rho_4 = 0$. Because we are using four lags, the effective number of observations is 71. Also, the unadjusted R^2 for the auxiliary regression was 0.699, which makes the TR^2 statistic 49.636 whose p-value is below 0.00001. There is thus a very strong evidence of fourth-order serial correlation. The model was then estimated by the Generalized Cochrane–Orcutt Procedure discussed in Section 9.5 and the results are presented below with t-statistics in parentheses.

$$\widehat{LKWH} = 0.168 + 0.182LY - 0.093LPRICE + 0.0002181CDD + 0.0002379HDD$$
$$\quad\;\;\; (1.0) \quad\;\; (1.5) \qquad\quad (-3.4) \qquad\qquad (7.5) \qquad\qquad\quad (9.5)$$

$$\bar{R}^2 = 0.907 \qquad \text{d.f.} = 66 \qquad \hat{\sigma} = 0.02469$$

Although the coefficients are sensible, the model is seriously misspecified because it is unreasonable to expect that the structure is stable over the 1972–1990 period, especially because of the two "energy crises." We therefore turn our attention to a more complete model formulation and analysis which incorporates possible structural shifts in the parameters.

Modeling Structural Change

During the periods 1973–1974 and 1978–1979, the price of crude oil escalated dramatically and conservation became the watchword for reducing demand. Buildings were better insulated, more energy-efficient appliances and machinery were built, and automobiles became more fuel efficient. One might therefore expect that the relationship between electricity consumption and its determinants has changed. The dramatic increase in price did not continue forever, however. As can be seen from Figure 9.7, starting from 1983, the real price of electricity has decreased. We may therefore want to test whether further structural change has taken place since 1983.

To allow for a change in the structure, three dummy variables were defined.

$$D74 = 1 \text{ for } 1974.1 \text{ onward, } 0 \text{ otherwise}$$
$$D79 = 1 \text{ for } 1979.1 \text{ onward, } 0 \text{ otherwise}$$
$$D83 = 1 \text{ for } 1983.3 \text{ onward, } 0 \text{ otherwise}$$

Next we let the regression coefficients depend on these dummy variables. For instance, in equation (9.14) we would have

$$\beta_2 = a_0 + a_1 D74 + a_2 D79 + a_3 D83$$

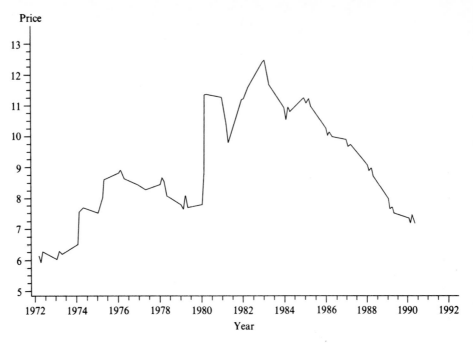

Figure 9.7 Real price of electricity (cents/kwh) for SDG&E

The income elasticities for the four periods, starting from 1972.2, would be a_0, $a_0 + a_1$, $a_0 + a_1 + a_2$ and $a_0 + a_1 + a_2 + a_3$. Thus, a_1 is the *change* in income elasticity (relative to the period 1972.2–1973.4) attributable to the 1974 structural change, and a_2 is the *additional change* due to the 1979 change in the structure, and similarly for others. In addition to this change, the sensitivity of a weather measure (β_4 and β_5) might also depend on the price of electricity. If, for instance, the price is high, then customers might postpone turning the airconditioner or heater on in order to save money. This possible effect can be captured by letting $\beta_4 = b_0 + b_1 \text{LPRICE} + \cdots$. Because there are numerous terms, we have not written down the complete model, but instead present a list of the variables in Table 9.7.

The formulation of a model with complete interactions with all the dummy variables is in the spirit of the Hendry approach of going from a general to a simpler model. The Lagrange Multiplier test is more cumbersome to apply here because it involves regression of the residuals from the transformed model in equation (9.11) against similarly transformed variables from the general model. Instead, we estimate the unrestricted model first and then attempt to make it simpler. Table 9.8 has the OLS estimates of a completely general model (see Practice Computer Session 9.9 for commands to duplicate those results). The Durbin–Watson statistic for the unrestricted model was 2.003, which indicates that there is no serial correlation. We can therefore apply OLS and obtain estimates with desirable properties. It is interesting to note that while the basic model specification suffered from the problem

TABLE 9.7 Definitions of Transformed Variables

Name	Definition
LKWH	ln(RESKWH/NOCUST)
LPRICE	ln(100 * PRICE/CPI)
LY	ln[100 * INCOME/(CPI * POP)]
LYD74	LY * D74
LYD79	LY * D79
LYD83	LY * D83
LPRD74	LPRICE * D74
LPRD79	LPRICE * D79
LPRD83	LPRICE * D83
D74CDD	D74 * CDD
D79CDD	D79 * CDD
D83CDD	D83 * CDD
D74HDD	D74 * HDD
D79HDD	D79 * HDD
D83HDD	D83 * HDD
LPRCDD	LPRICE * CDD
LPRHDD	LPRICE * HDD

of autocorrelation, the more complete model is free of it. However, as can be seen from Table 9.8, most of the regression coefficients have high p-values, indicating insignificance. This is not surprising because, with so many explanatory variables that are cross-products, we can expect high multicollinearity among them. To improve the precision of the estimates, insignificant variables with the highest p-

TABLE 9.8 OLS Estimates of the Completely General Model

Variable	Coefficient	Std. Error	t-stat	Prob $t > |T|$
CONSTANT	−0.75464	5.83367	−0.129	0.8976
D74	−0.96138	5.84958	−0.164	0.8701
D79	1.83334	0.70328	2.607	0.0118**
D83	−0.13811	0.79877	−0.173	0.8634
LY	−2.59852	6.81082	−0.382	0.7043

TABLE 9.8 *(Continued)*

Variable	Coefficient	Std. Error	*t*-stat	Prob $t > |T|$
LYD74	3.55357	6.81945	0.521	0.6045
LYD79	−0.68698	0.49454	−1.389	0.1706
LYD83	−0.19196	0.53624	−0.358	0.7218
LPRICE	2.19203	1.86751	1.174	0.2457
LPRD74	−1.87959	1.86975	−1.005	0.3193
LPRD79	−0.42905	0.14386	−2.982	0.0043***
LPRD83	0.13914	0.08792	1.583	0.1195
CDD	0.00124	0.00053	2.349	0.0226**
D74CDD	−2.59123e−04	3.72113e−04	−0.696	0.4892
D79CDD	−6.31416e−05	1.02108e−04	−0.618	0.5390
D83CDD	6.56797e−05	6.73552e−05	0.975	0.3339
LPRCDD	−3.08549e−04	2.11685e−04	−1.458	0.1509
HDD	8.39156e−04	4.59633e−04	1.826	0.0735*
D74HDD	−2.97733e−04	3.24407e−04	−0.918	0.3629
D79HDD	−5.27103e−05	8.97125e−05	−0.588	0.5593
D83HDD	−3.54196e−05	6.94792e−05	−0.510	0.6123
LPRHDD	−4.93960e−05	1.85356e−04	−0.266	0.7909

Mean of dep. var.	0.32876	S.D. of dep. variable	0.08182
Error Sum of Sq (ESS)	0.06924	Std Err of Resid. (sgmahat)	0.03614
Unadjusted *R*-squared	0.860	Adjusted *R*-squared	0.805
F-statistic (21, 53)	15.534	Probability *F* > 15.534 is <0.00001	
Durbin–Watson Stat.	2.003	First-order auto corr coeff	−0.004

MODEL SELECTION STATISTICS

SGMASQ	0.001306	AIC	0.00166	FPE	0.00169
HQ	0.002177	SCHWARZ	0.003276	SHIBATA	0.001465
GCV	0.001849	RICE	0.002233		

*Three *s indicate significance (two-tailed) at 1 percent, two *s indicate significance at levels between 1 and 5 percent, and one * indicates significance at levels between 5 and 10 percent.*

values were omitted one or two at a time and the model was reestimated. The "final" model results are given in Table 9.9. It will be noted that this model is also free from serial correlation. Furthermore, all the regression coefficients are significant at levels at or below 5 percent, and the model selection statistics are considerably better than the general model.

TABLE 9.9 OLS Estimates of the Final Model

Variable	Coefficient	Std. Error	t-Stat.	Prob $t > |T|$
constant	-1.11016	0.31195	-3.559	0.0007***
D79	0.84077	0.26614	3.159	0.0024***
LYD74	0.57435	0.19854	2.893	0.0053***
LYD83	-0.31348	0.09607	-3.263	0.0018***
LPRICE	0.66925	0.16990	3.939	0.0002***
LPRD74	-0.40025	0.13484	-2.968	0.0043***
LPRD79	-0.37653	0.12621	-2.983	0.0041***
LPRD83	0.13123	0.05213	2.517	0.0144**
CDD	8.96136e$-$04	2.42722e$-$04	3.692	0.0005***
D83CDD	9.16690e$-$05	3.67058e$-$05	2.497	0.0152**
LPRCDD	-2.98973e$-$04	1.06910e$-$04	-2.796	0.0069***
HDD	5.07992e$-$04	6.26447e$-$05	8.109	<0.0001***
D74HDD	-1.36025e$-$04	6.00382e$-$05	-2.266	0.0270**

Mean of dep. var.	0.32876	S.D. of dep. variable	0.08182
Error Sum of Sq (ESS)	0.07638	Std Err of Resid. (sgmahat)	0.03510
Unadjusted R-squared	0.846	Adjusted R-squared	0.816
F-statistic (12, 62)	28.341	Probability $F > 28.341$ is <0.00001	
Durbin–Watson Stat.	1.982	First-order auto corr coeff	-0.003

MODEL SELECTION STATISTICS

SGMASQ	0.001232	AIC	0.00144	FPE	0.001446
HQ	0.001691	SCHWARZ	0.002153	SHIBATA	0.001372
GCV	0.00149	RICE	0.001559		

*Three *s indicate significance (two-tailed) at 1 percent and two *s indicate significance at levels between 1 and 5 percent.*

Interpretation of the Results

The esitmated models for the four time periods are as follows:

1972.2–1973.4: LKWH $= -1.110 + 0.669$LPRICE
$+ 0.0008961$CDD $+ 0.00050799$HDD
$- 0.00029897$LPRICE $*$ CDD

1974.1–1978.4: LKWH $= -1.110 + 0.574$LY $+ 0.269$LPRICE
$+ 0.0008961$CDD $- 0.00029897$LPRICE $*$ CDD
$+ 0.00037197$HDD

$$1979.1\text{--}1982.2: \quad LKWH = -0.269 + 0.574LY - 0.108LPRICE$$
$$+ 0.0008961CDD + 0.00037197HDD$$
$$- 0.00029897LPRICE * CDD$$

$$1983.3\text{--}1990.4: \quad LKWH = -0.269 + 0.261LY + 0.024LPRICE$$
$$+ 0.0009878CDD + 0.00037197HDD$$
$$- 0.00029897LPRICE * CDD$$

It should be pointed out that the control period 1972.2–1973.4 has only seven observations and hence the model results for this period should not be taken too seriously. For instance, income elasticity was statistically insignificant during this period. During the period of rising electricity prices (1974.1–1983.2) income elasticity was 0.574; it dropped to 0.261 during the last period even though real electricity price was declining during this period. One possible explanation is that it takes time to adjust the stock of appliances and buildings in response to a substantial increase in price. When prices are escalating, consumers will switch to more efficient appliances and will demand homes with better insulation. Once this adjustment has taken place, the usage of electricity will be reduced thus rationalizing the observed reduction in the income elasticity.

The price elasticity showed even more dramatic structural change from period to period. The elasticity was as follows:

1972.2–1973.4:	$0.669 - 0.00029897CDD$
1974.1–1978.4:	$0.269 - 0.00029897CDD$
1979.1–1983.2:	$-0.108 - 0.00029897CDD$
1983.3–1990.4:	$0.024 - 0.00029897CDD$

There is interaction between cooling degree days and electricity price. Cooling degree days have varied from almost zero to nearly a thousand. During the first period, when electricity price was rising slowly, price elasticity was *positive*, which is contrary to standard economic theory. This might be because electricity consumption grew steadily as a result of growth in income and population, and this dominating trend might have been captured in the regression with a positive sign. It should be noted that when prices started to rise, the positive effect was considerably reduced; and since 1979 consumers have responded with a reduction in the quantity demanded, although this behavior was starting to be reversed by 1983 when the real price of electricity began to decline.

In an earlier discussion we had argued that the weather effect might depend on the price of electricity, and we see evidence to support that. The marginal effect of cooling degree days is given as follows:

1972.2–1973.4:	$0.0008961 - 0.00029897LPRICE$
1974.1–1978.4:	$0.0008961 - 0.00029897LPRICE$

$$1979.1-1983.2: \qquad 0.0008961 - 0.00029897 \text{LPRICE}$$

$$1983.3-1990.4: \qquad 0.0009878 - 0.00029897 \text{LPRICE}$$

It is evident that the marginal effect of the weather depends negatively on the price of electricity. In other words, an increase of one cooling degree day results in a smaller increase in electricity usage if the price of electricity is high. It is interesting to note that during the last period of the study, the marginal effect was larger. This is not surprising because since 1983, the real price of electricity has been declining.

Heating degree days also have the expected positive effect, although there is no significant interaction with price. In 1974 there was a significant reduction in the marginal HDD effect, but no further significant changes are evident.

- -

SUMMARY

In this chapter we have explored the impact of *serial correlation* (or *autocorrelation*), that is, correlation among the residual terms of a regression model. The consequences of ignoring serial correlation were first examined. Two tests for the presence of autocorrelation were next discussed. Assuming serial correlation of the first order, we presented two estimation procedures. Finally, we discussed the case of higher order serial correlation, both testing and estimation.

In the presence of autocorrelation, OLS estimates and forecasts based on them are still unbiased and consistent, but they are not BLUE and are hence inefficient. Furthermore, if the exogenous variables have been growing over time, and serial correlation is positive (which is frequently the case), the estimated residual variance will be an underestimate and the value of $\bar{R}^2$ will be an overestimate. This means that the goodness of fit will be exaggerated and the estimated t-statistics will be larger than the true values. Most seriously, if serial correlation is ignored and the OLS procedure is applied, the tests of hypotheses will not be valid.

The plot of the estimated residuals is a useful guide that signals the presence of serial correlation. If serial correlation is present, successive residuals will tend to be clustered together.

First-order serial correlation can be tested by the *Durbin–Watson test*. The procedure is to estimate the model by OLS and compute the estimated residuals $\hat{u}_t$. The Durbin–Watson statistic (d) is next calculated using equation (9.6). For a one-tailed test for positive serial correlation, two values, denoted by d_L and d_U, are read from Table A.5b in Appendix A. If $d \geq d_U$, we conclude that there is no serial correlation. If $d \leq d_L$ we conclude that there is significant first-order autocorrelation. If d lies between d_L and d_U, the test is inconclusive. A two-tailed test is carried out to test whether serial correlation is zero or not. The procedure is identical except that the critical d_L and d_U are obtained from Table A.5a instead.

An alternative test that is conclusive in all cases is based on the Lagrange multiplier (LM) test described in Chapter 7. This consists of running an auxiliary regression of $\hat{u}_t$ against $\hat{u}_{t-1}$ and all the explanatory variables in the model. Under the null hypothesis of zero autocorrelation, the value of $(T-1)R^2$ is distributed as chi-square with 1 d.f. If this exceeds the critical value, the conclusion is that there is significant first-order serial correlation.

The LM test can be applied to test higher order serial correlations also. The procedure is to regress $\hat{u}_t$ against $\hat{u}_{t-1}, \hat{u}_{t-2}, \ldots, \hat{u}_{t-p}$ (usually up to the periodicity of the data set), in addition to the variables originally in the model. The value of $(T-p)R^2$ from this auxiliary regression is compared against the critical value in a chi-square distribution with degrees of freedom equal to the number of lagged residuals used in the auxiliary regression (which is $\hat{p}$ here).

If first-order serial correlation is identified, the *Hildreth–Lu (HILU) search procedure* may be used to correct for it. The procedure is to choose a value of ρ, the first-order autocorrelation coefficient, between -1 and $+1$. Then obtain the transformed variables, $Y_t - \rho Y_{t-1}$ and $X_t - \rho X_{t-1}$ for each X in the model. The transformed dependent variable is regressed against the transformed independent variables and the error sum of squares (ESS) of this regression is computed. Next ρ is changed to a new value and the whole procedure repeated. By searching for the value of ρ that gives the lowest ESS, we obtain the Hildreth–Lu estimates, which are consistent and asymptotically more efficient than OLS estimates.

An alternative estimating method is the *Cochrane–Orcutt (CORC) iterative procedure*. In this method, the OLS residuals $\hat{u}_t$ are used to obtain an estimate of ρ using equation (9.7). This value is used to transform the variables as above and a transformed regression run. The estimates obtained this way are used to recompute $\hat{u}_t$. The procedure is then repeated until two successive ρ-values do not change by more than some prespecified level. This iterative procedure has been found to converge fairly quickly and needs much less computation time than the Hildreth–Lu procedure. However, by searching over the entire range -1 to $+1$, the Hildreth–Lu technique selects the global minimum for ESS. If there are several local minima of ESS, the Cochrane–Orcutt procedure might iterate to a local minimum, which is not a global minimum. Cochrane–Orcutt estimates are also consistent and asymptotically more efficient than OLS estimates. A more desirable procedure is to search in broader steps using the HILU procedure and then fine-tune it using the CORC technique.

The Cochrane–Orcutt iterative procedure can be extended to higher order serial correlation case also. The procedure is to regress the OLS residuals $\hat{u}_t$ against $\hat{u}_{t-1}, \hat{u}_{t-2}, \hat{u}_{t-3}$, and so on, and obtain $\hat{\rho}_1, \hat{\rho}_2$, and so on. Next transform the dependent variable as $Y_t - \hat{\rho}_1 Y_{t-1} - \hat{\rho}_2 Y_{t-2} - \cdots$, and similarly for each of the Xs. Regress the transformed Y against the transformed Xs. Use the estimates of this transformed regression to recompute $\hat{u}_t$. Repeat the procedure until the error sum of squares of the transformed regression does not change by more than a prespecified percent.

When forecasting in the presence of autocorrelated errors, more efficient forecasts may be obtained by using the error structure.

KEY TERMS

ARCH	Generalized differencing
AR(1)	Hildreth–Lu (HILU) search
AR(p)	procedure
Autocorrelation	pth-order autoregressive process
Autocorrelation function	Quasi-differencing
Autoregressive Conditional	Random walk
Heteroscedasticity	Residual plot
Cochrane–Orcutt (CORC) iterative	Serial correlation
procedure	Serial independence
Durbin–Watson (DW) test	Stationarity
First difference	Stationary time series
First-order autocorrelation coefficient	Unit roots
First-order autoregressive process	White noise series
First-order serial correlation	

REFERENCES

Cochrane, D., and Orcutt, G. H. "Application of Least Squares Regressions to Relationships Containing Autocorrelated Error Terms." *J. Amer. Stat. Assoc.*, Vol. 44 (1949): 32–61.

Durbin, J., and Watson, G. S. "Testing for Serial Correlation in Least Squares Regression." *Biometrica*, Vol. 37 (1950): 409–428, and Vol. 38 (1951): 159–178.

Engle, R. F. "Wald, Likelihood Ratio, and Lagrangian Multiplier Tests in Econometrics," *Handbook of Econometrics*, ed. Z. Griliches and M. D. Intriligator. New York: North-Holland, 1984.

Fama, Eugene F. "A Pricing Model for the Municipal Bond Market." Manuscript. University of Chicago, 1977.

Granger, C. W. J. *Forecasting in Business and Economics*. New York: Academic Press, 1989.

Heaton, Hal. "The Relative Yields on Taxable and Non-taxable Debt." *J. Money, Credit, and Banking* (November 1986): 482–494.

Hildreth, C., and Lu, J. Y. "Demand Relations with Autocorrelated Disturbances." *Technical Bulletin 276*. Michigan State University (November 1960).

Kmenta, Jan. *Elements of Econometrics*. New York: Macmillan, 1986.

Prais, S. J., and Winsten, C. B. "Trend Estimators and Serial Correlation." *Cowles Commission Discussion Paper 383*, Chicago, 1954.

Taylor, Lester. "The Demand for Electricity: A Survey." *The Bell Journal*, Vol. 6, No. 1 (1975).

Trzcinka, Charles. "The Pricing of Tax-exempt Bonds and the Miller Hypothesis." *J. Finance* (September 1982): 907–923.

PRACTICE COMPUTER SESSIONS

9.1 Use the data file *data3-6 and the input file ps9-1.inp* to verify Example 9.1.

9.2 Example 9.2 can be reproduced using the data file *data4-14* and the input file *ps9-2.inp*.

9.3 Example 9.3 also uses the data in *data3-6*, but the input commands are in *ps9-3.inp*.

9.4 To verify Example 9.4, you need *data4-14* and *ps9-4.inp*.

9.5 Example 9.5 can be duplicated with the data in *data9-1* and the command file *ps9-5.inp*.

9.6 The data in *data4-14* in conjunction with *ps9-6.inp* can be used to reproduce Example 9.6.

9.7 Example 9.7 requires *data9-2* and *ps9-7.inp*.

9.8 Example 9.8 illustrating how HILU and CORC procedures may yield different results can be verified using *data4-10* and *ps9-8.inp*.

9.9 The results presented in the application Section 9.8 can be duplicated using the data set *data9-10* and the input file *ps9-9.inp*. Because the application covers a variety of topics, the computer session might take quite some time to do.

EXERCISES

†**9.1** Consider the following model estimated earlier by OLS with annual data for the years 1963–1985 for the United States as a whole:

$$\widehat{LH} = -4.759 + 1.873LG - 1.229LR$$
$$\quad\quad (-1.4) \quad\quad (3.8) \quad\quad (-4.0)$$
$$\bar{R}^2 = 0.386 \quad\quad T = 23 \quad\quad DW\ d = 0.794$$

where LH is the logarithm of housing starts, LG is the logarithm of the gross national product, and LR is the logarithm of the mortgage rate. The values in parentheses are *t*-statistics.

a. Test the model for first-order serial correlation under the alternative most common in economics. Be sure to state the null and alternative hypotheses. Based on your conclusions, list the properties of the estimates and associated statistics, and the validity of the tests of hypotheses.
b. Describe step by step how you would apply the LM test for first-order autocorrelation. Your answers must be specific to the above model.
c. Describe the procedures for applying the Cochrane–Orcutt and Hildreth–Lu methods of estimating the parameters. Again your answer should be specific to the above model. What are the statistical properties of these estimates?
d. Using your regression program and the data in Table 4.11 verify the above estimates. Next plot the residuals against time. Do you observe any clustering of residuals that indicates the presence of serial correlation?
e. Estimate the model by CORC and HILU procedures. Do the two methods give similar estimates? Based on your intuition and knowledge of the

underlying behavior, would you say that the estimates and associated statistics are sensible?

9.2 Use the data in Table 4.11 (at the end of the chapter) and generate the variables lph = log(housing/pop), lpcgnp = log(gnp/pop), and lr = log(intrate). Then estimate the following model by OLS.

$$\text{lph} = \beta_1 + \beta_2 \text{lpcgnp} + \beta_3 \text{lr} + u$$

Test the model for first-order serial correlation using both the Cochrane–Orcutt and Lagrange Multiplier tests, and indicate your conclusions. Based on your conclusions what can you say about the properties of the OLS estimates in terms of unbiasedness, consistency, and efficiency?

If there is significant serial correlation, estimate the model by the mixed HILU–CORC procedure. Does serial correlation persist? Next test the model for AR(3) errors. If present, obtain the estimates by the Generalized CORC procedure and interpret the results.

9.3 The planning department of a city obtained the following estimated double-log relationship by OLS, with t-statistics in parentheses:

$$\widehat{\text{LH}_t} = 1.12 + 1.141\text{LY}_t + 0.961\text{LP}_t$$
$$\quad\quad\quad (0.8) \quad\quad (10.7) \quad\quad (1.5)$$

$$\bar{R}^2 = 0.98 \quad\quad T = 27 \quad\quad \text{DW } d = 0.65$$

where LH is the logarithm of the number of single family dwellings, LY is the logarithm of the city's total income in constant dollars, and LP is the logarithm of the city's population. From the DW statistic what conclusion would you draw about the residuals of the model? What are the implications on (a) bias, if any, of estimates and forecasts; (b) standard errors, goodness of fit, and t-statistics; and (c) validity of tests? If necessary, suggest an alternative procedure of estimating the model. Explain why it might be superior in terms of estimates and their properties (explain what you mean by "superior").

†9.4 A study on industrial employment in San Diego estimated the following model by OLS, using annual data for 22 years:

$$\widehat{\text{LEMP}} = -3.89 + 0.51\text{LINCM} - 0.25\text{LWAGE} + 0.62\text{LG}$$
$$\quad\quad\quad (-0.56) \quad\quad (2.3) \quad\quad\quad (-1.7) \quad\quad\quad (5.8)$$

$$\bar{R}^2 = 0.996 \quad\quad \text{DW } d = 1.147$$

EMP is total employment, INCM is total income, WAGE is the average hourly wage rate, and G is the total expenditure of the local governments in the area, all in logarithmic terms. Verify that the DW test for first-order autocorrelation is inconclusive. Describe step by step how the LM test will be applied in the above case. Next describe how the Cochrane–Orcutt procedure can be used to obtain the estimates. Again your descriptions should be specific to the model.

9.5 Let C_t be real per capita consumption in the United States at time t, and Y_t be the real per capita disposable income, both measured in billions of dollars.

The following model was estimated by OLS, using annual data for 32 years (LY is the logarithm of Y):

$$\hat{C}_t = -21151 + 2989.9 LY_t$$
$$\quad\;\; (-39.3) \qquad\quad (45.0)$$

$$\bar{R}^2 = 0.985 \qquad DW\; d = 0.207$$

Test the model for first-order serial correlation. Be sure to state the assumption on the error terms, and the null and alternative hypotheses. Based on your result would you say that we are justified in feeling that the fit is excellent and the regression coefficients extremely significant? Why or why not?

9.6 Using data for a number of employees of a firm, a labor economist estimated the following model by OLS (t-values in parentheses):

$$\widehat{\ln E} = 7.71 + 0.094S + 0.023N - 0.000325N^2$$
$$\quad\;\; (6.8) \quad\;\; (18.8) \quad\;\; (2.6) \qquad (-1.7)$$

$$R^2 = 0.337 \qquad T = 60 \qquad DW\; d = 0.53$$

where ln E is the natural logarithm of earnings, S is the number of years of schooling, and N is the number of years of experience. "Because the Durbin–Watson test rejects the null hypothesis of zero first-order serial correlation, the t-tests are invalid, and the above R^2 is an overestimate of the true R^2." Do you agree with the statement in quotations? Explain.

9.7 Using the data in Table 9.11 and your regression program estimate the following model by ordinary least squares:

$$PROFITS = \alpha + \beta SALES + u$$

Save the residuals, obtain the residual plot, and examine whether it exhibits signs of serial correlation. Test your model for first-order autocorrelation using both the DW and LM tests. If it is significant, reestimate the model using both CORC and HILU procedures. Retest the model for serial correlation. Are your results meaningful? If not, what modifications do you suggest?

†9.8 Use the data in Table 9.2 and estimate the following double-log model by OLS (prefix L denotes logarithms):

$$LDEMAND_t = \beta_0 + \beta_1 LPRICE_t + \beta_2 LINCOME_t$$
$$+ \beta_3 LTEMP_t + u_t$$

a. Test the model for first-order serial correlation using both the Durbin–Watson and Lagrange multiplier tests. Be sure to (i) write down the assumption about the error term u_t, (ii) state the null and alternative hypotheses, and (iii) state the test criterion and your conclusion.
b. Based on your conclusion above, are your estimates (i) unbiased, (ii) consistent, (iii) efficient? (Be sure to define each term.) Carefully justify your answer.

    c. Describe step by step how you will go about obtaining "better" estimates than OLS. Explain what you mean by "better."

9.9   Table 9.12 contains data on the number of new cars sold in the United States and a number of variables that it might be related to.

    a. Estimate the double-log model (prefix L denotes logs) by OLS.

$$LQNC = \beta_1 + \beta_2 LPRICE + \beta_3 LINCOME + \beta_4 LPRIME$$
$$+ \beta_5 LUNEMP + \beta_6 SPRING + \beta_7 STRIKE + u$$

    (The STOCK variable is ignored in this formulation.)

    b. Compute the correlation coefficients for the independent variables. Is multicollinearity a problem in the data set? If yes, what can you say about the statistical properties of your estimates, t-values, and so on?

    c. Perform the LM test for first-order autocorrelation. Is there evidence of significant serial correlation? In light of your findings what can you say about the properties of the OLS estimates and associated statistics?

    d. Based on your results modify the model and reestimate if necessary. Are the model selection statistics better? Check the new model for autocorrelation.

    e. Because the data are quarterly, fourth-order serial correlation is suspected. Test the model for fourth-order serial correlation. What do you conclude? Does your conclusion suggest a "better" method (explain what you mean by "better")? If yes, apply that method and get revised estimates. Are they improved? If not, what other suggested models and/or estimation procedures would you recommend?

9.10   According to basic macroeconomic theory, the equilibrium gross national product (Yt) depends on a number of policy and other exogenous variables, in particular on the money supply (Mt), government expenditure (Gt), taxes (Tt), and exports (Xt).

    a. Using the data in Table 9.13 estimate the following model by ordinary least squares:

$$Yt = \beta_1 + \beta_2 Mt + \beta_3 Gt + \beta_4 Tt + \beta_5 Xt + ut$$

    b. What signs would you expect for each of the regression coefficients (ignore the constant)? Justify your answers. Do the observed estimates agree with your intuition? If not, do you have any explanations for them?

    c. Test the model for first-order serial correlation using both the DW and LM tests. What do your results indicate about the unbiasedness, consistency, and efficiency of your estimates?

    d. Describe the steps necessary to obtain Cochrane–Orcutt estimates of the above model. Your answers should not repeat what is in the book but should be specific to the above model. Use your regression program to obtain CORC estimates. Are they improved compared to OLS estmates? Explain what you mean by "improved."

e. Because the data are quarterly, fourth-order serial correlation is suspected. Test the model for fourth-order serial correlation. What do you conclude? Does your conclusion suggest a "better" method (explain what you mean by "better")? If yes, apply that method and get revised estimates. Are they improved? If not, what other suggested models and/or estimation procedures would you recommend?

9.11 Consider the model $E_t = \alpha + \beta T_t + u_t$, relating electricity consumption at time t and temperature T. We would expect β to be positive in the summer and negative in the winter (explain why). An investigator decides to fit a piece-wise linear relationship between E and T, using as break points 45, 60, and 70 degrees. You are hired as a research assistant to carry it out. Describe step by step how you would go about estimating such a relationship. Then describe how you would test the model for serial correlation so that a conclusive result is obtained. Suppose you do find significant serial correlation [for simplicity assume that it is AR(1)]. What procedures would you adopt to get "better" estimates? Explain what you mean by "better."

9.12 Table 9.14 has annual data for the following variables:

$$POP = \text{Population in millions}$$
$$RPM = \text{Revenue air passenger miles (domestic) in billions}$$
$$NOP = \text{Number of operators (airlines)}$$
$$OPREV = \text{Operating revenue from passengers in millions of dollars}$$
$$GNP = \text{Gross national product of the United States in billions of dollars}$$
$$ACCID = \text{Number of American planes in an accident}$$
$$FATAL = \text{Number of fatalities from aircraft accidents}$$
$$REGU = \text{Dummy variable for airline regulation/deregulation, 0 for 1945–1979, and 1 for 1979 onward}$$

First estimate the following model by OLS.

$$\ln(RPM/POP) = \beta_1 + \beta_2 REGU + \beta_3 \ln(OPREV/RPM)$$
$$+ \beta_4 \ln(GNP/POP) + \beta_5 \ln(ACCID/RPM)$$
$$+ \beta_6 FATAL + u$$

RPM/POP is the per capita revenue passenger miles, GNP/POP is per capita income, OPREV/RPM measures the average price per mile, and ACCID/PRM measures the accident rate per passenger mile of travel. The model is double-log except for the fact that REGU and FATAL are not expressed in log form. This is because there are zero entries in the data for these variables. Use both the Durbin–Watson and LM tests for first-order autocorrelation. Given your results, what can you say about the properties of OLS estimates, the goodness of fit, and tests of hypotheses?

Next estimate the model by both CORC and the mixed HILU–CORC procedures and compare the results. Suppose we want to test whether the intercept and slope coefficients (some of which are elasticities) depend on the variable REGU. In other words, there might have been a structural change when deregulation went into effect. Formulate another model with complete interaction terms and indicate what the null hypothesis of no structural change means. Estimate appropriate models to test for this and carry out such a test. Again use the mixed HILU–CORC procedure to estimate a general model and then use relevant tests to reduce it to one in which coefficients are significant so that more efficient estimates could be obtained.

Finally, test the model for third-order serial correlation and, if called for, use Generalized Cochrane–Orcutt technique to estimate the model with an appropriate error specification.

9.13   Table 9.15 has annual data for indices of U.S. farm inputs and output with 1977 as the base year. The specific variables are the following:

OUTPUT = Farm output

LABOR = Farm labor

LAND = Farm real estate

MACHINES = Mechanical power and machinery

FERT = Agricultural chemicals used

SEEDFEED = Seed, feed, and livestock purchases

Estimate a double-log model relating the log of output to the log of each of the inputs. Test the model for serial correlation of first and third orders. If significant autocorrelation is present, estimate the models by the CORC, mixed HILU–CORC, and generalized CORC procedures. Eliminate insignificant variables and reestimate the resulting models. Choose your "final" model (justify your choice) and interpret the results.

9.14   The data used in the application section 6.8 is time series. Check the model presented there for serial correlation [both AR(1) and higher orders]. If it is significant, redo the analysis using the mixed HILU–CORC procedure and see if your results are the same.

†9.15   Table 9.16 has quarterly U.S. data for the following variables for the period 1976.1 through 1985.4:

NUMCARS = Number of new car sales of U.S. dealers in thousands

PRICE = New car price index

INCOME = Per capita disposable personal income in 1982 dollars

POP = Estimated population obtained by interpolating from annual data (millions)

INTRATE = Prime interest rate charged by banks

UNEMP = Unemployment rate for all workers

Estimate the relationship between per capita new car sales (NUMCARS/POP) and its determinants; price, income, interest rate, and unemployment rate. Formulate the model so that the regression coefficients are all elasticities. Carry out the analysis in three stages. First estimate the model by OLS and test for first-order serial correlation using both the DW and LM tests. If present, estimate the model by CORC and mixed HILU–CORC. Do they give the same results? Eliminate insignificant variables and reestimate the model using appropriate techniques. In the final model, test whether the demand for new car sales is elastic or inelastic with respect to price and income.

In the second stage, test for seasonal effects (omit the unemployment rate variable for the rest of the analysis). In particular, estimate a relevant model assuming that the constant term is different across seasons. Again test the new model for serial correlation and use appropriate estimation techniques to obtain more efficient estimates.

In the third stage, test the model you started with in the second stage for serial correlation of orders 1 through 4. If present, use generalized CORC to estimate the model. Once again omit insignificant variables. Choose the model that, in your opinion, best approximates the data-generating process and interpret the results of this model.

TABLE 9.10 Data for Electricity Demand and Its Determinants

PERIOD	RESKWH	NOCUST	PRICE	CPI	INCOME	CDD	HDD	POP
1972.2	586.608	459.903	2.250	36.540	1815.148	75.335	285.451	1422.640
1972.3	625.797	467.130	2.207	36.984	1863.625	581.389	3.015	1434.922
1972.4	704.154	476.188	2.370	37.486	1915.929	103.646	402.203	1447.842
1973.1	817.206	483.329	2.295	37.900	1967.750	0.435	833.673	1462.783
1973.2	667.642	489.866	2.454	38.639	2020.041	57.923	397.441	1475.720
1973.3	661.827	498.285	2.487	39.733	2077.095	410.773	6.798	1487.269
1973.4	732.839	506.800	2.526	40.354	2138.914	117.642	365.674	1497.428
1974.1	796.876	512.824	2.712	41.448	2202.625	0.374	826.140	1502.213
1974.2	655.335	517.733	3.254	42.896	2264.497	40.035	325.475	1512.336
1974.3	692.599	524.639	3.394	44.315	2329.736	514.421	5.572	1526.462
1974.4	768.172	531.437	3.494	45.380	2398.341	140.399	328.867	1544.589
1975.1	877.881	535.785	3.497	46.473	2462.662	1.399	950.170	1568.375
1975.2	722.124	539.371	3.646	46.946	2531.149	13.105	557.091	1586.568
1975.3	697.671	545.028	3.829	48.040	2607.868	344.041	44.112	1603.196
1975.4	804.178	551.368	4.193	48.750	2692.821	149.864	392.326	1618.261
1976.1	880.008	556.996	4.349	49.459	2783.068	11.815	759.206	1632.120

(continued)

TABLE 9.10 (*Continued*)

PERIOD	RESKWH	NOCUST	PRICE	CPI	INCOME	CDD	HDD	POP
1976.2	763.618	562.832	4.455	50.051	2868.182	62.011	340.030	1647.173
1976.3	790.428	569.214	4.446	50.878	2957.082	564.732	9.828	1661.827
1976.4	860.741	577.596	4.417	51.410	3049.768	310.182	183.902	1676.080
1977.1	946.673	585.285	4.385	52.209	3128.320	9.415	655.552	1689.320
1977.2	793.593	593.077	4.464	53.391	3220.589	23.149	433.728	1703.565
1977.3	820.803	600.232	4.522	54.426	3331.884	564.823	8.986	1718.422
1977.4	876.286	610.294	4.561	55.165	3462.207	200.742	190.146	1733.892
1978.1	993.199	618.782	4.741	56.214	3610.249	14.334	543.892	1750.456
1978.2	842.539	625.529	4.991	57.796	3741.214	159.433	228.523	1765.936
1978.3	893.369	634.131	5.123	60.368	3875.558	578.080	6.444	1780.940
1978.4	998.721	643.019	5.006	62.024	4013.279	261.622	379.944	1795.468
1979.1	1135.091	649.268	5.005	64.477	4146.769	4.131	921.737	1811.355
1979.2	901.289	655.771	5.144	67.493	4284.350	105.130	290.166	1825.895
1979.3	942.471	662.934	5.694	70.434	4430.241	655.935	6.148	1838.570
1979.4	1024.852	672.787	5.627	73.258	4584.440	246.199	252.745	1849.381
1980.1	1068.690	678.791	5.893	75.726	4740.678	8.908	507.824	1857.086
1980.2	914.884	683.517	6.909	79.732	4894.944	59.813	319.841	1867.879
1980.3	930.812	687.818	9.082	80.072	5056.558	632.576	9.812	1879.896
1980.4	969.382	693.819	9.370	82.511	5225.521	149.297	262.378	1893.138
1981.1	1028.968	698.543	9.644	85.852	5431.957	23.108	519.092	1908.541
1981.2	883.718	702.322	9.501	87.951	5602.093	171.909	189.776	1921.797
1981.3	958.449	706.307	9.470	91.542	5741.343	843.172	0.038	1934.128
1981.4	980.453	710.868	9.254	94.987	5849.707	165.298	255.815	1945.534
1982.1	1062.744	714.317	10.617	94.913	5919.064	7.118	686.491	1956.446
1982.2	887.136	716.701	10.940	97.322	6026.718	66.692	272.422	1967.849
1982.3	933.269	718.679	11.129	97.618	6141.202	609.145	11.222	1978.801
1982.4	978.160	721.649	11.001	95.105	6262.516	208.839	317.704	1989.304
1983.1	1020.435	723.832	11.952	96.435	6363.223	6.480	610.247	1997.640
1983.2	917.487	726.287	12.235	98.150	6484.145	79.510	275.726	2008.131
1983.3	975.387	730.103	12.065	99.865	6633.636	793.841	2.070	2020.346
1983.4	998.109	735.890	11.823	101.195	6811.696	350.759	231.407	2034.284
1984.1	1015.545	741.208	11.232	102.806	7015.020	8.369	544.615	2049.802

TABLE 9.10 (Continued)

PERIOD	RESKWH	NOCUST	PRICE	CPI	INCOME	CDD	HDD	POP
1984.2	919.639	746.641	10.959	104.358	7193.724	155.497	161.922	2063.751
1984.3	1040.188	753.684	11.444	104.713	7377.877	978.149	1.672	2077.874
1984.4	1082.732	761.885	11.591	107.521	7567.479	268.416	342.204	2092.173
1985.1	1164.663	768.456	12.177	108.393	7771.606	4.422	887.923	2104.190
1985.2	945.277	777.619	12.099	110.005	7961.563	83.583	280.598	2118.474
1985.3	1062.046	787.210	12.420	110.877	8142.478	670.318	11.208	2135.242
1985.4	1079.565	797.610	12.254	112.045	8314.353	161.970	357.074	2154.494
1986.1	1137.534	807.725	11.494	112.503	8466.333	15.201	557.210	2175.757
1986.2	992.370	816.428	11.295	113.168	8638.207	85.650	256.515	2195.027
1986.3	1087.314	827.405	11.505	113.671	8821.862	476.717	13.059	2214.835
1986.4	1107.644	839.905	11.411	114.557	9017.298	55.421	270.461	2235.180
1987.1	1263.671	851.421	11.419	115.994	9211.409	7.875	815.183	2255.779
1987.2	1054.402	862.399	11.252	117.113	9406.817	84.765	260.703	2276.126
1987.3	1107.669	875.061	11.421	117.642	9616.429	334.274	22.457	2296.774
1987.4	1214.441	885.997	11.441	118.954	9840.245	209.056	301.720	2317.721
1988.1	1335.147	895.657	10.966	121.057	10068.894	10.255	791.362	2338.321
1988.2	1122.214	903.766	10.836	122.737	10292.817	86.570	288.234	2359.266
1988.3	1238.305	914.192	11.114	124.125	10527.287	503.150	19.489	2380.872
1988.4	1233.677	924.501	10.887	125.869	10772.302	121.276	307.070	2403.141
1989.1	1432.962	933.047	10.212	127.982	11076.538	12.383	915.367	2427.867
1989.2	1156.211	940.333	9.906	129.812	11379.382	105.908	235.876	2450.158
1989.3	1276.944	948.572	10.128	131.436	11566.177	468.688	16.749	2470.646
1989.4	1279.626	956.610	10.000	133.158	11792.947	158.125	239.111	2489.329
1990.1	1485.453	963.867	9.999	135.813	12082.537	2.167	828.817	2507.403
1990.2	1206.455	969.334	9.936	138.283	12243.461	92.788	250.563	2526.082
1990.3	1394.055	974.530	10.464	139.992	12486.069	642.757	3.707	2543.518
1990.4	1336.979	979.510	10.293	142.265	12746.299	191.233	284.108	2559.711

Source: San Diego Gas and Electric Company, courtesy of Larry Schelhorse, Gregory Katsapis, and Robert Dye.

TABLE 9.11 Data on Profits and Sales of the U.S. Manufacturing Sector

Year	Profits	Sales	Year	Profits	Sales
1950	12.9	181.9	1970	28.6	708.8
1951	11.9	245.0	1971	31.0	751.1
1952	10.7	250.2	1972	36.5	849.5
1953	11.3	265.9	1973	48.1	1017.2
1954	11.2	248.5	1974	58.7	1060.6
1955	15.1	278.4	1975	49.1	1065.2
1956	16.2	307.3	1976	64.5	1203.2
1957	15.4	320.0	1977	70.4	1328.1
1958	12.7	305.3	1978	81.1	1496.4
1959	16.3	338.0	1979	98.7	1741.8
1960	15.2	345.7	1980	92.6	1912.8
1961	15.3	356.4	1981	101.3	2144.7
1962	17.7	389.4	1982	70.9	2039.4
1963	19.5	412.7	1983	85.8	2114.3
1964	23.2	443.1	1984	107.6	2335.0
1965	27.5	492.2	1985	87.6	2331.4
1966	30.9	554.2	1986	83.1	2220.9
1967	29.0	575.4	1987	115.6	2378.2
1968	32.1	631.9	1988	154.6	2596.2
1969	33.2	694.6			

Source: Economic Report of the President, 1990, Table C-90.

TABLE 9.12 Data on Automobile Demand and Its Determinants

Data are quarterly for the periods 1970.1 through 1979.4.
Entries in a row correspond to successive periods.

QNC: Quantity of New Cars Sold in Thousands

2054	2533	1979	1827	2339	2727	2425	2747	2441
2955	2599	2943	2936	3249	2670	2581	2137	2507
2343	1866	1923	2165	2198	2328	2381	2788	2416
2513	2617	3195	2668	2688	2540	3337	2713	2710
2739	2942	2571	2396					

TABLE 9.12 (*Continued*)

		PRICE:	Average Real Price of 12 New Car Models in Dollars					
3150	3106	3346	3279	3256	3230	3199	3167	3106
3045	3127	3060	2962	2881	3484	3406	3354	3296
3265	3207	3184	3135	3238	3207	3137	3075	3207
3160	3097	3010	3204	3147	3054	2948	3097	3010
2987	2933	3053	2996					
		INCOME:	Real Disposable Income in Billions of Dollars					
737.4	752.5	760.1	756.2	771.1	779.9	780.7	785.2	792
798.7	812.4	838.1	855.2	862.3	867.9	873.3	860.2	859.7
859.4	850.8	845.1	891.4	878.2	885.1	899.5	904.1	908.9
914.6	919.5	933.9	952.2	965.9	973.4	982.8	994.2	1004.8
1011.1	1011.7	1019.8	1020.1					
		PRIME:	Prime Interest Rate in Percent					
8.46	8	7.94	7.23	5.88	5.39	5.97	5.54	4.89
5.01	5.34	5.76	6.11	7.03	9.13	9.81	9.26	10.94
11.99	11	8.98	7.32	7.56	7.58	6.83	6.9	7.09
6.54	6.25	6.47	6.9	7.67	7.98	8.3	9.14	10.81
11.75	11.72	12.12	15.08					
		UNEMP:	Unemployment Rate in Percent					
4.4	4.7	5.5	6	6	5.6	6	6.1	5.9
5.5	5.5	5.2	5	4.8	4.8	4.9	5.1	5.2
5.8	7.4	8.7	8.6	8.3	8.3	7.5	7.5	7.8
7.9	7.3	7.1	6.9	6.3	6.2	5.8	5.9	5.9
5.7	5.7	5.8	5.9					
		SPRING = 1	For the Second Quarter					
		0	Otherwise					
0	1	0	0	0	1	0	0	0
1	0	0	0	1	0	0	0	1
0	0	0	1	0	0	0	1	0
0	0	1	0	0	0	1	0	0
0	1	0	0					

(*continued*)

TABLE 9.12 (*Continued*)

STRIKE = 1 for Fourth Quarter of 1970 When There Was a General Motors Strike								
0	0	0	1	0	0	0	0	0
0	0	0	0	0	0	0	0	0
0	0	0	0	0	0	0	0	0
0	0	0	0	0	0	0	0	0
0	0	0	0					

STOCK: Total Number of Cars on the Road in Millions								
79.231	79.915	80.449	80.976	81.651	82.438	83.138	83.982	84.732
85.640	86.439	87.279	88.116	89.043	89.805	90.561	91.187	91.921
92.608	92.524	93.145	93.845	95.241	95.846	96.456	97.190	97.818
98.294	98.791	99.397	99.904	100.631	101.319	102.222	102.957	103.896
104.845	105.864	106.755	107.585					

Source: Data compiled by Mark Palandri.

TABLE 9.13 U.S. Data on GNP and Its Determinants

Data are quarterly for the periods 1959.1 through 1984.4.
Entries in a row correspond to successive periods.
All variables in billions of constant 1979 dollars.

Y_t: Gross National Product								
485.1	497.8	498	502.4	516.1	514.5	517.7	513	517.4
527.9	538.5	551.5	564.4	572.2	579.2	582.8	592.1	600.3
613.1	622.1	636.9	645.6	656	660.6	682.7	695	710.7
732	754.8	764.6	777.7	790.9	799.7	805.9	822.9	837.1
862.9	886.7	903.6	917.4	943.8	957.6	976.4	978	994.2
1008.9	1027.9	1030.9	1075.2	1094.3	1113.9	1127.3	1166.5	1197.2
1223.9	1263.5	1311.6	1342.9	1369.4	1413.3	1426.2	1459.1	1489.1
1516.8	1524.6	1563.5	1627.4	1678.2	1730.9	1761.8	1794.7	1843.7
1899.1	1968.9	2031.6	2062.4	2111.4	2230.3	2289.5	2367.6	2420.5
2474.5	2546.1	2591.5	2673	2672.2	2734	2848.6	2978.8	3017.7
3099.6	3114.4	3112.6	3159.5	3179.4	3212.5	3268.7	3365.1	3437.5
3535	3676.5	3757.5	3812.2	3852.5				

M_t: Money Stock, Including Liquid Assets								
1125.7	1141.6	1161.8	1166.2	1172.4	1179.6	1195.1	1207.9	1224.1
1243.3	1262	1284.2	1310.7	1337.9	1359.2	1385.7	1417.3	1443.9
1472.5	1502.5	1526.3	1551.8	1581	1612.8	1640.8	1671.2	1706

TABLE 9.13 (*Continued*)

Mt: Money Stock, Including Liquid Assets

1742.1	1774	1800.8	1813.9	1835.2	1868.1	1903.2	1946.3	1987.3
2028.9	2068.2	2121.6	2172.5	2210.1	2235.2	2245.5	2276.4	2300.5
2330.3	2381.4	2433.2	2492.3	2557.4	2625.2	2686.7	2761.7	2840
2929.6	3031.9	3134.7	3227.9	3323.8	3400.1	3492.7	3587.6	3662.8
3727.9	3782.7	3863.9	3963.7	4070	4177.4	4288.1	4390	4505.2
4634.9	4770	4911.6	5062.4	5207.8	5347.1	5488.9	5662.3	5821.4
6007.2	6201.5	6326.3	6457.2	6570	6722.7	6908.9	7116.5	7289.5
7505.7	7731.8	7941.4	8125.701	8326.7	8517.7	8750.2	8962.5	9197.4
9408.101	9662.4	9966.9	10268.601	10517.601				

Gt: Government Expenditures

91.3	90.7	92.3	92.6	91	93.1	95	96.5	99.7
102.7	103.7	105.3	109.9	110.2	111.7	113.9	114.6	113.3
115.2	118.1	119.6	120.1	119	119.3	119.6	121.9	127.6
132.1	137.5	141.6	148.6	153.6	161.8	162.9	167.2	171.1
175.6	183.3	185.1	187.7	186.8	189.8	192.6	195.9	197.2
210.7	209.3	214.1	217.3	224.8	226.6	230.3	240.3	249.4
242.6	263.8	265.5	269	267.2	275.7	285.8	301.6	311.3
323.2	341.2	361.7	371.9	382.1	382.3	385	399.1	408.2
410.8	421.6	438.7	449.3	454.7	460.2	476.3	491.8	497.8
504.9	503.8	551	577.2	599.5	630.3	653.6	675.7	685
714.9	737.7	745.9	754	789.1	835.7	824.2	835.8	839.4
850.6	867.2	884.9	905.2	934.7				

Tt: Federal Government Receipts

88.3	92.3	90.5	91.1	98.6	97.2	96.5	95.4	95.4
97.6	99.8	103.2	104.3	106.1	108.5	109.9	112.7	115.3
116.4	117.8	116.6	113.4	116.6	118.3	124.2	125.8	124.6
128.7	138.1	142.9	145.4	147.7	149	149.7	153.6	158.1
165.9	171.2	182.5	188	198.2	201.3	199.2	200.3	195.9
197.6	194.3	193.6	198.8	201.2	202.8	208.1	227.6	228.9
232.4	240.1	256.7	260.2	264.2	273.9	281.4	291	303.4
299.8	294.2	261.7	307.3	316.3	328.5	336.4	344.2	351.4
371.6	379.6	386.7	398.4	407.2	434.9	452.1	471.4	488
498.9	510.8	522.4	539.4	535	555.3	585.6	628.2	635.8
652.4	641.7	636.7	641.1	630.3	633.1	636.3	665.2	659.7
671.1	709.4	721.8	727.1	742.1				

(*continued*)

TABLE 9.13 (*Continued*)

X_t:	U.S. Exports of Merchandise, Except for Military Aid							
3.895	3.983	4.358	4.197	4.63	4.915	5.032	4.989	5.085
4.836	5.062	5.247	5.15	5.446	5.357	5.07	6.084	5.663
5.715	5.948	6.196	6.238	6.451	6.727	5.589	6.94	6.92
7.09	7.181	7.216	7.431	7.575	7.745	7.739	7.764	7.763
8.028	8.465	9.019	8.581	7.615	9.765	9.889	10.019	10.327
10.798	10.848	10.757	11.085	11.049	11.726	9.745	11.767	11.673
12.442	13.333	15.337	16.783	18.327	20.413	22.324	24.077	25.086
26.508	27.016	25.708	27.039	27.934	27.065	28.681	29.654	29.82
29.728	30.559	31.094	29.834	30.963	35.687	37.247	39.666	41.225
42.923	47.303	50.392	52.669	54.654	56.182	57.183	59.968	58.435
57.871	57.202	55.659	54.952	52.843	48.87	50.234	48.709	50.325
51.394	53.002	53.204	55.487	55.948				

Source: Data compiled by David Arroyo.

TABLE 9.14 Annual Data for Modeling Domestic Revenue Passenger Miles

Year	POP	RPM	NOP	OPREV	GNP	ACCID	FATAL	REQU
1947	144.083	6.1	40	256	232.2	52	255	0
1948	146.73	6	44	312	257.3	67	158	0
1949	149.304	6.7	50	389	257.3	43	110	0
1950	152.271	8	54	445	284.8	41	165	0
1951	154.878	10.6	50	591	328.2	55	210	0
1952	157.553	12.5	48	695	345.4	56	157	0
1953	160.184	14.8	46	804	363.2	43	105	0
1954	163.026	16.8	47	906	361.2	54	23	0
1955	165.931	19.9	47	1065	398	46	225	0
1956	168.903	22.4	43	1193	419.2	53	156	0
1957	171.984	25.4	44	1348	442.8	51	78	0
1958	174.882	25.3	45	1432	444.5	63	149	0
1959	177.83	29.3	45	1722	482.8	69	310	0

TABLE 9.14 *(Continued)*

Year	POP	RPM	NOP	OPREV	GNP	ACCID	FATAL	REQU
1960	180.671	30.6	49	1860	507	67	378	0
1961	183.691	31.1	41	1951	520.1	58	135	0
1962	186.538	33.6	45	2167	560.3	43	183	0
1963	189.242	38.5	45	2374	589.2	49	145	0
1964	191.889	44.1	44	2701	628.7	53	226	0
1965	194.303	51.9	49	3142	691	63	253	0
1966	196.56	60.6	49	3534	749.9	54	72	0
1967	198.712	75.5	44	4260	793.5	51	255	0
1968	200.706	87.5	37	4913	865.7	54	298	0
1969	202.677	102.7	37	5943	932.3	48	152	0
1970	205.052	104.1	36	6359	1015.5	39	3	0
1971	207.661	106.4	38	6736	1063.4	41	194	0
1972	209.896	118.1	35	7565	1171	43	186	0
1973	211.909	126.3	33	8379	1307	32	217	0
1974	213.854	129.7	31	9903	1434	43	460	0
1975	215.973	131.7	35	10290	1598.4	29	122	0
1976	218.035	145.3	32	12104	1783	21	36	0
1977	220.239	156.6	32	13772	1991	18	75	0
1978	222.585	182.7	36	15753	2250	19	16	0
1979	225.055	208.9	52	18930	2508	18	352	1
1980	227.757	200.8	63	23317	2732	15	0	1
1981	230.138	198.7	98	25504	3052.6	25	4	1
1982	232.52	210.1	98	25440	3166	15	233	1
1983	234.799	226.9	96	27346	3405.7	22	15	1
1984	237.001	243.7	95	31437	3772.2	12	4	1
1985	239.279	270.6	106	33343	4014.9	17	197	1
1986	241.613	302.1	93	33814	4240.3	20	0	1
1987	243.915	324.5	93	37309	4526.7	31	231	1

Source: Statistical Abstract of United States, 1945–1989. Data compiled by Graham Rushall.

TABLE 9.15 Indices of U.S. farm Inputs and Output (with 1977 = 100)

Year	OUTPUT	LABOR	LAND	MACHINES	FERT	SEEDFEED
1948	63	285	107	62	16	52
1949	62	285	108	68	18	56
1950	61	265	109	72	19	58
1951	63	251	109	77	21	62
1952	66	237	108	81	23	63
1953	66	220	108	82	24	63
1954	66	214	108	82	24	65
1955	69	220	108	83	26	66
1956	69	212	106	84	27	69
1957	67	196	105	83	27	68
1958	73	182	104	83	28	73
1959	74	183	105	84	32	77
1960	76	177	103	83	32	77
1961	76	167	103	80	35	81
1962	77	163	104	80	38	83
1963	80	155	104	79	43	83
1964	79	148	104	80	46	85
1965	82	144	103	80	49	86
1966	79	132	102	82	56	89
1967	83	128	104	85	66	92
1968	85	124	102	86	69	89
1969	85	118	102	86	73	93
1970	84	112	105	85	75	96
1971	92	108	103	87	81	102
1972	91	110	102	86	86	104
1973	93	109	100	90	90	107
1974	88	109	99	92	92	99
1975	95	106	97	96	83	93
1976	97	100	98	98	96	101
1977	100	100	100	100	100	100
1978	104	100	100	104	107	108
1979	111	99	103	104	123	115
1980	104	96	103	101	123	114
1981	118	96	104	98	129	108
1982	116	93	102	92	118	108

TABLE 9.15 *(Continued)*

Year	OUTPUT	LABOR	LAND	MACHINES	FERT	SEEDFEED
1983	96	97	101	88	105	110
1984	112	92	97	84	121	106
1985	118	85	95	80	123	106
1986	111	80	93	75	110	103
1987	110	78	92	72	111	111
1988	102	75	91	71	113	107

Source: Economic Report of the President, 1990, Tables C-96 and C-97.

TABLE 9.16 Quarterly Data on U.S. New Car Sales and Their Determinants

Period	New Car Sales (thousands)	New Car Price Index	Per Capita Income	Population (millions)	Prime rate (%)	Unemp rate (%)
1976.1	2053.919	134.3	8932	218.035	6.75	7.6
1976.2	2410.397	134.5	8964	218.808	6.88	7.5
1976.3	1996.812	134.3	8997	219.447	7.13	7.8
1976.4	2145.445	139.2	9073	220.086	6.50	7.9
1977.1	2162.622	140.9	9097	220.239	6.25	6.8
1977.2	2574.504	141.2	9219	221.334	6.50	6.4
1977.3	2114.055	141.4	9332	221.971	6.92	6.0
1977.4	2253.273	148.1	9488	222.608	7.75	5.7
1978.1	2055.718	151.1	9638	222.585	8.00	5.4
1978.2	2775.774	152.4	9706	223.640	8.25	5.2
1978.3	2176.929	153.7	9786	224.285	9.25	5.2
1978.4	2299.577	157.0	9884	224.928	10.81	5.1
1979.1	2184.622	162.1	9753	225.055	11.75	5.8
1979.2	2261.607	165.5	9738	226.252	11.75	5.7
1979.3	1993.980	166.5	9795	226.890	12.17	5.8
1979.4	1887.846	169.9	9784	227.528	15.00	5.9
1980.1	1849.142	174.7	9788	227.757	16.46	6.2
1980.2	1550.025	178.1	9640	228.827	16.90	7.3
1980.3	1514.511	180.7	9712	229.462	11.67	7.5
1980.4	1664.574	183.6	9756	230.095	16.58	7.5
1981.1	1732.469	184.3	9806	230.138	19.50	7.4

(continued)

TABLE 9.16 (*Continued*)

Period	New Car Sales (thousands)	New Car Price Index	Per Capita Income	Population (millions)	Prime rate (%)	Unemp rate (%)
1981.2	1575.560	189.7	9819	231.126	19.00	7.4
1981.3	1617.414	191.9	9858	231.767	20.25	7.4
1981.4	1280.413	194.9	9864	232.407	17.17	8.4
1982.1	1400.688	195.8	9700	232.520	16.21	8.3
1982.2	1534.134	197.2	9743	233.659	16.50	9.3
1982.3	1327.771	198.3	9728	234.298	14.67	9.8
1982.4	1494.065	198.9	9758	234.936	12.00	10.5
1983.1	1456.922	201.2	9802	234.799	10.83	10.2
1983.2	1878.104	201.4	9856	235.895	10.50	9.9
1983.3	1646.131	202.1	9993	236.543	10.75	9.2
1983.4	1814.142	205.8	10157	237.191	11.00	8.4
1984.1	1994.609	207.2	10371	237.019	11.08	7.8
1984.2	2251.734	207.6	10413	238.326	12.25	7.4
1984.3	1854.253	208.1	10466	238.977	12.96	7.3
1984.4	1850.927	211.0	10457	239.626	11.67	7.1
1985.1	2042.281	213.7	10429	239.283	10.54	7.2
1985.2	2272.546	214.4	10617	240.634	10.17	7.2
1985.3	2217.673	214.6	10468	241.291	9.50	7.0
1985.4	1672.204	218.0	10504	241.947	9.50	6.9

Source: Wards Automotive Year Book 1977. Economic Report of the President, various years.

9.A APPENDIX

Miscellaneous Derivations

9.A.1 Proof That the DW d Is Approximately $2(1 - \hat{\rho})$

The Durbin–Watson d given in equation (9.6) can be expanded as follows:

$$d = \frac{\sum\limits_{t=2}^{t=T} \hat{u}_t^2 + \sum\limits_{t=2}^{t=T} \hat{u}_{t-1}^2 - 2\sum\limits_{t=2}^{t=T} \hat{u}_t \hat{u}_{t-1}}{\sum\limits_{t=1}^{t=T} \hat{u}_t^2} \tag{9.A.1}$$

Because the residuals $\hat{u}_t$ are generally small, the summations from 2 to T or from 1 to $T - 1$ are both approximately equal to (denoted by the symbol $\simeq$) the summation from 1 to T. Therefore

$$\sum_{t=2}^{t=T} \hat{u}_t^2 \simeq \sum_{t=2}^{t=T} \hat{u}_{t-1}^2 \simeq \sum_{t=1}^{t=T} \hat{u}_t^2$$

We note from this that the first two terms of (9.A.1) approximately cancel with the denominator, giving 2. Also the third term is the same as equation (9.7), giving $2\hat{\rho}$. It follows from this that d is approximately equal to $2(1 - \hat{\rho})$.

9.A.2 Properties of u_t When It Is AR(1)

Substituting repeatedly from equation (9.2) we get

$$u_t = \rho u_{t-1} + \epsilon_t = \epsilon_t + \rho(\epsilon_{t-1} + \rho u_{t-2}) = \epsilon_t + \rho\epsilon_{t-1} + \rho^2(\epsilon_{t-2} + \rho u_{t-3})$$
$$= \epsilon_t + \rho\epsilon_{t-1} + \rho^2\epsilon_{t-2} + \cdots$$

Because $E(\epsilon_t) = 0$, we have $E(u_t) = 0$. Also, by the independence of the ϵs,

$$\sigma_u^2 = \mathrm{Var}(u_t) = \mathrm{Var}(\epsilon_t) + \rho^2\mathrm{Var}(\epsilon_{t-1}) + \rho^4\mathrm{Var}(\epsilon_{t-2}) + \cdots$$

$$= \sigma_\epsilon^2(1 + \rho^2 + \rho^4 + \cdots) = \frac{\sigma_\epsilon^2}{1 - \rho^2} \tag{9.A.2}$$

Note that the infinite series will sum to a finite value only if $|\rho| < 1$. Thus, a necessary condition for stationarity is that the first-order autocorrelation be strictly less than 1 in absolute value. If $\rho = 1$, the error process becomes $u_t = u_{t-1} + \epsilon_t$. The value of u at time t is therefore equal to its value in the previous period plus a purely random effect. This process is known as the *random walk model* and is frequently used in modeling stock price behavior using the "efficient markets" theory, which states that the change in a price from one period to the next is purely random. The covariance between u_t and u_{t-s}, for $s \neq 0$, is given by

$$E(u_t u_{t-s}) = E[(\epsilon_t + \rho_{t-1} + \rho^2 \epsilon_{t-2} + \cdots)(\epsilon_{t-s} + \rho \epsilon_{t-s-1} + \rho^2 \epsilon_{t-s-2} + \cdots)]$$

All the cross-product terms of the type $\epsilon_t \epsilon_{t-s}$, $\epsilon_{t-1} \epsilon_{t-s}$, and so on have zero expectations because ϵ_t and ϵ_{t-s} are, by assumption, independent. Only the square terms ϵ_{t-s}^2, ϵ_{t-s-1}^2, and so on remain. Therefore

$$\begin{aligned}
E(u_t u_{t-s}) &= E(\rho^s \epsilon_{t-s}^2 + \rho^{s+2} \epsilon_{t-s-1}^2 + \rho^{s+4} \epsilon_{t-s-2}^2 + \cdots) \\
&= \rho^s \sigma_\epsilon^2 (1 + \rho^2 + \rho^4 + \cdots) \\
&= \frac{\rho^s \sigma_\epsilon^2}{1 - \rho^2} = \rho^s \sigma_u^2
\end{aligned}$$

(9.A.3)

The coefficient of correlation between u_t and u_s [denoted by $r(s)$] is known as the **autocorrelation function** and is given by

$$r(s) = \frac{\text{Cov}(u_t, u_{t-s})}{\text{Var}(u_t)} = \rho^s$$

Since $|\rho| < 1$, as s increases (which means that as you move further into the past) the autocorrelation function decreases in absolute value, the rate of decline being dependent on the numerical value of ρ. At any rate, the error terms are correlated, violating the OLS assumption that they are not.

9.A.3   Treatment of the First Observation Under AR(1)

In describing the Cochrane–Orcutt procedure we transformed the first observation as follows:

$$Y_1^* = Y_1(1 - \rho^2)^{1/2} \quad \text{and} \quad X_{1i}^* = X_{1i}(1 - \rho^2)^{1/2} \quad (9.A.4)$$

To see the justification for this, note that the first observation is

$$Y_1 = \beta_1 + \beta_2 X_2 + \beta_3 X_3 + \cdots + \beta_k X_{1k} + u_1 \quad (9.A.5)$$

Equation (9.2) is not defined for the first observation because u_0 is undefined. From equation (9.A.2) the variance of u_t is $\sigma_\epsilon^2/(1 - \rho^2)$. Suppose we define u_1 to be equal to $\epsilon_1/(1 - \rho^2)^{1/2}$. Then

$$\text{Var}(u_1) = \frac{1}{1 - \rho^2} \text{Var}(\epsilon) = \frac{\sigma_\epsilon^2}{1 - \rho^2}$$

which is in conformity with equation (9.A.2). Equation (9.A.5) now becomes

$$Y_1 = \beta_1 + \beta_2 X_2 + \beta_3 X_3 + \cdots + \beta_k X_{1k} + \frac{\epsilon_1}{(1 - \rho^2)^{1/2}} \qquad (9.A.6)$$

Multiplying through by $(1 - \rho^2)^{1/2}$ and using (9.A.4), we get equation (9.8) for $t = 1$ also. We therefore see that this treatment of the first observation enables us to include it in the estimation, but with a slightly different transformation for the first observation.

PART V

SPECIAL TOPICS

This part covers a number of more advanced topics. Instructors can choose from these topics depending on interest and availability of time. Chapter 10 describes how one models the effects of lags in economic behavior that arise because the effects of policy changes are not instantaneous. Problems associated with modeling such lagged behavior are also addressed here. Chapter 11 discusses in detail how forecasts of economic variables can be generated. Both the econometric and time series approaches to forecasting are discussed, as well as the techniques for optimally combining forecasts from different models. The treatment of binary dependent variables and limited dependent variables (e.g., variables that take only positive values or that lie between 0 and 1) are covered in Chapter 12. Chapter 13 is concerned with special problems that arise when a relationship that a researcher is interested in estimating is actually part of a system of several relationships. In other words, the model *specification involves several simultaneous equations. In this*

chapter a detailed analysis of two-equation models is presented

with a brief introduction to extensions for lagged models.

CHAPTER 10

Distributed Lag Models

■ The impact of policy changes is almost never instantaneous but requires some time to be felt. As was illustrated in Section 4.6, the gross national product in a given quarter depends on the money supply and government expenditure not only in that quarter but on those values in previous quarters as well. Similarly, the lagged dependent variable might appear as a regressor. For example, consumption at time t might depend on consumption at time $t - 1$, partly because of habit formation and typical consumer resistance to radical changes in life styles. To capture this lag in behavior, the specification of time series models often includes lagged values of the dependent and independent variables. The inclusion of lagged variables as regressors often creates problems. This chapter examines these problems and suggests solutions to them. The cases of lagged independent variables and lagged dependent variables are treated separately.

10.1 Lagged Independent Variables

Suppose the model under consideration is

$$Y_t = \alpha + \beta_0 X_t + \beta_1 X_{t-1} + \cdots + \beta_p X_{t-p} + u_t \qquad (10.1)$$

In this model, called a **distributed lag model**, only current and lagged values of X—that is, **lagged independent variables**—are used to predict Y_t. As an example, let Y_t be the consumption of electricity at the tth hour of a day and X_t be the temperature at that hour. In the summer, if the temperatures during successive hours are high, the interiors of buildings heat up (this is called the "heat build-up effect"); and hence electricity consumption is likely to depend not only on the current temperature but also on recent past temperatures. The coefficient β_0 is the weight attached to X_t; it is also $\Delta Y_t / \Delta X_t$, the average increase in Y_t when X_t is increased by one unit. β_0 is known as the **impact multiplier**—that is, it is the marginal effect of X on Y in the same time period. β_i is $\Delta Y_t / \Delta X_{t-i}$, the average increase in Y_t for a unit increase in X_{t-i}, that is, for a unit increase in X made i periods prior to t. It is also the average increase in Y an i number of periods from now when X is increased now by one unit. β_i is known as the **interim multiplier of order i**. These points are illustrated in the following example.

Example 10.1

From basic macroeconomic theory it is known that changes in the money supply induce changes in the interest rate. However, we would expect the changes to take place over a period of time. For simplicity, let us assume that other variables, such as government expenditure, do not significantly affect interest rates. The following specification assumes a fourth-order lag in behavior:

$$R_t = \alpha + \beta_0 M_t + \beta_1 M_{t-1} + \beta_2 M_{t-2} + \beta_3 M_{t-3} + \beta_4 M_{t-4} + u_t \quad (10.2)$$

where R is the interest rate and M is the money supply. Table 10.1 has quarterly data for the United States on these two variables for the 100 quarters 1960.1 through 1984.4. When the model was estimated using the OLS procedure, the Durbin–Watson statistic was 0.502. It is evident from Tables A.5a and A.5b that such a low DW statistic indicates the presence of serial correlation. The model was therefore estimated by the mixed Hildreth–Lu and Cochrane–Orcutt procedure for first-order autocorrelation. The estimated model is as follows (see Practice Computer Session 10.1):

$$\hat{R}_t = 4.312 + 0.019 M_t - 0.026 M_{t-1} + 0.030 M_{t-2} - 0.022 M_{t-3} - 0.002 M_{t-4}$$
$$\phantom{\hat{R}_t =} (3.5) \quad (2.5) \quad\quad (-2.4) \quad\quad (2.8) \quad\quad (-2.0) \quad\quad (-0.2)$$

Other things being equal, an increase in money supply is expected to decrease the interest rate. We note, however, that some of the coefficients are positive, which is contrary to expectation. The main reason for such coefficients is the strong multicollinearity among the lagged money supply variables. In fact the correlation between every pair of explanatory variables is over 0.999. We saw in Chapter 5 that multicollinearity can cause a reversal of signs. The impact multiplier is 0.019 and the other coefficients are the interim multipliers; but because other determinants of the interest rate are not in the model, these numbers should not be taken seriously. □

Suppose the economy were in a **steady state** (also known as the **long-run equilibrium**) in which all the variables were constant over time. Denoting the long-run value with an asterisk, the steady-state relation becomes ($u_t = 0$ in the steady state)

$$Y^* = \alpha + \beta_0 X^* + \beta_1 X^* + \cdots + \beta_p X^* = \alpha + X^*(\beta_0 + \beta_1 + \cdots + \beta_p)$$

This gives the cumulative effect over time as $\Delta Y^* / \Delta X^* = \beta_0 + \beta_1 + \cdots + \beta_p$, which is known as the **long-run multiplier**. In Example 10.1, the sum of the multipliers is given by -0.001. The long-run monetary multiplier is therefore quite small.

TABLE 10.1 Data on U.S. Interest Rate and Money Supply

Data are quarterly for the United States for the period 1960.1 through 1984.4.
Entries in a row are for consecutive periods.

R_t: Interest Rate in Percent

4.02	3.36	3.07	2.86	2.88	3.06	3.06	3.18	3.06
3.03	3.06	3.01	3.03	3.2	3.57	3.81	3.91	3.83
3.84	4.02	4.06	3.99	4.2	4.72	4.97	4.97	5.82
5.2	4.35	4.48	5.24	5.71	5.58	5.98	5.44	6.19
6.34	7.04	7.82	8.17	6.97	7.55	6.73	5	3.69
5.64	5.41	4.6	4.67	4.93	5.52	5.52	6.85	7.31
8.31	7.27	7.76	8.67	8.87	7.31	6.11	6.29	7.75
6.6	6.21	6.52	5.84	4.89	5.5	5.8	6.53	6.96
7.31	8.09	8.64	10.3	10.25	9.57	10.84	11.98	15.82
8.16	11.52	14.88	13.71	14.86	16.52	12.85	13.95	14.07
10.85	8.91	9.04	9.66	10.16	10.11	10.59	12.08	11.58
9.33								

M_t: Money Supply in Billions of 1979 Dollars

1172.4	1179.6	1195.1	1207.9	1224.1	1243.3	1262	1284.2	1310.7
1337.9	1359.2	1385.7	1417.3	1443.9	1472.5	1502.5	1526.3	1551.8
1581	1612.8	1640.8	1671.2	1706	1742.1	1774	1800.8	1813.9
1835.2	1868.1	1903.2	1946.3	1987.3	2028.9	2068.2	2121.6	2172.5
2210.1	2235.2	2245.5	2276.4	2300.5	2330.3	2381.4	2433.2	2492.3
2557.4	2625.2	2686.7	2761.7	2840	2929.6	3031.9	3134.7	3227.9
3323.8	3400.1	3492.7	3587.6	3662.8	3727.9	3782.7	3863.9	3963.7
4070	4177.4	4288.1	4390	4505.2	4634.9	4770	4911.6	5062.4
5207.8	5347.1	5488.9	5662.3	5821.4	6007.2	6201.5	6326.3	6457.2
6570	6722.7	6908.9	7116.5	7289.5	7505.7	7731.8	7941.4	8125.701
8326.7	8517.7	8750.2	8962.5	9197.4	9408.101	9662.4	9966.9	10,268.601
10,517.601								

Source: City base data series.

From the β's we can construct a weighted average of these lags to get a **mean lag**, or **average lag**. The general expression is as follows:

$$\text{mean lag} = \frac{\sum_{i=0}^{i=p} i\beta_i}{\sum_{i=0}^{i=p} \beta_i} = \frac{\beta_1 + 2\beta_2 + 3\beta_3 + \cdots + p\beta_p}{\beta_0 + \beta_1 + \beta_2 + \cdots + \beta_p} \tag{10.3}$$

If we used quarterly data and specified four lags, the mean lag would take the form $(\beta_1 + 2\beta_2 + 3\beta_3 + 4\beta_4)/(\beta_0 + \beta_1 + \beta_2 + \beta_3 + \beta_4)$. If the mean lag were 3.4, then, on average, the lag would be between three and four periods. It is easy to verify that the mean lag for the preceding example is 40, which is unrealistically high. When some of the estimated β's are negative, as in our case, the mean lag is not a very useful concept.

Because $X_t, X_{t-1}, \ldots, X_{t-p}$ are all uncorrelated with u_t, the least squares procedure will give estimates that are BLUE and consistent. Nevertheless, several difficulties are commonly encountered here. The value of p, the largest lag, is often unknown. In this case we may be tempted to specify a large value for p. But this creates multicollinearity problems because of close relations among $X_t, X_{t-1}, \ldots,$ X_{t-p}. We encountered severe multicollinearity even when only four lags were used. Second, a large value for p means a considerable loss in degrees of freedom because we can only use the observations in the range $p + 1$ through T. As we know, lower degrees of freedom imply a worsening in the precision of the estimates (that is, their efficiency) and a reduction in the power of tests of hypotheses. It is therefore desirable to devise methods that will alleviate these difficulties. The typical approach is to impose some structure on the β's and reduce from $p + 1$ to a few the number of parameters to be estimated. Only two of the methods are presented here. Details on additional methods are available from the books by Kmenta (1986) and Judge, Griffiths, Hill, and Lee (1985).

Koyck Lag (or Geometric Lag)

Koyck (1954) proposed a geometrically declining scheme for the β's, a scheme now known as the **Koyck** (or **geometric**) **lag**. More specifically, he assumed that $\beta_i = \lambda\beta_{i-1}$, with $0 < \lambda < 1$. Thus, the weight for period i is a fraction of the weight for the previous period. By repeated substitution we get $\beta_i = \beta_0\lambda^i$, which gives a geometrically decreasing set of weights. Making the largest lag ($_p$) infinitely large, we have

$$Y_t = \alpha + \beta_0 X_t + \beta_0\lambda X_{t-1} + \beta_0\lambda^2 X_{t-2} + \cdots + u_t$$

Note that the coefficients decline geometrically (see Figure 10.1) and that there are only three unknown parameters: α, β_0, and λ. The assumption is that the biggest impact of X is felt immediately and that subsequent effects gradually decline to zero. However, because the series is infinite, we cannot use it to estimate β_0 and λ directly. To simplify it, first write down the series for Y_{t-1}:

$$Y_{t-1} = \alpha + \beta_0 X_{t-1} + \beta_0\lambda X_{t-2} + \beta_0\lambda^2 X_{t-3} + \cdots + u_{t-1}$$

Next multiply it term by term by λ, subtract from the above, and cancel common terms. We then get

$$Y_t - \lambda Y_{t-1} = \alpha(1 - \lambda) + \beta_0 X_t + u_t - \lambda u_{t-1}$$

or

$$Y_t = \alpha^* + \lambda Y_{t-1} + \beta_0 X_t + v_t \qquad (10.4)$$

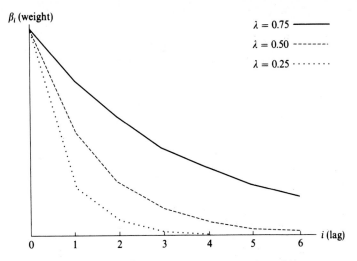

β_i (weight)

$\lambda = 0.75$ ———

$\lambda = 0.50$ --------

$\lambda = 0.25$ ·······

i (lag)

0 1 2 3 4 5 6

Figure 10.1 Koyck (or geometric) distributed lag

where $\alpha^* = \alpha(1 - \lambda)$. Thus, the Koyck lag procedure is a convenient way to reduce the number of parameters in a distributed lag model, provided the declining geometric approximation is reasonable. In the electricity consumption example this is sensible, because we would expect the largest impact to be due to the temperature at the time period t, with smaller impacts due to temperatures at time periods $t - 1$, $t - 2$, and so on. The mean lag for this case depends only on λ and is given by

$$\text{mean geometric lag} = \frac{\lambda\beta_0 + 2\lambda^2\beta_0 + 3\lambda^3\beta_0 + \cdots}{\beta_0 + \lambda\beta_0 + \lambda^2\beta_0 + \cdots} = \frac{\lambda}{1 - \lambda}$$

Note that equation (10.4) now has Y_{t-1}, which is a lagged dependent variable. Furthermore, the error term is not autocorrelated but has a different structure, known as a **moving average**, that will be discussed in detail in the next chapter. The estimation of this model creates a number of problems that are discussed in Section 10.2.

Practice Problems

10.1   Verify that the long-run multiplier is $\beta_0/(1 - \lambda)$.

Almon Lag (or Polynomial Lag)

An alternative procedure is the **Almon** (or **polynomial**) **lag**. Proposed by Almon (1965), it assumes that the coefficient β_i can be approximated by a polynomial in i, so that

$$\beta_i = f(i) = \alpha_0 + \alpha_1 i + \alpha_2 i^2 + \cdots + \alpha_r i^r$$

Because continuous functions can generally be approximated by a polynomial, this procedure is quite flexible. Figure 10.2 illustrates two commonly assumed

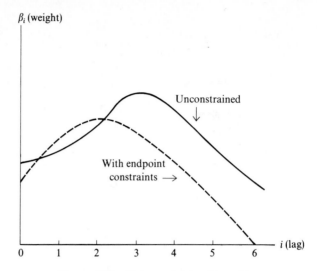

Figure 10.2 Polynomial (or Almon) lag

shapes that are reasonable in many circumstances. In one of them, endpoint constraints such as $\beta_{-1} = \beta_{p+1} = 0$ are imposed; the other is unconstrained. When there has been a change in government policy (for example, the enactment of a new tax law), we might expect the immediate effect to be negligible. The main effect may be felt in two or three quarters, and thereafter the effect might decline again. A second- or third-degree polynomial is often adequate to capture the shape underlying this behavior. The Almon procedure, however, requires the prior selection of the degree of polynomial (r) and the period of the largest lag used in the model (p). Unlike in the Koyck lag procedure, p in the Almon procedure must be finite. Suppose we choose $r = 3$ and $p = 4$—that is, a cubic polynomial and a lag of four periods. We then have

$$\beta_0 = f(0) = \alpha_0$$
$$\beta_1 = f(1) = \alpha_0 + \alpha_1 + \alpha_2 + \alpha_3$$
$$\beta_2 = f(2) = \alpha_0 + 2\alpha_1 + 4\alpha_2 + 8\alpha_3$$
$$\beta_3 = f(3) = \alpha_0 + 3\alpha_1 + 9\alpha_2 + 27\alpha_3$$
$$\beta_4 = f(4) = \alpha_0 + 4\alpha_1 + 16\alpha_2 + 64\alpha_3$$

Substituting these in the model and grouping terms we get

$$
\begin{aligned}
Y_t ={}& \alpha + \alpha_0 X_t + (\alpha_0 + \alpha_1 + \alpha_2 + \alpha_3)X_{t-1} + (\alpha_0 + 2\alpha_1 + 4\alpha_2 + 8\alpha_3)X_{t-2} \\
&+ (\alpha_0 + 3\alpha_1 + 9\alpha_2 + 27\alpha_3)X_{t-3} + (\alpha_0 + 4\alpha_1 + 16\alpha_2 + 64\alpha_3)X_{t-4} + u_t \\
={}& \alpha + \alpha_0(X_t + X_{t-1} + X_{t-2} + X_{t-3} + X_{t-4}) \\
&+ \alpha_1(X_{t-1} + 2X_{t-2} + 3X_{t-3} + 4X_{t-4}) \\
&+ \alpha_2(X_{t-1} + 4X_{t-2} + 9X_{t-3} + 16X_{t-4}) \\
&+ \alpha_3(X_{t-1} + 8X_{t-2} + 27X_{t-3} + 64X_{t-4}) + u_t
\end{aligned}
$$

The unknown α's, and hence the β's, are readily estimated because the variables in parentheses can be obtained through appropriate transformations. If α_3 is insignificiant, we may use a second-degree polynomial. If we wish to include additional terms, we may easily do this also. We may change r and p and choose those that maximize $\bar{R}^2$.

Example 10.2

The polynomial lag approach was used by Almon to estimate the relation between capital expenditures in manufacturing industries and past appropriations in those industries. Quarterly observations were used for the period 1953– 1961. The model was

$$E_t = \alpha_1 S_{t1} + \alpha_2 S_{t2} + \alpha_3 S_{t3} + \alpha_4 S_{t4} + \beta_0 A_t + \beta_1 A_{t-1} + \cdots + \beta_p A_{t-p} + u_t$$

where E_t is capital expenditures at time t (in millions of dollars); A_t, A_{t-1}, and so on are appropriations at time periods t, $t-1$, and so on (also in millions of dollars); and S_{t1}, S_{t2}, S_{t3}, and S_{t4} are seasonal dummies. Almon chose to include all the seasonal dummies without a constant term. The estimated model for all manufacturing industries is (standard errors in parentheses)

$$\hat{E}_t = -283 S_{t1} + 13 S_{t2} - 50 S_{t3} + 320 S_{t4} + \underset{(0.023)}{0.048} A_t + \underset{(0.016)}{0.099} A_{t-1}$$

$$+ \underset{(0.013)}{0.141} A_{t-2} + \underset{(0.023)}{0.165} A_{t-3} + \underset{(0.023)}{0.167} A_{t-4} + \underset{(0.013)}{0.146} A_{t-5} + \underset{(0.016)}{0.105} A_{t-6}$$

$$+ \underset{(0.024)}{0.053} A_{t-7}$$

$$\bar{R}^2 = 0.922 \qquad \text{DW } d = 0.890$$

The model was estimated under the endpoint constraints $\beta_{-1} = \beta_8 = 0$. Figure 10.3 graphs the estimated weights. Although the goodness of fit is very good,

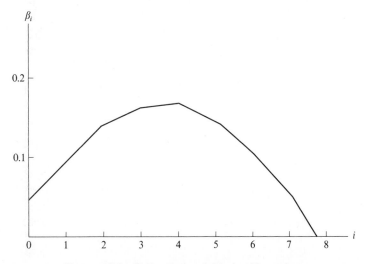

Figure 10.3 Estimated weights for Almon lags

it may be misleading because the Durbin–Watson statistic indicates the presence of serial correlation. Almon tried a number of variations of the model, the details of which may be found in the paper. The standard errors in parentheses indicate that the weights for the lagged capital appropriations are significant. The mean lag is computed as

$$\frac{0.099 + 2(0.141) + 3(0.165) + 4(0.167) + 5(0.146) + 6(0.105) + 7(0.053)}{0.048 + 0.099 + 0.141 + 0.165 + 0.167 + 0.146 + 0.105 + 0.053}$$

which comes to 3.544. Thus, the average lag is almost four quarters.

Practice Problem

10.2   Assume that $r = 2$ and $p = 4$ (that is, a quadratic distributed lag) and derive the estimable econometric model. Describe how you will estimate the relevant parameters.

Other Types of Lag Structures

A number of other schemes for reducing the number of parameters in a distributed lag model have also been proposed. We list them here without any discussion. They include *Pascal lag*, *rational lag*, *gamma lag*, *LaGuerre lag*, and *Shiller lag*. Kmenta (1986) gives an excellent treatment of these approaches.

Empirical Example: The Monetary-Fiscal Policy Debate

Over the past several decades, there has been an ongoing debate regarding the relative effectiveness of monetary and fiscal policies. "Monetarists" argue that the money supply is more important in determining the level of economic activity than government expenditure and taxes. "Keynesians" or "Fiscalists" contend that fiscal policy (as measured by government expenditure and taxes) is more effective in determining GNP, employment, interest rate, and so on. Numerous empirical studies have tried to resolve the debate but with mixed results. Many of these studies used the Almon lag technique to measure the impact of policy variables. Schmidt and Waud (1973) have pointed out a number of pitfalls in using this procedure. They have also reexamined two studies of the relative importance of monetary and fiscal policy and argued that insufficient attention to model specification and estimation can lead to misleading results. In this section we present a portion of the Schmidt–Waud paper.

One of the models estimated is of the following form:

$$\Delta GNP_t = \alpha + \beta_0 \Delta M_t + \beta_1 \Delta M_{t-1} + \cdots + \beta_3 \Delta M_{t-4}$$
$$+ \gamma_0 \Delta E_t + \cdots + \delta_0 \Delta R_t + \cdots + u_t$$

where Δ denotes the change in a variable from period $t - 1$ to t (for example, $\Delta M = M_t - M_{t-1}$), GNP is gross national product, M is money supply (currency plus demand deposits), E is federal expenditure, and R is federal tax receipts. The model was originally estimated by Andersen and Jordan (1968) using quarterly data for the period 1952.1 through 1968.2. They assumed that $r = 4$ and $p = 3$ and used the endpoint constraints that $\beta_{-1} = 0$ and $\beta_4 = 0$. Table 10.2 shows their

TABLE 10.2 Andersen–Jordan (Constrained) and Schmidt–Waud
(Constrained) Estimates (1952.1–1968.2)

	Regression Coefficients (t-statistics)					
	Constrained A–J			Constrained S–W		
Lag	ΔM	ΔE	ΔR	ΔM	ΔE	ΔR
0	1.95 (2.66)	0.41 (1.31)	0.12 (0.41)	1.13 (2.75)	0.74 (3.19)	0.02 (0.09)
1	1.37 (2.43)	0.53 (2.15)	0.05 (0.21)	1.46 (4.48)	0.48 (2.58)	−0.11 (−0.51)
2	1.07 (1.91)	−0.04 (−0.15)	0.00 (0.00)	1.29 (4.65)	−0.05 (−0.33)	−0.23 (−0.91)
3	1.34 (1.90)	−0.72 (−2.48)	0.01 (0.02)	0.87 (2.53)	−0.39 (−2.06)	−0.25 (−0.96)
4	0	0	0	0.40 (1.34)	−0.34 (−2.06)	−0.16 (−0.66)
5				0.05 (0.15)	0.01 (0.04)	0.00 (0.01)
6				−0.10 (−0.28)	0.33 (1.64)	0.12 (0.47)
7				0	0	0
Sum	5.74 (6.84)	0.19 (0.38)	0.18 (0.25)	5.09 (4.03)	0.76 (1.00)	−0.62 (−0.55)
Const.	1.94 (1.75)			3.27 (2.07)		
S.E.	4.17			3.85		
$\bar{R}^2$	0.59			0.62		
D.W.	1.84			2.16		

ΔM, ΔE, and ΔR are the changes in the narrow money stock, high employment federal expenditures, and high employment federal receipts, respectively.
Source: Schmidt and Waud (1973), Table 1, p. 15. Reprinted with the permission of the American Statistical Association.

results. Andersen and Jordan concluded that fiscal policy is not an important determinant of aggregate economic activity. Schmidt and Waud allowed for more lags (that is, varied p) and chose the one that maximized $\bar{R}^2$ (or equivalently, minimized $\hat{\sigma}^2$). Table 10.2 shows their results also. Note that the Schmidt–Waud estimates do not support Andersen–Jordan's contention that fiscal policy is ineffective.

Corrigan (1970) criticized the Andersen–Jordan study on two grounds: first that they did not maximize $\bar{R}^2$ by letting both p and r vary, and second that the manner in which they measured changes in fiscal policy was not proper. Corrigan argued that not all of government receipts and expenditures are exogenous. Part of them, especially tax receipts, are automatic responses to changes in aggregate economic activity. He constructed different measures (called "initial stimulus") for expenditures and receipts. In this reexamination, however, Corrigan used only a second-degree polynomial but searched over lags for many periods and assumed different lags for the independent variables. His conclusion (see Table 10.3) was that fiscal policy does indeed matter in determining GNP. Schmidt and Waud extended the analysis further by letting both p and r vary and by dropping the endpoint constraints. Their results are also presented in Table 10.3.

The findings show that fiscal policy can neither be ruled out as ineffectual nor be claimed to have a strong influence on changes in GNP. Also, the signs of regression coefficients switch in all three independent variables. Schmidt–Waud's analysis emphasizes how important it is to pay attention to methodological issues and how sensitive the results can be to model specifications.

TABLE 10.3 Corrigan and Schmidt–Waud (Minimum s.e.) Estimates (1952.1–1968.2)

	Corrigan's Min. s.e., Second-Degree Polynomial			S–W Min. s.e., Fourth-Degree Polynomial		
Lag	ΔM	ΔCE	ΔCR	ΔM	ΔCE	ΔCR
0	1.1 (2.2)	0.3 (1.2)	0.0 (0.2)	2.11 (2.76)	−0.01 (−0.05)	−0.27 (−0.78)
1	1.2 (6.0)	0.4 (2.7)	0.3 (1.9)	0.72 (0.83)	0.55 (1.87)	0.16 (0.31)
2	1.1 (3.7)	0.4 (1.8)	0.4 (3.6)	1.58 (2.68)	0.63 (2.08)	−0.08 (−0.22)
3	0.7 (2.6)		0.5 (4.0)	1.53 (2.89)	−0.44 (−1.51)	−0.28 (−0.73)
4			0.6 (4.0)	0.10 (0.11)	−0.67 (−2.44)	−0.12 (−0.30)
5			0.5 (3.8)	−0.40 (−0.48)		0.36 (1.01)
6			0.4 (3.7)			0.72 (1.32)
7			0.2 (3.6)			0.16 (0.41)
8						
Sum	4.1	1.1	3.1	5.64 (5.07)	0.05 (0.12)	0.65 (0.40)
Const.	(No Figure Reported)			2.87 (3.23)		
S.E.	4.1			3.75		
$\bar{R}^2$	0.6			0.64		
D.W.	1.5			1.92		

ΔM is as in Table 9.2. ΔCE is Corrigan's initial stimulus government spending component. ΔCR is Corrigan's initial stimulus tax component.
Source: Schmidt and Waud (1973), Table 5, p. 17. Reprinted with the permission of the American Statistical Association.

10.2   Lagged Dependent Variables

As mentioned earlier, the presence of the **lagged dependent** (or endogenous) **variable** as a regressor is quite common in economics. In the Koyck lag transformation used previously, Y_{t-1} appears as a regressor. Two other common specifications involving lagged dependent variables are given in the following sections.

Partial Adjustment Model

Suppose Y_t^* is the desired level of inventories of a firm, Y_t is the actual level, and X_t is the sales. Assume that the desired level of inventories depends on sales as

$$Y_t^* = \alpha + \beta X_t \tag{10.5}$$

Because of "frictions" in the market, the gap between the actual and desired levels cannot be closed instantaneously but only with some lag and random shocks. Suppose only a fraction of the gap is closed each period. In this case, the inventory at time t would equal that at time $t - 1$, plus an adjustment factor, plus a random error term. More formally,

$$Y_t = Y_{t-1} + \lambda(Y_t^* - Y_{t-1}) + u_t \qquad 0 < \lambda < 1 \tag{10.6}$$

This model is called the **partial adjustment model**. The parameter λ is called the **adjustment coefficient** and $1/\lambda$ is called the **speed of adjustment**. The adjustment coefficient approximates the fraction of the gap closed in one period. The speed of adjustment approximates the number of periods it takes for most of the adjustment to take place. Thus, if $\hat{\lambda} = 0.25$, approximately 25 percent of the gap will be closed in one period, and the number of periods of adjustment is 4. If the desired inventories Y_t^* exceed the actual inventories at the end of the time period $t - 1$, we would expect part of that gap to close in the period t, and hence Y_t will go up by $\lambda(Y_t^* - Y_{t-1})$ plus an unpredictable random shock. Combining (10.5) and (10.6) we get the model

$$\begin{aligned} Y_t &= \alpha\lambda + (1 - \lambda)Y_{t-1} + \beta\lambda X_t + u_t \\ &= \beta_0 + \beta_1 Y_{t-1} + \beta_2 X_t + u_t \end{aligned} \tag{10.7}$$

Practice Problem

10.3   Suppose $\hat{\beta}_1 = 0.667$ and $\beta_2 = 0.3$. Estimate β and λ from this. What is the marginal effect of sales on (a) desired and (b) actual inventories? What is the average number of periods required for the gap between desired and actual inventories to be closed?

Adaptive Expectations Model

Another model that has a lagged dependent variable is the **adaptive expectations model**. Suppose Y_t is consumption, X_t^* is expected income, and X_t is actual income. Consumption is assumed to be related not to current income but to expected income. Thus

$$Y_t = \alpha + \beta X_t^* + u_t \tag{10.8}$$

β is the marginal propensity to consume out of expected income. This equation cannot be estimated in practice because X_t^* is typically unobservable and hence there are no data on it. We therefore need to impose additional structure on the model. Assume that consumers revise their expectations based on how well their earlier expectations were realized. The change in expectation, $X_t^* - X_{t-1}^*$, is assumed to depend on the gap between X_{t-1} and X_{t-1}^*, as follows:

$$X_t^* - X_{t-1}^* = \lambda(X_{t-1} - X_{t-1}^*) \qquad 0 < \lambda < 1 \qquad (10.9)$$

If actual income in period $t - 1$ exceeds expectations, we would expect consumers to revise their expectation upward. Equation (10.9) thus becomes

$$X_t^* = \lambda X_{t-1} + (1 - \lambda)X_{t-1}^*$$

We can solve equation (10.8) for X_t^* in terms of Y_t as $X_t^* = (Y_t - \alpha - u_t)/\beta$. Substituting this in the above equation and rearranging terms, we get

$$\frac{Y_t - \alpha - u_t}{\beta} = \lambda X_{t-1} + (1 - \lambda)\left(\frac{Y_{t-1} - \alpha - u_{t-1}}{\beta}\right)$$

Multiplying throughout by β, keeping only Y_t on the left-hand side, and grouping terms, we obtain the following estimable econometric model:

$$\begin{aligned} Y_t &= \alpha\lambda + (1 - \lambda)Y_{t-1} + \lambda\beta X_{t-1} + u_t - (1 - \lambda)u_{t-1} \\ &= \beta_0 + \beta_1 Y_{t-1} + \beta_2 X_{t-1} + v_t \end{aligned} \qquad (10.10)$$

where $\beta_0 = \alpha\lambda$, $\beta_1 = 1 - \lambda$, $\beta_2 = \lambda\beta$, and $v_t = u_t - (1 - \lambda)u_{t-1}$. The error term in equation (10.10) is of the moving average form, encountered in equation (10.4), which is examined more closely in this chapter in the section on estimation procedures as well as in Chapter 11 on forecasting. Once estimates of the β's have been obtained, α, β, and λ can be estimated as follows:

$$\hat{\lambda} = 1 - \hat{\beta}_1, \qquad \hat{\alpha} = \frac{\hat{\beta}_0}{\hat{\lambda}}, \qquad \hat{\beta} = \frac{\hat{\beta}_2}{\hat{\lambda}}$$

It is interesting to note that we are able to estimate the marginal propensity to consume out of expected income even though there are no data on expected income. This illustrates how one can incorporate unobserved variables in a model and still estimate unknown parameters, provided additional structure is imposed.

The regression coefficient β_2 is $\Delta Y_t/\Delta X_{t-1}$ and is hence the one-period interim multiplier of X on Y. To get the long-run multiplier, set $u_t = 0$, $Y_t = Y^*$, and $X_t = X^*$ for all t. We then have $\hat{Y}^* = \hat{\beta}_0 + \hat{\beta}_1 \hat{Y}^* + \hat{\beta}_2 X^*$. The estimated long-run relation becomes $\hat{Y}^* = (\hat{\beta}_0 + \hat{\beta}_2 X^*)/(1 - \hat{\beta}_1)$. It follows that the estimated long-run multiplier is

$$\frac{\Delta\hat{Y}^*}{\Delta X^*} = \frac{\hat{\beta}_2}{1 - \hat{\beta}_1} = \hat{\beta} \qquad (10.11)$$

Practice Problem

10.4 Using the same estimates of β_1 and β_2 as in Practice Problem 10.3, estimate the impact multiplier, the long-run multiplier, and the interim multiplier for two, three, and four periods (the interim multiplier for period i is $\Delta Y_t / \Delta X_{t-i}$).

Consequences of Ignoring Lagged Dependent Variables

Why should we be concerned about the presence of lagged dependent variables as regressors? Why not treat them as any other lagged variable? In other words, why not regress Y_t against a constant, Y_{t-1}, and X_t; then obtain $\hat{\beta}_0$, $\hat{\beta}_1$, and $\hat{\beta}_2$; and finally solve for α, β, and λ? This question is examined with the following simple model. The results generalize to more complicated models.

$$Y_t = \beta Y_{t-1} + u_t \qquad (10.12)$$

in which u_t is assumed to satisfy all the assumptions made in Chapter 3. In particular, we assume that $E(Y_{t-1} u_t) = 0$—that is, that Y_{t-1} is uncorrelated with u_t. This assumption is quite sensible because the current disturbance u_t cannot affect last period's value of the dependent variable.

The least squares estimate of β is

$$\hat{\beta} = \frac{\displaystyle\sum_{t=2}^{t=T} Y_t Y_{t-1}}{\displaystyle\sum_{t=2}^{t=T} Y_t^2}$$

Substituting for Y_t from the model and separating the β term, we get

$$\hat{\beta} = \beta + \frac{\displaystyle\sum_{t=2}^{t=T} u_t Y_{t-1}}{\displaystyle\sum_{t=2}^{t=T} Y_t^2}$$

$$= \beta + \frac{u_2 Y_1 + u_3 Y_2 + \cdots + u_T Y_{T-1}}{Y_2^2 + Y_3^2 + \cdots + Y_T^2}$$

Even though Y_{t-1} and u_t may be uncorrelated, Y_{t-1} depends on u_{t-1} [because $Y_{t-1} = \beta Y_{t-2} + u_{t-1}$, from equation (10.12)] and hence many of the terms in the numerator are correlated with terms in the denominator. The second term on the right-hand side will therefore not have zero expectation. It follows that $E(\hat{\beta}) \neq \beta$, which means that $\hat{\beta}$ is biased. Thus, the application of ordinary least squares to a model with lagged dependent variables leads to biased estimates. Because the error term u_t is uncorrelated with all other u's and with Y_{t-1}, by Property 3.2 $\hat{\beta}$ is consistent even though biased in small samples. If the disturbance term u_t is also normally distributed, then large-sample tests are valid because standard errors can be estimated consistently. We thus have the following property.

Property 10.1	If lags of the dependent variable are present as regressors but the disturbance term u_t satisfies Assumptions 3.2 through 3.7, then a. OLS estimates of the parameters will be biased in small samples but will be consistent and asymptotically efficient. b. Estimates of residuals and standard errors are consistent, and hence the tests of hypotheses are valid for large samples. In small samples, however, tests are invalid.

Random Walks and Testing for a Unit Root

In the previous chapter we briefly discussed the **random walk model** and the problem created by a unit root. Although, the problem was discussed in the context of a serially correlated error term, it can, and often does, occur in distributed lag models with lagged dependent variables. Consider the autoregressive model $Y_t = \rho Y_{t-1} + u_t$ in which u_t is "well-behaved" (that is, is *white noise*). If ρ is exactly equal to 1, then the equation reduces to $Y_t = Y_{t-1} + u_t$, or equivalently, $\Delta Y_t = u_t$. Thus, the *change* in Y_t is independently and identically distributed with zero mean, constant variance, and zero covariance. This is the simplest random walk model, one that has frequently been used to describe the behavior of stock market prices.

An extension of this is the **random walk model with drift** which has the form $Y_t = Y_{t-1} + d + u_t$, where d is the drift component. In this modified formulation, the change in Y_t is determined by a trend and a stochastic shock. As an example, suppose the population (P_t) of a region is growing exponentially at some constant rate. Thus

$$P_t = P_0 e^{gt + u_t}$$

where g is the constant growth rate and u_t is a random error term. Taking logarithms of both sides, we get

$$\ln(P_t) = \ln(P_0) + gt + u_t$$

It follows from this that

$$\ln(P_t) - \ln(P_{t-1}) = gt - g(t-1) + u_t - u_{t-1} = g + v_t$$

If v_t is white noise, this has the form of a random walk model with $Y_t = \ln(P_t)$ and the drift term $d = g$.

A general form that captures the above as special cases is given below:

$$Y_t = \alpha + \beta t + \sum_{i=1}^{i=p} \gamma_i Y_{t-i} + u_t$$

which can be expressed in the equivalent form

$$\Delta Y_t = \alpha + \beta t + (\rho - 1)Y_{t-1} + \sum_{i=1}^{i=p} \theta_i \Delta Y_{t-i} + u_t \qquad (10.13)$$

TABLE 10.4   Critical Values for the Dickey–Fuller Test

Sample size (n)	Probability To the Right of Critical Value							
	0.99	0.975	0.95	0.90	0.10	0.05	0.025	0.01
25	0.74	0.90	1.08	1.33	5.91	7.24	8.65	10.61
50	0.76	0.93	1.11	1.37	5.61	6.73	7.81	9.31
100	0.76	0.94	1.12	1.38	5.47	6.49	7.44	8.73
250	0.76	0.94	1.13	1.39	5.39	6.34	7.25	8.43
500	0.76	0.94	1.13	1.39	5.36	6.30	7.20	8.34
∞	0.77	0.94	1.13	1.39	5.34	6.25	7.16	8.27

Source: Dickey and Fuller (1981). Reprinted with the permission of the Econometric Society.

As mentioned in Chapter 9, when $\rho = 1$, the variance of Y_t goes to infinity as t goes to infinity. This is the *unit root problem*, and it would be useful to test for it. Dickey and Fuller (1979, 1981) proposed a test for the joint hypothesis $\beta = 0$ and $\rho = 1$ that implies a unit root. The **Dickey–Fuller test** consists of estimating the unrestricted model in equation (10.13) and the restricted model

$$\Delta Y_t = \alpha + \sum_{i=1}^{i=p} \theta_i \Delta Y_{t-i} + u_t$$

and then constructing the usual F-statistic

$$F_c = \frac{(ESSR - ESSU)/2}{ESSU/(T-k)}$$

where ESSR and ESSU are the sum of squared residuals for the restricted and unrestricted models, T is the number of observations used in the unrestricted model [equation (10.13)], and k is the number of parameters estimated in the unrestricted model [$p + 3$ in equation (10.13)]. The usual F-test is not applicable here because, when $\rho = 1$, F_c does not have the well-known F-distribution. Dickey and Fuller have derived the distribution of F_c when $\rho = 1$ and tabulated the critical values (see Table 10.4) for it. It is easily verified that the critical values in Table 10.4 are much higher than those in the standard F table. This implies that a test statistic rejected by the standard F-test may not be rejected by the Dickey–Fuller test. In other words, the standard F-test might lead one to conclude that there is no unit root when in fact there might be a unit root (for example, the model might be a random walk).

Example 10.3

Table 10.8 at the end of the chapter has monthly data on the exchange rate of deutsche marks per dollar (January 1973 through January 1986), which is

Marks per dollar

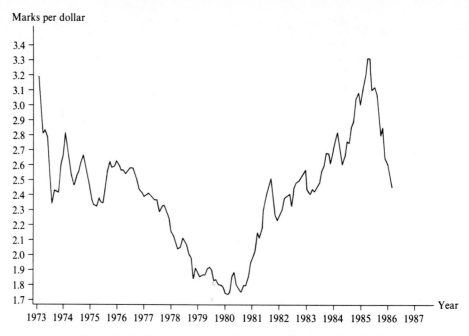

Figure 10.4 Exchange rate of Deutsche Mark per U.S. Dollar

graphed in Figure 10.4. We first estimated the following unrestricted model (see Practice Computer Session 10.2).

$$\Delta\text{EXCHRATE}_t = 0.06988 + 0.00014714t - 0.03503\text{EXCHRATE}_{t-1}$$
$$+ 0.28881\,\Delta\text{EXCHRATE}_{t-1}$$

with ESS = 0.73844. The estimated restricted model was

$$\Delta\text{EXCHRATE}_t = -0.00235 + 0.29559\,\Delta\text{EXCHRATE}_{t-1}$$

which had ESS = 0.76526. The corresponding Wald F-statistic is 2.7425. The critical value for the traditional F-test (with d.f. 2 and 151) is slightly less than 3.07 at 5 percent and below 2.35 at 10 percent. We note that the null hypothesis that there is no unit root will be rejected at 10 percent but not at 5 percent (the p-value is 0.068). In contrast, the Dickey–Fuller test will not reject the null hypothesis even at the 10 percent level. Thus a traditional Wald test would have concluded that there is no unit root.

If the Dickey–Fuller test cannot reject a unit root, then one can use the difference formulation described in the previous chapter. □

Lagged Dependent Variables and Serial Correlation

Properties 10.1a and 10.1b do not hold if the disturbance term u_t depends on u_{t-1}, either as in equation (10.4) (that is, the moving average form) or when u_t is serially correlated (that is, the autoregressive form). The combination of lagged dependent variables and serial correlation destroys the consistency property. Furthermore, the Durbin–Watson test for serial correlation is invalid. The DW value tends to be closer to 2 (when $\rho > 0$), and hence we may erroneously conclude that there is no serial correlation.

If $u_t = \rho u_{t-1} + \epsilon_t$, then Cochrane–Orcutt and Hildreth–Lu procedures will give consistent estimates but they will be biased in small samples. It can be shown [see Johnston (1972), Section 10-3] that if the OLS procedure is used, the large-sample limits for the parameters are as follows:

$$\hat{\beta} \to \beta + \frac{\rho(1 - \beta^2)}{1 + \beta\rho}$$

$$\hat{\rho} \to \rho - \frac{\rho(1 - \beta^2)}{1 + \beta\rho}$$

$$d \to 2(1 - \rho) + \frac{2\rho(1 - \beta^2)}{1 + \beta\rho}$$

We therefore see that even with a large sample, the OLS estimate $\hat{\beta}$ does not converge to the true value, estimated autocorrelation coefficient does not converge to the true ρ, and the estimated Durbin–Watson statistic does not converge to $2(1 - \rho)$. We thus have the following property.

Property 10.2

If lags of the dependent variable are present as regressors, but the disturbance term u_t depends on u_{t-1}, u_{t-2}, and so on, then

a. OLS estimates of the parameters, and forecasts based on them, will be biased and inconsistent.
b. Estimates of residuals and standard errors will also be inconsistent, and hence hypotheses tests are no longer valid even for large samples.
c. The Durbin–Watson test for first-order serial correlation is no longer valid.

The Durbin-*h* Test   Durbin (1970) has developed a large-sample test, the **Durbin-*h* test**, for first-order serial correlation when lagged dependent variables are present. The steps for the test are as follows:

Step 1   Estimate the model by OLS and obtain the residuals ($\hat{u}_t$).
Step 2   Estimate the first-order autocorrelation coefficient as

$$\hat{\rho} = \frac{\sum \hat{u}_t \hat{u}_{t-1}}{\sum \hat{u}_t^2}$$

or as $(2 - d)/2$, where d is the Durbin–Watson statistic.

Step 3 Construct the following statistic, known as the Durbin-h statistic ($T' = T - 1$, the number of observations used):

$$h = \hat{\rho} \left[\frac{T'}{1 - T's_{\hat{\beta}}^2} \right]^{1/2}$$

where $s_{\hat{\beta}}^2$ is the estimated variance of $\hat{\beta}$, the coefficient of Y_{t-1} in the model. In large samples h has a normal distribution.

Step 4 Reject the null hypothesis of $\rho = 0$ against the alternative $\rho \neq 0$ when $h < -z^*$ or $h > z^*$, where z^* is the point on standard normal $N(0, 1)$ such that the area to the right is 2.5 percent (or 0.5 percent for a 1 percent test).

Lagrange Multiplier Test Note that the Durbin-h test will fail if $T's_{\hat{\beta}}^2 > 1$ because then the denominator will be the square root of a negative number. Also, the Durbin-h test is not applicable when terms such as Y_{t-2}, Y_{t-3}, and so on are present, or when autocorrelation is of a higher order. A better alternative is to use a Lagrange multiplier test procedure, which is similar to the one used in Chapter 9. The steps for the LM test are as follows:

Step 1 The model is assumed to be

$$Y_t = \beta_0 + \beta_1 Y_{t-1} + \beta_2 Y_{t-2} + \cdots + \beta_p Y_{t-p} + \beta_{p+1} X_t + \cdots + u_t$$
$$u_t = \rho_1 u_{t-1} + \rho_2 u_{t-2} + \cdots + \rho_m u_{t-m} + \epsilon_t$$

where p is the order of the lagged dependent variable and m is the order of the autoregressive error term (it is assumed that $p > m$).

Step 2 Estimate the model by OLS and obtain the residuals ($\hat{u}_t$).

Step 3 Regress $\hat{u}_t$ on $\hat{u}_{t-1}, \hat{u}_{t-2}, \ldots, \hat{u}_{t-m}$ and all the explanatory variables in the model, including the lagged dependent variables $Y_{t-1}, Y_{t-2}, \ldots, Y_{t-p}$, and obtain the unadjusted R^2.

Step 4 Compute $(T - p)R^2$ and reject H_0: all $\rho_i = 0$ against H_1: not all the ρ's are zero, if it exceeds $\chi_m^2(0.05)$, the point on χ_m^2 such that the area to the right is 5 percent. ($T - p$ is used because the number of observations actually used is $T - p$.)

The LM test can also be used to test whether lagged dependent variables should even be present. Suppose the model formulated is $Y_t = \alpha + \beta X_t + u_t$ and we want to test whether $Y_{t-1}, Y_{t-2}, \ldots$ should be included. The LM test for this is exactly the same as the test for adding new variables in the model (discussed in Section 7.1). The first step is to regress Y_t against a constant and X_t, and save the residual $\hat{u}_t$. Next regress $\hat{u}_t$ against a constant, $X_t, Y_{t-1}, Y_{t-2}, \ldots$, and Y_{t-p}. As in Step 4, $(T - p)R^2$ is used as a test statistic.

Estimation Procedures

Several procedures are available to estimate models involving lagged dependent variables. The method depends on the properties of the random disturbance terms.

A Model with "Well-behaved" Error Terms   As mentioned in Chapter 3, if the disturbance terms (u_t) satisfy Assumptions 3.2 through 3.7, they are often referred to as **well-behaved error** terms. Consider the model

$$Y_t = \beta_0 + \beta_1 Y_{t-1} + \beta_2 X_t + u_t \tag{10.13}$$

with well-behaved errors. We have seen that the partial adjustment model leads to an equation of this form. As stated in Property 10.1, the OLS procedure gives consistent and asymptotically efficient estimates of the parameters and their standard errors. Furthermore, tests of hypotheses are valid for large samples. Hence OLS is applicable, provided the sample size is large enough (usually over 30). Small-sample bias will, however, persist and we cannot get estimates that are BLUE. It should be pointed out that the Durbin–Watson statistic printed by regression packages should not be used to test for serial correlation. Either the Durbin-h test or, preferably, the LM test described in the previous section should be applied.

A Model with Autocorrelated Disturbances   If the error terms follow the AR(1) process, the model is of the form

$$Y_t = \beta_0 + \beta_1 Y_{t-1} + \beta_2 X_t + u_t \tag{10.14}$$

$$u_t = \rho u_{t-1} + \epsilon_t \tag{10.15}$$

where the new error term ϵ_t is assumed to be well-behaved. We know from Property 10.2 that because u_t depends on u_{t-1}, Y_{t-1} and u_t are directly correlated, and hence applying the OLS procedure to (10.14) will lead to biased and inconsistent estimates. The Cochrane–Orcutt (CORC) procedure is, however, applicable here with a slight modification. The steps are as follows:

Step 1   Estimate the parameters β_0, β_1, and β_2 by OLS and save the residuals $\hat{u}_t = Y_t - \hat{\beta}_0 - \hat{\beta}_1 Y_{t-1} - \hat{\beta}_2 X_t$.

Step 2   Regress $\hat{u}_t$ against $\hat{u}_{t-1}$ (using observations 2 through T) and obtain $\hat{\rho}$.

Step 3   Transform the variables as follows: $Y_t^* = Y_t - \hat{\rho} Y_{t-1}$, $Y_{t-1}^* = Y_{t-1} - \hat{\rho} Y_{t-2}$, and $X_t^* = X_t - \hat{\rho} X_{t-1}$.

Step 4   Regress Y_t^* against a constant, Y_{t-1}^*, and X_t^* (using observations 3 through T because Y_t^* is defined only from period 3 onward).

Step 5   Using the estimates of the β's obtained from Step 4, compute a second round set of residuals $\hat{u}_t$. Next go back to Step 2 and iterate until successive $\hat{\rho}$ estimates do not differ by more than some desired value.

These five steps are identical to those for the CORC method. Although these estimates are consistent even in the presence of lagged dependent variables and autocorrelated errors, the standard errors obtained from that procedure are inconsistent. Consistent standard errors may be obtained by carrying out a final step.

Step 6   Use the final estimates of the β's from Step 4 and compute the residuals of the transformed model; that is, obtain $\hat{\epsilon}_t$. Next regress $\hat{\epsilon}_t$ against a constant, Y_{t-1}^*, X_t^*, and $\hat{u}_{t-1}$ (not $\hat{\epsilon}_{t-1}$). The standard errors of the regression coefficients and that of $\hat{\rho}$ obtained from this step are consistent.

Further details on this technique may be found in Harvey (1981).

A Model with Moving Average Error Terms In equations (10.4) and (10.10) the error term was of the form $u_t - \lambda u_{t-1}$, where λ is the adjustment coefficient ($0 < \lambda < 1$). Such an error term is called a **moving average (MA) error**. It is clear that because Y_{t-1} and u_{t-1} are correlated, OLS estimates will be biased and inconsistent. In this case we may proceed as follows. First, we reproduce equation (10.10):

$$Y_t = \alpha\lambda + (1 - \lambda)Y_{t-1} + \lambda\beta X_{t-1} + [u_t - (1 - \lambda)u_{t-1}] \tag{10.16}$$

Next we define $W_t = Y_t - u_t$. It follows from this that

$$
\begin{aligned}
W_t - (1 - \lambda)W_{t-1} &= (Y_t - u_t) - (1 - \lambda)(Y_{t-1} + u_{t-1}) \\
&= Y_t - (1 - \lambda)Y_{t-1} - [u_t - (1 - \lambda)u_{t-1}] \\
&= \alpha\lambda + \lambda\beta X_{t-1} = \beta_0 + \beta_1 X_{t-1} \tag{10.17}
\end{aligned}
$$

where $\beta_0 = \alpha\lambda$ and $\beta_1 = \lambda\beta$. We thus have

$$W_t = (1 - \lambda)W_{t-1} + \beta_0 + \beta_1 X_{t-1}$$

By repeated substitution for W_{t-1}, W_{t-2}, and so on, and by setting $\gamma = 1 - \lambda$, we get

$$
\begin{aligned}
W_t &= \gamma^t W_0 + \beta_0(1 + \gamma + \gamma^2 + \cdots + \gamma^{t-1}) + \beta_1(X_{t-1} + \gamma X_{t-2} + \cdots + \gamma^{t-2}X_1) \\
&= \gamma^t W_0 + \beta_0 \frac{1 - \gamma^t}{1 - \gamma} + \beta_1 Z_t \tag{10.18}
\end{aligned}
$$

where

$$Z_t = X_{t-1} + \gamma X_{t-2} + \cdots + \gamma^{t-2}X_1$$

Because $W_t = Y_t - u_t$, equation (10.18) can be rewritten as

$$
\begin{aligned}
Y_t = W_t + u_t &= \gamma^t W_0 + \beta_0 \frac{1 - \gamma^t}{1 - \gamma} + \beta_1 Z_t + u_t \\
&= \alpha_0 + \alpha_1 \gamma^t + \beta_1 Z_t + u_t \tag{10.19}
\end{aligned}
$$

where

$$\alpha_0 = \frac{\beta_0}{1 - \gamma} \quad \text{and} \quad \alpha_1 = W_0 - \frac{\beta_0}{1 - \gamma}$$

Because γ lies between 0 and 1 (by assumption), we can use a search procedure similar to that used by Hildreth–Lu. Fix values of γ (at 0.05 or 0.01 intervals from 0 to 1) and for each γ estimate equation (10.19) by regressing Y_t against a constant, γ^t, and Z_t. Pick the value of γ for which the error sum of squares of (10.19) is minimum, and obtain the full estimates for that γ.

Several other procedures are available but are not presented here. The reader is referred to Johnston (1984) and Kmenta (1986).

Practice Problem

10.5 Show that if u_t is autoregressive, with the special form $u_t = (1 - \lambda)u_{t-1} + \epsilon_t$, where ϵ_t is well-behaved (that is, is white noise), then the OLS estimates of the parameters in equation (10.16) will be consistent. Explain why you cannot assert that the estimates are also BLUE. Carefully justify your answers, giving references to assumptions and properties listed in earlier chapters.

Empirical Example: Inflation and the Savings Rate

It has been frequently observed that high rates of inflation and high rates of personal savings are closely related. Davidson and MacKinnon (1983) have examined two competing theories on the effect of inflation on the savings rate. The first states that when the rate of inflation increases, interest payments also increase so as to compensate asset holders for the loss in real value of assets. Consumers wishing to maintain the real value of their wealth will refrain from increasing consumption, even though measured income has gone up, because the increase in income is simply an inflation premium. Observed savings will therefore go up. Thus, measured savings and income tend to overestimate real savings and real income. A second theory argues that when inflation is unanticipated, consumers will reduce consumption demand, which thus results in increased involuntary savings.

Davidson and MacKinnon have constructed an econometric model that incorporates both of these theories, and have estimated it separately for the United States and Canada. They used quarterly data for 1954.1 to 1979.4. The basic model is

TABLE 10.5 Estimates of the Davidson–MacKinnon Models

	United States			Canada		
	IIa	IIb	IIab	Ia	Ib	Iab
a_0 or b_0	0.6476 (0.0452)	0.6728 (0.0650)	0.6310 (0.0662)	0.2485 (0.0437)	0.4861 (0.0785)	0.2976 (0.0830)
b_1	0.6387 (0.0464)	0.6669 (0.0670)	0.6209 (0.0686)	0.2179 (0.0453)	0.4594 (0.0820)	0.2690 (0.0859)
α	0.3935 (0.1019)	—	0.2708 (0.1230)	0.5339 (0.0722)	—	0.5909 (0.1151)
d_2	—	0.7202 (0.1503)	0.3223 (0.2296)	—	0.8077 (0.2127)	−0.1641 (0.2932)
d_1	—	0.0228 (0.0534)	0.0528 (0.0539)	—	−0.2603 (0.0882)	−0.0683 (0.0910)
Coefficient on $t(\times 1000)$	−0.1721 (0.0412)	−0.1541 (0.0398)	−0.1911 (0.0423)	−0.3550 (0.1716)	−0.3535 (0.1938)	−0.3264 (0.1755)
Coefficient on t^2 $(\times 100\,000)$	—	—	—	0.4036 (0.1368)	0.4230 (0.1584)	0.3722 (0.1438)
Coefficient on S_{t-2}/Y_t	0.1828 (0.0617)	0.2178 (0.0617)	0.1894 (0.0617)	—	—	—
log L	380.04	378.95	381.88	343.92	333.65	344.65
Standard error	0.00673	0.00684	0.00669	0.00986	0.01095	0.00991
AR(1)	0.9213 (+)	0.4193 (+)	0.5968 (−)	0.9490 (+)	0.0128 (−)	0.2727 (−)
AR(4)	0.0382 (−)	0.0286 (−)	0.0201 (−)	0.5923 (−)	0.8144 (−)	0.4497 (−)
AR(1, 2, 3, 4)	0.2339 (− − − −)	0.1982 (+ − − −)	0.1444 (− − − −)	0.7504 (+ + + −)	0.1495 (− − + −)	0.6214 (− + + −)

Source: Davidson and MacKinnon, 1983. Reprinted with the permission of Chapman and Hall, Ltd.

as follows (for the theory behind this equation refer to the Davidson–MacKinnon paper):

$$\frac{S_t}{Y_t} = a_0 + (1 - a_0)\alpha \frac{Z_t}{Y_t} + b_1\left[\frac{S_{t-1} - Y_{t-1}}{Y_t}\right] + d_1 \ln\left[\frac{Y_t}{Y_{t-1}}\right] + d_2 \pi_t + u_t$$

where S_t is real savings, Y_t is real disposable income, π_t is the inflation rate, and Z_t is the loss in real value of wealth due to inflation. Z_t is measured as $\pi_t I_t / r_t$, where I_t is the real value of interest and dividend payments, and r_t is the nominal rate of interest.

If the overmeasurement hypothesis holds, we would expect α to be between zero and one. If the involuntary savings hypothesis is true, d_1 and d_2 should both be positive. Davidson and MacKinnon estimated the model along with a variety of modifications including seasonal dummies, time trends, and their powers. Table 10.5 presents estimates of the various models with standard errors in parentheses. The results do not support the theory that unanticipated inflation leads to involuntary savings (for both Canada and the United States). There is, however, tentative support for the first theory that inflation leads to higher measured savings rates. Davidson and MacKinnon also tested the model for the presence of serial correlation of orders up to 4. Although they found some serial correlation, the models were not reestimated with the more general method presented in Chapter 9.

10.3 Error Correction Models

The partial adjustment mechanism is a way of allowing for adjustment costs and/or incomplete information. In recent years, another class of distributed lag models, known as **error correction models**, have gained popularity. The principle behind these models is that there often exists a long-run equilibrium relationship between two economic variables (for example, consumption and income, wages and prices, and so on). In the short run, however, there may be disequilibrium. With the error correction mechanism, a proportion of the disequilibrium in one period is corrected in the next period. For instance, the change in price in one period may depend on the excess demand in the previous period. The error correction process is thus a means to reconcile short-run and long-run behavior. Notable contributions in this area have been made by Sargan (1964), Davidson, Hendry, Srba, and Yeo (1989), Currie (1981), Dawson (1981), Salmon (1982), Hendry (1984), Engle and Granger (1987), among others. In this section we develop the econometric framework for error correction models and illustrate it with an empirical example.

Suppose that the long-run relation between Y_t and X_t is of the form

$$Y_t = KX_t \tag{10.20}$$

where K is a fixed constant. As an example, Friedman (1957) formulated the "permanent income hypothesis," which states that consumption (Y_t) is proportional to "permanent income" (X_t). He approximated permanent income by a distributed lag process. Another example is the "life-cycle hypothesis" [see Ando and

Modigliani (1963)], which argues that, in the long run, consumption is a constant fraction of wealth. As another example, wages and prices might have nearly equal long-run growth rates although in the short run their rates of growth might diverge.

Taking logarithms of both sides of equation (10.20) we obtain

$$\ln Y_t = \ln K + \ln X_t \qquad \text{or} \qquad y_t = k + x_t \qquad (10.21)$$

where the lowercase letters are used to denote logarithms. Because $y_{t-1} = k + x_{t-1}$, we have,

$$\Delta y_t = \Delta x_t \qquad (10.22)$$

where Δ denotes the change in a variable from period $t-1$ to t. A general short-run model with lagged adjustment is of the following form:

$$y_t = \beta_0 + \beta_1 x_t + \beta_2 x_{t-1} + \alpha_1 y_{t-1} + u_t \qquad (10.23)$$

Under what conditions will the short-run model be consistent with the long-run model? To examine this question, let $y_t = y^*$ and $x_t = x^*$ for all t. Equation (10.23) now becomes (setting $u_t = 0$ in the long run)

$$y^*(1 - \alpha_1) = \beta_0 + (\beta_1 + \beta_2)x^*$$

For this to be compatible with equation (10.21) we need the condition

$$1 - \alpha_1 = \beta_1 + \beta_2$$

which will give $y^* = k^* + x^*$, where $k^* = \beta_0/(1 - \alpha_1)$. Suppose $1 - \alpha_1 = \gamma = \beta_1 + \beta_2$. Then $\alpha_1 = 1 - \gamma$ and $\beta_2 = \gamma - \beta_1$. Substituting these in (10.23) we get

$$y_t = \beta_0 + \beta_1 x_t + (\gamma - \beta_1)x_{t-1} + (1 - \gamma)y_{t-1} + u_t$$

or

$$y_t - y_{t-1} = \beta_0 + \beta_1(x_t - x_{t-1}) + \gamma(x_{t-1} - y_{t-1}) + u_t$$

That is,

$$\Delta y_t = \beta_0 + \beta_1 \Delta x_t + \gamma(x_{t-1} - y_{t-1}) + u_t \qquad (10.24)$$

The above equation is the structure of the simplest error correction model. It relates the change in one variable to the change in another variable plus the gap between the two variables in the previous period. It is important to note that the equation captures the short-run adjustment, but at the same time, it is guided by long-run theory. The term $x_{t-1} - y_{t-1}$ provides the short-run disequilibrium adjustment. A test on γ is therefore a test for this disequilibrium component.

The general specification of the error correction model is as follows:

$$\Delta y_t = \beta_0 + \beta_1 \Delta x_t + \gamma_1 x_{t-1} + \gamma_2 y_{t-1} + u_t \qquad (10.24a)$$

Note that the general formulation does not assume that $\gamma_2 = -\gamma_1$; in fact we can test for it. A test on γ_1 and γ_2 is therefore a test for the disequilibrium adjustment term.

The most general version of the error correction model has a second equation relating changes in x_t to those in y_t and lagged values. We thus have

$$\Delta x_t = \pi_0 + \pi_1 \Delta y_t + \theta_1 x_{t-1} + \theta_2 y_{t-1} + v_t \qquad (10.24b)$$

The error correction framework described in this section is very closely related to the concept of **cointegration** introduced by Granger (1981) and developed in detail by Engle and Granger (1987). This topic is discussed in the next chapter.

Empirical Example: Wages and Prices in the United Kingdom

Although Phillips (1954) introduced the error correction model, the earliest paper to adopt the approach was that by Sargan (1964). In a study of the relationship between wages and prices in the United Kingdom, he formulated a large variety of models, several of which had the error correction formulation. Here we present only a few selected models. You are encouraged to read the original article as well as the other papers previously cited.

Using quarterly data, Sargan estimated the following model (values in parentheses are t-statistics):

$$\widehat{w_t - w_{t-1}} = \underset{(-0.058)}{-0.005}(p_{t-1} - p_{t-4}) - \underset{(-2.234)}{0.0143}U_{t-1} - \underset{(-2.904)}{0.395}(w_{t-1} - p_{t-1})$$
$$+ \underset{(1.149)}{0.00085}F_t + \underset{(3.216)}{0.00119}t$$

where w_t is the logarithm of a wage index, p is the logarithm of a price index, U is the logarithm of the unemployment rate, and F is a dummy variable (which took the value 0 up to the fourth quarter of 1951 and 1 thereafter, to incorporate a wage freeze in the earlier period). The model included a time trend to capture the fact that relative wages have been growing over time because of technical progress. The dependent variable is the rate of change of the wage rate (because it is the change in logarithms). Sargan used the rate of change in prices over a whole year rather than over one quarter. The term $w_{t-1} - p_{t-1}$ is the error correction disequilibrium adjustment discussed earlier. The unemployment term captures the business cycle effect. In periods of high unemployment we would not expect wages to rise much.

We note that the rate of price change and the wage freeze factor are insignificant, but the error correction term is significant. When insignificant terms were omitted, the estimated model became the following:

$$\widehat{w_t - w_{t-1}} = \underset{(-2.069)}{-0.0120}U_{t-1} - \underset{(-3.712)}{0.271}(w_{t-1} - p_{t-1}) + \underset{(3.694)}{0.00133}t$$

The significance of the disequilibrium adjustment term is higher. As can be expected, when unemployment rises, wages tend to grow more slowly. Similarly, a rise in real wages reduces the rate of growth of wages. A rise in productivity would cause the wage rate to grow faster. Sargan tried other variations, including longer lags for the explanatory variables, real profits instead of the time trend, and so on. From one of these models Sargan estimated that the average lag for prices was 4.02 quarters and the mean lag for unemployment was 7.02 quarters.

10.4 Application: An Error Correction Model of U.S. Defense Expenditures

Ramanathan and Blackburn (1991) have applied the error correction approach to modeling U.S. defense expenditures. They argue that although the rate of change of military and total government expenditures might diverge in the short run, they have a stable long-run relationship (see Figure 10.5). This long-run relationship can be derived from a simple static model of utility maximization. Suppose the government has the Cobb–Douglas "objective function"

$$U(M, N) = M^{\alpha}N^{1-\alpha}$$

where M and N are the "quantities" of military and nonmilitary expenditures and α is a fixed parameter. We want to maximize U with respect to M and N, subject to the government budget constraint $G = p_M M + p_N N$. G is the total government expenditure, p_M is the price index of military goods, and p_N is the price index of nonmilitary goods. Using the procedure discussed in Appendix Section 2.A.2, it is easy to show that the "optimum" expenditure on M is $p_M M = \alpha G$, which has the form in equation (10.20).

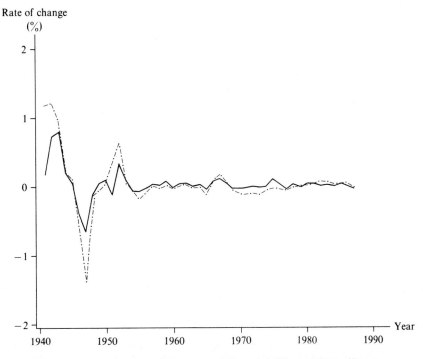

Figure 10.5 Rate of change of government and military expenditures (1940–1987) (Solid line denotes government and broken line denotes military)

The error correction formulation derived from this simple long run relationship is given by

$$\Delta m_t = \alpha + \beta \Delta g_t + \gamma(g_{t-1} - m_{t-1}) + u_t \qquad (10.25)$$

where m_t is the logarithm of military expenditures and g_t is the logarithm of total government expenditures. Thus the rate of change in military expenditures is determined by the rate of change in total government expenditure in the same period and the difference between the logarithms of total expenses and the military budget in the previous period. The null hypothesis that $\gamma = 0$ tests for the short-run disequilibrium error correlation term. It will be noted that by letting g_{t-1} and m_{t-1} have coefficients that are equal in value but opposite in sign, we have imposed the constraint $\gamma_2 = -\gamma_1$ in equation (10.24a). This is to simplify the analysis. Interested readers can relax this assumption and test for it using the data provided. As mentioned in Section 10.3, the general structure of the error correction model would also have a second equation relating g_t to m_t and their lagged values, but as such an equation is not meaningful in our context, it has not been specified.

In the empirical analysis, the data used were annual for the period 1940 through 1987, which gives effectively 47 observations. Table 10.9 at the end of the chapter has data on the following variables:

UG = unadjusted annual government outlays expressed in billions of dollars for the years 1940–87

EM = total U.S. military outlays expressed in billions of dollars

GNPDEF = annual implicit gnp deflator for federal government purchases of goods and services, base year 1972

SDEM = percent of democrats in the senate

HDEM = percent of democrats in the house of representatives

PRES = party of the president in office, Rep = 1, Demo = 0

ELECT = 1 for the year in which the president might have an incentive to increase and decrease military expenditure as a means of stabilizing the government

REAGAN = 1 for the years during which President Reagen was in office

OPP = 1 denotes a year in which the majority party in the senate is of the opposing party with respect to the president in office, 0 otherwise

WW2 = World War II period, 1941–1945

KWAR = Korean War period, 1951–1953

VWAR = Vietnam War period, 1965–1969

WARSAW = 1 for the years when the Warsaw Pact was in effect, 1955 onward

KRUS = 1 for the years during which Kruschev may have changed Soviet military policy

GORB = 1 for the years during which Soviet leader Gorbachav may have changed Soviet military policy

SALT = the structural change possibly brought about by the SALT I treaty, 0 = before, 1 = after

Both military and total expenditures are in current dollars and should be converted to real terms. We then need the change in their logarithms. This gives

$$\text{REALMIL} = \text{UM} * 100/\text{GNPDEF}$$

$$\text{REALG} = \text{UG} * 100/\text{DNPDEF}$$

$$\text{MILIT} = \ln(\text{REALMIL}_t) - \ln(\text{REALMIL}_{t-1})$$

$$\text{GOVT} = \ln(\text{REALG}_t) - \ln(\text{REALG}_{t-1})$$

MILIT is the dependent variable representing the difference in the logarithms of total military outlays between the periods t and $t - 1$. In terms of the previous notation, this is Δm_t and measures the instantaneous rate of growth of expenditure on defense. Military expenditures are in billions of constant 1972 dollars. GOVT is Δg_t, the difference between the logarithms of total government expenditure in periods t and $t - 1$. It represents the rate of growth in the total government budget. These data were also in constant 1972 dollars (billions). LONGDEF is $g_{t-1} - m_{t-1}$, the error correction adjustment.

We note from Figure 10.5 that the rates of change of military and total expenditures deviate substantially from one another during the World War II and Korean War periods, but over the longer run the relationship is more stable.

Ordinary Least Squares estimates of the coefficients in equation (10.25) are presented below with t-statistics in parentheses (use Practice Computer Session 10.3 to reproduce the results of this section):

$$\text{MILIT} = \underset{(-2.8)}{-0.172} + \underset{(12.9)}{1.579\text{GOVT}} + \underset{(2.8)}{0.169\text{LONGDEF}}$$

$$\text{d.f.} = 44 \qquad \bar{R}^2 = 0.792 \qquad \hat{\sigma} = 0.17241$$

where $\text{MILIT} = \Delta m_t$, $\text{GOVT} = \Delta g_t$, and $\text{LONGDEF} = g_{t-1} - m_{t-1}$.

The Effects of Other Variables

Although all the regression coefficients are statistically significant and the model explains 79.2 percent of the variation in the growth rate of the military budget, tests for first-order serial correlation indicate the presence of autocorrelation in the model. Therefore, the estimates are inefficient and the significance of the regression coefficients is questionable. Although one can use a method such as the Cochrane–Orcutt iterative procedure to correct for serial correlation, this was not done because the basic model relates the military expenditure to only total government expenditure and has to be modified to account for changes due to other variables. We can expect that the short-run adjustment coefficient γ will be related to a number of economic and political variables. To allow for these effects, the authors assume that γ depends on a number of other variables. In particular,

$$
\begin{aligned}
\gamma = \gamma_0 &+ \gamma_1 \text{PRES} + \gamma_2 \text{ELECT} + \gamma_3 \text{REAGAN} + \gamma_4 \text{OPP} + \gamma_5 \text{HDEM} \\
&+ \gamma_6 \text{SDEM} + \gamma_7 \text{WW2} + \gamma_8 \text{KWAR} + \gamma_9 \text{VWAR} + \gamma_{10} \text{KRUS} \\
&+ \gamma_{11} \text{GORB} + \gamma_{12} \text{SALT}
\end{aligned} \tag{10.26}
$$

The variables on the right-hand side are described below. One might want to test whether α and β are also related to these other variables, but because the focus here is on the error correction term, this was not done. Furthermore, that would have added 24 more coefficients to estimate and, as the effective number of observations is only 47, there will be a substantial decrease in the precision of the estimates and the power of tests.

From the above we obtain the following unrestricted model, which includes the interactions between the variables in equation (10.26) and those in the basic model.

$$
\begin{aligned}
\text{MILIT}_t = \alpha &+ \beta \text{GOVT}_t + \text{LONGDEF}_t (\gamma_0 + \gamma_1 \text{PRES}_t \\
&+ \gamma_2 \text{ELECT}_t + \gamma_3 \text{REAGAN}_t + \gamma_4 \text{OPP}_t + \gamma_5 \text{HDEM}_t \\
&+ \gamma_6 \text{SDEM}_t + \gamma_7 \text{WW2}_t + \gamma_8 \text{KWAR}_t + \gamma_9 \text{VWAR}_t \\
&+ \gamma_{10} \text{KRUS}_t + \gamma_{11} \text{GORB}_t + \gamma_{12} \text{SALT}_t) + u_t
\end{aligned} \tag{10.27}
$$

We now turn our attention to a description of the new variables in the model.

The Political Variables

To test for the presence of a political business cycle, Ramanathan and Blackburn use the binary variable, ELECT, which will have the value of 1 for an election year and the year immediately preceding it, and zero for the other two years following a Presidential election. If the political business cycle is present, we would expect this variable to have a positive marginal effect on military expenditures.

To test for the effects of party affiliation, a number of variables were included. The first is PRES, which was given the value of 1 for each year a Republican president was in office. OPP represents a dummy variable assigned the value 1 whenever the President and Senate majority are from opposing parties. Also included are HDEM and SDEM, which represent the percentage of seats held by Democrats in the House and Senate, respectively. A dummy variable called REAGAN is also included, with the value 1 from 1981 onward and zero prior to that. This variable is introduced because President Reagan pursued an aggressive policy toward the military budget. To the extent that this was the case, we expect the regression coefficient to be positive.

International Variables

Understandably, several past studies have indicated that a number of exogenous international factors influence levels of defense expenditures. Two factors that have received substantial empirical support are the occurrence of war and changes in peace-time relations between the United States and the Soviet Union [Rattinger (1975), Ostrom (1978), Zuk and Woodbury (1986)]. Therefore, a number of international variables have been included.

To measure the effects of war, WW2, KWAR, and VWAR were included in the model. All three are binary variables with values of 1 for World War II, the Korean War, and the Vietnam War, respectively. International tension has usually been measured in the form of a tension metric based on events that are concerned with the relations of two nations (Rattinger, 1975). Because this study is not bilateral but takes account of conflicts with other countries as well (Korea, Vietnam, and indirectly China), other variables have been used, which, it is hoped, would capture this broad spectrum of international tension.

Krushchev conducted a more aggressive policy that culminated in actions such as the building of the Berlin Wall and, more notably, the Cuban Missile crisis, both of which contributed to the Cold War between the United States and Soviet Union. Gorbachav was chosen because of his initiation of perestroika in an attempt to improve relations. The final variable included is SALT, which was included to test for any structural changes that may have resulted from the signing and ratification of the SALT I arms reduction treaty. This variable was chosen because it represents a culmination of the detente era in U.S.–Soviet relations.

Empirical Results

Equation (10.27) was first estimated by the OLS procedure. The model was then tested for first-order serial correlation coefficient. Because of the presence of the lagged dependent variable, the Durbin–Watson test is not applicable. Therefore, the authors used the Lagrange Multiplier test (see Chapters 7 and 9). Basically, the procedure is to regress the estimated residuals $\hat{u}_t$ on $\hat{u}_{t-1}$ and all the variables in equation (10.27), and compute the test statistic TR^2, where T is the number of observations used in the above regression and R^2 is the *unadjusted R*-squared value from the same regression. Under the null hypothesis that the first-order serial correlation coefficient is zero, TR^2 has the χ^2 distribution with one degree of freedom. In our example, $T = 46$ (the first observation is lost because of the $\hat{u}_{t-1}$ term) and $R^2 = 0.138$. Therefore, $TR^2 = 6.348$, which is significant at the 1.2 percent level, thus implying serial correlation. Equation (10.27) was then estimated by a mixed Hildreth–Lu (HILU) and Cochrane–Orcutt (CORC) procedure. This consists of first using the HILU search procedure to obtain an estimate of the first-order serial correlation coefficient, and then fine tuning it using the CORC iterative procedure. We can expect this procedure to converge to the global maximum likelihood estimates. Table 10.6 presents the estimates and associated statistics.

It is unrealistic to expect all the estimated coefficients to be statistically significant. We note that many terms are insignificant. In order to improve the precision of the remaining estimates, these were then omitted one or two at a time, and the resulting model was estimated by the mixed HILU–CORC procedure. Additional diagnostic tests were also performed on this model [Lagrange Multiplier (LM) test for the presence of a lagged dependent variable, ARCH test for time-varying variances, and LM test for higher order serial correlation], but no evidence was found to support any of them (see Chapters 7, 8, and 9 for a discussion of these diagnostic tests). Table 10.7 contains the estimates and associated statistics for the final model. We note that in the final model, most of the regression coefficients are significant at the 1 percent level.

TABLE 10.6 HILU–CORC Estimates of the General Model in Equation (10.27)

Variable	Coefficient	Std. Error	t-stat	Prob $t > |T|$
CONSTANT	−0.19814	0.03679	−5.386	<0.0001***
GOVT	1.31688	0.07033	18.725	<0.0001***
LONGDEF	0.29021	0.22232	1.305	0.2014
LONGDEF * PRES	0.03553	0.06429	0.553	0.5844
LONGDEF * ELECT	−0.00137	0.02722	−0.050	0.9602
LONGDEF * REAGAN	−0.02705	0.07806	−0.347	0.7313
LONGDEF * OPP	−0.05306	0.06448	−0.823	0.4168
LONGDEF * HDEM	$1.95561e{-}06$	$4.03108e{-}03$	0.000	0.9996
LONGDEF * SDEM	−0.00299	0.00502	−0.595	0.5563
LONGDEF * WW2	0.46665	0.09747	4.788	<0.0001***
LONGDEF * KWAR	0.41699	0.06549	6.367	<0.0001***
LONGDEF * VWAR	0.12367	0.06619	1.868	0.0712*
LONGDEF * KRUS	0.14522	0.06031	2.408	0.0222**
LONGDEF * GORB	0.02471	0.04328	0.571	0.5722
LONGDEF * SALT	−0.00534	0.04176	−0.128	0.8991

d.f. = 31 $\bar{R}^2 = 0.943$ $\hat{\sigma} = 0.08178$

*Three *'s indicate significance at 1 percent, two *'s indicate significance between 1 and 5 percent, and one * indicates significance between 5 and 10 percent. $\bar{R}^2$ and $\hat{\sigma}$ are based on the estimated residuals for equation (10.27) using the mixed estimation procedure described earlier.*

TABLE 10.7 HILU–CORC Estimates for the Final Model

Variable	Coefficient	Std. Error	t-stat	Prob $t > |T|$
CONSTANT	−0.20750	0.02992	−6.935	0.0001***
GOVT	1.34260	0.06467	20.762	0.0001***
LONGDEF	0.35268	0.09435	3.738	0.0006***
LONGDEF * SDEM	−0.00413	0.00164	−2.526	0.0158**
LONGDEF * WW2	0.46914	0.07794	6.019	0.0001***
LONGDEF * KWAR	0.42589	0.04811	8.853	0.0001***
LONGDEF * VWAR	0.14121	0.04228	3.340	0.0019***
LONGDEF * KRUS	0.15773	0.04237	3.722	0.0006***

d.f. = 38 $\bar{R}^2 = 0.951$ $\hat{\sigma} = 0.07577$

*Three *'s indicate significance at 1 percent, two *'s indicate significance between 1 and 5 percent, and one * indicates significance between 5 and 10 percent. $\bar{R}^2$ and $\hat{\sigma}$ are based on the estimated residuals for equation (10.27) using the mixed estimation procedure described earlier.*

Interpretation of the Results

The variables included in the final model explain 95.1 percent of the variance of the rate of growth of military expenditures, which is considerably higher than that of the basic model. The explanatory variables are classified as follows according to whether they are significant at the 1 or 5 percent levels or are insignificant:

1 percent	GOVT, LONGDEF, LONGDEF * WW2, LONGDEF * KWAR, LONGDEF * VWAR, and LONGDEF * KRUS
5 percent	LONGDEF * SDEM
Insignificant	LONGDEF * PRES, LONGDEF * ELECT, LONGDEF * REAGAN, LONGDEF * OPP, LONGDEF * HDEM, LONGDEF * GORB, and LONGDEF * SALT

As can be seen by the significance of GOVT, military expenditures grew at a significant rate over the sample period with a marginal effect of 1.343. Thus a 1 percent increase in government expenditures resulted in a greater increase of 1.343 percent in military expenditures, indicating that military expenditures have become a greater portion of government expenditures. This is confirmed by the significance of the short-run error correction term, LONGDEF.

Most of the variables significant at the 1 percent level are international variables indicating that, relatively, they have greater influence than the chosen domestic variables. All three of the war variables are significantly positive as expected, although, as can be seen by the differences in their coefficients, World War II and the Korean War had greater marginal effects upon military expenditure than did the Vietnam War.

World War II	0.469 LONGDEF
Korean War	0.426 LONGDEF
Vietnam War	0.141 LONGDEF

This result is plausible since both of the earlier wars involved greater degrees of mobilization in terms of troops and intensity of fighting. KRUS also has a positive marginal effect, 0.158 LONGDEF, which again is as would be expected from the consequences of his aggressive foreign policy.

The only significant domestic variable was SDEM seeming to indicate that party affiliation in the Senate is indicative of voting patterns on military appropriations. This should not be taken as absolute proof, however, since as can be observed from the magnitude of the effect, -0.00413 LONGDEF, this effect is a small one. In addition, the insignificance of HDEM, PRES, and OPP lead us to the conclusion that party affiliation is not a significant sign of military voting patterns. The significance of SDEM then should be that party affiliation, in the Senate at least, is probably at most an occasional short-run trend that is an insignificant factor in comparison to other events such as war or sensitivity to voting patterns of constituents (Majeski and Jones, 1981).

The insignificance of ELECT seems to indicate that there is no manipulation of defense expenditures in the name of political gain. This does not imply that government expenditures are not used in times of recession for the sake of macroeconomic policy. It is likely in this case that a larger government budget will only in part be supplemented by an augmented military budget, resulting in no significant proportional change. Another possibility is that government spending is used in the same fashion originally suggested for military expenditure.

The insignificance of both GORB and SALT isn't all that surprising either. In the case of GORB it is most likely due to the relatively few years that he was in power with respect to the sample of this study. The fact that SALT is not significant is possibly because it resulted in only a reduction in nuclear arms and that it was part of a general reduction in military expenditures. It could also be so because military funds were redistributed to other portions of the military budget.

Concluding Remarks

The error correction framework used in this study has provided some unique insights to the variation in military expenditure in the United States during World War II and later periods. There is considerable evidence of interaction between the error correction effect and some of the economic and political variables in determining the rates of growth of the military budget. In particular, the short-run adjustment term (LONGDEF) interacts significantly with several policy variables. The scope of this study is limited, however, by the limited degrees of freedom. In spite of this, the error correction model has provided a useful benchmark with which to work. Even if the assumption of a stable relationship between two variables is at best a tenuous one, the error correction approach may still provide researchers a powerful instrument with which to carry out studies. This approach is powerful because its unique structure describes a relationship between two related variables and makes short-run and long-run behavior consistent.

SUMMARY

This chapter has examined the consequences of using lagged variables in a model—both lagged explanatory and lagged dependent (or endogenous) variables. Models involving lags from several periods are known as *distributed lag models*.

A distributed lag model with only lagged explanatory variables is of the form

$$Y_t = \alpha + \beta_0 X_t + \beta_1 X_{t-1} + \cdots + \beta_p X_{t-p} + u_t$$

The partial effect $\Delta Y_t/\Delta X_t$ is known as the *impact multiplier*—that is, it is the marginal effect of X on Y in the same time period. The partial effect $\Delta Y_t/\Delta X_{t-i}$ is known as the *interim multiplier of order i*, that is, the marginal effect of changes in X made at the present time on Y i periods hence. *Long-run equilibrium* (or *steady state*) is attained when all the variables are constant over time. We denote the long-run values by Y^* and X^*. The partial effect $\Delta Y^*/\Delta X^*$ then is known as the *long-run multiplier*, the effect of X on Y after all the adjustments have taken place and a long-run equilibrium has been attained.

If we apply ordinary least squares to this model, the estimates are still BLUE and consistent, because none of the assumptions is violated. However, because $X_t, X_{t-1}, \ldots$, will generally be highly correlated, multicollinearity problems arise. Furthermore, the larger the value of p the more the number of parameters to be estimated and the fewer the degrees of freedom. This worsens the precision of the estimates and reduces the powers of tests of hypotheses.

One way to reduce the number of parameters to be estimated is to use the *Koyck lag* (or *geometric lag*) scheme proposed by Koyck. The procedure assumes that the weight for the period i is a fraction of the weight for the previous period. Thus $\beta_i = \lambda \beta_{i-1}$, where $0 < \lambda < 1$. This assumption is reasonable in cases in which most of the impact of X is immediate, with diminished effects as time goes on. The model can now be transformed as

$$Y_t = \alpha(1 - \lambda) + \lambda Y_{t-1} + \beta_0 X_t + u_t$$

which has only three parameters to be estimated.

An alternative procedure to reduce the number of parameters is the *Almon lag* (or *polynomial lag*) proposed by Almon. In this scheme each coefficient is assumed to be a polynomial in the lags. For instance,

$$\beta_i = \alpha_0 + \alpha_1 i + \alpha_2 i^2 + \cdots + \alpha_r i^r$$

The model can now be transformed to one involving the estimation of the α's. Because the degree of the polynomial is usually no more than 3, the number of parameters to be estimated is limited. The choice of the largest lag (p) and the degree of the polynomial (r) may be made by choosing various combinations and then selecting the one that maximizes $\bar{R}^2$.

The Koyck lag transformation converts a distributed lag model to one involving the lagged dependent variable term Y_{t-1}. Other schemes such as a *partial adjustment* or *adaptive expectations* can also result in lag dependent variables as regressors. If a model has lagged dependent variables and the OLS procedure is used to estimate the parameters, then (1) the estimates and forecasts based on them are biased in small samples, but are consistent and asymptotically efficient; and (2) estimated standard errors are consistent and tests of hypotheses are valid for large samples, *provided the error terms are well-behaved—that is, they satisfy Assumptions 3.2 through 3.7.*

If the coefficient for the lag-dependent variable is exactly 1, then we have the *unit root problem* in which the variance of the dependent variable goes to infinity with the sample size. It is possible to use the *Dickey–Fuller test* to check whether there is a unit root. The procedure is basically to estimate a restricted and an unrestricted model and compute the F-statistic in the usual way. However, the critical value for the test should not be obtained from the traditional F-table because the distribution is not F. Instead, use the critical values obtained by Dickey and Fuller.

If the error terms are serially correlated or follow a *moving average* in which the errors are linear combinations of other well-behaved random errors, then OLS estimates and forecasts will be biased and inconsistent. Estimated standard errors will also be inconsistent, and hence tests of hypotheses are invalid. Finally, the Durbin–Watson test for serial correlation is not applicable if lagged dependent variables are present in the model. An alternative test is a *Durbin-h test*, but it has limitations. The Lagrange multiplier test is a better one. The procedure is first to estimate the model by OLS and save the residuals ($\hat{u}_t$). Next regress $\hat{u}_t$ against $\hat{u}_{t-1}$, $\hat{u}_{t-2}, \ldots, \hat{u}_{t-m}$, and all the explanatory variables in the model, *including the lagged dependent regressors Y_{t-1}, $Y_{t-2}, \ldots, Y_{t-p}$*, and compute the unadjusted R^2. The LM test statistic is $(T - p)R^2$, which, under the null hypothesis of zero serial correlation, has a χ^2_m distribution (m is the order of the serial correlation and $T - p$ is the number of observations actually used in estimating the auxiliary regression). If $(T - p)R^2 > \chi^2_m(0.05)$, the null hypothesis is rejected at the 5 percent level.

Several estimation procedures are available when lagged dependent variables are present. If the errors are well-behaved, then the OLS procedure gives desirable properties for large samples (usually of sizes 30 or more). If the errors are serially correlated, the Cochrane–Orcutt procedure will give consistent estimates, but the standard errors will be inconsistent. A slight modification to the CORC procedure will yield consistent standard errors also. If the errors follow a moving average scheme, then the model can be transformed and a search procedure used to get consistent estimates.

Another way of incorporating short-run adjustments in a model is to use the *error correction mechanism*. The error correction model has the following general structure:

$$\Delta y_t = \beta_0 + \beta_1 \Delta x_t + \beta_2(y_{t-1} - x_{t-1}) + u_t$$

where

$$\Delta y_t = \ln(Y_t) - \ln(Y_{t-1}) \qquad \text{and} \qquad \Delta x_t = \ln(X_t) - \ln(X_{t-1})$$

are the respective rates of change. The term $y_{t-1} - x_{t-1}$ allows for a short-run disequilibrium adjustment that leads to a long-run situation in which Y_t and X_t grow at the same constant rate. The error correction model is closely related to *cointegration* discussed in the next chapter.

KEY TERMS

Adaptive expectations model	Durbin-*h* test
Adjustment coefficient	Error correction model
Almon lag	Geometric lag
Average lag	Impact multiplier
Cointegration	Interim multiplier of order *i*
Dickey–Fuller test	Koyck lag
Distributed lag model	Lagged dependent variable

Laged independent variable

Long-run equilibrium

Long-run multiplier

Mean lag

Moving average

Moving average (MA) error

Partial adjustment model

Polynomial lag

Random walk

Random walk with drift

Speed of adjustment

Steady state

Unit root test

Well-behaved errors

REFERENCES

Almon, S. "The Distributed Lag Between Capital Appropriations and Expenditures." *Econometrica*, Vol. 30 (January 1965): 178–196.

Andersen, L. C., and Jordan, J. L. "Monetary and Fiscal Policy Actions: A Test of Their Relative Importance in Economic Stabilization." *Review of the Federal Reserve Bank of St. Louis* (November 1968): 11–24.

Ando, A., and Modigliani, F. "The 'Life-Cycle' Hypothesis of Saving: Aggregate Implications and Tests." *American Economic Review*, Vol. 53 (1963): 55–84.

Barro, R. J. "Unanticipated Money Growth and Economic Activity in the United States." In *Money, Expectations, and the Business Cycle*, ed. Robert Barro. New York: Academic Press, 1981. Pp. 137–169.

Corrigan, E. G. "The Measurement and Importance of Fiscal Policy Changes." *Monthly Review, Federal Reserve Bank of New York* (June 1970): 133–145.

Currie, D. "Some Long-Run Features of Dynamic Time-Series Models." *Economic Journal*, Vol. 91 (1981): 704–715.

Davidson, J. E. H.: Hendry, D. F.; Srba, F.; and Yeo, S. "Economic Modelling of the Aggregate Time-series Relationship Between Consumer's Expenditure and Income in the United Kingdom." *Economic Journal*, Vol. 88 (1978); 661–692.

Davidson, R., and MacKinnon, J. G. "Inflation and the Savings Rate." *Applied Economics*, Vol. 15 (December 1983): 731–743.

Dawson, A. "Sargan's Wage Equation: A Theoretical and Empirical Reconstruction." *Applied Economics*, Vol. 13 (1981): 351–363.

Dickey, David A., and Fuller, Wayne A. "Distribution of the Estimators for Autoregressive Time Series with a Unit Root." *J. Am. Stat. Assoc.*, 14 (June 1979): 427–431.

Dickey, D. A., and Fuller, W. A. "Likelihood Ratio Statistics for Autoregressive Time Series with a Unit Root." *Econometrica*, 49 (July 1981): 1057–1072.

Durbin, J. "Testing for Serial Correlation in Least Squares Regression When Some of the Regressors Are Lagged Dependent Variables." *Econometrica*, Vol. 38 (May 1970): 410–421.

Dutkowsky, D. H. "Unanticipated Money Growth, Interest Rate Volatility, and Unemployment in the United States." *Rev. Econ. and Stat.*, Vol. 69 (February 1987): 144–148.

Economic Report of the President. Washington, D.C.: U.S. Government Printing Office, 1991.

Engle, R. F., and Granger, C. W. J. "Co-integration and Error Correction: Representation, Estimation, and Testing." *Econometrica*, Vol. 55 (March 1987): 251–276.

Friedman, M. *A. Theory of the Consumption Function.* Princeton, N.J.: Princeton University Press, 1957.

Granger, C. W. J. "Some Properties of Time Series Data and Their Use on Econometric Model Specification." *Journal of Econometrics*, 16 (1981): 121–130.

Harvey, A. C. *The Econometric Analysis of Time Series.* New York: J. Wiley & Sons, 1981.

Hendry, D. F. "Econometric Modelling of House Prices in the United Kingdom." In *Econometrics and Quantitative Economics* ed. D. F. Hendry and K. F. Wallis. Oxford: Basil Blackwell, 1984.

Johnston, J. *Econometric Methods.* New York: McGraw-Hill, 1972 and 1984.

Judge, G. G.; Griffiths, W. E.; Hill, R. C.; and Lee, T. C. *The Theory and Practice of Econometrics.* New York: J. Wiley & Sons, 1985.

Kmenta, Jan. *Elements of Econometrics.* New York: Macmillan, 1986.

Koyck, L. M. *Distributed Lags and Investment Analysis.* New York: North-Holland, 1954.

Majeski, S. J., and Jones, D. L. "Arms Race Modeling, Causality Analysis and Model Specification." *Journal of Conflict Resolution*, 25 (1981): 259–288.

Ostrom, C. "A Reactive Linkage Model of the U.S. Defense Expenditure Policy Making Process." *American Political Science Review*, 72 (1978): 941–956.

Phillips, P. C. B. "Time Series Regression with a Unit Root." *Econometrica*, Vol. 50 (March 1987): 277–302.

Rattinger, H. "Arms, Detente, and Bureaucracy, the Case of the Arms Race in Europe." *Journal of Conflict Resolution*, 19 (1975): 571–595.

Ramanathan, Ramu, and Blackburn, Jan. "U.S. Defense Expenditures: An Error Correction (Cointegration) Approach," DISCUSSION PAPER 91–13, University of California, San Diego, 1991.

Salmon, M. "Error Correction Mechanisms." *Economic Journal*, Vol. 92 (1982): 615–629.

Sargan, J. D. "Wages and Prices in the United Kingdom: A Study in Econometric Methodology." In Hart, P. E., Millis, G., and Whittaker, J. K. (eds.) *Econometric Analysis for National Economic Planning.* London: Butterworths, 1964. Also reprinted in *Econometrics and Quantitative Economics*, ed. D. F. Hendry and K. F. Wallis. Oxford: Basil Blackwell, 1984.

Schmidt, P., and Waud, R. N. "Almon Lag Technique and the Monetary Versus Fiscal Debate." *J. Amer Stat. Assoc.*, Vol. 68 (March 1973): 11–19.

Zuk, G., and Woodbury, N. R. "U.S. Defense Spending, Electoral Cycles and Soviet–American Relations." *Journal of Conflict Resolution*, 30 (1986): 445–468.

PRACTICE COMPUTER SESSIONS

10.1 To reproduce Example 10.1, use the ECSLIB commands in *ps10 − 1.inp* and the data file *data10 − 1*.

10.2 For the Dickey–Fuller test in Example 10.2, the ECSLIB commands are in *ps10 – 2.inp* and the data set is *data10 – 8*.

10.3 For the application in Section 10.4, the commands in *ps10 – 3.inp* will be very useful. The data for this are in *data10 – 9*. Because the steps to arrive at a final model are numerous, this session will take a considerable amount of time.

EXERCISES

†**10.1** Suppose the demand for money is given by the relation $M_t = \alpha + \beta Y_t^* + \gamma R_t$, where M_t is real cash balances, Y_t^* is "expected" real income and R_t is the interest rate, at time t. Expectations are revised according to the adaptive rule $Y_t^* = \lambda Y_{t-1} + (1 - \lambda) Y_{t-1}^* + u_t$, $0 < \lambda < 1$. You have data on Y_t, M_t, and R_t but none on Y_t^*.
   a. Formulate an econometric model that, in principle, can be used to derive estimates of α, β, γ, and λ. (These estimates won't be unique but you may ignore that problem here.)
   b. Suppose $E(u_t) = 0$, $E(u_t^2) = \sigma^2$, $E(u_t, u_{t-s}) = 0$ for $s \neq 0$ and Y_{t-1}, R_t, M_{t-1}, R_{t-1} are all uncorrelated with u_t. Are the OLS estimates (i) unbiased, (ii) consistent? Why or why not?
   c. Suppose, instead, that $u_t = \rho u_{t-1} + \epsilon_t$, with ϵ_t having properties similar to those in part b. Are the OLS estimates (i) unbiased, (ii) consistent, in this case? Explain.

10.2 Actual business expenditure for new plant and equipment (Y_t) is given by the relation $Y_t = e^\alpha (X_t^*)^\beta e^{u_t}$, where X_t^* is expected sales, α and β are unknown coefficients, and u_t is a random variable. Because X_t^* is not observable, we postulate the adaptive rule $X_t^*/X_{t-1}^* = (X_{t-1}/X_{t-1}^*)^\gamma$, where X_t is actual sales and γ is the adjustment coefficient.
   a. Derive a relationship that can be used to estimate α, β, and γ from data on X_t and Y_t.
   b. State the assumptions on u_t needed to ensure that the OLS estimates of the model you obtained in part a are consistent. Explain why your assumptions imply consistency.
   c. Under the assumptions stated by you, are the OLS estimates also unbiased? Why or why not?
   d. Suppose u_t has the normal distribution with mean zero, constant variance, and zero covariance. Are the OLS estimates consistent? Explain why or why not.

10.3 A firm has a desired level of inventories I_t^* that is given by $I_t^* = \alpha + \beta S_t$, where S_t is the sales at time t. Because of market frictions and random shocks, actual inventories I_t differ from the desired I_t^*, according to the relation

$$I_t = I_{t-1} + \lambda(I_{t-1}^* - I_{t-1}) + u_t$$

where u_t is a random error term whose properties are unspecified at this point. You have data on I_t and S_t but none on I_t^*.

a. State the signs and other restrictions you would expect for the unknown parameters α, β, and λ. Explain our reasoning.

b. Derive a relationship that can be used to estimate α, β, and λ. (Ignore assumptions on u_t here.)

c. State all the assumptions on u_t that will make OLS estimates of the model you got in part b also consistent. Under the assumptions just stated, are the estimates also BLUE? Why or why not?

d. Are α, β, and λ estimable? If not, explain why not? If yes, describe how they can be estimated? That is, express $\hat{\alpha}$, $\hat{\beta}$, and $\hat{\lambda}$ in terms of the estimates of the model you obtained in part b.

$^†10.4$ Let C_t be real per capita consumption in the United States at time t, and Y_t be real per capita disposable income, both measured in billions of dollars. Using annual data for 32 years, the following model was obtained:

$$\hat{C}_t = -21151 + 2989.9 \ln(Y_t)$$
$$\underset{(-39.3)}{} \quad \underset{(45.0)}{}$$

$$\bar{R}^2 = 0.985 \qquad d = 0.207$$

The values in parentheses are t-statistics and d is the Durbin–Watson statistic.

a. Test the model for first-order serial correlation at the 5 percent level using the alternative most common in economics.

b. Based on your conclusion, what can you say about the properties of the OLS estimates just given, in terms of (i) unbiasedness, (ii) BLUE, and (iii) the validity of tests of hypotheses?

c. Describe, step by step, an estimation procedure that will give "better" estimates than OLS. Explain why your procedure is superior to OLS.

It is hypothesized that C_t depends on the consumption in the previous period but is adjusted for changes in disposable income. The following model was obtained using OLS (t-values in parentheses):

$$\hat{C}_t = -21.83 + 1.01 C_{t-1} + 0.769[Y_t - Y_{t-1}]$$
$$\underset{(-0.78)}{} \quad \underset{(107.5)}{} \quad \underset{(7.8)}{}$$

$$\bar{R}^2 = 0.998 \qquad d = 2.11 \qquad \hat{\rho} = -0.07$$

d. Are these estimates unbiased? Explain.

e. Test the model for first-order serial correlation. Write down the null and alternative hypotheses. [*Note*: you have all the information you need to carry out this test.]

f. Based on your results in part e, are the OLS estimates (i) unbiased, (ii) consistent? Explain.

g. If you found significant serial correlation, describe how you can get "better" estimates than those by OLS. Explain what you mean by "better."

10.5* Let S_t^* be the desired savings of a household and Y_t^* be its expected income. The relationship between these two variables is of the form $S_t^* = \alpha + \beta Y_t^*$. Consumers revise their desires and expectations according to the partial adjustment and adaptive expectations rules.

$$S_t = S_{t-1} + \lambda(S_{t-1}^* - S_{t-1})$$
$$Y_t^* = Y_{t-1}^* + \mu(Y_{t-1} - Y_{t-1}^*)$$

where S_t is actual saving and Y_t is actual income. You have data on only S_t and Y_t, and none on S_t^* and Y_t^*.

a. State the signs and other restrictions you would expect for the unknown parameters α, β, λ, and μ. Explain your reasoning.

b. Derive a relationship that can be used to estimate α, β, λ, and μ (add an error term u_t at the end).

c. State all the assumptions on u_t that will make OLS estimates of the model you got in part b also consistent. Under the assumptions just stated, are the estimates also BLUE? Why or why not?

d. Are α, β, λ, and μ estimable? If not, explain why not? If yes, describe how they can be estimated? That is, express, $\hat{\alpha}$, $\hat{\beta}$, $\hat{\lambda}$, and $\hat{u}$ in terms of the estimates of the model you obtained in part b.

10.6 Table 10.10 has annual data on per capital consumption (C_t) and personal disposable income (Y_t), both in constant 1982 dollars. Estimate a model similar to equation (10.1), choosing your own lag period. Test the model for serial correlation and, if it is present, use the mixed HILU–CORC procedure to obtain new estimates. Compute the long-run multiplier for this model and check to see if it is meaningful.

10.7 Suppose consumption is determined not by current income but by "expected income" (Y_t^*). Also assume that consumers revise their expectations according to the adaptive expectations scheme described in Section 10.2. We then have the following two equations (ignoring error terms):

$$C_t = \alpha + \beta Y_t^*$$
$$Y_t^* = \lambda Y_{t-1} + (1 - \lambda)Y_{t-1}^*$$

By proceeding as we did in Section 10.2, derive an estimable econometric formulation. Use the data set in Table 10.10 and estimate the model you obtained. Test it for autocorrelation and correct for it if needed. From your estimates, obtain estimates of the unknown parameters. Compute the long-run multiplier in this example also. Do you get sensible results?

10.8 Use a purely autoregressive framework to relate the logarithm of consumption to its past values only. Estimate this model with the data in Table 10.10 and test for a unit root. Reestimate the model if appropriate. Carry out a similar exercise using the income series.

10.9 Construct an error correction model for the consumption function used in the previous three exercises and estimate it using the same data set. Is the short-run adjustment term significant?

10.10 Table 10.12 has annual data on the population (P_t) of the State of California. Estimate an appropriate log-linear model and test it for a unit root. Carry out a similar exercise with the population data in Tables 3.11 and 3.12.

10.11 Table 9.1 has annual data on the farm population (Y_t) in the United States. Estimate the following models which involve only lagged dependent variables and a time trend. Which of the models is "better"? Explain what you mean by "better."

$$Y_t = \beta_0 + \beta_1 Y_{t-1} + \beta_2 Y_{t-2} + \alpha t + u_t$$
$$Y_t = \beta_0 + \beta_1 Y_{t-1} + \alpha t + u_t$$

Use the Durbin-h and LM tests for first-order serial correlation. Based on your results what do you conclude about the consistency of the OLS estimates obtained?

10.12 In each of the following questions, a statement has been made in quotations. Carefully prove or provide adequate explanations whether or not the statement is valid. If it is not valid, state the correct version of the assertion. Justify your answers.

a. "When it comes to unbiasedness, consistency, and efficiency of the estimates of the parameters of a multiple regression model (with no lagged dependent variable), high multicollinearity, ignoring serial correlation, and adding an irrelevant variable, all have similar results."

b. Consider two models using time series data:

(A) $Y_t = \alpha + \beta X_t + u_t$
(B) $Y_t = \alpha + \beta X_t + \gamma Y_{t-1} + u_t$

"Model B is likely to have a higher $\bar{R}^2$ than Model A."

c. "If a model has a lagged dependent variable as a regressor and the DW statistic d using OLS estimates is less than d_L, then we can reject the null hypothesis that $\rho = 0$, where $u_t = \rho u_{t-1} + \epsilon_t$."

10.13 Table 9.13 has quarterly data for the United States on the gross national product (GNP), money supply, government expenditure, taxes, and exports. In Exercise 9.10 you estimated a static model that related GNP to the other variables.

a. Estimate a new model with lagged variables M_{t-1}, M_{t-2}, M_{t-3}, M_{t-4}, G_{t-1}, and so on. Use lags up to four quarters but no lagged GNP. Do the model selection statistics improve compared to the results for Exercise 9.10? Is multicollinearity a problem here? Test the model for serial correlation. If present, obtain Cochrane–Orcutt estimates. Are they sensible? Are the signs of the regression coefficients sensible?

b. Use the Almon lag technique to reformulate the model and estimate it. Try polynomials of degrees 2 and 3, with lags up to four periods. How do these results compare with those in part a?

c. Use the LM test to test whether lagged GNP terms belong in the model. If yes, add them and reestimate, being sure to test for serial correlation.

d. For each of the models, calculate the long-run multiplier for each exogenous variable.

e. Which of the models and estimates do you consider "best"? Explain what you mean by "best."

10.14 Table 9.12 contains data on the demand for automobiles and its determinants. Suppose that the desired purchase of new cars in a given period is a function of the cars' average price, consumer income, the prime interest rate (a proxy for auto loan rates), the unemployment rate, a dummy for a General Motors strike, and a dummy for the spring quarter. Actual purchase follows the partial adjustment mechanism described in Section 10.2. Use that to formulate an econometric model (in double-log terms). Next estimate this model and compare the results with those in Exercise 9.9. Also compute the long-run multipliers for each of the exogenous variables. Are the results sensible?

10.15 Redo Exercise 10.14 using the stock variable in Table 9.12 as the dependent variable. In other words, you are modeling the desired stock rather than the desired purchase of new cars.

10.16 According to the theory of economic growth, the long-run rate of inflation equals the rate of growth of the money supply minus the rate of growth of the population. This implies a long-run relationship of the form $P_t = KM_t/N_t$, where P_t is the price index, M_t is money supply, and N_t is the size of the population.

a. Show that the result translates to $p_t = k + m_t - n_t$, where the lowercase variable are the logarithms of the corresponding uppercase variables.

b. Consider the short-run relation

$$p_t = \beta_0 + \beta_1 p_{t-1} + \beta_2 m_t + \beta_3 m_{t-1} + \beta_4 n_t + \beta_5 n_{t-1} + u_t$$

Show that if $\beta_1 = 1 - \gamma$, $\beta_3 = \gamma - \beta_2$, and $\beta_5 = -\gamma - \beta_4$, then this short-run relation is consistent with the long-run behavior postulated above.

c. Derive an error correction model of the change in log price.

d. Table 10.11 has annual data for the United States for the period 1959–1985. N_t is the population in millions; M_t is money supply (in billions of current dollars), defined as M_3 in the Economic Report of the President; and P_t is the consumer price, with 1982 as the base year. Using those data estimate the error correction model you formulated in part c, and interpret the results.

TABLE 10.8   Data on the Exchange Rate of Deutsche Marks per Dollar

Period	Marks	Period	Marks	Period	Marks
1973.01	3.196	1975.10	2.581	1978.07	2.056
1973.02	3.005	1975.11	2.589	1978.08	1.997
1973.03	2.813	1975.12	2.622	1978.09	1.969
1973.04	2.837	1976.01	2.602	1978.10	1.837
1973.05	2.79	1976.02	2.562	1978.11	1.904
1973.06	2.578	1976.03	2.56	1978.12	1.879
1973.07	2.335	1976.04	2.538	1979.01	1.85
1973.08	2.426	1976.05	2.562	1979.02	1.857
1973.09	2.424	1976.06	2.577	1979.03	1.86
1973.10	2.414	1976.07	2.574	1979.04	1.896
1973.11	2.58	1976.08	2.529	1979.05	1.908
1973.12	2.657	1976.09	2.489	1979.06	1.884
1974.01	2.815	1976.10	2.429	1979.07	1.824
1974.02	2.714	1976.11	2.413	1979.08	1.829
1974.03	2.617	1976.12	2.383	1979.09	1.794
1974.04	2.526	1977.01	2.393	1979.10	1.789
1974.05	2.461	1977.02	2.405	1979.11	1.771
1974.06	2.525	1977.03	2.392	1979.12	1.734
1974.07	2.553	1977.04	2.374	1980.01	1.725
1974.08	2.618	1977.05	2.359	1980.02	1.748
1974.09	2.661	1977.06	2.356	1980.03	1.851
1974.10	2.593	1977.07	2.282	1980.04	1.876
1974.11	2.51	1977.08	2.317	1980.05	1.791
1974.12	2.45	1977.09	2.324	1980.06	1.767
1975.01	2.364	1977.10	2.278	1980.07	1.747
1975.02	2.327	1977.11	2.241	1980.08	1.79
1975.03	2.319	1977.12	2.151	1980.09	1.789
1975.04	2.376	1978.01	2.118	1980.10	1.842
1975.05	2.35	1978.02	2.077	1980.11	1.919
1975.06	2.34	1978.03	2.033	1980.12	1.97
1975.07	2.471	1978.04	2.042	1981.01	2.011
1975.08	2.574	1978.05	2.105	1981.02	2.139
1975.09	2.618	1978.06	2.084	1981.03	2.106

(*continued*)

TABLE 10.8 (*Continued*)

Period	Marks	Period	Marks	Period	Marks
1981.04	2.164	1982.12	2.419	1984.07	2.849
1981.05	2.294	1983.01	2.389	1984.08	2.886
1981.06	2.378	1983.02	2.428	1984.09	3.031
1981.07	2.44	1983.03	2.411	1984.10	3.068
1981.08	2.501	1983.04	2.44	1984.11	2.998
1981.09	2.352	1983.05	2.467	1984.12	3.104
1981.10	2.254	1983.06	2.549	1985.01	3.171
1981.11	2.229	1983.07	2.591	1985.02	3.303
1981.12	2.258	1983.08	2.674	1985.03	3.298
1982.01	2.294	1983.09	2.668	1985.04	3.095
1982.02	2.366	1983.10	2.603	1985.05	3.109
1982.03	2.38	1983.11	2.685	1985.06	3.064
1982.04	2.397	1983.12	2.75	1985.07	2.908
1982.05	2.313	1984.01	2.811	1985.08	2.794
1982.06	2.429	1984.02	2.698	1985.09	2.838
1982.07	2.466	1984.03	2.597	1985.10	2.645
1982.08	2.481	1984.04	2.647	1985.11	2.595
1982.09	2.505	1984.05	2.748	1985.12	2.512
1982.10	2.532	1984.06	2.74	1986.01	2.438
1982.11	2.554				

Source: Citibase data series.

TABLE 10.9 Data on U.S. Military Expenditure and Its Determinants

YEAR	UG	UM	GNPDEF	HDEM	SDEM	PRES	ELECT	REAGAN	OPP	WW2	KWAR	VWAR	KRUS	GORB	SALT
1940	9.589	1.504	22.7	60.138	71.875	0	1	0	0	0	0	0	0	0	0
1941	13.98	6.062	27.8	61.609	68.75	0	0	0	0	1	0	0	0	0	0
1942	34.5	23.97	33	61.609	68.75	0	0	0	0	1	0	0	0	0	0
1943	78.909	63.212	34	50.698	60.417	0	1	0	0	1	0	0	0	0	0
1944	93.956	76.874	33.1	50.698	60.417	0	1	0	0	1	0	0	0	0	0
1945	95.184	81.585	31.9	55.76	58.333	0	0	0	0	1	0	0	0	0	0
1946	61.738	44.731	30.2	55.76	58.333	0	0	0	0	0	0	0	0	0	0
1947	36.931	13.059	35	43.318	46.875	0	1	0	1	0	0	0	0	0	0
1948	36.493	13.015	39	43.318	46.875	0	1	0	1	0	0	0	0	0	0
1949	40.57	13.907	41.4	60.46	56.25	0	0	0	0	0	0	0	0	0	0
1950	43.147	13.119	39.6	60.46	56.25	0	0	0	0	0	0	0	0	0	0
1951	45.757	22.544	46.6	53.917	51.042	0	1	0	0	0	1	0	0	0	0
1952	67.692	44.015	48.9	53.917	51.042	0	1	0	0	0	1	0	0	0	0
1953	76.769	50.413	50.1	48.618	48.958	1	0	0	0	0	1	0	0	0	0
1954	70.89	46.645	49.1	48.618	48.958	1	0	0	0	0	0	0	0	0	0
1955	68.509	40.245	50.4	53.333	50	1	1	0	1	0	0	0	1	0	0
1956	70.46	40.305	52.9	53.333	50	1	1	0	1	0	0	0	1	0	0
1957	76.741	42.76	55.1	53.811	51.042	1	0	0	1	0	0	0	1	0	0
1958	82.575	44.371	57.7	53.811	51.042	1	0	0	1	0	0	0	1	0	0
1959	92.104	46.617	59	64.989	65	1	1	0	1	0	0	0	1	0	0
1960	92.223	45.908	59.4	64.989	65	1	1	0	1	0	0	0	1	0	0
1961	97.795	47.381	60.2	60.183	65	0	0	0	0	0	0	0	1	0	0
1962	106.813	51.097	62	60.183	65	0	0	0	0	0	0	0	1	0	0
1963	111.311	52.257	63.5	59.31	67	0	1	0	0	0	0	0	1	0	0
1964	118.584	53.591	65.1	59.31	67	0	1	0	0	0	0	0	1	0	0

TABLE 10.9 (Continued)

YEAR	UG	UM	GNPDEF	HDEM	SDEM	PRES	ELECT	REAGAN	OPP	WW2	KWAR	VWAR	KRUS	GORB	SALT
1965	118.43	49.578	67.1	67.816	68	0	0	0	0	0	0	1	0	0	0
1966	134.652	56.785	70	67.816	68	0	0	0	0	0	0	1	0	0	0
1967	158.254	70.708	72.7	56.912	64	0	1	0	0	0	0	1	0	0	0
1968	178.833	80.517	76.5	56.912	64	0	1	0	0	0	0	1	0	0	0
1969	184.548	81.232	80.1	55.862	57	1	0	0	1	0	0	1	0	0	0
1970	196.588	80.295	86.6	55.862	57	1	0	0	1	0	0	0	0	0	0
1971	210.172	77.497	92.7	58.525	54	1	1	0	1	0	0	0	0	0	1
1972	230.681	77.645	100	58.525	54	1	1	0	1	0	0	0	0	0	1
1973	245.707	75.033	106.3	55.324	56	1	0	0	1	0	0	0	0	0	1
1974	269.359	77.864	114.9	55.324	56	1	0	0	1	0	0	0	0	0	1
1975	332.332	84.852	126	66.897	60	1	1	0	1	0	0	0	0	0	1
1976	371.779	87.917	133.5	66.897	60	1	1	0	1	0	0	0	0	0	1
1977	409.203	95.147	150.2	67.126	61	0	0	0	0	0	0	0	0	0	1
1978	458.729	102.259	160.7	67.126	61	0	0	0	0	0	0	0	0	0	1
1979	503.464	113.605	175.3	63.741	58	0	1	0	0	0	0	0	0	0	1
1980	590.92	130.912	195.2	63.741	58	0	1	0	0	0	0	0	0	0	1
1981	678.209	153.868	213.2	55.862	46	1	0	1	0	0	0	0	0	0	1
1982	745.706	180.714	228.3	55.862	46	1	0	1	0	0	0	0	0	0	1
1983	808.327	204.41	237.4	61.982	46	1	1	1	0	0	0	0	0	0	1
1984	851.781	220.928	244.9	61.982	46	1	1	1	0	0	0	0	0	0	1
1985	946.316	245.154	257.1	58.065	47	1	0	1	0	0	0	0	0	0	1
1986	990.258	265.48	263.2	58.065	47	1	0	1	0	0	0	0	0	1	1
1987	1004.586	273.966	270.5	59.31	55	1	1	1	1	0	0	0	0	1	1

Source: History of American Statistics from Colonial Times; Historical Tables: Budget of the U.S. Government.

TABLE 10.10 Data on Per Capita Consumption and Personal Disposable Income for the United States (in 1982 dollars)

YEAR	CONS	INCOME	YEAR	CONS	INCOME	YEAR	CONS	INCOME
1947	4625	4820	1962	5729	6271	1977	8551	9381
1948	4650	5000	1963	5855	6378	1978	8808	9735
1949	4661	4915	1964	6099	6727	1979	8904	9829
1950	4834	5220	1965	6362	7027	1980	8783	9722
1951	4853	5308	1966	6607	7280	1981	8794	9769
1952	4915	5379	1967	6730	7513	1982	8818	9725
1953	5029	5515	1968	7003	7728	1983	9139	9930
1954	5066	5505	1969	7185	7891	1984	9489	10419
1955	5287	5714	1970	7275	8134	1985	9840	10625
1956	5349	5881	1971	7409	8322	1986	10123	10905
1957	5370	5909	1972	7726	8562	1987	10311	10946
1958	5357	5908	1973	7972	9042	1988	10580	11368
1959	5531	6027	1974	7826	8867	1989	10678	11531
1960	5561	6036	1975	7926	8944	1990	10668	11508
1961	5579	6113	1976	8272	9175			

Source: Economic Report of the President, 1991.

TABLE 10.11 Data for U.S. Population, Money Supply, and GNP Deflator

YEAR	N	M	P	YEAR	N	M	P
1959	177.83	299.8	30.4	1975	215.973	1172.2	59.3
1960	180.671	315.3	30.9	1976	218.035	1311.8	63.1
1961	183.691	341	31.2	1977	220.239	1472.6	67.3
1962	186.538	371.4	31.9	1978	222.585	1646.6	72.2
1963	189.242	406	32.4	1979	225.055	1803.2	78.6
1964	191.889	442.5	32.9	1980	227.757	1987.5	85.7
1965	194.303	482.2	33.8	1981	230.138	2234.2	94
1966	196.56	505.1	35	1982	232.52	2441.9	100
1967	198.712	557.1	35.9	1983	234.799	2693.4	103.9
1968	200.706	606.2	37.7	1984	237.001	2982.8	107.7
1969	202.677	615	39.8	1985	239.279	3202.1	110.9
1970	205.052	677.5	42	1986	241.625	3494.5	113.8
1971	207.661	776.2	44.43	1987	243.942	3678.7	117.4
1972	209.896	886	46.5	1988	246.307	3918.3	121.3
1973	211.909	985	49.5	1989	248.762	4044.3	126.3
1974	213.854	1070.4	54	1990	251.394	4094	131.5

Source: Economic Report of the President, 1991.

TABLE 10.12   Population of the State of
California (in millions)

Year	Population	Year	Population
1960	15.863	1975	21.538
1961	16.412	1976	21.936
1962	16.951	1977	22.352
1963	17.53	1978	22.836
1964	18.026	1979	23.257
1965	18.464	1980	23.78
1966	18.831	1981	24.267
1967	19.1747	1982	24.786
1968	19.432	1983	25.309
1969	19.7447	1984	25.78
1970	20.039	1985	26.358
1971	20.346	1986	26.999
1972	20.585	1987	27.655
1973	20.869	1988	28.323
1974	21.174	1989	29.063

Source: 1990 Economic Report of the Governor of the State of
California.

CHAPTER 11

Forecasting

■ An important reason for formulating an econometric model is to generate forecasts of one or more economic variables. In Chapter 1 we presented a number of examples of forecasting, and in Section 3.11 we used the simple regression model to illustrate the basic principles of forecasting.[1] In this chapter we take up the issue of forecasting in more detail. We describe the various approaches to it, as well as the methods of evaluating forecasts and combining the predictions generated by different models. Because the subject of forecasting is so wide-ranging, however, this chapter will serve only to introduce the issues involved. Numerous books have been written on the topic and readers are referred to them for further details.

Although the term **forecasting** (or the equivalent term **prediction**) is generally used in the context of trying to predict the future, the principles apply equally well to predicting cross-section variables. For instance, in the real estate example used in Chapters 3, 4, 6, and 7, one could obtain the predicted average price, given the characteristics of a house.

In categorizing forecasting methodologies, two broad approaches can be distinguished. **Econometric forecasting** is based on a regression model that relates one or more dependent variables to a number of independent variables. This approach has gained enormous popularity because of its ability to explain changes in the dependent variables in terms of changes in economic and other behavioral variables—in particular, changes in policy variables. In contrast to the econometric approach, **time series forecasting** is most commonly based on attempts to predict the values of a variable from past values of the same variable.

· · · · · · ·

[1] *It will be useful to reread Section 3.11 at this point.*

These categories are very broad and the line between them is not clear-cut. For example, while some econometric models are formulated in terms of only past values of the dependent variable, some pure time series (noneconometric) models relate one variable to the values of other variables (such models are known as **vector autoregressive**). The time series approach has generally been found to be superior to the econometric approach when very short-run predictions are made. Econometric models are better suited to modeling longer term effects. Models that synthesize these two general approaches offer potentially improved short- and long-run forecasts. Section 11.6 discusses econometric forecasting and Section 11.7 gives an introduction to time series forecasting.

11.1   Fitted Values, Ex-post, and Ex-ante Forecasts

In a forecasting environment three time periods are of interest. An investigator first uses the data for the period T_1 through T_2 (for example, 1948 through 1982) to estimate one or more models. From these estimates **fitted values** (sometimes referred to as **in-sample forecasts**) are obtained; that is, forecasts are made for the sample period T_1 through T_2 (1948 through 1982 in our example). As an example, consider the following regression model:

$$Y_t = \beta_1 + \beta_2 X_{t2} + \beta_3 X_{t3} + \cdots + \beta_k X_{tk} + u_t \tag{11.1}$$

The fitted value for time period t is

$$\hat{Y}_t = \hat{\beta}_1 + \hat{\beta}_2 X_{t2} + \hat{\beta}_3 X_{t3} + \cdots + \hat{\beta}_k X_{tk} \tag{11.2}$$

Out-of-sample forecasts are generated next for time periods $T_2 + 1$ onward. This **post-sample period** can be divided into two parts: periods $T_2 + 1$ through T_3 (say, 1983 through 1991), for which the actual values of Y and all the X's are known; and period $T_3 + 1$ onward (say, 1992 onward), for which the values of the X's and Y are

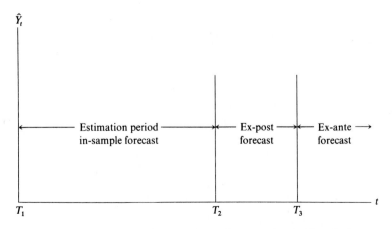

Figure 11.1   In-sample, ex-ante, and ex-post forecast periods

unknown. Forecasts generated for the period $T_2 + 1$ through T_3 are known as **ex-post forecasts** and those for $T_3 + 1$ onward are known as **ex-ante forecasts**. Figure 11.1 illustrates these three forecasting periods. Since Y_t is known for $T_2 + 1$ through T_3, the forecasts can be compared with these actual values and the out-of-sample performance of the model evaluated (more on that in the next section). Because the data for the ex-post forecast period have not been used to obtain the estimates of the parameters, ex-post forecasts provide a true test of the model's forecasting ability. Ex-ante forecasts are for periods for which neither the dependent nor the independent variables are known and are hence predictions about the unknown future.

Example 11.1

As an example, consider an analyst in the load forecasting department of a utility who is interested in forecasting total residential sales. The analyst has several monthly models that relate residential electricity consumption to weather patterns during the month as well as to other seasonal effects, the price of electricity, the stock of appliances, household income, and so on. Suppose that the forecaster has monthly data for 10 years (120 observations). To compare the forecasting ability of the different models, the investigator might first use observations 1 through 100 to estimate the models (this is the *in-sample* period). She then uses the estimated models to generate *ex-post* forecasts of electricity consumption for the period 101 through 120, *with the known values of the independent variables*. As the values of the dependent variable are also known with certainty in the post-sample period, forecasts can be judged against these known values and one of the models selected as the "best." The model finally selected is then reestimated using the entire sample (all 120 observations in our example) and *ex-ante* forecasts (based on this reestimated model) generated for periods beyond 120. These ex-ante forecasts will be the basis on which future electricity-generating capacity is planned and electricity rates set. □

11.2 Evaluation of Models

Most forecasters evaluate their models in terms of the models' ability to forecast. Several approaches are used in evaluating forecasting performance. In Section 3.11 the **mean squared error** (**MSE**) was introduced as a measure for comparing forecasts from different models. For a general model with k regression coefficients, MSE is defined as follows:

$$\text{MSE} = \frac{\sum (Y_t^f - Y_t)^2}{T - k}$$

where T is the number of observations, Y_t is the actual value of the dependent variable, and Y_t^f is the value predicted from a model. In the sample period, MSE is the same as $\hat{\sigma}^2$, the estimate of the variance of the error term u_t.

The model selection criteria discussed in Section 4.4 can also be used to evaluate forecast performance. The procedure is to use each of the competing models to predict the values of Y *during the ex-post period*. Next compute the sum of squared errors (ESS) as $\sum (Y_t^f - Y_t)^2$ and then use the model selection criteria in Table 4.3. A model with lower values of these criterion statistics would be judged superior in terms of the forecasting ability.

A third approach used to judge a model is based on the estimation of the following simple linear regression between the forecast and the observed Y:

$$Y_t = a + bY_t^f + e_t$$

If the forecast is perfect for all t, then we would expect $\hat{a}$ to be zero and $\hat{b}$ to be one. This can be formally tested using an appropriate t-test.

11.3 Conditional and Unconditional Forecasts

In considering ex-post or ex-ante forecasts, it is important to distinguish between *conditional and unconditional* forecasts. A **conditional forecast** is obtained when a dependent variable is predicted under the assumption that the independent variables have specific values (which could be known values). As a simple example of a conditional forecast, consider the following model:

$$H_t = \alpha + \beta P_t + u_t \tag{11.3}$$

where H_t is the number of housing units in a certain city and P_t is the city's population. As was noted in Section 3.11, the conditional forecast of H given P, say as P_0, is $\hat{H} = \hat{\alpha} + \hat{\beta}P_0$. Suppose that the population at time $T + 1$ is given as P_{T+1}. Then the conditional forecast for H given that $P = P_{T+1}$ is $\hat{H}_{T+1} = \hat{\alpha} + \hat{\beta}P_{T+1}$. Thus, assuming that next period's population is P_{T+1}, we obtain the conditional prediction for next period's housing units to be $\hat{\alpha} + \hat{\beta}P_{T+1}$.

Unconditional forecasts are obtained when the values of the exogenous variables are not given a priori but are generated from the model itself or from an auxiliary model. Thus, the independent variables are not measured with certainty but are subject to uncertainty. In the housing unit example, the future population of the city is unknown. An auxiliary model of population migration, births, and deaths may be used to obtain a forecast of the population in the time period $T + 1$ (call it $\hat{P}_{T+1}$). Forecasts of housing units obtained by combining the econometric model with the population model are unconditional. We would thus have $\hat{H}_{T+1} = \hat{\alpha} + \hat{\beta}\hat{P}_{T+1}$, where $\hat{P}_{T+1}$ is the forecast of population obtained from an auxiliary model.

Fitted values generated for the in-sample period are conditional (because the values of the X's are given), but forecasts for the ex-ante period are unconditional because they require that the independent variables be predicted before the dependent variable is predicted. Forecasts for the ex-post period can be either conditional or unconditional depending on how they were obtained.

At this time it is useful to point out some inconsistencies in the literature regarding the use of the terms *conditional* and *unconditional*. Some authors define these terms in exactly the opposite way to the definitions presented here. This is erroneous. The term *conditional* comes from the terminology in probability theory in which we consider the *conditional distribution*, denoted as $P(Y|X)$ in Chapter 2, of one random variable *given* the value of another random variable. The *conditional mean* of this distribution is $E(Y|X)$. A forecast of Y is an estimate of $E(Y|X)$ and will depend on X. Therefore, the forecast of Y for a given value of X is a *conditional forecast*. The *unconditional mean* of Y, denoted as $E(Y)$, is the expected value of Y over the joint probability density $f(x, y)$ and does not depend on X. An estimate of $E(Y)$ is the *unconditional forecast* in which X is also treated as a random variable.

Example 11.2

The "weather normalization" of sales carried out by electric utilities is a good example of conditional forecasting. In order to set the rates for electricity, utilities are routinely asked by public utilities commissions to obtain "weather-adjusted series" for electricity sales. Such series are obtained by asking the question "What would electricity consumption have been if the weather had been normal?" Normal weather is typically measured by taking the average values for temperature, humidity, wind speed, and so on over a 10-year (or longer) period. The "normal weather" values are then substituted for the weather variables and a forecast is generated. The difference between the forecast of consumption with actual weather and that corresponding to "normal weather" is the weather adjustment. Clearly, there is no such thing as a unique "normal weather." Ten-year averages of weather measures and 20-year averages of weather measures will generate two different weather adjustments. The forecasts are thus conditional on the definition of "normal weather." If we also forecast the weather and use it to forecast electricity consumption, we obtain unconditional forecasts.

□

11.4 Forecasting from Time Trends

Most time series of aggregate variables exhibit a steadily increasing or decreasing pattern, known as a **trend**. One can fit a **smooth curve** to an underlying trend. The fitted curve can then be extrapolated to generate forecasts of the dependent variable. This approach to forecasting is called **trend line fitting**. There is no underlying behavioral econometric model or theory involved, just the simple assumption that past patterns will continue in the future. In order to decide what type of trend line to fit, an investigator graphs the dependent variable over time and identifies whether the trend is linear, quadratic, or exponential, or has other patterns. We list below a number of commonly used trend lines.

(A) Straight line: $Y_t = \beta_1 + \beta_2 t + u_t$

(B) Quadratic: $Y_t = \beta_1 + \beta_2 t + \beta_3 t^2 + u_t$

(C) Cubic: $Y_t = \beta_1 + \beta_2 t + \beta_3 t^2 + \beta_4 t^3 + u_t$

(D)   Linear-log: $Y_t = \beta_1 + \beta_2 \ln(t) + u_t$

(E)   Reciprocal: $Y_t = \beta_1 + \beta_2(1/t) + u_t$

(F)   Log-linear: $\ln(Y_t) = \beta_1 + \beta_2 t + u_t$

(G)   Double-log: $\ln(Y_t) = \beta_1 + \beta_2 \ln(t) + u_t$

(H)   Logistic: $\ln\left[\dfrac{Y_t}{1 - Y_t}\right] = \beta_1 + \beta_2 t + u_t$

The first five formulations have Y_t as the dependent variable, the next two have $\ln(Y_t)$ as the dependent variable, and the last has a logistic transformation on Y_t. It should be emphasized that the values of $\bar{R}^2$ are comparable only between two models with the same dependent variable. Also, the log transformation requires Y_t and $Y_t/(1 - Y_t)$ to be positive. The logistic curve is a useful functional form when Y_t is between 0 and 1 or when Y_t is a percent. As was stated in Section 4.6, the logistic curve ensures that the forecasted value is always between 0 and 1 (or 0 to 100 if the dependent variable is a percent).

We noted in Chapters 3 and 4 that if the dependent variable is in logarithmic form, then forecasts are biased. To explore this further, exponentiate the double-log model above. We get

$$e^{\ln Y_t} = Y_t = e^{\beta_1 + \beta_2 \ln(t) + u_t} = e^{\beta_1} t^{\beta_2} e^{u_t}$$

Taking the expected value of both sides gives

$$E(Y_t) = e^{\beta_1} t^{\beta_2} E[e^{u_t}] \neq e^{\beta_1} t^{\beta_2}$$

because $E(u_t) = 0$ does not imply that $E[e^{u_t}] = 1$. However, it is possible to estimate $E[e^{u_t}]$ by using the fact that $E[e^{u_t}] = e^{\sigma^2/2}$ (not proved). An estimate of $e^{\sigma^2/2}$ is $e^{\hat{\sigma}^2/2}$. Therefore, a corrected prediction of Y_t is

$$\hat{Y}_t = e^{\hat{\beta}_1} t^{\hat{\beta}_2} e^{\hat{\sigma}^2/2}$$

To generate forecasts from trend lines, the following relations are used (setting the unpredictable error u_t to zero):

Straight line: $\hat{Y}_t = \hat{\beta}_1 + \hat{\beta}_2 t$

Quadratic: $\hat{Y}_t = \hat{\beta}_1 + \hat{\beta}_2 t + \hat{\beta}_3 t^2$

Cubic: $\hat{Y}_t = \hat{\beta}_1 + \hat{\beta}_2 t + \hat{\beta}_3 t^2 + \hat{\beta}_4 t^3$

Linear-log: $\hat{Y}_t = \hat{\beta}_1 + \hat{\beta}_2 \ln(t)$

Reciprocal: $\hat{Y}_t = \hat{\beta}_1 + \hat{\beta}_2(1/t)$

Log-linear: $\hat{Y}_t = e^{\hat{\beta}_1 + \hat{\beta}_2 t + (\hat{\sigma}^2/2)}$

Double-log: $\hat{Y}_t = e^{\hat{\beta}_1} t^{\hat{\beta}_2} e^{(\hat{\sigma}^2/2)}$

Logistic: $\hat{Y}_t = \dfrac{1}{1 + e^{-[\hat{\beta}_1 + \hat{\beta}_2 t + (\hat{\sigma}^2/2)]}}$

If the trend line exhibits serial correlation in the residuals, improved forecasts can be obtained by exploiting the residual structure, as was described in the previous chapter.

A common use of trend lines is to remove an underlying trend (known as **detrending**) and then examine the deviation of the observed dependent variable from the fitted trend line. In this case, an analyst first fits one of the curves listed above and then obtains the residuals $\hat{u}_t$. The values of these residuals can then be related to variables that might explain the fluctuations around the trend. This approach is often used by business cycle analysts. They first fit a long-term trend for the dependent variable of interest (stock prices, gross national product, unemployment, or whatever), remove the trend and obtain $\hat{u}_t$, and then relate the residuals to very short run variables such as the season, government policy announcements, extraordinary international events, and so on.

It should be emphasized that fitting a trend line is generally not an end in itself; but it would be useful as part of a broader modeling strategy in which a dependent variable is related to several independent variables, including perhaps trends. Simple curve fitting is not based on any underlying mechanism but on the assumption, often found to be false, that past behavior will continue.

Practice Problem

11.1   In the log-linear, double-log, and logistic curves above, solve for Y_t explicitly as a function of time, and verify the given forecasts. Then graph $\hat{Y}_t$ under various assumptions about the signs of the $\hat{\beta}$'s. What different shapes can the curves capture?

Application: Fitting Trend Lines for the Wage Rate in California

Table 11.1 has annual data on the average hourly earnings in California. Figure 11.2 graphs this over time, showing that the wage rate was very stable until 1965, when it increased at a substantial rate for two decades and then moderated. All eight of the trend lines presented earlier were estimated. Because there was strong evidence of serial correlation, the parameters were estimated by the mixed HILU–CORC procedure described in Chapter 9. In-sample forecasts were then generated after allowing for the serial correlation adjustment to the forecast as well as the bias in forecast for the logarithmic formulations. The regression $Y_t = a + bY_t^f + e_t$, which relates the actual value to the predicted value of the dependent variable, was estimated next. Table 11.2 presents the estimates $\hat{a}$ and $\hat{b}$ along with the eight-model selection statistics described in Table 4.3 (Practice Computer Session 11.1 provides the details to reproduce these results). When the forecast is good, we would expect $\hat{a}$ to be close to zero and $\hat{b}$ to be close to 1. We note that the cubic relation (Model C) is best both in this regard and in terms of the AIC and other selection criteria. The next best model was Model B, which is quadratic.

TABLE 11.1 Hourly Wage Rates in California
1960–1989

Year	Wage Rate	Year	Wage Rate
1960	2.62	1975	5.22
1961	2.72	1976	5.59
1962	2.79	1977	6.00
1963	2.88	1978	6.43
1964	2.96	1979	7.03
1965	3.05	1980	7.70
1966	3.16	1981	8.56
1967	3.29	1982	9.24
1968	3.44	1983	9.52
1969	3.62	1984	9.77
1970	3.80	1985	10.12
1971	4.02	1986	10.36
1972	4.25	1987	10.75
1973	4.44	1988	10.80
1974	4.76	1989	11.16

Source: Economic Report of the Governor, State of California, 1990.

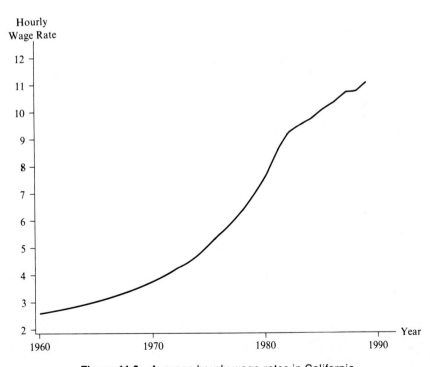

Figure 11.2 Average hourly wage rates in California

TABLE 11.2 Comparison of Forecast Performance of Trend Lines

	Model A	Model B	Model C	Model D	Model E	Model F	Model G	Model H
$\hat{a}$	−0.002250	−0.005650	0.001450	−0.121160	−0.190790	0.116290	0.103800	0.030610
$\hat{b}$	1.000370	1.000920	0.999760	1.019800	1.031180	0.979680	0.981860	0.995470
SGMASQ	0.026346	0.024179	0.015712	0.037962	0.044446	0.042708	0.036026	0.025882
AIC	0.028156	0.026660	0.017848	0.040571	0.047501	0.045643	0.038502	0.027661
FPE	0.028162	0.026680	0.017879	0.040580	0.047511	0.045653	0.038511	0.027677
HQ	0.029000	0.027868	0.018934	0.041787	0.048925	0.047011	0.039656	0.028490
SCHWARZ	0.030941	0.030711	0.021552	0.044583	0.052198	0.050157	0.042310	0.030396
SHIBATA	0.027912	0.026162	0.017281	0.040219	0.047088	0.045247	0.038168	0.027421
GCV	0.028297	0.026968	0.018226	0.040774	0.047738	0.045872	0.038695	0.027799
RICE	0.028453	0.027332	0.018705	0.040999	0.048002	0.046125	0.038908	0.027953

Practice Problem

11.2 Redo the above analysis using data only for the period 1960–1985. Then obtain the predictions for 1986–1989 (be sure to correct for the serial correlation in errors and forecast bias in the logarithmic formulations). Then compute the mean squared forecast errors for each of the models. Which model does best in terms of post-sample predictions?

Smoothing an Economic Time Series

When a series is plotted over time, one might notice that there are fluctuations around a smooth trend line. An investigator interested only in the underlying trend might want to **smooth** the series by reducing the short-term volatility of the series. This is accomplished in a number of ways. One method is to compute a **moving average** of the form

$$Y_t = \frac{1}{n}\sum(X_t + X_{t-1} + \cdots + X_{t-n+1})$$

where X_t is the original series and Y_t is the new series obtained by averaging n successive terms. For example, when $n = 3$ we would average the first three observations, then average observations 2, 3, and 4, then average 3, 4, and 5, and so on. The extent of smoothness depends on the size of n; the larger n is, the smoother the resulting series. In using Y_t in a regression, however, it should be remembered that Y_t is defined only in the range (n, T), and hence we would lose $n - 1$ observations.

Another approach is **exponential smoothing** in which the new series is obtained as a weighted average of present and past values of series with geometrically declining weights. We would thus have

$$Y_t = \lambda[X_t + (1 - \lambda)X_{t-1} + (1 - \lambda)^2 X_{t-2} + \cdots]$$

with $0 < \lambda < 1$. This can be expressed in a simpler form by noting that for $t - 1$

$$Y_{t-1} = \lambda[X_{t-1} + (1 - \lambda)X_{t-2} + (1 - \lambda)^2 X_{t-3} + \cdots]$$

from which the following equation is easily derived.

$$Y_t = \lambda X_t + (1 - \lambda)Y_{t-1}$$

If λ is close to 1, X_t is given a heavy weight and hence the resulting series will be as unsmooth as X_t. It follows that the smaller the value of λ, the smoother Y_t will be. Note that exponential smoothing causes only one observation to be lost.

TABLE 11.3 Monthly Data on Total Nonagricultural Employment in the United States (in hundred thousands)

Period	Employment	Period	Employment
1983.01	94,341	1985.01	101,514
1983.02	94,399	1985.02	101,857
1983.03	95,023	1985.03	102,859
1983.04	95,655	1985.04	102,946
1983.05	96,032	1985.05	103,503
1983.06	97,836	1985.06	104,185
1983.07	99,144	1985.07	105,144
1983.08	99,179	1985.08	105,116
1983.09	98,825	1985.09	104,692
1983.10	99,252	1985.10	105,318
1983.11	99,866	1985.11	105,362
1983.12	99,852	1985.12	105,254
1984.01	98,463	1986.01	104,140
1984.02	99,104	1986.02	104,021
1984.03	99,898	1986.03	104,744
1984.04	100,437	1986.04	105,080
1984.05	101,567	1986.05	105,695
1984.06	102,932	1986.06	107,218
1984.07	103,536	1986.07	108,176
1984.08	102,982	1986.08	108,075
1984.09	102,247	1986.09	106,963
1984.10	102,994	1986.10	107,666
1984.11	103,019	1986.11	107,673
1984.12	103.037	1986.12	107,762

Data Compiled by William Ryburn.

Employment
(× 100)

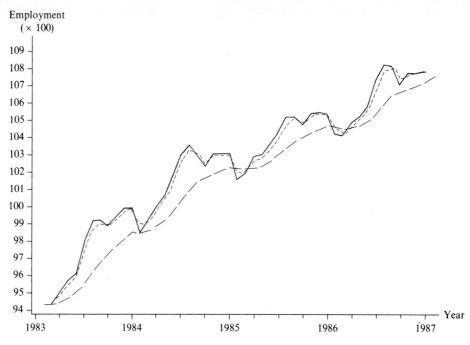

Figure 11.3 Actual and exponentially smoothed employment series (solid line is actual, broken line is $\lambda = 0.7$, dashed line is $\lambda = 0.2$)

Example 11.3

Table 11.3 shows monthly data on total nonagricultural employment in the United States, measured in hundred thousands. Figure 11.3 presents this series and two exponentially smoothed series with $\lambda = 0.2$ and 0.7 (Practice Computer Session 11.2 provides the steps to generate the actual numbers). Note that the plot for $\lambda = 0.2$ is smoother than the other two series plots. □

Adaptive Forecasts Using Exponentially Weighted Errors

Exponential smoothing is also useful when adjusting forecasts to allow for prediction errors made in the recent past. More specifically, let Y_t be the actual value of Y at time t and Y_t^a be the forecast generated by some model (labeled a). The error in forecast is then $e_t^a = Y_t - Y_t^a$. Also let Y_{t+1}^a be the forecast for the time period $t + 1$ using Model a. The **adaptive forecast** Y_{t+1}^b for the time period $t + 1$ is given by

$$Y_{t+1}^b - Y_{t+1}^a = (Y_t^b - Y_t^a) + \lambda e_t^a$$

where the adjustment factor λ is often chosen to be a small number. To start the process, it is usually assumed that $Y_1^a = Y_1^b$. This method thus has a built-in learning process by which most recent prediction errors are used to adjust a subsequent period's forecasts.

11.5 Combining Forecasts

In empirical research, the common procedure adopted by analysts is to estimate a number of alternative models, subject them to several tests of hypotheses, and finally choose one as the "best" for whatever purpose the model is intended. If the goal is forecasting, the typical approach is to reserve a part of the available data for postsample forecasting exercises, obtain forecasts from different models, and choose that model which has the best forecasting performance in the postsample period. In the previous section, we used several alternative models to forecast wage rates and concluded that the cubic model was the best from the point of view of forecasting. Models that are judged inferior from a forecasting point of view are usually discarded.

Bates and Granger pointed out in 1969, however, that discarded models do still contain information about the underlying behavior of the dependent variable and argued that **combining forecasts** from several models would outperform those from a single model. As a simple example, suppose f_1 and f_2 are forecasts from two different models or approaches. For simplicity of exposition assume they are independent with the same variance σ^2. Consider an arithmetic average of these two forecasts, $f = \frac{1}{2}(f_1 + f_2)$. The variance of the combined forecast f is $\sigma^2/2$, which is less than the variance of each individual forecast. It is therefore clear that there may be some merit in obtaining combinations of forecasts. In the application of Section 11.2 we found that the quadratic and logistic models gave reasonably good forecasts. Combining these forecasts might be useful, but the other models generated very poor forecasts and should be discarded.

In this section we discuss a number of approaches to combining forecasts and study the properties of such combinations. We consider only linear combinations of forecasts here. The question of interest is how to construct optimum weights for the different forecasts. The steps are as follows:

Step 1 Use the sample period data to estimate the various models.
Step 2 Predict the values of the dependent variable during the sample period.
Step 3 Use the fitted values and actual values of the dependent variable to construct a set of weights for combining the forecasts.
Step 4 Generate out-of-sample forecasts from individual models.
Step 5 Combine these forecasts using the weights obtained in Step 3. If the models are to be evaluated for forecast performance in the postsample period, we need the actual values of the dependent variable.

We present three different methods of combining forecasts and compare their relative merits. The analysis presented here is drawn from a paper by Granger and Ramanathan (1984).

Method A

Let Y_t be the actual value, at time t, of a dependent variable, and $f_{t1}, f_{t2}, \ldots, f_{tk}$ be forecasts generated by k alternative approaches or models. Some of these forecasts may be from econometric models, others from time series models, and yet others from the "expert opinion" of analysts knowledgeable about the behavior of Y. An intuitively obvious approach is to obtain a weighted average of these forecasts, the weights to be determined from some optimality property. Thus, the combined forecast will be $f_t = \beta_1 f_{t1} + \beta_2 f_{t2} + \cdots + \beta_k f_{tk}$.

In the first method, we assume that the weights sum to unity; that is, $\sum \beta_i = 1$. The error in the combined forecast is $u_t = Y_t - f_t$. The sum of squared forecast errors is therefore $\sum u_t^2 = \sum (Y_t - f_t)^2$, where the summation is for the periods 1 through T, for which both forecasts and the actual values of Y are available. The "optimum" method of combining is to choose the weights β_i so that the sum of squared forecast errors is a minimum. It is easily shown that the weights can be estimated using any regression program. To see this, note that

$$Y_t = f_t + u_t = \beta_1 f_{t1} + \beta_2 f_{t2} + \cdots + \beta_k f_{tk} + u_t \tag{11.4}$$

with $\beta_1 + \beta_2 + \cdots + \beta_k = 1$, or $\beta_k = 1 - \beta_1 - \beta_2 - \cdots - \beta_{k-1}$. Substituting this in (11.4) we get

$$Y_t = \beta_1 f_{t1} + \beta_2 f_{t2} + \cdots + \beta_{k-1} f_{t,k-1} + (1 - \beta_1 - \beta_2 - \cdots - \beta_{k-1}) f_{tk} + u_t$$

Taking f_{tk} to the left side and grouping the β_i terms, we obtain

$$Y_t - f_{tk} = \beta_1 (f_{t1} - f_{tk}) + \beta_2 (f_{t2} - f_{tk}) + \cdots + \beta_{k-1} (f_{t,k-1} - f_{tk}) + u_t \tag{11.5}$$

We readily see that the β's can be estimated by regressing $Y_t - f_{tk}$ against $f_{t1} - f_{tk}$, $f_{t2} - f_{tk}, \ldots, f_{t,k-1} - f_{tk}$, with no constant term in the estimation. β_k is estimated as $1 - \hat{\beta}_1 - \hat{\beta}_2 - \cdots - \hat{\beta}_{k-1}$. Note that the estimated weights could be negative.

Will the mean value of the forecast error ($\hat{u}_t$) due to f be zero? That is, will $(1/T)\sum \hat{u}_t = 0$?

$$\sum \hat{u}_t = \sum (Y_t - \hat{f}_t) = \sum (Y_t - \hat{\beta}_1 f_{t1} - \hat{\beta}_2 f_{t2} - \cdots - \hat{\beta}_k f_{tk}) \tag{11.6}$$

Suppose each of the individual forecasts has zero mean forecast error; that is, suppose that $\sum (Y_t - f_{ti}) = 0$, for each i. Then $\sum f_{ti} = \sum Y_t$. Substituting this in (11.6) we get

$$\sum \hat{u}_t = \sum Y_t - \hat{\beta}_1 \sum Y_t - \hat{\beta}_2 \sum Y_t - \cdots - \hat{\beta}_k \sum Y_t$$
$$= (\sum Y_t)(1 - \hat{\beta}_1 - \hat{\beta}_2 - \cdots - \hat{\beta}_k) = 0 \tag{11.7}$$

because the sum of the estimated weights is 1. Therefore, a sufficient condition for zero mean combined forecast error is that each forecast have zero mean forecast error. In general, there is no assurance that individual forecasts are unbiased—that is, that they neither overpredict nor underpredict, on average. For this reason, the combined forecast is likely to have nonzero mean forecast error.

Method B

There is nothing inviolable about requiring that the weights for individual forecasts add up to 1. Suppose we do not impose that restriction. Can we get "better" combined forecasts? The answer is yes, provided the criterion for "better" is minimum mean squared forecast error. We see from equation (11.4) that the procedure now is to regress Y against $f_1, f_2, \ldots, f_k$, again with no constant term, but with no constraints. Because we are minimizing the unconstrained sum of squared forecast errors, the minimum value will be no more than that obtained by Method A. Thus, if ESS_A is the estimated error sum of squares in equation (11.5) and ESS_B is the same for Method B, then $ESS_B \leq ESS_A$, the gain being $ESS_A - ESS_B$. Will the combined forecast error average to zero in this case? We see that here also

$$\sum \hat{u}_t = \left(\sum Y_t \right)(1 - \hat{\beta}_1 - \hat{\beta}_2 - \cdots - \hat{\beta}_k)$$

if each individual forecast has zero mean error. But, unless the estimated weights happen to sum to unity, the mean forecast error will not be zero. Therefore, although we gain on MSE, we may obtain a combined forecast that has nonzero error mean even though each individual forecast has zero error mean. Note that if any of the individual forecasts is biased, the combined forecast is likely to be biased also.

Is it possible to have the best of both worlds; that is, is it possible to have the lowest mean squared error and zero mean error, even if some of the individual forecasts have nonzero error means? Granger and Ramanathan (1984) have derived such a method of combining forecasts. This is described next.

Method C

If individual forecasts are biased, then their weighted average is also likely to be biased. Suppose we could obtain an estimate of this bias. Then by subtracting this estimated bias we could perhaps get an unbiased forecast of the dependent variable, even though some of the individual forecasts may be biased. This is the motivation behind the Granger–Ramanathan (GR) approach. The trick is to add a constant term to the forecast and let the estimated constant term adjust for the bias. The modified forecast would therefore be $f_t = \beta_0 + \beta_1 f_{t1} + \beta_2 f_{tk} + \cdots + \beta_k f_{tk}$. No constraints are imposed on any of the β's. The forecast error is $u_t = Y_t - f_t$. The formulation thus becomes the familiar multiple regression model

$$Y_t = \beta_0 + \beta_1 f_{t1} + \beta_2 f_{tk} + \cdots + \beta_k f_{tk} + u_t \tag{11.8}$$

Note that Method B is a special case of this with the constraint $\beta_0 = 0$, and Method A is a special case of this with $\beta_0 = 0$ and $\beta_1 + \beta_2 + \cdots + \beta_k = 1$. The procedure for estimating the weights is to regress Y_t against a constant, $f_{t1}, f_{t2}, \ldots,$ and f_{tk}, with no constraints. Because an unconstrained minimum is no greater than a constrained minimum, we have $ESS_C \leq ESS_B \leq ESS_A$. Hence Method C is the best in terms of minimum mean squared forecast error. Is the mean combined forecast error zero? To answer this, note that

$$\sum \hat{u}_t = \sum (Y_t - \hat{f}_t) = \sum (Y_t - \hat{\beta}_0 - \hat{\beta}_1 f_{t1} - \hat{\beta}_2 f_{t2} - \cdots - \hat{\beta}_k f_{tk}) \tag{11.9}$$

But the minimization of the mean squared forecast error $\sum \hat{u}_t^2$ with respect to $\hat{\beta}_0$ gives the normal equation

$$\sum (Y_t - \hat{\beta}_0 - \hat{\beta}_1 f_{t1} - \hat{\beta}_2 f_{t2} - \cdots - \hat{\beta}_k f_{tk}) = \sum \hat{u}_t = 0$$

It follows from this that $\sum \hat{u}_t = 0$ and hence the mean combined forecast error is zero. Note that we did not stipulate that any of the individual forecast errors have zero mean. Therefore, Method C is the best because it gives the smallest mean squared forecast error and has an unbiased combined forecast *even if individual forecasts are biased.* For this reason Granger and Ramanathan advocate that "the common practice of obtaining a weighted average of alternative forecasts should be abandoned in favor of an unrestricted linear combination *including a constant term.*"

Example 11.3

Bessler and Brandt (1981) combined forecasts for quarterly hog prices from an econometric model, a time series model called ARIMA (described in Section 10.7), and from expect opinions, for the period 1976.1 to 1979.2. Granger and Ramanathan applied each of the three methods to 16 observations from this data set and obtained optimum weights. They then subjected the methods to a postsample forecast exercise for the periods 17 through 24. They also did an in-sample comparison with all 24 observations to estimate the weights. Table 11.4

TABLE 11.4   Weights and In-Sample Forecast Errors for Hog Price Data

Forecast	Mean Error	Sum of Squared Errors	Weights for			
			Const.	Econ.	ARIMA	Expert
Original						
Econometric	−1.71	610.4	—	1.00	—	—
ARIMA	−0.03	420.7	—	—	1.00	—
Expert opinion	0.59	522.7	—	—	—	1.00
Combined Method A (no constant, weights sum to 1)						
All three	−0.26	334.7	0.00	0.30	0.27	0.43
Econ. & ARIMA	−0.35	409.8	0.00	0.19	0.81	0.00
ARIMA & expert	0.21	360.8	0.00	0.00	0.45	0.55
Expert & Econ.	−0.44	344.6	0.00	0.62	0.00	0.38
Combined Method B (unconstrainted, no constant term)						
All three	0.06	331.4	0.00	0.35	0.22	0.43
Econ. & ARIMA	0.11	403.4	0.00	0.26	0.73	0.00
ARIMA & expert	0.14	360.7	0.00	0.00	0.62	0.38
Expert & Econ.	0.06	337.4	0.00	0.51	0.00	0.48
Combined Method C (unconstrained with constant)						
All three	0.00	319.6	7.57	0.19	0.26	0.38
Econ. & ARIMA	0.00	372.6	11.80	0.03	0.70	0.00
ARIMA & expert	0.00	325.4	10.65	0.00	0.42	0.34
Expert & Econ.	0.00	327.8	6.80	0.36	0.00	0.48

Source: Granger and Ramanathan (1984).

TABLE 11.5 Weights and Out-of-Sample Forecast Errors for Hog Price Data

Forecast	Mean Error	Sum of Squared Errors	Weights for			
			Const.	Econ.	ARIMA	Expert
Original						
Econometric	−0.95	322.8	—	1.00	—	—
ARIMA	0.78	245.1	—	—	1.00	—
Expert opinion	−2.13	160.2	—	—	—	1.00
Combined Method A (no constant, weights sum to 1)						
All three	−1.14	199.1	0.00	0.47	0.15	0.38
Econ. & ARIMA	0.51	238.6	0.00	0.16	0.84	0.00
ARIMA & expert	0.32	212.2	0.00	0.00	0.84	0.16
Expert & Econ.	−1.47	206.6	0.00	0.55	0.00	0.45
Combined Method B (unconstrainted, no constant term)						
All three	−0.59	199.8	0.00	0.50	0.16	0.33
Econ. & ARIMA	1.16	246.1	0.00	0.30	0.68	0.00
ARIMA & expert	0.56	217.3	0.00	0.00	0.86	0.14
Expert & Econ.	−0.94	205.0	0.00	0.59	0.00	0.40
Combined Method C (unconstrained with constant)						
All three	−0.86	193.4	3.50	0.45	0.13	0.34
Econ. & ARIMA	0.96	233.5	2.89	0.25	0.66	0.00
ARIMA & expert	−0.32	180.2	7.72	0.00	0.63	0.20
Expert & Econ.	−1.17	198.8	3.79	0.51	0.00	0.39

Source: Granger and Ramanathan (1984).

gives the weights and forecast errors for the 24 in-sample periods, and Table 11.5 shows the out-of-sample forecast errors for the period 17 through 24. Table 11.4 indicates that the original forecast methods produced somewhat biased forecasts, although these biases did not contribute much to the MSE. The best individual forecast was by the time series ARIMA method. We also note that any kind of combined forecast substantially improved the MSE. As the theory predicts. Method C has zero mean forecast error and the lowest MSE. Further, as the postsample exercise in Table 11.5 indicates, mean errors are no longer zero if the weights estimated from period 1 through 16 are used to predict prices for the period 17 through 24. Although Method C is consistently superior to the other methods, combining three forecasts is not always superior to combining just a pair. □

It should be emphasized that the example result may not hold in general for other data sets. It is quite possible that MSE and mean error may be worse in the postsample period than in the in-sample period. Bohara, McNown, and Batts (1987) have shown that, in some cases, individual forecasts for the postsample period might outperform the Granger–Ramanathan method of combining forecasts using Model C, although in the in-sample period the GR method will always be superior. Other studies have found that the GR method outperforms other methods in post-sample situations also. As Granger (1989) has pointed out, the combining of forecasts should be especially fruitful when radically different methods, such as econometric and time series, are used to generate the forecasts. The *Journal of Forecasting* (1989) and the *International Journal of Forecasting* (1989) have each devoted an entire issue to combining forecasts. They contain a number of interesting articles, some using advanced methods.

11.6 Forecasting from Econometric Models

The econometric approach to forecasting consists first of formulating an econometric model that relates a dependent variable to a number of independent variables that are expected to affect it. The model is then estimated and used to obtain conditional and/or unconditional forecasts of the dependent variable. The models are generally formulated on both economic and statistical grounds.

Consider, as an example, the problem of forecasting the monthly electricity sales of a utility. Economic theory tells us that consumers make selections on appliances (including home heating, cooling, and water heating appliances) based on their level of income, the prices of the appliances, and other characteristics such as the demographic composition of the household. The actual usage of these appliances typically varies with the weather as well as with other seasonal effects such as weekdays or weekends, vacations, and holidays. An econometric model of electricity sales would therefore relate monthly electricity sales to weather measures, such as the number of cooling and heating degree days encountered (see the application in Section 9.8), monthly dummy variables that allow for other seasonal effects, income, stock of appliances, and the price of electricity. If different models and approaches are to be evaluated, a forecaster typically obtains conditional forecasts based on the known values of the independent variables for a postsample period. Conditional forecasts are also often obtained under different scenarios of the future: a fast growth in population and income, a medium growth in the economic/demographic variables, or a slow growth. Alternative time paths for the price of electricity can also be selected. To obtain unconditional forecasts of electricity sales, a utility analyst would have to model the behavior of the independent variables themselves. Common approaches used are fitting time trends or using purely time series methods such as those discussed in the next section.

The following are several alternative formulations commonly used in forecasting.

Econometric forecasting with no lagged dependent variables or serially correlated errors This is the simplest case of econometric forecasting. The underlying model is of the form in equation (11.1) in which the errors are well-behaved and satisfy Assumptions 3.2 through 3.7. A forecast for the time period $T + h$ (that is, *h* steps-ahead forecast) is given by

$$\hat{Y}_{T+h} = \hat{\beta}_1 + \hat{\beta}_2 X_{T+h,2} + \hat{\beta}_3 X_{T+h,3} + \cdots + \hat{\beta}_k X_{T+h,k} \tag{11.10}$$

As mentioned previously, the forecast will be conditional if the values for $X_{T+h,i}$ are assumed to be given from some exogenous mechanism.

Econometric forecasting with no lagged dependent variables but serially correlated errors We saw in Chapter 9 that if the errors of a regression model are serially correlated, we can obtain improved predictions by using that information. In equation (11.2) suppose that u_t follows the first-order autoregressive process (ϵ_t are assumed to be well-behaved):

$$u_t = \rho u_{t-1} + \epsilon_t \tag{11.11}$$

If $\hat{\rho}$ is an estimate of the serial correlation coefficient, we have

$$\hat{u}_{T+1} = \hat{\rho}\hat{u}_T, \qquad \hat{u}_{T+2} = \hat{\rho}\hat{u}_{T+1} = \hat{\rho}^2\hat{u}_T, \qquad \hat{u}_{T+h} = \hat{\rho}^h\hat{u}_T$$

Because $\hat{u}_T$ is obtainable from the sample, we can obtain a better prediction of the forecast error *h* steps ahead and hence obtain the following revised forecast of Y_{T+h}:

$$\hat{Y}_{T+h} = \hat{\beta}_1 + \hat{\beta}_2 X_{T+h,2} + \hat{\beta}_3 X_{T+h,3} + \cdots + \hat{\beta}_k X_{T+h,k} + \hat{\rho}^h\hat{u}_T \tag{11.12}$$

In the general case of a *q*th-order autoregressive error structure

$$u_t = \rho_1 u_{t-1} + \rho_2 u_{t-2} + \cdots + \rho_q u_{t-q} + \epsilon_t \tag{11.13}$$

a one-step-ahead forecast error is estimated as

$$\hat{u}_{T+1} = \hat{\rho}_1\hat{u}_T + \hat{\rho}_2\hat{u}_{T-1} + \cdots + \hat{\rho}_q\hat{u}_{T+1-q} \tag{11.14}$$

The one-step-ahead forecast of Y_{T+1} is therefore

$$\hat{Y}_{T+1} = \hat{\beta}_1 + \hat{\beta}_2 X_{T+1,2} + \hat{\beta}_3 X_{T+1,3} + \cdots + \hat{\beta}_k X_{T+1,k} + \hat{u}_{T+1} \tag{11.15}$$

Subsequent forecasts would be generated in a similar way.

Econometric forecasting with lagged dependent variables and serially correlated errors The most general econometric formulation of a single dependent variable is the one with both lagged dependent variables and autocorrelated errors:

$$Y_t = \alpha_0 + \alpha_1 Y_{t-1} + \cdots + \alpha_p Y_{t-p} + \beta_1 X_{t1} + \cdots + \beta_k X_{tk} + u_t \tag{11.16}$$

$$u_t = \rho_1 u_{t-1} + \rho_2 u_{t-2} + \cdots + \rho_q u_{t-q} + \epsilon_t \tag{11.17}$$

The procedure for estimating a simpler version of this model was described in Section 10.2. For given values $X_{T+1,1}, X_{T+1,2}, \ldots, X_{T+1,k}$, a one-step-ahead forecast is given by

$$\begin{aligned} \hat{Y}_{T+1} = {}& \hat{\alpha}_0 + \hat{\alpha}_1 Y_T + \hat{\alpha}_2 Y_{T-1} + \cdots + \hat{\alpha}_p Y_{T+1-p} \\ & + \hat{\beta}_1 X_{T+1,1} + \hat{\beta}_2 X_{T+1,2} + \cdots + \hat{\beta}_k X_{T+1,k} + \hat{u}_{T+1} \end{aligned} \tag{11.18}$$

where

$$\hat{u}_{T+1} = \hat{\rho}_1\hat{u}_T + \hat{\rho}_2\hat{u}_{T-1} + \cdots + \hat{\rho}_q\hat{u}_{T+1-q} \tag{11.19}$$

For higher steps, this procedure will be repeated with $\hat{Y}_{T+1}$ instead of Y_{T+1}.

Empirical Example: Short-Term Forecasts of Electricity Sales

Engle and Granger (1986) carried out a comparative analysis of several alternative models and methodologies for forecasting monthly electricity sales. A portion of their study is presented here. For details refer to their paper. The data refer to monthly series for 1964 through 1981 for California. The estimation was done for 168 periods (approximately 1964–1977) and ex-post forecasts were obtained for 36 periods during 1978–1980. Table 11.6 presents the estimates for one of the models used and Table 11.7 presents LM test statistics for a number of types of model specifications. The dependent variable is residential electricity consumption per customer. CDD and HDD are the cooling and heating degree days defined in the application of Section 9.8. In Table 11.7 RPINC/C is real per capita income and RELCP750 is the real average price of electricity. The model also includes monthly dummy variables (MAY is omitted to avoid exact multicollinearity). AUTO refers

TABLE 11.6 Diagnostic Tests for California Model Auto-A

Test Stat.	d.f.	% of Dist.	Test	Test Dist.
2.749	1	90.269	AUTO1	CHI-SQ
1.998	1	84.254	AUTON	CHI-SQ
18.600	10	95.436	AUTO1-N	CHI-SQ
0.898	1	65.668	AUTO MAX	CHI-SQ
4.019	1	95.501	YLAGD1	CHI-SQ
2.669	1	89.769	YLAGDN	CHI-SQ
9.320	12	32.468	YLAG1-N	CHI-SQ
0.627	1	57.186	Y-MAX	CHI-SQ
13.765	1	99.979	ARCH1	CHI-SQ
0.308	1	42.153	ARCHN	CHI-SQ
19.761	12	92.826	ARCH1-N	CHI-SQ
26.913	24	69.147	ARCH1-2N	CHI-SQ
1.212	1	72.918	TIME TND	CHI-SQ
12.175	2	99.773	CDDMA*TIME, HDDMA*TIME	
9.597	6	85.733	$CDD^2, HDD^2, CDD(-1)^2,$ $HDD(-1)^2, CDD(-2)^2, HDD(-2)^2$	
6.368	2	95.859	RELCP250, RELCP500	
4.432	3	78.158	TIME, D70, T70	
7.466	3	94.156	TIME, D72, T72	
20.915	3	99.989	TIME, D74, T74	
2.7491	1	90.269	AUTO-2	
3.8405	3	72.079	AUTO-3, AUTO-4, AUTO-6	

Source: Engle and Granger, 1986. Reprinted with the permission of the Electric Power Research Institute.

TABLE 11.7 California Estimates of Model Auto-A

DEPENDENT VARIABLE = DELC/C
SUM OF SQUARED RESIDUALS = 11245
MEAN OF DEPENDENT VARIABLE = 394.63
STANDARD DEVIATION = 64.732
STANDARD ERROR OF THE REGRESSION = 8.806
R-SQUARED = 0.983
ADJUSTED R-SQUARED = 0.981
F-STATISTIC (22,145) = 403.55
NUMBER OF OBSERVATIONS = 168

Variable	Lag	Beta/Rho	Std. Error	t-stat
CDD	0	0.123	0.028	4.406
CDD	1	0.171	0.028	6.047
CDD	2	0.102	0.027	3.672
HDD	0	0.063	0.012	4.952
HDD	1	0.010	0.013	7.418
HDD	2	0.032	0.013	2.522
RPINC/C	0	13.492	36.630	0.368
RELCP750	0	−8.780	4.716	−1.861
JAN	0	77.899	11.159	6.980
FEB	0	38.327	10.277	3.729
MAR	0	23.834	8.599	2.771
APR	0	3.743	6.043	0.619
JUN	0	17.025	6.559	2.595
JUL	0	32.158	10.978	2.929
AUG	0	29.562	14.513	2.036
SEP	0	35.415	15.522	2.281
OCT	0	26.262	13.761	1.908
NOV	0	33.551	11.741	2.857
DEC	0	53.550	11.100	4.824
CONST	0	516.190	247.140	2.088
AUTO	1	0.709	0.061	11.603
AUTO	12	0.580	0.072	7.962
AUTO	13	−0.315	0.083	−3.789

Source: Engle and Granger, 1986. Reprinted with the permission of the Electric Power Research Institute.

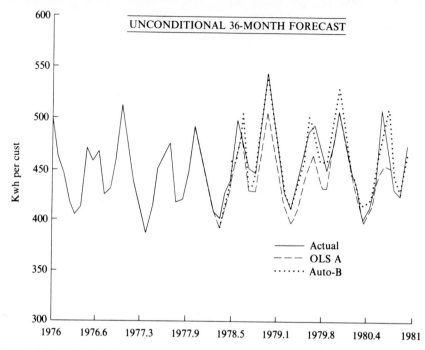

Figure 11.4 California forecast comparison

Source: Engle and Granger, 1986. Reprinted with the permission of the Electric Power Research Institute.

to serial correlation terms (lags 1, 12, and 13 were used). The values labeled "% of dist" (Table 11.5) are probabilities in the chi-square distribution to the *left* of the observed chi-square (100 minus the level of significance). Entries over 95 percent indicate significance at 5 percent. The interactions between CDD and time as well as HDD and time were the only significant ones. Engle and Granger reestimated the model including these interaction terms.

Unconditional forecasts obtained from this model (labeled AUTO-B) and a simple model with no serial correlation (labeled OLSA) are graphed in Figure 11.4. The root mean squared error (RMSE) for a one-step-ahead forecast was 15.4 for OLSA and 13.6 for AUTO-B. Both the figure and the RMSE values show that the model with autoregressive error terms performed better. Engle and Granger also estimated a variety of other models for ten different states. These are discussed in their paper.

11.7 Forecasting from Time Series Models

As mentioned earlier, econometric models are generally based on some underlying behavior of the agents involved in an economic system. A widely used alternative class of models, however, especially for short-run forecasting, is known as *time series models*. These typically relate a dependent variable to its past values and to random errors that may be serially correlated. Time series models are generally not based on any underlying economic behavior. Until about 30 years ago, time series models were most common in engineering and the physical sciences. In the last two decades, however, the time series approach has gained enormous popularity in economics, especially for short-run forecasting for which time series models have proven to be better suited than econometric models. In this section we present a brief introduction to the issues involved in the time series approach. For an excellent treatment of time series models and forecasting at the undergraduate level, refer to the book by Granger (1989).

A time series is often modeled as the sum (or product) of three components: (1) a **trend term**, (2) a **seasonal term**, and (3) a **random** (or **stochastic**) term. We thus have

$$Y_t = T_t + S_t + u_t \qquad \text{or} \qquad Y_t = T_t S_t u_t$$

where Y is the dependent variable, T is the trend component, S is the seasonal component, and u is the random error term. An example of a simple linear time trend is $T_t = \alpha + \beta t$. In Section 11.4 several other forms of trends were fitted. If Y_t has been growing exponentially, it should be converted first to logarithms. As the name indicates, a seasonal component is one that is due to a regularly occurring seasonal phenomenon such as the month or a quarter, week, day, hour, public holidays, and so on. We have seen many examples in which seasonal dummies can be used to estimate seasonal patterns. Very sophisticated techniques were developed to estimate these components, but by the 1930s investigators were disenchanted with the methods, and a different structure was formulated for time series variables. This is discussed next.

The Structure of Time Series Models

Autoregressive (AR) Models   A purely autoregressive time series model [which is a special case of equation (11.16)] has the following structure:

$$Y_t = \alpha_1 Y_{t-1} + \alpha_2 Y_{t-2} + \cdots + \alpha_p Y_{t-p} + u_t \tag{11.20}$$

where Y_t is the tth observation on the dependent variable *after subtracting its mean*, and u_t is a well-behaved error term with zero mean and constant variance that is uncorrelated with u_s for $t \neq s$ (such a term is known as **white noise**). The constant term is omitted because Y_t is expressed as a deviation from the mean. Readers should readily recognize that this is a special case of the distributed lag model discussed in Chapter 10 and a special case of equation (11.16) with all the β's set to zero. In other words, Y_t is modeled only with its own past and not with other independent variables. These are **autoregressive**, or **AR, models**, and the one in equation (11.20) is referred to as an AR(p) model, p being the order of the autoregressive structure.

Moving Average (MA) Models   The following model is referred to as a **moving average**, or **MA, model** of order q, denoted by MA(q):

$$Y_t = v_t - \beta_1 v_{t-1} - \beta_2 v_{t-2} - \cdots - \beta_q v_{t-q} \tag{11.21}$$

where v_t is a white noise error series. Y_t is thus a linear combination of white noise random variables. We encountered such an error term in Section 10.2.

ARMA Models A mixture of the autoregressive and moving average formulations is known as an **ARMA model**. Thus, an ARMA (p, q) model is of the general form

$$Y_t = \alpha_1 Y_{t-1} + \alpha_2 Y_{t-2} + \cdots + \alpha_p Y_{t-p}$$
$$+ v_t - \beta_1 v_{t-1} - \beta_2 v_{t-2} - \cdots - \beta_q v_{t-q}$$
(11.22)

The Autocorrelation Function and the Correlogram

Consider the correlation coefficient $r(s)$ between u_t and u_{t-s} for values of s from 0 to $t-1$. This function is called the **autocorrelation function**. The autocorrelation function is thus defined as

$$r(s) = \text{Cor}(u_t, u_{t-s}) = \frac{\text{Cov}(u_t, u_{t-s})}{\text{Var}(u_t)} = \frac{E(u_t u_{t-s})}{E(u_t^2)}$$

which can be estimated by the sample correlation coefficient between u_t and u_{t-s}

The **correlogram** is the graph of $r(s)$ against s, for $s = 0, 1, 2, \ldots, t-1$. It is a useful guide for determining how correlated the error term (u_t) is to the past errors $u_{t-1}, u_{t-2}, \ldots$.

It is shown in Appendix 11.A that in the case of the first-order autoregressive process [AR(1)] given by equation (9.2), the autocorrelation function takes the form $r(s) = \rho^s$. The correlogram for AR(1) is presented in Figure 11.5 for $\rho = 0.3, 0.6$, and 0.9 for $s = 1$ through 10. Figure 11.6 presents the same for negative values of ρ. Note that $r(s)$ is independent of t. Also, if $|\rho| < 1$, the variance of u_t will be finite (proved in Appendix 11.A) Hence, the AR(1) process is stationary provided the autoregressive coefficient ρ does not exceed 1 in absolute value. If ρ is negative, $r(s)$ will alternate in sign. If ρ is high, then the correlogram for AR(1) declines slowly over time, whereas

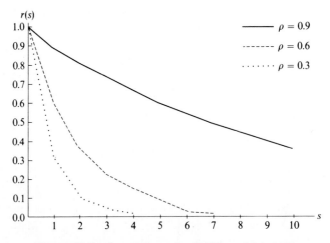

Figure 11.5 Correlogram for AR(1) model ($\rho > 0$)

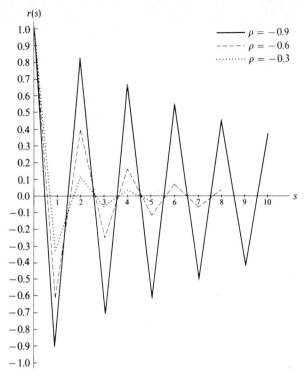

Figure 11.6   Correlogram for AR(1) model ($\rho < 0$)

for a low ρ, the function quickly decreases to zero. The usefulness of the auto-correlation function and the correlogram is discussed in more detail later in this chapter.

Stationarity

In this chapter we restrict ourselves only to the case in which the autocorrelation function $r(s)$ is independent of t, the time period from which current and past residual correlations are measured, and depends only on the distance (s) between the time period t and the period ($t - s$) for which the correlation is calculated. Furthermore, u_t is assumed to have a finite variance. This property is known as **stationarity**, and any time series obeying this is called a **stationary time series**. Thus, the process that generates the stochastic disturbances is time-invariant. Under stationarity, $\text{Var}(u_{t-s})$ and $\text{Var}(u_t)$ are the same. For more details on the correl-ogram, stationarity, and autoregressive formulations, see Granger (1989).

Nonstationarity, Differencing, and ARIMA Models   We just saw that stationarity has the property that the correlation between a variable at time $t(Y_t)$ and its value at time $s(Y_s)$ depends only on the distance $t - s$ between the two time periods. A stationary series has a constant (not necessarily zero) mean and variance that does not change through time. The process that generates the series is thus time-invariant. Most economic series, however, have **nonstationarity** because they steadily grow over time. For instance, if Y_t has a linear or exponential time trend, it will not be stationary. Estimation of the ARMA process requires that Y_t be a stationary time series. What can one do in such a case? It is possible to convert most nonstationary time series to stationary form through the process of **differencing**. Consider a linear trend of the form $Y_t = \alpha + \beta t$. The **first difference** of Y_t is defined as $\Delta Y_t = Y_t - Y_{t-1}$. We see that

$$\Delta Y_t = \alpha + \beta t - \alpha - \beta(t - 1) = \beta$$

which is constant and hence stationary. Thus, a linear trend can be removed by differencing once. If a series is growing exponentially at a constant rate, the logarithm $\ln(Y_t)$ has a linear trend that can be differenced. It is easily shown that a quadratic trend can be removed by differencing twice. The **second difference** (denoted as $\Delta^2 Y$) is defined as the first difference of the first difference. Thus,

$$\Delta^2 Y_t = (Y_t - Y_{t-1}) - (Y_{t-1} - Y_{t-2}) = Y_t - 2Y_{t-1} + Y_{t-2} \qquad (11.23)$$

Another form in which nonstationarity often arises is seasonality. Nonstationarity in monthly and quarterly series can often be removed by taking appropriate differencing: $\Delta_4 = Y_t - Y_{t-4}$ for quarterly data and $\Delta_{12} = Y_t - Y_{t-12}$ for monthly series.

Practice Problem

11.3 a. Show that the quadratic trend $Y_t = \alpha + \beta t + \gamma t^2$ can be removed with a second difference.

   b. Show that the quarterly differencing $\Delta_4 = Y_t - Y_{t-4}$ also removes a linear trend, and similarly for Δ_{12}.

Suppose a nonstationary time series can be converted to a stationary one by differencing d times. Then the series is said to be **integrated of order d** and is written as $I(d)$. The differenced stationary series can then be modeled as an ARMA(p, q). In this case the process that generates the series Y_t is called an **autoregressive integrated moving average**, and the models are **ARIMA models**, denoted as ARIMA(p, d, q).

Estimation and Forecasting with an ARIMA Model

Box and Jenkins (1970) proposed a specific approach to time series modeling, which consists of three stages:

1. **Identification**, which is the specification of p, d, and q.
2. **Estimation**, which consists of estimating the parameters in equation (11.22) in which the left-hand side is the series differenced d times.
3. **Diagnostic checking**, which consists of applying a variety of tests to see whether the estimated model fits the data adequately. If the model is found to be inadequate, the process is repeated.

Identification   Because most economic time series vary over time in a systematic way, the first step in identification is to choose d, the number of times to difference a series to make it approximately stationary. A plot of the series over time often gives a clue as to the nature of the series. If the series appears to grow exponentially, first take the logarithm and plot it against time. If a linear trend is apparent, difference the series (or its logarithm) once and plot the differenced series. If this also exhibits a trend, a second differencing might be required. Economic time series rarely require differencing more than twice.

A second way to identify whether differencing is required is to calculate the autocorrelation function (ACF) defined earlier and plot the correlogram. The correlogram is a plot of the coefficients of correlation between a series and its past values. If this plot declines slowly (as for $\rho = 0.9$ in Figure 11.4), then differencing is indicated. Next plot the correlogram of the first differences. If this plot also declines slowly, a second difference is indicated.

Nonstationarity due to seasonal effects is handled by **deseasonalizing** the series. A simple way to take out the seasonal component in a monthly data series is to obtain the difference $Y_t - Y_{t-12}$. Alternatively, we could regress Y_t against seasonal dummy variables and then obtain the residuals of the fitted equation, which would be free of seasonal effects. Other more sophisticated methods are discussed in Granger (1989) and Granger and Newbold (1986). If seasonal effects are present, the ACF will have "spikes" at regular intervals (see Figure 11.7 for an illustration with monthly data). The difference $Y_t - Y_{t-12}$ often removes the seasonal and linear trend effects (see Figure 11.8 for an illustration with the same monthly data).

The initial choices of the order of the autoregressive and moving average terms (p and q) are usually made simultaneously. For large values of the lag (denoted

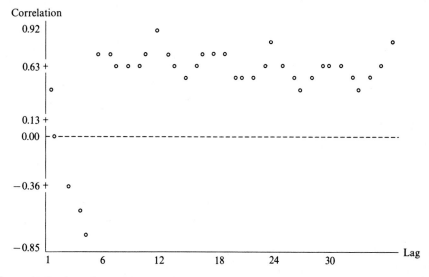

Figure 11.7   Correlogram for monthly electricity sales data

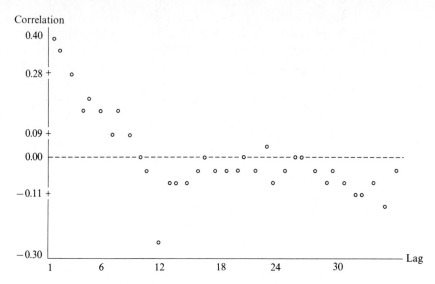

Figure 11.8 Correlogram for 12-month differenced data

by k), the theoretical ACF of the AR(p) model is approximately of the form $A\rho^k$ (with $-1 < \rho < 1$). If ρ is positive, the ACF will steadily decline (see Figure 11.5). If ρ is negative, the function will be bounded by a pair of curves, as in Figure 11.9. For the MA(q) model, the theoretical correlogram is zero for all lags greater than q but has no particular shape before q (see Figure 11.10). The estimated correlogram can be used as a guide to choosing a value of q. If the correlogram remains near zero after a particular lag, then that lag will be a good choice for q.

To choose the initial value of p, another function, called the **partial autocorrelation function (PACF)**, and the associated graph, called the **partial correlogram**, are used. Suppose we fit a first-order autoregressive model of the form $Y_t = a_{11} Y_{t-1} + u_t$ and estimate a_{11} by OLS (the constant term is omitted by letting Y_t be the devia-

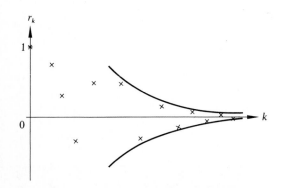

Figure 11.9 Correlogram for AR(p).

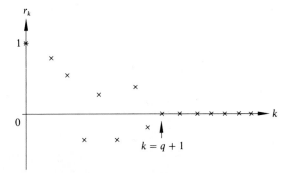

Figure 11.10 Correlogram for MA(q).

tion from the mean of the series). Next we estimate an AR(2) model of the form $Y_t = a_{21} Y_{t-1} + a_{22} Y_{t-2} + u_t$, and obtain $\hat{a}_{22}$. By proceeding in this way, we can obtain $\hat{a}_{kk}$, the estimated regression coefficient of Y_{t-k} when a kth-order autoregressive model is estimated. The plot of $\hat{a}_{kk}$ is the partial correlogram. It is the correlation between Y_t and Y_{t-k}, after the effects of the other Y's have been removed. The theoretical partial correlogram has the property that, if the order of autoregression is p, then $a_{kk} = 0$ for all $k > p$. The estimated partial correlogram can therefore be used as a guide in choosing a value of p. If the partial correlogram remains near zero after a particular lag, then that lag will be a good choice for p. The guidelines for identifying an initial time series model can be summarized as follows:

1. If the correlogram remains near zero after a certain lag, say q, then the appropriate choice for the order of MA is q.
2. If the partial correlogram remains near zero after a certain lag, say p, then the appropriate choice for the order of AR is p.
3. If neither of these happens but both plots eventually decline to zero, we could start with a simple ARMA(1, 1) model.

Estimation The procedure for estimating the parameters of a time series model is quite complicated and involves solving a set of nonlinear equations. Many computer programs that compute correlograms and partial correlograms used in identifying a model, and then automatically carry out the estimation process are available (FORECAST MASTER, FORECAST PRO, TSP, Micro TSP, to name a few).

Diagnostic Checking The diagnostic checking stage consists of subjecting the estimated model to a variety of tests to make sure that it fits the data adequately. The best way to examine whether a model is adequate is to conduct a postsample exercise—that is, reserve a part of the sample (which will not be used in the estimation) for ex-post forecasting and then compare the forecasted values with the known values of Y. Commonly used summary statistics are the mean squared error and the Akaike information criterion (see Section 4.4). Another simple approach is to *overfit* the model—that is, fit a slightly higher order model and then test whether the extra parameters are significantly different from zero.

In any case, if the model fits the data well, the residuals from the model [$\hat{v}_t$ in equation (11.22)] should be white noise. The usual procedure is to compute the residuals and their autocorrelation function and then examine whether the residuals approximate a white noise series. Box and Pierce (1970) have proposed a formal test for this. The procedure is to compute the **Box-Pierce statistic**:

$$Q = T \sum_{k=1}^{k=K} r_k^2 \qquad (11.24)$$

where r_k is the kth-order autocorrelation of the residuals ($\hat{v}_t$), T is the number of observations, and K is a preselected number of autocorrelations (say 20 or more).

If the residual series is white noise, then Q will have a chi-square distribution with K-p-q degrees of freedom. If Q is larger than a critical value of chi-square, we conclude that the residual series is not white noise. A more recent test now in common use is by Ljung and Box (1978). The **Ljung-Box test statistic** is given by

$$\text{LJB} = T'(T' + 2)\sum_{k=1}^{k=K}\left[\frac{r_k^2}{T' - k}\right] \tag{11.25}$$

where $T' = T - d$, the number of observations used after the series has been differenced d times. Under the null hypothesis that the residuals are indeed white noise, LJB has a chi-square distribution with K-p-q degrees of freedom. The criterion for acceptance or rejection of the test is similar to that of the Box–Pierce test.

Forecasting The final step is to obtain the actual forecasts. We see from equation (11.22) that a one-step-ahead forecast is given by (setting v_{T+1} to 0)

$$\hat{Y}_{T+1} = \hat{\alpha}_1 Y_T + \hat{\alpha}_2 Y_{T-1} + \cdots + \hat{\alpha}_p Y_{T+1-p}$$
$$- \hat{\beta}_1 \hat{v}_T - \hat{\beta}_2 \hat{v}_{T-1} - \cdots - \hat{\beta}_q \hat{v}_{T+1-q} \tag{11.26}$$

If the series had to be differenced in order to make it stationary, then this forecast would have been for $\Delta\hat{Y}_{T+1} = \hat{Y}_{T+1} - \hat{Y}_T$, from which $\hat{Y}_{T+1}$ is obtained as $\hat{Y}_T + \Delta\hat{Y}_{T+1}$. If the series had been differenced twice, we would have had, from equation (11.23).

$$\hat{Y}_{T+1} = 2Y_T - Y_{T-1} + \Delta^2\hat{Y}_{T+1}$$

Empirical Example: Forecasting Monthly Electricity Sales

Gunel (1987) has carried out a comparative study of a number of different approaches to forecasting Ontario Hydro Electric Company's monthly system energy demand: one of these approaches was the Box–Jenkins method described here. Figure 11.11 is a graph of the total system energy demand for the period January 1970 to April 1984. The graph indicates both strong seasonality and an upward trend. The AIC criterion and the root mean squared error (RMSE) are presented here for four different ARMA models:

ARMA Order	AIC	RMSE
(1, 1)	1930	320
(4, 1)	1927	312
(1, 4)	1926	311
(0, 4)	1924	311

ARMA(0, 4) is the best, but Gunel found strong seasonality indicated by the ACF. To remove the nonstationarity due to seasonal effects, Gunel regressed the

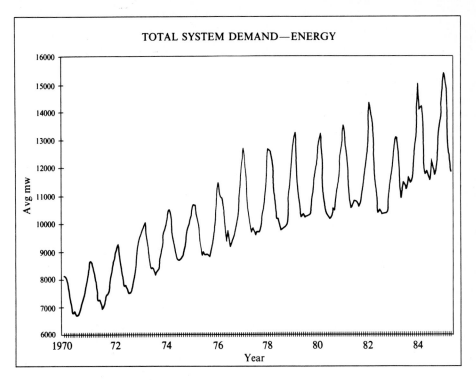

Figure 11.11 Total system energy demand

Source: Gunel, 1987. Reprinted with the permission of the Electric Power Research Institute.

energy series against a constant and 11 monthly dummy variables and computed the residuals. The residuals were then modeled using the Box–Jenkins methodology. ARIMA(0, 1, 4) appeared to be superior to a number of alternatives the author tried. Postsample forecasts were made through June 1985. Figure 11.12 is a comparison of a number of different models. Although the graph doesn't show it very clearly, the above model (labeled BJ7 in the graph) does well in forecast performance. The statistical measures also indicated that the model has no serial correlation and the lowest forecast error.

11.8   Cointegration

In Chapter 10 we introduced the *error correction model* which related changes in one variable to changes in another variable as well as to the past levels of the two variables. The formulation was based on an underlying long-run relationship between the two variables. This notion is closely related to the concept of **cointegration** introduced by Granger (1981). Suppose X_t and Y_t are two random walks and hence are not stationary (in particular, their variances increase with t). In

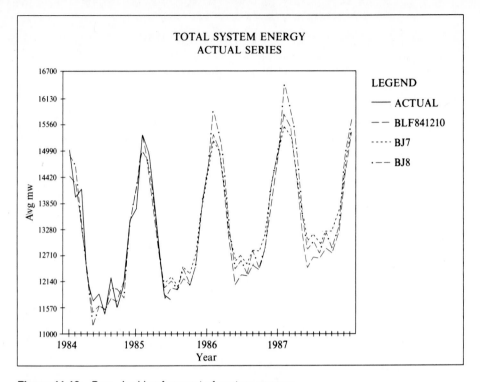

Figure 11.12   Box–Jenkins forecast of system energy

Source: Gunel, 1987. Reprinted with the permission of the Electric Power Research Institute.

general, we would expect that a linear combination of X_t and Y_t would also be a random walk. Yet, the two series may have the property that a particular linear combination of them $(X_t - aY_t)$ is stationary. Thus, X_t and Y_t may each be integrated of order 1 [that is, $I(1)$], but there may exist an a such that $X_t - aY_t$ is stationary [that is, $I(0)$ with a finite variance]. If such a property holds, then we say that X_t and Y_t are **cointegrated**. Two cointegrated series will thus not drift too far apart over the long run. Examples of possibly cointegrated series are short-term and long-term interest rates, prices of two close substitutes, and prices and wages in two related markets.

Testing for Cointegration

Because the type of model to be estimated might depend on whether a "dependent variable" may be cointegrated with an "independent" variable, it is important to test whether two (or more) variables are cointegrated. Engle and Granger (1987) considered a variety of tests for cointegration, of which we discuss the two recommended by them. To motivate the tests, consider two variables X_t and Y_t which are integrated of order 1.

TABLE 11.8 Critical Values for Testing for Cointegration

Level of significance (%)	DW statistic	Augmented DF *t*-statistic
1	0.511	3.77
5	0.386	3.17
10	0.322	2.84

Source: Engle, R. F., and Granger, C. W. J. "Co-integration and Error Correction, Representation, Estimation, and Testing" from *Econometrica*, March 1987, Vol. 55, pp. 251–276.

Cointegrating Regression DW Test   This is the simplest test for cointegration. The procedure is first to estimate the following equation called the **cointegrating regression**.

$$Y_t = \alpha + \beta X_t + u_t$$

The Durbin–Watson statistic for this is given by

$$DW = \frac{\sum (\hat{u}_t - \hat{u}_{t-1})^2}{\sum \hat{u}_t^2}$$

As mentioned earlier, in general one would expect u to be $I(1)$ if X and Y are $I(1)$. If this were so, the DW statistic will be close to zero and the two series will *not be cointegrated*. Thus, one way of testing for the lack of cointegration is to see if DW is close to zero. If DW is significantly positive, then we would suspect that the two series are cointegrated. The standard tables for the DW test used in Chapter 9 are not applicable here because there the null hypothesis was that $DW = 2$, rather than that $DW = 0$. Engle and Granger did a simulation study and obtained the critical values presented in Table 11.8 for a sample of 100 observations.

Augmented Dickey–Fuller Test   Here also a cointegration regression is first run. Next obtain the error terms

$$\hat{u}_t = Y_t - \hat{\alpha} - \hat{\beta} X_t$$

Then estimate the following **Dickey–Fuller regression**

$$\Delta \hat{u}_t = -\phi \hat{u}_{t-1} + \sum_1^p b_i \Delta \hat{u}_{t-i} + \epsilon_t$$

where p is the preselected order of lags for the residuals. The test statistic is the t-statistic for ϕ but the t-distribution is not appropriate. For this case also Engle and Granger have provided critical values using a simulation procedure for 100 observations (see Table 11.8).

Example 11.4

Table 11.9 provides annual data on the average hourly wage rates for California and for the United States as a whole, for the period 1969–1989, and Figure 11.13

TABLE 11.9 Hourly Wage Rates in the United States and California 1960–1989

Year	California	United States	Year	California	United States
1960	2.62	2.26	1975	5.22	4.83
1961	2.72	2.32	1976	5.59	5.22
1962	2.79	2.38	1977	6.00	5.67
1963	2.88	2.45	1978	6.43	6.17
1964	2.96	2.53	1979	7.03	6.70
1965	3.05	2.61	1980	7.70	7.27
1966	3.16	2.72	1981	8.56	7.99
1967	3.29	2.82	1982	9.24	8.49
1968	3.44	3.01	1983	9.52	8.83
1969	3.62	3.19	1984	9.77	9.19
1970	3.80	3.35	1985	10.12	9.54
1971	4.02	3.57	1986	10.36	9.73
1972	4.25	3.82	1987	10.75	9.91
1973	4.44	4.09	1988	10.80	10.18
1974	4.76	4.43	1989	11.16	10.47

Source: Economic Report of the Governor, State of California, 1990.

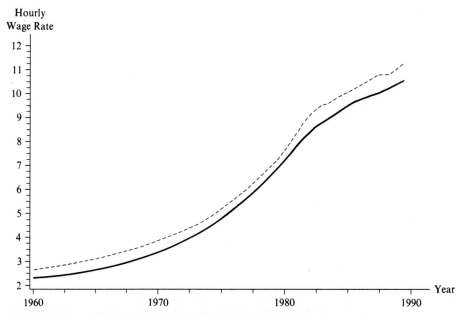

Figure 11.13 Hourly wage rates in the United States and California (the solid line represents the United States; the broken line, California)

shows this data graphed. Note that the curves are practically identical except for the fact that the graph for California is consistently above that for the United States. A natural question that arises is whether the two wage rates are cointegrated. Before examining that, however, we should determine whether the two series follow random walks. This was first done with the Dickey–Fuller test described in the previous chapter. The unrestricted model was (W refers to a wage rate)

$$\Delta W_t = \beta_1 + \beta_2 t + \beta_3 W_{t-1} + \beta_4 \Delta W_{t-1} + u_t$$

The null hypothesis that the series is a random walk is $\beta_2 = 0$ and $\beta_3 = 0$. The F-statistics for this were 3.724 and and 3.1304 for the United States and California, respectively (see Practice Computer Session 11.3 to reproduce the results of this example). From the Dickey–Fuller table of critical values presented in Table 10.4 we note that the random walk hypothesis cannot be rejected even at a 10 percent level. To apply the DW test for cointegration, we obtained the following cointegrating regression:

$$CALWAGE_t = 0.28887 + 1.03405\,USWAGE$$
$$T = 30 \qquad DW = 0.712$$

The DW statistic is well above all the critical values in Table 11.8 and supports the hypothesis that the two wage rates are cointegrated. It should be pointed out, however, that the critical values were based on simulations for 100 observations whereas we have only 30 observations. The proper critical values for other sample sizes are not presently available, and the evidence in favor of cointegration is therefore only suggestive.

To apply the augmented Dickey–Fuller test, we saved the residuals from the above regression and obtained the following Dickey–Fuller Regression, assuming a fourth-order lag process:

$$\Delta \hat{u}_t = -0.36489 \hat{u}_{t-1} + 0.0567 \Delta \hat{u}_{t-1} + 0.24509 \Delta \hat{u}_{t-2}$$
$$- 0.50435 \Delta \hat{u}_{t-3} + 0.21878 \Delta \hat{u}_{t-4}$$

In view of the lags specified, the effective data period is 1965–1989. The computed t-statistic for the coefficient of $-\hat{u}_{t-1}$ was 1.543, which is considerably below the critical values in Table 11.8. We therefore cannot reject the null hypothesis of no cointegration (the caveat about the smallness of the sample size applies here also).   □

• •

SUMMARY

One of the major applications of an econometric model is that of *forecasting* or *prediction*. There are two broad approaches to forecasting: *econometric* and *time series*. *Econometric forecasting* is based on a regression model that relates one or more dependent variables to several independent variables. *Time series forecasting* relates a dependent variable to its past values and attempts to use the relationship to predict the dependent variable.

A forecasting environment consists of three time periods. An investigator uses a sample of observations and estimates the model. The predicted values of the dependent variable during this *in-sample* period are also known as *fitted values*. *Out-of-sample* forecasts can be either ex-post or ex-ante. *Ex-post* forecasts are for the period during which actual values of the dependent and independent variables are known. Such forecasts are often compared with the actual values to evaluate the forecasting performance of a model. *Ex-ante* forecasts are predictions of the future with values of the independent variables predicted from other models.

Forecasts can be conditional or unconditional. When the values of the independent variables are given (or known) we obtain *conditional forecasts. Unconditional forecasts* are generated when the values of the exogenous variables are not given a priori but are generated from the model itself or from an auxiliary model.

The evaluation of the forecasting ability of a model is done in a number of ways. First we withhold a portion of the sample and not use it for estimation purposes. Next we generate forecasts for the withheld sample (this is the ex-post forecast) and compute prediction errors and the sum of squared prediction errors (ESS). This can be used to calculate the model selection statistics presented in Table 4.3. A model that has lower values for most of the criterion statistics is judged to be superior. In addition, we regress the predicted value against a constant and the actual value. If the forecast is perfect we would expect the estimated constant term to be near zero and the estimated slope term to be near one.

Trend line fitting is a commonly used forecasting technique that expresses the dependent variable as a function of just time. The assumed functional form could be linear, quadratic, linear-log, reciprocal, log-linear, double-log, or logistic.

An investigator interested only in the underlying trend of a time series rather than in fluctuations around the trend might *smooth* the data using either an average of several successive terms (called the *moving average*) or an exponential smoothing, which obtains a weighted average of current and past values of the series, the weights declining exponentially as we move back in time. The technique can be used on forecast errors in order to obtain *adaptive forecasts.*

When several alternative models appear to generate reasonably good forecasts, it is better to combine the forecasts rather than select one model as the "best" and discard the others. The optimum method of combining forecasts is to regress (using sample period data or ex-post data) the actual values against a constant and the forecasts generated by the alternative models. The estimated coefficients are then used as weights to combine forecasts. In the sample period, the combined forecast has the lowest sum of squared errors with zero mean forecast error, *even if individual forecasts are biased.*

In econometric models, forecasts are generated by substituting predicted or assumed values for the independent variables. If there is serial correlation in the residuals, the errors can be modeled with an autoregressive process and the information used in obtaining more efficient forecasts.

As mentioned earlier, time series models relate a dependent variable to its own past values. A purely autoregressive time series (*AR model*) would relate the dependent to its past values with white noise errors. A moving average model (*MA model*) relates a dependent variable to a linear combination of white noise error terms. An *ARMA model* combines the AR and MA features into a single model.

The *correlogram* is a useful diagram for identifying patterns in correlation among series. It plots the *autocorrelation function*, which gives the coefficient of correlation between the values of a series at time t and those at time $t-s$, for different values of s.

The property of *stationarity* has the feature that the series has a time-invariant mean and variance, and the correlation between a variable at time t and that at time $s(t \neq s)$ depends only on the distance $t-s$ between the two periods. A nonstationary series can often be differenced (by obtaining the change from one period to the next) to make it stationary. Sometimes it may have to be differenced many times or converted to logarithms before differencing. A linear trend can be removed by differencing once, a quadratic trend can be removed by differencing twice, and so on. Quarterly and monthly data often exhibit seasonal effects that can be removed by differences of order 4 or 12—that is, by $Y_t - Y_{t-4}$ or $Y_t - Y_{t-12}$. *ARIMA models* are models that are first differenced many times to produce stationarity and then an ARMA model fitted to it.

The estimation of a time series model consists of three steps: (1) identification, (2) estimation, and (3) diagnostic checking. Identification is the process of specifying the orders of differencing, autoregressive modeling, and moving average modeling. Correlograms and partial correlograms are used in identifying models. Diagnostic checking is the process of subjecting the model to tests to see whether it fits adequately. Two tests frequently used here are the *Box–Pierce test* and the *Ljung–Box test*. Once the model has been judged adequate, forecasts are generated from the estimated model.

The concept of *cointegration* is closely related to that of an *error correction model* introduced in the previous chapter. If two series are integrated of order 1, but a particular linear combination of them is stationary, the two series are said to be *cointegrated*. Two cointegrated series will generally not drift too far apart. To test for cointegration, one can use a modified Durbin–Watson test or the *augmented Dickey–Fuller test*.

REFERENCES

Bates, J. M., and Granger, C. W. J. "The Combination of Forecasts." *Operations Research Quarterly*, Vol. 20 (1969): 451–469.

Bessler, D. A., and Brandt, J. A. "Forecasting Livestock Prices with Individual and Composite Methods." *Applied Economics*, Vol. 13 (1981): 513–522.

Bohara, A.; McNown, R.; and Batts, J. T. "A Re-evaluation of the Combination and Adjustment of Forecasts." *Applied Economics*, Vol. 19 (1987): 437–455.

Box, G. E. P., and Jenkins, G. M. *Time Series Analysis, Forecasting, and Control*. San Francisco: Holden Day, 1970.

Box, G. E. P., and Pierce, D. A. "Distribution of Residual Autocorrelations in Autoregressive Integrated Moving Average Time Series Models." *J. Amer. Stat. Assoc.*, Vol. 65 (1970): 1509–1526.

Economic Report of the President. Washington, D.C.: U.S. Government Printing Office, 1987.

Engle, R. F., and Granger, C. W. J. *Forecasting Electricity Sales Over the Short Term: A Comparison of New Methodologies*, Section 2. Electric Power Research Institute, EM-4772, September 1986.

Engle, R. F., and C. W. J. "Co-integration and Error Correction: Representation, Estimation and Testing." *Econometrica*, Vol. 55 (March 1987): 251–276.

Granger, C. W. J. "Some Properties of Times Series Data and Their Use in Econometric Model Specification." *J. Econometrics*, Vol. 16 (May 1981): 121–130.

Granger, C. W. J. "Combining Forecasts—Twenty Years Later." *Journal of Forecasting*, 1989.

Granger, C. W. J. *Forecasting in Business and Economics.* New York: Academic Press, 1989.

Granger, C. W. J., and Newbold, P. *Forecasting Economic Time Series.* Orlando: Academic Press, 1986.

Granger, C. W. J., and Ramanathan, Ramu. "Improved Methods of Combining Forecasts." *Journal of Forecasting*, Vol. 3 (1984): 197–204.

Gunel, I. "Forecasting System Energy Demand." *Forecast Master Program Case Studies.* Electric Power Research Institute, EM-5114, April 1987.

International Journal of Foreccasting, Special section on combining forecasts, November 1989.

Journal of Forecasting. Special issue on combining forecasts, July 1989.

Ljung, G. M., and Box, G. E. P. "On a Measure of Lack of Fit in Time Series Models." *Biometrika*, Vol. 65 (1978): 297–303.

KEY TERMS

Adaptive forecast
ARIMA models
ARMA models
Autocorrelation function
Augmented Dickey–Fuller test
Autoregressive integrated moving average
Autoregressive (AR) models
Box-Pierce statistic
Cointegrating regression
Combining forecasts
Conditional forecast
Correlogram
Deseasonalization

Detrending
Diagnostic checking
Differencing
Econometric forecasting
Estimation
Ex-ante forecast
Exponential smoothing
Ex-post forecast
First difference
Fitted value
Forecasting
Identification
In-sample forecast
Ljung–Box test statistic

Mean squared error (MSE)
Moving average (MA) model
Nonstationarity
Out-of-sample forecast
Partial autocorrelation function
  (PACF)
Partial correlogram
Post-sample period
Prediction
Random term
Seasonal term
Second difference

Smoothing
Smooth curve
Stationarity
Stochastic term
Time series forecasting
Trend
Trend line fitting
Trend term
Unconditional forecast
Vector autoregression
White noise

PRACTICE COMPUTER SESSIONS

11.1 The application on fitting trend lines for the wage rate in California can be duplicated using the data file *data11-1* and the ECSLIB command input file *ps11-1.inp*.

11.2 Example 11.3 on exponential smoothing uses the data file *data11-3* and the input file *ps11-2.inp*.

11.3 To reproduce Example 11.4, use the input file *ps11-3.inp* and the data in *data11-9*.

EXERCISES

11.1 Define each of the following terms and provide examples to illustrate them: fitted values, conditional, unconditional, ex-post forecast, ex-ante forecast.

11.2 Describe step by step how you would go about evaluating the forecasts from a model.

11.3 Suppose you have forecasts from three different approaches: the econometric approach, the time series approach, and expert opinion. Y_t is the dependent variable and the forecasts are f_{t1}, f_{t2}, and f_{t3}. Describe the exact steps for combining the forecasts using the Granger–Ramanathan method, Method C.

11.4 You have quarterly sales for a company for several years. Describe how the dummy variable approach can be used to "deseasonalize" the series (define the term in quotes).

11.5 Describe how you would "detrend" a series Y_t (define *detrending*).

†11.6 Consider the model $Y_t = \alpha + \beta X_t + u_t$, with $u_t = \rho u_{t-1} + \epsilon_t$. Describe how you would use the estimated models to generate forecasts, taking account

of the serial correlation. Suppose the error structure was $u_t = \rho_1 u_{t-1} + \rho_3 u_{t-3} + \epsilon_t$. What is the forecasting procedure in this case?

11.7   Suppose the error term of a regression model is $MA(1)$, so that $u_t = \epsilon_t - \lambda \epsilon_{t-1}$, where ϵ_t is white noise. Derive an expression for the autocorrelation function $r(s) = \text{cor}(u_t, u_{t-s})$, $t \neq s$.

†11.8   You have monthly data for electricity sales for a utility for a number of years. It exhibits both seasonal variation and exponential growth over the years. Describe how you would formulate econometric and time series models to capture these effects.

11.9   Suppose $Y_t = Y_0 e^{\lambda t}$; that is, Y is growing exponentially. Show that the first difference in log of Y becomes stationary (define the term *stationary*).

†11.10   Consider an adaptive expectations model derived in Section 10.2. Explain whether the model is AR, MA, ARMA, or ARIMA.

11.11   You have quarterly data for several years for a company. Describe how you would use the time series approach to model the series.

11.12   In many of the previous chapters time series data were used to relate a dependent variable to its determinants. For each case, withhold the last 10 or 15 observations and estimate a linear and a double-log model with the rest of the data. Next use the models to generate forecasts for the last 10 or 15 periods, using the known values of the independent variables. Compare the forecasts for the observed values (derive appropraite criterion statistics for this) and evaluate the forecasting ability of the models. Also use the Granger–Ramanathan method, Method C, to combine the forecasts and then evaluate them.

11.13   Chapters 9 and 10 have several data series that can be used to model the corresponding dependent variable using the time series approach. Use the Dickey–Fuller test to check them for unit root (in some cases, you may have to take a logarithm first).

11.14   Table 9.13 contains quarterly data for the United States for a number of variables. First test whether GNP and money supply are random walks (try levels as well as logarithms). Then test them for cointegration.

11.15   Application Section 10.4 presented an error correlation model of U.S. military expenditures. Test military and total government expenditures for random walks and cointegration. Do the same analysis for military and nonmilitary expenditures.

11.A APPENDIX

Miscellaneous Derivations

11.A.1 Properties of u_t When It Is AR(1)

Substituting repeatedly from equation (9.2) we get

$$u_t = \rho u_{t-1} + \epsilon_t = \epsilon_t + \rho(\epsilon_{t-1} + \rho u_{t-2}) = \epsilon_t + \rho\epsilon_{t-1} + \rho^2(\epsilon_{t-2} + \rho u_{t-3})$$
$$= \epsilon_t + \rho\epsilon_{t-1} + \rho^2\epsilon_{t-2} + \cdots$$

Because $E(\epsilon_t) = 0$, we have $E(u_t) = 0$. Also, by the independence of the ϵ's,

$$\sigma_u^2 = \text{Var}(u_t) = \text{Var}(\epsilon_t) + \rho^2\,\text{Var}(\epsilon_{t-1}) + \rho^4\,\text{Var}(\epsilon_{t-2}) + \cdots$$

$$= \sigma_\epsilon^2(1 + \rho^2 + \rho^4 + \cdots) = \frac{\sigma_\epsilon^2}{1 - \rho^2}$$

Note that the infinite series will sum to a finite value only if $|\rho| < 1$. Thus, a necessary condition for stationarity is that the first-order autocorrelation be strictly less than 1 in absolute value. If $\rho = 1$, the error process becomes $u_t = u_{t-1} + \epsilon_t$. The value of u at time t is therefore equal to its value in the previous period plus a purely random effect. This process is known as the *random walk model* and is frequently used in modeling stock price behavior using the "efficient markets" theory, which states that the change in a price from one period to the next is purely random. The covariance between u_t and u_{t-s}, for $s \neq 0$, is given by

$$E(u_t u_{t-s}) = E[(\epsilon_t + \rho_{t-1} + \rho^2\epsilon_{t-2} + \cdots)(\epsilon_{t-s} + \rho\epsilon_{t-s-1} + \rho^2\epsilon_{t-s-2} + \cdots)]$$

All the cross-product terms of the type $\epsilon_t\epsilon_{t-s}$, $\epsilon_{t-1}\epsilon_{t-s}$, and so on have zero expectations because ϵ_t and ϵ_{t-s} are, by assumption, independent. Only the square terms ϵ_{t-s}^2, ϵ_{t-s-1}^2, and so on remain. Therefore

$$E(u_t u_{t-s}) = E(\rho^s\epsilon_{t-s}^2 + \rho^{s+2}\epsilon_{t-s-1}^2 + \rho^{s+4}\epsilon_{t-s-2}^2 + \cdots)$$
$$= \rho^2\sigma_\epsilon^2(1 + \rho^2 + \rho^4 + \cdots)$$

$$= \frac{\rho^2\sigma_\epsilon^2}{1 - \rho^2} = \rho^s\sigma_u^2$$

It is now easy to prove that the autocorrelation function (defined in Section 11.7) is $r(s) = \rho^s$ for the AR(1) model. Substituting the variance and covariance just derived, we get

$$r(s) = \frac{\text{Cov}(u_t, u_{t-s})}{\text{Var}(u_t)} = \rho^s$$

Since $|\rho| < 1$, as s increases (which means that as you move further into the past) the autocorrelation function decreases in absolute value, the rate of decline being dependent on the numerical value of ρ. At any rate, the error terms are correlated, violating the OLS assumption that they are not.

CHAPTER 12

Qualitative and Limited Dependent Variables

■ In all the topics discussed so far, we have treated the values of a dependent variable as if they varied continuously. Many situations arise, however, in which this is not the case. Suppose, for instance, we wish to model the purchasing decision of a household, and in particular, the decision whether to buy a car. In a given survey period, a typical family either bought a car or it did not. In this situation, we have a **qualitative dependent variable**—that is, one that takes the value 1 if the household purchased a car and the value 0 if it did not. Other household decisions such as whether to buy a house, or furniture, appliances, or other durable goods are examples in which the dependent variable might be a dummy variable. In the labor market, whether to enter the labor force, strike an employer, or join a union are examples of binary dependent variables. In these cases, the interpretation of the dependent variable is that it is a probability measure for which the *realized value* is 0 or 1, although the *theoretical value* could be any intermediate value.

In Chapter 6, we introduced dummy (or binary) variables and demonstrated their usefulness in capturing the effects of qualitative independent variables on the dependent variable. Special problems arise when the dependent variable is binary. Models involving dependent variables of this type are referred to as **discrete choice models**, or as **qualitative response models**.

The dependent variable might also take other forms in which it is not continuous. For instance, in the car purchase example, suppose we related the expenditure on a car, in a given period, to a number of determinants such as household income and family size. In such a case, the dependent variable will be continuous, *but with a big jump from* 0—expenditure will be zero if a family did not buy a car. Thus, the sample might contain a number of observations with zero values along with observations with values in the thousands. This situation also calls for a special type of analysis. Dependent variables of this type are known as **limited dependent variables**. This chapter examines the special problems created by qualitative and limited dependent variables and the techniques needed to address those problems.

12.1 Linear Probability (or Binary Choice) Models

In the car purchase example, let Y_t be the probability that a particular household (tth in the sample) will purchase a car in a given year. Let X_t be the household income. Consider the simple regression model $Y_t = \alpha + \beta X_t + u_t$. Although the interpretation of Y_t is as a probability, the *observed* value for a given household will either be 1 or 0 because, in the survey period, the household either bought the car or it did not. Hence, the dependent variable takes a binary form here. Such models are known as **linear probability** or **binary choice** models. Why should that cause any problems? Why not estimate α and β by regressing the dummy variable Y against a constant and income? The answer is that, as will be shown presently, in the case of a dummy dependent variable, the residuals will be heteroscedastic, and hence the application of OLS will yield inefficient estimates.

Let p_t be the probability that $Y_t = 1$, or equivalently, that $u_t = 1 - \alpha - \beta X_t$ (see Table 12.1). Then $1 - p_t$ is the probability that $Y_t = 0$, or that $u_t = -\alpha - \beta X_t$. The random variable u_t is therefore not normally distributed but has the binomial distribution (refer to Section 2.1) with only two outcomes. The expected value of u_t must be zero, and hence we have

$$0 = E(u_t) = p_t(1 - \alpha - \beta X_t) + (1 - p_t)(-\alpha - \beta X_t)$$

Solving this equation for p_t we have $p_t = \alpha + \beta X_t$. The variance of $u_t(\sigma_t^2)$ is $E(u_t^2)$ because $E(u_t) = 0$. By definition,

$$\sigma_t^2 = p_t(1 - \alpha - \beta X_t)^2 + (1 - p_t)(-\alpha - \beta X_t)^2$$
$$= p_t(1 - p_t)^2 + (1 - p_t)p_t^2 = p_t(1 - p_t)$$

which makes use of the fact that $\alpha + \beta X_t = p_t$. Hence $\sigma_t^2 = (1 - \alpha - \beta X_t)(\alpha + \beta X_t)$, which varies with t, thus establishing the heteroscedasticity of the residuals u_t.

Even though the normality assumption of u_t is violated, OLS estimates of α and β are unbiased and consistent, but inefficient because of the heteroscedasticity. The tests of hypotheses critically depend on normality. However, we can invoke the central limit theorem (Property 2.12b), which states that if several random variables are identically distributed, their mean will be asymptotically normal even if the

TABLE 12.1 Probability Distribution of u_t

u_t	Probability
$1 - \alpha - \beta X_t$	p_t
$-\alpha - \beta X_t$	$1 - p_t$

random variables were originally not normal. Because OLS estimates are linear combinations of such random variables, the normality holds for large samples. However, because heteroscedasticity invalidates tests, they are no longer valid. We saw in Chapter 8 that we can get asymptotically efficient estimates by applying the weighted least squares (WLS) procedure here, provided we can obtain suitable estimates of σ_t^2. Using the OLS estimates $\hat{\alpha}$ and $\hat{\beta}$, we can estimate the residual variance as

$$\hat{\sigma}_t^2 = (\hat{\alpha} + \hat{\beta}X_t)(1 - \hat{\alpha} - \hat{\beta}X_t) = \hat{Y}_t(1 - \hat{Y}_t)$$

We can now set $w_t = 1/\hat{\sigma}_t$ and apply weighted least squares in the manner described in Chapter 8. However, a potential problem arises when the predicted value $\hat{Y}_t$ is 0 or 1, or is outside the interval 0 to 1. In this case, $\hat{\sigma}_t^2$ will not be positive. There is no assurance that OLS will not make such unacceptable predictions. When it does happen, however, we can modify the procedure slightly. If the predicted σ_t^2 was not positive, set w_t to zero. This is basically equivalent to omitting such observations. The steps for estimating a linear probability model are as follows:

Step 1 Estimate the model by the ordinary least squares (OLS) procedure and obtain the predicted values of the dependent variable ($\hat{Y}_t$).

Step 2 Estimate the residual variance as $\hat{\sigma}_t^2 = \hat{Y}_t(1 - \hat{Y}_t)$.

Step 3 Construct the weight for the tth observation as $w_t = 1/\hat{\sigma}_t$, provided $\hat{\sigma}_t^2$ is positive. If $\hat{\sigma}_t^2$ is 0 or negative, set w_t to zero.

Step 4 Obtain weighted least squares (WLS) estimates (see Section 8.3) using w_t as the weight for the tth observation.

As mentioned above, because the predicted values are not guaranteed to be between 0 and 1, this model is not used much today.

12.2 The Probit Model

An alternative to the linear probability model described in the previous section is the **Probit Model**. To illustrate that it does not have the drawbacks of the former model, consider the example of an employee of a company who has to decide whether or not to join a union. The assumption underlying probit analysis is that there is a response function of the form $Y_t^* = \alpha + \beta X_t + u_t$, where X_t is observable but where Y_t^* is an unobservable variable. What we observe in practice is Y_t, which takes the value 1 if $Y_t^* > 0$ and 0 if otherwise. We thus have

$$Y_t = 1 \qquad \text{if } \alpha + \beta X_t + u_t > 0$$
$$Y_t = 0 \qquad \text{if } \alpha + \beta X_t + u_t \leq 0$$

If we denote by $F(z)$ the cumulative distribution function of the normal distribution, that is, $F(z) = P(Z \leq z)$, then

$$P(Y_t = 1) = P(u_t > -\alpha - \beta X_t) = 1 - F\left(\frac{-\alpha - \beta X_t}{\sigma}\right)$$

$$P(Y_t = 0) = P(u_t \leq -\alpha - \beta X_t) = F\left(\frac{-\alpha - \beta X_t}{\sigma}\right)$$

The joint probability density of the sample of observations (called the *likelihood function* in the Chapter 2 appendix) is therefore given by

$$L = \prod_{Y_t=0} F\left(\frac{-\alpha - \beta X_t}{\sigma}\right) \prod_{Y_t=1} \left[1 - F\left(\frac{-\alpha - \beta X_t}{\sigma}\right)\right]$$

The parameters α and β are estimated by maximizing the above expression, which is highly nonlinear in the parameters and cannot be estimated by conventional regression programs. Programs such as PROBIT, MIDAS, and SAS can perform the specialized nonlinear optimization needed here.

An Empirical Example: A Probit Model of Television Station Behavior

Foster and Hull (1986) used probit analysis to model the decision as to whether a television station should subscribe to the Television Code of the National Association of Broadcasters (NAB). The sample data were for 89 U.S. commercial television stations sold betwen January 1976 and March 1982 when the NAB suspended the Code's advertising provisions.

Let Y_t^* be the index of incentive for Station t to abide by the code, which depends on a number of characteristics. The model used by Foster and Hull is as follows (omitting the t subscript):

$$Y^* = \beta_1 + \beta_2 A + \beta_3 Ca + \beta_4 Nc + \beta_5 Y + \beta_6 V + \beta_7 N$$
$$+ \beta_8 CPo + \beta_9 \% \Delta CP + \beta_{10} T + u_t$$

with $Y = 1$ if $Y^* > 0$ and 0 otherwise. The explanatory variables are (refer to the original paper for details about these variables as well as for a variety of other models estimated by the authors):

 A = Station audience size

 Ca = Percentage of designated market area (DMA) households wired for cable

 Nc = Number of large commercial stations viewable

 Y = Per capita income of the area

 V = 1 if station has VHF channel, 0 otherwise

 N = 1 if station was network affiliate, 0 otherwise

 CPo = Index of potential cartel effectiveness

 CP = Another index of potential cartel effectiveness

 T = Number of months between sale date and March 1982

The estimated model was (with absolute values of t-ratios in parentheses)

$$\hat{C}^* = -3.281 + 0.015A + 0.008Ca - 0.113Nc + 0.380Y - 0.551V$$
$$\quad (1.22) \quad (3.02) \quad (0.55) \quad (1.29) \quad (1.90) \quad (1.42)$$
$$+ 1.081N - 0.002CPo + 0.0003\% \Delta CP + 0.004T$$
$$\quad (2.12) \quad (0.11) \quad (0.02) \quad (0.42)$$

If cartel effects are important, we would expect CPo, $\%\Delta CP$, and T to have significant positive effects on the probability of subscribing to the Television Code, that is, β_8, β_9, and β_{10} would be positive. However, when the authors tested the null hypothesis that $\beta_8 = \beta_9 = \beta_{10} = 0$, it could not be rejected at the 10 percent level. If all the insignificant variables are dropped from the specification, the estimated model is the following:

$$\hat{C}^* = -3.450 + 0.013A + 0.347Y + 0.982N$$
$$\quad\;\;(2.45)\quad\;\,(2.93)\quad\;\;(1.92)\quad\;\;(2.57)$$

12.3 The Logit Model

In Section 4.6, we introduced the **logit model** (also known as the *logistic model*) and pointed out its usefulness when the dependent variabe takes values only between 0 and 1 (or between 0 and 100, if it is in percentage form). The logistic model has the following functional form:

$$\ln\left[\frac{P}{1-P}\right] = \alpha + \beta X + u \tag{12.1}$$

where P is the value of the dependent variable between 0 and 1. The rationale for this form can be seen by solving the equation for P (by first exponentiating both sides). We then obtain the probability that the dependent variable takes the value P, as follows:

$$P = \frac{1}{1 + e^{-(\alpha + \beta X + u)}} \tag{12.2}$$

It is easy to see that if $\beta X = +\infty$, P is 1, and when $\beta X = -\infty$, P takes the value 0. Thus, P can never be outside the range $[0, 1]$.

The estimation procedure depends on whether the observed P is between 0 and 1, or whether it is binary and takes the value 0 or the value 1. In the case in which P is strictly between 0 and 1 (for example, P is the fraction of households purchasing a car), the method is simply to transform P and obtain $Y = \ln[P/(1 - P)]$. Then regress Y against a constant, and X (more explanatory variables are easily added). If, however, P is binary, then the logarithm of $P/(1 - P)$ is undefined when P is either 0 or 1. The procedure used in such a case is the maximum likelihood method discussed in Sections 2.A.3 and 3.A.4.

The marginal effect of X on P is calculated by taking the partial derivative of P with respect to X. The estimated marginal effect is given as follows:

$$\frac{\Delta\hat{P}}{\Delta X} = \frac{\hat{\beta}e^{-(\hat{\alpha}+\hat{\beta}X)}}{[1 + e^{-(\hat{\alpha}+\hat{\beta}X)}]^2} = \hat{\beta}\hat{P}(1 - \hat{P})$$

There are a number of computer programs that estimate the logit model in more general contexts. They include SAS, MLOGIT, and QUAIL. Refer to Amemiya's 1981 survey for more details on this.

Example 12.1

In this example we use the logistic model to estimate the relation between women's labor force participation rates and their determinants. The estimated model using the data in Table 4-12 (see Practice Computer Session 12.1)

$$\ln\left[\frac{WLFP}{1 - WLFP}\right] = \underset{(-2.90)}{-0.506} + \underset{(6.22)}{0.000202 YF} + \underset{(4.88)}{0.0099 EDUC} - \underset{(-3.89)}{0.04204 UE}$$
$$- \underset{(-1.82)}{0.00199 URB} - \underset{(-3.52)}{0.00494 WH}$$

Because the dependent variable here is not WLFP, the regression coefficients are not comparable, nor are the adjusted R^2 values. It is interesting to note, however, that the t-values are similar. □

One way of comparing the goodness of fit of a linear model with that of a logit is to use the latter to forecast WLFP and then compute the error sum of squares and the model selection statistics. When this was done, we found that the linear model is better. See Practice Computer Session 12.1 for details.

Empirical Example: Career Interruptions Following Childbirth

Even (1987) has used the logit model to examine the effect of childbirth on the probability that a woman will return to work.[1] The basic assumption behind the model he uses is that "a woman will resume employment in the first time period following childbirth in which her full wage (W) exceeds the value of her time in the home or her reservation wage (R)." The data used were from the 1973 National Survey of Family Growth, for 866 white married women who had at least one child and who worked sometime during their most recent pregnancy. The explanatory variables are the following:

s = number of time periods after childbirth

KIDS = number of children in the family

DKIDS = the variable KIDS multiplied by the number of quarters of career interruptions since childbirth

AGE = mother's age at the most recent birth

HINC = father's income reported at the time of interview

MQPRIOR = number of months that the mother ceased employment prior to her most recent childbirth

EXP = number of years of labor market experience

DEXP = the variable EXP multiplied by the number of quarters of nonemployment since childbirth

· · · · · · ·

[1] *More specifically, what is modeled is the hazard rate, the conditional probability of returning to work at time t, given that the woman has not returned prior to t.*

OCC = 1 if the mother's occupation is professional or technical, 0 otherwise

EDUC = number of years of education

DEDUC = the variable EDUC multiplied by the number of quarters of non-employment since childbirth

Table 12.2 presents the estimated coefficients (with t-statistics in parentheses) for a number of alternative model specifications, the dependent variable being the

TABLE 12.2   Estimated Logit Models

	(1)	(2)	(3)	(4)	(5)	(6)
Constant	−0.286 (0.69)	−0.45 (1.08)	0.095 (0.18)	0.34 (0.66)	0.75 (1.44)	0.97 (1.80)
s	*	*	−0.12 (1.62)	−0.28 (4.01)	−0.58 (6.31)	−0.79 (5.45)
s^2	*	*	*	0.0097 (7.02)	0.050 (6.13)	0.096 (3.67)
$s^3/100$	*	*	*	*	−0.13 (4.90)	−0.47 (2.54)
$s^4/1000$	*	*	*	*	*	0.077 (1.88)
DKIDS	*	0.018 (2.29)	0.023 (2.78)	0.015 (2.03)	0.013 (1.82)	0.013 (1.82)
DEXP	*	−0.0080 (2.77)	−0.0074 (2.49)	−0.0053 (2.03)	−0.0055 (2.23)	−0.0055 (2.23)
DEDUC	*	−0.010 (5.21)	−0.0019 (0.34)	−0.0031 (0.65)	−0.0026 (0.54)	−0.0025 (0.53)
KIDS	0.082 (1.70)	0.026 (0.41)	0.0010 (0.02)	0.047 (0.76)	0.051 (0.81)	0.051 (0.81)
AGE	−0.046 (2.87)	−0.046 (2.78)	−0.045 (2.73)	−0.044 (2.67)	−0.044 (2.66)	−0.045 (2.69)
HINC	−0.027 (3.83)	−0.016 (2.27)	−0.016 (2.28)	−0.015 (2.12)	−0.015 (2.13)	−0.015 (2.12)
MQPRIOR	−0.148 (8.06)	−0.12 (6.63)	−0.12 (6.55)	−0.12 (6.30)	−0.12 (6.16)	−0.12 (6.11)
EXP	0.033 (2.26)	0.076 (3.84)	0.073 (3.66)	0.063 (3.30)	0.063 (3.29)	0.064 (3.30)
OCC	0.311 (2.45)	0.28 (2.12)	0.29 (2.20)	0.27 (2.02)	0.25 (1.90)	0.25 (1.97)
EDUC	−0.025 (0.92)	0.025 (0.89)	−0.014 (0.38)	−0.0090 (0.26)	−0.0091 (0.26)	−0.0089 (0.25)
L	−1806.8	−1698.1	−1696.8	−1674.8	−1661.6	−1659.9
Goodness-of-fit statistics	459.65 (0)	98.84 (2.2E − 11)	97.14 (4.4E − 11)	61.34 (2.0E − 5)	37.82 (0.027)	33.91 (0.066)

Source: Adapted from Even, 1987, Table 2, p. 266. Reprinted with the permission of the University of Chicago Press.

probability of returning to work. We note that EDUC is not statistically significant in any of the models, whereas a priori we would have expected a positive effect on wages. An explanation that Even offers for this is that a high wage might also induce a woman to demand a high child quality and, consequently, she might quit her job to improve child quality. The insignificance of the interaction term DEDUC indicates that the marginal effect of EDUC does not depend on the number of quarters of nonemployment since childbirth.

The coefficient for KIDS is insignificant, but that for the interaction DKIDS is significantly positive (at the 5 percent level of significance). This means that additional children have a negligible effect on the probability immediately after childbirth, but the marginal effect increases as time passes. This might be due to older children requiring less attention, and to the fact that their presence might increase the demand for market goods.

AGE has the expected negative sign and is significant. Similarly, the higher the husband's income, the lower the probability of returning to work. Experience has the expected positive effect on the probability, as does the dummy variable for professional women.

The variable MQPRIOR, which is the number of months that the mother ceased employment prior to childbirth, has a very strong negative effect. Thus, quitting earlier during pregnancy increases the probability that the woman will not (or will not be able to) return to work.

12.4   Limited Dependent Variables

As mentioned in the introduction to this chapter, the observed values of an independent variable sometimes have a discrete jump at zero. For instance, if we take a random sample of women and record their wages, we may observe many zero values because recorded wages are available only for working women. Thus, in the simple regression model $Y_t = \alpha + \beta X_t + u_t$, we observe the dependent variable only when $Y_t > 0$. As another example, if we obtain a random sample of households and record their expenditure on durable goods, some of the entries may be zero while others are positive. We therefore never observe negative values. What are the consequences of disregarding this fact and regressing Y against a constant and X? We note that, in this situation, the residuals will not satisfy the condition $E(u_t) = 0$, which is required for the unbiasedness of estimates. A dependent variable with the property that it has a discrete jump at zero (or any other threshold value) is known as a *limited dependent variable*. One of the first applications (in economics) of the limited dependent variable model was given by Tobin (1958). He applied it to model household expenditure on automobiles. Such models are referred to as **Tobit models** or as **Censored Regressions**.

The Tobit Model (or Censored Regressions)

In the Tobit model, there is an asymmetry between observations with positive values of Y and those with negative values. In this case, the model becomes

$$Y_t = \begin{cases} \alpha + \beta X_t + u_t & \text{if } Y_t > 0 \quad \text{or} \quad u_t > -\alpha - \beta X_t \\ 0 & \text{if } Y_t \le 0 \quad \text{or} \quad u_t \le -\alpha - \beta X_t \end{cases}$$

The basic assumptions behind this model is that there exists an index function $I_t = \alpha + \beta X_t + u_t$ for each economic agent being studied. If $I_t \le 0$, the value of the dependent variable is set to zero. If $I_t > 0$, the value of the dependent variable is set to I_t. Suppose u has the normal distribution with mean zero and variance σ^2. We note that $Z = u/\sigma$ is a standard normal random variable. Denote by $f(z)$ the probability density of the standard normal variable Z, and by $F(z)$ its cumulative density—that is, $P[Z \le z]$. Then the joint probability density for those observations for which Y_t is positive is given by (see Section 3.A.4) the following expression:

$$P_1 = \prod_{i=1}^{i=m} \frac{1}{\sigma} f\left[\frac{Y_i - \alpha - \beta X_i}{\sigma} \right]$$

where $\prod$ denotes the product and m is the number of observations in the subsample for which Y is positive. For the second subsample (of size n) for which the observed Y is zero, the random variable $u \le -\alpha - \beta X$. The probability for this event is

$$P_2 = \prod_{j=1}^{j=n} P[u_j \le -\alpha - \beta X_j]$$

$$= \prod_{j=1}^{j=n} F\left[\frac{-\alpha - \beta X_j}{\sigma} \right]$$

The joint probability for the entire sample is therefore given by $L = P_1 P_2$. Because this is nonlinear in α and β, the OLS procedure is not applicable here. The procedure for obtaining estimates of α and β is to maximize L with respect to the parameters. This is the maximum likelihood procedure described in Section 3.A.4.

Among others, the computer programs LIMDEP, SAS, and TSP have procedures for estimating the Tobit model.

Empirical Example: A Tobit Model of Charitable Contributions

Reece (1979) has carried out a study of charitable contributions using a Tobit model. Although he examined a number of components of charitable contributions, here we focus on just three: total of all contributions, contributions to charities, and a category called "CONTRIB," which excludes from the total gifts support to nonhousehold members and certain miscellaneous contributions. Most of the data were obtained (for a large number of households) from the Consumer Expenditure Survey of the Bureau of Labor Statistics, for 1972 and 1973. Households were from a number of Standard Metropolitan Statistical Areas (SMSAs). Other sources of data were the U.S. Bureau of the Census and the Department of Health, Education, and Welfare. Table 12.3 presents the estimated elasticities implied by the coefficients of the index function, the coefficients themselves, and the corresponding t-statistics.

TABLE 12.3 Estimated Tobit Models

	Equations		
	(1) Charity + Deducted	(2) All	(3) Contrib
PRICE	−0.976	−1.401	−1.192
	−114.60 (−2.67)	−787.88 (−4.63)	−396.71 (−4.15)
INCOME	1.423	0.550	0.877
	0.0095 (9.99)	0.0176 (4.87)	0.0166 (8.01)
AGE	0.309	0.484	0.380
	0.8808 (1.44)	6.60 (2.79)	3.06 (2.30)
ASSISTANCE	−0.097	−0.186	0.102
	−0.0108 (−0.29)	−0.0996 (−0.67)	0.0322 (0.39)
RECIPIENT	−0.138	0.327	0.351
	−0.0017 (−0.37)	0.0190 (1.06)	0.0121 (1.20)
COL	−1.511	0.518	−0.542
	−0.1420 (−1.21)	0.2329 (0.51)	−0.1443 (−0.57)
SECOND	−0.016	0.005	−0.012
	−3.42 (−0.27)	5.32 (0.11)	−7.30 (−0.26)
CONSTANT	124.70 (0.95)	113.33 (0.22)	183.61 (0.64)
$1 - e'e/s^2$	0.342	0.175	0.282
$1 - e'e/y'y$	0.466	0.405	0.529

Note: The elasticity, coefficient, and t-statistic (in parentheses) are given for each variable.
Source: Adapted from Reece, 1979, Table 1, p. 147. Reprinted with the permission of the America Economic Association.

The independent variables are as follows:

PRICE = price of contributions

INCOME = average of current and previous years' family income (before taxes) plus net return from home ownership

ASSISTANCE = average public assistance

RECIPIENT = lower quintile family income for the SMSA

COL = an index of family budget for the SMSA

AGE = age of the head of the household

SECOND = 1 for the sample from 1973, 0 for the sample from 1972

Reece defines the price of a dollar of contribution to be the amount of consumption foregone by the household in making the contribution. Because of the tax deductibility of the contributions, the price will generally be less than 1. For more details on the exact measure used, those interested should refer to the original paper. In order to take account of differences in the price of consumption goods across households, a cost of living index variable (COL) is used. The variable RECIPIENT is used to approximate the effect of the social environment. The assumption is that, aside from themselves, households are concerned mostly about other families living in the same geographical area (this is the "utility interdependence" hypothesis). If the other families' average income is low, the household might be more generous with its contributions. The income below which 20 percent of the families reside in the area (the lower quintile) is used as RECIPIENT.

The last two rows of Table 12.3 show two goodness-of-fit measures. Although they are not very high, they are reasonable, considering the fact that it is difficult to get high goodness-of-fit measures in cross-section data (especially one for a large number of households). The dependent variable CHARITY + DEDUCTED includes all charitable contributions, whether they were deducted from pay or not. The PRICE and INCOME variables are statistically significant and have the expected signs. The social environment variables ASSISTANCE and RECIPIENT have insignificant negative coefficients. This suggests a lack of support for the "utility interdependence" hypothesis. The coefficient for SECOND is negative and significant. This indicates that contributions decreased, on average, in 1973 as compared to 1972. This result is to be expected because 1972 was an election year. The results also indicate that (1) the tax deductibility of contributions to charity is an important element in determining the amount of contributions made, and (2) religious organizations gain even more when contributions are tax deductible.

SUMMARY

This chapter has been concerned with the special treatment needed when the dependent variable (Y) either takes a binary form or has a discrete jump at zero. Whenever an economic agent's decision takes the form of whether or not to pursue a particular course of action (for example, buy a car or house, strike against an employer, return to work after childbirth, vote for a particular candidate, and so on), the observed values of Y is 1 or 0. Models that address this type of dependent variable are known as *discrete choice models*. *Linear probability models, probit models*, and *logit models* are examples of discrete choice models. OLS is not applicable to a model with a binary dependent variable because the error terms are heteroscedastic. Using a binomial framework, it is possible to estimate the heteroscedasticity and apply weighted least squares. However, there is no guarantee that the predicted value of the dependent variable (which is interpreted as a probability measure) will be between 0 and 1. To avoid this difficulty, logit models are often used. The dependent variable now takes the form $\ln[P/(1 - P)]$, where P is the observed fraction of times a particular decision is favored and $\ln$ is the natural logarithm. The logit model has the property that the predicted value of P is always between 0 and 1. If Y is not the observed fraction but is binary (taking the values 0 and 1 only), then a probit model is appropriate.

In many situations, Y may be bounded by zero (or some other threshold value). Thus, the observed value of Y might always be positive or zero, but never negative. Endogenous variables of this type are known as *limited dependent variables*. The *Tobit model* is frequently used to address limited dependent variables. OLS is not applicable here either because the condition $E(u) = 0$ (u is the error term), needed for unbiasedness of estimates, is not satisfied. The appropriate procedure here is the maximum likelihood method.

KEY TERMS

Binary choice models	Logit models
Censored regressions	Qualitative dependent variable
Discrete choice models	Qualitative response models
Limited dependent variable	Tobit models
Linear probability models	

REFERENCES

The references given here include a number of excellent surveys on the topics.

Amemiya, T. "Qualitative Response Models: A Survey." *Journal of Economic Literature*, Vol. 19 (December 1981): 1488–1536.

Amemiya, T. "Tobit Models: A Survey." *Journal of Econometrics*, Vol. 24 (January/February 1984): 3–61.

Even, William. "Career Interruptions Following Childbirth." *Journal of Labor Economics*, Vol. 5 (April 1987): 255–277.

Foster, Carroll, B., and Hull, Brooks. "An OPEC in Fantasyland: The NAB Television Code as Cartel," University of Michigan-Dearborn. Working Paper No. 41, 1986.

Ham, John C., and Rea, Jr., Samuel A. "Unemployment Insurance and Male Unemployment Duration in Canada." *Journal of Labor Economics*, Vol. 5 (July 1987): 325–353.

Maddala, G. S. *Limited Dependent and Qualitative Variables in Econometrics*. Cambridge: Cambridge University Press, 1983.

Reece, William S. "Charitable Contributions: New Evidence on Household Behavior." *American Economic Review*, Vol. 69 (March 1979): 142–151.

Tobin, James. "Estimation of Relationships for Limited Dependent Variables." *Econometrica*, Vol. 26 (1958): 24–36.

Tracy, Joseph. "An Empirical Test of an Asymmetric Information Model of Strikes." *Journal of Labor Economics*, Vol. 5 (April 1987): 149–173.

PRACTICE COMPUTER SESSION

12.1 Example 12.1 can be reproduced using the data file *data 4 — 12* and the command input file *ps12 — 1. inp.*

EXERCISES

†12.1 A company did a survey of employees between 55 and 65 years of age who had either retired recently or were eligible for retirement but had not yet retired. Let *P* be probability of retirement, *A* be the age of the employee or retiree, *N* be the number of years employed, and *S* be the salary at the present time or at retirement. The observed values of *P* are either 0 or 1. Describe how you would formulate a linear probability model for the probability of retirement. Next describe the estimation procedure. What signs would you expect for each of the explanatory variables? Justify your answers carefully.

†12.2 Suppose you have a sample of companies for which you have data on the following variables:

> *P* = the fraction of employees between 55 and 65 years of age
> who have recently retired
> *A* = the median age of employees or recent retirees
> *N* = the median number of years employed
> *S* = the median salary

Formulate a logit model of the probability of retirement and explain how you would estimate it.

12.3 Let *H* be the fraction of households in a given SMSA that purchased a house in a certain period, *Y* be the median income of the SMSA, *P* be the median price of a single family house in the area, and *R* be the average mortgage rate prevailing in the city. To model the probability of purchasing a house, is a linear probability model or a logit model more appropriate? Formulate a model and describe how you would estimate it.

12.4 A union wants to model the relationship between the probability that an employee will join the union, and a number of characteristics of the employee. It hires you to conduct a survey and construct appropriate models. What kind of survey would be appropriate here: a survey of individual employees in a company or a survey of employees in several companies? Describe the kind of data you would obtain and the model you would formulate. For the model you construct, describe the estimation procedure.

12.5 An analyst for the Justice Department obtains a random sample of the names of persons arrested for a crime and gathers the following information: whether the person was convicted, the annual income, number of years of schooling, race, male or female, and the number of previous arrests.

Formulate an appropriate model for the probability of conviction and describe how you would estimate it. Do you have any prior notion of what sign to expect for each of the independent variables? Explain.

12.6 A labor economist draws a random sample of women, both employed and unemployed but in the labor force, and gathers the following data: monthly wages (which will be zero if the woman is unemployed), age of the woman, number of years of education, skill status (unskilled, clerical or equivalent, and professional), race (white or nonwhite), and the number of years of prior experience. What is the appropriate framework for modeling the wages? Describe how you would estimate the model you formulate.

CHAPTER 13

Simultaneous Equation Models

■ All the econometric models discussed so far have been concerned with a single dependent variable. In many economic models, however, several endogenous (that is, dependent) variables are determined simultaneously. Estimating demand and supply equations is an example of this type of formulation; here the price and quantity are jointly determined. Macroeconomic models are also examples of simultaneous equation specification. In this chapter we study the special problems that arise when simultaneous equation models are estimated. Only the basics of simultaneous equation models are presented, however. The reader is referred to the bibliography at the end of this chapter for more details and generalizations.

13.1 Structure and Reduced Forms of Simultaneous Equation Models

Structural Equations

Consider the following equations representing the demand and supply of wheat (for simplicity, the t-subscript is omitted):

$$q_d = \alpha_0 + \alpha_1 p + \alpha_2 y + u \tag{13.1}$$

$$q_s = \beta_0 + \beta_1 p + \beta_2 r + v \tag{13.2}$$

$$q_d = q_s \tag{13.3}$$

where q_d is the quantity of wheat demanded, q_s is the supply of wheat, p is the price, y is income, r is the amount of rainfall, and u and v are stochastic disturbance terms. The first equation is the demand relation in which the quantity demanded is related to price and income. Equation (13.2) specifies the quantity supplied as a function of price and the amount of rainfall. Although other variables such as the amount of fertilizer, machines used, and so on, are important determinants of supply, they have been excluded in order to simplify the exposition. Equations (13.1) and (13.2) are known as **behavioral equations** (because they are determined by the behavior of economic agents). Basic economic theory tells us that the equilibrium price and quantity sold are determined by the equality of supply and demand. Equation (13.3) is thus the equilibrium condition that determines price and quantity sold. The simultaneous equation system therefore consists of two behavioral equations and one equilibrium condition.

Equations (13.1), (13.2), and (13.3) are known as the **structural equations** of the simultaneous equation model, and the regression coefficients—the α's and β's— are known as the **structural parameters**. Because price and quantity are jointly determined, they are both **endogenous variables**. We note that price influences quantity and vice versa. This is known as a **feedback**, a feature common among simultaneous equation models. Income and rainfall are not determined by the specified model but are given exogenously, and hence they are the **exogenous variables**. In single-equation models we used the terms *exogenous variable* and *explanatory variable* interchangeably. In simultaneous equation modeling this is no longer possible. In equation (13.1), price is an explanatory variable but is not an exogenous variable.

Although there are three equations in the model just specified, by setting $q_d = q_s = q$, we can reduce the model to a two-equation specification. The simultaneous equation model therefore consists of two equations in two endogenous variables (p and q) and three exogenous variables (a constant term, income, and rainfall). The number of equations in a system (which is the same as the number of endogenous variables) is denoted by G, and the number of exogenous variables by K.

A simultaneous equation model might also have other types of equations and variables. These are best understood with an example. Consider the following simple macro model:

$$C_t = \alpha_0 + \alpha_1 DY_t + \alpha_2 DY_{t-1} + u_t \tag{13.4}$$

$$I_t = \beta_0 + \beta_1 DY_t + \beta_2 DY_{t-1} + v_t \tag{13.5}$$

$$DY_t = Y_t - T_t \tag{13.6}$$

$$Y_t = C_t + I_t + G_t \tag{13.7}$$

where C is consumption expenditure, I is investment, Y is the gross national product (GNP), G is government expenditure, T is total taxes, and DY is disposable income. Equation (13.6) defines disposable income as GNP less taxes. This equation is thus an *identity*. Equations (13.4) and (13.5) are the behavioral equations, and equation (13.7) is the equilibrium condition, well known in macro models. The model thus consists of four structural equations in the four endogenous variables Y_t, C_t, I_t, and DY_t (that is, $G = 4$). The variable DY_{t-1} is disposable income in the previous period. At time t, this lagged endogenous variable is known and is hence predetermined. We therefore see that a simultaneous equation model consists of endogenous variables whose behavior we are trying to explain, exogenous variables whose values are given outside the system, and **predetermined variables** that consist of lagged endogenous variables. To avoid confusion, we henceforth include all exogenous variables under the category *predetermined*. A model will thus consist of endogenous variables (G in number) and predetermined variables (K in number). In the macro example, G is 4 and K is also 4 (G_t, T_t, DY_{t-1}, and a constant).

Another type of equation, not specified in the examples given previously, is a **technical equation**. For example, we could have added a production function to the macro model, relating the aggregate supply (Q) to inputs such as the capital stock (K) and labor (L). The types of equations encountered in simultaneous equation models are thus behavioral, technical, equilibrium conditions, and identities.

Reduced Form Equations

Equating (13.1) and (13.2) and solving for p, we obtain the following relation:

$$p = \frac{\beta_0 - \alpha_0}{\alpha_1 - \beta_1} - \frac{\alpha_2}{\alpha_1 - \beta_1} y + \frac{\beta_2}{\alpha_1 - \beta_1} r + \frac{v - u}{\alpha_1 - \beta_1} \tag{13.8}$$

which can be written in the form

$$p = \lambda_0 + \lambda_1 y + \lambda_2 r + \epsilon_1 \tag{13.9}$$

Substituting this in equation (13.1), we get (q is the equilibrium quantity sold):

$$q = (\alpha_0 + \alpha_1 \lambda_0) + (\alpha_1 \lambda_1 + \alpha_2)y + \alpha_1 \lambda_2 r + \epsilon_2 = \mu_0 + \mu_1 y + \mu_2 r + \epsilon_2 \tag{13.10}$$

ϵ_1 and ϵ_2 are new error terms that depend on u and v. Equations (13.9) and (13.10) specify each of the endogenous variables in terms of only the predetermined variables, the parameters of the model, and the stochastic disturbance terms. Note that the right-hand sides of (13.9) and (13.10) do not contain any endogenous variables. These two equations are known as the **reduced form equations**, and the λ's and μ's are known as the **reduced form parameters**. Reduced form equations are obtained by solving each of the endogenous variables in terms of the predetermined variables, the unknown parameters, and the disturbance terms. We readily see that a *reduced form equation will generally contain the error terms from all the equations.* Thus, the reduced form equation for GNP in the macro model will depend on a constant, G_t, T_t, DY_{t-1}, all the structural parameters, and the error terms u_t and v_t.

Practice Problem

13.1   Derive the reduced form for the macro model in equations (13.4)–(13.7).

13.2   Causality

When we identify one variable as the "dependent" variable (Y) and another as the "explanatory" variable (X), we have made an implicit assumption that changes in the explanatory variable induce changes in the dependent variable. This is the notion of **causality** in which information about X is expected to affect the conditional distribution of the future values of Y. If X causes Y and Y causes X, then there is a **feedback**, which means that the two variables are **jointly determined** (the price of a commodity and the quantity of goods sold are examples of this feedback effect). In many cases, the apparent direction of causality is not clear. For instance, does the money supply cause changes in the interest rate or is it the other way around? It is therefore of considerable interest to test for causal directions between two variables.

The Granger Test for Causality

The first attempt at testing for the direction of causality was by Granger (1969). The intuition behind the test is quite straightforward. Suppose X **Granger-causes** Y but Y does not Granger-cause X, then past values of X should be able to help predict future values of Y, but past values of Y should not be helpful in forecasting X. More specifically, consider the following model in which X and Y are expressed as deviations from the respective means.

$$(U) \qquad Y_t = \sum_{i=1}^{p} \alpha_i Y_{t-i} + \sum_{j=1}^{q} \beta_j X_{t-j} + u_t \qquad (13.11)$$

where u_t is white-noise, p is the order of the lag for Y, and q is the order of the lag for X. The null hypothesis that X does not Granger-cause Y is that $\beta_j = 0$ for $i = 1, 2, \ldots, q$. The restricted model is therefore

$$(R) \qquad Y_t = \sum_{i=1}^{p} \alpha_i Y_{t-i} + v_t \qquad (13.12)$$

The test statistic is the standard Wald F-statistic

$$F_c = \frac{(\text{ESSR} - \text{ESSU})/q}{\text{ESSU}/(T - p - q)}$$

where T is the number of observations used in the unrestricted model in equation (13.11), ESSU is the error sum of squares for equation (13.11), and ESSR is the error sum of squares for the restricted model (13.12). Under the null hypothesis of X not Granger-causing Y, F_c has the F-distribution with q d.f. for the numerator and $T - p - q$ d.f. for the denominator. The test is carried out in the usual way. Although equations (13.11) and (13.12) do not have other explanatory variables, the procedure is the same when such variables are included in the models. The order of the lags (p and q) are arbitrary and are usually chosen to be large. Alternatively, one could carry out the test for different values of the lags and make sure that conclusions are robust and not model dependent. The same determination could also have been made with a Lagrange Multiplier Test.

It should be noted that the above procedure tests only for the causal direction from X to Y. Thus, a rejection of the null hypothesis indicates that X Granger-causes Y. To test for causality from Y to X, the variables X and Y will be interchanged in equations (13.11) and (13.12) and a corresponding test statistic derived.

If both tests reject the null hypotheses, then we can conclude that there is a lagged feedback effect.

Since the publication of Granger's paper, a vareity of alternatives have been proposed [see Sims (1972), Geweke, Meese, and Dent (1983), Haugh (1976), Pierce (1977), Pierce and Haugh (1977), and Nelson and Schwert (1982)].

Example 13.1

To illustrate the Granger-causality test we examine the direction of causation between money supply and the interested rate. The unrestricted models are the following.

$$r_t = \sum_{i=1}^{6} \alpha_i r_{t-i} + \sum_{j=1}^{6} \beta_j m_{t-j} + u_t$$

$$m_t = \sum_{i=1}^{6} \alpha_i m_{t-i} + \sum_{j=1}^{6} \beta_j r_{t-j} + u_t$$

To carry out the analysis, we have used the quarterly data for the United States provided in Table 10.1 (see Practice Computer Session 13.1 for the commands to reproduce the empirical results presented here). r_t is the interest rate minus its average over the sample period and similarly m_t is the money supply minus its average.

For the interest rate equation, the Wald F-statistic for the omission of the money supply variables is 4.304 and the corresponding p-value is 0.000809. This implies that the null hypothesis that past money supply values do not influence future interest rates is rejected at levels well below 0.01 percent. For the money supply equation, the Wald F was 2.3533 with a p-value of 0.037956. The hypothesis that past interest rates do not affect future money supply is rejected at levels below 4 percent. There is thus strong evidence of causality in both directions, indicating lagged feedback effects. □

13.3 Consequences of Ignoring Simultaneity

Suppose we treat each of the equations in a simultaneous equation model as a separate single-equation model and estimate the parameters, if any, by OLS. What are the properties of the estimates? In particular, are they unbiased, consistent, efficient, BLUE, and so on? For example, to estimate equation (13.4), suppose we regress C_t against a constant, DY_t, and DY_{t-1}. It is useful to know the properties of these estimates. This issue is examined next with a simple macroeconomic model. The conclusions, however, generalize to models with many equations.

Consider the following well-known income determination model presented in introductory courses on macroeconomics:

$$C_t = \alpha + \beta Y_t + u_t \qquad 0 < \beta < 1 \tag{13.13}$$

$$Y_t = C_t + I_t \tag{13.14}$$

where C_t is consumption expenditure, Y_t is net national product, and I_t is net investment. The only modification made here is the addition of u_t, a stochastic disturbance term. Equation (13.13) is the familiar consumption function and equation (13.14) is the equilibrium condition. In this model, investment is treated as exogenous (and hence I_t and u_t are uncorrelated by assumption). The endogenous variables are C_t and Y_t, and the predetermined variables are the constant term and I_t.

Substituting for Y_t from equation (13.14) into equation (13.13) and solving for C_t, we obtain the reduced form for C_t:

$$C_t = \frac{\alpha}{1-\beta} + \frac{\beta I_t}{1-\beta} + \frac{u_t}{1-\beta} \tag{13.15}$$

Similarly, substituting for C_t from equation (13.11) into equation (13.12) and solving for Y_t, we obtain the reduced form for Y_t:

$$Y_t = \frac{\alpha}{1-\beta} + \frac{I_t}{1-\beta} + \frac{u_t}{1-\beta} \tag{13.16}$$

Let us now examine the consequences of estimating equation (13.13), ignoring the fact that it is part of a simultaneous equation system. First of all, we can readily see that the estimates will be biased. Property 3.1 states that the least squares procedure yields unbiased estimates provided u_t has zero mean and is uncorrelated with the independent variables. This means that u_t should be uncorrelated with Y_t. But, as is seen from the reduced form equation for Y_t, this assumption is false. It is evident that Y_t depends on u_t, and hence applying ordinary least squares will give biased estimates. This is true for models with more equations. The simultaneity implies that endogenous variables appearing on the right-hand side of a given equation will be correlated with the corresponding residual, thus making OLS estimates biased.

Will the estimates be at least consistent; that is, will the bias be small in large samples and the estimates converge to the true values when the sample size is increased indefinitely? To answer this we need some formal analysis. The limit of the OLS estimate $\hat{\beta}$ as the number of observations T increases indefinitely is derived in the chapter appendix as follows:

$$\lim_{T \to \infty} \hat{\beta} = \frac{\beta\sigma_I^2 + \sigma_u^2}{\sigma_I^2 + \sigma_u^2} = \beta + \frac{(1-\beta)\sigma_u^2}{\sigma_I^2 + \sigma_u^2} \tag{13.17}$$

where σ_I^2 and σ_u^2 are, respectively, the variances of I and u. Because $\beta \neq 1$ and $\sigma_u^2 \neq 0$, we see that $\hat{\beta}$ does not converge to the true β. Therefore, $\hat{\beta}$ is not only biased but is also inconsistent. The bias in $\hat{\beta}$ is known as the **least squares bias** or as the **simultaneous equation bias**. Even with a large sample the bias does not become small but is positive, giving an overestimate of β. It is interesting to note that even though there are no unknown coefficients or stochastic error terms in equation (13.14), the very fact that it implies a feedback effect causes bias and inconsistency. Standard errors of the estimates are also biased, and hence tests of hypotheses are invalid. The consequences of ignoring simultaneity are summarized in Property 13.1.

Property 13.1

> If simultaneity among variables is ignored and the OLS procedure is applied to estimate the parameters of a system of simultaneous equations, the estimates will be biased and inconsistent. Forecasts based on them will also be biased and inconsistent. Furthermore, tests of hypotheses on parameters will be invalid.

In Section 4.7 we estimated a relationship between housing starts and GNP. Although changes in GNP affect housing starts, there is also a feedback effect because housing starts affect the equilibrium level of GNP. They are thus jointly determined by other factors. The estimates presented in Section 4.7 therefore suffer from least squares bias.

13.4   The Identification Problem

The reduced form equation (13.9) expresses price as a function of the predetermined variables: constant, income, and rainfall. Because the predetermined variables are not endogenous, and hence are uncorrelated with the error terms, OLS can be applied to the reduced form to yield unbiased, consistent, and efficient estimates of the reduced form parameters (λ's and μ's in the example used here), provided the reduced form errors are "well behaved." A natural question is whether we can obtain consistent estimates of the original parameters of the structural equations (α's and β's in our example). When an investigator obtains the estimates of the reduced form equations and then attempts to go back and solve for the structural parameters, he or she finds one of three situations: (1) It is not possible to go from the reduced form back to the structure, (2) it is possible to go back in a unique way, and (3) there is more than one way to go back. This problem of being able to go back and reconstruct estimates of the structural parameters from estimates of the reduced form coefficients is known as the **identification problem**. The first type, in which it is not possible to go from the reduced form to the structure, is known as the **unidentified equation** or **underidentification**. The second case, the unique situation, is called **exact identification**. The final case, in which more than one structural estimate is obtainable, is called **overidentification**. We examine each of these cases with a number of models of demand and supply equations.

Model 1

Consider the following supply and demand model (say for wheat) presented in elementary textbooks (for simplicity the t-subscript is omitted) without random error terms:

Structure:

$$q_d = \alpha_0 + \alpha_1 p + u \qquad \text{(demand equation)}$$
$$q_s = \beta_0 + \beta_1 p + v \qquad \text{(supply equation)}$$
$$q_d = q_s = q \qquad \text{(equilibrium condition)}$$

Reduced form (obtained by solving separately for p and q):

$$p = \frac{\beta_0 - \alpha_0}{\alpha_1 - \beta_1} + \frac{v - u}{\alpha_1 - \beta_1} = \lambda_0 + \epsilon_1$$

$$q = \frac{\alpha_1 \beta_0 - \alpha_0 \beta_1}{\alpha_1 - \beta_1} + \frac{\alpha_1 v - \beta_1 u}{\alpha_1 - \beta_1} = \mu_0 + \epsilon_2$$

where u and v are random error terms and $q = q_d = q_s$. Applying OLS to the reduced forms gives the following two equations:

$$\hat{\lambda}_0 = \bar{p} \qquad \text{or} \qquad \frac{\beta_0 - \alpha_0}{\alpha_1 - \beta_1} = \bar{p}$$

$$\hat{\mu}_0 = \bar{q} \qquad \text{or} \qquad \frac{\alpha_1 \beta_0 - \alpha_0 \beta_1}{\alpha_1 - \beta_1} = \bar{q}$$

where $\bar{p}$ and $\bar{q}$ are the sample means of price and quantity. As there are only two equations in the four unknowns $\alpha_0, \alpha_1, \beta_0$, and β_1, we cannot obtain their estimates. We are thus faced with the problem of not being able to go back to the structure from the reduced form estimates. This is the case of underidentification.

Why the simple demand and supply curves are not estimable can be explained intuitively. Note that the observations (p_t, q_t) are equilibrium points and hence are the intersections of the demand and supply curves at various points. Suppose for argument that the supply curve is fixed over time but the demand curve is shifting. The intersection points (which are also the observations) would be as in Figure 13.1. The observed values of p and q would then trace the supply curve, but we may erroneously conclude that it is the demand curve with a wrong slope. Similarly, if we are interested in the supply curve, which in actuality has shifted while the demand curve has remained fixed, we would estimate not the supply curve but the demand curve. In practice, however, both the demand and supply curves shift with the intersection points, as in Figure 13.2. The observation points trace neither the

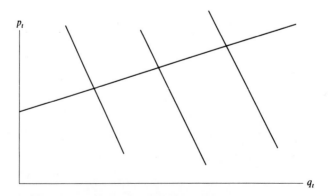

Figure 13.1 Demand curve shifting but supply curve fixed

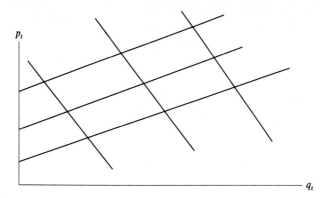

Figure 13.2 Both demand and supply curves shifting

demand curve nor the supply curve. Thus, without additional information as to how these curves are shifting, these relations are not identifiable.

Model 2

Let us modify Model 1 to take shifts explicitly into account as follows:

$$\text{Demand:} \quad q = \alpha_0 + \alpha_1 p + \alpha_2 y + u$$

$$\text{Supply:} \quad q = \beta_0 + \beta_1 p + v$$

where y is income and is exogenous. We have thus assumed that the supply curve is fixed whereas the demand curve shifts with income. As we saw in Figure 13.1, in this situation the supply curve can be estimated, but the demand curve cannot. Let us verify this formally. The reduced form is

$$p = \frac{\beta_0 - \alpha_0}{\alpha_1 - \beta_1} - \frac{\alpha_2}{\alpha_1 - \beta_1} y + \frac{v - u}{\alpha_1 - \beta_1}$$

$$= \lambda_0 + \lambda_1 y + \epsilon_1$$

$$q = (\beta_0 + \beta_1 \lambda_0) + \beta_1 \lambda_1 y + \epsilon_2$$

$$= \mu_0 + \mu_1 y + \epsilon_2$$

Since y is exogeneous and hence is independent of ϵ_1 and ϵ_2, we can apply OLS to the reduced form and obtain $\hat{\lambda}_0, \hat{\lambda}_1$ by regressing p against y and the constant term, and $\hat{\mu}_0, \hat{\mu}_1$ by regressing q against y and the constant. Note that $\hat{\beta}_1 = \hat{\mu}_1/\hat{\lambda}_1$ and $\hat{\beta}_0 = \hat{\mu}_0 - \hat{\lambda}_0 \hat{\beta}_1$, and hence the supply curve is identified. But the demand curve is not identified because

$$\hat{\lambda}_0 = \frac{\hat{\beta}_0 - \alpha_0}{\alpha_1 - \hat{\beta}_1} \qquad \hat{\lambda}_1 = \frac{-\alpha_2}{\alpha_1 - \hat{\beta}_1}$$

are only two equations in the three unknowns α_0, α_1, and α_2. We are therefore unable to go back to the structure of the demand equation from the reduced form, but can uniquely go back to the supply equation.

In a two-equation model, if one of the equations has an omitted variable, then it is identified. In Model 2, for example, the income variable is absent from the supply equation and hence is identified. This result is not proved. A similar condition must be satisfied in multiequation models. How can the demand equation be identified? By the rule, one of the variables present in the supply equation must be absent from the demand equation. This is so in the next model.

Model 3

Let r be the rainfall and consider the following model, used earlier:

$$\text{Demand:} \quad q = \alpha_0 + \alpha_1 p + \alpha_2 y + u$$
$$\text{Supply:} \quad q = \beta_0 + \beta_1 p + \beta_2 r + v$$

The exogenous variables are y, r, and the constant, and the endogenous variables are p and q. The reduced form is

$$p = \frac{\beta_0 - \alpha_0}{\alpha_1 - \beta_1} - \frac{\alpha_2}{\alpha_1 - \beta_1} y + \frac{\beta_2}{\alpha_1 - \beta_1} r + \epsilon_1$$
$$= \lambda_0 + \lambda_1 y + \lambda_2 r + \epsilon_1$$
$$q = (\alpha_0 + \alpha_1 \lambda_0) + (\alpha_1 \lambda_1 + \alpha_2)y + \alpha_1 \lambda_2 r + \epsilon_2$$
$$= \mu_0 + \mu_1 y + \mu_2 r + \epsilon_2$$

Note that the reduced form consists of exogenous variables from all the equations. We can run a regression of p on the constant, y, and r to get $\hat{\lambda}_0$, $\hat{\lambda}_1$, and $\hat{\lambda}_2$, and run a regression of q on the constant, y, and r to get $\hat{\mu}_0$, $\hat{\mu}_1$, and $\hat{\mu}_2$. From these, the structural parameters are obtained as follows:

$$\hat{\alpha}_1 = \frac{\hat{\mu}_2}{\hat{\lambda}_2} \qquad\qquad \hat{\alpha}_2 = \hat{\mu}_1 - \hat{\alpha}_1 \hat{\lambda}_1$$

$$\hat{\alpha}_0 = \hat{\mu}_0 - \hat{\alpha}_1 \hat{\lambda}_0 \qquad \hat{\beta}_1 = \hat{\alpha}_1 + \left(\frac{\hat{\alpha}_2}{\hat{\lambda}_1}\right)$$
$$\hat{\beta}_2 = \hat{\lambda}_2(\hat{\alpha}_1 - \hat{\beta}_1) \qquad \hat{\beta}_0 = \hat{\alpha}_0 + \hat{\lambda}_0(\hat{\alpha}_1 - \hat{\beta}_1)$$

Thus, all the structural parameters can be estimated unambiguously.

Model 4

We now present a model that is overidentified:

$$\text{Demand:} \quad q = \alpha_0 + \alpha_1 p + \alpha_2 y + u$$
$$\text{Supply:} \quad q = \beta_0 + \beta_1 p + \beta_2 r + \beta_3 f + v$$

where f is the amount of fertilizer used and is another exogenous variable. The difference between this and Model 3 is that two of the exogenous variables (r, f) are absent from the demand equation. The reduced form is

$$p = \frac{\beta_0 - \alpha_0}{\alpha_1 - \beta_1} - \frac{\alpha_2 y}{\alpha_1 - \beta_1} + \frac{\beta_2 r}{\alpha_1 - \beta_1} + \frac{\beta_3 f}{\alpha_1 - \beta_1} + \epsilon_1$$

$$= \lambda_0 + \lambda_1 y + \lambda_2 r + \lambda_3 f + \epsilon_1$$

$$q = (\alpha_0 + \alpha_1 \lambda_0) + (\alpha_1 \lambda_1 + \alpha_2) y + \alpha_1 \lambda_2 r + \alpha_1 \lambda_3 f + \epsilon_2$$

$$= \mu_0 + \mu_1 y + \mu_2 r + \mu_3 f + \epsilon_3$$

First regress p and q on all the exogenous variables y, r, f, and the constant to obtain the λ's and μ's. As $\alpha_1 \lambda_2 = \mu_2$, we can estimate α_1 as $\hat{\mu}_2/\hat{\lambda}_2$. However, we also have $\alpha_1 \lambda_3 = \mu_3$. Therefore, $\hat{\alpha}_1 = \hat{\mu}_3/\hat{\lambda}_3$ is another estimate of $\hat{\alpha}_1$. Only by a rare coincidence will we find the two estimates to be the same. Depending on which of these we choose, we will get different estimates of the parameters. Thus, there is more than one way to go back to the structure, and we have overidentification.

To summarize, we can assign any given structural equation to one of three identification categories:

1. *Unidentified*: There is no way to go back to the structure from the reduced form. Both equations of Model 1 and the demand equation of Model 2 are unidentified.
2. *Exactly identified*: There is a unique way to go back, as in Model 3.
3. *Overidentified*: There is more than one way to go back to the structure from the reduced form, as in Model 4. Note from Model 4 that there is an implicit nonlinear restriction among the parameters, namely, $\mu_2/\lambda_2 = \mu_3/\lambda_3$. These are known as the **overidentifying restrictions**.

To determine the identifiability of a system of equations, two sets of conditions are checked: the *order condition* and the *rank condition*. The order condition is only a necessary condition and is not sufficient; that is, if the order condition is not satisfied, the model is not identified. However, the fact that the order condition is satisfied does not guarantee the model's identifiability. The rank condition is also needed. The order condition can be stated in three different forms.

Property 13.2

> For the order condition of identifiability, the number of variables excluded (that is, absent) from an equation must be greater than or equal to $G - 1$, where G is the number of structural equations. Alternatively, the number of predetermined variables (which consist of exogenous variables and all lagged variables, including lagged endogenous variables) excluded from an equation must be greater than or equal to the number of included endogenous variables minus 1. In general, the number of prior restrictions on the parameters should not be less than the number of equations in the model minus 1 ($G - 1$).

Example 13.2

Consider the following three-equation model, in which the Y's are the endogenous variables and the X's and the constant term are the predetermined variables:

$$Y_1 = \alpha_0 + \alpha_1 Y_2 + \alpha_2 Y_3 + \alpha_4 X_1 + \alpha_5 X_2 + u_1$$
$$Y_2 = \beta_0 + \beta_1 Y_3 + \beta_2 X_1 + u_2$$
$$Y_3 = \gamma_0 + \gamma_1 Y_2 + u_3$$

Because G equals 3 here, for the order condition to be satisfied, at least two variables should be absent from each equation. In the first equation all the variables are present; that is, none are absent. This equation is therefore not identified. In the second equation Y_1 and X_2 are absent, and hence the order condition is satisfied. In the third equation Y_1, X_1, and X_2 are absent, and therefore this equation also satisfies the order condition.   □

The statement of the rank condition requires a knowledge of matrix algebra and is beyond the scope of this book. Readers familiar with linear algebra are referred to the books listed at the end of this chapter.

Practice Problem

13.2 Derive the reduced form equations for the above system and indicate whether you can go back and reconstruct structural parameters from those of the reduced form.

13.5 Estimation Procedures

Indirect Least Squares

We have seen that if a model is exactly identified, then there is a unique way to obtain the structural estimates from the reduced form estimates. This procedure is called the **indirect least squares (ILS) procedure** and is illustrated with the simple macro model presented in Section 13.3.

The reduced form for C_t can be rewritten as

$$C_t = \lambda_0 + \lambda_1 I_t + \epsilon_t \tag{13.18}$$

where $\lambda_0 = \alpha/(1 - \beta)$, $\lambda_1 = \beta/(1 - \beta)$, and $\epsilon_t = u_t/(1 - \beta)$. The exogenous variable I_t is uncorrelated with u_t, and hence OLS is applicable to the reduced form. This property generalizes to a multiequation model. Thus, the error terms in the reduced form of a simultaneous equation model always satisfy the assumptions for applying OLS to the reduced form. *OLS estimates of the reduced form parameters (λ_0 and λ_1 in our example) are therefore BLUE.* Applying OLS to equation (13.18) and using the notation in equations (13.A.2) and (13.A.3) in the chapter appendix, we can obtain estimates of α and β (denoted by ˜).

$$\frac{\tilde{\beta}}{1 - \tilde{\beta}} = \tilde{\lambda}_1 = \frac{S_{CI}}{S_{II}} \quad \text{or} \quad \tilde{\beta} = \frac{S_{CI}}{S_{CI} + S_{II}}$$

and

$$\tilde{\alpha} = (1 - \tilde{\beta})\tilde{\lambda}_0$$

Because transformations of consistent estimates are also consistent, $\tilde{\alpha}$ and $\tilde{\beta}$ are consistent. They are, however, not unbiased because the transformations are nonlinear. The procedure, then, consists of first applying OLS to the reduced form equations and then using them to solve indirectly for the structural parameters.

Instrumental Variable Technique and the Two-Stage Least Squares

The ILS procedure is applicable only when a structural equation is exactly identified. If a system is overidentified, we need other estimation techniques. We have seen that the reason why OLS estimates of a structural equation are not consistent is that the right-hand side endogenous variable (call it Y_2) is correlated with the error term. Suppose we find a variable (call it Z) that has the following properties: (1) Z_t is uncorrelated with the error term, and (2) Z_t is highly correlated with the right-hand side endogenous variable Y_2. Z will then serve as a good substitute variable for Y_2. Estimates obtained using Z will be consistent because it is uncorrelated with the error term. Such a variable is called an **instrumental variable**, and the method just described, in which the instrumental variable is used as a substitute for the endogenous variable causing least squares bias, is called the **instrumental variable technique (IV)**.

How can we find an instrument that satisfies the two conditions just stated? In the context of simultaneous equation models, a frequently used instrumental variable technique is the **two-stage least squares (TSLS) method**. The procedure can be applied to obtain a unique set of estimates that are consistent. This technique is useful in the case of exact identification also, and will give the same estimates as those given by the ILS procedure. Therefore, it can be applied whether a model is exactly identified or overidentified. TSLS is easy to apply and is illustrated here for Model 4. An empirical example and a "walk-through" example are presented later.

Stage 1 First estimate the reduced form for all the endogenous variables that appear on the right-hand side. In Model 4, p is the only endogenous variable appearing on the right-hand side. So regress p on y, r, f, and the constant. Then save $\hat{p}$, the predicted values of p as obtained from the reduced form estimates. Thus, $\hat{p} = \hat{\lambda}_0 + \hat{\lambda}_1 y + \hat{\lambda}_2 r + \hat{\lambda}_3 f$.

Stage 2 Estimate the structural equation but use as instruments the predicted endogenous variables obtained in the first stage. In Model 4 this means that we regress q on the constant, $\hat{p}$, and y for the demand equation. Regress q on the constant, $\hat{p}, r$, and f for the supply equation. Thus, we are estimating the structural equations but are replacing p by $\hat{p}$. $\hat{p}$ is the instrumental variable here. In computing standard errors, however, the original p will be used. It can be shown that this procedure leads to consistent estimates.

Another procedure, known as the **three-stage least squares method**, takes into account the covariances between the error terms of different equations. This procedure and other procedures such as limited information maximum likelihood and full information maximum likelihood are beyond the scope of this book. Interested readers with a background in matrix algebra are referred to the bibliography at the end of this chapter.

Lagrange Multiplier Test for Omitted Variables

In Chapter 7, we discussed the procedure to use the LM test for adding variables to a single-equation model. The test is also applicable in the context of a simultaneous equation, but requires some modification. Wooldridge (1990) has shown that the test procedure used for a single equation model is not applicable because the distribution of the TR^2 statistic calculated in the usual way is unknown even for a large sample. He proposed, instead, the following procedure:

Step 1 Let the general model be $Y_t = \beta_1 X_{t1} + \beta_2 X_{t2} + u_t$, in which the goal is to test the null hypothesis $\beta_2 = 0$. X_{t1} and X_{t2} are used generically to represent a basic set of variables and an added set of variables, respectively (X_{t1} will include a constant term also). Denote by Z_t the variables in the reduced form which will be used as instruments.

Step 2 Estimate the restricted model $Y_t = \beta_1 X_{t1} + u_t$ by TSLS and save the corresponding residuals as $\tilde{u}_t$.

Step 3 Regress X_{t1} against Z_t and obtain the "fitted" values $\tilde{X}_{t1}$.

Step 4 Do the same with X_{t2} and denote the fitted values by $\hat{X}_{t2}$.

Step 5 Regress $\tilde{u}_t$ against $\tilde{X}_{t1}$ and $\hat{X}_{t2}$ and compute the test statistic TR^2. Under the null hypothesis that $\beta_2 = 0$, and for large samples, this will have an approximate $\chi^2_{k_2}$ distribution with d.f. k_2 equal to the number of restrictions in $\beta_2 = 0$. This can be used in the usual way to test the null hypothesis.

Wooldridge also presents an F-statistic analog to the Wald test statistic in single equation models.

Serial Correlation in a Simultaneous Equation Model*

If time series data are used to estimate a simultaneous equation model, it is very likely that the disturbance terms are serially correlated. The LM test can be used to test for serial correlation, but it to requires modification similar to the one made earlier [see Wooldridge (1991)]. The steps are

Step 1 Estimate the model $Y_t = \beta X_t + u_t$ by TSLS and save the residuals $\hat{u}_t$.

Step 2 Regress X_t by Z_t, the variables in the reduced form that serve as instruments, and obtain the fitted values $\hat{X}_t$.

Step 3 Regress $\hat{u}_t$ against $\hat{X}_t$ and $\hat{u}_{t-1}, \hat{u}_{t-2}, \ldots, \hat{u}_{t-p}$ and compute $(T - p)R^2$. Serial correlation of order p can be tested with this using the χ^2 distribution with p degrees of freedom.

If serial correlation is present, using the standard TSLS procedure is questionable, and a modified procedure may be required. This modified method is described with the following two-equation model, but the principle is the same for models with more equations:

$$Y_{t1} = \alpha_{12} Y_{t2} + \beta_{11} X_{t1} + \beta_{12} X_{t2} + u_t \tag{13.19}$$

$$Y_{t2} = \alpha_{21} Y_{t1} + \beta_{21} X_{t1} + \beta_{23} X_{t3} + v_t \tag{13.20}$$

$$u_t = \rho_1 u_{t-1} + \epsilon_{t1} \tag{13.21}$$

$$v_t = \rho_2 v_{t-1} + \epsilon_{t2} \tag{13.22}$$

where Y_1 and Y_2 are the endogenous variables, and X_1, X_2, and X_3 are the predetermined variables. The structural disturbances are assumed to follow an AR(1) process, with the ϵ's being white noise. The quasi-differenced version of equation (13.19) is given by

$$Y_{t1} - \rho_1 Y_{t-1,1} = \alpha_{12}(Y_{t2} - \rho_1 Y_{t-1,2}) + \beta_{11}(X_{t1} - \rho_1 X_{t-1,1}) \\ + \beta_{12}(X_{t2} - \rho_1 X_{t-1,2}) + \epsilon_{t1} \tag{13.23}$$

The Hildreth–Lu search procedure and the Cochrane–Orcutt iterative procedure are applicable here, but note that because the modified reduced form for Y_{t2} will contain lags of X_1, X_2, and X_3, the first stage must include these as regressors. The steps for estimating equation (13.19) are therefore the following:

Step 1 Regress Y_{t2} against $X_{t1}, X_{t2}, X_{t3}, X_{t-1,1}, X_{t-1,2}$, and $X_{t-1,3}$, and save the predicted value $\hat{Y}_{t2}$.

Step 2 Choose a value for ρ_1 and estimate equation (13.23) by OLS using $\hat{Y}_{t2}$ as an instrument for Y_{t2}.

Step 3 Repeat Step 2 for various values of ρ_1 between -1 and $+1$ and choose that ρ_1 for which the error sum of squares of equation (13.23) is minimum. This is the modified Hildreth–Lu search procedure. The Cochrane–Orcutt technique is also similar to the one in Chapter 9. The only difference is that $\hat{Y}_{t2}$ is used instead of Y_{t2}.

If the model has lagged dependent variables as predetermined variables, then the first-stage regression for Y_{t2} should include $Y_{t-1,1}$ and $Y_{t-2,1}$ (as well as, possibly, $Y_{t-1,2}$ and $Y_{t-2,2}$) as regressors. To see this, suppose that X_{t1} was really $Y_{t-1,1}$. Then we see that equation (13.23) will have $Y_{t-1,1}$ and $Y_{t-2,1}$ on the right-hand side, and hence these must be included as regressors in the first-stage regression. Fair (1970) has shown that this procedure gives consistent estimates of the structural equations.

13.6 Empirical Example: Regulation in the Contact Lens Industry

In a recent study, Hass-Wilson (1987) has examined the effects of state restrictions prohibiting the fitting of contact lenses by independent opticians on the price and quality of contact lenses. A two-equation model is used to relate the price and quality of contact lenses, and the parameters are estimated by two-stage least squares. Before looking at the empirical formulation let us examine the background.

The purchase of contact lenses involves three steps: (1) a visit to an ophthalmologist or optometrist for examination and prescription, (2) a fitting examination to measure the radius of curvature of the cornea, and (3) purchase and evaluation of the lenses. The contact lens industry is characterized by oligopoly, in which many sellers have some degree of market power. In a number of states there are tying requirements (that is, requirements that the purchase of one product, such as contact lenses, must be accompanied by the purchase of another product, such as the services of an optometrist or ophthalmologist) that prohibit the fitting of contact lenses by independent opticians. The question for examination is whether the tying requirements result in an increase in the price of contact lenses and if so by how much.

Hass–Wilson formulates an oligopoly model in which sellers maximize profits with respect to price. Without going through the intermediate steps for the econometric specification (details are in the paper), we simply give here the two equations formulated:

$$P = f(\text{QUALW, SOFT, FITOPH, FITOPTOM, EXOPH, Y,}$$
$$\text{INPUT, R-FIT, LIC, R-AD, REG})$$

$$\text{QUALW} = g(\text{P, FITOPH, FITOPTOM, SEX, AGE, FAIL. WEARTIME,}$$
$$\text{HOURS, DIRT, DAMAGE, WARP, SOFT, R-FIT,}$$
$$\text{R-AD, LIC, REG})$$

where

$$P = \text{price of contact lenses}$$
$$\text{QUALW} = \text{a weighted index of eye health}$$
$$\text{SOFT} = 1 \text{ for soft contact lenses, 0 otherwise}$$
$$\text{FITOPH} = 1 \text{ if fitting was done by an ophthalmologist}$$
$$\text{FITOPTOM} = 1 \text{ if fitting was done by an optometrist}$$
$$\text{EXOPH} = 1 \text{ if examined by an ophthalmologist}$$
$$Y = \text{income}$$
$$\text{INPUT} = \text{price of inputs}$$
$$\text{R-FIT} = 1 \text{ if the consumer's state has restrictions on fitting by opticians}$$
$$\text{R-AD} = 1 \text{ if the consumer's state restricts advertising}$$
$$\text{LIC} = 1 \text{ if the state requires licenses for opticians}$$
$$\text{REG} = \text{index of other commercial practice restrictions}$$
$$\text{SEX} = 1 \text{ for male}$$
$$\text{AGE} = \text{age of consumer}$$

$$\text{FAIL} = 1 \text{ if consumer was unsuccessful in wearing}$$
$$\text{contact lenses before}$$
$$\text{WEARTIME} = \text{wear time prior to the exam}$$
$$\text{HOURS} = \text{average hours worn per day}$$
$$\text{DIRT} = 1 \text{ if lenses were dirty}$$
$$\text{DAMAGE} = 1 \text{ if lenses were damaged}$$
$$\text{WARP} = 1 \text{ if lenses were warped}$$

This model was estimated with 354 observations obtained by the Federal Trade Commission during the period 1976–1979 from consumers in 18 urban areas. Two-stage least squares estimates of the parameters are as follows (standard errors are in parentheses):

$$\hat{P} = \underset{(43.3)}{167.30} - \underset{(0.9)}{0.64\text{QUALW}} + \underset{(6.5)}{53.92\text{SOFT}} + \underset{(10.8)}{17.87\text{FITOPH}} + \underset{(13.9)}{2.72\text{FITOPTOM}}$$

$$+ \underset{(13.8)}{28.48\text{EXOPH}} - \underset{(0.0)}{0.01Y} - \underset{(39.0)}{18.52\text{INPUT}} + \underset{(7.9)}{17.29\text{R-FIT}} - \underset{(7.3)}{4.45\text{LIC}}$$

$$R^2 = 0.29 \qquad T = 354 \qquad F = 12.73$$

$$\widehat{\text{QUALW}} = \underset{(9.1)}{8.02} - \underset{(0.1)}{0.08P} + \underset{(2.7)}{3.39\text{FITOPH}} - \underset{(2.0)}{0.06\text{FITOPTOM}} + \underset{(1.6)}{3.61\text{SEX}}$$

$$- \underset{(0.1)}{0.07\text{AGE}} - \underset{(1.9)}{283\text{FAIL}} - \underset{(0.3)}{0.83\text{WEARTIME}} - \underset{(0.5)}{0.83\text{HOURS}}$$

$$- \underset{(1.0)}{1.65\text{DIRT}} + \underset{(0.9)}{1.03\text{DAMAGE}} + \underset{(1.1)}{0.07\text{WARP}} + \underset{(4.1)}{7.85\text{SOFT}}$$

$$- \underset{(1.5)}{0.10\text{R-FIT}} + \underset{(2.3)}{0.06\text{R-AD}} - \underset{(1.3)}{0.53\text{LIC}} + \underset{(0.7)}{0.53\text{REG}}$$

$$R^2 = 0.14 \qquad T = 354 \qquad F = 3.51$$

The null hypothesis of main interest is that the coefficient for R-FIT is zero in the price equation. This hypothesis is rejected at the 5 percent level, indicating that the tying requirements do significantly affect the price of contact lenses. In states that restrict contact lens prescriptions by opticians, prices are expected to be higher, on average, by \$17.29. The author also used a double-log model for the price, and estimated that contact lens prices were 8 percent higher in states with restrictions. The results suggest, too, that quality, measured as eye health, does not significantly affect price. Other types of restrictions, such as those on the use of trade names and the number of branch offices an optometrist may operate, are also associated with higher contact lens prices. The quality equation estimates suggest that tying requirements do not significantly affect quality. Finally, the quality provided by opticians is not significantly different from that provided by optometrists or ophthalmologists. Advertising and other restrictions do not appear to affect quality significantly.

13.7 Application: A Simple Keynesian Model

We use a simple Keynesian model to illustrate the principles discussed in this chapter. The discussion here is, however, not exhaustive. Extensions to the analysis are suggested in the exercises. The reader is encouraged to use the data provided to formulate other variations and estimate them. The structural equations of the model are the following:

$$C_t = \alpha_0 + \alpha_1 DY_t + u_{t1}$$
$$I_t = \beta_0 + \beta_1 DY_t + \beta_2 r_t + u_{t2}$$
$$r_t = \gamma_0 + \gamma_1 Y_t + \gamma_2 M_t + u_{t3}$$
$$DY_t = Y_t - T_t$$
$$Y_t = C_t + I_t + G_t + X_t$$

where C is aggregate consumption expenditure, I is investment, Y is GNP, DY is disposable income (GNP less taxes), G is government expenditure, M is the money supply, X is net exports, r is the interest rate, and the u's are stochastic error terms. All financial variables are in real terms (billions of 1982 dollars). The jointly determined endogenous variables are C, I, Y, DY, and r. The predetermined variables are the constant term, G, T, X, and M. The first equation is the consumption function, which relates consumption to disposable income. The second equation is the investment function, and the third equation determines the interest rate and is derived from equilibrium in the money market.

Let the money demand function (also known as the *liquidity preference function*) be $M_d = L(Y, r)$. In equilibrium, this will equal the money supply M (money demand and supply are measured as real balances). Solving the equation $M = L(Y, r)$ for r in terms Y and real M, we get the third equation (which is the well-known LM curve). The fourth equation is an identity that defines disposable income. The last equation is the condition for equilibrium in the goods market.

Note that this model is purely Keynesian because there is no price determination. Table 13.1 has annual data for the 32 years, from 1959 to 1990, for a number of aggregate variables. These have to be appropriately transformed, if necessary, to obtain the variables in the model. $M2$ is money supply measured as M_2, which is the sum of currency, demand deposits, checking and saving account balances, overnight repurchase agreements, and Eurodollars. P is the GNP deflator, a price index measure. As mentioned in Chapter 1, there is no such thing as a single interest rate. In the investment equation the corporate bond rate seems appropriate. Because the goods market clearing condition must be exactly met, we have not used independent data series for Y, C, I, G, and X. Instead, C_t is obtained as $Y_t - I_t - G_t - X_t$. It can be verified, however, that this is almost identical to the published values for C_t, "statistical discrepancies" accounting for the difference. Total taxes are calculated as $T_t = 100*(\text{PERSTAX}_t + \text{CORPTAX}_t)/P_t$—that is, as the sum of personal and corporate taxes divided by the price index (to convert to real terms). Disposable income is then derived as $Y_t - T_t$. Real money supply

TABLE 13.1 Aggregate Annual Data for the United States for 1959–1990

Year	Y_t	I_t	G_t	X_t	PERSTAX$_t$	CORPTAX$_t$	$M2_t$	P_t	r_t	POP$_t$
1959	1629.1	270.3	397.7	−18.2	46.1	23.6	297.8	30.4	4.38	177.830
1960	1665.3	260.5	403.7	−4.0	50.5	22.7	312.4	30.9	4.41	180.671
1961	1708.7	259.1	427.1	−2.7	52.2	22.8	335.5	31.2	4.35	183.691
1962	1799.4	288.6	449.4	−7.5	57.0	24.0	362.7	31.9	4.33	186.538
1963	1873.3	307.1	459.8	−19	60.5	26.2	393.3	32.4	4.26	189.242
1964	1973.3	325.9	470.8	5.9	58.8	28.0	424.8	32.9	4.40	191.889
1965	2087.6	367.0	487.0	−2.7	65.2	30.9	459.4	33.8	4.49	194.303
1966	2208.3	390.5	532.6	−13.7	74.9	33.7	480.0	35.0	5.13	196.560
1967	2271.4	374.4	576.2	−16.9	82.4	32.7	524.4	35.9	5.51	198.712
1968	2365.6	391.8	597.6	−29.7	97.7	39.4	566.4	37.7	6.18	200.706
1969	2423.3	410.3	591.2	−34.9	116.3	39.7	589.6	39.8	7.03	202.677
1970	2416.2	381.5	572.6	−30.0	116.2	34.4	628.1	42.0	8.04	205.052
1971	2484.8	419.3	566.5	−39.8	117.3	37.7	712.7	44.4	7.39	207.661
1972	2608.5	465.4	570.7	−49.4	142.0	41.9	805.2	46.5	7.21	209.896
1973	2744.1	520.8	565.3	−31.5	152.0	49.3	861.0	49.5	7.44	211.909
1974	2729.3	481.3	573.2	0.8	171.8	51.8	908.6	54.0	8.57	213.854
1975	2695.0	383.3	580.9	18.9	170.6	50.9	1023.3	59.3	8.83	215.973
1976	2826.7	453.5	580.3	−11.0	198.7	64.2	1163.7	63.1	8.43	218.035
1977	2958.6	521.3	589.1	−35.5	228.1	73.0	1286.7	67.3	8.02	220.239
1978	3115.2	576.9	604.1	−26.8	261.1	83.5	1389.0	72.2	8.73	222.585
1979	3192.4	575.2	609.1	3.6	304.7	88.0	1497.1	78.6	9.63	225.055
1980	3187.1	509.3	620.5	57.0	340.5	84.8	1629.9	85.7	11.94	227.757
1981	3248.8	545.5	629.7	49.4	393.3	81.1	1793.5	94.0	14.17	230.138
1982	3166.0	447.3	641.7	26.3	409.3	63.1	1953.1	100.0	13.79	232.520
1983	3279.1	504.0	649.0	−19.9	410.5	77.2	2186.5	103.9	12.04	234.799
1984	3501.4	658.4	677.7	−84.0	440.2	93.9	2371.6	107.7	12.71	237.001
1985	3618.7	637.0	731.2	−104.3	486.6	96.4	2570.6	110.9	11.37	239.279
1986	3717.9	639.6	761.6	−129.7	512.9	106.3	2814.2	113.8	9.02	241.625
1987	3845.3	669.0	779.1	−118.5	571.6	126.9	2913.2	117.4	9.38	243.942
1988	4016.9	705.7	780.5	−75.9	591.6	136.2	3072.4	121.3	9.71	246.307
1989	4117.7	716.9	798.1	−54.1	658.8	135.1	3221.6	126.3	9.26	248.762
1990	4155.8	690.3	820.8	−37.5	699.8	134.1	3323.3	131.5	9.32	251.394

Sources: Economic Report of the President, 1991, Tables B-2, B-26, B-87, B-67, B-3, B71, B-31.

is calculated using the transformation, $M_t = 100\ M2_t/P_t$. The OLS estimates of the structural parameters are as follows: (see Practice Computer Session 13.2):

$$\hat{C}_t = -227.654 + 0.831DY_t \qquad\qquad \bar{R}^2 = 0.997$$
$$\phantom{\hat{C}_t = } \underset{(-11.3)}{}\ \underset{(101.4)}{}$$

$$\hat{I}_t = -40.851 + 0.238DY_t - 6.616r_t \qquad \bar{R}^2 = 0.947$$
$$\phantom{\hat{I}_t = } \underset{(-1.8)}{}\ \underset{(16.3)}{}\ \underset{(-2.1)}{}$$

$$\hat{r}_t = -0.175 + 0.010Y_t - 0.011M_t \qquad \bar{R}^2 = 0.636$$
$$\phantom{\hat{r}_t = } \underset{(-0.1)}{}\ \underset{(3.0)}{}\ \underset{(-2.1)}{}$$

Although the t-statistic and adjusted R^2 are presented, because of the simultaneity they are invalid. To obtain consistent estimates of the parameters and their standard errors, we apply the two-stage least squares (TSLS) procedure. The estimated equations are as follows:

$$\hat{C}_t = -228.780 + 0.832DY_t \qquad\qquad \bar{R}^2 = 0.997$$
$$\phantom{\hat{C}_t = } \underset{(-11.3)}{}\ \underset{(101.3)}{}$$

$$\hat{I}_t = -41.951 + 0.255DY_t - 11.511r_t \qquad \bar{R}^2 = 0.942$$
$$\phantom{\hat{I}_t = } \underset{(-1.8)}{}\ \underset{(11.1)}{}\ \underset{(-2.0)}{}$$

$$\hat{r}_t = -0.178 + 0.010Y_t - 0.012M_t \qquad \bar{R}^2 = 0.636$$
$$\phantom{\hat{r}_t = } \underset{(-0.1)}{}\ \underset{(2.8)}{}\ \underset{(-2.0)}{}$$

The first stage in estimating the consumption function consists of regressing DY against a constant G, T, X, and M, and saving the predicted value $\widehat{DY}_t$ for use as an instrumental variable. In the second stage, C_t is regressed against a constant and $\widehat{DY}_t$. In calculating the residuals and standard errors, however, actual DY_t is used. The TSLS procedure for the other two equations is similar. We note that the goodness of fit of all the equations is fairly high. Also, the t-statistics indicate high significance in all cases. Furthermore, the estimates for the consumption and interest rate equations are quite close to those by OLS, but they differ considerably for the investment function.

Economic theory tells us that as the interest rate rises, investment will fall. We note that this is supported empirically. Macro theory also tells us that an increase in the money supply will reduce the equilibrium interest rate. We note that the coefficient for M in the interest rate equation is significantly negative. Because it would take time for changes in the money supply to cause changes in the interest rate, a model with lagged variables would be more appropriate. In a similar manner, we can expect lagged impact of interest rate changes on investment. These variations are suggested in the exercises.

Serial Correlation

The Durbin–Watson statistics for the three structural equations are 0.818 for the consumption function, 1.548 for the investment equation, and 0.282 for the interest rate equation. It is easy to verify that these indicate that there is significant first-order serial correlation in the consumption and interest rate equations, but almost none in the investment equation. This makes the use of the standard TSLS procedure questionable for the consumption and interest rate equations. Serial correlation in simultaneous equation models requires a modified Cochrane–Orcutt procedure in conjunction with two-stage least squares. As in Chapter 8, we would use a quasi-differenced model such as $C_t - \hat{\rho}C_{t-1}$ against a constant and $DY_t - \hat{\rho}DY_{t-1}$. The first stage will now consist of regressing DY_t against a constant, G_t, G_{t-1}, T_t, T_{t-1}, and so on. The predicted values from this first stage are then used as instruments in the quasi-differenced structural equation. In the first stage of the interest rate equation, Y_t will be regressed against G_t, G_{t-1}, T_t, T_{t-1}, and so on.

Reduced Form and the Multipliers

It would be useful to obtain the estimates of the reduced form for GNP using the TSLS estimates just obtained. The reduced form parameters obtained this way are known as the **implied reduced form estimates**. The reduced form for GNP would relate it to the predetermined variables in the system—namely, a constant, G, T, X, and M. The implied reduced form for Y_t is obtained as follows (∗ is multiplication):

$$
\begin{aligned}
Y_t &= C_t + I_t + G_t + X_t \\
&= -228.780 + 0.832(Y_t - T_t) - 41.951 \\
&\quad + 0.255(Y_t - T_t) - 11.511(-0.178 + 0.010Y_t \\
&\quad - 0.012M_t) + G_t + X_t \\
&= -228.780 - 41.951 + (11.511 \times 0.178) \\
&\quad + Y_t[0.832 + 0.255 - (11.511 \times 0.010)] \\
&\quad + (11.511 \times 0.012)M_t + G_t + X_t \\
&\quad - (0.832 + 0.255)T_t \\
&= -268.682 + 0.972Y_t + 0.138M_t \\
&\quad + G_t + X_t - 1.087T_t
\end{aligned}
$$

Bringing all the Y_t terms to the left and solving for Y_t, we get the implied reduced form as

$$
\begin{aligned}
Y_t &= -9595.786 + 4.929M_t + 35.714G_t \\
&\quad + 35.714X_t - 38.821T_t
\end{aligned}
$$

The partial derivative of Y_t with respect to a given variable is the multiplier for that variable. We note that, in this simple model, the government expenditure multiplier is much higher than the monetary multiplier.

SUMMARY

This chapter has been concerned with the special problems that arise when a regression equation of interest is part of a system of simultaneous equations. A simultaneous equation system consists of a number of *structural equations* involving several *endogenous variables* whose values are determined within the specified system. Their values also depend on several *exogenous variables* whose values are specified outside the system, and also on lagged values of variables, known as *predetermined variables*. To avoid confusion, exogenous variables are also considered predetermined. Structural equations can be behavioral, technical, identities, or equilibrium conditions. If each of the endogenous variables is solved in terms of the exogenous and predetermined variables, we obtain a system of *reduced form equations*. These equations will not contain any endogenous variables but will depend on the stochastic terms of all the equations.

It is possible to test for the direction of *causality* using the *Granger Causality Test*. This involves testing whether past values of one variable significantly affect the present and future values of another variable.

If the simultaneity is ignored and ordinary least squares applied, the estimates will be biased and inconsistent. Consequently, forecasts will be biased and inconsistent. In addition, tests of hypotheses will no longer be valid.

Because the exogenous and predetermined variables are independent of all the error terms, OLS can be applied to the reduced form to obtain estimates that are BLUE and consistent. The natural question that arises at this point is "Why not apply OLS to the reduced form and then solve backwards for the structural coefficients?" Unfortunately, this is not always possible. This is the *identification problem*. If it is not possible to solve for the coefficients of a structural equation from estimates of the coefficients of the reduced form equation, we have a model that is *unidentified* or *underidentified*. If a unique set of structural estimates can be estimated, we have an *exactly identified* equation. If more than one structural estimate is possible. we have an *overidentified* specification.

If an equation is exactly identified, we can apply *indirect least squares* by first estimating the reduced form and solving backwards for the structural coefficients. This procedure, however, is cumbersome, especially if there are several equations. A better method that gives consistent estimates is the *instrumental variable technique*, in which one finds a substitute variable (say Z) for an endogenous variable with the following properties: (1) Z is uncorrelated with the error term, and (2) Z is highly correlated with the endogenous variable. The variable Z (known as an *instrumental variable*) is used in place of the endogenous variable, and the structural equation is estimated. A frequently used instrumental variable technique is the *two-stage least squares procedure*, which is especially appropriate when an equation is overidentified. In the first stage, each of the reduced form equations is estimated, and the predicted values of the endogenous values saved. These are then used in place of the endogenous variables, and the structural equation estimated. In calculating residuals and standard errors, however, the actual values of the endogenous values are used instead of the predicted values.

Once the structural estimates have been obtained, we can use them to get the *implied reduced form estimates* by solving each of the endogenous variables in terms of the exogenous and predetermined variables. Because TSLS estimates take account of overidentifying restrictions, the implied reduced form estimates obtained from them are more efficient than direct reduced form estimates.

From the implied (or direct) reduced form estimates we can obtain the multipliers of the endogenous variables with respect to the exogenous variables, many of which will be policy variables.

KEY TERMS

Behavioral equations
Causality
Endogenous variable
Exact identification
Exogenous variable
Feedback
Granger causality
Identification problem
Implied reduced form estimates
Reduced form equation
Reduced form parameter
Simultaneous equation bias
Structural equations
Structural parameters

Technical equation
Indirect least squares (ILS) procedure
Instrumental variable
Instrumental variable technique (IV)
Least squares bias
Overidentification
Overidentifying restrictions
Predetermined variables
Three-stage least squares method
Two-stage least squares (TSLS)
  method
Underidentification
Unidentified equation

REFERENCES

Economic Report of the President. Washington, D.C.: U.S. Government Printing Office, 1991.

Fair, Ray C. "The Estimation of Simultaneous Equation Models with Lagged Endogenous Variables and First Order Serially Correlated Errors." *Econometrica,* Vol. 38 (May 1970): 507–516.

Geweke, J., Meese, R., and Dent. W. "Comparing Alternative Tests of Causality in Temporal Systems," *J. Econometrics,* Vol. 77 (1982), 161–194.

Granger, C. W. J. "Investigating Causal Relations by Econometric Models and Cross-spectral Models," *Econometrica,* Vol. 37 (1969), 424–438.

Haas-Wilson, Deborah. "Tying Requirements in Markets with Many Sellers: The Contact Lens Industry." *Review of Economics and Statistics,* Vol. 69 (February 1987): 170–175.

Haugh, L. D. "Checking the Independence of Two Covariance-stationary time series: a Univariate Residual Cross-correlation Approach," *J. Amer. Stat. Assoc.,* Vol. 71 (1976), 378–385.

Johnston, J. *Econometric Methods.* New York: McGraw-Hill, 1984.

Judge, G. G., Griffiths, W. E., Hill, R. C., and Lee, T. *The Theory and Practice of Econometrics.* New York: John Wiley & Sons, 1985.

Kmenta, Jan. *Elements of Econometrics.* New York: Macmillan, 1986.

Nelson, C. R., and Schwert, G. W. "Tests for Predictive Relationships between Time Series Variables: a Monte Carlo Investigation." *J. Amer. Stat. Assoc.,* Vol. 77 (1982), 11–18.

Pindyck, R. S., and Rubenfeld, D. L. *Econometric Models and Economic Forecasts.* New York: McGraw-Hill, 1976.

Peirce, D. A. "Relationships—and the Lack Thereof—between Economic Time Series, with Special Reference to Money and Interest Rates," *J. Amer. Stat. Assoc.,* Vol. 72 (1977), 11–22.

Pierce, D. A., and Haugh, L. D. "Causality in Temporal System: Characterizations and a Survey," *J. Econometrics*, Vol. 5 (1977), 265–294.

Sims, C. "Money, Income, and Causality," *Amer. Econ. Rev.*, Vol. 62 (1972), 540–552.

Wooldridge, J. "A Note on the Lagrange Multiplier and F-Statistics for Two-Stage Least Squares Regression," *Economics Letters*, Vol. 34 (1990), 151–155.

Wooldridge, J. "On the Application of Robust Regression-rooted Diagnostics to Models of Conditional Means and Conditional Variables," *J. Econometrics*, Vol. 47 (1991), 5–46.

PRACTICE COMPUTER SESSIONS

13.1 The data file *data10 – 1* and the ECSLIB input command file *ps13 – 1.inp* are needed to verify Example 13.1.

13.2 To reproduce the results of the application section, use *ps13 – 2.inp* and the data file *data13 – 1*.

13.3 Use *data13 – 2* and *ps13 – 3.inp* as a starting point for Exercise 13.10.

EXERCISES

†**13.1** Twenty-fiive years ago it was possible to write papers estimating the consumption function $C_t = \alpha + \beta Y_t + u_t$ using the OLS assumptions on u_t.

a. Based on what you have learned so far, give alternative reasons as to why this model may be misspecified, either in the deterministic part (that is, in the $\alpha + \beta Y_t$ part) or in the error structure (that is, in assumptions on u_t). State clearly the nature of the misspecification in each case.

b. Choose two of the reasons, one for the deterministic part and one for the error structure, and in each case examine the OLS estimates of this consumption function from the point of view of (i) unbiasedness, (ii) BLUE, and (iii) consistency. State, with adequate reasons, whether these properties hold.

13.2 This question refers to the macro model presented in Section 13.3 and the ILS procedure discussed in Section 13.5. Using the relation $Y = C + I$, first show that $S_{YI} = S_{CI} + S_{II}$. Then write the reduced form for GNP as $Y_t = \mu_0 + \mu_1 I_t + v_t$, and show that the OLS estimates $\tilde{\mu}_0$ and $\tilde{\mu}_1$ are given by

$$\hat{\mu}_0 = \bar{Y} - \hat{\mu}_1 \bar{I} \qquad \hat{\mu}_1 = \frac{S_{YI}}{S_{II}}$$

Finally, estimate α and β indirectly from these, and show that they are identical to those obtained earlier. Thus, in this example, it does not matter which reduced form is used to obtain indirect least squares estimates of the structural parameters.

†**13.3** The structural form of a two-equation model is as follows (the *t*-subscript is

omitted):

$$P = \alpha_1 + \alpha_2 N + \alpha_3 S + \alpha_4 A + u$$
$$N = \beta_1 + \beta_2 P + \beta_2 M + v$$

where P and N are endogenous and S, A, and M are exogenous.

a. For each equation, examine whether it is under-, over-, or exactly identified.

b. What explanatory variables, if any, are correlated with u? What explanatory variables, if any, are correlated with v?

c. What happens if OLS is used to estimate the α's and the β's?

d. Can the α's be estimated by ILS? If yes, derive the estimates. Answer the same equation about the β's.

e. Explain step by step how the TSLS method can be applied on the second equation.

13.4   Consider the following simple three-equation model:

$$A = X - M \qquad\qquad \text{Endogenous: } A, M, X$$
$$M = \alpha_1 + \alpha_2 Y + \alpha_3 P + \alpha_4 U + u \qquad \text{Exogenous: } Y, P, U$$
$$X = \beta_1 + \beta_2 P + \beta_3 A + v \qquad\qquad \text{Error terms: } u, v$$

a. Check whether the order condition is satisfied for the second and third equations. What is your conclusion?

b. Derive the reduced form equations.

c. How would you use the TSLS estimation procedure on the third equation?

d. Explain why we can use the OLS method on the second equation. What properties do the estimates have?

e. Suppose we had used OLS to estimate the third equation. What properties will those estimates have?

13.5   Consider the following three-equation model relating crime in a city to a number of determinants:

$$\text{PROPCRIME} = \alpha_1 + \alpha_2 \text{MEDHOME} + \alpha_3 \text{POPDEN} + \alpha_4 \text{UNEMP}$$
$$+ \alpha_5 \text{POLICE} + u$$
$$\text{VIOLNTCRIME} = \beta_1 + \beta_2 \text{POLICE} + \beta_3 \text{DEATH} + \beta_4 \text{MEDAGE} + v$$
$$\text{POLICE} = \gamma_1 + \gamma_2 \text{PROPCRIME} + \gamma_3 \text{VIOLNTCRIME} + w$$

where PROPCRIME is property crime, VIOLNTCRIME is violent crime, POLICE is the expenditure on police, DEATH is a dummy variable that takes the value 1 if the city is in a state that allows the death penalty, MEDHOME is median value of homes, POPDEN is the density of population (number of people per square mile), UNEMP is the unemployment rate, and MEDAGE is the median age of the city's population.

a. What signs would you expect a priori for each of the coefficients?

b. Check the order conditions on each equation.

c. Describe step by step how you would use TSLS to estimate each of the equations.

13.6　Use the data presented in Table 13.1 and the transformations presented in Section 13.7, and obtain T_t and M_t in constant dollars. Next estimate the reduced form for Y_t directly by regressing Y_t against a constant, G_t, T_t, X_t, and M_t. Compare the coefficients derived in this way to the TSLS estimates obtained in Section 13.7. Explain why the implied reduced form estimates (from TSLS structural estimates) would be more efficient than the OLS estimates. [*Hint*: the TSLS method takes account of overidentifying restrictions that the OLS estimation procedure ignores.]

13.7　Redo the analysis of Section 13.7 using per capita values for all financial variables. Table 13.1 has the U.S. population in millions.

13.8　Extend the analysis of Section 13.7 to include dynamic behavior. Consider the following dynamic model, in which one-period lags have been added:

$$C_t = \alpha_0 + \alpha_1 D Y_t + \alpha_2 D Y_{t-1} + u_{t1}$$
$$I_t = \beta_0 + \beta_1 D Y_t + \beta_2 D Y_{t-1} + \beta_3 r_t + \beta_4 r_{t-1} + u_{t2}$$
$$r_t = \gamma_0 + \gamma_1 Y_t + \gamma_2 Y_{t-1} + \gamma_3 M_t + \gamma_4 M_{t-1} + u_{t3}$$
$$D Y_t = Y_t - T_t$$
$$Y_t = C_t + I_t + G_t + X_t$$

The dynamic form of the consumption function can be rationalized by noting that consumers tend to maintain past consumption patterns, but would adjust them based on changes in income levels. A plausible formulation is therefore

$$C_t = a + b D Y_{t-1} + c(D Y_t - D Y_{t-1}) + u_{t1} \qquad a, b, c > 0$$

The $D Y_{t-1}$ term reflects the component based on the previous period's disposable income, and the term involving $D Y_t - D Y_{t-1}$ is the marginal effect of a change in disposable income from the previous period. If income falls (that is, if $D Y_t - D Y_{t-1}$ is negative), consumers are likely to adjust their consumption downwards. Setting $\alpha_0 = a$, $\alpha_1 = c$, and $\alpha_2 = b - c$, we get the earlier specification. The investment and interest rate equations can be derived similarly. Estimate this model first by OLS and then by TSLS and compare the results. Next derive the impact, interim, and long-run multipliers for monetary and fiscal policy variables.

13.9　Redo the analysis in Exercise 13.8 in per capita terms.

13.10　Is money supply really exogenous as standard macro theory says? Examine this question using the monthly data for money supply (M2), unemployment rate, and inflation rate provided in the file *data13−2* in the diskette accompanying the book. Generate lagged variables for up to 12 months. Then use the Granger-causality Test to test wether past unemployment and inflation rates affect the money supply. [Use Practice Computer Session 13.3 as a starting point.]

Derivation of the Limits for OLS Estimates

In this appendix we compute the limit of the OLS estimate of β ($\hat{\beta}$) for equation (13.13), and show that it is not equal to the true value, thus proving that the estimate is inconsistent. Applying the OLS procedure to equation (13.13), we obtain the following expression for $\hat{\beta}$ [see equations (3.7), (3.8), and (3.9)].

$$\hat{\beta} = \frac{S_{CY}}{S_{YY}} \tag{13.A.1}$$

where

$$S_{CY} = \sum (C_t - \bar{C})(Y_t - \bar{Y}) \tag{13.A.2}$$

$$S_{YY} = \sum (Y_t - \bar{Y})^2 \tag{13.A.3}$$

From the reduced forms of the model [equations (13.15) and (13.16)] we have

$$C_t - \bar{C} = \frac{\beta}{1 - \beta}(I_t - \bar{I}) + \frac{u_t - \bar{u}}{1 - \beta} \tag{13.A.4}$$

$$Y_t - \bar{Y} = \frac{I_t - \bar{I}}{1 - \beta} + \frac{u_t - \bar{u}}{1 - \beta} \tag{13.A.5}$$

where the bar above a variable represents the sample mean. Multiplying the left-hand sides of equations (13.A.4) and (13.A.5) and summing, we have

$$S_{CY} = \frac{\beta}{(1 - \beta)^2} S_{II} + \frac{1}{(1 - \beta)^2} S_{uu} + \frac{1 + \beta}{(1 - \beta)^2} S_{Iu}$$

where S_{II}, S_{uu}, and S_{Iu} are defined similarly to S_{CY} and S_{YY}. As $T \to \infty$, S_{uu}/T converges to the variance σ_u^2 (by the law of large numbers in Property 2.12), S_{Iu}/T converges to 0 because I_t and u_t are uncorrelated, and S_{II}/T converges to the variance σ_I^2. Therefore, S_{CY}/T converges to $(\beta\sigma_I^2 + \sigma_u^2)/(1 - \beta)^2$. Similarly,

$$S_{YY} = \frac{S_{II}}{(1 - \beta)^2} + \frac{S_{uu}}{(1 - \beta)^2} + \frac{2S_{Iu}}{(1 - \beta)^2}$$

and hence S_{YY}/T converges to $(\sigma_I^2 + \sigma_u^2)/(1 - \beta)^2$. Thus, the asymptotic limit of $\hat{\beta}$ is as follows:

$$\lim_{T \to \infty} \hat{\beta} = \frac{\beta\sigma_I^2 + \sigma_u^2}{\sigma_I^2 + \sigma_u^2} = \beta + \frac{(1 - \beta)\sigma_u^2}{\sigma_I^2 + \sigma_u^2}$$

This establishes equation (13.17).

PART VI

PRACTICE

This part, which contains only one chapter, takes the reader through the various steps involved in carrying out an empirical project and in preparing a report. It also provides details that will help in choosing a topic, obtaining sources for review of existing literature, and looking for data. If students are expected to conduct an empirical study, this chapter should be assigned early in the course.

CHAPTER 14

Carrying Out an Empirical Project

■ In Chapter 1, we gave a brief description of the various stages of an empirical study, from formulating the problem to be studied to interpreting the results. Although most of the chapters have presented illustrative applications in the form of mini projects, a student will learn more about econometrics from a complete empirical project than from dozens of lectures. A student can also assert to a prospective employer that he or she has conducted a project from start to finish. In this chapter, each of the steps presented in Chapter 1 is elaborated further. If an instructor is requiring an empirical project, this chapter should be studied earlier, especially the parts about formulating a research question, specifying an initial model in general form, and gathering the data.

As one might easily infer, there is no unique way to conduct an empirical study, and no magic formula one can apply. Practice is the only way to really learn the steps involved in applied research and to develop the intuition needed to judge results and draw conclusions. This chapter, therefore, can offer only general guidelines and suggestions for approaches.

14.1 Selecting a Topic

If you are a professional researcher, the problem for study is usually dictated by the requirements of the job and/or assigned by your superiors. For instance, one of the major tasks of an analyst in the load forecasting department of an electric utility is to estimate the relationship between the demand for electricity and its various determinants, such as weather and seasonal patterns, the price of electricity, income, stock of appliances, industrial and demographic mix of the utility service area, and so on. The estimated relation is then used to generate load forecasts. These forecasts are evaluated by the state's public utilities commission to determine what the new rate structure should be and whether any new power plants are required to service the area's demand. In this example, the research question is easily posed as that of relating the demand for electricity to its determinants and that of generating forecasts.

If you are a student in a course on econometrics, however, the instructor might require that you carry out an empirical project, and not assign any specific problem to be examined. The first task then is to select a topic for study, which naturally raises the question "What do I do and how do I get started?" To answer this, consider the following. Before taking a course in econometrics you undoubtedly took other economics courses, some of which might be at the upper-division level. You would have studied many theories about the behavior of economic agents and the relationships among economic variables. So ask yourself now which of the theoretical relationships you studied would be worth empirically estimating and which bodies of theories can be put to empirical tests. In the courses you took, there might have been a discussion of an equation or of someone's study that interested you. This would be worth following up. Your former professors might be willing to help you focus on one of the problems of interest, but don't impose on them or take advantage of their generosity. Some possible topic areas are the following:[1]

1. *Macroeconomics*: Estimate a consumption or investment or money demand function. These usually require time series analysis and two-stage least squares. You might try to estimate a Phillips curve, either with international data for many countries or with time series data for a given country. Macro topics have the advantage that the data are relatively easy to come by.
2. *Microeconomics*: Estimating production, cost, supply, and demand functions are obvious choices, but data are generally hard to obtain.
3. *Urban and regional economics*: Estimate the demand for housing, transportation, schools and other public facilities, and so on for a city, county, or state. Measure the sensitivity of industrial location to differences across regions in tax rates, energy prices, zoning laws, degree of unionization, availability of skilled labor, and so on.
4. *International economics*: Estimate import and export functions for a given country over time or across many countries. Relate exchange rates to their determinants.
5. *Development economics*: Measure the determinants of per capita income (GNP) across countries.

. . . . . .

[1] *This list is drawn from a similar list provided to me by Carrol Foster.*

6. *Labor economics*: Test theories on unionization, early retirement, labor force participation rates, wage differentials among women, minorities, young workers, and so on.

7. *Industrial organization*: Measure the effects of advertising on sales and profits, or on the concentration (that is, market share) in industries. Estimate the relationship between expenditures on research and development (R&D) and employee productivity. Study the relationship between industry concentration and profitability due to merger activity.

8. *Public finance*: Estimate the relationship between local government tax revenue and its characteristics, such as population, demographic and industrial mix, wages, income, and so on. Also relate the expenditures on health, roads, education, and so on to their determinants.

9. *Socioeconomics*: Explain variations across cities, counties, and states in crime, poverty, divorce rates, family size, and so on.

10. *Politics*: Relate voter turnout to a number of characteristics of precincts, candidates, and so on. Explain the vote obtained by a politician in different districts.

A systematic way to approach the problem of choosing a specific topic is to make effective use of a classification system adopted by the *Journal of Economic Literature* (*JEL*), which is a quarterly publication that presents a classified list of books and journal articles published in the preceding quarter (see Table 14.1 for a copy of this list). As an example, if you are interested in studying labor mobility, first look up the entry in Table 14.1 under "Manpower; Labor; Population" and note that the relevant classification number is 823. Next turn to the "Subject Index of Articles in Current Periodicals," which contains a detailed list of recent articles published under the various classifications, and make a list of those that interest you. The journal also lists the contents of current periodicals and has abstracts on selected books and articles. The abstracts will help you learn more about particular topics, and help you decide whether a paper is too theoretical for your tastes.

Journals such as *Applied Economics, Review of Economics and Statistics, International Monetary Fund Staff Papers,* and the *Brookings Paper on Economic Activity* are predominantly application-oriented and would be useful starting points. Some journals specialize in certain fields (for example, *Journal of Human Resources, Journal of Urban Economics, Journal of Regional Science*). These can be identified from a list of journals that the *JEL* uses for abstracts (Table 14.2 has a partial listing). If you have a general field in mind, these specialized journals might be helpful in narrowing down a specific research question. Be sure to write down the names and other references for books and journals that relate to the topic of your choice. Take a quick look at the papers to see if you wish to pursue the topic further. Bibliographical citations in these papers are also worth looking into. The list you compile at this stage will be indispensable in future stages. After selecting a topic, prepare a statement of the problem you intend to study.

TABLE 14.1 Journal of Economic Literature Classification System

---

000 General Economics; Theory; History; Systems
    010 General Economics
        011 General economics
        012 Teaching of economics
    020 General Economic Theory
        021 General equilibrium and disequilibrium theory
        022 Microeconomic theory
        023 Macroeconomic theory
        024 Welfare theory
        025 Social choice
        026 Economics of uncertainty and information; game theory and bargaining theory
        027 Economics of centrally planned economies
    030 History of Economic Thought; Methodology
        031 History of economic thought
        036 Economic methodology
    040 Economic History
        041 Economic history: general
        042 Economic history: United States and Canada
        043 Economic history: ancient and medieval (until 1453)
        044 Economic history: Europe
        045 Economic history: Asia
        046 Economic history: Africa
        047 Economic history: Latin America and Caribbean
        048 Economic history: Oceania
    050 Economic Systems
        051 Capitalist economic systems
        052 Socialist aand communist economic systems
        053 Comparative economic systems

100 Economic Growth; Development; Planning; Fluctuations
    110 Economic Growth; Development; and Planning Theory and Policy
        111 Economic growth theory and models
        112 Economic development models and theories
        113 Economic planning theory and policy
        114 Economics of war, defense, and disarmament
    120 Country Studies
        121 Economic studies of developing countries
        122 Economic studies of developed countries
        123 Comparative studies of developing, developed, and/or centrally planned economies
        124 Economic studies of centrally planned economies
    130 Economic Fluctuations; Forecasting; Stabilization; and Inflation
        131 Economic fluctuations
        132 Forecasting; econometric models
        133 General outlook and stabilization theories and policies
        134 Inflation and deflation

TABLE 14.1 *(Continued)*

200   Quantitative Economic Methods and Data
    210   Econometric, Statistical, and Mathematical Methods and Models
        211   Econometric and statistical methods and models
        212   Construction, analysis, and use of econometric models
        213   Mathematical methods and models
        214   Computer programs
        215   Experimental economic methods
    220   Economic and Social Statistical Data and Analysis
        221   National income accounting
        222   Input-output
        223   Financial accounts
        224   National wealth and balance sheets
        225   Social indicators: data and analysis
        226   Productivity and growth: Theory and data
        227   Prices
        228   Regional statistics
        229   Microdata and database analysis

300   Domestic Monetary and Fiscal Theory and Institutions
    310   Domestic Monetary and Financial Theory and Institutions
        311   Domestic monetary and financial theory and policy
        312   Commercial banking
        313   Capital markets
        314   Financial intermediaries
        315   Credit to business, consumer, etc. (including mortgages)
    320   Fiscal Theory and Policy; Public Finance
        321   Fiscal theory and policy
        322   National government expenditures and budgeting
        323   National taxation, revenue, and subsidies
        324   State and local government finance
        325   Intergovernmental financial relationships

400   International Economics
    410   International Trade Theory
        411   International trade theory
    420   Trade Relations; Commercial Policy; International Economic Integration
        421   Trade relations
        422   Commercial policy
        423   Economic integration
430   International Finance
        431   Open economy macroeconomics; exchange rates
        432   International monetary arrangements
        433   Private international lending
440   International Investment and Foreign Aid
        441   International investment and long-term capital movements
        442   International business
        443   International lending and aid (public)

(continued)

TABLE 14.1 *(Continued)*

500 Administration; Business Finance; Marketing; Accounting
    510 Administration
        511 Organization and decision theory
        512 Managerial economics
        513 Business and public administration
        514 Goals and objectives of firms
    520 Business Finance and Investment
        521 Business finance
        522 Business investment
    530 Marketing
        531 Marketing and advertising
    540 Accounting
        541 Accounting

600 Industrial Organization; Technological Change; Industry Studies
    610 Industrial Organization and Public Policy
        611 Market structure: industrial organization and corporate strategy
        612 Public policy toward monopoly and competition
        613 Regulation of public utilities
        614 Public enterprises
        615 Economics of transportation
        616 Industrial policy
        619 Economics of regulation
    620 Economics of Technological Change
        621 Technological change; innovation; research and development
    630 Industry Studies
        631 Industry studies: manufacturing
        632 Industry studies: extractive industries
        633 Industry studies: distributive trades
        634 Industry studies: construction
        635 Industry studies: services and related industries
        636 Nonprofit industries: theory and studies
    640 Economic Capacity
        641 Economic capacity

700 Agriculture; Natural Resources
    710 Agriculture
        711 Agricultural supply and demand analysis
        712 Agricultural situation and outlook
        713 Agricultural policy, domestic and international
        714 Agricultural finance
        715 Agricultural markets and marketing
        716 Farm management
        717 Land reform and land use
        718 Rural economics
    720 Natural Resources
        721 Natural resources
        722 Conservation and pollution
        723 Energy

TABLE 14.1 *(Continued)*

730 Economic Geography
    731 Economic geography

800 Manpower; Labor; Population
    810 Manpower Training and Allocation; Labor Force and Supply
        811 Manpower training and development
        812 Occupation
        813 Labor force
    820 Labor Markets; Public Policy
        821 Labor economics
        822 Public policy; role of government
        823 Labor mobility; national and international migration
        824 Labor market studies; wages, employment
        825 Productivity studies: labor, capital, and total factor
        826 Labor markets: demographic characteristics
    830 Trade Unions; Collective Bargaining; Labor-Management Relations
        831 Trade unions
        832 Collective bargaining
        833 Labor-management relations
    840 Demographic Economics
        841 Demographic economics
    850 Human Capital; Value of Human Life
        851 Human capital; value of human life

900 Welfare Programs; Consumer Economics; Urban and Regional Economics
    910 Welfare, Health, and Education
        911 General welfare programs
        912 Economics of education
        913 Economics of health (including medical subsidy programs)
        914 Economics of poverty
        915 Social security
        916 Economics of law and crime
        917 Economics of minorities; economics of discrimination
        918 Economics of aging
    920 Consumer Economics
        921 Consumer economics; levels and standards of living
    930 Urban Economics
        931 Urban economics and public policy
        932 Housing economics
        933 Urban transportation economics
    940 Regional Economics
        941 Regional economics

Source: Journal of Economic Literature, September 1987. Reprinted with the permission of the American Economic Association.

TABLE 14.2 A Selected List of Periodicals

American Journal of Agricultural Economics	*Journal of Economics and Business*
American Journal of Economics and Sociology	*Journal of Finance*
Annals of Regional Science	*Journal of Financial and Quantitative Analysis*
Antitrust Bulletin	*Journal of Financial Economics*
Applied Economics	*Journal of Financial Research*
Australian Economic Review	*Journal of Health Economics*
Brookings Papers on Economic Activity	*Journal of Human Resources*
Cambridge Journal of Economics	*Journal of Industrial Economics*
Canadian Journal of Agricultural Economics	*Journal of International Economics*
Canadian Journal of Economics	*Journal of Law and Economics*
Eastern Economic Journal	*Journal of Macroeconomics*
Economica	*Journal of Monetary Economics*
Economic Analysis and Worker's Management	*Journal of Money, Credit, and Banking*
Economic Enquiry	*Journal of Political Economy*
Economic Journal	*Journal of Public Economics*
Economic Modeling	*Journal of Quantitative Economics*
Economic Record	*Journal of Regional Science*
Economics of Education Review	*Journal of Urban Economics*
Economic Studies Quarterly	*Managerial and Decision Economics*
Empirical Economics	*Manchester School of Economics and Social Studies*
Energy Economics	*Marine Resource Economics*
European Economic Review	*Monthly Labor Review*
Federal Reserve Bank Reviews	*National Tax Journal*
Federal Reserve Bulletin	*Natural Resources Journal*
Financial Review	*Oxford Bulletin of Economics and Statistics*
Indian Economic Journal	*Quarterly Journal of Business and Economics*
Indian Economic Review	*Quarterly Journal of Economics*
Industrial Relations	*Quarterly Review of Economics and Business*
International Labor Review	*Rand Journal of Economics*
Journal of Agricultural Economics	*Regional Science and Urban Economics*
Journal of Applied Econometrics	*Review of Income and Wealth*
Journal of Business	*Review of Social Economy*
Journal of Business and Economic Statistics	*Social Science Quarterly*
Journal of Consumer Research	*Southern Economic Journal*
Journal of Economic Issues	*Survey of Current Business*

14.2   Review of Literature

The next step after choosing a topic and formulating a research question is to find out what other researchers have done on that topic. This bibliographic search is crucial because you will not only learn how models have been formulated and estmated, but also what the data sources are. The starting point for the literature review is, again, the *Journal of Economic Literature*. In the process of selecting a topic, you will have compiled a list of relevant papers and/or books on the subject. First read each of these quickly to see if it is worth devoting more time to. In particular, note the bibliography items for other papers on the same topic. Another useful reference source is the *Social Science Citation Index*. This periodical provides a list (typically by authors' names) of journals, books, and so on that have cited a particular research work. If a selected reference item looks interesting, read it carefully and take notes. In particular, identify the dependent and independent variables, the types of models formulated, the techniques of estimation and tests of hypotheses used, and the data sources and measures. Next prepare a three- to five-page summary of each article or book chapter that relates to your research question. It is recommended that at least four such summaries be prepared.

14.3   Formulating a General Model

Based on the literature review you should construct a general formulation of your own model. This might require an optimizing framework such as utility maximization, profit maximization, or cost minimization. The initial model will be stated in broad terms, and will identify the dependent and independent variables for which you would like to get data. You should also decide at this stage whether a simultaneous equation model is called for. If your variables have feedback effects (that is, X affects Y and Y affects X), your model should be a simultaneous equation model, unless you are interested only in the reduced form described in Chapter 13. Whether cross-section or time series data are appropriate for your stated objectives should also be decided at this stage. If your goal is to explain what makes the values of the dependent variable change over time, then the relevant data will be time series. If, on the other hand, you wish to investigate why different groups (such as different countries, states, counties, firms, industries, employment groups) behave differently at a given point in time, then cross-section data are called for. The relationships estimated with cross-section data might not be stable over time. To examine this issue you need pooled data. Prepare a write-up explaining why you believe the independent variables you have chosen are likely to affect the dependent variable(s). Describe the hypotheses you plan to test and the expected nature of the effect of independent variables. In particular, discuss the expected signs of regression coefficients, whether nonlinearity might be present, what kinds of interactions among independent variables you should look for, and so on.

14.4 Collecting the Data

Now come the long, and often tedious, tasks of gathering the data, organizing them in a form that computers can process, and finally entering them on a computer for future analysis. How much data should one obtain, and what are the sources from which data can be gathered? We have seen that the higher the degrees of freedom, the better the precision of an estimate and the greater the power of tests of hypotheses. Increasing the degrees of freedom means having more observations relative to the number of independent variables. In the wage determination application of Section 7.3, the number of independent variables was quite large (see Table 7.4) because of the numerous interaction terms. We saw in Chapters 9 and 10 that if a time series model has many lag terms and/or higher order serial correlation, we lose several initial observations. To compensate for this we need more observations. Finally, the Lagrange multiplier test and tests for heteroscedasticity are large-sample tests that suggest the need for more observations. A rule of thumb is to have at least 30 degrees of freedom.

Data Sources

Where does one look for data sources? If your study refers to a problem about the local economy, a visit to the government or private agency that obtains relevant data might be fruitful. Many professional investigators (such as a utility forecaster or an economist working for the Federal Reserve) may have ready-made data from their own institution. In this computer age many data series are already available in machine-readable form. Some libraries provide selected data series in microfiche form. Numerous government as well as private agencies sell data tapes or floppy disks with data. In addition, more and more academic institutions are compiling **online databases** that can readily be accessed by anyone with a computer account and either a terminal or a microcomputer. Microcomputers are capable of **downloading** and **uploading** data. Downloading is the process of accessing a **mainframe computer** (a centrally located machine available to many users simultaneously through remote terminals) and transferring data (or text) to a microcomputer. Uploading is the reverse, the process of transferring text and data from the microcomputer to the mainframe computer.

A variety of statistical abstracts provides valuable information in printed form. The *Economic Report of the President* is a useful source of aggregate annual time series data for the United States as a whole. Similar economic reports are available from the office of the governor in most states. These contain countywide data also. The *U.S. Statistical Abstract* is rich in data for the United States as a whole as well as in data across states and SMSAs (Standard Metropolitan Statistical Areas). Individual states also have their own statistical abstracts. Yearbooks such as the *United Nations Yearbook* and the *Demographic Yearbook* are also useful data sources. The Bureau of the Census provides considerably detailed data based on the decennial census. Other censuses, such as the *Census of Manufacturing* and the

Census of Population and Housing, provide data more frequently. Monthly and/or quarterly data on a variety of economic and business indicators can be obtained from the *Survey of Current Business* or from publications from Dun and Bradstreet. A number of the data series are available by industries classified by **SIC codes** (*Standard Industrial Classification codes*). The *Federal Reserve Bulletin* is a valuable source for financial statistics, as are the Standard and Poors and Moody's ratings of securities and other financial information. Information relating to agriculture is available from *Agricultural Statistics*. For statistics on education, a variety of sources is available: *Digest of Education Statistics, Financial Statistics of Institutions of Higher Education, Admissions Testing Program Summary Reports*, publications by the National Center for Education Statistics, and so on.

Although these data sources can provide a researcher with a starting point, the amount of published data is so voluminous that it is impossible to list them all here. Fortunately, however, compendia are available that, like the *Journal of Economic Literature*, provide a classified listing of data sources. The most valuable of these is the *Statistical Reference Index* compiled by the Congressional Information Service. As its cover page indicates, it is a "selective guide to American statistical publications from private organizations and state government sources." There are three parts to this index: (1) an index volume that lists the publications, with minimal detail about the exact data series; (2) an abstracts volume, which provides considerable information about each of the data series; and (3) microfiche containing selected recent data.

Work Sheets

If the data you seek are available in printed form rather than in machine-readable form, you have the task of copying them down and then making them machine-readable. This is accomplished through **work sheets**. The work sheet might be prepared so that the data are arranged by observations (as in Table 6.1, for example) or by variables (as in Table 6.9). The choice is largely a matter of convenience and the way the published data are arranged. For each series be sure to note the exact data source (with page and table numbers, name and year of publication, the agency that publishes the data, and so on). This is important because you may wish to go back later to verify entries or look for additional data. It is also crucial that the units of measurement be noted. As we have seen, interpreting the numerical values of regression coefficients depends critically on the units in which the variables are measured. Finally, check whether there have been any changes in the definitions of variables or in the base periods for price and other indices. If there were changes, you may have to adjust the data accordingly.

Because computers can do all the arithmetic calculations, there is no need for you to convert data manually to suit your model. For instance, if your model calls for per capita real income, gather information about nominal income, a price index, and population. Then let the computer perform the appropriate transformation to obtain per capita real income.

Entering the Data on a Computer

Next comes the task of entering the data into a computer for access by a regression program. How they are entered depends very much on the regression package you plan to use to analyze them. In order to do this you need a **text editor**, which is basically a word processing program. You may also use a **spread sheet** program (such as Lotus 1-2-3) to enter the data. Most regression programs expect the data to be in **ASCII** form. ASCII stands for the *American Standard Code for Information Interchange* and is a widely used standard for entering data and text. If your word processing program does not store the data in ASCII form, it is likely to give you the option of preparing an ASCII version of the data. Be sure to choose this option if your regression program will not accept non-ASCII files. Many regression programs have their own built-in editors. Before you actually attempt to enter the data on the computer, study the data input requirements of the regression program you plan to use.

Generating New Variables

In carrying out empirical analyses, an analyst often works with transformed variables rather than with the original variables for which the data were assembled. We have seen many examples of this. Double-log models require that all the variables be transformed into logarithms. Quadratic and interaction terms require the multiplication of variables. To convert variables to real terms, the nominal variables need to be divided by a price index. To calculate percentage change, the transformation $100(X_t - X_{t-1})/X_{t-1}$ is required. To calculate the "instantaneous rate of change," use the transformation $\ln(X_t) - \ln(X_{t-1})$—that is, the difference in the logarithm between two successive observations. Regression packages have the capability of transforming data internally. Take advantage of this capability.

Computers vary in the precision with which numerical calculations are made. Some programs and machines are more subject to round-off errors than others. It is generally a good practice to avoid using large values in the actual analysis. The sum of squares associated with such large values may be astronomically large, causing bad round-off errors. For instance, rather than enter population as 2,157,899, convert it to ten-thousandths, and enter it as 215.7899. It is also generally a good practice to scale variables so that the entered values are in the range 1 to 1000.

14.5 Empirical Analysis

Analysis is obviously the most important stage of an empirical study. It consists of first putting the data through some preliminary checking, then estimating the models formulated initially, performing appropriate tests, and, if necessary, reformulating them and reestimating them.

Preliminary Data Analysis

Before actually using the data to estimate models it is important that the data be subjected to some preliminary analysis in order to catch typing errors, **outliers** (which are extreme values), and lack of variation in the data. Some common typing mistakes are: using an "el" instead of a "one" (possibly an old habit from using typewriters that did not have a separate key for unity) and using an "oh" for a "zero." A raw listing of the data is very useful in spotting obvious mistakes.

The next step is to plot each series against the observation number. In other words, plot X_t against t for each series. Outliers are easier to identify with this plot. If t stands for time, the graph will be a time series plot and will give you an idea of the time path of the variable and the underlying growth rate. A common temptation is to graph the values of the dependent variable against values of each independent variable in order to see whether some nonlinearity can be identified. Although such graphs might be useful in some cases, they can also be misleading. The graph between observed Y and observed X *does not hold other variables constant.* Thus, what appears to be a nonlinear relation between Y and X might really be a series of linear relationships that are being shifted by the movement of a third variable Z. Such "data mining" to identify relationships should be avoided. Instead, use theory about behavior to formulate models and perform appropriate tests for model specification, including nonlinearity.

In addition to a plot of the data to identify outliers, it is useful to obtain summary statistics such as the mean, standard deviation, and the coefficient of variation, which is the ratio of the standard deviation to the mean. Although there is no hard and fast rule about the coefficient of variation, a low value such as 0.05 indicates that the standard deviation is only about 5 percent of the mean. This means that the variable in question does not vary much and might not exhibit any significance if used as an independent variable in a regression (refer to the discussion in Chapter 3 on Assumption 3.3).

Finally, obtain the matrix of correlation coefficients—that is, the correlation coefficients for every pair of variables used in the analysis. A high correlation between the dependent variable and a given independent variable is clearly desirable. A high correlation between two independent variables might cause multicollinearity problems and is worth noting ahead of time. Be cautioned, however, that a low correlation between two independent variables does not mean that multicollinearity need not arise. This point was discussed in detail in Chapter 5.

Model Estimation and Hypothesis Testing

We are now ready to estimate the general model formulated in Section 14.3. Estimate the model and examine the F-statistic and $\bar{R}^2$. What percent of the variation in the dependent variable does the model capture? The first model estimated often has disappointing results. Signs of some of the regression coefficients might be contrary to prior expectations, t-statistics might indicate insignificance of variables, adjusted $\bar{R}^2$ might be low, serial correlation might be present if time series data are used, and so on. Here again there is no general formula as to how to proceed. A considerable amount of judgment is required at each stage, and researchers differ a great deal on the approaches.

Certain general guidelines are, nevertheless, useful. A fundamental lesson is to avoid hasty conclusions without subjecting the model to more analysis. The approach that is recommended is to formulate models based on some theoretical framework and an understanding of the underlying behavior, and then perform a battery of diagnostic tests to assure yourself that the conclusions are robust—that is, that they are not too sensitive to model specification. We have seen throughout that the Wald and Lagrange multiplier tests are extremely useful in testing for the inclusion of omitted variables, nonlinearities, interactions, the presence of lagged dependent variables, serial correlation of higher orders, and whether new variables should be added to the specification. When several similar models are formulated, the model selection criteria can be used to judge the superiority of one model over another. If a certain variable is insignificant under alternative formulations, you can safely conclude that perhaps it is redundant, and its omission might not result in serious misspecification.

Check the correlations among explanatory variables and see if high values can explain unexpected signs and/or insignificant coefficients. If serial correlation is found to be present with time series data, reformulate the model to see if serial correlation can be eliminated. If necessary, apply Cochrane–Orcutt and/or Hildreth–Lu methods. Similarly, if heteroscedasticity is found, the weighted least squares procedure described in Chapter 8 would be appropriate. For simultaneous equation models the two-stage least squares procedure should be adopted to avoid least squares bias and the inconsistency of estimates. The estimation and diagnostic testing of models often involves several stages of reestimation and retesting.

Writing a Report

The final stage of the study is to write a report describing the various steps and interpreting the results. First, prepare a brief title for the study that describes the nature of the question examined. In writing the report keep the style simple and straightforward. Sedulously eschew all polysyllabic profundities (in other words, don't use big words). A suggested outline for the final report is

1. Statement of the Problem
2. Review of Literature
3. Formulation of a General Model
4. Data Sources and Description
5. Model Estimation and Hypothesis Testing
6. Interpretation of the Results and Conclusions
7. Limitations of the Study and Possible Extensions
8. Acknowledgements
9. References

Statement of the Problem: In a paragraph to a page, describe the problem you have studied, the questions you asked, and the broad hypotheses you have tested. You can also give a brief indication of your conclusions.

Review of Literature: Assemble the literature review you conducted earlier and attach it here. As mentioned in Section 14.2, this section will contain a summary of each paper and book you read that relates to your study, with the models and methods used, the data sources, and the conclusions arrived at by the author(s).

Formulation of a General Model: Describe here the initial model you formulated in Section 14.3. Point out the differences between your approach and those of others who have studied similar problems.

Data Sources and Description: Present a table of variable names and their definitions. Be sure to specify the units of measurement. List the data sources and attach a copy of the raw data. Include in the table the transformations that generated the variables actually used in estimation (see Table 9.7 for an example).

Model Estimation and Hypothesis Testing: Present the regression results in one or more tables similar to Table 4.2. Although many authors present standard errors in parentheses below regression coefficients, it is recommended that the *t*-statistics be presented instead, with possible asterisks to identify significant coefficients. Also present useful summary statistics such as adjusted R^2, the Durbin–Watson statistic, model selection criteria, the F-statistic, degrees of freedom, and so on. In the text, describe the models you estimated, the various tests you carried out, and the results. The extent to which the actual econometric analysis should be described depends very much on the audience. If you are submitting a term paper to an instructor, it might be important to be informative about every stage of the analysis. If the audience is not likely to be very technically oriented, it is desirable to move such technical details to appendices.

Interpretation of the Results and Conclusions: State what you observe in terms of the original hypotheses and expectations. If you found unexpected results, present some rationalization for them. The interpretation of results sections in the applications, Sections 4.9, 7.3, and 9.8, are useful guides here. Provide some concluding remarks regarding your study and put it in perspective with other studies.

Limitations of the Study and Possible Extensions: It is important to recognize your study's limitations. Such limitations might be due to a lack of available data or of computer programs for a specific method you deem appropriate, or to other reasons. Suggest where one can go from here and what possible extensions would be interesting.

Acknowledgements: During the course of conducting the empirical study, you might have received the help of a number of persons: professors, teaching assistants, personnel in the library who helped you with the bibliography, people who helped you obtain the data, and so on. It is common courtesy to acknowledge their help.

References: Attach an alphabetical list of the references you compiled earlier in preparing for the analysis. The list should include the bibliography for the literature review as well as the references for your data sources. Avoid numbering the bibliography items and using corresponding numerical references in the text because if you add a bibliographical citation later, you will have to renumber the references and make numerous text changes. If you list the bibliography alphabetically and make text references to it by authors' names and perhaps year of publication, you will need to make only minor, if any, alterations to handle subsequent changes. The format used in this book is a useful one.

■ ■

KEY TERMS

ASCII
Downloading
Mainframe computer
On-line database
Outliers

SIC code
Spread sheet
Text editor
Uploading
Work sheet

APPENDIX A

Statistical Tables

TABLE A.1   Areas Under the Standard Normal Curve from 0 to z

z	0.00	0.01	0.02	0.03	0.04	0.05	0.06	0.07	0.08	0.09
0.0	0.0000	0.0040	0.0080	0.0120	0.0160	0.0199	0.0239	0.0279	0.0319	0.0359
0.1	0.0398	0.0438	0.0478	0.0517	0.0557	0.0596	0.0636	0.0675	0.0714	0.0753
0.2	0.0793	0.0832	0.0871	0.0910	0.0948	0.0987	0.1026	0.1064	0.1103	0.1141
0.3	0.1179	0.1217	0.1255	0.1293	0.1331	0.1368	0.1406	0.1443	0.1480	0.1517
0.4	0.1554	0.1591	0.1628	0.1664	0.1700	0.1736	0.1772	0.1808	0.1844	0.1879
0.5	0.1915	0.1950	0.1985	0.2019	0.2054	0.2088	0.2123	0.2157	0.2190	0.2224
0.6	0.2257	0.2291	0.2324	0.2357	0.2389	0.2422	0.2454	0.2486	0.2518	0.2549
0.7	0.2580	0.2612	0.2642	0.2673	0.2704	0.2734	0.2764	0.2794	0.2823	0.2852
0.8	0.2881	0.2910	0.2939	0.2967	0.2995	0.3023	0.3051	0.3078	0.3106	0.3133
0.9	0.3159	0.3186	0.3212	0.3238	0.3264	0.3289	0.3315	0.3340	0.3365	0.3389
1.0	0.3413	0.3438	0.3461	0.3485	0.3508	0.3531	0.3554	0.3577	0.3599	0.3621
1.1	0.3643	0.3665	0.3686	0.3708	0.3729	0.3749	0.3770	0.3790	0.3810	0.3830
1.2	0.3849	0.3869	0.3888	0.3907	0.3925	0.3944	0.3962	0.3980	0.3997	0.4015
1.3	0.4032	0.4049	0.4066	0.4082	0.4099	0.4115	0.4131	0.4147	0.4162	0.4177
1.4	0.4192	0.4207	0.4222	0.4236	0.4251	0.4265	0.4279	0.4292	0.4306	0.4319
1.5	0.4332	0.4345	0.4357	0.4370	0.4382	0.4394	0.4406	0.4418	0.4429	0.4441
1.6	0.4452	0.4463	0.4474	0.4484	0.4495	0.4505	0.4515	0.4525	0.4535	0.4545
1.7	0.4554	0.4564	0.4573	0.4582	0.4591	0.4599	0.4608	0.4616	0.4625	0.4633
1.8	0.4641	0.4649	0.4656	0.4664	0.4671	0.4678	0.4686	0.4693	0.4699	0.4706
1.9	0.4713	0.4719	0.4726	0.4732	0.4738	0.4744	0.4750	0.4756	0.4761	0.4767
2.0	0.4772	0.4778	0.4783	0.4788	0.4793	0.4798	0.4803	0.4808	0.4812	0.4817
2.1	0.4821	0.4826	0.4830	0.4834	0.4838	0.4842	0.4846	0.4850	0.4854	0.4857
2.2	0.4861	0.4864	0.4868	0.4871	0.4875	0.4878	0.4881	0.4884	0.4887	0.4890
2.3	0.4893	0.4896	0.4898	0.4901	0.4904	0.4906	0.4909	0.4911	0.4913	0.4916
2.4	0.4918	0.4920	0.4922	0.4925	0.4927	0.4929	0.4931	0.4932	0.4934	0.4936
2.5	0.4938	0.4940	0.4941	0.4943	0.4945	0.4946	0.4948	0.4949	0.4951	0.4952
2.6	0.4953	0.4955	0.4956	0.4957	0.4959	0.4960	0.4961	0.4962	0.4963	0.4964
2.7	0.4965	0.4966	0.4967	0.4968	0.4969	0.4970	0.4971	0.4972	0.4973	0.4974
2.8	0.4974	0.4975	0.4976	0.4977	0.4977	0.4978	0.4979	0.4979	0.4980	0.4981
2.9	0.4981	0.4982	0.4982	0.4983	0.4984	0.4984	0.4985	0.4985	0.4986	0.4986
3.0	0.49865	0.4987	0.4987	0.4988	0.4988	0.4989	0.4989	0.4989	0.4990	0.4990
4.0	0.49997									

If z = 0.93, p(0 ≤ Z ≤ z) = 0.3238.

Source: *Statistical Analysis for Decision Making*, Morris Hamburg, 4th edition, 1987. Reprinted with the permission of Harcourt Brace Jovanovich, Inc.

TABLE A.2   Percentage Points of the *t*-Distribution

d.f.	1 T = 0.4 2 T = 0.8	0.25 0.5	0.1 0.2	0.05 0.1	0.025 0.05	0.01 0.02	0.005 0.01	0.0025 0.005	0.001 0.002	0.0005 0.001
1	0.325	1.000	3.078	6.314	12.706	31.821	63.657	127.32	318.31	636.62
2	.289	0.816	1.886	2.920	4.303	6.965	9.925	14.089	22.327	31.598
3	.277	.765	1.638	2.353	3.182	4.541	5.841	7.453	10.214	12.924
4	.271	.741	1.533	2.132	2.776	3.747	4.604	5.598	7.173	8.610
5	0.267	0.727	1.476	2.015	2.571	3.365	4.032	4.773	5.893	6.869
6	.265	.718	1.440	1.943	2.447	3.143	3.707	4.317	5.208	5.959
7	.263	.711	1.415	1.895	2.365	2.998	3.499	4.029	4.785	5.408
8	.262	.706	1.397	1.860	2.306	2.896	3.355	3.833	4.501	5.041
9	.261	.703	1.383	1.833	2.262	2.821	3.250	3.690	4.297	4.781
10	0.260	0.700	1.372	1.812	2.228	2.764	3.169	3.581	4.144	4.587
11	.260	.697	1.363	1.796	2.201	2.718	3.106	3.497	4.025	4.437
12	.259	.695	1.356	1.782	2.179	2.681	3.055	3.428	3.930	4.318
13	.259	.694	1.350	1.771	2.160	2.650	3.012	3.372	3.852	4.221
14	.258	.692	1.345	1.761	2.145	2.624	2.977	3.326	3.787	4.140
15	0.258	0.691	1.341	1.753	2.131	2.602	2.947	3.286	3.733	4.073
16	.258	.690	1.337	1.746	2.120	2.583	2.921	3.252	3.686	4.015
17	.257	.689	1.333	1.740	2.110	2.567	2.898	3.222	3.646	3.965
18	.257	.688	1.330	1.734	2.101	2.552	2.878	3.197	3.610	3.922
19	.257	.688	1.328	1.729	2.093	2.539	2.861	3.174	3.579	3.883
20	0.257	0.687	1.325	1.725	2.086	2.528	2.845	3.153	3.552	3.850
21	.257	.686	1.323	1.721	2.080	2.518	2.831	3.135	3.527	3.819
22	.256	.686	1.321	1.717	2.074	2.508	2.819	3.119	3.505	3.792
23	.256	.685	1.319	1.714	2.069	2.500	2.807	3.104	3.485	3.767
24	.256	.685	1.318	1.711	2.064	2.492	2.797	3.091	3.467	3.745
25	0.256	0.684	1.316	1.708	2.060	2.485	2.787	3.078	3.450	3.725
26	.256	.684	1.315	1.706	2.056	2.479	2.779	3.067	3.435	3.707
27	.256	.684	1.314	1.703	2.052	2.473	2.771	3.057	3.421	3.690
28	.256	.683	1.313	1.701	2.048	2.467	2.763	3.047	3.408	3.674
29	.256	.683	1.311	1.699	2.045	2.462	2.756	3.038	3.396	3.659
30	0.256	0.683	1.310	1.697	2.042	2.457	2.750	3.030	3.385	3.646
40	.255	.681	1.303	1.684	2.021	2.423	2.704	2.971	3.307	3.551
60	.254	.679	1.296	1.671	2.000	2.390	2.660	2.915	3.232	3.460
120	.254	.677	1.289	1.658	1.980	2.358	2.617	2.860	3.160	3.373
∞	.253	.674	1.282	1.645	1.960	2.326	2.576	2.807	3.090	3.291

1 T = area under one tail; 2 T = area under both tails.
For 25 degrees of freedom (d.f.), $P(t > 2.060) = 0.025$ *and* $P(t < -2.060$ *or* $t > 2.060) = 0.05$.
Source: Biometrika Tables for Statisticians, Vol. I. Edited by E. S. Pearson and H. O. Hartley, 3rd edition, 1966. Reprinted with the permission of the Biometrika Trustees.

TABLE A.3 Upper Percent Points of the Chi-Square Distribution (v is the Degrees of Freedom and Q is the Area in the Right Tail)

Q v	0.250	0.100	0.050	0.025	0.010	0.005	0.001
1	1.32330	2.70554	3.84146	5.02389	6.63490	7.87944	10.828
2	2.77259	4.60517	5.99146	7.37776	9.21034	10.5966	13.816
3	4.10834	6.25139	7.81473	9.34840	11.3449	12.8382	16.266
4	5.38527	7.77944	9.48773	11.1433	13.2767	14.8603	18.467
5	6.62568	9.23636	11.0705	12.8325	15.0863	16.7496	20.515
6	7.84080	10.6446	12.5916	14.4494	16.8119	18.5476	22.458
7	9.03715	12.0170	14.0671	16.0128	18.4753	20.2777	24.322
8	10.2189	13.3616	15.5073	17.5345	20.0902	21.9550	26.125
9	11.3888	14.6837	16.9190	19.0228	21.6660	23.5894	27.877
10	12.5489	15.9872	18.3070	20.4832	23.2093	25.1882	29.588
11	13.7007	17.2750	19.6751	21.9200	24.7250	26.7568	31.264
12	14.8454	18.5493	21.0261	23.3367	26.2170	28.2995	32.909
13	15.9839	19.8119	22.3620	24.7356	27.6882	29.8195	34.528
14	17.1169	21.0641	23.6848	26.1189	29.1412	31.3194	36.123
15	18.2451	22.3071	24.9958	27.4884	30.5779	32.8013	37.697
16	19.3689	23.5418	26.2962	28.8454	31.9999	34.2672	39.252
17	20.4887	24.7690	27.5871	30.1910	33.4087	35.7185	40.790
18	21.6049	25.9894	28.8693	31.5264	34.8053	37.1565	42.312
19	22.7178	27.2036	30.1435	32.8523	36.1909	38.5823	43.820
20	23.8277	28.4120	31.4104	34.1696	37.5662	39.9968	45.315
21	24.9348	29.6151	32.6706	35.4789	38.9322	41.4011	46.797
22	26.0393	30.8133	33.9244	36.7807	40.2894	42.7957	48.268
23	27.1413	32.0069	35.1725	38.0756	41.6384	44.1813	49.728
24	28.2412	33.1962	36.4150	39.3641	42.9798	45.5585	51.179
25	29.3389	34.3816	37.6525	40.6465	44.3141	46.9279	52.618
26	30.4346	35.5632	38.8851	41.9232	45.6417	48.2899	54.052
27	31.5284	36.7412	40.1133	43.1945	46.9629	49.6449	55.476
28	32.6205	37.9159	41.3371	44.4608	48.2782	50.9934	56.892
29	33.7109	39.0875	42.5570	45.7223	49.5879	52.3356	58.301
30	34.7997	40.2560	43.7730	46.9792	50.8922	53.6720	59.703
40	45.6160	51.8051	55.7585	59.3417	63.6907	66.7660	73.402
50	56.3336	63.1671	67.5048	71.4202	76.1539	79.4900	86.661
60	66.9815	74.3970	79.0819	83.2977	88.3794	91.9517	99.607
70	77.5767	85.5270	90.5312	95.0232	100.425	104.215	112.317
80	88.1303	96.5782	101.879	106.629	112.329	116.321	124.839
90	98.6499	107.565	113.145	118.136	124.116	128.299	137.208
100	109.141	118.498	124.342.	129.561	135.807	140.169	149.449
X	+0.6745	+1.2816	+1.6449	+1.9600	+2.3263	+2.5758	+3.0902

For 25 d.f., $P(\chi^2 > 37.6525) = 0.05$.
For $v > 100$ take

$$\chi^2 = v\left\{1 - \frac{2}{9v} + X\sqrt{\frac{2}{9v}}\right\}^3 \quad \text{or} \quad \chi^2 = \tfrac{1}{2}\{X + \sqrt{(2v-1)}\}^2,$$

according to the degree of accuracy required. X is the standardized normal deviate corresponding to $P = 1 - Q$ and is shown in the bottom line of the table.

Source: Biometrika Tables for Statisticians, Vol. I. Edited by E. S. Pearson and H. O. Hartley, 3rd edition, 1966. Reprinted with the permission of the Biometrika Trustees.

TABLE A.4a Upper 1% Points of the F-Distribution

n \ m	1	2	3	4	5	6	7	8	9	10	12	15	20	24	30	40	60	120	∞
1	4052	4999.5	5403	5625	5764	5859	5928	5981	6022	6056	6106	6157	6209	6235	6261	6287	6313	6339	6366
2	98.50	99.00	99.17	99.25	99.30	99.33	99.36	99.37	99.39	99.40	99.42	99.43	99.45	99.46	99.47	99.47	99.48	99.49	99.50
3	34.12	30.82	29.46	28.71	28.24	27.91	27.67	27.49	27.35	27.23	27.05	26.87	26.69	26.60	26.50	26.41	26.32	26.22	26.13
4	21.20	18.00	16.69	15.98	15.52	15.21	14.98	14.80	14.66	14.55	14.37	14.20	14.02	13.93	13.84	13.75	13.65	13.56	13.46
5	16.26	13.27	12.06	11.39	10.97	10.67	10.46	10.29	10.16	10.05	9.89	9.72	9.55	9.47	9.38	9.29	9.20	9.11	9.02
6	13.75	10.92	9.78	9.15	8.75	8.47	8.26	8.10	7.98	7.87	7.72	7.56	7.40	7.31	7.23	7.14	7.06	6.97	6.88
7	12.25	9.55	8.45	7.85	7.46	7.19	6.99	6.84	6.72	6.62	6.47	6.31	6.16	6.07	5.99	5.91	5.82	5.74	5.65
8	11.26	8.65	7.59	7.01	6.63	6.37	6.18	6.03	5.91	5.81	5.67	5.52	5.36	5.28	5.20	5.12	5.03	4.95	4.86
9	10.56	8.02	6.99	6.42	6.06	5.80	5.61	5.47	5.35	5.26	5.11	4.96	4.81	4.73	4.65	4.57	4.48	4.40	4.31
10	10.04	7.56	6.55	5.99	5.64	5.39	5.20	5.06	4.94	4.85	4.71	4.56	4.41	4.33	4.25	4.17	4.08	4.00	3.91
11	9.65	7.21	6.22	5.67	5.32	5.07	4.89	4.74	4.63	4.54	4.40	4.25	4.10	4.02	3.94	3.86	3.78	3.69	3.60
12	9.33	6.93	5.95	5.41	5.06	4.82	4.64	4.50	4.39	4.30	4.16	4.01	3.86	3.78	3.70	3.62	3.54	3.45	3.36
13	9.07	6.70	5.74	5.21	4.86	4.62	4.44	4.30	4.19	4.10	3.96	3.82	3.66	3.59	3.51	3.43	3.34	3.25	3.17
14	8.86	6.51	5.56	5.04	4.69	4.46	4.28	4.14	4.03	3.94	3.80	3.66	3.51	3.43	3.35	3.27	3.18	3.09	3.00
15	8.68	6.36	5.42	4.89	4.56	4.32	4.14	4.00	3.89	3.80	3.67	3.52	3.37	3.29	3.21	3.13	3.05	2.96	2.87
16	8.53	6.23	5.29	4.77	4.44	4.20	4.03	3.89	3.78	3.69	3.55	3.41	3.26	3.18	3.10	3.02	2.93	2.84	2.75
17	8.40	6.11	5.18	4.67	4.34	4.10	3.93	3.79	3.68	3.59	3.46	3.31	3.16	3.08	3.00	2.92	2.83	2.75	2.65
18	8.29	6.01	5.09	4.58	4.25	4.01	3.84	3.71	3.60	3.51	3.37	3.23	3.08	3.00	2.92	2.84	2.75	2.66	2.57
19	8.18	5.93	5.01	4.50	4.17	3.94	3.77	3.63	3.52	3.43	3.30	3.15	3.00	2.92	2.84	2.76	2.67	2.58	2.49
20	8.10	5.85	4.94	4.43	4.10	3.87	3.70	3.56	3.46	3.37	3.23	3.09	2.94	2.86	2.78	2.69	2.61	2.52	2.42
21	8.02	5.78	4.87	4.37	4.04	3.81	3.64	3.51	3.40	3.31	3.17	3.03	2.88	2.80	2.72	2.64	2.55	2.46	2.36
22	7.95	5.72	4.82	4.31	3.99	3.76	3.59	3.45	3.35	3.26	3.12	2.98	2.83	2.75	2.67	2.58	2.50	2.40	2.31
23	7.88	5.66	4.76	4.26	3.94	3.71	3.54	3.41	3.30	3.21	3.07	2.93	2.78	2.70	2.62	2.54	2.45	2.35	2.26
24	7.82	5.61	4.72	4.22	3.90	3.67	3.50	3.36	3.26	3.17	3.03	2.89	2.74	2.66	2.58	2.49	2.40	2.31	2.21
25	7.77	5.57	4.68	4.18	3.85	3.63	3.46	3.32	3.22	3.13	2.99	2.85	2.70	2.62	2.54	2.45	2.36	2.27	2.17
26	7.72	5.53	4.64	4.14	3.82	3.59	3.42	3.29	3.18	3.09	2.96	2.81	2.66	2.58	2.50	2.42	2.33	2.23	2.13
27	7.68	5.49	4.60	4.11	3.78	3.56	3.39	3.26	3.15	3.06	2.93	2.78	2.63	2.55	2.47	2.38	2.29	2.20	2.10
28	7.64	5.45	4.57	4.07	3.75	3.53	3.36	3.23	3.12	3.03	2.90	2.75	2.60	2.52	2.44	2.35	2.26	2.17	2.06
29	7.60	5.42	4.54	4.04	3.73	3.50	3.33	3.20	3.09	3.00	2.87	2.73	2.57	2.49	2.41	2.33	2.23	2.14	2.03
30	7.56	5.39	4.51	4.02	3.70	3.47	3.30	3.17	3.07	2.98	2.84	2.70	2.55	2.47	2.39	2.30	2.21	2.11	2.01
40	7.31	5.18	4.31	3.83	3.51	3.29	3.12	2.99	2.89	2.80	2.66	2.52	2.37	2.29	2.20	2.11	2.02	1.92	1.80
60	7.08	4.98	4.13	3.65	3.34	3.12	2.95	2.82	2.72	2.63	2.50	2.35	2.20	2.12	2.03	1.94	1.84	1.73	1.60
120	6.85	4.79	3.95	3.48	3.17	2.96	2.79	2.66	2.56	2.47	2.34	2.19	2.03	1.95	1.86	1.76	1.66	1.53	1.38
∞	6.63	4.61	3.78	3.32	3.02	2.80	2.64	2.51	2.41	2.32	2.18	2.04	1.88	1.79	1.70	1.59	1.47	1.32	1.00

m = degrees of freedom for the numerator
n = degrees of freedom for the denominator

Source: *Handbook of Tables for Mathematics*, edited by Robert C. West and Samuel M. Selby, 1970. Reprinted with the permission of the CRC Press, Inc.

TABLE A.4b Upper 5% Points of the *F*-Distribution

n \ m	1	2	3	4	5	6	7	8	9	10	12	15	20	24	30	40	60	120	∞
1	161.4	199.5	215.7	224.6	230.2	234.0	236.8	238.9	240.5	241.9	243.9	245.9	248.0	249.1	250.1	251.1	252.2	253.3	254.3
2	18.51	19.00	19.16	19.25	19.30	19.33	19.35	19.37	19.38	19.40	19.41	19.43	19.45	19.45	19.46	19.47	19.48	19.49	19.50
3	10.13	9.55	9.28	9.12	9.01	8.94	8.89	8.85	8.81	8.79	8.74	8.70	8.66	8.64	8.62	8.59	8.57	8.55	8.53
4	7.71	6.94	6.59	6.39	6.26	6.16	6.09	6.04	6.00	5.96	5.91	5.86	5.80	5.77	5.75	5.72	5.69	5.66	5.63
5	6.61	5.79	5.41	5.19	5.05	4.95	4.88	4.82	4.77	4.74	4.68	4.62	4.56	4.53	4.50	4.46	4.43	4.40	4.36
6	5.99	5.14	4.76	4.53	4.39	4.28	4.21	4.15	4.10	4.06	4.00	3.94	3.87	3.84	3.81	3.77	3.74	3.70	3.67
7	5.59	4.74	4.35	4.12	3.97	3.87	3.79	3.73	3.68	3.64	3.57	3.51	3.44	3.41	3.38	3.34	3.30	3.27	3.23
8	5.32	4.46	4.07	3.84	3.69	3.58	3.50	3.44	3.39	3.35	3.28	3.22	3.15	3.12	3.08	3.04	3.01	2.97	2.93
9	5.12	4.26	3.86	3.63	3.48	3.37	3.29	3.23	3.18	3.14	3.07	3.01	2.94	2.90	2.86	2.83	2.79	2.75	2.71
10	4.96	4.10	3.71	3.48	3.33	3.22	3.14	3.07	3.02	2.98	2.91	2.85	2.77	2.74	2.70	2.66	2.62	2.58	2.54
11	4.84	3.98	3.59	3.36	3.20	3.09	3.01	2.95	2.90	2.85	2.79	2.72	2.65	2.61	2.57	2.53	2.49	2.45	2.40
12	4.75	3.89	3.49	3.26	3.11	3.00	2.91	2.85	2.80	2.75	2.69	2.62	2.54	2.51	2.47	2.43	2.38	2.34	2.30
13	4.67	3.81	3.41	3.18	3.03	2.92	2.83	2.77	2.71	2.67	2.60	2.53	2.46	2.42	2.38	2.34	2.30	2.25	2.21
14	4.60	3.74	3.34	3.11	2.96	2.85	2.76	2.70	2.65	2.60	2.53	2.46	2.39	2.35	2.31	2.27	2.22	2.18	2.13
15	4.54	3.68	3.29	3.06	2.90	2.79	2.71	2.64	2.59	2.54	2.48	2.40	2.33	2.29	2.25	2.20	2.16	2.11	2.07
16	4.49	3.63	3.24	3.01	2.85	2.74	2.66	2.59	2.54	2.49	2.42	2.35	2.28	2.24	2.19	2.15	2.11	2.06	2.01
17	4.45	3.59	3.20	2.96	2.81	2.70	2.61	2.55	2.49	2.45	2.38	2.31	2.23	2.19	2.15	2.10	2.06	2.01	1.96
18	4.41	3.55	3.16	2.93	2.77	2.66	2.58	2.51	2.46	2.41	2.34	2.27	2.19	2.15	2.11	2.06	2.02	1.97	1.92
19	4.38	3.52	3.13	2.90	2.74	2.63	2.54	2.48	2.42	2.38	2.31	2.23	2.16	2.11	2.07	2.03	1.98	1.93	1.88
20	4.35	3.49	3.10	2.87	2.71	2.60	2.51	2.45	2.39	2.35	2.28	2.20	2.12	2.08	2.04	1.99	1.95	1.90	1.84
21	4.32	3.47	3.07	2.84	2.68	2.57	2.49	2.42	2.37	2.32	2.25	2.18	2.10	2.05	2.01	1.96	1.92	1.87	1.81
22	4.30	3.44	3.05	2.82	2.66	2.55	2.46	2.40	2.34	2.30	2.23	2.15	2.07	2.03	1.98	1.94	1.89	1.84	1.78
23	4.28	3.42	3.03	2.80	2.64	2.53	2.44	2.37	2.32	2.27	2.20	2.13	2.05	2.01	1.96	1.91	1.86	1.81	1.76
24	4.26	3.40	3.01	2.78	2.62	2.51	2.42	2.36	2.30	2.25	2.18	2.11	2.03	1.98	1.94	1.89	1.84	1.79	1.73
25	4.24	3.39	2.99	2.76	2.60	2.49	2.40	2.34	2.28	2.24	2.16	2.09	2.01	1.96	1.92	1.87	1.82	1.77	1.71
26	4.23	3.37	2.98	2.74	2.59	2.47	2.39	2.32	2.27	2.22	2.15	2.07	1.99	1.95	1.90	1.85	1.80	1.75	1.69
27	4.21	3.35	2.96	2.73	2.57	2.46	2.37	2.31	2.25	2.20	2.13	2.06	1.97	1.93	1.88	1.84	1.79	1.73	1.67
28	4.20	3.34	2.95	2.71	2.56	2.45	2.36	2.29	2.24	2.19	2.12	2.04	1.96	1.91	1.87	1.82	1.77	1.71	1.65
29	4.18	3.33	2.93	2.70	2.55	2.43	2.35	2.28	2.22	2.18	2.10	2.03	1.94	1.90	1.85	1.81	1.75	1.70	1.64
30	4.17	3.32	2.92	2.69	2.53	2.42	2.33	2.27	2.21	2.16	2.09	2.01	1.93	1.89	1.84	1.79	1.74	1.68	1.62
40	4.08	3.23	2.84	2.61	2.45	2.34	2.25	2.18	2.12	2.08	2.00	1.92	1.84	1.79	1.74	1.69	1.64	1.58	1.51
60	4.00	3.15	2.76	2.53	2.37	2.25	2.17	2.10	2.04	1.99	1.92	1.84	1.75	1.70	1.65	1.59	1.53	1.47	1.39
120	3.92	3.07	2.68	2.45	2.29	2.17	2.09	2.02	1.96	1.91	1.83	1.75	1.66	1.61	1.55	1.50	1.43	1.35	1.25
∞	3.84	3.00	2.60	2.37	2.21	2.10	2.01	1.94	1.88	1.83	1.75	1.67	1.57	1.52	1.46	1.39	1.32	1.22	1.00

m = degrees of freedom for the numerator

n = degrees of freedom for the denominator

Source: *Handbook of Tables for Mathematics*, edited by Robert C. West and Samuel M. Selby, 1970. Reprinted with the permission of the CRC Press, Inc.

TABLE A.4c Upper 10% Points of the F-Distribution

n \ m	1	2	3	4	5	6	7	8	9	10	12	15	20	24	30	40	60	120	∞
1	39.86	49.50	53.59	55.83	57.24	58.20	58.91	59.44	59.86	60.19	60.71	61.22	61.74	62.00	62.26	62.53	62.79	63.06	63.33
2	8.53	9.00	9.16	9.24	9.29	9.33	9.35	9.37	9.38	9.39	9.41	9.42	9.44	9.45	9.46	9.47	9.47	9.48	9.49
3	5.54	5.46	5.39	5.34	5.31	5.28	5.27	5.25	5.24	5.23	5.22	5.20	5.18	5.18	5.17	5.16	5.15	5.14	5.13
4	4.54	4.32	4.19	4.11	4.05	4.01	3.98	3.95	3.94	3.92	3.90	3.87	3.84	3.83	3.82	3.80	3.79	3.78	3.76
5	4.06	3.78	3.62	3.52	3.45	3.40	3.37	3.34	3.32	3.30	3.27	3.24	3.21	3.19	3.17	3.16	3.14	3.12	3.10
6	3.78	3.46	3.29	3.18	3.11	3.05	3.01	2.98	2.96	2.94	2.90	2.87	2.84	2.82	2.80	2.78	2.76	2.74	2.72
7	3.59	3.26	3.07	2.96	2.88	2.83	2.78	2.75	2.72	2.70	2.67	2.63	2.59	2.58	2.56	2.54	2.51	2.49	2.47
8	3.46	3.11	2.92	2.81	2.73	2.67	2.62	2.59	2.56	2.54	2.50	2.46	2.42	2.40	2.38	2.36	2.34	2.32	2.29
9	3.36	3.01	2.81	2.69	2.61	2.55	2.51	2.47	2.44	2.42	2.38	2.34	2.30	2.28	2.25	2.23	2.21	2.18	2.16
10	3.29	2.92	2.73	2.61	2.52	2.46	2.41	2.38	2.35	2.32	2.28	2.24	2.20	2.18	2.16	2.13	2.11	2.08	2.06
11	3.23	2.86	2.66	2.54	2.45	2.39	2.34	2.30	2.27	2.25	2.21	2.17	2.12	2.10	2.08	2.05	2.03	2.00	1.97
12	3.18	2.81	2.61	2.48	2.39	2.33	2.28	2.24	2.21	2.19	2.15	2.10	2.06	2.04	2.01	1.99	1.96	1.93	1.90
13	3.14	2.76	2.56	2.43	2.35	2.28	2.23	2.20	2.16	2.14	2.10	2.05	2.01	1.98	1.96	1.93	1.90	1.88	1.85
14	3.10	2.73	2.52	2.39	2.31	2.24	2.19	2.15	2.12	2.10	2.05	2.01	1.96	1.94	1.91	1.89	1.86	1.83	1.80
15	3.07	2.70	2.49	2.36	2.27	2.21	2.16	2.12	2.09	2.06	2.02	1.97	1.92	1.90	1.87	1.85	1.82	1.79	1.76
16	3.05	2.67	2.46	2.33	2.24	2.18	2.13	2.09	2.06	2.03	1.99	1.94	1.89	1.87	1.84	1.81	1.78	1.75	1.72
17	3.03	2.64	2.44	2.31	2.22	2.15	2.10	2.06	2.03	2.00	1.96	1.91	1.86	1.84	1.81	1.78	1.75	1.72	1.69
18	3.01	2.62	2.42	2.29	2.20	2.13	2.08	2.04	2.00	1.98	1.93	1.89	1.84	1.81	1.78	1.75	1.72	1.69	1.66
19	2.99	2.61	2.40	2.27	2.18	2.11	2.06	2.02	1.98	1.96	1.91	1.86	1.81	1.79	1.76	1.73	1.70	1.67	1.63
20	2.97	2.59	2.38	2.25	2.16	2.09	2.04	2.00	1.96	1.94	1.89	1.84	1.79	1.77	1.74	1.71	1.68	1.64	1.61
21	2.96	2.57	2.36	2.23	2.14	2.08	2.02	1.98	1.95	1.92	1.87	1.83	1.78	1.75	1.72	1.69	1.66	1.62	1.59
22	2.95	2.56	2.35	2.22	2.13	2.06	2.01	1.97	1.93	1.90	1.86	1.81	1.76	1.73	1.70	1.67	1.64	1.60	1.57
23	2.94	2.55	2.34	2.21	2.11	2.05	1.99	1.95	1.92	1.89	1.84	1.80	1.74	1.72	1.69	1.66	1.62	1.59	1.55
24	2.93	2.54	2.33	2.19	2.10	2.04	1.98	1.94	1.91	1.88	1.83	1.78	1.73	1.70	1.67	1.64	1.61	1.57	1.53
25	2.92	2.53	2.32	2.18	2.09	2.02	1.97	1.93	1.89	1.87	1.82	1.77	1.72	1.69	1.66	1.63	1.59	1.56	1.52
26	2.91	2.52	2.31	2.17	2.08	2.01	1.96	1.92	1.88	1.86	1.81	1.76	1.71	1.68	1.65	1.61	1.58	1.54	1.50
27	2.90	2.51	2.30	2.17	2.07	2.00	1.95	1.91	1.87	1.85	1.80	1.75	1.70	1.67	1.64	1.60	1.57	1.53	1.49
28	2.89	2.50	2.29	2.16	2.06	2.00	1.94	1.90	1.87	1.84	1.79	1.74	1.69	1.66	1.63	1.59	1.56	1.52	1.48
29	2.89	2.50	2.28	2.15	2.06	1.99	1.93	1.89	1.86	1.83	1.78	1.73	1.68	1.65	1.62	1.58	1.55	1.51	1.47
30	2.88	2.49	2.28	2.14	2.05	1.98	1.93	1.88	1.85	1.82	1.77	1.72	1.67	1.64	1.61	1.57	1.54	1.50	1.46
40	2.84	2.44	2.23	2.09	2.00	1.93	1.87	1.83	1.79	1.76	1.71	1.66	1.61	1.57	1.54	1.51	1.47	1.42	1.38
60	2.79	2.39	2.18	2.04	1.95	1.87	1.82	1.77	1.74	1.71	1.66	1.60	1.54	1.51	1.48	1.44	1.40	1.35	1.29
120	2.75	2.35	2.13	1.99	1.90	1.82	1.77	1.72	1.68	1.65	1.60	1.55	1.48	1.45	1.41	1.37	1.32	1.26	1.19
∞	2.71	2.30	2.08	1.94	1.85	1.77	1.72	1.67	1.63	1.60	1.55	1.49	1.42	1.38	1.34	1.30	1.24	1.17	1.00

m = degrees of freedom for the numerator
n = degrees of freedom for the denominator
Source: *Handbook of Tables for Mathematics*, edited by Robert C. West and Samuel M. Selby, 1970. Reprinted with the permission of the CRC Press, Inc.

TABLE A.5a Durbin–Watson Statistic (d): 5% Significance Points of d_L and d_U in Two-tailed Tests

n	k' = 1 d_L	d_U	k' = 2 d_L	d_U	k' = 3 d_L	d_U	k' = 4 d_L	d_U	k' = 5 d_L	d_U
15	0.95	1.23	0.83	1.40	0.71	1.61	0.59	1.84	0.48	2.09
16	0.98	1.24	0.86	1.40	0.75	1.59	0.64	1.80	0.53	2.03
17	1.01	1.25	0.90	1.40	0.79	1.58	0.68	1.77	0.57	1.98
18	1.03	1.26	0.93	1.40	0.82	1.56	0.72	1.74	0.62	1.93
19	1.06	1.28	0.96	1.41	0.86	1.55	0.76	1.72	0.66	1.90
20	1.08	1.28	0.99	1.41	0.89	1.55	0.79	1.70	0.70	1.87
21	1.10	1.30	1.01	1.41	0.92	1.54	0.83	1.69	0.73	1.84
22	1.12	1.31	1.04	1.42	0.95	1.54	0.86	1.68	0.77	1.82
23	1.14	1.32	1.06	1.42	0.97	1.54	0.89	1.67	0.80	1.80
24	1.16	1.33	1.08	1.43	1.00	1.54	0.91	1.66	0.83	1.79
25	1.18	1.34	1.10	1.43	1.02	1.54	0.94	1.65	0.86	1.77
26	1.19	1.35	1.12	1.44	1.04	1.54	0.96	1.65	0.88	1.76
27	1.21	1.36	1.13	1.44	1.06	1.54	0.99	1.64	0.91	1.75
28	1.22	1.37	1.15	1.45	1.08	1.54	1.01	1.64	0.93	1.74
29	1.24	1.38	1.17	1.45	1.10	1.54	1.03	1.63	0.96	1.73
30	1.25	1.38	1.18	1.46	1.12	1.54	1.05	1.63	0.98	1.73
31	1.26	1.39	1.20	1.47	1.13	1.55	1.07	1.63	1.00	1.72
32	1.27	1.40	1.21	1.47	1.15	1.55	1.08	1.63	1.02	1.71
33	1.28	1.41	1.22	1.48	1.16	1.55	1.10	1.63	1.04	1.71
34	1.29	1.41	1.24	1.48	1.17	1.55	1.12	1.63	1.06	1.70
35	1.30	1.42	1.25	1.48	1.19	1.55	1.13	1.63	1.07	1.70
36	1.31	1.43	1.26	1.49	1.20	1.56	1.15	1.63	1.09	1.70
37	1.32	1.43	1.27	1.49	1.21	1.56	1.16	1.62	1.10	1.70
38	1.33	1.44	1.28	1.50	1.23	1.56	1.17	1.62	1.12	1.70
39	1.34	1.44	1.29	1.50	1.24	1.56	1.19	1.63	1.13	1.69
40	1.35	1.45	1.30	1.51	1.25	1.57	1.20	1.63	1.15	1.69
45	1.39	1.48	1.34	1.53	1.30	1.58	1.25	1.63	1.21	1.69
50	1.42	1.50	1.38	1.54	1.34	1.59	1.30	1.64	1.26	1.69
55	1.45	1.52	1.41	1.56	1.37	1.60	1.33	1.64	1.30	1.69
60	1.47	1.54	1.44	1.57	1.40	1.61	1.37	1.65	1.33	1.69
65	1.49	1.55	1.46	1.59	1.43	1.62	1.40	1.66	1.36	1.69
70	1.51	1.57	1.48	1.60	1.45	1.63	1.42	1.66	1.39	1.70
75	1.53	1.58	1.50	1.61	1.47	1.64	1.45	1.67	1.42	1.70
80	1.54	1.59	1.52	1.62	1.49	1.65	1.47	1.67	1.44	1.70
85	1.56	1.60	1.53	1.63	1.51	1.65	1.49	1.68	1.46	1.71
90	1.57	1.61	1.55	1.64	1.53	1.66	1.50	1.69	1.48	1.71
95	1.68	1.62	1.56	1.65	1.54	1.67	1.52	1.69	1.50	1.71
100	1.59	1.63	1.57	1.65	1.55	1.67	1.53	1.70	1.51	1.72

n = number of observations
k' = number of explanatory variables excluding constant
Source: J. Durbin and G. S. Watson, "Testing for Serial Correlation in Least Squares Regression," *Biometrika*, Vol. 38 (1951), pp. 159–177. Reprinted with permission of the Biometrika Trustees.

TABLE A.5b   Durbin–Watson Statistic (d): 5% Significance Points of d_L and d_U in One-tailed Tests

	$k' = 1$		$k' = 2$		$k' = 3$		$k' = 4$		$k' = 5$	
n	d_L	d_U	d_L	d_U	d_L	d_U	d_L	d_U	d_L	d_U
15	1.08	1.36	0.95	1.54	0.82	1.75	0.69	1.97	0.56	2.21
16	1.10	1.37	0.98	1.54	0.86	1.73	0.74	1.93	0.62	2.15
17	1.13	1.38	1.02	1.54	0.90	1.71	0.78	1.90	0.67	2.10
18	1.16	1.39	1.05	1.53	0.93	1.69	0.82	1.87	0.71	2.06
19	1.18	1.40	1.08	1.53	0.97	1.68	0.86	1.85	0.75	2.02
20	1.20	1.41	1.10	1.54	1.00	1.68	0.90	1.83	0.79	1.99
21	1.22	1.42	1.13	1.54	1.03	1.67	0.93	1.81	0.83	1.96
22	1.24	1.43	1.15	1.54	1.05	1.66	0.96	1.80	0.86	1.94
23	1.26	1.44	1.17	1.54	1.08	1.66	0.99	1.79	0.90	1.92
24	1.27	1.45	1.19	1.55	1.10	1.66	1.01	1.78	0.93	1.90
25	1.29	1.45	1.21	1.55	1.12	1.66	1.04	1.77	0.95	1.89
26	1.30	1.46	1.22	1.55	1.14	1.65	1.06	1.76	0.98	1.88
27	1.32	1.47	1.24	1.56	1.16	1.65	1.08	1.76	1.01	1.86
28	1.33	1.48	1.26	1.56	1.18	1.65	1.10	1.75	1.03	1.85
29	1.34	1.48	1.27	1.56	1.20	1.65	1.12	1.74	1.05	1.84
30	1.35	1.49	1.28	1.57	1.21	1.65	1.14	1.74	1.07	1.83
31	1.36	1.50	1.30	1.57	1.23	1.65	1.16	1.74	1.09	1.83
32	1.37	1.50	1.31	1.57	1.24	1.65	1.18	1.73	1.11	1.82
33	1.38	1.51	1.32	1.58	1.26	1.65	1.19	1.73	1.13	1.81
34	1.39	1.51	1.33	1.58	1.27	1.65	1.21	1.73	1.15	1.81
35	1.40	1.52	1.34	1.58	1.28	1.65	1.22	1.73	1.16	1.80
36	1.41	1.52	1.35	1.59	1.29	1.65	1.24	1.73	1.18	1.80
37	1.42	1.53	1.36	1.59	1.31	1.66	1.25	1.72	1.19	1.80
38	1.43	1.54	1.37	1.59	1.32	1.66	1.26	1.72	1.21	1.79
39	1.43	1.54	1.38	1.60	1.33	1.66	1.27	1.72	1.22	1.79
40	1.44	1.54	1.39	1.60	1.34	1.66	1.29	1.72	1.23	1.79
45	1.48	1.57	1.43	1.62	1.38	1.67	1.34	1.72	1.29	1.78
50	1.50	1.59	1.46	1.63	1.42	1.67	1.38	1.72	1.34	1.77
55	1.53	1.60	1.49	1.64	1.45	1.68	1.41	1.72	1.38	1.77
60	1.55	1.62	1.51	1.65	1.48	1.69	1.44	1.73	1.41	1.77
65	1.57	1.63	1.54	1.66	1.50	1.70	1.47	1.73	1.44	1.77
70	1.58	1.64	1.55	1.67	1.52	1.70	1.49	1.74	1.46	1.77
75	1.60	1.65	1.57	1.68	1.54	1.71	1.51	1.74	1.49	1.77
80	1.61	1.66	1.59	1.69	1.56	1.72	1.53	1.74	1.51	1.77
85	1.62	1.67	1.60	1.70	1.57	1.72	1.55	1.75	1.52	1.77
90	1.63	1.68	1.61	1.70	1.59	1.73	1.57	1.75	1.54	1.78
95	1.64	1.69	1.62	1.71	1.60	1.73	1.58	1.75	1.56	1.78
100	1.65	1.69	1.63	1.72	1.61	1.74	1.59	1.76	1.57	1.78

n = number of observations
k' = number of explanatory variables excluding constant
Source: J. Durbin and G. S. Watson, "Testing for Serial Correlation in Least Squares Regression," *Biometrika*, Vol. 38 (1951), pp. 159–177. Reprinted with permission of the Biometrika Trustees.

TABLE A.6 Cumulative Terms For the Binomial Distribution $\sum_{x'}^{n} \binom{n}{x} p^{x'}(1-p)^{n-x'}$

						p					
n	x'	0.5	.10	.15	.20	.25	.30	.35	.40	.45	.50
2	1	.0975	.1900	.2775	.3600	.4375	.5100	.5775	.6400	.6975	.7500
	2	.0025	.0100	.0225	.0400	.0625	.0900	.1225	.1600	.2025	.2500
3	1	.1426	.2710	.3859	.4880	.5781	.6570	.7254	.7840	.8336	.8750
	2	.0072	.0280	.0608	.1040	.1562	.2160	.2818	.3520	.4252	.5000
	3	.0001	.0010	.0034	.0080	.0156	.0270	.0429	.0640	.0911	.1250
4	1	.1855	.3439	.4780	.5904	.6836	.7599	.8215	.8704	.9085	.9375
	2	.0140	.0523	.1095	.1808	.2617	.3483	.4370	.5248	.6090	.6875
	3	.0005	.0037	.0120	.0272	.0508	.0837	.1265	.1792	.2415	.3125
	4	.0000	.0001	.0005	.0016	.0039	.0081	.0150	.0256	.0410	.0625
5	1	.2262	.4095	.5563	.6723	.7627	.8319	.8840	.9222	.9497	.9688
	2	.0226	.0815	.1648	.2627	.3672	.4718	.5716	.6630	.7438	.8125
	3	.0012	.0086	.0266	.0579	.1035	.1631	.2352	.3174	.4069	.5000
	4	.0000	.0005	.0022	.0067	.0156	.0308	.0540	.0870	.1312	.1875
	5	.0000	.0000	.0001	.0003	.0010	.0024	.0053	.0102	.0185	.0312
6	1	.2649	.4686	.6229	.7379	.8220	.8824	.9246	.9533	.9723	.9844
	2	.0328	.1143	.2235	.3447	.4661	.5798	.6809	.7667	.8364	.8906
	3	.0022	.0158	.0473	.0989	.1694	.2557	.3529	.4557	.5585	.6562
	4	.0001	.0013	.0059	.0170	.0376	.0705	.1174	.1792	.2553	.3438
	5	.0000	.0001	.0004	.0016	.0046	.0109	.0223	.0410	.0692	.1094
	6	.0000	.0000	.0000	.0001	.0002	.0007	.0018	.0041	.0083	.0156
7	1	.3017	.5217	.6794	.7903	.8665	.9176	.9510	.9720	.9848	.9922
	2	.0444	.1497	.2834	.4233	.5551	.6706	.7662	.8414	.8976	.9375
	3	.0038	.0257	.0738	.1480	.2436	.3529	.4677	.5801	.6836	.7734
	4	.0002	.0027	.0121	.0333	.0706	.1260	.1998	.2898	.3917	.5000
	5	.0000	.0002	.0012	.0047	.0129	.0288	.0556	.0963	.1529	.2266
	6	.0000	.0000	.0001	.0004	.0013	.0038	.0090	.0188	.0357	.0625
	7	.0000	.0000	.0000	.0000	.0001	.0002	.0006	.0016	.0037	.0078
8	1	.3366	.5695	.7275	.8322	.8999	.9424	.9681	.9832	.9916	.9961
	2	.0572	.1869	.3428	.4967	.6329	.7447	.8309	.8936	.9368	.9648
	3	.0058	.0381	.1052	.2031	.3215	.4482	.5722	.6846	.7799	.8555
	4	.0004	.0050	.0214	.0563	.1138	.1941	.2936	.4059	.5230	.6367
	5	.0000	.0004	.0029	.0104	.0273	.0580	.1061	.1737	.2604	.3633
	6	.0000	.0000	.0002	.0012	.0042	.0113	.0253	.0498	.0885	.1445
	7	.0000	.0000	.0000	.0001	.0004	.0013	.0036	.0085	.0181	.0352
	8	.0000	.0000	.0000	.0000	.0000	.0001	.0002	.0007	.0017	.0039
9	1	.3698	.6126	.7684	.8658	.9249	.9596	.9793	.9899	.9954	.9980
	2	.0712	.2252	.4005	.5638	.6997	.8040	.8789	.9295	.9615	.9805
	3	.0084	.0530	.1409	.2618	.3993	.5372	.6627	.7682	.8505	.9102
	4	.0006	.0083	.0339	.0856	.1657	.2703	.3911	.5174	.6386	.7461
	5	.0000	.0009	.0056	.0196	.0489	.0988	.1717	.2666	.3786	.5000
	6	.0000	.0001	.0006	.0031	.0100	.0253	.0536	.0994	.1658	.2539
	7	.0000	.0000	.0000	.0003	.0013	.0043	.0112	.0250	.0498	.0898
	8	.0000	.0000	.0000	.0000	.0001	.0004	.0014	.0038	.0091	.0195
	9	.0000	.0000	.0000	.0000	.0000	.0000	.0001	.0003	.0008	.0020

(continued)

TABLE A.6   (*Continued*)

n	x'	0.5	.10	.15	.20	.25	.30	.35	.40	.45	.50
10	1	.4013	.6513	.8031	.8926	.9437	.9718	.9865	.9940	.9975	.9990
	2	.0861	.2639	.4557	.6242	.7560	.8507	.9140	.9536	.9767	.9893
	3	.0115	.0702	.1798	.3222	.4744	.6172	.7384	.8327	.9004	.9453
	4	.0010	.0128	.0500	.1209	.2241	.3504	.4862	.6177	.7340	.8281
	5	.0001	.0016	.0099	.0328	.0781	.1503	.2485	.3669	.4956	.6230
	6	.0000	.0001	.0014	.0064	.0197	.0473	.0949	.1662	.2616	.3770
	7	.0000	.0000	.0001	.0009	.0035	.0106	.0260	.0548	.1020	.1719
	8	.0000	.0000	.0000	.0001	.0004	.0016	.0048	.0123	.0274	.0547
	9	.0000	.0000	.0000	.0000	.0000	.0001	.0005	.0017	.0045	.0107
	10	.0000	.0000	.0000	.0000	.0000	.0000	.0000	.0001	.0003	.0010
11	1	.4312	.6862	.8327	.9141	.9578	.9802	.9912	.9964	.9986	.9995
	2	.1019	.3026	.5078	.6779	.8029	.8870	.9394	.9698	.9861	.9941
	3	.0152	.0896	.2212	.3826	.5448	.6873	.7999	.8811	.9348	.9673
	4	.0016	.0185	.0694	.1611	.2867	.4304	.5744	.7037	.8089	.8867
	5	.0001	.0028	.0159	.0504	.1146	.2103	.3317	.4672	.6029	.7256
	6	.0000	.0003	.0027	.0117	.0343	.0782	.1487	.2465	.3669	.5000
	7	.0000	.0000	.0003	.0020	.0076	.0216	.0501	.0994	.1738	.2744
	8	.0000	.0000	.0000	.0002	.0012	.0043	.0122	.0293	.0610	.1133
	9	.0000	.0000	.0000	.0000	.0001	.0006	.0020	.0059	.0148	.0327
	10	.0000	.0000	.0000	.0000	.0000	.0000	.0002	.0007	.0022	.0059
	11	.0000	.0000	.0000	.0000	.0000	.0000	.0000	.0000	.0002	.0005
12	1	.4596	.7176	.8578	.9313	.9683	.9862	.9943	.9978	.9992	.9998
	2	.1184	.3410	.5565	.7251	.8416	.9150	.9576	.9804	.9917	.9968
	3	.0196	.1109	.2642	.4417	.6093	.7472	.8487	.9166	.9579	.9807
	4	.0022	.0256	.0922	.2054	.3512	.5075	.6533	.7747	.8655	.9270
	5	.0002	.0043	.0239	.0726	.1576	.2763	.4167	.5618	.6956	.8062
	6	.0000	.0005	.0046	.0194	.0544	.1178	.2127	.3348	.4731	.6128
	7	.0000	.0001	.0007	.0039	.0143	.0386	.0846	.1582	.2607	.3872
	8	.0000	.0000	.0001	.0006	.0028	.0095	.0255	.0573	.1117	.1938
	9	.0000	.0000	.0000	.0001	.0004	.0017	.0056	.0153	.0356	.0730
	10	.0000	.0000	.0000	.0000	.0000	.0002	.0008	.0028	.0079	.0193
	11	.0000	.0000	.0000	.0000	.0000	.0000	.0001	.0003	.0011	.0032
	12	.0000	.0000	.0000	.0000	.0000	.0000	.0000	.0000	.0001	.0002
13	1	.4867	.7458	.8791	.9450	.9762	.9903	.9963	.9987	.9996	.9999
	2	.1354	.3787	.6017	.7664	.8733	.9363	.9704	.9874	.9951	.9983
	3	.0245	.1339	.2704	.4983	.6674	.7975	.8868	.9421	.9731	.9888
	4	.0031	.0342	.0967	.2527	.4157	.5794	.7217	.8314	.9071	.9539
	5	.0003	.0065	.0260	.0991	.2060	.3457	.4995	.6470	.7721	.8666
	6	.0000	.0009	.0053	.0300	.0802	.1654	.2841	.4256	.5732	.7095
	7	.0000	.0001	.0013	.0070	.0243	.0624	.1295	.2288	.3563	.5000
	8	.0000	.0000	.0002	.0012	.0056	.0182	.0462	.0977	.1788	.2905
	9	.0000	.0000	.0000	.0002	.0010	.0040	.0126	.0321	.0698	.1334
	10	.0000	.0000	.0000	.0000	.0001	.0007	.0025	.0078	.0203	.0461

(*continued*)

TABLE A.6 (Continued)

							p				
n	x'	0.5	.10	.15	.20	.25	.30	.35	.40	.45	.50
13	11	.0000	.0000	.0000	.0000	.0000	.0001	.0003	.0013	.0041	.0112
	12	.0000	.0000	.0000	.0000	.0000	.0000	.0000	.0001	.0005	.0017
	13	.0000	.0000	.0000	.0000	.0000	.0000	.0000	.0000	.0000	.0001
14	1	.5123	.7712	.8972	.9560	.9822	.9932	.9976	.9992	.9998	.9999
	2	.1530	.4154	.6433	.8021	.8990	.9525	.9795	.9919	.9971	.9991
	3	.0301	.1584	.3521	.5519	.7189	.8392	.9161	.9602	.9830	.9935
	4	.0042	.0441	.1465	.3018	.4787	.6448	.7795	.8757	.9368	.9713
	5	.0004	.0092	.0467	.1298	.2585	.4158	.5773	.7207	.8328	.9102
	6	.0000	.0015	.0115	.0439	.1117	.2195	.3595	.5141	.6627	.7880
	7	.0000	.0002	.0022	.0116	.0383	.0933	.1836	.3075	.4539	.6047
	8	.0000	.0000	.0003	.0024	.0103	.0315	.0753	.1501	.2586	.3953
	9	.0000	.0000	.0000	.0004	.0022	.0083	.0243	.0583	.1189	.2120
	10	.0000	.0000	.0000	.0000	.0003	.0017	.0060	.0175	.0426	.0898
	11	.0000	.0000	.0000	.0000	.0000	.0002	.0011	.0039	.0114	.0287
	12	.0000	.0000	.0000	.0000	.0000	.0000	.0001	.0006	.0022	.0065
	13	.0000	.0000	.0000	.0000	.0000	.0000	.0000	.0001	.0003	.0009
	14	.0000	.0000	.0000	.0000	.0000	.0000	.0000	.0000	.0000	.0001
15	1	.5367	.7941	.9126	.9648	.9866	.9953	.9984	.9995	.9999	1.0000
	2	.1710	.4510	.6814	.8329	.9198	.9647	.9858	.9948	.9983	.9995
	3	.0362	.1841	.3958	.6020	.7639	.8732	.9383	.9729	.9893	.9963
	4	.0055	.0556	.1773	.3518	.5387	.7031	.8273	.9095	.9576	.9824
	5	.0006	.0127	.0617	.1642	.3135	.4845	.6481	.7827	.8796	.9408
	6	.0001	.0022	.0168	.0611	.1484	.2784	.4357	.5968	.7392	.8491
	7	.0000	.0003	.0036	.0181	.0566	.1311	.2452	.3902	.5478	.6964
	8	.0000	.0000	.0006	.0042	.0173	.0500	.1132	.2131	.3465	.5000
	9	.0000	.0000	.0001	.0008	.0042	.0152	.0422	.0950	.1818	.3036
	10	.0000	.0000	.0000	.0001	.0008	.0037	.0124	.0338	.0769	.1509
	11	.0000	.0000	.0000	.0000	.0001	.0007	.0028	.0093	.0255	.0592
	12	.0000	.0000	.0000	.0000	.0000	.0001	.0005	.0019	.0063	.0176
	13	.0000	.0000	.0000	.0000	.0000	.0000	.0001	.0003	.0011	.0037
	14	.0000	.0000	.0000	.0000	.0000	.0000	.0000	.0000	.0001	.0005
	15	.0000	.0000	.0000	.0000	.0000	.0000	.0000	.0000	.0000	.0000
16	1	.5599	.8147	.9257	.9719	.9900	.9967	.9990	.9997	.9999	1.0000
	2	.1892	.4853	.7161	.8593	.9365	.9739	.9902	.9967	.9990	.9997
	3	.0429	.2108	.4386	.6482	.8029	.9006	.9549	.9817	.9934	.9979
	4	.0070	.0684	.2101	.4019	.5950	.7541	.8661	.9349	.9719	.9894
	5	.0009	.0170	.0791	.2018	.3698	.5501	.7108	.8334	.9147	.9616
	6	.0001	.0033	.0235	.0817	.1897	.3402	.5100	.6712	.8024	.8949
	7	.0000	.0005	.0056	.0267	.0796	.1753	.3119	.4728	.6340	.7228
	8	.0000	.0001	.0011	.0070	.0271	.0744	.1594	.2839	.4371	.5982
	9	.0000	.0000	.0002	.0015	.0075	.0257	.0671	.1423	.2559	.4018
	10	.0000	.0000	.0000	.0002	.0016	.0071	.0229	.0583	.1241	.2272

(continued)

TABLE A.6   (*Continued*)

n	x'	0.5	.10	.15	.20	.25	.30	.35	.40	.45	.50
16	11	.0000	.0000	.0000	.0000	.0003	.0016	.0062	.0191	.0486	.1051
	12	.0000	.0000	.0000	.0000	.0000	.0003	.0013	.0049	.0149	.0384
	13	.0000	.0000	.0000	.0000	.0000	.0000	.0002	.0009	.0035	.0106
	14	.0000	.0000	.0000	.0000	.0000	.0000	.0000	.0001	.0006	.0021
	15	.0000	.0000	.0000	.0000	.0000	.0000	.0000	.0000	.0001	.0003
	16	.0000	.0000	.0000	.0000	.0000	.0000	.0000	.0000	.0000	.0000
17	1	.5819	.8332	.9369	.9775	.9925	.9977	.9993	.9998	1.0000	1.0000
	2	.2078	.5182	.7475	.8818	.9499	.9807	.9933	.9979	.9994	.9999
	3	.0503	.2382	.4802	.6904	.8363	.9226	.9673	.9877	.9959	.9988
	4	.0088	.0826	.2444	.4511	.6470	.7981	.8972	.9536	.9816	.9936
	5	.0012	.0221	.0987	.2418	.4261	.6113	.7652	.8740	.9404	.9755
	6	.0001	.0047	.0319	.1057	.2347	.4032	.5803	.7361	.8529	.9283
	7	.0000	.0008	.0083	.0377	.1071	.2248	.3812	.5522	.7098	.8338
	8	.0000	.0001	.0017	.0109	.0402	.1046	.2128	.3595	.5257	.6855
	9	.0000	.0000	.0003	.0026	.0124	.0403	.0994	.1989	.3374	.5000
	10	.0000	.0000	.0000	.0005	.0031	.0127	.0383	.0919	.1834	.3145
	11	.0000	.0000	.0000	.0001	.0006	.0032	.0120	.0348	.0826	.1662
	12	.0000	.0000	.0000	.0000	.0001	.0007	.0030	.0106	.0301	.0717
	13	.0000	.0000	.0000	.0000	.0000	.0001	.0006	.0025	.0086	.0245
	14	.0000	.0000	.0000	.0000	.0000	.0000	.0000	.0005	.0019	.0064
	15	.0000	.0000	.0000	.0000	.0000	.0000	.0000	.0001	.0003	.0012
	16	.0000	.0000	.0000	.0000	.0000	.0000	.0000	.0000	.0000	.0001
	17	.0000	.0000	.0000	.0000	.0000	.0000	.0000	.0000	.0000	.0000
18	1	.6028	.8499	.9464	.9820	.9944	.9984	.9996	.9999	1.0000	1.0000
	2	.2265	.5497	.7759	.9009	.9605	.9858	.9954	.9987	.9997	.9999
	3	.0581	.2662	.5203	.7287	.8647	.9400	.9764	.9918	.9975	.9993
	4	.0109	.0982	.2798	.4990	.6943	.8354	.9217	.9672	.9880	.9962
	5	.0015	.0282	.1206	.2836	.4813	.6673	.8114	.9058	.9589	.9846
	6	.0002	.0064	.0419	.1329	.2825	.4656	.6450	.7912	.8923	.9519
	7	.0000	.0012	.0118	.0513	.1390	.2783	.4509	.6257	.7742	.8811
	8	.0000	.0002	.0027	.0163	.0569	.1407	.2717	.4366	.6085	.7597
	9	.0000	.0000	.0005	.0043	.0193	.0596	.1391	.2632	.4222	.5927
	10	.0000	.0000	.0001	.0009	.0054	.0210	.0597	.1347	.2527	.4073
	11	.0000	.0000	.0000	.0002	.0012	.0061	.0212	.0576	.1280	.2403
	12	.0000	.0000	.0000	.0000	.0002	.0014	.0062	.0203	.0537	.1189
	13	.0000	.0000	.0000	.0000	.0000	.0003	.0014	.0058	.0183	.0481
	14	.0000	.0000	.0000	.0000	.0000	.0000	.0003	.0013	.0049	.0154
	15	.0000	.0000	.0000	.0000	.0000	.0000	.0000	.0002	.0010	.0038
	16	.0000	.0000	.0000	.0000	.0000	.0000	.0000	.0000	.0001	.0007
	17	.0000	.0000	.0000	.0000	.0000	.0000	.0000	.0000	.0000	.0001
	18	.0000	.0000	.0000	.0000	.0000	.0000	.0000	.0000	.0000	.0000

(*continued*)

TABLE A.6   (Continued)

n	x'	0.5	.10	.15	.20	.25	.30	.35	.40	.45	.50
							p				
19	1	.6226	.8649	.9544	.9856	.9958	.9989	.9997	.9999	1.0000	1.0000
	2	.2453	.5797	.8015	.9171	.9690	.9896	.9969	.9992	.9998	1.0000
	3	.0665	.2946	.5587	.7631	.8887	.9538	.9830	.9945	.9985	.9996
	4	.0132	.1150	.3159	.5449	.7369	.8668	.9409	.9770	.9923	.9978
	5	.0020	.0352	.1444	.3267	.5346	.7178	.8500	.9304	.9720	.9904
	6	.0002	.0086	.0537	.1631	.3322	.5261	.7032	.8371	.9223	.9682
	7	.0000	.0017	.0163	.0676	.1749	.3345	.5188	.6919	.8273	.9165
	8	.0000	.0003	.0041	.0233	.0775	.1820	.3344	.5122	.6831	.8204
	9	.0000	.0000	.0008	.0067	.0287	.0839	.1855	.3325	.5060	.6762
	10	.0000	.0000	.0001	.0016	.0089	.0326	.0875	.1861	.3290	.5000
	11	.0000	.0000	.0000	.0003	.0023	.0105	.0347	.0885	.1841	.3238
	12	.0000	.0000	.0000	.0000	.0005	.0028	.0114	.0352	.0871	.1796
	13	.0000	.0000	.0000	.0000	.0001	.0006	.0031	.0116	.0342	.0835
	14	.0000	.0000	.0000	.0000	.0000	.0001	.0007	.0031	.0109	.0318
	15	.0000	.0000	.0000	.0000	.0000	.0000	.0001	.0006	.0028	.0096
	16	.0000	.0000	.0000	.0000	.0000	.0000	.0000	.0001	.0005	.0022
	17	.0000	.0000	.0000	.0000	.0000	.0000	.0000	.0000	.0001	.0004
	18	.0000	.0000	.0000	.0000	.0000	.0000	.0000	.0000	.0000	.0000
	19	.0000	.0000	.0000	.0000	.0000	.0000	.0000	.0000	.0000	.0000
20	1	.6415	.8784	.9612	.9885	.9968	.9992	.9998	1.0000	1.0000	1.0000
	2	.2642	.6083	.8244	.9308	.9757	.9924	.9979	.9995	.9999	1.0000
	3	.0755	.3231	.5951	.7939	.9087	.9645	.9879	.9964	.9991	.9998
	4	.0159	.1330	.3523	.5886	.7748	.8929	.9556	.9840	.9951	.9987
	5	.0026	.0432	.1702	.3704	.5852	.7625	.8818	.9490	.9811	.9941
	6	.0003	.0113	.0673	.1958	.3828	.5836	.7546	.8744	.9447	.9793
	7	.0000	.0024	.0219	.0867	.2142	.3920	.5834	.7500	.8701	.9423
	8	.0000	.0004	.0059	.0321	.1018	.2277	.3990	.5841	.7480	.8684
	9	.0000	.0001	.0013	.0100	.0409	.1133	.2376	.4044	.5857	.7483
	10	.0000	.0000	.0002	.0026	.0139	.0480	.1218	.2447	.4086	.5881
	11	.0000	.0000	.0000	.0006	.0039	.0171	.0532	.1275	.2493	.4119
	12	.0000	.0000	.0000	.0001	.0009	.0051	.0196	.0565	.1308	.2517
	13	.0000	.0000	.0000	.0000	.0002	.0013	.0060	.0210	.0580	.1316
	14	.0000	.0000	.0000	.0000	.0000	.0003	.0015	.0065	.0214	.0577
	15	.0000	.0000	.0000	.0000	.0000	.0000	.0003	.0016	.0064	.0207
	16	.0000	.0000	.0000	.0000	.0000	.0000	.0000	.0003	.0015	.0059
	17	.0000	.0000	.0000	.0000	.0000	.0000	.0000	.0000	.0003	.0013
	18	.0000	.0000	.0000	.0000	.0000	.0000	.0000	.0000	.0000	.0002
	19	.0000	.0000	.0000	.0000	.0000	.0000	.0000	.0000	.0000	.0000
	20	.0000	.0000	.0000	.0000	.0000	.0000	.0000	.0000	.0000	.0000
21	1	.6594	.8906	.9671	.9908	.9976	.9994	.9999	1.0000	1.0000	1.0000
	2	.2830	.6353	.8450	.9424	.9810	.9944	.9996	.9997	.9999	1.0000
	3	.0849	.3516	.6295	.8213	.9255	.9729	.9914	.9976	.9994	.9999
	4	.0189	.1520	.3887	.6296	.8083	.9144	.9669	.9890	.9969	.9993
	5	.0032	.0522	.1975	.4140	.6326	.8016	.9076	.9630	.9874	.9967

(continued)

TABLE A.6   (*Continued*)

n	x′	0.5	.10	.15	.20	.25	.30	.35	.40	.45	.50
							p				
21	6	.0004	.0144	.0827	.2307	.4334	.6373	.7991	.9043	.9611	.9867
	7	.0000	.0033	.0287	.1085	.2564	.4495	.6433	.7998	.9036	.9608
	8	.0000	.0006	.0083	.0431	.1299	.2770	.4635	.6505	.8029	.9054
	9	.0000	.0001	.0020	.0144	.0561	.1477	.2941	.4763	.6587	.8083
	10	.0000	.0000	.0004	.0041	.0206	.0676	.1632	.3086	.4883	.6682
	11	.0000	.0000	.0001	.0010	.0064	.0264	.0772	.1744	.3210	.5000
	12	.0000	.0000	.0000	.0002	.0017	.0087	.0313	.0849	.1841	.3318
	13	.0000	.0000	.0000	.0000	.0004	.0024	.0108	.0352	.0908	.1917
	14	.0000	.0000	.0000	.0000	.0001	.0006	.0031	.0123	.0379	.0946
	15	.0000	.0000	.0000	.0000	.0000	.0001	.0007	.0036	.0132	.0392
	16	.0000	.0000	.0000	.0000	.0000	.0000	.0001	.0008	.0037	.0133
	17	.0000	.0000	.0000	.0000	.0000	.0000	.0000	.0002	.0008	.0036
	18	.0000	.0000	.0000	.0000	.0000	.0000	.0000	.0000	.0001	.0007
	19	.0000	.0000	.0000	.0000	.0000	.0000	.0000	.0000	.0000	.0001
	20	.0000	.0000	.0000	.0000	.0000	.0000	.0000	.0000	.0000	.0000
	21	.0000	.0000	.0000	.0000	.0000	.0000	.0000	.0000	.0000	.0000
22	1	.6765	.9015	.9720	.9926	.9982	.9966	.9999	1.0000	1.0000	1.0000
	2	.3018	.6608	.8633	.9520	.9851	.9959	.9990	.9998	1.0000	1.0000
	3	.0948	.3800	.6618	.8455	.9394	.9793	.9399	.9984	.9997	.9999
	4	.0222	.1719	.4248	.6680	.8376	.9319	.9755	.9924	.9980	.9996
	5	.0040	.0621	.2262	.4571	.6765	.8355	.9284	.9734	.9917	.9978
	6	.0006	.0182	.0999	.2674	.4832	.6866	.8371	.9278	.9729	.9915
	7	.0001	.0044	.0368	.1330	.3006	.5058	.6978	.8416	.9295	.9738
	8	.0000	.0009	.0114	.0561	.1615	.3287	.5264	.7102	.8482	.9331
	9	.0000	.0001	.0030	.0201	.0746	.1865	.3534	.5460	.7236	.8569
	10	.0000	.0000	.0007	.0061	.0295	.0916	.2084	.3756	.5650	.7383
	11	.0000	.0000	.0001	.0016	.0100	.0387	.1070	.2281	.3963	.5841
	12	.0000	.0000	.0000	.0003	.0029	.0140	.0474	.1207	.2457	.4159
	13	.0000	.0000	.0000	.0001	.0007	.0043	.0180	.0551	.1328	.2617
	14	.0000	.0000	.0000	.0000	.0001	.0011	.0058	.0215	.0617	.1431
	15	.0000	.0000	.0000	.0000	.0000	.0002	.0015	.0070	.0243	.0669
	16	.0000	.0000	.0000	.0000	.0000	.0000	.0003	.0019	.0080	.0262
	17	.0000	.0000	.0000	.0000	.0000	.0000	.0001	.0004	.0021	.0085
	18	.0000	.0000	.0000	.0000	.0000	.0000	.0000	.0001	.0005	.0022
	19	.0000	.0000	.0000	.0000	.0000	.0000	.0000	.0000	.0001	.0004
	20	.0000	.0000	.0000	.0000	.0000	.0000	.0000	.0000	.0000	.0001
	21	.0000	.0000	.0000	.0000	.0000	.0000	.0000	.0000	.0000	.0000
	22	.0000	.0000	.0000	.0000	.0000	.0000	.0000	.0000	.0000	.0000

(*continued*)

TABLE A.6 (Continued)

n	x′	| 0.5	.10	.15	.20	.25	.30	.35	.40	.45	.50
23	1	.6926	.9114	.9762	.9941	.9987	.9997	1.0000	1.0000	1.0000	1.0000
	2	.3206	.6849	.8796	.9602	.9884	.9970	.9993	.9999	1.0000	1.0000
	3	.1052	.4080	.6920	.8668	.9508	.9843	.9957	.9990	1.0000	1.0000
	4	.0258	.1927	.4604	.7035	.8630	.9462	.9819	.9948	.9988	.9998
	5	.0049	.0731	.2560	.4993	.7168	.8644	.9449	.9810	.9945	.9987
	6	.0008	.0226	.1189	.3053	.5315	.7312	.8691	.9460	.9814	.9947
	7	.0001	.0058	.0463	.1598	.3463	.5601	.7466	.8760	.9490	.9827
	8	.0000	.0012	.0152	.0715	.1963	.3819	.5864	.7627	.8848	.9534
	9	.0000	.0002	.0042	.0273	.0963	.2291	.4140	.6116	.7797	.8950
	10	.0000	.0000	.0010	.0089	.0408	.1201	.2592	.4438	.6364	.7976
	11	.0000	.0000	.0002	.0025	.0149	.0546	.1425	.2871	.4722	.6612
	12	.0000	.0000	.0000	.0006	.0046	.0214	.0682	.1636	.3135	.5000
	13	.0000	.0000	.0000	.0001	.0012	.0072	.0283	.0813	.1836	.3388
	14	.0000	.0000	.0000	.0000	.0003	.0021	.0100	.0349	.0937	.2024
	15	.0000	.0000	.0000	.0000	.0001	.0005	.0030	.0128	.0411	.1050
	16	.0000	.0000	.0000	.0000	.0000	.0001	.0008	.0040	.0153	.0466
	17	.0000	.0000	.0000	.0000	.0000	.0000	.0002	.0010	.0048	.0173
	18	.0000	.0000	.0000	.0000	.0000	.0000	.0000	.0002	.0012	.0053
	19	.0000	.0000	.0000	.0000	.0000	.0000	.0000	.0000	.0002	.0013
	20	.0000	.0000	.0000	.0000	.0000	.0000	.0000	.0000	.0000	.0002
	21	.0000	.0000	.0000	.0000	.0000	.0000	.0000	.0000	.0000	.0000
	22	.0000	.0000	.0000	.0000	.0000	.0000	.0000	.0000	.0000	.0000
	23	.0000	.0000	.0000	.0000	.0000	.0000	.0000	.0000	.0000	.0000
24	1	.7080	.9202	.9798	.9953	.9990	.9998	1.0000	1.0000	1.0000	1.0000
	2	.3391	.7075	.8941	.9669	.9910	.9978	.9995	.9999	1.0000	1.0000
	3	.1159	.4357	.7202	.8855	.9602	.9881	.9970	.9993	.9999	1.0000
	4	.0298	.2143	.4951	.7361	.8850	.9576	.9867	.9965	.9992	.9999
	5	.0060	.0851	.2866	.5401	.7534	.8889	.9578	.9866	.9964	.9992
	6	.0010	.0277	.1394	.3441	.5778	.7712	.8956	.9600	.9873	.9967
	7	.0001	.0075	.0572	.1889	.3926	.6114	.7894	.9040	.9636	.9887
	8	.0000	.0017	.0199	.0892	.2338	.4353	.6425	.8081	.9137	.9680
	9	.0000	.0003	.0059	.0362	.1213	.2750	.4743	.6721	.8270	.9242
	10	.0000	.0001	.0015	.0126	.0547	.1528	.3134	.5109	.7009	.8463
	11	.0000	.0000	.0003	.0038	.0213	.0742	.1833	.3498	.5461	.7294
	12	.0000	.0000	.0001	.0010	.0072	.0314	.0942	.2130	.3849	.5806
	13	.0000	.0000	.0000	.0002	.0021	.0115	.0423	.1143	.2420	.4194
	14	.0000	.0000	.0000	.0000	.0005	.0036	.0164	.0535	.1341	.2706
	15	.0000	.0000	.0000	.0000	.0001	.0010	.0055	.0217	.0648	.1537
	16	.0000	.0000	.0000	.0000	.0000	.0002	.0016	.0075	.0269	.0758
	17	.0000	.0000	.0000	.0000	.0000	.0000	.0004	.0022	.0095	.0320
	18	.0000	.0000	.0000	.0000	.0000	.0000	.0001	.0005	.0028	.0113
	19	.0000	.0000	.0000	.0000	.0000	.0000	.0000	.0001	.0007	.0033
	20	.0000	.0000	.0000	.0000	.0000	.0000	.0000	.0000	.0001	.0008

(continued)

TABLE A.6   (*Continued*)

n	x'	0.5	.10	.15	.20	.25	.30	.35	.40	.45	.50
							p				
24	21	.0000	.0000	.0000	.0000	.0000	.0000	.0000	.0000	.0000	.0001
	22	.0000	.0000	.0000	.0000	.0000	.0000	.0000	.0000	.0000	.0000
	23	.0000	.0000	.0000	.0000	.0000	.0000	.0000	.0000	.0000	.0000
	24	.0000	.0000	.0000	.0000	.0000	.0000	.0000	.0000	.0000	.0000
25	1	.7226	.9282	.9828	.9962	.9992	.9999	1.0000	1.0000	1.0000	1.0000
	2	.3576	.7288	.9069	.9726	.9930	.9984	.9997	.9999	1.0000	1.0000
	3	.1271	.4629	.7463	.9018	.9679	.9910	.9979	.9996	.9999	1.0000
	4	.0341	.2364	.5289	.7660	.9038	.9668	.9903	.9976	.9995	.9999
	5	.0072	.0980	.3179	.5793	.7863	.9095	.9680	.9905	.9977	.9995
	6	.0012	.0334	.1615	.3833	.6217	.8065	.9174	.9706	.9914	.9980
	7	.0002	.0095	.0695	.2200	.4389	.6593	.8266	.9264	.9742	.9927
	8	.0000	.0023	.0255	.1091	.2735	.4882	.6939	.8464	.9361	.9784
	9	.0000	.0005	.0080	.0468	.1494	.3231	.5332	.7265	.8660	.9461
	10	.0000	.0001	.0021	.0173	.0713	.1894	.3697	.5754	.7576	.8852
	11	.0000	.0000	.0005	.0056	.0297	.0978	.2288	.4142	.6157	.7878
	12	.0000	.0000	.0001	.0015	.0107	.0442	.1254	.2677	.4574	.6550
	13	.0000	.0000	.0000	.0004	.0034	.0175	.0604	.1538	.3063	.5000
	14	.0000	.0000	.0000	.0001	.0009	.0060	.0255	.0778	.1827	.3450
	15	.0000	.0000	.0000	.0000	.0002	.0018	.0093	.0344	.0960	.2122
	16	.0000	.0000	.0000	.0000	.0000	.0005	.0029	.0132	.0440	.1148
	17	.0000	.0000	.0000	.0000	.0000	.0001	.0008	.0043	.0174	.0539
	18	.0000	.0000	.0000	.0000	.0000	.0000	.0002	.0012	.0058	.0216
	19	.0000	.0000	.0000	.0000	.0000	.0000	.0000	.0003	.0016	.0073
	20	.0000	.0000	.0000	.0000	.0000	.0000	.0000	.0001	.0004	.0020
	21	.0000	.0000	.0000	.0000	.0000	.0000	.0000	.0000	.0001	.0005
	22	.0000	.0000	.0000	.0000	.0000	.0000	.0000	.0000	.0000	.0001
	23	.0000	.0000	.0000	.0000	.0000	.0000	.0000	.0000	.0000	.0000
	24	.0000	.0000	.0000	.0000	.0000	.0000	.0000	.0000	.0000	.0000
	25	.0000	.0000	.0000	.0000	.0000	.0000	.0000	.0000	.0000	.0000
30	1	.7854	.9576	.9924	.9988	.9998	1.0000	1.0000	1.0000	1.0000	1.0000
	2	.4465	.8163	.9520	.9895	.9980	.9997	1.0000	1.0000	1.0000	1.0000
	3	.1878	.5886	.8486	.9558	.9894	.9979	.9997	1.0000	1.0000	1.0000
	4	.0608	.3526	.6783	.8773	.9626	.9907	.9981	.9997	1.0000	1.0000
	5	.0156	.1755	.4755	.7448	.9021	.9698	.9925	.9985	.9998	1.0000
	6	.0033	.0732	.2894	.5725	.7974	.9234	.9767	.9943	.9989	.9998
	7	.0006	.0258	.1526	.3930	.6519	.8405	.9414	.9828	.9960	.9993
	8	.0001	.0078	.0698	.2392	.4857	.7186	.8762	.9565	.9879	.9974
	9	.0000	.0020	.0278	.1287	.3264	.5685	.7753	.9060	.9688	.9919
	10	.0000	.0005	.0097	.0611	.1966	.4112	.6425	.8237	.9306	.9786

(*continued*)

TABLE A.6 (*Continued*)

n	x′	0.5	.10	.15	.20	.25	.30	.35	.40	.45	.50
							p				
30	11	.0000	.0001	.0029	.0256	.1057	.2696	.4922	.7085	.8650	.9506
	12	.0000	.0000	.0008	.0095	.0507	.1593	.3452	.5689	.7673	.8998
	13	.0000	.0000	.0002	.0031	.0216	.0845	.2198	.4215	.6408	.8192
	14	.0000	.0000	.0000	.0009	.0082	.0401	.1263	.2855	.4975	.7077
	15	.0000	.0000	.0000	.0002	.0027	.0169	.0652	.1754	.3552	.5722
	16	.0000	.0000	.0000	.0001	.0008	.0064	.0301	.0971	.2309	.4278
	17	.0000	.0000	.0000	.0000	.0002	.0021	.0124	.0481	.1356	.2923
	18	.0000	.0000	.0000	.0000	.0001	.0006	.0045	.0212	.0714	.1808
	19	.0000	.0000	.0000	.0000	.0000	.0002	.0014	.0083	.0334	.1002
	20	.0000	.0000	.0000	.0000	.0000	.0000	.0004	.0029	.0138	.0494
	21	.0000	.0000	.0000	.0000	.0000	.0000	.0001	.0009	.0050	.0214
	22	.0000	.0000	.0000	.0000	.0000	.0000	.0000	.0002	.0016	.0081
	23	.0000	.0000	.0000	.0000	.0000	.0000	.0000	.0000	.0004	.0026
	24	.0000	.0000	.0000	.0000	.0000	.0000	.0000	.0000	.0001	.0007
	25	.0000	.0000	.0000	.0000	.0000	.0000	.0000	.0000	.0000	.0002
	26	.0000	.0000	.0000	.0000	.0000	.0000	.0000	.0000	.0000	.0000
	27	.0000	.0000	.0000	.0000	.0000	.0000	.0000	.0000	.0000	.0000
	28	.0000	.0000	.0000	.0000	.0000	.0000	.0000	.0000	.0000	.0000
	29	.0000	.0000	.0000	.0000	.0000	.0000	.0000	.0000	.0000	.0000
	30	.0000	.0000	.0000	.0000	.0000	.0000	.0000	.0000	.0000	.0000
35	1	.8339	.9750	.9966	.9996	1.0000	1.0000	1.0000	1.0000	1.0000	1.0000
	2	.5280	.8776	.9757	.9960	.9995	.9999	1.0000	1.0000	1.0000	1.0000
	3	.2542	.6937	.9130	.9810	.9967	.9995	.9999	1.0000	1.0000	1.0000
	4	.0958	.4690	.7912	.9395	.9864	.9976	.9997	1.0000	1.0000	1.0000
	5	.0290	.2693	.6193	.8565	.9590	.9909	.9984	.9998	1.0000	1.0000
	6	.0073	.1316	.4311	.7279	.9024	.9731	.9942	.9990	.9999	1.0000
	7	.0015	.0552	.2652	.5672	.8080	.9350	.9830	.9966	.9995	.9999
	8	.0003	.0200	.1438	.4007	.6777	.8674	.9581	.9898	.9981	.9997
	9	.0000	.0063	.0689	.2550	.5257	.7659	.9110	.9740	.9943	.9991
	10	.0000	.0017	.0292	.1457	.3737	.6354	.8349	.9425	.9848	.9970
	11	.0000	.0004	.0110	.0747	.2419	.4900	.7284	.8877	.9646	.9917
	12	.0000	.0001	.0037	.0344	.1421	.3484	.5981	.8048	.9271	.9795
	13	.0000	.0000	.0011	.0142	.0756	.2271	.4577	.6943	.8656	.9552
	14	.0000	.0000	.0003	.0053	.0363	.1350	.3240	.5639	.7767	.9123
	15	.0000	.0000	.0001	.0018	.0158	.0731	.2109	.4272	.6624	.8447
	16	.0000	.0000	.0000	.0005	.0062	.0359	.1256	.2997	.5315	.7502
	17	.0000	.0000	.0000	.0001	.0022	.0160	.0682	.1935	.3976	.6321
	18	.0000	.0000	.0000	.0000	.0007	.0064	.0336	.1143	.2751	.5000
	19	.0000	.0000	.0000	.0000	.0002	.0023	.0150	.0615	.1749	.3679
	20	.0000	.0000	.0000	.0000	.0001	.0008	.0061	.0300	.1016	.2498
	21	.0000	.0000	.0000	.0000	.0000	.0002	.0022	.0133	.0536	.1553

(*continued*)

TABLE A.6   *(Continued)*

n	x'	0.5	.10	.15	.20	.25	.30	.35	.40	.45	.50
						p					
35	22	.0000	.0000	.0000	.0000	.0000	.0001	.0007	.0053	.0255	.0877
	23	.0000	.0000	.0000	.0000	.0000	.0000	.0002	.0019	.0109	.0448
	24	.0000	.0000	.0000	.0000	.0000	.0000	.0001	.0006	.0042	.0205
	25	.0000	.0000	.0000	.0000	.0000	.0000	.0000	.0002	.0014	.0083
	26	.0000	.0000	.0000	.0000	.0000	.0000	.0000	.0000	.0004	.0030
	27	.0000	.0000	.0000	.0000	.0000	.0000	.0000	.0000	.0001	.0009
	28	.0000	.0000	.0000	.0000	.0000	.0000	.0000	.0000	.0000	.0003
	29	.0000	.0000	.0000	.0000	.0000	.0000	.0000	.0000	.0000	.0001
	30	.0000	.0000	.0000	.0000	.0000	.0000	.0000	.0000	.0000	.0000
	31	.0000	.0000	.0000	.0000	.0000	.0000	.0000	.0000	.0000	.0000
	32	.0000	.0000	.0000	.0000	.0000	.0000	.0000	.0000	.0000	.0000
	33	.0000	.0000	.0000	.0000	.0000	.0000	.0000	.0000	.0000	.0000
	34	.0000	.0000	.0000	.0000	.0000	.0000	.0000	.0000	.0000	.0000
	35	.0000	.0000	.0000	.0000	.0000	.0000	.0000	.0000	.0000	.0000
40	1	.8715	.9852	.9985	.9999	1.0000	1.0000	1.0000	1.0000	1.0000	1.0000
	2	.6009	.9195	.9879	.9985	.9999	1.0000	1.0000	1.0000	1.0000	1.0000
	3	.3233	.7772	.9514	.9921	.9990	.9999	1.0000	1.0000	1.0000	1.0000
	4	.1381	.5769	.8698	.9715	.9953	.9994	.9999	1.0000	1.0000	1.0000
	5	.0480	.3710	.7367	.9241	.9840	.9974	.9997	1.0000	1.0000	1.0000
	6	.0139	.2063	.5675	.8387	.9567	.9914	.9987	.9999	1.0000	1.0000
	7	.0034	.0995	.3933	.7141	.9038	.9762	.9956	.9994	.9999	1.0000
	8	.0007	.0419	.2441	.5629	.8180	.9447	.9876	.9979	.9998	1.0000
	9	.0001	.0155	.1354	.4069	.7002	.8890	.9697	.9939	.9991	.9999
	10	.0000	.0051	.0672	.2682	.5605	.8041	.9356	.9844	.9973	.9997
	11	.0000	.0015	.0299	.1608	.4161	.6913	.8785	.9648	.9926	.9989
	12	.0000	.0004	.0120	.0875	.2849	.5594	.7947	.9291	.9821	.9968
	13	.0000	.0001	.0043	.0432	.1791	.4228	.6857	.8715	.9614	.9917
	14	.0000	.0000	.0014	.0194	.1032	.2968	.5592	.7888	.9249	.9808
	15	.0000	.0000	.0004	.0079	.0544	.1926	.4279	.6826	.8674	.9597
	16	.0000	.0000	.0001	.0029	.0262	.1151	.3054	.5598	.7858	.9231
	17	.0000	.0000	.0000	.0010	.0116	.0633	.2022	.4319	.6815	.8659
	18	.0000	.0000	.0000	.0003	.0047	.0320	.1239	.3115	.5609	.7852
	19	.0000	.0000	.0000	.0001	.0017	.0148	.0699	.2089	.4349	.6821
	20	.0000	.0000	.0000	.0000	.0006	.0063	.0363	.1298	.3156	.5627
	21	.0000	.0000	.0000	.0000	.0002	.0024	.0173	.0744	.2130	.4373
	22	.0000	.0000	.0000	.0000	.0000	.0009	.0075	.0392	.1331	.3179
	23	.0000	.0000	.0000	.0000	.0000	.0003	.0030	.0189	.0767	.2148
	24	.0000	.0000	.0000	.0000	.0000	.0001	.0011	.0083	.0405	.1341
	25	.0000	.0000	.0000	.0000	.0000	.0000	.0004	.0034	.0196	.0769
	26	.0000	.0000	.0000	.0000	.0000	.0000	.0001	.0012	.0086	.0403
	27	.0000	.0000	.0000	.0000	.0000	.0000	.0000	.0004	.0034	.0192
	28	.0000	.0000	.0000	.0000	.0000	.0000	.0000	.0001	.0012	.0083
	29	.0000	.0000	.0000	.0000	.0000	.0000	.0000	.0000	.0004	.0032

(continued)

TABLE A.6   (Continued)

n	x'	0.5	.10	.15	.20	.25	.30	.35	.40	.45	.50
40	30	.0000	.0000	.0000	.0000	.0000	.0000	.0000	.0000	.0001	.0011
	31	.0000	.0000	.0000	.0000	.0000	.0000	.0000	.0000	.0000	.0003
	32	.0000	.0000	.0000	.0000	.0000	.0000	.0000	.0000	.0000	.0001
	33	.0000	.0000	.0000	.0000	.0000	.0000	.0000	.0000	.0000	.0000
	34	.0000	.0000	.0000	.0000	.0000	.0000	.0000	.0000	.0000	.0000
	35	.0000	.0000	.0000	.0000	.0000	.0000	.0000	.0000	.0000	.0000
	36	.0000	.0000	.0000	.0000	.0000	.0000	.0000	.0000	.0000	.0000
	37	.0000	.0000	.0000	.0000	.0000	.0000	.0000	.0000	.0000	.0000
	38	.0000	.0000	.0000	.0000	.0000	.0000	.0000	.0000	.0000	.0000
	39	.0000	.0000	.0000	.0000	.0000	.0000	.0000	.0000	.0000	.0000
	40	.0000	.0000	.0000	.0000	.0000	.0000	.0000	.0000	.0000	.0000
45	1	.9006	.9913	.9993	1.0000	1.0000	1.0000	1.0000	1.0000	1.0000	1.0000
	2	.6650	.9476	.9940	.9995	1.0000	1.0000	1.0000	1.0000	1.0000	1.0000
	3	.3923	.8410	.9735	.9968	.9997	1.0000	1.0000	1.0000	1.0000	1.0000
	4	.1866	.6711	.9215	.9871	.9984	.9999	1.0000	1.0000	1.0000	1.0000
	5	.0729	.4729	.8252	.9618	.9941	.9993	.9999	1.0000	1.0000	1.0000
	6	.0239	.2923	.6858	.9098	.9821	.9974	.9997	1.0000	1.0000	1.0000
	7	.0066	.1585	.5218	.8232	.9554	.9920	.9990	.9999	1.0000	1.0000
	8	.0016	.0757	.3606	.7025	.9059	.9791	.9967	.9996	1.0000	1.0000
	9	.0003	.0320	.2255	.5593	.8275	.9529	.9909	.9988	.9999	1.0000
	10	.0001	.0120	.1274	.4120	.7200	.9066	.9780	.9964	.9996	1.0000
	11	.0000	.0040	.0651	.2795	.5911	.8353	.9531	.9906	.9987	.9999
	12	.0000	.0012	.0302	.1741	.4543	.7380	.9104	.9784	.9964	.9996
	13	.0000	.0003	.0127	.0995	.3252	.6198	.8453	.9554	.9910	.9988
	14	.0000	.0001	.0048	.0521	.2159	.4912	.7563	.9164	.9799	.9967
	15	.0000	.0000	.0017	.0250	.1327	.3653	.6467	.8570	.9591	.9920
	16	.0000	.0000	.0005	.0110	.0753	.2538	.5248	.7751	.9238	.9822
	17	.0000	.0000	.0002	.0044	.0395	.1642	.4017	.6728	.8698	.9638
	18	.0000	.0000	.0000	.0017	.0191	.0986	.2887	.5564	.7944	.9324
	19	.0000	.0000	.0000	.0006	.0085	.0549	.1940	.4357	.6985	.8837
	20	.0000	.0000	.0000	.0002	.0035	.0283	.1215	.3214	.5869	.8144
	21	.0000	.0000	.0000	.0001	.0013	.0135	.0708	.2223	.4682	.7243
	22	.0000	.0000	.0000	.0000	.0005	.0060	.0382	.1436	.3526	.6170
	23	.0000	.0000	.0000	.0000	.0001	.0024	.0191	.0865	.2494	.5000
	24	.0000	.0000	.0000	.0000	.0000	.0009	.0089	.0483	.1650	.3830
	25	.0000	.0000	.0000	.0000	.0000	.0003	.0038	.0250	.1017	.2757
	26	.0000	.0000	.0000	.0000	.0000	.0001	.0015	.0120	.0582	.1856
	27	.0000	.0000	.0000	.0000	.0000	.0000	.0005	.0053	.0308	.1163
	28	.0000	.0000	.0000	.0000	.0000	.0000	.0002	.0021	.0150	.0676
	29	.0000	.0000	.0000	.0000	.0000	.0000	.0001	.0008	.0068	.0362
	30	.0000	.0000	.0000	.0000	.0000	.0000	.0000	.0003	.0028	.0178

(continued)

TABLE A.6   *(Continued)*

n	x'						p				
		0.5	.10	.15	.20	.25	.30	.35	.40	.45	.50
45	31	.0000	.0000	.0000	.0000	.0000	.0000	.0000	.0001	.0010	.0080
	32	.0000	.0000	.0000	.0000	.0000	.0000	.0000	.0000	.0004	.0033
	33	.0000	.0000	.0000	.0000	.0000	.0000	.0000	.0000	.0001	.0012
	34	.0000	.0000	.0000	.0000	.0000	.0000	.0000	.0000	.0000	.0004
	35	.0000	.0000	.0000	.0000	.0000	.0000	.0000	.0000	.0000	.0001
	36	.0000	.0000	.0000	.0000	.0000	.0000	.0000	.0000	.0000	.0000
	37	.0000	.0000	.0000	.0000	.0000	.0000	.0000	.0000	.0000	.0000
	38	.0000	.0000	.0000	.0000	.0000	.0000	.0000	.0000	.0000	.0000
	39	.0000	.0000	.0000	.0000	.0000	.0000	.0000	.0000	.0000	.0000
	40	.0000	.0000	.0000	.0000	.0000	.0000	.0000	.0000	.0000	.0000
	41	.0000	.0000	.0000	.0000	.0000	.0000	.0000	.0000	.0000	.0000
	42	.0000	.0000	.0000	.0000	.0000	.0000	.0000	.0000	.0000	.0000
	43	.0000	.0000	.0000	.0000	.0000	.0000	.0000	.0000	.0000	.0000
	44	.0000	.0000	.0000	.0000	.0000	.0000	.0000	.0000	.0000	.0000
	45	.0000	.0000	.0000	.0000	.0000	.0000	.0000	.0000	.0000	.0000

Linear interpolation will be accurate at most to two decimal places.
Source: Handbook of Tables for Mathematics, The Chemical Rubber Co., Fourth Edition, 1970.

APPENDIX B

Details about the ECSLIB Program

■ The best way to reinforce understanding of the theoretical concepts and procedures introduced in this book is to gain some "hands-on" experience. A great deal of empirical econometrics requires judgment, which can best be acquired by practice. Students are therefore strongly encouraged to use a statistical software package to duplicate the results presented here and to carry out further analysis with the data provided.

Instructors who have adopted this textbook can obtain a free diskette containing the data used in all the examples and empirical applications (except those based on other people's research). The files are in ASCII form (MS–DOS only) and can be read directly by most standard regression packages or uploaded to a mainframe computer. Associated with each data file is a second file containing information about the sources of data, units of measurement, periodicity of data, and starting and ending dates for time series data.

Description of ECSLIB

Also included on the diskette is the regression program ECSLIB, developed by the author and some associated documentation and help files. ECSLIB is an easy-to-use program (the basic steps can be learned in ten minutes) that reads a data series and performs correlation and regression analysis, including ordinary and two-stage least squares, Hildreth–Lu and Cochrane–Orcutt estimations (including higher order serial correlation), weighted least squares, heteroscedasticity estimation, mean, standard deviation, coefficient of variation (s.d./mean), correlation coefficients, minimum, maximum, median, skewness and kurtosis measures, graph, plot, frequency distribution, generation of new variables through transformations and forecasts, and also printing and storing the series. ECSLIB also provides several criteria for selecting among models, a feature generally not found in most other regression packages. Probability values associated with several test statistics are also provided, so that statistical tables need not be referred to. The output from the program is in ASCII form and can be edited and incorporated into research reports.

How to obtain the Program and Data Diskette

Instructors who have adopted the book for class use can order a copy of a diskette (only MS-DOS version is available) by writing to the publisher or by calling the toll-free number (800) 237-2665 or by sending a Fax [(619) 699-6320] to the attention of the microcomputer editor. The standard diskette is in a 3.5-inch, low density format (other formats can be requested). Instructors are permitted to reproduce the program for distribution (free of charge) to students enrolled in the course. Others can obtain the program by sending a check or money order on a U.S. bank for $35 ($50 for countries other than Canada), payable to Ramu Ramanathan at the following address (be sure to indicate whether a 3.5-inch or 5.25-inch format is required):

Dr. Ramu Ramanathan
Department of Economics
University of California, San Diego
La Jolla, CA 92093-0508

ECSLIB is written in the C programming language and the complete source code may be obtained from the author for $500.

ECSLIB Program License Agreement

The following terms and conditions should be read carefully. Opening the diskette package implies acceptance of the terms of this license by the user.

License
a. Instructors who have adopted the book are permitted to reproduce the program diskette for distribution to students enrolled in the course. Others may reproduce the program for personal backup copies only. Students who receive a copy of the ECSLIB program are also bound by this agreement.
b. The program may not be moved electronically over a network without written permission from the author.
c. The program may not be sublicensed, rented, or assigned, nor may the program be incorporated, in whole or in part, into another program.

Limited Warranty

THE PROGRAM IS PROVIDED "AS IS" WITHOUT WARRANTY OF ANY KIND, EITHER EXPRESSED OR IMPLIED, INCLUDING, BUT NOT LIMITED TO, ANY WARRANTY OF PERFORMANCE OR ANY IMPLIED WARRANTY OF MERCHANTABILITY OR FITNESS FOR ANY PARTICULAR PURPOSE. THE ENTIRE RISK OF USING THE PROGRAM IS ASSUMED BY THE USER.

Equipment Needed

The minimum equipment needed to run the ECSLIB program is the following:

IBM PC, XT, AT or a compatible system
Monochrome monitor
Two disk drives (a hard disk is strongly recommended)
512 K memory (640 K is recommended)
DOS 3.3 or later version (contact the author for earlier DOS Versions)

Although the program will run without a printer, you will need one to obtain hard copies of the output. A mathematics coprocessor (8087 chip) is optional. The program senses its presence and uses it if it is available.

Background

Before using ECSLIB you should read your computer manual and familiarize yourself with certain commands of the disk-operating system (known as DOS commands, which are executed from the DOS prompt, usually >). Useful DOS commands are *CD*, *COPY*, *FORMAT*, *RENAME*, *DELETE*, *PATH*, *SET*, and *DIR*. You should also read the sections on files, directories, batch files, and path names, and learn how to format disks and make back-up copies of files.

It is essential to understand the difference between a DOS command and an ECSLIB command. A DOS command gives instructions to your disk-operating system about executing the command. This has nothing to do with ECSLIB. Once you are in ECSLIB, however, only commands that ECSLIB can recognize will be acceptable.

Documentation for the Program

Because ECSLIB is constantly being improved, any manual presented in the book becomes obsolete virtually as soon as the book is published. For this reason, no documentation is included here. Instead, the ECSLIB diskette has several files that provide the necessary documentation. To print these, place the ECSLIB disk in drive A or B, as appropriate, and change drive to it. Set your printer paper so that the top of the page is just above the ribbon and turn it on. Then use the following DOS commands one after the other to get a number of documentations:

LPR UPDATE > PRN
LPR LPR.DOC > PRN
LPR CAT.DOC > PRN
LPR EDIT.DOC PRN
LPR ECSLIB.DOC > PRN
LPR ECSLIB.HLP > PRN

Read the section "A QUICK INTRODUCTION TO ECSLIB" in ECSLIB.DOC and try the practice sessions described there (which should not take more than 15 minutes). Also read the manual for the program EDIT which is an extremely simple ASCII text editor.

ECSLIB Commands

The following is a list of commands that ECSLIB will accept. The help file ECSLIB.HLP has details about each of the commands.

Operation	List of commands
Exiting from ECSLIB	quit
Help on commands	help; and help commandname
List of variables	list
Executing a batch file	run
Editing a DOS text file	edit textfilename
Executing a DOS command	dos DOS command
Summarizing the data	summary, corr, freq
Changing the sample range	smpl
Displaying data	print, graph, plot
Generating new variables	logs, lags, square, rhodiff, genr, fcast, sim
Storing variables	store
Estimation procedures	ols, omit, add, corc, hilu, ar, tsls, wls, hccm, hsk
Miscellaneous commands	corrgm, criteria, lmtest, pvalue

APPENDIX C

Answers to
Selected Problems

■ This appendix sketches the answers to selected practice problems and end-of-chapter exercises. Because Chapters 2, 3, and 4 are fundamental to a good understanding of econometric methodology, answers are provided for more of the problems in these chapters. In later chapters, many of the questions involve empirical analysis and have no single answer.

Chapter 2

Practice Problems

2.3   Let S = alarm set and T = on time. Given $P(S) = 0.7$, $P(T\,|\,S) = 0.99$, and $P(T\,|\,\bar{S}) = 0.6$. Because T must occur either with S or $\bar{S}$, $P(T) = P(T \cap S) + P(T \cap S)$. By the definition of conditional probability, $P(T \cap S) = P(T\,|\,S)P(S)$ and $P(T \cap S) = P(T\,|\,\bar{S})P(\bar{S})$. Therefore, $P(T) = (0.99 \times 0.7) + (0.6 \times 0.3) = 0.873$.

2.5   Let X be the number of persons preferring brand A to brand B, out of a sample of 18. Also, $p = 0.60$ is the probability that a person drawn at random will prefer brand A. The claim will be rejected if $X \leq 8$.

$$P(X \leq 8) = \sum_{x=0}^{x=8} \binom{18}{x} 0.6^x 0.4^{18-x}$$

Table A.6 tabulates cumulative probability values only for $p \leq 0.5$. To obtain what we want, let $y = 18 - x$. Noting that $\binom{18}{x} = \binom{18}{y}$, we have

$$P(X \leq 8) = \sum_{y=10}^{y=18} \binom{18}{y} 0.4^y 0.6^{18-y}$$

From Table A.6 this is 0.1347. There is therefore a 13.47 percent chance of rejecting a true claim.

2.11   Given that $X = 1, 2, \dots, 5$ with probability 0.2, we want the correlation coefficient between X and X^2. First we need the following:

$$\text{Cov}(X, X^2) = E(X^3) - E(X)E(X^2)$$
$$V(X) = E(X^2) - [E(X)]^2 \qquad V(X^2) = E(X^4) - [E(X^2)]^2$$

These can be calculated as follows:

$$E(X) = 0.2(1 + 2 + \cdots + 5) = 3$$
$$E(X^2) = 0.2(1^2 + 2^2 + \cdots + 5^2) = 11$$
$$E(X^3) = 0.2(1^3 + 2^3 + \cdots + 5^3) = 45$$
$$E(X^4) = 0.2(1^4 + 2^4 + \cdots + 5^4) = 195.8$$
$$\text{Cov}(X, X^2) = 45 - (3 \times 11) = 12$$
$$V(X) = 11 - 9 = 2$$
$$V(X^2) = 195.8 - 121 = 74.8$$

The correlation coefficient between X and X^2 is therefore given by

$$\frac{2}{\sqrt{(2 \times 74.8)}} = 0.9811, \text{ which is slightly below 1.}$$

Exercises

2.4   Let X be the number of persons who do not show up, out of 23 reservations. The probability of a "no show" is $p = 0.1$. The company can accommodate every one if no more than 20 people wish to board the plane, that is, if at least 3 people do not arrive. Thus, we need $P(X \geq 3)$, when $n = 23$ and $p = 0.1$. From Table A.6 this is given as 0.4080.

2.6   a. $E(X - \mu) = \sum f(x_i)(x_i - \mu) = \sum x_i f(x_i) - \mu \sum f(x_i)$. Because $\sum f(x_i) = 1$ and the first term is $E(X) = \mu$, the above expression becomes $E(X) - \mu = 0$.
    b. $E(c) = c \sum f(x_i) = c$.
    c. $E[cg(X)] = \sum cg(x_i)f(x_i) = c \sum g(x_i)f(x_i) = cE[g(X)]$.
    d. $E[u(X) + v(X)] = \sum [u(x_i) + v(x_i)]f(x_i) = \sum u(x_i)f(x_i) + \sum v(x_i)f(x_i) = E[u(X)] + E[v(X)]$.

2.9   Because each of the elementary outcomes is equally likely, the density function is

$$f(x) = 1/n, \quad \text{for } x = 1, 2, \ldots, n.$$

$$E(X) = \frac{1}{n}(1 + 2 + \cdots + n) = (n + 1)/2.$$

$$E(X^2) = \frac{1}{n}(1^2 + 2^2 + \cdots + n^2)$$

$$= (n + 1)(2n + 1)/6.$$

$$\text{Therefore,} \quad V(X) = E(X^2) - [E(X)]^2 = \frac{(n + 1)(2n + 1)}{6} - \frac{(n + 1)^2}{4}$$

$$= (n^2 - 1)/2.$$

2.11   Let $\bar{X}$ be the average income. Then, by Property 2.10, $\bar{X} \sim N(\mu, \sigma^2/n) = N(26, 1.44)$. We need $P(17 \le \bar{X} \le 33)$. If we subtract the mean and divide by the standard deviation, the resulting random variable has the standard normal distribution (Z). Therefore, the probability is equal to

$$P\left(\frac{17 - 26}{1.2} \le Z \le \frac{33 - 26}{1.2}\right) = P(-7.5 \le Z \le 5.83)$$

Using the symmetry of the distribution, we have

$$P(-7.5 \le Z \le 5.83) = P(0 \le Z \le 7.5) + P(0 \le Z \le 5.83)$$

which is almost equal to 1. Thus, the average income will almost certainly lie between \$17,000 and \$33,000.

2.14   Given that $V(X_i) = \sigma_i^2 (i = 1, 2)$ and $\text{COV}(X_1, X_2) = \sigma_{12}$

$$\begin{aligned}
^{\text{COV}}(X_1 + X_2, X_1 - X_2) &= \text{COV}(X_1, X_1) - \text{COV}(X_1, X_2) \\
&\quad - \text{COV}(X_2, X_1) + \text{COV}(X_2, X_2) \\
&= V(X_1) - V(X_2) = \sigma_1^2 - \sigma_2^2
\end{aligned}$$

Y and Z will be uncorrelated if and only if $\sigma_1 = \sigma_2$.

2.17   Given $n = 13$, $\bar{x} = .031$, and $s = 0.01$. The null hypothesis is $H_0: \mu = \mu_0 = 0$ and the alternative is $H_1: \mu \ne 0$. The test statistic is $t_c = \sqrt{n}(\bar{x} - \mu_0)/s = \sqrt{13}$ $0.031/0.01 = 11.1772$. We see from the t-table that for 12 d.f. all the critical values (t^*) in the table are below t_c. Therefore H_0 is rejected at all the tabulated values implying that the excess rate of return is significantly different from zero. The 95 percent confidence interval is $\bar{x} \pm (t^*s/\sqrt{n}) = .031 \pm (2.179 \times 0.01/\sqrt{13}) = (0.025, 0.037)$.

2.19   The first step is to get the combined variance as

$$s^2 = \frac{(m-1)s_x^2 + (n-1)s_y^2}{m+n-2} = \frac{426 \times 0.541^2 + 426 \times 0.42^2}{952} = 0.23454$$

Therefore, $s = 0.484$. The test statistic here is

$$|t_c| = \frac{|\bar{x} - \bar{y}|}{s\left[\dfrac{1}{m} + \dfrac{1}{n}\right]^{1/2}} = \frac{3.558 - 2.786}{0.484\left[\dfrac{2}{427}\right]^{1/2}} = 23.306$$

It is clear from the t-table that such a large test statistic would reject the null hypothesis that the mean scores are equal even at the 0.1 percent level of significance. The conclusion, therefore, is that the mean squares are significantly different.

CHAPTER 3

Practice Problems

3.1   In figure d, the last scatter diagram, successive observations tend to be clustered; that is, if one of the points is above (below) the regression line, the next is also likely to be above (below). This suggests that u_t and $u_s (t \neq s)$ are not uncorrelated, as Assumption 3.6 requires.

3.3   On paper, copy Figure 3.1 and then add a straight line to show $\hat{Y} = \hat{\alpha} + \hat{\beta}X$, the fitted regression line. The deviation of the observation point (X_t, Y_t) from $\alpha + \beta X_t$ is the *true error* u_t, and the deviation from $\hat{\alpha} + \hat{\beta}X_t$ is the *estimated error* $\hat{u}_t$. It is now easy to see why equations (c), (d), and (e) are incorrect. For equations (f) and (g), the summation is over the sample observations. There is no reason why the true errors u_t should average to zero in the sample (they will, however, average to zero in the population because of Assumption 3.2). The estimated errors $(\hat{u}_t)$ will average to zero in the sample because of the normal equation (3.2).

3.5   Unbiasedness (Property 3.1) and consistency (Property 3.2) both require Assumptions 3.2, 3.3 and 3.4. (See the proofs of these properties for details.) BLUE is established by the Gauss–Markov Theorem, which requires Assumptions 3.5 and 3.6 also. Normality of the estimates requires Assumption 3.7 as well.

3.6   From equation (3.3), $\hat{\alpha} = \bar{Y} - \hat{\beta}\bar{X}$. $E(\hat{\alpha}) = E(\bar{Y}) - E(\hat{\beta}\bar{X}) = E(\bar{Y}) - \bar{X}E(\hat{\beta})$ because, X_t being nonrandom (Assumption 3.4), $\bar{X}$ can be taken out of the expectation. Because $\hat{\beta}$ is unbiased (Property 3.1), $E(\hat{\beta}) = \beta$. The expected value of $\bar{Y}$ is given by

$$E(\bar{Y}) = E\left(\frac{\sum Y_t}{T}\right) = \frac{\sum E(Y_t)}{T} = \left(\frac{1}{T}\right)\sum E(\alpha + \beta X_t + u_t)$$

Because X_t is nonrandom, $E(X_t) = X_t$. Also, $\sum \alpha$ is equal to $T\alpha$ because there are T terms and each is α. Therefore,

$$E(\bar{Y}) = \left(\frac{1}{T}\right)(T\alpha) + \left(\frac{1}{T}\right)\beta \sum X_t + \left(\frac{1}{T}\right)\sum E(u_t)$$

$$= \alpha + \beta\bar{X} + \left(\frac{1}{T}\right)\sum E(u_t)$$

By Assumption 3.2, $E(u_t) = 0$. Therefore, $E(\bar{Y}) = \alpha + \beta\bar{X}$. It follows that $E(\hat{\alpha}) = E(\bar{Y}) - \beta\bar{X} = \alpha$, which implies that α is also unbiased.

3.9   We sketch the proof for a one-tailed test only. If a coefficient is significant at the 1 percent level, then $t_c > t^*_{T-2}(0.01)$, where t^* is the point on the t-distribution with $T - 2$ d.f. such that the area to the right is 0.01. Note that the critical t^* for a higher level (say 0.05) must be such that $t^*_{T-2}(0.01) > t^*_{T-2}(0.05)$. It follows that $t_c > t^*_{T-2}(0.05)$, which implies that the coefficient is significant at the 5 percent level also.

3.17   Let P be price and S be square feet. Then the estimated elasticity (η) of price with respect to square feet is $\eta = (S/\hat{P})(d\hat{P}/dS)$.

For the estimated linear model, $d\hat{P}/dS = 0.09386$, and $\hat{P} = 22.601 + 0.09386S$. Substituting these into the expression for elasticity, we get

$$\eta = \frac{0.09386S}{22.601 + 0.09386S}$$

This can now be calculated for any value of S. It is easy to verify, numerically and algebraically, that the elasticity increases as S increases.

For the linear-log model, $\hat{P} = -1069.577 + 168.895 \ln(S)$. The derivative of $\ln(S)$ with respect to S is $1/S$. Therefore, $d\hat{P}/dS = 168.895(1/S)$. The expression for elasticity now becomes

$$\eta = \frac{168.895}{-1069.577 + 168.895 \ln(S)}$$

which can be calculated for any value of S.

Exercises

3.1   In the scatter diagram drawn here, we first compute the slope of each of the straight lines and then obtain the average slope. The slope of the straight line connecting (X_1, Y_1) and (X_t, Y_t) is given by $(Y_t - Y_1)/(X_t - X_1)$. Noting that there are $T - 1$ such straight lines, we have

$$\hat{\beta} = \frac{1}{T-1} \sum_{t=2}^{t=T} \left[\frac{Y_t - Y_1}{X_t - X_1}\right]$$

$$E\left[\frac{Y_t - Y_1}{X_t - X_1}\right] = E\left[\frac{(\alpha + \beta X_t + u_t) - (\alpha + \beta X_1 + u_1)}{X_t - X_1}\right]$$

$$= \beta + E\left[\frac{u_t - u_1}{X_t - X_1}\right] = \beta$$

because the X's are nonrandom and $E(u_t) = 0$. This means that each of the terms in the summation has expectation β and hence the average will also have the same expectation, thus implying unbiasedness. By the Gauss–Markov Theorem, $\tilde{\beta}$ is inferior because it is less efficient than the OLS estimator of β.

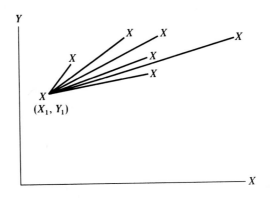

3.4   a. The simple method in Section 3.2 yields two conditions, $\sum \hat{u}_t = 0$ and $\sum X_t \hat{u}_t = 0$. For the model given here, the first equation gives $\sum (Y_t - \tilde{\beta} \sum X_t) = 0$, or $\sum Y_t = \tilde{\beta} \sum X_t$. Solving this, we have $\tilde{\beta} = \bar{Y}/\bar{X}$. (Note that this requires that $\bar{X}$ not be zero.) The second equation is $\sum X_t(Y_t - \hat{\beta} X_t) = 0$, or $\sum X_t Y_t = \hat{\beta} \sum X_t^2$, which gives $\hat{\beta} = (\sum X_t Y_t)/(\sum X_t^2)$.

   b. $E(\hat{\beta}) = E(\sum X_t Y_t / \sum X_t^2)$. Because X_t is nonrandom (Assumption 3.4), $\sum X_t^2$ is also nonrandom and hence can be taken out of the expectation. Also, the expectation of a sum is the sum of expectations. Therefore,

$$E(\hat{\beta}) = \left(\frac{1}{\sum X_t^2}\right) \sum E(X_t Y_t) = \left(\frac{1}{\sum X_t^2}\right) \sum E[X_t(\beta X_t + u_t)]$$

$$= \left(\frac{1}{\sum X_t^2}\right) \beta \sum (X_t^2) + \left(\frac{1}{\sum X_t^2}\right) \sum X_t E(u_t) = \beta$$

because $E(u_t) = 0$ by Assumption 3.2. Hence $\hat{\beta}$ is unbiased. The proof for $\tilde{\beta}$ is similar.

   c. For the fitted line $\hat{Y} = \hat{\beta} X$ to go through the point $(\bar{X}, \bar{Y})$, $\hat{\beta}\bar{X}$ must be equal to $\bar{Y}$. However,

$$\hat{\beta}\bar{X} = \frac{\sum X_t Y_t}{\sum X_t^2} \bar{X}$$

which will generally not be equal to $\bar{Y}$. This means that the point $(\bar{X}, \bar{Y})$ is not likely to lie on the straight line $\hat{Y} = \hat{\beta}X$. In contrast, however, $\tilde{\beta}\bar{X} = \bar{Y}$ and hence the straight line $\hat{Y} = \tilde{\beta}X$ passes through the point $(\bar{X}, \bar{Y})$.

d. The OLS procedure minimizes the error sum of squares

$$\text{ESS} = \sum \hat{u}_t^2 = \sum (Y_t - \hat{\beta}X_t)^2$$

with respect to $\hat{\beta}$. Taking the partial derivative with respect to $\hat{\beta}$ (see the chapter appendix, Section 3.A.1), we get

$$\frac{\partial \text{ESS}}{\partial \hat{\beta}} = \sum \left[2\hat{u}_t \left(\frac{\partial \hat{u}_t}{\partial \hat{\beta}} \right) \right] = 2 \sum (Y_t - \hat{\beta}X_t)(-X_t) = 0$$

Solving this for $\hat{\beta}$ we obtain the same expression as in part a.

e. To establish this, proceed exactly as in Section 3.A.2, expect set α to zero throughout.

f. Gauss–Markov Theorem states that the OLS estimate $(\hat{\beta})$ is BLUE; that is, it is most efficient, with the lowest variance among all linear unbiased estimates. Thus, any other linear unbiased estimate, in particular $\tilde{\beta}$, is less efficient. Therefore $\hat{\beta}$ is superior to $\tilde{\beta}$.

3.8 This question is answered in Section 3.12.

3.9 All the procedures require Assumption 3.1 and need at least two observations. Additional assumptions are as follows:

a. This procedure requires Assumptions 3.2, 3.3, and 3.4.

b. Only Assumption 3.3 is required by OLS.

c. Assumptions 3.2 through 3.6 are required for the Gauss–Markov Theorem, which states that OLS estimators are BLUE.

d. The maximum likelihood procedure requires all the assumptions listed in Table 3.2.

3.12 The model is $E = \alpha + \beta N + u$, where E is the starting salary and N is the number of years of college attended.

a. $\alpha + \beta N$ is the population average starting salary for a person with N years of college education. If N is zero, then the average salary is α. Thus, α is the average starting salary for a person with no college education. β is the change in E per unit change in N — that is, dE/dN. Thus, β is the extra starting salary for each extra year of college education.

b. We require that the error terms be normally distributed only when the statistical distributions of $\hat{\alpha}$ and $\hat{\beta}$ are derived for hypothesis testing. Therefore, the properties of unbiasedness, consistency, efficiency (BLUE) are valid, provided Assumptions 3.1 through 3.6 hold. If the distribution of u_t is unknown, then all tests of hypotheses are invalid.

c. Let E^* be the salary measured in hundreds of dollars. Then $E = 100E^* = \alpha + \beta N + u$. It follows that $E^* = (\alpha/100) + (\beta/100)N + (u/100)$ is the new model, with E^* as the dependent variable. If α^* and β^* are the parameters of the new model, we have $\alpha^* = \alpha/100$ and $\beta^*/100$.

Therefore, the new regression coefficients will be one-hundredths of the regression coefficients of the original model. Similarly, the new standard errors will be one-hundredths of the old standard errors. Because R^2, t-, and F-statistics are ratios, they are independent of the scale of units and hence will be unchanged.

3.16   This question is answered for log-linear and double-log models only. In all these questions, the procedure is to (1) state the algebraic relation between a variable in the old units of measurement and another in the new units of measurement, (2) substitute the new variable for the old variable in the model, and (3) note the algebraic relations between the new regression coefficients and the old ones. R^2, t, and F are independent of scale. Only the coefficients and their standard errors will be affected.

Consider the log-linear case first. Let $\ln Y = \alpha + \beta X + u$ be the model. Suppose X is measured in thousandths; that is, $X^* = X/1000$. Then the revised model is $\ln Y = \alpha + 1000\beta X^* + u = \alpha + \beta^* X^* + u$. The new slope coefficient is therefore $\beta^* = 1000\beta$. The intercept and the error terms are unaffected. Therefore, the only change is in the estimated coefficient for X, which will be multiplied by a factor of 1000. Its standard error will also be multiplied by the same factor. R^2, t-, and F-statistics will be unaffected.

Suppose now that the model is double-log: $\ln Y = \alpha + \beta \ln X + u$. The revised model is $\ln Y = \alpha + \beta \ln(1000\ X^*) + u = \alpha + \beta \ln 1000 + \beta \ln X^* + u = \alpha^* + \beta \ln X^* + u$, where $\alpha^* = \alpha + \beta \ln 1000$. The slope coefficient is now unchanged but the intercept term becomes $\alpha^* = \alpha + \beta \ln 1000$. An estimate of α is obtained as $\hat{\alpha} = \bar{\alpha}^* - \hat{\beta} \ln 1000$.

Next assume that X is unchanged but Y is measured in thousandths; that is, $Y^* = Y/1000$. The log-linear model is now $\ln(1000\ Y^*) = \alpha + \beta X + u$. This gives $\ln Y^* = -\ln 1000 + \alpha + \beta X + u = \alpha^* + \beta X + u$. Here also only the intercept is changed. We have $\hat{\alpha} = \hat{\alpha}^* + \ln 1000$. Finally, let the model be double-log and $Y^* = Y/1000$. We then have $\ln(1000\ Y^*) = \alpha + \beta \ln X + u$. The new model is $\ln Y^* = -\ln 1000 + \alpha + \beta \ln X + u = \alpha^* + \beta \ln X + u$. Here also, $\hat{\alpha} = \hat{\alpha}^* + \ln 1000$. [Redo this analysis when both X and Y are measured in thousandths.]

3.19   The t-ratio is the coefficient divided by its standard error. Use the values given for two of them and solve for the third, $\hat{\sigma}^2 = \text{ESS}/(T - 2) = 305.96/(22 - 2) = 15.298$. $R^2 = 1 - (\text{ESS}/\text{TSS})$. We therefore need TSS. But, from equation (2.17),

$$S_v^2 = \frac{1}{(T - 1)} \sum (V_t - \bar{V})^2 = \frac{1}{(T - 1)} \text{TSS}$$

We can therefore solve for TSS as $(T - 1)s_v^2$. R^2 is now readily obtained. From equation (3.3), $\bar{V} = \hat{\alpha} + \hat{\beta}\bar{P}$. From Section 3.A.8, $r_{vp}^2 = R^2$. The square root of this is r_{vp}. The confidence interval for β is derived in Section 3.9 as $\hat{\beta} \pm t^* s_{\hat{\beta}}$, where $s_{\hat{\beta}}$ is the standard error of $\hat{\beta}$ and t^* is the point on the t-distribution with 20 d.f. ($= T - 2$) such that the area to the right is 0.025.

Chapter 4

Practice Problems

4.3 Let ESS be the error sum of squares of equation (4.1') and ESS* be the error sum of squares of equation (4.1*). We note that u_t^* can be derived from u_t as $u_t^* = (u_t - \hat{u})/s_y$, where s_y is the standard deviation of Y. Therefore, ESS* = ESS$/s_y^2$.

4.6 ESS is already compared in Practice Problem 4.3. R^2 is independent of scale and is hence unaffected.

4.7 Part of a Property 4.3 is not applicable, but part b is because AIC decreases when variables are dropped. The SCHWARZ criterion is therefore redundant. Because we have only 14 observations, we cannot say anything about HQ. Part c is not applicable.

4.8 From Property 4.2, $\hat{\beta}_i^* = \beta_i s_{x_i}/s_y$. Therefore, the standard error of $\hat{\beta}_i^*$ is obtained by multiplying the standard error of $\hat{\beta}_i$ by s_{x_i}/s_y. The t-statistics, however, will be the same.

4.12 *Method 1:* First, regress ln Q_t against a constant, ln K_t, and ln L_t, and compute the unrestricted error sum of squares ESS$_U$. Next, impose the restriction $\alpha + \beta = 1$; that is, let $\beta = 1 - \alpha$. The restricted model is ln $Q_t = \beta_1 + \alpha \ln K_t + (1 - \alpha) \ln L_t + u_t = \beta_1 + \alpha(\ln K_t - \ln L_t) + \ln L_t + u_t$. Bringing the term ln L_t, which has no unknown coefficient, to the left, we have

$$\ln Q_t - \ln L_t = \beta_1 + \alpha(\ln K_t - \ln L_t) + u_t$$

Regress the left-hand side against a constant and (ln K_t − ln L_t), and obtain ESS$_R$, the restricted error sum of squares. The test is the standard Wald F-test with 1 d.f. for the numerator and $T - 3$ d.f. for the denominator [see equation (4.3)].

Method 3: This method depends on a t-statistic for $\hat{\alpha} + \hat{\beta} - 1$. The t-statistic to compute is

$$t_c = \frac{\hat{\alpha} + \hat{\beta} - 1}{[\widehat{\text{Var}(\hat{\alpha})} + \widehat{\text{Var}(\hat{\beta})} + 2\,\widehat{\text{Cov}(\hat{\alpha}, \hat{\beta})}]^{1/2}}$$

Under the null hypothesis that $\alpha + \beta = 1$, this has a t-distribution with d.f. $T - 3$. Reject the null hypothesis (at the 5 percent level) if $|t_c| > t_{T-3}^*(0.025)$, where t^* is the point in the t-distribution with an area of 0.025 on each tail.

4.15 Differentiating PRICE partially with respect to SQFT we get

$$\frac{\partial \text{PRICE}}{\partial \text{SQFT}} = \beta_2 + 2\beta_3 \text{SQFT}$$

This means that if β_3 is zero, the marginal effect of SQFT on PRICE is a constant for all SQFT. If β_3 is negative, then the marginal effect decreases as SQFT increases. In other words, as SQFT increases, the extra price for each extra square foot of living area decreases. Thus, the slope of the relation between price and square feet decreases as square feet increase.

4.17   The estimated coefficient is $\hat{\beta} = [\sum(X_t Y_t)/\sum X_t^2]$ (see Exercise 3.2 part d for proof). Substitute for Y_t from the true model to obtain

$$\hat{\beta} = \frac{\sum[X_t(\alpha + \beta X_t + u_t)]}{\sum X_t^2} = \alpha \frac{\sum X_t}{\sum X_t^2} + \beta + \frac{\sum X_t u_t}{\sum X_t^2}$$

The expected value of the third term is zero because $E(u_t) = 0$. But, for $\hat{\beta}$ to be unbiased, the first term must also be zero. Thus, unless $\sum X_t = 0$, which means that unless the sample mean of X is zero, the estimate will be biased.

4.19   We have seen that by changing the scale of the units of measurement, the numerical value of a coefficient can be made large or small. It is therefore a mistake to look only at the magnitude of a coefficient; to see if the coefficient is statistically significant, we must look also at the t-statistic. The coefficient 0.000024 multiplies Y^2, which is a large number. Thus, the contribution of the quadratic term is not negligible even though the coefficient appears to be small.

Exercises

4.2   Before answering this question study the first empirical example in Section 4.8. The marginal propensity to consume is $\partial C/\partial Y$. For this to decrease as income increases, we need $\partial^2 C/\partial Y^2 < 0$. A simple way to allow for this is to assume that $\partial C/\partial Y = a + bY$. The second derivative being negative means that $b < 0$. In order for the first derivative to depend on Y, we need $C = aY + (bY^2/2) + $ other terms. The effect of family size is similar. Therefore, $C = cN + (dN^2/2) + $ other terms. Combining these we get the following model:

$$C = \beta_0 + \beta_1 Y + \beta_2 Y^2 + \beta_3 N + \beta_4 N^2 + u$$

The required tests are, $\beta_2 = 0$ against $\beta_2 < 0$, and $\beta_4 = 0$ against $\beta_4 < 0$. We could also use the logarithmic function to test the hypotheses. An alternative version is

$$C = \alpha_0 + \alpha_1 Y + \alpha_2 \ln Y + \alpha_3 N + \alpha_4 \ln N + v$$

The partial derivatives are $\partial C/\partial Y = \alpha_1 + (\alpha_2 Y)$ and $\partial C/\partial N = \alpha_3 + (\alpha_4/N)$. The relevant tests are $\alpha_2 = 0$ against $\alpha_2 > 0$, and $\alpha_4 = 0$ against $\alpha_4 > 0$.

4.6   The true model is $Y_t = \beta X_t + u_t$ and the estimated model is $Y_t = \beta Z_t + v_t$. The estimated regression coefficient is (see the answer to Exercise 3.4, part d) $\beta = (\sum Y_t Z_t)/(\sum Z_t^2)$. The expected value of this is

$$E(\hat{\beta}) = E\left[\frac{\sum Y_t Z_t}{\sum Z_t^2}\right] = \frac{1}{\sum Z_t^2} E(\sum Y_t Z_t) = \frac{1}{\sum Z_t^2} \sum E(Y_t Z_t)$$

making use of the facts that Z_t is nonrandom and that the expectation of a summation is the sum of the expectations. Because the true process that generates Y_t is given by $\beta X_t + u_t$, and because $E(u_t) = 0$, we have

$$E(Y_t Z_t) = E[Z_t(\beta X_t + u_t)] = \beta Z_t X_t$$

Therefore, $E(\hat{\beta}) = \beta(\sum Z_t X_t / \sum Z_t^2)$, which will be equal to β only if the expression in parentheses is equal to 1. The same condition is needed for consistency also.

4.9 a. Calcium is supposed to improve the bone structure, and it is not clear whether it has any effect on CHD. The sign could be either positive or negative. Cigarette smokers have been shown to have a higher incidence of coronary problems. Thus, we would expect the coefficient for CIG to be positive. This is the case in all the models. Unemployment puts stress on a worker and, in turn, can lead to heart problems. Hence, we expect a positive sign for this variable. Higher consumption of fats has been shown to affect the arteries and hence increase the risk of death due to heart disease. Thus, this coefficient would be expected to be positive, and it is so in all the models. Meat contains animal fat and hence the same argument applies. Alcoholic drinks have a mixed effect. Doctors say that moderate drinkers have a lower incidence of heart problems but that both non-drinkers and heavy drinkers have problems. Because heavy drinkers have a much higher incidence of heart disease, we would expect positive signs for SPIRITS, BEER, and WINE. The observed signs differ from this expectation. The unexpected signs can be rationalized by *multicollinearity*, a topic discussed in Chapter 5.

b. The values of $\bar{R}^2$ range from 0.645 to 0.672. Considering that the data are time series, we would expect higher R^2. The F-statistics reported in Table 4.12 test the null hypothesis that every regression coefficient except the constant term is zero. The alternative hypothesis is that at least one of them is nonzero. Under the null hypothesis, the calculated F has an F-distribution with degrees of freedom for the numerator equal to the number of restrictions in the null hypothesis (eight for Model A) and the degrees of freedom for the denominator equal to the number of observations minus the number of regression coefficients *including the constant* $(34 - 9 = 25$ here). From Table A.4b, $F_{8,25}^*(0.05)$ is 2.34. Because the observed F (8.508) $> F^*$, we reject the null hypothesis (at the 5 percent level) and conclude that at least one of the regression coefficients is nonzero. This result is not surprising because we note that many of the t-values appear significant (using the rule of thumb value of 2). The tests for Models B and C are similar.

c. Here also the tests are conducted for Model A only and for two-sided alternatives. To test a single regression coefficient for significance we use the t-test. The d.f. is 25 $(34 - 9)$. For a 5 percent level of significance, $t_{25}^*(0.025) = 2.06$. For statistical significance, the calculated t must be greater than t^* in absolute value. According to this criterion, the regression coefficients for SPIRITS and BEER are significant (at 5 percent level) but those for the other variables are not. The other variables are thus candidates to be dropped. However, we must not be hasty and drop them simultaneously (recall the omitted variable bias discussed in Section 4.7). It is quite possible that if we eliminate the most insignificant one (which is WINE because it has the lowest t-value), some of the other coefficients will become significant.

d. Suppose we eliminate all the variables with t-values below 0.5 in absolute value. We would then exclude UNEMP, MEAT, and WINE from the model. This results in Model B. We could then perform a joint F-test (the Wald test) for these coefficients. Treating Model A as the unrestricted model and Model B as the restricted one, we get the following calculated F:

$$F_c = \frac{(\text{ESS}_B - \text{ESS}_A)/3}{\text{ESS}_A/25} = 0.2525$$

From Table A.4c, $F^*_{3,25}(0.1) = 2.32$. Therefore, these three regression coefficients are not jointly significant even at the 10 percent level. This suggests that all three of them can be dropped.

e. One should use a variety of criteria to determine whether one model is better than another. The model selection criteria given in Section 4.4 will certainly help. According to the values in Table 4.12, Model C is the "best" (has the smallest value for most of the criteria). The significance of the coefficients is another factor to consider. In Model A many coefficients are insignificant. In Model B calcium is insignificant, but in Model C all the regression coefficients, except the constant term, are significant. Because the constant term captures the average effect of omitted variables, it should always be retained.

f. It would have been desirable to obtain data on exercise, diet patterns, weight patterns, and so on. A cross-section study with data on individuals would have been even better.

4.15 a. We use a t-test for each regression coefficient. The degrees of freedom are $27 - 3 = 24$. The critical values for the 1, 5, and 10 percent levels are (for two-tailed tests) 2.797, 2.064, and 1.711, respectively. At these three levels of significance, only the t-statistic for log Y_t is significant.

b. Let the original model be written as

$$\widehat{\log H_t} = \hat{\beta}_0 + \hat{\beta}_1 \log Y_t + \hat{\beta}_2 \log P_t$$

Suppose we had used $Y_t^* = Y_t/P_t$ instead of Y_t. The new model would be

$$\begin{aligned}
\widehat{\log H_t} &= \hat{\alpha}_0 + \hat{\alpha}_1 \log Y_t^* + \hat{\alpha}_2 \log P_t \\
&= \hat{\alpha}_0 + \hat{\alpha}_1 \log(Y_t/P_t) + \hat{\alpha}_2 \log P_t \\
&= \hat{\alpha}_0 + \hat{\alpha}_1 \log Y_t - \hat{\alpha}_1 \log P_t + \hat{\alpha}_2 \log P_t \\
&= \hat{\alpha}_0 + \hat{\alpha}_1 \log Y_t + (\hat{\alpha}_2 - \hat{\alpha}_1) \log P_t
\end{aligned}$$

We note that each version can be readily derived from the other and hence they are essentially the same. The estimates of the constant term and the coefficient for log Y_t are the same as before. $\hat{\alpha}_2$ is obtained from $\hat{\beta}_2 = \hat{\alpha}_2 - \hat{\alpha}_1$ as $\hat{\alpha}_2 = \hat{\beta}_2 + \hat{\beta}_1$.

c. The demand for a product would depend on its price and hence the price of a single family dwelling is an important variable. Similarly, the mortgage rate is important. If the price of condominiums is low, the demand for single family houses will decrease. Therefore, the price of condominiums might be relevant as well. Property 4.5 summarizes the consequences of omitting an important variable.

Chapter 5

Exercises

5.3 a. Other things being equal, the higher the San Diego population or the higher the number of houses, the greater will be the demand for water. We would therefore expect positive signs for SDHOUSE and SDPOP. Higher income persons may be expected to use more water, but we don't expect this to be strong. The expected sign for SDPCY is positive. If water is more expensive, users are likely to conserve its use and hence we expect the coefficient for PRWATER to be negative. If it rains heavily in San Diego, lawn and other garden or crop field requirements for water will be less. Hence, the coefficient for SDRAIN is likely to be negative. All the signs agree with intuition except SDPCY, which has an unexpected sign.

b. The t-statistic being insignificant means that the variable, by itself, does not appear to be significant. The F-statistic tests whether the variables are jointly significant. The degrees of freedom for a t-test are 9 (15−6). The critical t^* for a 10 percent level is 1.833. Note that all the t-values are below this in absolute value and are hence insignificant, even at a 10 percent level. The degrees of freedom for the numerator of the F-statistic is 5 and for the denominator is 9. For a 1 percent test, the critical F^* is 6.06. The observed F is larger than this, indicating joint significance of the regression coefficients. The conflicting result is due to multicollinearity. SDHOUSE, SDPOP, and SDPCY would all be highly correlated. This would lower their t's and could make them insignificant. PRWATER and SDRAIN could be insignificant for a different reason. If the values of a variable have not changed much over the sample period, then its effect cannot be measured well. These two variables may not have changed much over the years and hence their effects may be difficult to measure.

c. Multicollinearity is a problem with the observations of the independent variables and has no effect on the assumptions made in Chapter 3. Therefore, the properties of unbiasedness, consistency, efficiency, and BLUE still hold. However, the variances of the estimates will be larger than another case in which there is no multicollinearity.

d. The new dependent variable is consumption per household (=SDWATER/SDHOUSE). The water consumption by a household should be related to household characteristics. These are AVGFAMSIZE, FAMILY INCOME, PRWATER, and AVGRAIN. AVGFAMSIZE may be obtained by dividing SDPOP by SDHOUSE. Also, FAMILY INCOME = SDPCY * AVGFAMSIZE and AVGRAIN = SDRAIN/SDHOUSE. A model that would be appropriate (others are also possible is

$$\frac{\text{SDWATER}}{\text{SDHOUSE}} = \alpha_0 + \alpha_1 \frac{\text{SDPOP}}{\text{SDHOUSE}} + \alpha_2 \text{SDPCY} * \text{AVGFAMSIZE} + u$$

Chapter 6

Practice Problems

6.1   Define a new dummy variable $D^* = 1$ for non-democrats and 0 for others. The model is now $Y = a_0 + a_1 D^* + bX + u$. Because $D^* = 1 - D$, we have $Y = a_0 + a_1(1 - D) + bX + u = (a_0 + a_1) - a_1 D + bX + u$. Therefore the models are essentially the same. Note that $a_0 + a_1 = \alpha_0$, $-a_1 = \alpha_1$, and $b = \beta$. Hence, $\hat{a}_0 = \hat{\alpha}_0 + \hat{\alpha}_1$, $\hat{a}_1 = -\hat{\alpha}_1$, and $\hat{b} = \hat{\beta}$. R^2 and the F-statistic will be unchanged, but the standard error and t-statistic for $\hat{a}_0$ will be quite different.

6.5   Let $A_3 = 1$ for young households (under 25 years of age) and 0 for others. If the oldest group is the control, then the relevant dummy variables are A_3 and A_1 and the new model is

$$Y = a_0 + a_1 A_1 + a_2 A_3 + bX + u$$

Because $A_1 + A_2 + A_3 = 1$, $A_3 = 1 - A_1 - A_2$. Substituting this into the model we obtain

$$Y = a_0 + a_1 A_1 + a_2(1 - A_1 - A_2) + bX + u$$
$$= (a_0 + a_2) + (a_1 - a_2)A_1 - a_2 A_2 + bX + u$$

It follows from this that $\alpha_0 = a_0 + a_2$, $\alpha_1 = a_1 - a_2$, $-a_2 = \alpha_2$, and $b = \beta$. The coefficients of the new model can be derived from those of the previous model as follows:

$$\hat{b} = \hat{\beta}, \quad \hat{a}_2 = -\hat{\alpha}_2, \quad \hat{a}_1 = \hat{\alpha}_1 - \hat{\alpha}_2, \quad \text{and} \quad \hat{a}_0 = \hat{\alpha}_0 + \hat{\alpha}_2$$

The hypothesis that the senior age group behaves as a young household does is now tested with a t-test on a_2. The joint hypothesis $\alpha_1 = \alpha_2 = 0$ translates to $a_1 = a_2 = 0$ and can be tested with a Wald F-test. The hypothesis $\alpha_1 = \alpha_2$ now becomes $a_1 = 0$ and can be tested with a t-test on $\hat{a}_1$. We readily see that the two versions are basically equivalent, and hence it is immaterial which way the model is formulated.

6.7   Only part a is answered here; part b is left as an exercise. First write the saving relation for clerical workers and the same for skilled workers. The models are (ignoring the error term):

Clerical: $Y = (\beta_0 + \beta_8) + \beta_1 A_1 + \beta_2 A_2 + \beta_3 H$
$+ \beta_4 E_1 + \beta_5 E_2 + \beta_{10} X$

Skilled: $Y = (\beta_0 + \beta_7) + \beta_1 A_1 + \beta_2 A_2 + \beta_3 H$
$+ \beta_4 E_1 + \beta_5 E_2 + \beta_{10} X$

If the two groups behave identically, then β_7 must be equal to β_8. Therefore, the null hypothesis to test is $\beta_7 = \beta_8$. The unrestricted model is equation (6.13) and the restricted model is obtained by imposing the condition $\beta_7 = \beta_8$.

$$Y = \beta_0 + \beta_1 A_1 + \beta_2 A_2 + \beta_3 H + \beta_4 E_1 + \beta_5 E_2 + \beta_6 O_1 + \beta_7 O_2 + \beta_7 O_3$$
$$+ \beta_9 O_4 + \beta_{10} X + u$$

Combining the β_7 terms we get

$$Y = \beta_0 + \beta_1 A_1 + \beta_2 A_2 + \beta_3 H + \beta_4 E_1 + \beta_5 E_2 + \beta_6 O_1 + \beta_7 (O_2 + O_3)$$
$$+ \beta_9 O_4 + \beta_{10} X + u$$

Before estimating this restricted model, create a new variable $Z = O_2 + O_3$. The actual test procedure is the Wald F-test, described in Section 4.5.

6.9   The procedure here is very similar to that in Practice Problem 6.5.

6.11   The income elasticities in the three periods are γ_0, $\gamma_0 + \gamma_1$, and $\gamma_0 + \gamma_1 + \gamma_2$. These elasticitis will be the same only if $\gamma_1 = \gamma_2 = 0$. The test for this is the familiar Wald test. First estimate the unrestricted model given in Section 6.5. Next set γ_1 and γ_2 to 0 and estimate the restricted model. The relevant test statistic is F with 2 d.f. for the numerator and $T - 9$ d.f. for the denominator.

Exercises

6.4   The exercises in this chapter are similar to Exercise 6.4 and hence we provide detailed answers to this exercise only. The reader should use this as a sample to answer the remaining questions.

Model A: $COLGPA = \alpha + \beta HSGPA + \gamma VSAT + \delta MSAT + u$

The first step is to define a number of dummy variables as follows:

$D1 = 1$ if the student graduated from a public school, 0 otherwise

$D2 = 1$ if the student lived on campus, 0 otherwise

$D3 = 1$ if the student is a science major, 0 otherwise

$D4 = 1$ if the student is a social science major, 0 otherwise

$D5 = 1$ if the student is a humanities major, 0 otherwise

$D6 = 1$ if the student is an arts major, 0 otherwise

The avoid exact multicollinearity, we do not define a dummy for the undeclared major. It thus becomes the control group.

i. The hypothesis is that α is the same across categories. Let

$$\alpha = a0 + a1D1 + a2D2 + a3D3 + a4D4 + a5D5 + a6D6$$

Substituting this in Model A, we get Model B as

$$\begin{aligned}\text{COLGPA} &= a0 + a1D1 + a2D2 + a3D3 + a4D4 + a5D5 + a6D6\\ &= + \beta\text{HSGPA} + \gamma\text{VSAT} + \delta\text{MSAT} + u\end{aligned}$$

The null hypothesis is that α is not different for the different groups. Thus, H_0 is $a1 = a2 = a3 = a4 = a5 = a6 = 0$. The alternative hypothesis is H_1: at least one of these is nonzero. Estimate Models A and B and save their error sum squares as ESSA and ESSB. The Wald F-statistic then is

$$F_c = \frac{(\text{ESSA} - \text{ESSB})/(\text{DFA} - \text{DFB})}{\text{ESSB}/\text{DFB}}$$

where DFA is the degrees of freedom in Model A ($=427 - 4$) and DFB is the degrees of freedom in Model B ($=427 - 10$). Under the null hypothesis, this has an F-distribution with 6 d.f. in the numerator and 417 d.f. in the denominator. From the F-table look up $F^*(0.05)$ for the above degrees of freedom and reject the null hypothesis if F_c is greater than F^*. Otherwise accept the null hypothesis.

ii. The null hypothesis is that all the coefficients are the same across categories. Let

$$\alpha = a0 + a1D1 + a2D2 + a3D3 + a4D4 + a5D5 + a6D6$$
$$\beta = b0 + b1D1 + b2D2 + b3D3 + b4D4 + b5D5 + b6D6$$
$$\gamma = c0 + c1D1 + c2D2 + c3D3 + c4D4 + c5D5 + c6D6$$
$$\delta = d0 + d1D1 + d2D2 + d3D3 + d4D4 + d5D5 + d6D6$$

Substituting these in Model A, we get Model C as

$$\begin{aligned}\text{COLGPA} =\ & a0 + a1D1 + a2D2 + a3D3 + a4D4 + a5D5 + a6D6\\ & + (b0 + b1D1 + b2D2 + b3D3 + b4D4 + b5D5\\ & + b6D6)\text{HSGPA}\\ & + (c0 + c1D1 + c2D2 + c3D3 + c4D4 + c5D5\\ & + c6D6)\text{VSAT}\\ & + (d0 + d1D1 + d2D2 + d3D3 + d4D4 + d5D5\\ & + d6D6)\text{MSAT} + u\end{aligned}$$

To estimate this model, first create new variables $Z1 = D1 * \text{HSGPA}$, $Z2 = D2 * \text{HSGPA}$, and so on, and use these to estimate the unrestricted model. The null hypothesis is that α, β, γ, and δ are not different for the different groups. Thus H_0 is $a1 = a2 = a3 = a4 = a5 = a6 = b1 = b2 = b3 = b4 = b5 = b6 = c1 = c2 = c3 = c4 = c5 = c6 = d1 = d2 = d3 = d4 = d5 = d6 = 0$. The alternative is H_1: at least one of these is non-zero. A Wald F-test is carried out in a manner similar to that in part i.

Chapter 7

Exercises

7.4 The basic model is $S = a + bY + u$, where S is household savings and Y is household income. Let H be equal to 1 if the household owns its home and 0 otherwise, O_1 be equal to 1 if the head of household is in the managerial class (0 otherwise), O_2 be equal to 1 if the head is in the clerical group, O_3 be 1 if the head is a skilled worker and O_4 be 1 if the head is self-employed. The control group is unskilled workers. To allow for differences among the various groups we assume that $a = \alpha_0 + \alpha_1 H + \alpha_2 O_1 + \alpha_3 O_2 + \alpha_4 O_3 + \alpha_5 O_4$, and $b = \beta_0 + \beta_1 H + \beta_2 O_1 + \beta_3 O_2 + \beta_4 O_3 + \beta_5 O_4$. The complete model now becomes

$$S = \alpha_0 + \alpha_1 H + \alpha_2 O_1 + \alpha_3 O_2 + \alpha_4 O_3 + \alpha_5 O_4$$
$$+ Y(\beta_0 + \beta_1 H + \beta_2 O_1 + \beta_3 O_2 + \beta_4 O_3 + \beta_5 O_4) + u$$
$$= \alpha_0 + \alpha_1 H + \alpha_2 O_1 + \alpha_3 O_2 + \alpha_4 O_3 + \alpha_5 O_4$$
$$+ \beta_0 Y + \beta_1 HY + \beta_2 O_1 Y + \beta_3 O_2 Y + \beta_4 O_3 Y + \beta_5 O_4 Y + u$$

The steps for the LM test are as follows:

Step 1 Estimate the basic model by regressing S against a constant and Y, and save the residual as $\hat{u} = S - \hat{a} - \hat{b}Y$.

Step 2 Generate new variables $Z_1 = HY$, $Z_2 = O_1 Y$, and so on.

Step 3 Regress $\hat{u}$ against a constant, Y, H, O_1, O_2, O_3, O_4, and each of the Z's, and obtain the unadjusted R^2 for this auxiliary regression.

Step 4 Compute TR^2 (T being the number of observations). Under the null hypothesis that the savings function is the same for all groups (that is, that α_i and β_i are all zero for $i = 1, 2, \ldots, 5$), TR^2 has chi-square distribution with 10 d.f.

Step 5 Reject the null hypothesis if $TR^2 > \chi^2_{10}(0.05)$, the point on the chi-square distribution with 10 d.f., the area to the right of which is 0.05 (any other level of significance may be chosen).

Even if the LM test accepts the null hypothesis, the auxiliary regression provides useful information about possible candidates to be included in the model. Any variable with a t-value of 1 or higher (in absolute value) is a candidate to be included in the original model. A new model is then estimated. Insignificant variables may be omitted in the usual way.

7.7 This question refers to Exercise 6.4; read the answers to that first.
   i. The null hypothesis is that α is the same across all categories. First estimate Model A by regressing COLGPA against a constant, HSGPA, VSAT, and MSAT, and save the residual as UA. Next regress UA against a constant,

HSGPA, VSAT, MSAT, $D1$, $D2$, $D3$, $D4$, $D5$, and $D6$. Then compute the TR^2 statistic [T is the number of observations (427 here) and R^2 is the unadjusted R^2 from the auxiliary regression]. Finally, reject the null hypothesis that $\alpha_i = 0$ for $i = 1, 2, \ldots, 6$ if $TR^2 > \chi_6^2(0.05)$, where $\chi_6^2(0.05)$ is the point on the chi-square distribution with 6 d.f., the area to the right of which is 0.05.

ii. The null hypothesis is that all the coefficients are equal across categories. To perform the LM test, first estimate the basic Model A and save its residual as UA. Next regress UA against all the variables in Model C of Exercise 6.4, part 2—that is, against a constant, HSGPA, VSAT, MSAT, the six dummies, and all the interaction terms—$Z1$, $Z2$, and so on. Compute the R^2 from this auxiliary regression. The test statistic is TR^2, where $T = 427$. Under the null hypothesis, this has a chi-square distribution with 24 d.f. (the number of restrictions). From the chi-square table look up $\chi_{24}^2(0.05)$, the point on this distribution such that the area to the right is 0.05, and reject the null hypothesis if TR^2 is greater than this. Otherwise accept the null hypothesis that the savings function is the same across all categories.

Chapter 8

Exercises

8.1
$$Y_t = \beta_0 + \beta_1 X_{t1} + \beta_2 X_{t2} + u_t$$
$$\sigma_t^2 = \sigma^2 Z_t^2$$
$$\text{ESS} = \sum(w_t Y_t - \beta_0 w_t - \beta_1 w_t X_{t1} - \beta_2 w_t X_{t2})^2$$

a. $\partial\text{ESS}/\partial\beta_0 = 0$ gives $\sum(w_t Y_t - \beta_0 w_t - \beta_1 w_t X_{t1} - \beta_2 w_t X_{t2})w_t = 0$.
$\partial\text{ESS}/\partial\beta_1 = 0$ gives $\sum(w_t Y_t - \beta_0 w_t - \beta_1 w_t X_{t1} - \beta_2 w_t X_{t2})w_t X_{t1} = 0$.
$\partial\text{ESS}/\partial\beta_2 = 0$ gives $\sum(w_t Y_t - \beta_0 w_t - \beta_1 w_t X_{t1} - \beta_2 w_t X_{t2})w_t X_{t2} = 0$.

b. Equation (11.11) is reproduced here:

$$\frac{Y_t}{Z_t} = \beta_0 \frac{1}{Z_t} + \beta_1 \frac{X_{t1}}{Z_t} + \beta_2 \frac{X_{t2}}{Z_t} + \frac{u_t}{Z_t}$$

The corresponding normal equations are the following:

$$\sum\left[\frac{Y_t}{Z_t} - \beta_0 \frac{1}{Z_t} - \beta_1 \frac{X_{t1}}{Z_t} - \beta_2 \frac{X_{t2}}{Z_t}\right]\frac{1}{Z_t} = 0$$

$$\sum\left[\frac{Y_t}{Z_t} - \beta_0 \frac{1}{Z_t} - \beta_1 \frac{X_{t1}}{Z_t} - \beta_2 \frac{X_{t2}}{Z_t}\right]\frac{X_{t1}}{Z_t} = 0$$

$$\sum\left[\frac{Y_t}{Z_t} - \beta_0 \frac{1}{Z_t} - \beta_1 \frac{X_{t1}}{Z_t} - \beta_2 \frac{X_{t2}}{Z_t}\right]\frac{X_{t2}}{Z_t} = 0$$

c. It is readily seen that if w_t is replaced by $1/Z_t$, both sets of normal equations become identical.

8.3 $$Y_t = \beta X_t + u_t \qquad E(u_t) = 0 \qquad \sigma_t^2 = \sigma^2 X_t^2$$

a. The slope of the straight line joining (X_t, Y_t) to the origin is Y_t/X_t. The average of this is

$$\tilde{\beta} = \frac{1}{T} \sum_{t=1}^{T} \left(\frac{Y_t}{X_t} \right)$$

b. Since $Y_t/X_t = \beta + (u_t/X_t)$, then $\tilde{\beta} = \beta + (1/T)\sum(u_t/X_t)$. Because X_t is non-random, $E(u_t/X_t) = [E(u_t)]/X_t = 0$. Hence $\tilde{\beta}$ is unbiased.

c. $Y_t = \beta X_t + u_t$ and $\text{Var}(u_t) = \sigma^2 X_t^2$. Divide both sides of the model by X_t. We get $Y_t/X_t = \beta + u_t/X_t = \beta + v_t$. $E(v_t) = 0$ and $\text{Var}(v_t) = \text{Var}(u_t/X_t) = \sigma^2$. Therefore, v_t has all the properties for the application of OLS, including homoscedasticity. OLS can thus be applied to the transformed model to get an estimate of β that is BLUE. OLS estimate for β in this model is given by

$$\min_{\beta} \sum v_t^2 = \sum \left(\frac{Y_t}{X_t} - \beta \right)^2$$

This gives

$$\sum \left(\frac{Y_t}{X_t} - \beta \right) = 0 \qquad \text{or} \qquad \tilde{\beta} = \frac{1}{T} \sum \left(\frac{Y_t}{X_t} \right)$$

which is the same as that derived in part a. It follows that $\tilde{\beta}$ is BLUE for β, which means that any other unbiased estimate, such as the OLS estimate using the original model $Y_t = \beta X + u_t$, will have a variance at least as large as that of $\tilde{\beta}$. $\tilde{\beta}$ is therefore most efficient.

$$S_t = \alpha + \beta Y_t + \gamma A_t + u_t$$

8.11 a. If σ_t depends on the size of the population P_t, then the variance σ_t^2 will depend on P_t^2. Assume that $\sigma_t^2 = \alpha_0 + \alpha_1 P_t^2 + \epsilon_t$. The null hypothesis to test is $\alpha_1 = 0$. The steps are as follows:

Step 1 Estimate the model by OLS, save the residual $\hat{u}_t$, and square it to obtain $\hat{u}_t^2$.

Step 2 Regress $\hat{u}_t^2$ against a constant and P_t^2. (If the structure of the heteroscedasticity is unknown, the auxiliary regression is $\hat{u}_t^2$ against a constant, Y_t, A_t, Y_t^2, A_t^2, and $Y_t A_t$.)

Step 3 Compute TR^2, where T is the number of observations and R^2 is the unadjusted R^2 from the auxiliary regression of Step 2. Under the null hypothesis this has a chi-square distribution with 1 d.f. (5 d.f. in the case of the unknown heteroscedasticity structure).

Step 4 Reject the null hypothesis of homoscedasticity (at the 5 percent level) if $TR^2 > \chi_1^2(0.05)$, the point on the distribution such that the area to the right is 0.05.

b. If heteroscedasticity is ignored, OLS estimates are still unbiased and consistent, but are not efficient (that is, not BLUE). This is because the proofs of unbiasedness and consistency depend only on the assumptions $E(u_t) = 0$ and $E(X_t u_t) = 0$, which are unaffected by heteroscedasticty. BLUE, on the other hand, requires that the error terms have constant variance.

c. It is now given that $\sigma_t = \sigma P_t$. Divide the model by P_t:

$$\frac{S_t}{P_t} = \alpha \frac{1}{P_t} + \beta \frac{Y_t}{P_t} + \gamma \frac{A_t}{P_t} + \frac{u_t}{P_t}$$

Because $\mathrm{Var}(u_t/P_t)$ is σ^2, the OLS procedure can be applied to this transformed model giving estimates that are BLUE. The procedure is to regress S_t/P_t against $1/P_t$, Y_t/P_t, and A_t/P_t, without a constant term.

Chapter 9

Exercises

9.1 a. The assumption on the error term is that $u_t = \rho u_{t-1} + \epsilon_t$, where ϵ_t is well-behaved. The null hypothesis is that $\rho = 0$, and the alternative most common in economics is that $\rho > 0$. The number of observations is 23 and k' ($=k - 1$) is 2. From Table A.5b, the critical values are $d_L = 1.17$ and $d_U = 1.54$. Because the observed d is less than d_L, we reject the null hypothesis of no autocorrelation and conclude that there is significant first-order serial correlation. The OLS estimates are still unbiased and consistent, but are no longer efficient. Furthermore, all tests of hypotheses are invalid.

b. First regress LH against a constant, LG, and LR, and save the residual as $\hat{u}_t$. Next regress $\hat{u}_t$ against a constant, LG, LR, and $\hat{u}_{t-1}$, and compute the unadjusted R^2 of this auxiliary regression. Reject the null hypothesis if $22R^2 > \chi_1^2(0.05)$, where $\chi_1^2(0.05)$ is the point on the chi-square distribution with 1 d.f. such that the area to the right is 0.05.

c. First regress LH against a constant, LG, and LR, and save the residual as $\hat{u}_t$. For the Hildreth−Lu procedure, choose a ρ (call it ρ_1) and obtain $LH_t^* = LH_t - \rho_1 LH_{t-1}$, $LG_t^* = LG_t - \rho_1 LG_{t-1}$, and $LR_t^* = LR_t - \rho_1 LR_{t-1}$. Then regress LH_t^* against a constant, LG_t^*, and LR_t^*, and save the error sum of squares ESS of this regression. Next choose a different ρ_1 and repeat the process. By systematically searching from -1 to $+1$, we get a series of ESS values. The final estimate of ρ is the one that minimizes this ESS. This ρ is then used to transform the variables and a final regression run.

In the Cochrane−Orcutt procedure too the first step is to regress LH against a constant, LG, and LR, and save the residual as $\hat{u}_t$. Next compute $\hat{\rho} = (\sum \hat{u}_t \hat{u}_{t-1})/(\sum \hat{u}_t^2)$. Use this to obtain LH*, LG*, and LR* as in the Hildreth−Lu case. Then regress LH* against a constant, LG*, and LR*, and obtain new estimates of the regression coefficients. Use these then to obtain a second round of residuals $\hat{u}_t$. The process is repeated until two successive estimates of ρ do not differ by more than some specified value.

Estimates obtained by the Hildreth–Lu and Cochrane–Orcutt procedures are more efficient than OLS estimates.

9.4 For $n = 22$, $k' = k - 1 = 3$, $d_L = 1.05$, $d_U = 1.66$. Because d ($= 1.147$) is between these two values, the Durbin–Watson test is inconclusive. To apply the LM test, the first step is to regress $LEMP$, against a constant, $LINCM$, $LWAGE$, and LG, and save the residual $\hat{u}_t$. Next regress $\hat{u}_t$ against a constant, $LINCM$, $LWAGE$, LG, and $\hat{u}_{t-1}$, and compute R^2. The test statistic is $21R^2$ which, under the null hypothesis of zero first-order serial correlation, has a chi-square distribution with 1 d.f. Reject the null hypothesis at the 5 percent level if $21\,R^2 > \chi_1^2(0.05)$, the point such that the area to the right of it is 0.05. The steps for the Cochrane–Orcutt procedure are as follows:

Step 1 First estimate the model by OLS and obtain the residuals $\hat{u}_t = LEMP_t + 3.89 - 0.51LINCM + 0.25LWAGE - 0.62LG_t$

Step 2 Estimate $\hat{\rho} = \left(\sum \hat{u}_t \hat{u}_{t-1} \right) / \left(\sum \hat{u}_t^2 \right)$.

Step 3 Transform the data as follows:

$$Y^* = LEMP_t - \hat{\rho}LEMP_{t-1}$$

$$X_1^* = LINCM_t - \hat{\rho}LINCM_{t-1}$$

and similarly for $LWAGE$ and LG as X_2^* and X_3^*.

Step 4 Regress Y^* on a constant, X_1^*, X_2^* and X_3^*, using

$$Y^* = \alpha_0 + \alpha_1 X_1^* + \alpha_2 X_2^* + \alpha_3 X_3^* + \text{error}$$

Step 5 From these estimates, obtain $\hat{u}_t$ of the *original* model again. Next go back to Step 2. The iteration ends when two successive estimates of ρ do not differ by more than some prespecified value.

This procedure gives consistent estimates that are more efficient than OLS estimates, but they are not unbiased or BLUE.

Chapter 10

Exercises

10.1

$$M_t = \alpha + \beta Y_t^* + \gamma R_t$$
$$Y_t^* = \lambda Y_{t-1} + (1 - \lambda)Y_{t-1}^* + u_t$$

a. Multiplying the second equation by β, we have

$$\beta Y_t^* = \lambda \beta Y_{t-1} + (1 - \lambda)\beta Y_{t-1}^* + \beta u_t$$

Substituting this into the first equation we get

$$M_t - \alpha - \gamma R_t = \lambda \beta Y_{t-1} + (1 - \lambda)(M_{t-1} - \alpha - \gamma R_{t-1}) + \beta u_t$$
$$M_t = \alpha - \alpha(1 - \lambda) + \lambda \beta Y_{t-1} + \gamma R_t + (1 - \lambda)M_{t-1} - (1 - \lambda)\gamma R_{t-1} + \beta u_t$$
$$= \alpha\lambda + \lambda \beta Y_{t-1} + \gamma R_t + (1 - \lambda)M_{t-1} - (1 - \lambda)\gamma R_{t-1} + \beta u_t$$

which is estimable as

$$M_t = \beta_0 + \beta_1 Y_{t-1} + \beta_2 R_t + \beta_3 M_{t-1} + \beta_4 R_{t-1} + v_t$$

There is a problem here in that the estimates are not unique. For instance, $1 - \lambda = \beta_3$. Hence $\hat{\lambda} = 1 - \beta_3$. Also, $\beta_2 = \gamma$ and $\beta_4 = -(1 - \lambda)\gamma$. Therefore, $1 - \lambda = -\beta_4/\beta_2$ and, thus, $\tilde{\lambda} = 1 + (\hat{\beta}_4/\hat{\beta}_2)$. There is no reason to believe that $\tilde{\lambda}$ and $\hat{\lambda}$ will be the same. What is essentially happening is that there is a nonlinear restriction among the β's, namely, $\beta_2\beta_3 + \beta_4 = 0$. Any estimation procedure must take this into account.

b. Under the assumptions given, $E(u_t) = 0$ and u_t is not correlated with any of the independent variables. Therefore, OLS estimates are consistent. However, because M_{t-1} is on the right-hand side, we have a lagged dependent variable. This gives biased estimates in small samples.

c. If $u_t = \rho u_{t-1} + \epsilon_t$, then M_{t-1} and u_t are correlated. Hence $E(M_{t-1}u_t) \neq 0$. To get unbiased and consistent estimates we need u_t to be uncorrelated with M_{t-1}, R_{t-1}, R_t, and Y_t. As this is not the case here, we get biased and inconsistent estimates.

10.4 a. $H_0: \rho = 0$, $H_1: \rho > 0$, where ρ is the first-order serial correlation; $T = 32$, $k' = 1, d_L = 1.37$, and $d_u = 1.50$. Because $d = 0.207 < d_L$, we reject H_0. We thus conclude that there is significant serial correlation.

b. The proof of unbiasedness does not require ρ to be equal to 0. Hence, OLS estimates are still unbiased. BLUE requires serial independence of errors and hence the estimates are no longer BLUE. Tests of hypotheses are invalid if there is serial correlation.

c. If $u_t = \rho u_{t-1} + \epsilon_t$ is a good approximation to the error process, then the following procedure will "improve" the estimates:

Step 1 Use OLS on the model and get $\hat{u}_t$, the residuals.

Step 2 Compute $\hat{\rho} = (\sum \hat{u}_t\hat{u}_{t-1})/\sum(\hat{u}_t^2)$, an estimate of ρ.

Step 3 Transform the variables and obtain

$$C_t^* = C_t - \hat{\rho}C_{t-1} \quad \text{and} \quad Y_t^* = \ln Y_t - \hat{\rho} \ln Y_{t-1}$$

Step 4 Regress C^* against Y^* and a constant. From these obtain new estimates $\hat{u}_t$.

Step 5 Go back to Step 2 and iterate until two successive values of $\hat{\rho}$ differ by no more than a prespecified number (for example, 0.01).

By transforming the models, we get consistent and efficient estimates, and the tests of hypotheses are valid.

d. The new model has C_{t-1}, the lagged dependent variable. The presence of such a variable destroys the unbiasedness property. Therefore the estimates are biased.

e. $H_0: \rho = 0$, $H_1: \rho > 0$. Because there is a lagged dependent variable, the Durbin-h tests is the appropriate one:

$$h = \hat{\rho}\left[\frac{T'}{1 - T's_{\hat{\beta}}^2}\right]^{1/2} = -0.39$$

where $T' = T - 1 = 31$. To get $s_{\hat{\beta}}^2$, divide the regression coefficient of C_{t-1} by its t-value and then square it. Because $|h| < 1.645$, the 10 percent critical value of the standard normal distribution, we fail to reject the null hypothesis (even at a 10 percent level), and conclude that there is no serial correlation.

f. Even though there is no serial correlation, because of the presence of a lagged independent variable, OLS estimates are biased. However, $\rho = 0$ implies that they are consistent.

Chapter 11

Exercises

11.4 The case of the first-order serial correlation is presented in equation (8.4). If $u_t = \rho_1 u_{t-1} + \rho_3 u_{t-3} + \epsilon_t$, then the forecast at time t is $\hat{Y}_t = \hat{\alpha} + \hat{\beta} X_t + \hat{\rho}_1 \hat{u}_{t-1} + \hat{\rho}_3 \hat{u}_{t-3}$. This forecast is defined only for $t = 4$ onward. Setting $\hat{u}_1 = \hat{u}_2 = \hat{u}_3 = 0$, we have the following:

$$\hat{Y}_4 = \hat{\alpha} + \hat{\beta} X_4 \qquad\qquad \hat{u}_4 = Y_4 - \hat{Y}_4$$
$$\hat{Y}_5 = \hat{\alpha} + \hat{\beta} X_5 + \hat{\rho}_1 \hat{u}_4 \qquad\qquad \hat{u}_5 = Y_5 - \hat{Y}_5$$
$$\hat{Y}_6 = \hat{\alpha} + \hat{\beta} X_6 + \hat{\rho}_1 \hat{u}_5 \qquad\qquad \hat{u}_6 = Y_6 - \hat{Y}_6$$
$$\hat{Y}_7 = \hat{\alpha} + \hat{\beta} X_7 + \hat{\rho}_1 \hat{u}_6 + \hat{\rho}_3 \hat{u}_4 \qquad \hat{u}_7 = Y_7 - \hat{Y}_7$$

The remaining periods are similar to $t = 7$.

11.7 Seasonal variations can be captured by 11 monthly dummies. Growth can be modeled by first converting the dependent variable to logarithms. Thus, a possible model is the following:

$$\ln(\text{SALES}_t) = \beta_0 + \beta_1 D_{t1} + \beta_2 D_{t2} + \cdots + \beta_{11} D_{t11} + \lambda t + u_t$$
$$u_t = \rho_1 u_{t-1} + \rho_2 u_{t-2} + \cdots + \rho_{12} u_{t-12} + \epsilon_t$$

where λ is the exponential growth rate, and D_{ti} is the tth observation on the dummy variable for the ith month. The second equation could also be modeled as a moving average—that is, as $\alpha_1 \epsilon_{t-1} + \alpha_2 \epsilon_{t-2} + \cdots + \alpha_{12} \epsilon_{t-12}$.

11.9 Equation (9.9) has both a lagged dependent variable and a moving average error term, and hence the model is ARMA.

Chapter 12

Exercises

12.1 The linear probability model is $P_t = \beta_0 + \beta_1 A_t + \beta_2 N_t + \beta_3 S_t + u_t$, where t refers to the tth employee. The older an employee is, the greater is the probability of retirement. The longer the employee has been with the company, the greater is the probability of retirement. The higher the salary of the employee, the smaller the opportunity cost of not working and hence the higher the probability of retirement. We would therefore expect $\beta_1, \beta_2,$ and β_3 to be positive. The estimation procedure is to first regress the dummy variable

P_t against a constant, A_t, N_t, and S_t. Next obtain the predicted probability of retirement as $\hat{P}_t = \hat{\beta}_0 + \hat{\beta}_1 A_t + \hat{\beta}_2 N_t + \hat{\beta}_3 S_t$. If $\hat{\sigma}_t^2 = \hat{P}_t(1 - \hat{P}_t)$ is positive, set the weight for the tth observation to $w_t = 1/\hat{\sigma}_t$; otherwise, set w_t to zero. Obtain weighted least squares estimates by regressing $(w_t P_t)$ against w_t, $(w_t A_t)$, $(w_t N_t)$, and $(w_t S_t)$.

12.2   If P_t is the fraction of employees who have recently retired, then the logit model is to regress $\ln[P_t/(1 - P_t)]$ against a constant, A_t, N_t, and S_t.

Chapter 13

Exercises

13.1   The model is $C_t = \alpha + \beta Y_t + u_t$.
   a. *Functional form:*   The model assumes that the marginal propensity to consume (MPC) is a constant β at all income levels. This is erroneous. Evidence indicates that MPC decreases with income. Thus,

$$C_t = \alpha + \beta Y_t + \gamma Y_t^2 + u_t \quad \text{or} \quad C_t = \alpha + \beta \ln Y_t + u_t$$

   would be more appropriate.
   Omitted variables: The model assumes that income is the only determinant of consumption. This is also wrong. Other variables such as wealth, past consumption, family size, or population are also important. Thus, such crucial variables are omitted.
   Heteroscedasticity: In cross-section studies it has been found that consumption patterns are much more varied for high income groups than for low income groups. Thus, the assumption that $E(u_t^2) = \sigma^2$ is unrealistic. It is more likely that σ_t^2 increases with income.
   Serial correlation: In time series data, successive error terms are often correlated: that is, the assumption that $E(u_t u_s) = 0$ for $t \neq s$ is invalid in this case. Here also the error structure is misspecified. The assumption $u_t = \rho u_{t-1} + \epsilon_t$ is better.
   Simultaneous equation bias: At the aggregate level, $C_t = \alpha + \beta Y_t + u_t$ may be a part of a simultaneous equation model. For instance, $Y_t = C_t + I_t$ may be a second equation. Thus, there is a feedback effect from C to Y.
   b. *Functional form:*   Wrong functional form of the type specified is a misspecification in the deterministic part. $E(u_t) \neq 0$ here and hence estimates are biased. They can therefore not be BLUE. Estimates need not be consistent. F- and t-tests are therefore invalid.
   Omitted variables: Same as above.
   Heteroscedasticity: If heteroscedasticity is ignored, we still have $E(u_t) = 0$ and hence OLS estimates are unbiased. However, they are not BLUE because $E(u_t^2)$ is not a constant. As long as Y and u are uncorrelated, they will be consistent also.
   Serial correlation: $E(u_t) = 0$ still holds, and hence OLS estimates are unbiased here also. But because $E(u_t u_s) \neq 0$ for $t \neq s$, they will not be BLUE. If Y_t and u_t are uncorrelated, estimates will be consistent.

Simultaneous equations bias: Now Y_t and u_t are correlated. Therefore, the estimates are biased and not consistent. They cannot be BLUE.

13.3

$$P = \alpha_1 + \alpha_2 N + \alpha_3 S + \alpha_4 A + u$$
$$N = \beta_1 + \beta_2 P + \beta_3 M + v$$

Endogenous: P and N Exogeneous: S, A, and M

a. This model corresponds to Model 4 of Section 13.3. We noted that the model is overidentified.
b. Because S, A, and M are exogenous, they are uncorrelated with both u and v. P and N are endogenous and are correlated with both u and v.
c. OLS estimates are biased and inconsistent.
d. Because the model is overidentified, indirect least squares is not applicable here.
e. In the first stage, regress P against a constant, S, A, and M, and save the predicted value $\hat{P}$. Similarly, regress N against a constant, S, A, and M, and save the predicted value $\hat{N}$. In the second stage, regress P against a constant, $\hat{N}$, S, and A to obtain TSLS estimates of the first equation. Regress N against a constant, $\hat{P}$, and M to obtain TSLS estimates of the second equation.

COPYRIGHTS AND ACKNOWLEDGMENTS

Page 124   "Regional Variation in Banking Costs" adapted from "The Impact of Regulation on Inter- and Intra Regional Variation in Commercial Banking Costs" by Frederick W. Bell and Neil B. Murphy, from *Journal of Regional Science*, Vol. 9, 1969. Reprinted by permission of the Regional Science Research Institute.

Page 137   Table 3.7, "Assets and return on invested capital (1989) for 26 U.S. companies in the food processing industry" reprinted from April 13, 1990 issue of *Business Week* by special permission, copyright © 1991 by McGraw-Hill, Inc.

Page 137   Table 3.8, "Total sales and profits for discount and fashion retailing companies in the United States" reprinted from April 13, 1990 issue of *Business Week* by special permission, copyright © 1990 by McGraw-Hill, Inc.

Page 139   Table 3.10, "Business school tuition and average starting salary of MBAs" reprinted from October 29, 1990 issue of *Business Week* by special permission, copyright © 1990 by McGraw-Hill, Inc.

Page 192   Table 4.4, "Savings Behavior in India" adapted from "An Econometric Exploration of Indian Saving Behavior" by Ramu Ramanathan in *Journal of the American Statistical Association*, March 1969. Reprinted by permission of the American Statistical Association.

Page 194   Table 4.5, "Net Migration Rates and the Quality of Life" adapted from "Differential Net Migration and the Quality of Life" by Ben-Chieh Liu from *Review of Economics and Statistics*, August 1975. Reprinted by permission of the President and Fellows of Harvard College.

Page 376–78   Example 9.7 from "Demand Relations with Autocorrelated Disturbances," Technical Bulletin 276, by Clifford Hildreth and John Y. Lu. Reprinted by permission of Michigan State University, Agricultural Experiment Station.

Pages 387–89   Tables 9.4, 9.5 and 9.6 from "The Relative Yields on Taxable and Tax-Exempt Debt by Hal Heaton, *Journal of Money, Credit, and Banking*, Vol. 18, No. 4 (November 1986) are reprinted by permission. Copyright © 1986 by the Ohio State University Press. All rights reserved.

Pages 433–34 "The Monetary-Fiscal Policy Debate" adapted from "The Almon Lag Technique and the Monetary Fiscal Debate" by Peter Schmidt and Roger N. Waud for *Journal of the American Statistical Association*, March 1973. Reprinted by permission of the American Statistical Association.

Page 439 Table 10.4, "Critical Values for the Dickey-Fuller Test" by Dickey and Fuller. Reprinted with the permission of the Econometric Society.

Page 445 "Inflation and the Savings Rate" adapted from "Inflation and the Savings Rate" by Russell Davidson and James G. Mackinnon from *Applied Economics*, 1983. Reprinted by permission of Chapman & Hall, Ltd.

Page 503 Table 11.8, "Critical Values for Testing for Cointegration," reprinted by the permission of the Econometric Society.

Page 519 Table 12.2 "Career Interruptions Following Childbirth" adapted from "Career Interruptions Following Childbirth" by William Even in *Journal of Labor Economics*, Vol. 5, pp. 255–277. Copyright © by The University of Chicago. All rights reserved.

Pages 560–63 Table 14.1, "Classification System for Articles and Abstracts," from *Journal of Economic Literature*, September 1987. Reprinted with the permission of the American Economic Association.

Page 574 Table A.1 from *Statistical Analysis for Decision Making*, Fourth Edition by Morris Hamburg, copyright © 1987 by Harcourt Brace Jovanovich, Inc., reprinted by permission of the publisher.

Pages 582–93 Table A.6, "Cumulative Terms for the Binomial Distribution." Reprinted with permission from *Handbook of Tables for Mathematics*, Fourth Edition. Copyright © 1970 CRC Press, Inc. Boca Raton, FL.

AUTHOR INDEX

SUBJECT INDEX

Acceptance region, 50
Adaptive expectation, 435–36, 461
Adaptive forecast, 482–83
Adjusted R^2, see R^2
Adjustment coefficient, 435
AIC (Akaike information criterion), 167
Almon lag, 430–31
Alternative hypothesis, 50, 52
Analysis of covariance, 264–70
Analysis of variance (ANOVA), 107,
    263–64
AR models, see autoregressive models
AR(l), 364
AR(p), 381–82
ARCH test, 384–85
ARIMA models, 496
ARMA models, 494
ASCII, 568, 595
Asymptotic
    efficiency, 44
    normality, 45
    unbiasedness, 42
Augmented Dickey-Fuller test,
    503–504
Autocorrelation, see serial correlation
Autocorrelation function, 494, 511–12
Autoregressive
    conditional heteroscedasticity, 384–85
    integrated moving average, 435
    models, 493
    process, 493
Average lag, see mean lag

Behavioral equation, 528
Bernoulli distribution, 331
Best linear unbiased estimator, 48,
    73–74, 148–50
Beta coefficient, 162
Bias, 40
    least squares, 532
    omitted variable, 186, 230–31
    simultaneous equation, 532
Binary choice model, 514–15

Binary variables, 252
Binomial distribution, 17–18
Bivariate distribution, 25
BLUE, 48, 73–74, 148–50
Box-Cox transformation, 184–85
Box-Pierce statistic, 499
Breusch-Pagan test, 342–43

Causality, 115–17, 529–31
Central limit theorem, 45
Censored regression, 520–21
Chain rule, 69
Chi-square distribution, 33–34, 313
Chow-test, 274–75
Cobb-Douglas production function, 71,
    180
Cochrane-Orcutt iterative procedure,
    374–75, 383
Coefficient of multiple determination, 104
Cointegration, 448, 501–05
Combining forecasts, 483–88
Conditional
    density, 26
    forecast, 475–76
    mean, 32
    probability, 26
Confidence interval, 48–50, 113–15
Consistency, 43–44, 94–95
Constant returns to scale, 180
Constrained optimization, 72–73
Continuous random variable, 17
Control group, 253
Cooling degree days, 390–91
CORC, see Cochrane-Orcutt procedure
Correlation coefficient, 30, 46, 105–06,
    153–54
Correlogram, 494–95
Covariance, 29–31, 46, 86
Critical region, 50, 99
Cross-section data, 9
Cumulative
    density function (cdf), 17
    distribution function, 17

B 2
C 3
D 4
E 5
F 6
G 7
H 8
I 9
J 0

Durbin–Watson Statistic (d)
5 percent significance points of d_L and d_U in one-tailed tests

	$k' = 1$		$k' = 2$		$k' = 3$		$k' = 4$		$k' = 5$	
n	d_L	d_U	d_L	d_U	d_L	d_U	d_L	d_U	d_L	d_U
15	1.08	1.36	0.95	1.54	0.82	1.75	0.69	1.97	0.56	2.21
16	1.10	1.37	0.98	1.54	0.86	1.73	0.74	1.93	0.62	2.15
17	1.13	1.38	1.02	1.54	0.90	1.71	0.78	1.90	0.67	2.10
18	1.16	1.39	1.05	1.53	0.93	1.69	0.82	1.87	0.71	2.06
19	1.18	1.40	1.08	1.53	0.97	1.68	0.86	1.85	0.75	2.02
20	1.20	1.41	1.10	1.54	1.00	1.68	0.90	1.83	0.79	1.99
21	1.22	1.42	1.13	1.54	1.03	1.67	0.93	1.81	0.83	1.96
22	1.24	1.43	1.15	1.54	1.05	1.66	0.96	1.80	0.86	1.94
23	1.26	1.44	1.17	1.54	1.08	1.66	0.99	1.79	0.90	1.92
24	1.27	1.45	1.19	1.55	1.10	1.66	1.01	1.78	0.93	1.90
25	1.29	1.45	1.21	1.55	1.12	1.66	1.04	1.77	0.95	1.89
26	1.30	1.46	1.22	1.55	1.14	1.65	1.06	1.76	0.98	1.88
27	1.32	1.47	1.24	1.56	1.16	1.65	1.08	1.76	1.01	1.86
28	1.33	1.48	1.26	1.56	1.18	1.65	1.10	1.75	1.03	1.85
29	1.34	1.48	1.27	1.56	1.20	1.65	1.12	1.74	1.05	1.84
30	1.35	1.49	1.28	1.57	1.21	1.65	1.14	1.74	1.07	1.83
31	1.36	1.50	1.30	1.57	1.23	1.65	1.16	1.74	1.09	1.83
32	1.37	1.50	1.31	1.57	1.24	1.65	1.18	1.73	1.11	1.82
33	1.38	1.51	1.32	1.58	1.26	1.65	1.19	1.73	1.13	1.81
34	1.39	1.51	1.33	1.58	1.27	1.65	1.21	1.73	1.15	1.81
35	1.40	1.52	1.34	1.58	1.28	1.65	1.22	1.73	1.16	1.80
36	1.41	1.52	1.35	1.59	1.29	1.65	1.24	1.73	1.18	1.80
37	1.42	1.53	1.36	1.59	1.31	1.66	1.25	1.72	1.19	1.80
38	1.43	1.54	1.37	1.59	1.32	1.66	1.26	1.72	1.21	1.79
39	1.43	1.54	1.38	1.60	1.33	1.66	1.27	1.72	1.22	1.79
40	1.44	1.54	1.39	1.60	1.34	1.66	1.29	1.72	1.23	1.79
45	1.48	1.57	1.43	1.62	1.38	1.67	1.34	1.72	1.29	1.78
50	1.50	1.59	1.46	1.63	1.42	1.67	1.38	1.72	1.34	1.77
55	1.53	1.60	1.49	1.64	1.45	1.68	1.41	1.72	1.38	1.77
60	1.55	1.62	1.51	1.65	1.48	1.69	1.44	1.73	1.41	1.77
65	1.57	1.63	1.54	1.66	1.50	1.70	1.47	1.73	1.44	1.77
70	1.58	1.64	1.55	1.67	1.52	1.70	1.49	1.74	1.46	1.77
75	1.60	1.65	1.57	1.68	1.54	1.71	1.51	1.74	1.49	1.77
80	1.61	1.66	1.59	1.69	1.56	1.72	1.53	1.74	1.51	1.77
85	1.62	1.67	1.60	1.70	1.57	1.72	1.55	1.75	1.52	1.77
90	1.63	1.68	1.61	1.70	1.59	1.73	1.57	1.75	1.54	1.78
95	1.64	1.69	1.62	1.71	1.60	1.73	1.58	1.75	1.56	1.78
100	1.65	1.69	1.63	1.72	1.61	1.74	1.59	1.76	1.57	1.78

n = number of observations

k' = number of explanatory variables excluding constant

Source: J. Durbin and G. S. Watson, "Testing for Serial Correlation in Least Squares Regression," *Biometrika*, Vol. 38 (1951), pp. 159–177. Reprinted with permission of the Biometrika Trustees.